W9-ACE-519

VICTORIAN LITERATURE AND CULTURE

Volume 20

ADVISORY BOARD

Victorian Literature
and Culture

Volume 20

Formerly Browning Institute Studies: Volumes 1–18

EDITORS
JOHN MAYNARD
ADRIENNE AUSLANDER MUNICH

Review Editor: Winifred Hughes
Associate Editor: Sandra Donaldson
Special Effects Editor: Jeffrey Spear
Assistant Editor: Abigail Burnham Bloom

AMS PRESS
1992

For current subscription information or back orders for volumes 1–19, write to AMS Press, Inc, 56 East 13th Street, New York, NY 10003, USA

VICTORIAN LITERATURE AND CULTURE is a publication of the Browning Institute, Inc., a nonprofit organization. It is published through the generous support of New York University and the State University of New York at Stony Brook. The editors gratefully acknowledge our indebtedness to our editorial assistants Lisa Golmitz, Devoney Looser, and Mary Sullivan.

Manuscripts and editorial correspondence can be addressed to either editor: Adrienne Munich: Department of English, SUNY/Stony Brook, Stony Brook, NY 11794 (516 632 9176; fax: 516 632 6252). John Maynard: Department of English, NYU, 19 University Pl., Room 235, N.Y., NY 10003 (212 998 8835; fax: 212 995 4019).

Please submit two copies of manuscripts; articles should be double-spaced throughout and follow the new MLA style (with a list of Works Cited at the conclusion). Chapters of books submitted for the *Works in Progress* section may follow the author's chosen style in the book project.

Correspondence concerning review essays should be addressed to Winifred Hughes: 50 Wheatsheaf Lane, Princeton, NJ 08540 (609 921 1489).

Suggestions for reprints of Victorian materials, texts or illustrations, should be addressed to Jeffrey Spear, Department of English, NYU, 19 University Pl., Room 200, N.Y., NY 10003 (212 998 8820; fax: 212 995 4019).

CONTENTS

Browning Bibliography

ILLUSTRATIONS

PRIMITIVE MARRIAGE, CIVILIZED MARRIAGE: ANTHROPOLOGY, MYTHOLOGY, AND *THE EGOIST*

By Patricia O'Hara

Nothing, perhaps, gives a more instructive insight into the true condition of savages than their ideas on the subject of relationship and marriage; nor can the great advantages of civilisation be more conclusively proved than by the improvement which it has effected in the relation between the two sexes.

Sir John Lubbock, *The Origin of Civilisation and the Primitive Condition of Man* (1870)

Women have us back to the conditions of primitive man, or they shoot us higher than the topmost star. But it is as we please. . . . By [women's] state is our civilization judged: and if it is hugely animal still, that is because primitive men abound and will have their pasture.

George Meredith, *The Egoist* (1879)

THE CONNECTIONS BETWEEN simple and complex, animal and human, and primitive and civilized as traced by nineteenth-century biological and social evolutionary theories realigned the modern self in relation to the ancestral savage self. Although most Victorian biological and social evolutionists maintained confidence that a vast distance spanned primitive and civilized cultures, to a few minds evolution's mirror of the past reflected unsettling lineaments of the barbarian discernible in the civilized, an image that became particularly pronounced as the century neared its close. Although their premises, theories, and methodologies varied widely, Victorian ethnologists and anthropologists sought to reconstruct primitive culture and to systematize the progress from the primitive past to contemporary civilization. Emerging out of proliferating studies in comparative mythology, comparative religion, philology, mythography, ethnology, Darwinian evolution, geography, and positivism, the science of Victorian evolutionary anthropology necessarily encompasses a multitude of interlocking fields of inquiry into the "culture" of primitive man.[1] In

1

the opening of *Primitive Culture* (1871), E. B. Tylor defined "culture," traditionally taken as a founding concept of anthropology, as "that complex whole which includes knowledge, belief, art, morals, law, custom, and any other capabilities and habits acquired by man as a member of society" (1:1), and a cultural category that appeared to illustrate the great progress from savage to civilized was marriage and the organization of sexual relations. Appearing when the legal and moral foundations of the institution of marriage were beginning to come under vigorous assault, the British anthropological studies published in the 1860s and 1870s on the laws and customs of primitive marriage and sexual relations share progressivist assumptions about social development that consistently yield a conservative affirmation of the supremacy of patriarchy, and the moral and legal superiority of civilized marriage and the present order of sexual relations. Two highly influential studies of primitive marriage, J. F. McLennan's *Primitive Marriage* (1865) and Sir John Lubbock's *The Origin of Civilisation and the Primitive Condition of Man* (1870), present divergent theories about the structure and evolution of primitive marriage but both confirm the "great advantage" of civilized sexual relations over the original, or earliest, "natural" relations between the sexes.

Published in 1879, George Meredith's *The Egoist* mounts an attack on the progressivist assumptions of the anthropological reconstructions of primitive marriage of the 1860s and '70s and their affirmations of patriarchal social organization. With references to the discourse of anthropology woven into an elaborate web of mythological allusions that evoke a cluster of patriarchal attitudes toward women and marriage, the novel presents an alternative reading of social evolution and the moral progress of civilization, a reading that pivots squarely upon the degraded status of civilized women.[2] *The Egoist* qualifies the inferences of social anthropological theory by exhibiting "civilized" man conducting his courtship and marital negotiations with "civilized" woman in ways that are considerably more "primitive" than "advanced." The developmental distance between the "thousands of civilized males" (151; ch. 11) — represented by the egoist, Sir Willoughby Patterne — and our "ancestral satyr" (151; ch. 11) is delineated as a distinctly short one. Egoism, akin to natural selection,[3] is identified as the mechanism that drives both "primitive" and "civilized" man in his quest for a suitable mate. The novel's allusions expose the tenuousness of the nineteenth century's pretensions to moral and intellectual superiority over the savage "other" by designating as "primitive" and mythically recurrent the sexual possessiveness and deeply embedded misogyny of "civilized" man's marital customs and relationships with women. I need to draw a distinction here, however. The novel neither interrogates nor challenges the legitimacy of contemporary Victorian constructions of the "primitive" as savage, deficient, immoral, or bestial. Rather, the novel divests the "civilized" of what Meredith perceived as its egotistically aggrandized status and, in so doing, replicates Victorian formulations of the "primitive." At certain points in the novel Sir Willoughby's sense of racial entitlement and class privilege are presented as symptoms of a diseased civilized egoism; however, in satirizing the civilized British aristocracy by allusively portraying its behavior as "primitive," the novel retains the "primitive" as a stable category. I have to this point highlighted the words "primitive" and "civilized" in order to draw attention to them as Victorian constructions or conceptualizations, and to distinguish those Victorian constructions from our contemporary recognition of the problematic ethnocentric implications of the terms "primitive" and "civilized." Our self-consciousness about these terms, however, does not resolve the difficulties of articulation and conceptualization; as Marianna Torgivnick has observed: "When we put *primitive* into quotation marks, we in a sense wish away the heritage of the West's exploitation of non-Western peoples" (20).

In the 1860s and '70s, anthropological theory was widely disseminated, and the well-versed, "intellectual novelist," George Meredith, was certainly cognizant of the main currents of social evolutionary theory, although we have no extant proof (in letters or memoirs) that Meredith read Lubbock or McLennan. However, anthropological studies routinely appeared in the pages of Victorian periodicals like the *Fortnightly Review, Contemporary Review, Fraser's Magazine,* and *Quarterly Review. Vittoria,* Meredith's political romance of the Italian revolution, ran serially in the *Fortnightly Review* (from January through December of 1866), with essays such as E. B. Tylor's "On the Origin of Language" and "Religion of Savages," McLennan's "Kinship in Ancient Greece," and W. Walker Williams's "Were the Ancient British Savages?" *Beauchamps Career,* another political romance, was published throughout 1874 in the *Fortnightly Review* with articles about Herbert Spencer's theory of social evolution, G. H. Lewes and positivism, and Sir Henry Maine's "Early History of Institutions." A "free-thinking" writer whose novels dramatize the maladies of civilization by meticulously delineating the dynamics of gender and class in marriage, Meredith was at various points a proponent of positivism, domestic political reforms, Irish Home Rule, and the rights of women.[4] His advocacy of the rights of women, especially as it is formulated in *The Egoist,* bears the palpable influence of John Stuart Mill's *The Subjection of Women* (1869),[5] particularly Mill's discussions, in chapters 1 and 3, of the constructed artificiality of what was commonly regarded as woman's "nature," and Mill's assertions that the subjection of women represents a "relic of the past," an instance of "the primitive state of slavery lasting on, through successive mitigations and modifications" (17, 7). Here I want to focus on the way *The Egoist*'s narration of the marriage plot expresses Meredith's deep resistance to the politics of social evolution and its sanctification of "civilized" marriage and the patriarchal family. To do this it will be necessary to look briefly at some of the relevant anthropological writing of the time.

> His communal wives, at his ease,
> He would curb with occasional blows;
> Or his State had a queen, like the bees
> (As another philosopher trows).
>   Andrew Lang, "Double Ballade of Primitive Man" (1880)

BOTH McLENNAN AND LUBBOCK refuted Sir Henry Maine's patriarchal theory, in *Ancient Law* (1861), which proposed patriarchy as the universal and original developmental stage. While they dislodged the natural authority of patriarchy with accounts of other forms of antecedent social orders, ultimately their social evolutionary investigations into the power structure of primitive marriage and lineage reinstate the authority of patriarchy by demonstrating both the barbarism of that antecedent natural order as well as the universal and original political and physical inferiority of women. McLennan and Lubbock were not themselves field workers but rather theoreticians, synthesizers who analyzed historical and legal records of ancient civilization and who drew heavily upon the living evidence presented in recent explorers' and colonialists' accounts of modern savages — extant primitive tribes primarily in North America, Africa, India, and the South Pacific. Abundantly intertextual, Lubbock's and McLennan's works teem with marvelous and exotic narrations and are charged with a palpably enthusiastic conviction that the vast expanse of human social history was decipherable, classifiable, and subject to the laws of development. Yet the methodology and data of these early investigators of the science of culture are, of course, neither empirical nor unbiased, and, as cultural historians in the last twenty years have demonstrated,[6] the politics of gender and race of the Victorian anthropological enterprise reflected and, in turn, authorized imperialist expansion and paternalistic domestic policies.

Central to both McLennan's and Lubbock's theories of tribal organization and prohibition and the evolutionary stages of sexual organization (the specific details of which lie beyond the scope of this essay) are two postulates about socio-sexual origins: marriage by force and descent through the female line exclusively. Both men recognized the discomforting implications of a history of sexual relations that traces the origins of the institution of matrimony to brutal violence against women, and the origins of the patriarchal family to matrilineal descent, but the overarching progressivist framework of evolutionary anthropology mitigated the unsavoriness of these origins. At the same time, however, that very evolutionary continuum links civilized marriage ceremonies to primitive wife-capture, whose vestiges, or "survivals," are perceptible in contemporary marriage ceremonies. McLennan drew the connection between *de facto* wife-capture, a phase of society that "existed,

at some time or another, almost everywhere'' (xvi), and the symbolic
"forms'' of feigned ceremonies of wife-capture, whose origins in actual
primitive acts of force are "disguised under a variety of symbolical forms in
the higher layers of civilization'' (4). Although the spatial-geological metaphor of "higher-layers'' (the standard evolutionary trope) moderates the connection between *de facto* and symbolic marriage by force, *Primitive Marriage*
does draw back the layers of civilized marriage ceremonies to reveal their
primitive origins. Writing after *Primitive Marriage* was published, Lubbock
anticipated and acknowledged resistance to anthropology's construction of
the civilized ceremonies as symbolic recapitulation of the primitive. "It requires strong evidence . . . to satisfy us that the origin of marriage is independent of all sacred and social considerations; that it had nothing to do with
mutual affection or consent . . . and that it is to be symbolised . . . by brutal
violence and unwilling submission,'' but "the evidence is overwhelming''
(73). Again, the "mere symbols'' of force are construed as purely figurative
vestiges of brutality, without a literal referent in civilized society. The narratives of primitive behavior that serve as the evidence upon which McLennan's
and Lubbock's anthropological theories are based contain graphic descriptions
of actual, literal violence against women, and these descriptions of the brutal
rituals of primitive marriage implicitly emphasize the great advantages enjoyed by civilized woman in the marital arena. This contrast is illustrated
by Lubbock's description and accompanying drawing (see figure 1)[7] of an
Australian aboriginal marriage ritual: "The poor wretch is stolen upon in the
absence of her protectors. Being first stupefied with blows, inflicted with
clubs or wooden swords, on the head, back, and shoulders . . . [she is]
dragged through the woods by one arm. . . . The lover, or rather the ravisher,
is regardless of the stones or broken pieces of trees which may lie in his
route . . . when a scene ensues too shocking to relate'' (74). The accompanying illustration similarly stops short at the narrative scene "too shocking
to relate'' but effectively suggests the marriage ceremony's culmination in
rape and battery by picturing grotesquely leering aboriginal males tearing at
the arms and head of a wincing but physically passive woman.

While the anthropologists' constructions of primitive marriage by force
pictured civilized women as highly empowered relative to abjectly powerless
primitive women, McLennan's and Lubbock's investigations into primitive
marriage confronted a recurrent condition — the "curious practice'' of matrilineal descent — that raised the possibility of an earlier stage of female
supremacy and empowerment no longer accorded to women in the higher
levels of culture. Neither McLennan nor Lubbock entertained the possibility
of descent through the female as indicative of female social power. McLennan
built a theory that the original period of communal coupling (in which no

AUSTRALIAN ABORIGINAL MARRIAGE CEREMONY

Figure 1. "Australian Aboriginal Marriage Ceremony," from Sir John Lubbock's *The Origin of Civilisation and the Primitive Condition of Man: Mental and Social Condition of Savages* (New York: D. Appleton, 1870).

family ties were recognized) was followed by a stage of polyandry (wife-sharing), during which descent was reckoned through the female line because the paternity of any child was uncertain. Lubbock, who is far from precise or systematic in his thinking about inheritance through females, identifies the "milk-tie" between mother and child as one of the causes that tended "to strengthen the ties between parent and offspring" during the stage of communal marriage (he regarded polyandry as exceptional, not universal), in which the child "was regarded as related to the tribe, but not specially to any particular father or mother" (104). This recognition of the "milk-tie," however, is not accompanied by a recognition of any political rights of the woman. Thus, in the progress of social development toward monogamy and patriarchal descent, matrilineal descent is founded upon a condition in which women exist as shared sexual property. Again, civilized woman is shown to reap the benefits of patriarchy.

In 1861, the Swiss jurist, J. J. Bachofen had proposed a matriarchal theory, in *Das Mutterrecht (Mother-Right)*, a compendious survey of myth and religion, which held that an Amazonian revolt against "Haeterism" (the earliest stage in which no marriage ties are recognized, a stage McLennan and Lubbock do accept as antecedent to wife-capture and descent through females) led to a period of gynocracy, during which women were invested with political and religious powers. McLennan had not read Bachofen when he published *Primitive Marriage* in 1865, but in a later reprint of *Primitive Marriage* (in *Studies in Ancient History*, 1886), he appends a brief discussion of Bachofen. Lubbock does refer to Bachofen in *Origin of Civilisation*.

Both men reject Bachofen's theory. It is crucial to point out here that Bachofen's gynocracy, a "universal phenomenon," was not represented as an Amazonian Paradise Lost, a concept with some prestige among late nineteenth-century feminists as well as twentieth-century feminists and mythologists.[8] Rather, the movement from matriarchy to the "higher levels of culture" of patriarchy is understood as a progressive triumph of the spiritual over the material: "the triumph of paternity brings with it the liberation of the spirit from the manifestations of nature, a sublimation of human existence over the laws of material life. . . . Triumphant paternity partakes of the heavenly light, while childbearing motherhood is bound up with the earth that bears all things" (Bachofen 70, 109–10). His fundamental identification of the female with nature and materiality reproduces the Western classical heritage, and his larger progressivist developmental frame is ultimately consistent with that of the social evolutionists. However, Bachofen does repeatedly exalt gynocracy and thereby betrays an ambivalent spiritual nostalgia for the ascendancy of the female principle.[9] Furthermore, his matriarchal theory draws upon assumptions about mythology's historical authority and about women's capacities for power that radically oppose those of the British anthropologists.

McLennan and Lubbock rejected Bachofen's matriarchal theory on the basis of his euhemeristic methodology, which assumes that "the mythical tradition may be taken as a faithful reflection of the life of those times in which historical antiquity is rooted" (Bachofen 73). We should expect the Victorian anthropologists to take issue with Bachofen's euhemerism (even twentieth-century theories of matriarchy must depend upon myth as the central source, since no historical evidence exists to support the prior existence of matriarchy). However, their refutations also reflect Victorian culture's tightly held, and increasingly scientifically-sanctioned, convictions about innate gender difference and the universal, original physical and intellectual inferiority of women. In *Studies in Ancient History*, McLennan observes that Bachofen "saw *the fact* that kinship was anciently traced through women only, but not why it was the fact; . . . surely it is a pure dream of the imagination that they effected this by force of arms" and were "victorious in a war with men" (323-24). Similarly, Lubbock states flatly that "we do not find in history, as a matter of fact, that women do assert their rights, and savage women would, I think, be peculiarly unlikely to uphold their dignity in the manner supposed. On the contrary . . . it seems to me perfectly clear that the idea of marriage is founded on the rights, not of the woman, but of the man" (68). From this "scientific" vantage point, the power of women inscribed in mythological literature, a record of human consciousness, is not admissible into the historical record, and Bachofen's reading of the gynocratic past is derided as a "pure dream of the imagination," a phrase that might, in a non-scientific context, signify an exalted, intuitive apprehension of some truth of human existence. Their differing methodologies and epistemologies led the Victorian anthropologists and mythographers to opposing theories of the history of women's status, an opposition that we find articulated in the New Woman literature of late-nineteenth century and trippingly set forth by Andrew Lang in his "Double Ballade of Primitive Man" (quoted above), which pictures primitive woman as either "curb[ed] with occasional blows" or invested with the power of "a queen."

Although no simple generalizations encompass the breadth and diversity of the Victorians' understandings of mythology,[10] their literary appropriations of the mythic past were complicated by the physical and social sciences' reconstructions of "primitive culture." The Victorians' ability to value primitive mythopoesis as higher truth and to invest the ancient classics with the literary and heroic values of humanistic high culture was sorely compromised by anthropology's detailed portrait of primitive man.[11] At just such a point in time, when "ancient" connotatively shades off into "primitive" and "savage," new interpretative possibilities accrue to mythological allusion and its implicit analogy between present and ancient past. And it is at this historical moment that *The Egoist* superimposes the terms of anthropological discourse onto mythological allusions in order to display to the reader an analogical "inward mirror" of civilized man that is a palimpsest on which the earlier tracings of the primitive become visible in the "love season" of courtship and betrothal.

> The idea of compulsion — which is virtually the *raison d'etre* of marriage, in its legal aspect — is in itself an offence against morality. . . . It is the savage in the civilised man who scares us from attempting to honour the relation of man to woman as we believe, in our hearts, it ought to be honoured. . . . It is inconceivable that a people can go on progressing while they continue to cripple half their numbers . . . It is not beyond human power, though it may, in its first steps be terribly difficult, to destroy the survival of the old purchase-system that now desecrates the relations of the sexes.
> Mona Caird, "The Phases of Human Development, II" (1894)

THE MYTHOLOGICAL ALLUSIONS IN *The Egoist* work toward two different but related ends: they emphasize the violence of male dominance of women with images of female powerlessness, and they suggest a natural equality of the sexes with images of female power.[12] References to various mythological narratives, to isolated mythological figures, and to related images and symbols establish correspondences to characters and events at Patterne Hall that are multiple and overlapping, intersecting and divergent. Graeco-Roman myths are engraved onto an Oriental surface, the Blue Willow pattern of china, whose legend *The Egoist* reproduces.[13] The pattern's pictorial images (peach tree, birds, the enclosed estate) are refashioned into the symbolism of the novel, even merged with symbols (flowers, birds, trees) and references derived from classical mythology. Furthermore, the novel's references to "primitive" and "civilized" rituals of sexual relations dramatize the recurrent struggle for sexual power and the egoism of male dominance. The threads of various mythic and ethnological pasts are woven into a satire of Victorian marriage whose origins in the primitive and violent customs of wife-capture remain quite discernible beneath the veneer of civilized marriage.

Mona Caird's essay on human development (quoted above) illustrates how late Victorian feminism appropriated evolutionary discourse to argue for the moral imperative of the rights of women. Framing the issue of women's rights in social evolutionary terms, *The Egoist* in fact dramatizes opposing evolutionary perspectives. Sir Willoughby possesses an egoistic, ethnocentric evolutionary self-confidence that nature has "selected" him from "the pack": "A deeper student of Science than his rivals, he appreciated Nature's compliment in the fair one's choice of you" (71; ch. 5). He threatens to render "extinct" (128; ch. 10) those who "offend" him. His evolutionary self-regard collides with the narrator's depictions of the primitive instincts run rampant in men like Willoughby. "The Double-Blossom Wild Cherry Tree" chapter fuses the discourse of social anthropology with mythology and radically reverses contemporary theories of man's social evolution: civilized man is represented as displaying deeply primitive appetites and instincts, and civilized woman's inferiority and ignorance are understood as conditioned responses that mask her natural, primitive strength:

> The love season is the carnival of egoism, and it brings the touchstone to our natures. . . . Applied to Sir Willoughby, as to thousands of civilized males, the touchstone found him requiring to be dealt with by his betrothed as an original savage. She was required to play incessantly on the first reclaiming chord which led our ancestral satyr to the measures of the dance, the threading of the maze, and the setting conformably to his partner before it was accorded to him to spin her with both hands and a chirrup of his frisky heels. (150-51; ch. 11)

Man's behavior in love and courtship is construed as the "touchstone" that reveals that "thousands of civilized males" are in fact the "original savage." By 1879 social evolutionary theory had hardened the common semantic polarization of the terms "civilized" and "savage." This passage, however, collapses that polarization of "savage" and "civilized" at the very point upon which Lubbock had conclusively confirmed the "great advantages of civilisation": "relationship and marriage." The phrase, "our ancestral satyr," links mythology and evolution; "ancestral" invokes not only family pedigree but also the lineage of the race; and "satyr" holds up the legendary lascivious goat-man as our mythological evolutionary forebear. Furthermore, embedded in this multi-layered passage are allusions to Pan and Syrinx, and Ariadne and Theseus, both of which are tales about women who serve as the enabling agents for men to achieve power, and who become the victims of that male power. Syrinx escapes the rapacious pursuit by Pan, the goat-man, by being metamorphosed into a reed, which Pan in turn cuts and fashions into the pipes on which he plays his heavenly music. Syrinx's escape, like that of other metamorphosed women in myth (Daphne and Philomela, for example), is highly equivocal. Similarly, Ariadne "threaded the maze" for Theseus' escape from the labyrinth, but Theseus abandoned her after their marriage.

Male sexual possessiveness and mastery dissolve the boundary between savage and gentleman and past and present. The erotic appetite for female purity that turns women into objects for consumption[14] impels both ancient and contemporary man:

> [women] perceive, too, and it may be gratefully, that they address their performances less to the taming of the green and prankish monsieur of the forest than

to the pacification of a voracious aesthetic gluttony, craving them insatiably,
through all the tenses, with shrieks of the lamentable letter "I" for their purity.
Whether they see that it has its foundation in the sensual, and distinguish the
ultra-refined but lineally great-grandson of the Hoof in this vast and dainty
exacting appetite is uncertain. (151; ch. 11)

Again, anthropological postulates joined with mythological allusion yield a
revisionist evolutionary theory about the profoundly primitive nature of "ultra-refined" civilized man. "Green and prankish monsieur of the forest"
figures civilized man as a satyr in a smoking jacket. The "ultra-refined"
gentleman for whom women perform is not merely the "lineally great-grandson of the Hoof," he *is* the Hoof (which adds new shades of meaning to Mrs.
Mountstuart's epigram on Willoughby's coming of age, "You see he has a
leg" [43; ch. 2]). "The Egoist," the narrator later observes, "is our fountain-
head, primeval man: the primitive is born again, the elemental reconstituted.
Born again, into new conditions, the primitive may be highly polished of
men, and forfeit nothing save the roughness of his original nature. He is not
only his own father, he is ours; and he is also our son. We have produced
him, he us. Such were we, to such are we returning" (466; ch. 39). In the
metaphysics of consubstantiality, "The Egoist is the Son of Himself. He is
likewise the Father. And the son loves the father, the father the son" (465;
ch. 39). Egoists beget egoists, and the reproduction of egoism arrests the
past, present, and future into a condition of stasis. The tribesman, the satyr,
and the mythic gods and heroes with whom Willoughby is allusively associated throughout the narrative dissolve into the single greatest impediment to
the real progress of civilization — The Egoist. Thus the "dainty exacting
appetite" of contemporary man is the same one that sent Pan in pursuit of
Syrinx and primitive man to neighboring tribes to acquire a wife by, in
Lubbock's phrasing, "brutal violence and unwilling submission" (73).

Further, the novel claims for women an ancient strength and natural
equality that have degenerated into ornamental weakness through a process
of unnatural selection and modification. Logically, this claim creates an evolutionary contradiction: if primitive man dominated and subjugated primitive
woman, how does one account for her natural power and equality. This
fundamental contradiction confronted every nineteenth-century writer who
constructed an argument for equal rights for women in the present by drawing
upon the evidence of the historical past and who consulted both the mythological record of human consciousness, in which ancient woman's power is
frequently valorized, and the ethnological record, in which ancient woman's
abjection is universal. This paradox of ancient women, registered in Margaret
Fuller's *Woman in the Nineteenth Century* (1845), Mill's *The Subjection of
Women*, and the New Woman writing of the 1890s, lies at the heart of *The*

Egoist's attempts to forge a future for Clara Middleton, and for women in the nineteenth century. The novel glances back to an imagined earlier time when women were invested with individual and communal strength, a condition more fully elaborated in the mythological allusion and subtext of Meredith's later *Diana of the Crossways* (serially 1884; 1885). When Crossjay teases Clara that "you can't make soldiers or sailors of [girls]," she retorts with a recitation of women warriors that culminates with the mythic Amazons: "Have you never read of Mary Ambree? and Mistress Hannah Snell of Pondicherry? And there was the bride of the celebrated William Taylor. And what do you say to Joan of Arc? What do you say to Boadicea? I suppose you have never heard of the Amazons" (105; ch. 8). Donning the weakling's mask of blushing purity does not translate mortal woman to the celestial regions of the Angel in the House but rather drags her "ages back" to primitive degradation:

> [women have] suffered themselves to be dragged ages back . . . when it should have been their task to set the soul above the fairest fortune and the gift of strength in women beyond ornamental whiteness. Are they not of nature warriors, like men? — men's mates to bear them heroes instead of puppets? But the devouring male Egoist prefers them as inanimate overwrought polished pure-metal precious vessels, fresh from the hands of the artificer, for him to walk away with hugging, call all his own, drink of, and fill and drink of, and forget that he stole them. (152; ch. 11)

The proposition that women's natures are, like men's, strong and warrior-like, reverses the dominant perception of innate gender difference. Furthermore, it grants and values a natural strength that civilization has modified into an ornamental and artificial femininity.

The phrase, "inanimate overwrought polished pure-metal precious vessels," succinctly expresses what we now refer to as the objectification of women produced by the male gaze, and throughout the novel inscriptions of femininity attach themselves, by way of analogy, to Clara Middleton. Clara's arrival at Patterne Hall initiates an unofficial competition for the best description of her beauty, and the artificial objects to which she is compared express both the ornamental constructions of femininity and the post-evolutionary fear and disesteem of "the natural." Clara is likened to the "ladies of the Court of China, on rice-paper," whose images were made available for framing with the continued expansion of trade with China in the nineteenth century. Alternatively, she becomes one of the "bewitching silken shepherdesses who live though they never were," an elegant Dresden pastoral figurine, in vogue from the mid-eighteenth century. "The women of Leonardo, the angels of Luini" provide another fair analogy. One unnamed gauche individual "mentioned an antique statue of a figure breathing into a flute . . . but this comparison was repelled as grotesque" (76; ch. 5), a sly reference, I venture, to the goat-man Pan, typically represented playing the flute. However, the wise Mrs. Mountstuart Jenkinson, "our mother Nature" (42; ch. 2) renowned for her epigrams, coins the lasting phrase, "a dainty rogue in porcelain" (75, ch. 5) that Willoughby so loathes, for it contradicts "his original conclusion that [Clara] was essentially feminine, in other words, a parasite and a chalice." (78; ch. 5). Willoughby's interrogation of Mrs. Mountstuart leaves him unilluminated, but it reveals with clarity the civilized aversion to the natural in women:

> "Brittle would you say?"
> "I am quite unable to say."
> "An innocent naughtiness?"
> "Prettily moulded in a delicate substance."
> "You are thinking of some piece of Dresden you suppose her to resemble?"
> "I dare say."
> "Artificial?"
> "You would not have her *natural*?" (78–79; ch. 5, my emphasis)

"Our Mother Nature" comprehends well enough why the civilized egoist would not have his fiancee natural.

The Victorian anthropological association of the natural with the primitive and instinctive increased the worth of the artificial and the cultivated. The double-blossom cherry tree, a product of the horticultural art of modification, symbolizes that valuation of a produced, feminine ornamentality (or what Mill, in a rare metaphor, identified as the "hot-house and stove cultivation [that] has always been carried on of some of the capabilities of [women's] nature" (22). Like the tree's double-blossoms, the "ornamental whiteness" of Clara's objectified purity is shown to have originated in a natural whiteness — a mythic virginity that denotes the power of an inviolate, self-determined womanhood. Ironically, when Clara acts with the greatest self-determination, she appears most seductive to men: Clara is repulsed by the idea of kissing Willoughby, but the egoist reads her evasion of his kiss as a sign of her "purely, coldly, statue-like, Dian-like" (95; ch. 7) modesty, forgetting the vengeance Diana exacted upon Acteon for his violating gaze. Horace De Craye muses that "no person so seductive as Clara Middleton had he ever met. Her cry of loathing, 'Marriage!' coming from a girl, rang faintly clear of an ancient virginal aspiration of the sex to escape from their coil, and bespoke a pure, cold, savage pride that transplanted his thirst for her to higher fields" (274; ch. 22). Clara's ancient virginal aspirations, which constitute a kind of gendered collective unconscious, are stirred powerfully by her epiphanic identification with the double-blossom wild cherry tree.

Like the lovers pictured in the Blue Willow pattern, Clara and Vernon meet under a blossoming tree, the symbol in which converge the myths of the Blue Willow pattern, the narcissus flower, the Golden Bough, and the worship of the vestal Diana at Nemi. Dr. Middleton, a classicist, explains the horticultural evolution of the tree:

> "It is a gardener's improvement on the Vestal of the forest, the wild cherry," said Dr. Middleton, "and in this case we may admit the gardener's claim to be valid, though I believe that, with his gift of double-blossom, he has improved away the fruit. Call this the Vestal of civilization, then. . . . "
> "It is Vernon's Holy Tree the young rascal has been despoiling," said Sir Willoughby merrily.
> Miss Middleton was informed that this double-blossom wild cherry-tree was worshiped by Mr. Whitford. (114; ch. 9)

Like the phrase, "green monsieur of the forest," "the Vestal of civilization" yokes myth to social evolution to create an oxymoron that in this case encapsulates the contradiction of Victorian womanhood. The forcible, unnatural acts of grafting and pruning produce an "improved" tree that is, like Victorian woman, of greater ornamental value but, ironically, sterile. The "Vestal of the forest" alludes specifically to the mythic worship of Diana at the sacred grove at Nemi and the king of the wood who plucks the Golden Bough to succeed as priest (here humorously Crossjay, who has plucked cherry blossoms for Clara's bouquet) and generally to the primitive fetishistic and totemic worship of trees, a subject that McLennan and Tylor, among others, treated in the 1860s and 1870s.

The ancient, ritualized worship of virginity in secret forest groves locates Sir Willoughby's demand for "purity infinite" in the matrix of the past, but a natural, heroic, mythic virginity, like Diana's, suggests an ancient history of powerful and communal womanhood. The ancient virginal aspirations kindle in Clara as she gazes into the blinding light of the pure whiteness of the "virginal blossom" of the cherry tree, a vision forever lost when she recalls the image of Vernon under the tree and feels the stirrings of desire:

> She turned her face to where the load of virginal blossom, whiter than summer-cloud on the sky, showered and drooped and clustered so thick as to claim colour and seem, like higher Alpine snows in noon-sunlight, a flush of white. From deep to deeper heavens of white, her eyes perched and soared. Wonder lived in her. Happiness in the beauty of the tree pressed to supplant it, and was more mortal and narrower. Reflection came, contracting her vision and weighing her to earth. Her reflection was: "He must be good who loves to lie and sleep beneath the branches of this tree!" She would rather have clung to her first impression: wonder so divine, so unbounded, was like soaring into homes of angel-crowded space, sweeping through folded and on to folded white fountain-bow of wings, in innumerable wings, in innumerable columns; but the thought of it was no recovery of it; she might as well have striven to be a child. (154–55; ch. 11)

This whiteness speaks not of an absence of sexual stain, or of ignorant weakness, but of an uncorrupted essence. The ancient virginal aspirations for the integrity of the purest, blinding white are compromised by real men and sexual longing: by novel's end, Clara will metamorphose into Vernon's "Mountain Echo." She does not evolve into a New Woman (nor does Diana Warwich, in *Diana of the Crossways*), a creation beyond the limits of Meredith's advocacy of the cause of women,[15] although even the New Woman novelists of the 1890s were hard pressed to imagine a fully independent female character plausibly consistent with contingent social and political realities.

Clara does not evolve into something "new," but she does develop, altered by her vision of the virginal blossoms. Like so many nineteenth-century women whose access to education and learning provided them with a larger historical and evolutionary framework in which to view their personal plight, Clara comes to apprehend her private drama of entrapment and humiliation as a reenactment of the history of women. When Willoughby urges Clara to wear the Patterne pearls for a dinner party, she replies, "Forgive me, I cannot. And, Willoughby . . . does one not look like a victim decked for the sacrifice? — the garlanded heifer you see on Greek vases, in that array of jewellery?" (139; ch. 10). The association of marriage and death is the legacy of both primitive marriage by force and classical literature, and the novel contains a number of allusions to mythological seductions, abductions, and marriages (Psyche and Cupid, Apollo and Daphne, among others), too many to treat in detail here. However, the allusions to the myth of Demeter, Persephone, and Hades will serve to illustrate the ways in which mythological allusion in the novel not only recapitulates the ritual of primitive wife-capture, revealing the recurrent rapacious egoism of civilized man, but also communicates the powerful agency of the ancient female community, and thus embodies the paradox of ancient woman.

The mythological source features Hades' abduction of Persephone to the underworld and Demeter's maternal grief that wins the annual probation for her daughter. It records the dualism of woman as defenseless sexual object and creative maternal agent. When Clara begins to feel deep discontentment with Willoughby, she imagines a lifetime of marriage with him in terms that recall this mythological marriage by force. Contemplating the brief pre-nuptial vacation her father has reluctantly promised her, Clara thinks:

> To be fixed at the mouth of a mine, and to have to descend it daily, and not to discover great opulence below; on the contrary, to be chilled in subterranean sunlessness, without any substantial quality that she could grasp, only the mystery of the inefficient tallow-light in those caverns of the complacent talking-man: this appeared to her too extreme a probation for two or three weeks. How a life-time of it! (92; ch. 7)

Later, when urging Laetitia to accept Willoughby's proposal, Clara asks her to forget the day that she, Clara, opened Laetitia's eyes to Willoughby's egoism, and she again associates herself with Persephone: "Help me to forget it — that day, and those days, and all those days! I should be glad to think I passed a time beneath the earth, and have risen again" (579; ch. 48) (it is more than a little disturbing that she is sending Laetitia down into that inferno in her own place).[16] Throughout the novel, Clara contemplates her wedding day as the "the day of bells" (96; ch. 7), a funereal synecdoche[17] that Willoughby unwittingly reinforces with his arrogant assertion that "Most marriages ought to be celebrated with the funeral knell!" "I think so," Clara sadly agrees (190; ch. 15).

Taken as a body of literature, mythological narrative encodes a number of polarizations of female nature and power, and Dr. Middleton, the classical scholar and patriarch, functions as the learned authority on "all the contradictions and mutabilities ascribed to women from the beginning" (517; ch. 43). After Dr. Middleton grants the holiday probation, Willoughby circumvents Clara's escape by seducing Dr. Middleton to stay at Patterne Hall with the aged Patterne Port, a transaction negotiated in the wine cellar, the "cool vaulted cellar, and the central square block, or enceinte, where the thick darkness was not penetrated by the intruding lamp, but rather took it as an eye" (240; ch. 20). Clara's purity, or the absence of the stain of sexuality, is the commodity that gains Dr. Middleton access to the vinous treasure: " 'Mulier tum bene olet', you know. Most fragrant she that smells of naught," boasts Dr. Middleton, voicing the paradox of male desire. An unscented rose, Clara is prized because "she has no history. You are the first heading of the chapter" (244; ch. 20). Yet Dr. Middleton's capacity for venal paternal betrayal is not rooted in conscious malignity but rather in decades of professional study of the classics in which woman is construed as capricious and enigmatic. When Clara confronts her father with her desire to break the engagement to Willoughby, he spits out epithets in an effort to name the enigma and shame her into consistency. She is as "mad as Cassandra" (516; ch. 43), a "barbarian woman upon the evolutions of a serpent" (517; ch. 43), "a fantastical planguncula enlivened by the wanton tempers of a nursery chit" (518; ch. 43), and the "epitome . . . of all the contradictions and mutabilities ascribed to women from the beginning" (517; ch. 43). His paternal devotion to his daughter is compounded in ambivalence: "He loved his daughter and he feared her" (237; ch. 20). Clara Middleton is a young woman in dire need of a mother.

Ultimately, Clara is rescued, not by a competing suitor or a knightly hero but by a community of older women in the novel. However one reads Clara's ultimate marriage to Vernon Whitford, in this narrative of attempted wife-capture, the bride-to-be is saved from a forced marriage by the agency

of women. The oracular "witches" (52; ch. 3 and 456; ch. 37), Mrs. Mountstuart Jenkinson, the Ladies Busshe and Culmer, and the interchangeable
Aunts Eleanor and Isabel, variously predict, orchestrate, and preside over the
events at Patterne Hall. Their machinations, deliberate and otherwise, enable
Clara to escape marriage to Sir Willoughby. The Demetrian "mother Nature"
(42; ch. 2), Mrs. Mountstuart Jenkinson, rewards Clara's honesty about loving an unidentified someone else by stalling Willoughby for time and publiciz-
ing his clandestine proposal to Laetitia. Willoughby's Aunts Eleanor and
Isabel, "his shadows, his echoes" (112; ch. 8), unwittingly aid and abet
Clara in her escape from their nephew by embroidering a silken coverlet,
which conceals the sleeping Crossjay, who overhears Willoughby's proposal
to Laetitia, and thus provides Clara with "the loophole" (254; ch. 21) to slip
out of the engagement. "Meltingly feminine" (471; ch. 39), the aunts' coverlet is "sleek and warm, soft as hands of ladies, and redolent of them" (472;
ch. 40). Its assertion of a fragrant and intricately patterned femininity liberates
the captured Clara. Earlier in the novel, the narrator has noted that when
women behave like good "parasite[s]," they "one day gain for them[selves]
an inweaving and figurement — in the place of bees, ermine tufts, and
their various present decorations — upon the august great robes" of men
(176–77; ch. 14). The maiden aunts' silken coverlet empowers and releases
the unscented, inwoven woman — the "victim decked for the sacrifice" — from the urns, from the pages of mythology and anthropology,
and from the Blue Willow plate, where she has been trapped in the elaborate
pattern, frozen in the posture of pursuit.

> Here's a pot with a cot in a park,
> In a park where the peach-blossoms blew,
> Where the lovers eloped in the dark,
> Lived, died, and were changed into two
> Bright birds that eternally flew
> Through the boughs of the may, as they sang:
> 'Tis a tale was undoubtedly true
> In the reign of the Emperor Hwang
> Andrew Lang, "Ballade of Blue China" (1880)

THE MATERIAL OBJECT THAT MOST fully embodies the richness of the novel's
allusive mode and the substance of its ideological critique of civilized culture
is the Blue Willow pattern china. Beginning in the 1860s the Chinese Blue
Willow pattern of china, domestically produced by Staffordshire since the
late eighteenth century, gained a popularity with the Victorian middle classes
who could not afford the more expensive tastes of the collectors' "cult for
blue and white china" (Hillier 211), a cult whose members included Meredith's friends and literary acquaintances, like D. G. Rossetti, John Everett

Millais, Oscar Wilde, and Andrew Lang (Hillier 211–13, 290–91), whose "Ballade of Blue China" appeared with the "Double Ballade of Primitive Man" in his 1880 volume, *XXXII Ballades in Blue China*. The domestication of the Oriental and Eastern exotic in Victorian interior design and decoration during the rise of the Empire exemplifies what George Stocking, in a discussion of nineteenth-century anthropological museums, calls "the aestheticization" of "the material culture of non-Western peoples" (*Objects* 6). Whether in public galleries, like the British Museum, or in private homes, like Horace Walpole's "China Room" at Strawberry Hill and Lady Patterne's "India room" at Patterne Hall, the display of foreign objects made available by colonial expansion and acquisition manifests the ideology of Empire, founded upon assumptions of racial supremacy and entitlement — or, in the novel's terms, the egoism of gender, class, and race. The novel alludes to the Blue Willow pattern with Sir Willoughby Patterne's name, of course, as well as with a number of related images and symbols, and with a plot that virtually recapitulates the legend depicted in the Blue Willow pattern (see note 12 and figure 2), a legend that had worked its way into the popular culture of the 1870s, its appeal apparently as strong as in "the reign of the Emperor Hwang."

The Blue Willow pattern draws together the ethnological and mythological references to marriage by force, and in these allusions converge the politics of gender, race, and class of British civilized society. Sexual, racial, and class domination spring from the same source — primitive egoism — which is fully manifested in the man Clara Middleton orientally figures as an "obelisk lettered all over with hieroglyphics" (138; ch. 10). Throughout *The Egoist*, Sir Willoughby Patterne voices ethnocentric, classist positions on the subjects of British class structure and national stature. The Egoist who admits, "I own it, I do like the idea of living patriarchally" (143; ch. 11), explains to Clara that "Feudalism is not an objectionable thing if you can be sure of the lord" (123; ch. 9). During his grand tour with Vernon after being jilted by Constantia Durham, the ethnocentric Willoughby holds "an English review of his Maker's grotesques" in "America, Japan, China, Australia, nay, the continent of Europe" (58; ch. 4).

The mythological and social evolutionary allusions of *The Egoist* collapse its civilized present and future into the primitive and mythological pasts, and they expose the primitive egoism that survives in powerful ways in the drawing rooms and wine cellars of polite Victorian society. *The Egoist*'s evolutionary looking glass held up to Willoughby Patterne — the Everyman of Egoists — reflects back the visages of aboriginal wife-captors and wealthy mandarin suitors. The prognosis for humanity is not entirely grim, however. The novel's subtitle, "A Comedy in Narrative," promises a hopeful ending.[18] And as things turn out, nature has not selected Willoughby after

Figure 2. "The Blue Willow Pattern."

all: Laetitia Dale's faded health dims the prospect of Patterne heirs and increases the probability of the extinction of the line. The furies of the Comic Spirit, "our squatting imps in circle[,] grow restless on their haunches, as they bend eyes instantly, ears at full cock, for the commencement of the comic drama of the suicide" (37–38; Prelude). With its ironies etched in mythological and anthropological allusions, *The Egoist* optimistically predicts the inevitable extinction of the man of whom it is said: "He was highly civilized" (81; ch. 6).

Franklin & Marshall College

NOTES

I am most grateful to Franklin & Marshall College for a 1990–91 Faculty Research Grant that facilitated my revisions of this essay, especially by providing me with a research assistant, Elizabeth Lirio, whose hard work and good nature deserve mention. I would also like to thank George Levine for his invaluable responses to several drafts of this essay.

1. George W. Stocking Jr.'s *Victorian Anthropology* provides the single most valuable cultural-historical account of the developments of Victorian anthropology.

Especially relevant here are chapters 2–5. An earlier standard volume, Robert H. Lowie's *The History of Ethnological Theory,* remains useful. See also Burrow, Carneiro, and note 5, below.

2. My analysis of Meredith's allusive agenda, which might be identified as his "feminist" agenda (or, to be more historically accurate, an agenda in advocacy of the cause of women, as it was framed in Victorian period), coincides with Sandra Gilbert and Susan Gubar's analyses of the "submerged meanings" (72) buried in the mythological, Biblical, and literary appropriations of nineteenth-century women's writing that constitutes a radical revision of patriarchy's mythic "twin images of angel and monster" (44). Arguing from a somewhat different perspective, Nina Auerbach celebrates the animating and protean power of just such mythologies, which she perceives as "endowments," not oppressions (*Woman and the Demon*). Although I read Meredith's uses of mythology as a response to the palpable and powerful oppressiveness of the male classical ethos and patriarchal mythological constructions of an unnatural femininity, I nonetheless find Auerbach's analysis stimulating and wide-ranging.

3. The definitive discussion of evolution and *The Egoist* is Carolyn Williams's essay. Williams details how the plot "unravels the intimate principles of sexual selection, but Meredith's chief concern is to lay bare the spiritual forces inherent in this natural process. Willoughby's physical form, for example, belies his spiritual decay . . . whereas the seemingly old-fashioned scholar, Vernon Whitford, turns out to be 'a new kind of thing . . . produced in England of late' " (55). Although my focus on social evolutionary theory, mythology, and "the primitive" leads to a different reading of the novel, our readings are, nonetheless, complementary, and I am indebted to Williams's exemplary work on Meredith.

4. J. S. Stone's, *George Meredith's Politics,* provides the most thorough discussion of this subject available.

5. Drawing upon John Morley's *Recollections,* Stone notes that "Morley records that he did get Meredith excited about Mill's book, *The Subjection of Women,* a copy of which he brought to him in 1869" (48).

6. A considerable amount of work has been, and continues to be, published on the ideology of nineteenth-century anthropology. The authors whose works have informed my understanding of the sexual and racial politics of Victorian anthropology and have bearing on my reading of *The Egoist* include the following: Fee, Coward, Owen, Rainger, Stocking, Lorimer, and Brantlinger.

7. This illustration is reprinted in Stocking's *Victorian Anthropology* at the beginning of chapter six, "Victorian Cultural Ideology and the Image of Savagery" (186).

8. A comprehensive survey of feminist literary Amazonianism and matriarchalism from the 1880s to the present would span from George Gissing to Monique Wittig. Nina Auerbach's *Communities of Women: An Idea in Fiction* remains the best discussion of nineteenth-century literary female communities. Gilbert and Gubar offer specific discussions of Amazons and mythic mothers interspersed throughout their considerations of a multitude of mythic figures in nineteenth–century women's writing.

In the twentieth century, the most widely known advocates of pristine matriarchy are Eric Fromm and Joseph Campbell. See also Briffault, Neumann, Diner, and Gimbutas.

9. In Jonathan Fishbane's highly illuminating discussion of problems of interpreting Bachofen (in which he traces the ways in which Bachofen evoked "such powerful feelings among so many intellectuals who often worked in profoundly different

intellectual and ideological traditions'' [90]), Fishbane also identifies the tone in which Bachofen writes about matriarchy as contributing to ''a noticeable ambivalence toward the very cultural models he constructed. For example, he considered patriarchy a higher cultural form than matriarchy. Yet, his portrait of matriarchy is suffused with an almost melancholy longing to return to it'' (91).

10. The range of the Victorians' responses to and appropriations of mythology is reflected in Jenkyns, Bullen, and Kestner.

11. Recent commentators have corrected earlier twentieth-century denigrations (like that of Richard Chase in *Quest for Myth,* 1949) of the impoverished rationalism of Victorian mythography by demonstrating its open-minded humanism, or its ambivalence and keen sense of imaginative and spiritual loss at the expense of the gains of science. In ''Victorian Mythography and the Progress of the Intellect,'' Janet Burstein discusses in detail the ambivalence embodied in Victorian studies of mythology. James Kissane also offers useful background on this subject.

12. Although mythological allusions have been discussed in passing as part of larger discussions of the novels, no extensive study of Meredith's fictional uses of mythology has been undertaken. In his unpublished dissertation, Harvey Kerpneck does discuss mythological allusion in the novels; however, his discussion of mythical symbolism is largely thematic and does not anticipate my own. In '' 'Clio in Calliope': History and Myth in Meredith's *Diana of the Crossways,''* Jane Marcus relates Meredith's uses of mythology to the feminist issues in Diana, but the actual discussion of the mythologies of Diana is quite brief.

In his chapter, ''The Bower and the World: *The Egoist,''* Michael Wheeler discusses allusions to Diana of the Wood, as well as Pope's ''Rape of the Lock,'' Carlyle, and the Willow Pattern. He concludes with a certain irritation that ''rather than clarifying parallels and associations, symbols and analogies, for the reader, most of the literary echoes I have discussed are playfully poetic or referentially oblique'' (114). The limitations of Wheeler's work with allusion are made fairly clear by his conclusion.

13. Robert D. Mayo has provided a useful summary of the Willow story and its thematic and formal parallels. Since I take familiarity with the tale for granted in the text of my discussion, I reprint Mayo's summary here.

. . . the rich and influential mandarin who inhabited the stately mansion depicted on the right in the design was a widower possessed of a lovely daughter named Koong-see. He intended to marry his daughter to a wealthy suitor of high degree, but the maiden opposed her parent's wish. She had chosen for her lover a poor and honorable man serving as her father's secretary and had exchanged vows with him in clandestine meetings under the blossoming trees of the Willow Pattern. Suspecting his daughter's defection, the mandarin imprisoned her in a pavilion in his garden, and commanded her to marry the husband of his choice when the peach tree should be in blossom. Here Koong-see pined for her freedom, and prayed that she might find release. Her chosen lover found means to communicate with her, invaded her prison, and carried her off, while her father feted the promised bridegroom in the banquet hall. The lovers were hotly pursued by the mandarin (in some versions by Ta-jin, the rejected suitor), but they escaped over the Willow bridge. After further adventures the gods turned them into birds in token of their fidelity. (73)

14. Willoughby's vampirism is a recurrent metaphor: for an example see p. 206. Pruning is another metaphor with social evolutionary implications associated with Willoughby's actions. See Chapter 1, "A Minor Incident Showing an Hereditary Aptitude in the Use of the Knife," in which Willoughby refuses to admit his "hero," the "stumpy" Lieutenant Crossjay — an action that reveals his hypocrisy to Constantia Durham (who "jilts" him) and causes his demise with Clara when Crossjay Jr. (acting as his father's unwitting avenging angel) overhears Willoughby's proposal to Laetitia. Chapter 1 ends with the "ring of imps" feverish with delight as "They perceived in [Willoughby] a fresh *development* and very subtle manifestation of the *very old thing* from which he had sprung" (41). I have emphasized words in this quotation to illustrate that the narration of the novel abounds with evolutionary references. The ones I discuss in the body of this essay represent but a few examples.

15. Discussions of Meredith and the New Woman typically focus on Diana Warwick. Others have also suggested, though for reasons different from my own, that it is a mistake to read Diana Warwick as Meredith's version of a "New Woman." Judith Wilt for example, argues that Meredith "never did write the novel of the new woman, though. One feels he sensed he hadn't perfected his own reading yet. Who has?" (62). Donald D. Stone, however, puts Diana in the company of late Victorian New Women.

16. Arguing against the grain of surely almost every reader's uneasiness with Laetitia's fate in the novel, Richard C. Stevenson insists that Laetitia's marriage to Willoughby is optimistic and "plausible," and that she serves as Meredith's "spokesman" for the Comic Spirit (407).

17. In an interesting discussion of Meredith's use of synecdoche Daniel Smirlock identifies an "ironic ambivalence" in the novel, in which synecdoche is both adequate and inadequate to the enterprise of representation (316).

18. To my mind the most impressive reading of the "problematic" happy ending (which sends Clara from the arms of one man to another) is Carolyn Williams's "Unbroken Patterns: Gender, Culture, and Voice in *The Egoist*" which demonstrates how "an inherent ambivalence lies at the heart of Meredith's attempted integration of progressive, feminist goals with comedy as a genre; or, in other words, the choice to cast his feminist program of education in the form of comedy forecloses from the beginning many of its progressive possibilities" (48).

WORKS CITED

Auerbach, Nina. *Communities of Women: An Idea in Fiction*. Cambridge, MA: Harvard UP, 1978.

———. *Woman and the Demon: The Life of a Victorian Myth*. Cambridge, MA: Harvard UP, 1982.

Bachofen, J. J. *Mother Right: An Investigation of the Religious and Juridical Character of Matriarchy in the Ancient World*. 1861. Trans. Ralph Manheim. *Myth, Religion, and Mother Right: Selected Writings of J. J. Bachofen*. Intro. James Campbell. Princeton: Princeton UP, 1967.

Brantlinger, Patrick. *Rule of Darkness: British Literature and Imperialism, 1830–1914*. Ithaca: Cornell UP, 1988.

Briffault, Robert. *The Mothers: A Study of the Origins of Sentiments and Institutions*. 3 vols. New York: Macmillan, 1927.

Bullen, J.B., ed. *The Sun Is God: Painting, Literature and Mythology in the Nineteenth Century*. Oxford: Clarendon P, 1989.

Burstein, Janet. "Victorian Mythography and the Progress of the Intellect." *Victorian Studies* 18 (1975):309–24.

Burrow, J.W. "Evolution and Anthropology in the 1860's: The Anthropological Society of London, 1863–71." *Victorian Studies* 7 (1963): 137–54.

Caird, Mona. "The Phases of Human Development, II." *Westminster Review* 141 (1894): 162–79.

Campbell, Joseph. *The Masks of Gods*. 4 vols. New York: Viking, 1959–68.

Carneiro, Robert. "Classical Evolution." *Main Currents in Cultural Anthropology*. Ed. Raoul and Freda Naroll. New York: Appleton-Century-Crofts, 1973. 57–118.

Chase, Richard. *Quest for Myth*. 1949. New York: Greenwoood, 1969.

Coward, Rosalind. *Patriarchal Precedents: Sexuality and Social Relations*. London: Routledge & Kegan Paul, 1983.

Diner, Helen. *Mothers and Amazons: The First Feminine History of Culture*. New York: Julian P, 1965.

Fee, Elizabeth. "The Sexual Politics of Victorian Anthropology." *Clio's Consciousness Raised: New Perspectives on the History of Women*. Ed. Mary S. Hartman and Lois Banner. New York: Harper & Row, 1974. 86–102.

Fishbane, Jonathan. "The Bachofen Literature: The Problem of Interpretation." *Annals of Scholarship* 3.2 (1984–1986): 77–101.

Fowler, Lois Josephs. "*Diana of the Crossways*: A Prophecy for Feminism." *In Honor of Austin Wright*. Pittsburgh: Carnegie Mellon UP, 1972. 30–36.

Fromm, Erich. *The Crisis of Psychoanalysis*. New York: Holt, Rinehart, and Winston, 1970.

Gilbert, Sandra M., and Susan Gubar. *The Madwoman in the Attic: The Woman Writer and the Nineteenth-Century Literary Imagination*. New Haven: Yale UP, 1979.

Gimbutas, Marija. *The Language of the Goddess: Unearthing the Hidden Symbols of Western Civilization*. New York: Harper & Row, 1989.

Hillier, Bevis. *Pottery and Porcelain: 1700–1914*. New York: Meredith P, 1968.

Jenkyns, Richard. *The Victorians and Ancient Greece*. Cambridge, MA: Harvard UP, 1980.

Kerpneck, Harvey. "Image, Symbol and Myth in the Novels of George Meredith." Diss. U of Toronto, 1966.

Kestner, Joseph A. *Mythology and Misogyny: The Social Discourse of Nineteenth-Century British Classical-Subject Painting*. Madison: U of Wisconsin P, 1989.

Kissane, James. "Victorian Mythology." *Victorian Studies* 6 (1962): 5–28.

Lang, Andrew. *XXXII Ballades in Blue China*. 1880. London: Kegan Paul, Trench, 1883.

Lorimer, Douglas. "Theoretical Racism in Late-Victorian Anthropology, 1870–1900." *Victorian Studies* 31 (1988): 405–30.

Lowie, Robert H. *The History of Ethnological Theory*. New York: Rinehart, 1937.

Lubbock, Sir John. *The Origin of Civilisation and the Primitive Condition of Man: Mental and Social Condition of Savages*. New York: D. Appleton, 1870.

Maine, Henry. *Ancient Law*. 1861. London: Dent, 1917.

Marcus, Jane. " 'Clio in Calliope': History and Myth in Meredith's *Diana of the Crossways*." *Bulletin of the New York Public Library* 79 (1975–76): 167–92.

Mayo, Robert D. "*The Egoist* and the Willow Pattern." *ELH* 9 (1942): 71–78.

McLennan, J.F. *Primitive Marriage: An Inquiry Into the Origin of the Form of Capture in Marriage Ceremonies*. 1865. *Studies in Ancient History*. London: Macmillan, 1886.

Meredith, George. *The Egoist*. 1879. New York: Penguin, 1968.

Mill, John Stuart. *The Subjection of Women*. 1869. Cambridge, MA: M.I.T. P, 1970.

Neumann, Erich. *The Great Mother: An Analysis of the Archetype*. New York: Pantheon, 1955.

Owen, Rger. "Anthropology and Imperial Administration: Sir Alfred Lyall and the Official Use of Theories of Social Change Developed in India after 1857." *Anthropology and the Colonial Encounter*. 1973. Ed. Talal Asad. London: Ithaca P, 1975. 223–43.

Rainger, Ronald. "Race, Politics, and Science: The Anthropological Society of London in the 1860s." *Victorian Studies* 22 (1978): 51–70.

Smirlock, Daniel. "Rough Truth: Synedoche and Interpretation in *The Egoist*." *Nineteenth-Century Fiction* 31 (1976): 313–28.

Stevenson, Richard C. "Laetitia Dale and the Comic Spirit in *The Egoist*." *Nineteenth-Century Fiction* 26 (1972): 406–18.

Stocking, George W., Jr., ed. *Objects and Others: Essays on Museums and Material Culture*. Madison: U of Wisconsin P, 1985.

———. *Victorian Anthropology*. New York: Free P., 1987.

Stone, Donald D. "Victorian Feminism and the Nineteenth Century Novel." *Women's Studies* 1 (1972): 65–91.

Stone, J.S. *George Meredith's Politics: As Seen in His Life, Friendships, and Works*. Ontario: P.D. Meany, 1986.

Torgovnick, Marianna. *Gone Primitive: Savage Intellects, Modern Lives*. Chicago: U of Chicago P, 1990.

Tylor, E.B. *Primitive Culture*. 1871. 2nd ed. Vol. I. New York: Henry Holt, 1889. 2 vols.

Wheeler, Michael. *The Art of Allusion in Victorian Fiction*. New York: Barnes and Noble, 1979.

Williams, Carolyn. "Natural Selection and Narrative Form in *The Egoist*." *Victorian Studies* 27 (1983): 53–79.

———. "Unbroken Patternes: Gender, Culture, and Voice in *The Egoist*." *Browning Institute Studies* 13 (1985): 45–70.

Wilt, Judith. "Meredith's Diana: Freedom, Fiction, and the Female." *Texas Studies in Literature and Language* 18 (1976): 42–62.

EVOLUTIONARY SCIENCE AND THE WOMAN QUESTION

By Alan P. Barr

PERHAPS THE MOST PERVASIVE, unsettling, and enduring of the social and political upheavals to erupt in the late eighteenth century was the one benignly identified as the women's movement. The revolution in France lasted at most a quarter of a century, its terror was relatively short-lived, and it was contained within a single country. And yet, the outcries of Burke and Carlyle against it were stern and persuasive enough to encourage political retrenchment. By contrast, women's rights movements had implications for virtually every member of every class. Beheading a king evidently had far less consequence in the mundane life of *le citoyen moyen* than his sitting at table with his wife.

Given the implicit threat of this movement over time, it is not surprising that the (male) forces of the status quo, in summoning their armory, made capital use of science. Science was a central part of the nineteenth century's cultural world. Exciting, important, and very visible things were happening — rapidly — nor was there yet any sense that the educated laity was excluded from this other culture. Fossil collecting was a popular pastime for English gentlemen in the first half of the century, as was beetle collecting in the second. It was not just closet geologists and naturalists manqué who discussed Lyell and Darwin. The burgeoning world of popular journals (for example, *Cornhill, The Westminister Review, Blackwood's, Macmillan's, Popular Science Monthly,* and *Nature*) bristled with the current scientific essays. Public lectures in science — often to audiences of workingmen — became a popular art and a powerful form of education in the hands of masters like Huxley and Tyndall.

If the eighteenth-century empiricists had speculated in a comparatively rarified way that the world was basically rational, the age of Victoria was coming still closer to envisioning a world that could be solved, that was capable of scientific comprehension. Science could, it seemed, effectively address the most disparate of endeavors — from estimating the earth's age to determining ethical imperatives by calculating pleasure or gain, to laying track across Britain or cable across the Atlantic.

Science held out the admirable lure of objective, demonstrable certitude. Finally, theory, technique, and equipment could cooperate to settle the world's business. Not just in the practical matters of the physical machine, but in government, in education, and in psychology, science would unearth the various iron laws that operated and that determined reality. At least this was the heady form the new meliorism sometimes assumed.

Not surprisingly, the laudable march of science was frequently derailed by human fallibility, opacity, disingenuousness, opportunism, and even deceit. The more emotionally or philosophically loaded the subject under scrutiny, the more common, of course, were the human aberrations — and the more extreme the intellectual chicanery. The convergence of scientific discussions and the women's movement in the second half of the nineteenth century represents an illuminating chapter in intellectual history and in the history of science — for its breadth and audacity, for its (rare) nobility, and for its revelation of intrusive, human subjectivity.

A major aspect of the woman question involved determining the nature of woman, her relationship to man, and the consequent forms and rules that should surround (confine) her. The prospects were wonderful. If craniologists could measure her (generic) skull, it would be clear if she were educable, callibrating her menses would make her fitness to vote apparent, distinguishing her skeleton from man's would likewise settle her capacity for labor. These were obviously all seriously undertaken and pursued efforts. The mountain of imaginatively collected measurements by such scientists as Paul Broca, Léonce Manouvrier, and Gustave Le Bon attested to their hopes and to their seriousness. The woman question just kept getting more disturbing, reappearing, Hydra-like, in newer and — to some — more hideous forms: legal redress, employment opportunities, education, the vote and political power, equality of sexual expression. It was unremitting, even if it never assumed the urgency of a declaration of war. That the various branches of science might solve it was almost irresistibly attractive.

Craniologists, anatomists, physiologists, and in this century psychometrists and psychologists all fed the hope and contributed to the debate. None, however, stayed the course as long as the evolutionists. The idea of evolution of course long antedated Darwin. He simply brought to fruition the intellectual speculations of such figures as Erasmus Darwin, Robert Chambers, and Jean Baptiste Lamarck, consciously building on Lyell's model of gradual development. But evolution can also usefully, I think, be seen as part of a larger intellectual strain: meliorism. J. B. Bury, decades ago, traced the idea of progress back to the mid-eighteenth century (they had, after all, achieved a new age of Augustus). Where it really took hold, though, was in the nineteenth century, with the adamant Whiggism of Macaulay and his lesser-known but possibly even more adamant contemporary Henry Thomas Buckle. Macaulay's "State of England in 1685" famously demonstrated that the world was getting better and better; the evidence was in the numbers. The notion of evolution and Darwin's argument were biological corollaries of this ("scientist" and "biology" — like "agnostic" — were coined in the nineteenth century). The parallel, in fact, became treacherous when many Victorian science writers, beguiled by their belief in progress, carelessly or willfully lapsed into identifying evolution with improvement. Especially when he is being scrupulous, Darwin does not judge it in that sense; evolution merely describes adaptive change. To adjust to a changed climate or diet does not imply that you are a better or higher specimen.

Darwin himself wrote very little about women and evolution; there is one passage in *The Origin of Species* and three passages of perhaps seven or eight pages in *The Descent of Man* (1871). There were, however, scores of other scientists, social scientists, and polemicists who appropriated the evolutionary model into their discussions about the woman question. Many of these scientists and controversialists were obviously crack-pated, couching their incendiary assertions in the garb of science. These are interesting for their outrageous comic potential as well as for the lessons they contain about political and rhetorical discourse. Others are more complex in their relationship to scientific integrity, valiantly attempting to maintain a patina of logic and rigor — and then capitulating under the pressure of their own psychic demands. Finally, there is the group that may be the most interesting: those scientists who were consistently determined to be honest, logical, and open-minded — but whose personal preconceptions still, perhaps inevitably, colored their procedures and directed their conclusions.

A handful of critics in the 1970s — generally feminist — have commented on the skewed relationship between Victorian science and the political agenda for women. Elizabeth Fee, after acknowledging such rare figures as the exponents of "scientific socialism," who "supported the claims of female authority," determines that:

> the great bulk of Victorian scientists — overwhelmingly middle class and male — sought to use the calm, dispassionate truths of science to prove that the demands of feminist "agitators" were founded on unscientific claims about the capabilities of women. Scientists in areas as diverse as zoology, embryology, physiology, heredity, anthropology, and psychology had little difficulty in proving that the pattern of male-female relations that characterized the English middle classes was natural, inevitable, and progressive. ("Science" 180)

Susan Sleeth Mosedale identifies "a certain large corpus of scientific writing published in the later nineteenth and early twentieth centuries . . . [by] scientists opposed to the growing impetus for female emancipation in the Western world" (1) and speculates that this was part of a conservative reaction against a world in upheaval. Industrialization, commercial farming, and public education were among the factors altering society, dislocating women, and fueling the women's movement. These contributed to making the movement threatening to men and, Mosedale suggests, perhaps led them to try to secure that last remaining barn door: domestic arrangements. This pressure and the attendant biases led many "eminent biologists" to exceed the legitimate confines of their science to provide justifications for maintaining the female status quo. "Most of them," she reports,

> betray, by their uncritical acceptance of popular opinion about women, their emotional commitment to the *traditional* concept of the female's place in society. This commitment leads them to grasp at any fact, or alleged fact, of physiology, evolution, or anthropometry which might be worked into a system of evidence in support of woman's traditional role. (3)[1]

Lorna Duffin, with Herbert Spencer and then the eugenicists in mind, argues how, "In the hands of nineteenth-century writers the reconstruction of past evolutionary history became a polemical device for demonstrating that Victorian society was the most advanced and most civilised." But this contained a discomforting contradiction. Evolution was commonly interpreted — even if incorrectly — as an ongoing dynamic of progress: "Yet it is clear, if only in retrospect, that if Victorian society was the pinnacle of evolution, progress could not involve any radical changes in society. Evolutionary theory thus became a tool for arguing that change would be deleterious to future progress" (57). High among the social fixtures that it would be deleterious to tamper with was the place of women. The repeated studies of women's nature and appropriate sphere tended relentlessly and conveniently to assert the ideality of the existing arrangements.[2]

Although others have indicated the collusion of Victorian science with Victorian social conservatism, have suggested the waylaying of "Darwinism" that occurred in the debate about women, and of course have increasingly impugned the idea of science as value-free,[3] I would like to consider the extent to which the scientists and their fellow travellers who spoke for evolution participated in this controversy. As the dominant scientific adventure of the second half of the nineteenth century, evolution was a frequent, bellicose, and influential contributor to the increasingly disturbing and insistent question about woman's nature and place. From suffrage to education to law and politics to work and domestic roles, "science" had much to inform and pronounce. Every area where the movement for emancipation was challenging the established order proved an invitation for the putatively objective voice of scientific facticity. The breadth of involvement of figures from the Anthropological Society of London, Francis Galton and the eugenecists,

Spencer and the social Darwinists, and so on, was compelling, and the second-ary issue of how their cultural biases coerced their scientific rigor too is fascinating and instructive. The pages of the *Journal of the Anthropological Society* and of *Popular Science Monthly* for the 1870s and '80s, for example, make wonderful reading for the historians of science or of culture. As much as their readerships may have differed, the essays in these journals quickly convey how close the educated lay and the scientific audiences were assumed to be. Huxley and Arnold may have tilted over how much the new science curriculum should intrude itself into general education, but there was little evidence that in fact the two cultures had yet irrevocably diverged.

Nineteenth-century science tended to celebrate the splendor of facts. Fossils would provide the irrefutable map of biological development; more refined measurements and extrapolations would resolve the noisome issues of politics, including the demands of women. Facts were wonderful, instructive, definitive, and — from our perspective — wildly entertaining. As George Romanes confidently announced in the pages of *Nineteenth Century*, "We must look facts in the face." And one of the perhaps unpleasant facts he was gallantly willing to confront was that "it must take many centuries for heredity to produce the missing five ounces of the female brain" (666). His article, "Mental Differences Between Men and Women," is replete with such rhetori-cal assurances of factuality as: "it follows," "it is evident," "it is equally evident," and "Hence, also," driving him to discover woman's "deeply-rooted desire to please the opposite sex" (662–63).

Early in Romanes's essay is an illustration of how facts could be asserted and then, from the authority of those facts, conclusions could be inferred:

> Seeing that the average brain-weight of women is about five ounces less than that of men, on merely anatomical grounds we should be prepared to expect a marked inferiority of intellectual power in the former. Moreover, as the general physique of women is less robust than that of men — *and therefore* less able to sustain the fatigue of serious or prolonged brain action — we should also on physiological grounds be prepared to entertain a similar anticipation. *In actual fact* we find that the inferiority displays itself most conspicuously in a compara-tive absence of originality, and this more especially in the higher levels of intellectual work. (654-55; my emphases)

Romanes is here alluding to and building upon the quickly-accumulating research on brain measurements, something that in Paris had almost become an academic industry. Anatomists and anthropologists like Broca, Le Bon, and Manouvrier spent years zealously, compulsively callibrating skulls to determine the dimensions of brains and the mensurable differences between the brains of men and women and among the brains of different races. Broca's work was translated for the *Anthropological Review* as early as 1867, after which time the facts of brain measurement became an important component in the social-political arguments. If women's brains were demonstrably smaller than men's, then presumably they had distinctly different and lesser intellects, capacities, and functions. Even closer to the evolutionary paradigm was the construct explaining the increased divergence of male and female brains. In prehistoric times their brains were roughly equal — and presumably akin to those of contemporary "savages" — but in the course of human evolution they had diverged. Men's cranial capacity expanded — it would seem majestically — while that of women remained meagerly developed, at the level of uncivilized or child-like people (both comparisons were in vogue).

Broca, whose laboratory was supremely involved in cranial measurements, is actually surprisingly judicious in his review of the material that he provided for the Anthropological Society.[4] He urged the importance of studying the condition of women in society. His research is of course part of this necessary study. Even so, for all of his scientific openness, he prefaces his formulation of this question with the unexamined pronouncement that "In the normal condition of things, women's mission is not merely to bring forth children and to suckle them, but to attend to their early education, whilst the father must provide for the subsistence of the family." Anything that "affects this normal order necessarily induces a perturbance in the evolution of the races, and hence it follows that the condition of women in society must be most carefully studied by the anthropologist" (49–50). It is his expertise as a brain anatomist that has enabled Broca to unravel the right order of society and to appreciate how important this right order is.

Many others, as I will suggest, absorbed the findings of Broca and his group and transformed them into potent supports for the prevailing inegalitarianism. There were, however, unusual, minority opinions that strongly questioned the validity of cerebral distinctions and, more importantly, of the conclusions derived from these reputed differences. Helen Gardener, an important suffragist colleague of Elizabeth Cady Stanton, effectively tackled, in 1887, the issue of brain-weight-based assertions. If all the observational claims were true, she argued,

> it would surely be the easiest and simplest thing in the world to determine the sex of a subject by an examination of the brain alone. And if these "great and numerous differences" are natural, potential sex conditions, and not the results of difference in education, occupation, mental stimulus, and general environment, they would be as easily distinguished in the brains of infants . . . as in the brains of adults. . . .
>
> Now, I am assured by all of the brain experts and scientists to whom my questions were submitted, that the sex of two infants not only *could not* be "perceived at once," but could not be determined at all by these certainly sufficiently plain and numerous differences in brain size, matter, and condition

of which the doctor writes so confidently. . . . [further] no careful scientific observer could risk more than a mere *guess* as to the sex of *adult* brains, even upon the most careful and exhaustive examination.

And even more than this, it is a well-known fact that individual brain differences between persons of the same sex are greater and more numerous than any known to exist between the sexes, and that such a guess would, therefore, be worth very little to a scientific mind. ("Sex and Brain-Weight" 267)

So well did Gardener recognize the implications of the discussion about brain differences that she returned to it seven years later, as part of *Facts and Fictions of Life*, her monograph deploring the way biological arguments had been subverted by social biases. Because it was important to learn "just how far medical science and anthropology had really discovered demonstrable natural sex differences in the brains of men and women," she reported having resumed a program of interviews and researches (100). Her resource, "Dr. E. C. Spitzka, the celebrated New York brain specialist," a person none-too-congenial to the women's movement, openly proclaimed his ignorance of any distinction, declaring that you could not tell them apart, affirming, in fact, in very explicit terms, the impossibility of identifying a brain as "male" or "female" (124–25).

Far more common, however, were the rhetorically authoritative proclamations of investigators such as Frank Fernseed, who generally shared little of Broca's reticence or caution. Writing for the *Quarterly Journal of Science* in 1881, Fernseed built on the master: "Broca states the excess of [skull] size in men as compared with women, to be 150 c.c. for the French generally, but as much as 211 c.c. for the inhabitants of Paris" (743–44; this surely must be racism refined to the point of "cityism"). He closed his essay by extruding "the following conclusions" from "these data":

"The superiority of the female sex is witnessed only in the inferior races of mankind and in the young children of the higher, and marks an inferior stage of evolution.

"The same is the case with the equality of the sexes, which occurs merely in imperfectly developed varieties and species, in the young persons, in the decline of years, and in the lower classes of society.

"On the other hand, the pre-eminence of the male as compared with the female marks a higher stage of evolution. It occurs in the highest spheres and races, in the prime of life, and in the superior strata of society.

"Both morally and physically evolution appears to have traversed from a state of superiority of the female to a state of superiority of the male, equality of the sexes representing a transition or intermediate stage."

These results, I fear, will not be welcome to the successors of John Stuart Mill. But when did a "reformer" stoop to consider such trifles as biological facts? (744)

Fernseed here tidily combines the racist conclusions with the sexist ones, clearly viewing them all within an evolutionist framework, and ending with a final thrust preferring "facts" to the milque-toast reformism of Mill and those who suggested the potency of nurture.

But Fernseed and George Romanes were only two voices in the chorus confidently announcing the significant "Mental Differences Between Men and Women" (a title used by Romanes and others). Miss M. A. Hardaker, in an essay unflinchingly entitled "Science and the Woman Question," basically contended that because women are smaller and eat less — providing less energy for muscle and brain — they are necessarily feebler and stupider. From their greater cranial capacity and caloric stoking, "It follows, therefore, that *men will always think more than women.* . . . The distinction of exceptional women, of whom a list could be made, would add little to the general low average of feminine power" (583).[5]

The practical consequences of what could have been only an insulting, contorted description of women were quick to follow and not at all benign. One of the hotly contested issues involved the education of women. The growing demand for female education raised such questions as how long, how deeply, in what subjects, and under what circumstances women should be schooled. Physical anthropology, in this case the evolution of the skull and brain, provided one group of data in the debate. The prevailing view among anthropologists was that of Broca, Le Bon, and their English counterparts, that the brains of women had not evolved as far as those of men. Le Bon, for example, had declared, as part of the conclusion of his lengthy 1879 article on cerebral variations, that:

> Le sexe a une influence considérable sur le poids du cerveau. La femme a un cerveau beaucoup moins lourd que celui de l'homme, et cette infériorité subsiste à *âge égal*, à *poids égal* et à *taille égale*. L'étude des cerveaux féminins de diverses races montre que même dans les agglomérations les plus intelligentes, comme les Parisiens contemporains, il y a une notable proportion de la population féminine dont les crânes se rapprochent plus par le volume de ceux des gorilles que des crânes du sexe masculin les mieux développés. (102)
> (Sex has a considerable influence on the weight of the brain. Woman has a much lighter brain than that of man, and this inferiority remains — at equal ages, at equal weights, and at equal heights. The study of the brains of women of diverse races shows that even among the more intelligent groups, such as contemporary Parisians, there is a notable proportion of the female population whose skulls are closer in volume to those of gorillas than to the best developed male skulls.)

This intellectual inferiority seemed clearly to dictate a different capacity for learning and therefore a distinct educational program.

Few contested the findings of craniology: women, having evolved smaller, lighter brains than men, were not designed to be as intellectual. The most generous response to this axiom was that of people like Thomas Henry Huxley, who rejected the obnoxious conclusions commonly derived from these suppositions. Regarding education, he warned, "Granting the alleged defects of women, is it not somewhat absurd to sanction and maintain a system of education which would seem to have been specially contrived to exaggerate all these defects?" ("Emancipation" 71). His admonition continues:

> The possibility that the ideal of womanhood lies neither in the fair saint, nor in the fair sinner; that the female type of character is neither better nor worse than the male, but only weaker; that women are meant neither to be men's guides nor their playthings, but their comrades, their fellows, and their equals, so far as Nature puts no bar to that equality, does not seem to have entered into the minds of those who have had the conduct of the education of girls. (72)

He even concluded this essay on "Emancipation — Black and White" with a plea that if the burden of motherhood disadvantages woman in the race of life, it is "The duty of man . . . to see that not a grain is piled upon that load beyond what Nature imposes; that injustice is not added to inequality" (75).

Less generous but still relatively mild (or limited in their malevolence) were those whose response to the findings of craniology was that higher education for women was inappropriate and wasteful and who thus militated against it.[6] But the issue of women's education soon extended beyond cerebral measurements and became entangled with social attitudes and policy and with fretting about the health of the race generally. There was evidently substantial concern, particularly in America, about the feebleness of contemporary women.[7] In 1873, a Boston physician, Edward H. Clarke, published *Sex in Education; or, A Fair Chance for Girls*, which became a popular and influential treatise on the hazards of female education.

Clarke lamented the doleful prospects of trying to force female intellects. His pervasive theme is that during the crucial years from fourteen to eighteen a girl's physiological task — as nature has evolved it — is to develop her reproductive system. He pictures women as having a fixed or limited amount of energy overall. Any deflection of energy from the maturation of that system to brain work tends to countermand the design of evolution and can be catastrophic. He saw his generation of American women as feeble and attributed this to their being educated in the "boy's way": thinking and reciting standing up and during their "periodical disturbance." He was petrified by the spectre of infertility, which amounts to absolute evolutionary retrogression. He granted that many women have "graduated from school or college excellent scholars, but with undeveloped ovaries. Later, they married, and were sterile" (39). The important question "of woman's sphere" he would present not to the courts of Kant or Calvin, but to those of Agassiz and

Huxley. "The *quaestio vexata* of woman's sphere will be decided by her organization" (12–13). Because, in the "cultivated classes," education diminishes fertility, he warned that culture and progress will suffer (138). If we are not respectful of physiology and the lessons of evolutionary science (the courts of Agassiz and Huxley),

> [t]he stream of life that is to flow into the future will be Celtic rather than American: it will come from the collieries, and not from the peerage. Fortunately, the reverse of this picture is equally possible. The race holds its destinies in its own hands. The highest wisdom will secure the survival and propagation of the fittest. (140)

Clarke's arguments, assertions and strong admonitions against equal higher education for women may seem shrill and tediously misogynistic now, but his superficially clear and reasonable approach, particularly when laced with the awful case histories he appended — of wayward young women who excelled in college and seemed blooming, but subsequently (he implied consequently) became mad or sterile or both — could be devastatingly persuasive to concerned parents of the late Victorian period anxiously looking for an authority.

Though Clarke's views may have held sway, he did provoke impressive responses. Only months after his book was first released, Julia Ward Howe published *Sex and Education: A Reply to Dr. E. H. Clarke's "Sex in Education."* Incensed by Clarke's threat that women should not be educated along with men, that in fact higher education was an unhealthy pursuit for young women between fourteen and eighteen, Howe compiled and edited this volume of essays in refutation of the esteemed doctor. Howe objected to his tone ("The periodic function peculiar to women is a point upon which Dr. Clarke dwells with persistant irritation" 16) and to his dubious conclusions (she suggested that the frailer health of girls was more likely the result of their physical training, confinement, and dress than of their receiving "boys' " educations 27–28). Other contributors attacked his unscientific and biased spirit: T. W. Higginson found that he "by no means comes up to the recognized standard of science" (Howe 44), and "C" lashed out at his underlying desire to keep women in their place (Howe 123). Elizabeth Stuart Phelps scoffed: "Women sick because they study? Does it not look a little more as if women were sick because they *stopped* studying?" (Howe 134); "why a man would be made an invalid if subjected to the woman's life when the woman's education is over" (Howe 136). Despite the pointedness and ability of these essays and the "Testimonies" included from five colleges debunking Clarke's facts, the predisposition to see women as having evolved less capably (though more fitted than men for domesticity) was so strong that for some years Clarke's volume represented the dominant attitude.

Underlying much of the concern with women's education, as well as the larger discussions of the woman question and the interpretation of evolution, was the entrenched belief that woman's highest and most decorous function was maternity. Nature and natural selection apparently showed that men should think and work and women look beautiful and gestate. Broca was only one of the crowd that saw woman's mission as maternity and nurturance. His contention that because anything that "affects this normal order necessarily induces a perturbance in the evolution of the races" (which was why the condition of women in society had to be most carefully studied by the anthropologist; 49–50) was also commonly accepted. Less circumspect was Grant Allen. In "Woman's Place in Nature" he identified the male with the race and saw the female as merely reproducing: "She is the sex sacrificed to reproductive necessities" (258); "women, on the whole, are mostly told off as wives and mothers. . . . All the vast gains of our race in its progress toward civilization have been gains made for the most part by men alone" (260). Later in the same year, 1889, in "Plain Words on the Woman Question," he refined his views: "To the end of all time, it is mathematically demonstrable that most women must become the mothers of at least four children, or else the race must cease to exist" (173). Women must therefore (frankly) be trained to be wives and mothers (174).

Understanding evolution then led from a recognition of the limitations of women's educability to fashioning a proper scheme for educating them. The fear of the inadequately-educated woman co-existed with the horror of the blue-stocking unsexed by learning. The difficulty establishing women's colleges, the discussion over exactly what the curricula should be, and the question of necessary limits have all been elaborated by others.[8] I am only interested here in drawing the connection between the scientific description of woman's evolved nature and the selecting of subjects she should study. If nature constructed women to procreate and nurture, then they must be taught the necessary skills — and none that would deflect them from this purpose. How much arithmetic and how little history and science were simply fine tunings of the fundamental proposition.

The debates about suffrage and women's political possibilities involved the testimonies of anthropology and evolution in parallel ways. One of the most outrageous of the fine tuners, Luke Owen Pike, Fellow of the Anthropological Society of London, saw evidence that women should be excluded from politics. To such differences, he wrote, between women and men as "the smallness of the brain-case, the width of the pelvis, and the tendency to deposit adipose tissue, rather than muscular fibre . . . and other differences of structure, correspond numerous differences of function." The capacity and desire for muscular exertion as well as "for the prolonged study of abstruse subjects" are less in the female (83). Not surprisingly, he smugly observed, "women, on the average, prefer millinery to geology" (84). Moreover, "Woman naturally loves to teach the young. . . . She naturally loves to tend the sick of her family" (92). "It is not out of such qualities," he had already lamented, "that statesmanship can be developed or science advanced" (86). Worse yet, if women misguidedly devoted their energies to science and politics, they "would do violence to their physical organization" (87).

Function should follow morphology, and the man of science, Pike reassured, was not being tyrannical; rather, he "knows from observation and experience" the happiness that results from a structure's being healthily developed and fulfilled (90). To pervert woman's nature and put civilization at risk in this Hobbesian world where only the fittest survive would be folly. Perhaps in some fully-evolved, secure paradise women might venture into the arenas of political power:

> But, until then, until murder, theft, and villainy of every kind, shall have been extinguished, until that struggle for existence, which pervades all Nature and constitutes the only healthy check upon population, shall have been abolished, until every evil passion shall have been rooted out, [the humble anthropologist] may perhaps be permitted to raise his feeble protest against innovations which would not only subvert man's civilized customs but contradict Nature's first lessons. (94)

The prospects for women's empowerment were not bright.

Although reactions in the second half of the nineteenth century were generally apprehensive about female education, there were also those who thought the lessons of evolution did not contradict, but perhaps even advised it. Responding to the shortshrift she felt Darwin's *Descent* had given women, Antoinette Brown Blackwell included as a substantial part of her rebuttal, *The Sexes Throughout Nature* (1875), a plea for the education of women. She felt strong, intelligent women were needed to bequeath intellect, explicitly rejecting the common belief that it was through the father that intelligence was inherited.

> If anybody's *brain* requires to be sacrificed to those two Molochs, sewing-machine and cooking-stove, it is not hers! Nature's highest law is evolution, and no hereditary evolution is possible except through the prolonged maternal supervention. . . . the wisest man [cannot] bequeath intellect to children through the agency of a weak-minded or characterless mother. (116)

Blackwell denied that women were "incapable of appreciating the most highly complex fact or the most abstract principle" (134). She urged:

> Evolution has given and is still giving to woman an increasing complexity of development which cannot find a legitimate field for the exercise of all its

powers within the household. There is a broader, not a higher, life outside, which she is impelled to enter, taking some share also in its responsibilities. (135)

Confronting those who lamented the deterioration of family life, Blackwell saw evolution teaching "the lesson that the monogamic marriage is the basis of all progress" (136). As women (like men) evolved in complexity, this progress and marital harmony demanded better educated women. She insisted there was no evidence that women were the intellectual inferiors of men and that equal education was imperative, rejecting as "incredibly singular, blind, and perverse" the "dogmatism" that man's larger brain proves his superiority (177). As Marie Tedesco observes, Blackwell's critique of Darwin may have had its problems as rigorous science (especially in its contrived image of an elaborate balance of qualities between the sexes), but as a feminist tract it was firm in pushing to expand women's spheres — even as it upheld the sanctity of the home (64). Tedesco recognizes Blackwell's conception of evolution as dynamic, envisioning the continued development of the sexes and further progress of the race; her construct did not stop at the Victorian status quo, with its gender divisions (65).

M. Carey Thomas, the energetic and determined president of Bryn Mawr College from 1894 to 1922, was another forceful advocate of women's education. In her 1908 address to the college, she recalled the old uncertainty of the days of Clarke's *Sex in Education*, not really knowing whether women's health could stand the rigors of college education. Would the doctor's predictions of a crop of invalids be borne out? Happily, a few decades proved otherwise. Women evidently were constituted for it: "Women's college education has succeeded too well" (2:166), leaving them neither sterile nor dessicated (2:168).

The anxiety that educated women would be less fecund was only a part of the more general fears about declining birth rates and deteriorating families. Almost never were the ideals of maternity and family life questioned. Much more common were the lamentations about how these sacred cows were being devalued. Upon the success of the family and its procreativity depended the survival of the race. J. McGrigor Allan was fairly typical in the sentiments he conveyed to the Anthropological Society in 1869:

the women who discharge the conjugal and maternal functions properly — those women who are old-fashioned enough to find their happiness in
promoting the happiness of their husbands and families, are not only the finest
specimens of their sex in every point of view, but are working far more directly
and efficiently for the physical, mental, and moral progress of the human
species, than the superficial, flat-chested, thin-voiced Amazons, who are pouring forth sickening prate about the tyranny of man. . . . (ccxii)

He was reflecting the wave of panic about the increase in population control and the suspicion that education was counter-reproductive. Carroll Smith-Rosenberg and Charles Rosenberg identify these as "the warnings of 'race suicide' so increasingly fashionable in the late-nineteenth century," pointing out that, "A woman's willingness and capacity to bear children was a duty she owed not only to God and husband but to her 'race' as well" (351). It was not simply, as the Rosenbergs continue (thinking specifically of America), a fear of deliberate

> family limitation which resulted in small families; rather the increasingly unnatural life-style of the "modern American woman" had undermined her reproductive capacities so that even when she would, she could not bear adequate numbers of healthy children. Only if American women returned to the simpler life-styles of the eighteenth and early nineteenth centuries could the race hope to regain its former vitality; women must from childhood see their role as that of robust and self-sacrificing mothers. If not, their own degeneration and that of the race was inevitable. (353)

In the early part of this century, the eugenicists echoed the same worries: would middle class women reproduce at a rate sufficient to insure the fitness of the race (Duffin 76). It was the same story that we have already glimpsed regarding education: if the importance of the individual was subordinate to that of improving the race, and if education threatened women's fertlity, then women must clearly be sacrificed to the "progress" of the race. Motherhood must be emphasized (Duffin 76–85).

Although the overwhelming tendency was to laud the hearth and motherhood and to interpet evolution in ways that advanced them, there were the unusual figures who invoked evolutionary arguments to challenge these ideals. In 1894, Helen Gardener rejected the identification of man with "the race" and the relegation of woman to the role of maternal vehicle. She demanded: "Has a woman not the right to be a human being and count one in the economy of life before she is a mother — quite aside from her maternal capabilities?" After all, she complained, almost anticipating Existentialist cries, "Every man has and maintains the right to be a man first" (*Facts* 173).

Far more radical was the challenge of Charlotte Perkins Gilman, who, early in this century, used the language of evolutionary science both to argue for the advancement of women and to indict the family itself as retrogressive. At the center of her determined feminist campaign for economic egalitarianism was her discontent with the family and her rejection of maternal sacrifice. Her optimistic presumption was that "The period of women's economic dependence is drawing to a close, because its racial usefulness is wearing out" (137–38). Whatever may have been true in prior stages of human development, the relegation of half the species to the nursery, the kitchen, and environs, which was probably always ethically suspect, no longer made any scientific or economic sense. Gilman deflated the hypocrisies appended to motherhood, observing that, "the mere office of reproduction is as well performed by the laying of eggs to be posthumously hatched as by many years of exquisite devotion; but in the improvement of the species we come to other requirements" (178–79). She was incensed at the debasement this form of idolatry meant for women, finding "nothing in the achievements of human motherhood to prove that it is for the advantage of the race to have women give all their time to it." On the contrary, "The woman who works is usually a better reproducer than the woman who does not" (190–91). Her expropriation of social Darwinism discovered that "Neither the enormous percentage of children lost by death nor the low average health of those who survive, neither physical nor mental progress, give any proof of race advantage from the maternal sacrifice" (199). Far different from her sociological predecessor, Herbert Spencer, who came to favor so strongly the subordination of women in the service of motherhood and domesticity — for the sake of the race — Gilman announced, "The time has come when it is better for the world that women be economically independent" (316).[9]

Gilman's likening of domesticity to servitude, her economic emphasis, and her agitation for female independence can all be recognized as part of the movement to free women up to work outside of the home. The debate that surrounded this movement also had its evolutionary dimension. In its simplest biologically-couched form, the argument was, as George Ferrero — for one — relayed it, that the whole realm of nature shows females should not work. It diminished their capacity to gestate. He lectured:

> As it is a natural law that the man must labor and struggle to live, so is it a natural law that the woman should neither labor nor struggle for her existence.
> Biology clearly shows us, that the physiological prosperity of species depends on the division of labor between the sexes, for in exact ratio to this is the duration of life. This is the result of natural selection. (262–63)

For Ferrero there was a principle apparent in Nature that "the prosperity of a species increases, in exact proportion to the degree in which the male frees the female from the burdens and anxieties of life" (265). Besides, as he added almost gratuitously, "Another reason why woman should not work is the fact, that we wish her to be to us beautiful and attractive" (268) — no doubt to facilitate the mechanism of sexual selection.

Mary Sedgwick was only one of many who elaborated this argument. As men and women diverged, a division of labor became appropriate, each sex then becoming able to pursue its own specific capabilities. "Moreover," she reassured, "the women of to-day [1901] are gainers by this process of specialization, as we are free to fill our time with the occupations for which we are best suited'' (338). In actuality, this turned out to mean that women were incapable of respected and rewarded work outside of the home, where they were granted unchallenged competence. They were deemed physically unsuited for outside work, constantly thwarted by that signpost of nature, their "periodic disturbance," a disturbance which of course seemed never to impede the performance of menial labor no matter how exacting or onerous.

The division of labor and assigning of distinct work roles provided an equally prominent platform for the social evolutionists. Characteristically, the conception of progressive evolution led to the exclusion of women from the work force. As Cynthia Russett points out, citing such commentators as Milne-Edwards, W. K. Brooks, Spencer, and Geddes and Thomson, the increased division of labor left the "highly developed" female with the labor of reproduction as her task. Clearly, "Spencer considered division of labor the linchpin of the social, as of the biological, organism" (Russett 135–37). Much more important than the individual's possible relegation to a life of gilded desuetude was the satisfying image, for Spencer and the others, of a social order that was increasingly complex and specialized, with the anti-quated notion of completeness and self-sufficency yielding to one of greater fragmentation and interdependency. In theory this may have sounded seduc-tively modern and sophisticated; in practice it left women fixed on their pedestals, overlooking the nursery, kitchen, and laundry.

Russett finds a dimension absent in Spencer and his follower, William B. Carpenter, that was acknowledged by the more socialistic of the social Darwinists: "concern at the possibility, so apparent to Marx, that greater and greater division of labor, far from always conferring social benefits, might alienate the worker from his work and further social inequality" and that perceived this way such an account "does not provide women with much cause for cheering evolution on" (140). Karl Pearson and David Ritchie both saw an intimate connection between the question of women and the question of labor. They urged that until this linkage was accepted and women's labor encouraged, trained, and rewarded, resolutions were unlikely. They rejected the evolutionary model that defined a woman's function as exclusively mater-nal and domestic: "The home, whether we approve it or no, has ceased for ever to be the sole field of woman's activity" (Pearson, "Woman" 575). Ritchie complained that "The cultivation of separate sorts of virtues and separate ideals of duty [and work] in men and women has led to the whole social fabric being weaker and unhealthier than it need be" (72–73). Even if women were plunged — nominally equal — into the labor contest, they would suffer because of being so unequally prepared. But "There is another alternative, and that is the socialistic. The elevation of the *status* of women and the regulation of the conditions of labour are *ultimately* inseparable ques-tions" (75). Ritchie, in fact, was struck by the hypocrisy of denying women certain capacities, whether they be political, vocational, or intellectual, simply because through long centuries those incapacities had been "diligently cultivated" (69). One woman, Sarah Amos, writing for *The Contemporary Review* in 1894, went so far as to argue that it was not natural evolution that was misogynistic, but the evolution imposed by society that enfeebled women. "In the factory districts of England," she reminded a culture that had duplicitously denied that women had the ability to be productive, "machinery evolved the daughters long ago" (516).

In the struggle over suffrage, the last of the major aspects of the woman question I will examine, the same pattern repeats itself. The evidence of evolution could be cited by both camps, though it tended to be invoked much more frequently by what we would see as the repressive or illiberal parties. Sedgwick was particularly resolute in her argument against enfranchisement. She explained that anti-suffragists believed "woman suffrage would retard human progress — that it would introduce unforeseen complications into our social system" (333). She stressed the increasing divergence and specialization of the sexes across evolutionary history and the parallel divergence of occupations, activities, and educations. Racial development had produced a "division of labor which makes man an important member of a community instead of an isolated savage" (336). The lesson she would thus bring home was that: "Equality does not mean similarity of functions, and the suffrage agitation is a retrograde movement, which carried to its logical conclusions would take the race back towards the condition in which no sex characteristics existed" (337). It is not exactly clear how her pseudo-scientific rhetoric brought Sedgwick to the conclusion that voting would rescind sexual differentiation, but we are obviously in the familiar arena where women's advancement and sexual egalitarianism raised the horrifying spectre of unfeminine, asexual behavior. Besides, as Sedgwick — also familiarly — reminded impulsive reformers, "women are constantly handicapped by their peculiar physical limitations, a point which most suffragists ignore" (339). Menstruation, symbolic of both reproductivity and incapacity, then makes it as ill-advised for women to vote as it does for them to think and recite standing up or to compete with men professionally.

By contrast, Carrie C. Catt, delivering a speech in Chicago in 1893 to a Congress of Representative Women of the National American Woman Suffrage Association (NASA), unequivocally contended that the primary discovery of the nineteenth century, evolution, was on the side of suffrage. She was willing to accept the idea that women have evolved differently from men and even that they were superior in the humane and ministering virtues. But these virtues and the moral advance they represent were precisely what society needed (3). She felt women's competencies and votes were needed "because our civilization is strong and well-developed along all the lines of men's keenest interests, wealth and law and commerce. They are weak along the lines of women's keenest interests, protection of the individual and the home'' (5). The conscience woman has evolved ''sees misery and wants and wrongs on every side, and that conscience is constantly urging her to action'' (6). Denying women political power checkmated their moral and humane influence, a virtue the most intransigent of sexual separatists have conceded to them.

In essentially every battle that feminists were waging in their campaign for equality, an important factor was the voice of evolutionary science — whether emanating from Darwin or from Spencer. Darwin cautiously suggested ''it is probable that sexual selection has played a very important part'' in human evolution, that an inherent difference between the sexes is also ''at least probable,'' and that ''it is likely'' that woman should extend her maternal instincts (*Descent* 2:326), but this caution did not stop the concommitant suggestion of greater male variation from escalating into a contested issue in its own right.[10] Nor, as we have seen, did his relative temperance inhibit the rhetorical extravagances of some of his followers. At each political juncture, the data of science were enjoined in the service of political bias. In fact, the political component could occasionally prove more enduring than a particular scientific buttress. As the argument from variation and sexual selection became less persuasive, for example, a new scientific metaphor (as we would recognize it) emerged to verify the evolved differences between the sexes.

As early as 1879, W. K. Brooks had asserted in his evolutionary, specifically ''zoological,'' discussion of women, that the ''ovum is the conservative, and the male element the progressive or variable factor in the process of evolution'' (150). By 1889 Patrick Geddes and J. Arthur Thomson had elaborated this idea into the core of their influential book, *The Evolution of Sex*. It was metabolic rate that for them distinguished male cells from female. Geddes and Thomson described female cells as ''anabolic,'' basically passive, conserving, and safe (the cellular or metabolic analog to middling, unoriginal, and timid) and male cells as ''katabolic,'' more energetic, motile, and intrepid. The cloth out of which the new metaphor was cut may have been redyed, but the pattern was familiar enough. After presenting an array of statistics about muscle, fat, the number of red corpuscles, athletic prowess, endurance, and mortality, one of their followers, William Thomas, concluded, in ''On a Difference in the Metabolism of the Sexes,'' that woman has evolved a morphology and physiology — as expressed in her anabolic metabolism — that makes her more disposed to love offspring and ties of blood and to express herself in social concerns (61).

Man's katabolism predisposed him to activity and violence; woman's anabolism predisposed her to a stationary life. The first division of labor was, therefore, an expression of the characteristic contrast of the sexes. . . . This allotment of tasks was not made by the tyranny of man, but exists almost uniformly in primitive communities because it utilizes most advantageously the energies of both sexes . . . (62)[11]

While I have been interested primarily in displaying the extent to which the issues raised by the debate about women were engaged by Victorian evolutionists, I want also to indicate, even if cursorily, the range of subjective impedence or distortion among these scientists. No theme seems to animate Stephen J. Gould's essays for *Natural History* more than the tale of zealous and sincere scientists undone by their unconscious biases — or — conversely, of stalwarts whom the history of science subsequently dismissed because later prejudices were at odds with theirs or because later generations failed to appreciate older intellectual contexts. There is also, I think, little illusion left about science's being safely value free or of scientists proceeding in an ether removed from cultural contamination.[12]

More even than Victorian society in general, Victorian science was a male enterprise. Not only were the participants men (the Ethnographic Society refused even to admit women to its discussions), but the orientation, attitudes, and assumptions were preeminently masculine. Sometimes the prevailing social assumptions about gender were overt; often they were more subconscious and automatic. (It's one thing when someone blatantly declaims on the obvious physical, intellectual, and moral inferiority of women and quite another when a parent simply assumes his or her daughter is best off married, ensphered by domesticity, and untroubled by mathematics or politics.) Although there certainly were occasions when those who spoke from the podiums of science managed to overcome the biases of their culture, far more often these preconceptions coerced the investigators' conclusions. Three groups are discernible — and the divisions are very rough — that reflect distinct relationships between objectivity and the pressures of cultural prejudice.

The easiest group to recognize at a century's distance and the least interesting — though undeniably entertaining — are those figures whose invoking of evolution smacks of intellectual charlatanism. However sincere and rigorous and successful as scientists they may have been otherwise, it is hard to respect as intellectually honest the animadversions of, for example, Luke Owen Pike, George Romanes, J. McGrigor Allan, and Grant Allen. The snideness, coyness, unjustified or mis-justified assertions, and imposed moralisms that punctuate their essays that apply evolution to the woman question are sharply at odds with the care and objectivity appropriate to scientific discourse. Disinterestedness is the least suspected of qualities as we hear Allan villify the "superficial, flat-chested, thin-voiced Amazons, who are pouring forth sickening prate about the tyranny of men" (ccxii), or Grant

Allen rail against the "ideal of an unsexed woman" and the "deplorable accident" of spinsters (174, 178). When George Romanes discovered that in his test group the women read and comprehended more quickly than the men and then dismissed the discovery by adding, "that rapidity of perception as thus tested is no evidence of what may be termed the deeper qualities of mind — some of my slowest readers being highly distinguished men" (657), he surely was not holding to his customary scientific standards of reason and objectivity. And these were all members in good standing of the scientific community, usually of the Royal Society. Somehow when the focus was on woman's nature and place, it was easier to be caustic, irrascible, flippant, or dogmatic, that is, to slip into a rhetorical mode we assume to be more customary among politicians.

More striking is the instance of someone like Thomas Henry Huxley. Throughout his writings and his life it was obvious that Huxley held no virtue in higher esteem than honesty. In public, private, or professional dealings, he had little tolerance for any kind of duplicity. His essays, lectures, and letters repeatedly make this clear. His falling out with Richard Owen was precipitated by Owen's dishonesty in maintaining that the Hippocampus minor was exclusively present in humans. When Huxley himself blundered over the Bathybius, he had no trouble simply announcing he had been wrong. And yet, for all of his honest, open-minded willingness to see any truth that stumbled forth, Huxley was still able to read the evidence as demonstrating woman's intellectual and emotional inferiority. (His private life and letters to Henrietta Huxley do not suggest that, like Darwin, he had a strong emotional stake in maintaining a Victorian patriarchy.) As I have cited earlier, in "Emancipation — Black and White" he had no doubt women would prove unequal to men intellectually and physically in the race of life. Unlike the majority of his contemporaries, he argued this was no reason to handicap them socially and educationally, thereby adding injustice to inequality. Five years earlier, in 1860, he had expressed this same sentiment in a letter to Lyell:

> I am far from wishing to place any obstacle in the way of the intellectual advancement of women. On the contrary, I don't see how we are to make any permanent advancement when one-half of the race is sunk, as nine-tenths of women are, in mere ignorant parsonese superstitions; and to show you that my ideas are practical I have fully made up my mind, if I can carry out my own plans, to give my daughters the same training in physical science as their brother will get, so long as he is a boy. They, at any rate, shall not be got up as man-traps for the matrimonial market. If other people would do the like the next generation would see women fit to be the companions of men in all pur-suits — though I don't think that men have anything to fear from their competi-tion. But you know as well as I do that other people won't do the like, and five-sixths of women will stop in the doll stage of evolution to be the stronghold

of parsondom, the drag on civilisation, the degradation of every important
pursuit with which they mix themselves — "intrigues" in politics, and "fripon-
nes" in science. (Leonard Huxley 1:212)

Huxley's "advanced" views here, his demand that women be given
equal opportunities, contended with his clearly-held conviction that women
were just not as capable as men. As all of the fanfare about cerebral measurement indicated, it was indeed the exceptional nineteenth-century thinker (Mill,
for example) who could stand back and question the postulate of man's
intellectual superiority. Probably the closest Huxley ever came to such a
position was in a letter to *The Times* of London in 1874, where he charged:
"We have heard a great deal lately about the physical disabilities of women.
Some of these alleged impediments, no doubt, are really inherent in their
organisation, but nine-tenths of them are artificial — the products of their
modes of life" (Leonard Huxley 1:417). Characterisically, Huxley (the friend
and colleague of Spencer and Romanes!) genuinely saw the evidence as
indicating women's greater disabilities, but he also genuinely felt that these
deficits should certainly not be exaggerated and that they should however
possible be compensated for by education and support.[13]

Herbert Spencer exemplifies a third response to the collision of scientific
rigor, evolutionary findings, and personal responses to the woman question.
Spencer's metamorphosis from an early feminism to an increasing conservatism has been detailed by several critics. "The Rights of Women" chapter
in the 1851 *Social Statics* compares in its radicalism to the views of someone
like Mill. When, however, in 1867, as George Stocking, Jr., records in his
magnum opus on *Victorian Anthropology*, Harriet Taylor wanted to reprint it
with some feminist essays, Spencer refused, as he did when it came to
supporting the cry for suffrage (206). Carol Dyhouse traces in particular the
growing conservatism in Spencer's attitude toward female education. By
1867, in *The Principles of Biology*, and still more in *The Principles of Sociology* (1876), his reservations about supplying too much intellectual education
for women surfaced. He feared the "mental strain" would militate against
the central role of the monogamous nuclear family with its familiar contain-
ment of the wife in the home (Dyhouse, "Social" 43).[14]

In the course of tracing Spencer's change from the egalitarianism of
the first edition of *Social Statics* and early letters to his later hierarchical
conservatism, T. S. Gray persuasively argues that the transformation reflects
developments in Spencer's emotional life. Gray locates the beginnng of this
change in 1852, when he refused a romantic relationship with Marian Evans
(George Eliot). He parallels Spencer's increasing misogyny with his frustrations and even bitterness "at the hands of the opposite sex"(227) and his
intensified anxieties about whether he would ever successfully marry and

establish a home. Gray finds it particularly telling that Spencer's change here, unlike other attitudinal reversals in his writings, is (atypically) not framed logically. He seems to have deposited his frustrations and sense of inadequacy on women and the political threat that they represented.

Gray's argument needs no further elaborating. I would simply like to add that not only did Spencer abandon his characteristic tone and facade of rational, scientific discourse as he responded more and more to his own emotional pressures, but that his arguments on the woman question were consistently presented in the language of evolutionary science. He managed to turn coat, all the while using evolution as the jargon and substance of his argument. As an evolutionist before the appearance of *The Origin*, it is bracing to hear Spencer begin his chapter on women's rights declaring, "Equity knows no difference of sex. . . . The law of equal freedom manifestly applies to the whole race — female as well as male," and wonder, "why the differences of bodily organization, and those trifling mental variations which distinguish female from male, should exclude one-half of the race from the benefits" of a duly-ordained human happiness ("Rights" 173). His early evolutionary beliefs encouraged him to mock social and legal inequalities that, for example, allowed a man to beat his wife moderately, and to deny that women were intellectually inferior (175). He rejected as nonsensical the premise that woman's alleged weaker faculties meant that she should have less liberty to exercise them (177). At times he even sounded like Fournier or Mill, correlating a society's condition with its treatment of women and national despotism with domestic despotism (179), clearly identifying the evolution of society with the improvement in the situation of women.

Not only was Spencer to reverse these views, but he unwittingly described the supra-logical dynamic that would facilitate this reversal. In that same 1851 essay, he reflected metaphysically how:

> Belief always bears the impress of character — is, in fact, its product. Anthropomorphism sufficiently proves this. Men's wishes eventually get expressed in their faiths — their real faiths, that is; not their normal ones. Pull to pieces a man's Theory of Things, and you will find it based upon facts collected at the suggestion of his desires. A fiery passion consumes all evidence opposed to its gratification, and fusing together those that serve its purpose, casts them into weapons by which to achieve its end. (177)

This both poignantly describes the process I associated with Pike, Allan, and others and ironically anticipates Spencer's own change of mind.

By 1873, however, he was quite sure that the mental natures of men and women were different; he then sounded hauntingly like the chorus that insisted upon women's stunted development. The passage of two decades makes for a very different text:

> That men and women are mentally alike, is as untrue as that they are alike bodily. . . . To suppose that along with the unlikenesses between their parental activities there do not go unlikenesses of mental faculties, is to suppose that here alone in all Nature there is no adjustment of special powers to special functions. ("Psychology" 31)

In the seventies Spencer was very much a part of the group suggesting that women had evolved the desire to please and nurture and a finer intuition — all in the service of domestic efficiency. His chapters, "The *Status* of Women" and "Domestic Retrospect and Prospect," in the first volume of *Principles of Sociology* (1877), fully endorsed the popular anthropological or cultural evolutionary model of the greater proximity of primitive men and women and their subsequent divergence with the triumph of civilization. He proclaimed "the fact that the genesis of the family fulfils the law of Evolution under its leading aspects" (1:757). The early spokesman of reasoned independence and equality had metamorphosed into a defender of the status quo, all under the banner of evolution.

Although my principal interest has been to suggest the ways evolutionary science was impressed into service in the late Victorian period in the struggle against women's emancipation, I want also to recognize that there were some — if few — science writers who thought oppositely. I have already mentioned Blackwell's response to Darwin's *Descent, The Sexes Throughout Nature*,[15] and Helen Gardener's *Facts and Fictions of Life*, in which she exposed male prejudices and the egoistic distorting of science; previously-cited essays by Frances Emily White and Sarah Amos also make counter-claims.

In 1894 Elizabeth Burt Gamble published *The Evolution of Woman: An Inquiry Into the Dogma of Her Inferiority to Man* (revised in 1916 as *The Sexes in Science and History*). Not only did she interpret sexual selection oppositely from Darwin, deriving from it woman's evolved superiority, but she also subverted his valuation of greater variation, suggesting that the secondary sexual characteristic of hirsuteness indicated the male's lower stage of development.[16] Her point about the arbitrariness of Darwin's judgments is worth noticing. More trenchant was her attack on the evolutionists who denied the importance of nurture:

> It is a well understood fact that neither individuals nor classes which upon every hand have been thwarted and restrained, either by unjust and oppressive laws, or by the tyranny of custom, prejudice, or physical force, have ever made any considerable progress in the actual acquirement of knowledge or in the arts of life. Mr. Darwin's capacity for collecting and formulating facts seems not to have materially aided him in discerning the close connection existing at this stage of human progress between the masculinized conditions of human society and the necessary opportunities to succeed in the higher walks of life; in fact,

he seems to have forgotten that all the avenues to success have for thousands of years been controlled and wholly manipulated by men, while the activities of women have been distorted and repressed in order that the "necessities" of the male nature might be provided for. (*Sexes* 79)

Gamble was impatient with the traditional notions of male superiority that have associated male ascendancy with progress and female competition with weakness and ruin (*Sexes* 98–99). She likewise rejected as implausible Spencer's reading of anthropology: that prehistoric women were held as property (*Sexes* 134–36).[17] She even turned the tables on those who patronizingly relegated to women the evolved virtues of altruism and the finer feelings of sympathy and compassion. Unlike male energy, which had become "an actual hindrance to further progress" (*Sexes* 397), these female virtues were in fact crucial to the continued success of civilization.

Perhaps the most comprehensive of those who rebutted the anti-feminist use of evolution was Jean Finot, who published *Préjugé et problème des sexes* in 1912 (translated as *Problems of the Sexes* in 1913). Susan Mosedale, in the last section of "Science Corrupted" (41–54), excellently conveys Finot's analytical sharpness, his unmasking of prejudices, scientific sham, and illogic, and his sensitivity and psychological discernment. For my purposes I want only to recommend *Problems of the Sexes* as a solid and incisive attack on most of the "scientific" denigrations of women. Finot had a keen appreciation of the force of prejudice and of how it affected science. He obviously felt comfortable challenging the tradition I have been examining on its own turf and was able to do it lucidly and cogently.

With some choice exceptions, then, the evolutionists, like the theologians and lawyers of prior centuries and the physicians with whom they overlapped, claimed authority in the controversy about women. In the half century between the early writings of Spencer and Darwin and the social Darwinsts of the beginning of this century, there was a clear and important tendency for political priorities to impose themselves upon biological discussions. Science responded to the woman question, but in ways that revealed what Stephanie Shields identifies as a leitmotif in evolutionary discussions: the evolved supremacy of the white male (739). The late Victorian cultural imperatives strongly urged that whatever was was right, and these scientists were compliant enough handmaids in the face of that urging. Though I have concentrated on British sources, glances across to France and the United States suggest a similar, even collaborating intellectual climate. Evolutionary progress paradoxically became a conservative or even reactionary force for keeping women in their designated place.

Indiana University Northwest

NOTES

I would like to express my appreciation for the support that this essay had in its seminal stages from the National Endowment for the Humanities. It originated as a proposed project for an NEH faculty summer seminar in The Woman Question in an Age of Revolution, conducted by Karen Offen at Stanford University in 1989.

1. Stephanie Shields, in her critique of the American functionalist movement's use of Darwin to exploit women, similarly suggests: "The leitmotif of evolutionary theory as it came to be applied to the social sciences was the evolutionary supremacy of the Caucasian male. The notion of the supplementary, subordinate role of the female was ancillary to the development of that theme" (739).

2. See also Carroll Smith-Rosenberg and Charles Rosenberg, who report:

   Since at least the time of Hippocrates and Aristotle, the roles assigned women have attracted an elaborate body of medical and biological justification. This was especially true in the nineteenth century as the intellectual and emotional centrality of science increased steadily. Would-be scientific arguments were used in the rationalization and legitimization of almost every aspect of Victorian life, and with particular vehemence in those areas in which social change implied stress in existing arrangements. (332)

3. It is of course a theme woven through the essays of Stephen Jay Gould that scientists are ineluctably influenced by the predicates and biases of their own cultures. Evelleen Richards begins her discussion of "Darwin and the Descent of Women" by questioning the special status of science as objective and value free (57).

4. Of Broca's comparative moderation, Gould writes: "Of all his comparisons between groups, Broca collected most information on the brains of women versus men — presumably because it was most accessible, not because he held any special animus toward women. 'Inferior' groups are interchangeable in the general theory of biological determinism." Broca, Gould continues, "centered his argument about the biological status of women upon two sets of data; the large brains of men in modern societies and a supposed widening through time of the disparity in size between male and female brains" (103).

   It was "Topinard, Broca's chief disciple," Gould points out, who exemplified the scientific group that "explained the increasing discrepancy through time as a result of differing evolutionary pressures upon dominant men and passive women" (104). For a German counterpart of these French and English brain scientists, see J. P. Möbius, "The Physiological Mental Weakness of Woman."

5. The emphases are unabashedly Hardaker's. Nina Morais tellingly responded to Hardaker in the following issue of *Popular Science Monthly*, complaining: "To cover ancient prejudice with the palladium of scientific argument is to unite the strength of conservatism and of progress in one attack" (70). More particularly, she objected,

   thinkers will not infer the capacity of male and female brains from their products, until the different influences acting upon men and women can be eliminated. While anatomy is unable to solve for us the enigma of sexual brain-power, we may have recourse to comparison under similar environment as the key to our problem. This method of discovery Miss Hardaker, with a perversity remarkable in a disciple of modern science, is laboring zealously to prevent. (72)

Lamentably, Morais's voice proved comparatively inaudible in the judicious corridors of scientific debate.

For an elaborate and influential, scientifically dressed and delivered discussion of the "facts" of brain size and weight and their inexorable implications, see Le Bon's long article for the 1879 *Revue d'Anthropologie*. He reveled in the enlightenment of modern anthropology which had only recently learned to discount the traditional view which naively considered "tous les hommes comme doués d'une organisation et d'une intelligence égales et attribuaient leurs différences aux inégalities de l'éducation qu'ils reçoivent" (all men alike endowed with an equal [nervous] organization and intelligence, and attributes their differences to the inequalities of the education they receive, 27). This outmoded view that environment or nurture contributed to intellectual differences is, for him, happily supplanted by a congeries of measurements and computations clearly "proving" the superiority of civilized males generally and the preeminence of modern Parisian men in particular. His fourth section, on the variations in value and size of skulls, was especially hostile to the egalitarian hopes of feminists. Gould comments how, "In 1879 Gustave Le bon, chief misogynist of Broca's school, used these data to publish what must be the most vicious attack upon women in modern scientific literature" (104).

6. For discussions of "scientific" craniology see Elizabeth Fee's "Nineteenth-century Craniology" and Gould's *Mismeasure of Man*. An ancillary argument against higher education for women derives from the belief that males had greater variations as a group than females — more geniuses as well as more idiots. Cynthia Russett indicates how this led to the conclusion that if women lacked a genius level, graduate education was a waste (100).
7. Smith-Rosenberg and Rosenberg describe the fears about the comparative physical inferiority of American women and how co-education is weakening the race.

Since the beginnings of the nineteenth century, American physicians and social commentators generally had feared that American women were physically inferior to their English and Continental sisters. . . . Women could now, critics agonized, spend the entire period between the beginning of menstruation and the maturation of their ovarian systems in nerve-draining study. Their adolescence, as one doctor pointed out, contrasted sadly with those experienced by healthier, more fruitful forebears. (339, 341)

8. Dyhouse spells out the anxious suggestions of such enterprises as the Committee on Physical Deterioration's curricula ("Good Wives" 21–35). Two useful, contrasting opinions from the early years of this century were those of G. Stanley Hall and M. Carey Thomas.
9. See both Lois N. Magner and Maureen L. Egan for discussions of Gilman's conception of evolution as a force for feminism.
10. Frances Emily White (in 1875) was one of few early responders to *The Descent* who questioned the implication that greater variation meant male supremacy. She preferred "differences" (296). For a modern criticism of Darwin's theory of sexual selection in the context of sexism, see Sue V. Rosser and A. Charlotte

Hogsett. They see sexual selection as "a theory that assumes and provides a scientific explanation for female inferiority," one that "reflected and reinforced Victorian social sexual norms regarding the sexes" (43). They maintain that this relatively minor mechanism of evolution

> was necessary for Darwin in his attempt to arrest the consequences of his own metaphorical procedures, necessary because of his desire not to compare himself with beings (members of the other sex, members of other races) he could not consider his equals, and because of his repugnance in contemplating his ancestral ties with them. (51)

11. For further discussion of the emphasis on cell metabolism, see Jill Conway (she writes that for Geddes and Thomson, "The situation of women in society was not the result of acquired characteristics. It merely reflected the economy of cell metabolism and its parallel psychic differentiation between the sexes," 53) and Mosedale (32–41).

12. Richards begins "Darwin and the Descent of Woman" with an examination of the way scientific knowledge is refracted through its contemporary cultures (57). She suggests, then, how Darwin's science, especially sexual selection, is very much a result of Victorian cultural perspectives, perspectives comfortably reflected in his own household and marriage. Rosser and Hogsett arrive at a similar view of Darwin's biases.

13. For a developed discussion of Huxley and woman's place in Science see Evelleen Richards' 1989 essay. She is distinctly sceptical about his liberalism.

14. See also Mosedale for a discussion of Spencer's views (9–16). (A similar study could be made of Havelock Ellis's changing attitudes.)

15. For a good perspective on Blackwell's accomplishments as well as her scientific limitations see Marie Tedesco. The "modern" scientific spirit that prevailed among Darwin, Spencer, and their associates tended to dismiss J. S. Mill and those who urged the importance of environment. Blackwell interestingly observes that the old speculative methods of Mill — in recognizing the importance of nurture — got more modern, in the sense of valid, results than the scientific methods of Spencer that admitted only the influence of nature (Blackwell 213).

16. Gamble wrote:

> That hairiness denotes a low stage of development, Mr. Darwin incautiously admits, yet in dealing with this subject he is not disposed to carry his admission to its legitimate conclusion by treating its appearance on the body of man as a test in determining the comparative develpment of the female and male organisms. (*Sexes* 50–51)

17. Gamble pointedly spoofed the advance of evolution:

> Hypatia teaching Greek philosophy to the Alexandrians, and the early fathers in the Christian Church gravely arguing the question "Ought women to be called human beings?" indicate the extreme ideas relative to the position of women during the fourth century. As is well known, the latter gained ascendancy. (*Evolution* 341)

WORKS CITED

Allan, J. McGrigor. "On the Real Differences in the Minds of Men and Women." *Journal of the Anthropological Society* (London) 7 (1869): cxcv–ccxix.

Allen, Grant. "Plain Words on the Woman Question." *Popular Science Monthly* 36 (1889): 170–81.

———. "Woman's Place in Nature." *Forum* 7 (1889): 258–63.

Amos, Sarah M. "The Evolution of the Daughters." *Contemporary Review* 65 (1894): 515–20.

Blackwell, Antoinette Brown. *The Sexes Throughout Nature*. New York: G. P. Putnam's, 1875.

Broca, Paul. "Broca on Anthropology." *Anthropological Review* (London) 5 (1867): 193–205, continued in 6 (1868): 35–52.

Brooks, W. K. "The Condition of Women from a Zoölogical Point of View." *Popular Science Monthly* 15 (1879): 145–55 and 347–56.

Catt, Carrie C. "Evolution and Woman's Suffrage." Delivered at Department Meeting of N. A. S. A., May 18, 1893, during the Congress of Representative Women in Chicago. Berg Collection, New York Public Library.

Clarke, Edward H. *Sex in Education; or, A Fair Chance For Girls*. Boston: James R. Osgood, 1874.

Conway, Jill. "Stereotypes of Femininity in a Theory of Sexual Evolution." *Victorian Studies* 14 (1970): 47–62.

Darwin, Charles. *The Descent of Man, and Selection in Relation to Sex*. 1871. Princeton: Princeton UP, 1981.

Duffin, Lorna. "Prisoners of Progress: Women and Evolution." *Nineteenth-Century Woman: Her Cultural and Physical World*. Ed. Sara Delamont and Lorna Duffin. London: Croom Helm, 1978. 57–91.

Dyhouse, Carol. "Good Wives and Little Mothers: Social Anxieties and the Schoolgirl's Curriculum, 1890–1920." *Oxford Review of Education* 3 (1977): 21–35.

———. "Social Darwinistic ideas and the Development of women's education in England, 1880–1920." *History of Education* 5 (1976): 41–58.

Egan, Maureen L. "Evolutionary Theory in the Social Philosophy of Charlotte Perkins Gilman." *Hypatia* 4 (1989): 102–19.

Fee, Elizabeth. "Nineteenth-Century Craniology: The Study of the Female Skull." *Bulletin of the History of Medicine* 53 (1979): 415–33.

———. "Science and the Woman Problem: Historical Perspectives." *Sex Differences: Social and Biological Perspectives*. Ed. Michael S. Teitlebaum. Garden City, N.Y.: Anchor, 1976. 175–223.

———. "The Sexual Politics of Victorian Social Anthropology." *Clio's Consciousness Raised: New Perspectives on the History of Women*. Ed. Mary S. Hartman and Lois Banner. New York: Harper, 1974. 86–102.

Fernseed, Frank. "Sexual Distinctions and Resemblances" *Quarterly Journal of Science* 18 (1881): 741–44.

Ferrero, G. "The Problem of Woman, from a Bio-Sociological Point of View." *Monist* 4 (1894): 261–74.

Finot, Jean. *Problems of the Sexes*. Trans. Mary Safford. New York: G. P. Putnam's, 1913.

Gamble, Eliza Burt. *The Evolution of Woman: An Inquiry Into the Dogma of Her Inferiority to Man*, New York: G. P. Putnam's, 1894.

————. *The Sexes in Science and History: An Inquiry into the Dogma of Woman's Inferiroity to Man*. New York: G. P. Putnam's, 1916.

Gardener, Helen H. *Facts and Fictions of Life*. Chicago: Chas. H. Kerr, 1893.

————. "Sex and Brain-Weight." *Popular Science Monthly* 31 (1887): 266–68.

Geddes, Patrick, and J. Arthur Thomson. *The Evolution of Sex*. New York: Humboldt, 1889.

Gilman [Stetson], Charlotte Perkins. *Women and Economics: A Study of the Economic Relation Between Men and Women as a Factor in Social Evolution*. Boston: Small, Maynard, 1898.

Gould, Stephen J. *The Mismeasure of Man*. New York: Norton, 1981.

Gray, T. S. "Herbert Spencer on Women: A Study in Personal and Political Dissillusion." *International Journal of Women's Studies* 7 (1984): 217–31.

Hall, G. Stanley. *Adolescence: Its Psychology and Its Relations to Physiology, Anthropology, Sociology, Sex, Crime, Religion, and Education*. 1905. Rpt. in *Women, the Family, and Freedom*. Vol. 2. Ed. Susan Groag Bell and Karen M. Offen. Stanford: Stanford UP, 1983. 157–63.

Hardaker, Miss M. A. "Science and the Woman Question." *Popular Science Monthly* 20 (1882): 577–84.

Howe, Julia Ward. *Sex and Education: A Reply to Dr. E. H. Clarke's "Sex in Education."* 1874. New York: Arno, 1972.

Huxley, Leonard. *Life and Letters of Thomas Henry Huxley*. 2 vols. London: Macmillan, 1900.

Huxley, Thomas Henry. "Emancipation — Black and White." 1865. *Collected Essays*. vol. 3. New York: Greenwood, 1968. 66–75.

Le Bon, Gustave. "Récherches anatomiques et mathématiques sur les lois des variations du volume du cerveau et sur leurs relations avec l'intelligence." *Revue d'Anthropologie* 2nd ser. 2 (1879):27–104.

Magner, Lois N. "Women and the Scientific Idiom: Textual Episodes from Wollstonecraft, Fuller, Gilman, and Firestone." *Signs* 4 (1978): 61–80.

Möbius, J. P. "The Physiological Mental Weakness of Woman." Trans. by W. Alfred McCorn. *Alienist and Neurologist* 22 (July, 1901): 624–42.

Morais, Nina. "A Reply to Miss Hardaker on the Woman Question." *Popular Science Monthly* 21 (1882): 70–78.

Mosedale, Susan Sleeth. "Science Corrupted: Victorian Biologists Consider 'The Woman Question.' " *Journal of the History of Biology* 11 (1978): 1–55.

Pearson, Karl. "Woman and Labour." *Fortnightly Review* 329 (1894): 561–77.

————. "The Woman's Question." *The Ethic of Free Thought*. London: Unwin, 1888. 370–94.

Pike, Luke Owen. "Women and Political Power." *Popular Science Monthly* 1 (1872): 82–94.

Richards, Evelleen. "Darwin and the Descent of Women." *The Wider Domain of Evolutionary Thought*. Ed. David Oldroyd. London: D. Reidel, 1983. 57–111.

————. "Huxley and Women's Place in Science: The 'woman question' and the control of Victorian anthropology." *History, Humanity and Evolution: Essays for John C. Greene*. Ed. James R. Moore. New York: Cambridge UP, 1989.

Ritchie, David G. *Darwinism and Politics*. New York: Scribner's, 1901.

Romanes, George J. "Mental Differences Between Men and Women." *Nineteenth Century* 21 (1887): 654–72.

Rosenberg, Rosalind. "In Search of Woman's Nature:1850–1920." *Feminist Studies* 3 (1975):141–54.

Rosser, Sue V., and A. Charlotte Hogsett. "Darwin and Sexism: Victorian Causes, Contemporary Effects." *Feminist Visions: Toward a Transformation of the Liberal Arts Curriculum*. Ed. Diane L. Fowlkes and Charlotte S. McClure. University, AL: Alabama UP, 1984. 42–52.

Russett, Cynthia Eagle. *Sexual Science: The Victorian Construction of Womanhood*. Cambridge, MA.: Harvard UP, 1989.

Sedgwick, Mary K. "Some Scientific Aspects of the Woman Suffrage Question." *Gunton's Magazine* 20 (1901): 333–44.

Shields, Stephanie A. "Functionalism, Darwinism, and the Psychology of Women: A Study in Social Myth." *American Psychologist* 30 (1975): 739–54.

Smith-Rosenberg, Carroll, and Charles Rosenberg. "The Female Animal: Medical and Biological Views of Woman and Her Role in Nineteenth-Century America." *Journal of American History* 60 (1973): 333–56.

Spencer, Herbert. "Psychology of the Sexes." *Popular Science Monthly* 4 (1873): 30–38.

———. "The Rights of Women." *Social Statics, or, The Conditions Essential to Human Happiness*. 1851. New York: Appleton, 1890. 173–91.

———. "The *Status* of Women." *Principles of Sociology*. Vol 1. 1877. New York: Appleton, 1897. 725–44.

Stocking, Jr., George W. *Victorian Anthropology*. New York: Macmillan, 1987.

Tedesco, Marie. "A Feminist Challenge to Darwinism: Antoinette L. B. Blackwell on the Relations of the Sexes in Nature and Society." *Feminist Visions. Toward a Transformation of the Liberal Arts Curriculum*. Ed. Diane L. Fowlkes and Charlotte S. McClure. University, AL: Alabama UP, 1984. 53–65.

Thomas, M. Carey. "Present Tendencies in Women's College and University Education." 1908. Rpt. in *Women, the Family, and Freedom*. Vol. 2. Ed. Susan Groag Bell and Karen M. Offen. Stanford: Stanford UP, 1983. 163–69.

Thomas, William I. "On a Difference in the Metabolism of the Sexes." *American Journal of Sociology* 3 (1887): 31–63.

White, Frances Emily. "Woman's Place in Nature." *Popular Science Monthly* 6 (1875): 292–301.

PAYING UP: THE LAST JUDGMENT AND FORGIVENESS OF DEBTS

By John R. Reed

IN 1889, THE FAMOUS Baptist preacher Charles Haddon Spurgeon published a tract entitled *The Cheque Book of the Bank of Faith*, indicating by his easy updating of the metaphor how familiar the fundamental faith-as-currency trope was. The identification of moral investment and reward was not initiated by the Victorians, but they avidly seized upon the notion. Ultimately, the concept is traceable to various passages in the Bible, most notably in *Matthew* 6:19–21, which reads:

> Lay not up for yourselves treasures upon earth, where moths and rust doth corrupt, and where thieves break through and steal: But lay up for yourselves treasures in heaven, where neither moth nor rust doth corrupt and where thieves do not break through nor steal: For where your treasure is, there will your heart be also.

This and other passages in the Bible suggest that it is possible to build a savings account in heaven to cover debts of transgression in this world. That is not, of course, what the passage in *Matthew* says, but it is open to such an interpretation.

Perceiving sin as debt to be made up and thus forgiven was not unusual for an age fascinated by the accumulation of capital. At least since Max Weber we have been aware that many religious paradigms are closely related to commercial activities. God's forgiveness of man's debt of sin was a major concern in the nineteenth century, especially among evangelicals. Boyd Hilton has demonstrated the material connection between articles of faith and practical social and economic issues. Even the language of the evangelicals, he notes, reveals the intimate connection between faith and commerce. "Of course," Hilton says, "there had long been Christian overtones in the way that money and debt were described, as is clear from such words as 'redeem', 'convert', keeping 'faith' with creditors, and 'credit' itself, but it was in the nineteenth century that such phrases became staples of political debate"

(127). For the evangelicals, Christ's Atonement was the essential ingredient
of faith, for it was the one means for sinful man to achieve pardon and thus
enter heaven.

> Hilton explains "faith in the Atonement sanctifies the sinner as well as justifying
> him, and so prepares his heart for the Heaven which will be his home. This,
> in essence, was the evangelical 'scheme of salvation' . . . Its centrepiece was
> an 'economy of redemption' in which souls were bought in the cheapest market
> and sold in the dearest. (8)

But evangelicals were not the only ones to draw close connections between
financial and moral debt. As a young man serious about religion, Gladstone
wrote a memorandum to himself.

> We ought to care about money: as a means, to be utterly regardless of it, as an
> end. We ought to be careful 1. to spend it — always to have either a) a present
> or b) a prospective purpose for it. 2. *so* to spend it, that we may be the
> better able to open our books of pecuniary account, along with the rest of our
> proceedings, before God at the day of judgement. (Matthew 53–54)

Throughout the nineteenth century, attitudes toward a punitive God were
changing. F. D. Maurice, W. R. Greg, and Albert Barnes sought to replace
a vengeful with a forgiving God. But there could be immediate and material
consequences from changing attitudes about the deity's benignity. The middle
class, for example, lost a major excuse for holding itself above the lower
classes. As long as the accumulation of material goods was seen as a venture
risky to salvation, there was a compensation in being poor with a securer path
to redemption. That advantage disappeared with the onset of a forgiving God.

In *Family Prayers*, a very popular moral text at the beginning of the
nineteenth century, Henry Thornton considered the words "And forgive us
our debts as we forgive our debtors" from Matt. 6:12.

> By our trespasses we may be said to become debtors to God; for we incur a
> penalty proportioned to the sins which we commit. Now the debts, which we
> thus incur, we cannot pay. There is no hope that we shall ever pay them; for
> the future obedience of our whole lives, even if it should be perfect, can never
> cancel the trespasses, which are past: just as the paying regularly all our future
> debts can never cancel a debt, which is already standing out against us. We
> are, therefore, taught, in this prayer, to implore a free forgiveness; and we are
> in it likened to debtors who have nothing to pay; and who, therefore, can only
> ask a free discharge. (Thornton 70)

Elsewhere in Scripture, he says, we learn that it is Christ's death for our
sins that permits us to request this forgiveness. Others repeated Thornton's
insistence on human inability to repay the debt of sin and the consequent need

for Christ's Atonement. Albert Barnes declared in *The Atonement, in its Relations to Law and Moral Government* (1860): *"The atonement is something substituted in the place of the penalty of the law, which will answer the same ends as the punishment of the offender himself would. It is instead of his punishment"* (244). At the end of the century R. W. Dale was still insisting in *Christian Doctrine* (1895) that man may dismiss his resentment for an injury but cannot forgive another's sin. Only God can forgive sin and that forgiveness comes only through the Atonement. Nonetheless, if we are to receive forgiveness, we must make a "frank and sincere confession of sin, a humble submission to the righteousness of God in condemning and punishing it" (270).

Lay persons also concerned themselves with moral indebtedness. Explaining the concept of Christian forgiveness to young female friends, John Ruskin chooses the Lord's Prayer as his text.

> Forgive us — *As* we forgive — What power then have WE over other men's work? Perhaps you may see the meaning a little better by considering that the Lord's prayer says nothing about forgiving *Sin*, as respects *us*. Note the distinction in Luke: Forgive us our sins, as we forgive — those who are *indebted* to us. In Matthew it is "debts" in both cases. You know that "Sin" is especially an act against God. But debt may be to man. You can remit — or release a debt, cannot you. Quite a different thing from pardoning an offense. (240)

Ruskin goes on to explain that to forgive is to regard those who have offended "exactly as you would have regarded them had they *never* sinned, erred, or been in debt to you" (241). In referring to the Lord's Prayer, Ruskin uses the terms "sin" and "indebted," but the Church of England's *Book of Common Prayer* says "forgive us our trespasses as we forgive those who trespass against us. . . ." This version is shared by other Protestants, such as the Methodists, whereas the Catholic Church and some Nonconformist groups use the wording "forgive us our debts as we forgive our debtors. . . ." But, as Ruskin's reading indicates, no matter what the wording, those who used the Prayer seemed to agree that it implied a sense of obligation or indebtedness.

Believers in a retributive God did not yield easily to those who emphasized atonement and forgiveness over punishment. Witness the dismissal of Frederic Denison Maurice from his professorial chair at King's College, London, in 1853, because he ventured in *Theological Essays* (1852) to modify the prevailing image of an afterlife of eternal punishment for sinners. Geoffrey Rowell chronicles Victorian disputes about the life to come in *Hell and the Victorians*, and more recently Michael Wheeler has examined Victorian attitudes toward the four last things in *Death and the Future Life in Victorian Literature and Theology* (1990). There is a good deal for such scholars to record since the debate remained lively. Late in the century, Edward Bouverie

Pusey in *Sermons for the Church's Seasons from Advent to Trinity* (1883) could still assert that the terror of the Day of Judgment is that it *is* judgment (16). Furthermore, he indicated that it was likely to be a surprising judgment for those who, lacking self knowledge, unwisely supposed that they had accumulated valuable stores on earth only to discover that those stores were worthless in heaven (25).

The connection between actual debt and the metaphoric indebtedness of sin is clear and widespread in the Victorian period, as is the growing emphasis upon a loving rather than a punitive deity, and it should therefore come as no surprise that these same sentiments are evident in the literature of the time. In what follows I shall demonstrate how this relationship between material debt and moral indebtedness affects the nature of Charles Dickens's narratives.

A GOOD PART OF THE ENERGY in Dickens's novels derives from an extraordinary anticipatory movement toward a fictional destination. Contributing to this forceful narrative drive is Dickens's creation of an ultimate terminus for all action in the Last Judgment, an event that is referred to regularly, whether directly or indirectly, throughout his writings. For Dickens's contemporaries this constant reminder of a closure beyond the ending of his fictional worlds would have evoked a familiar anxiety about facing a final accounting along with a desire that the Great Accountant would be lenient concerning any imbalances. At an elementary level we are all aware of how frequently in Dickens's fiction imprisonment for debt represents a moral turning point for his characters, a secular prevision of what judgment hereafter might be. From Jingle and Pickwick to Arthur Clennam, physical imprisonment is an analogue for internal revelation. Other authors used the same shorthand: for example, the crucial episode of Rawdon Crawley's confinement in *Vanity Fair*. In these episodes the characters, whether wicked or virtuous, discover in debtor's prison the simple lesson that here mankind owes a moral debt to the savior of us all, a debt that may be mitigated but not forgiven by our charity toward the unfortunate among us. But the connection between material and moral debt is often far more subtle and complicated than this rudimentary situation suggests.

Dickens preached the high merits of forgiveness but was nonetheless inclined to see wickedness peremptorily punished. In his *The Life of Our Lord* (1934) Dickens approvingly records Christ's explanation to Simon that he forgave Mary Magdalene's sins because it is the greatest debtor who most appreciates the forgiveness of that debt (ch. 5, 48). Dickens instructs his children, for whom he wrote *The Life of Our Lord*, that they must themselves forgive if they hope to be forgiven, and he provides several more instances from Christ's teachings (ch. 6, 59). The parable of the workers in the vineyard, for example, indicates that even late in life those who truly repent can be forgiven their sins (ch. 6, 61–2). Set against all of this emphasis upon mercy and forgiveness is only one noteworthy account of punishment — the story of Judas. After his betrayal of Christ, Judas is overcome with remorse and returns to tell the chief priests that he cannot keep their money. "With those words, he threw the money down upon the floor, and rushing away, wild with despair, hanged himself. The rope, being weak, broke with the weight of his body, and it fell down on the ground, after death, all bruised and burst, — a dreadful sight to see!" (ch. 10, 101–2). In literally taking money to betray Christ, Judas has compounded his crime and become a debtor in both commercial and moral terms. He may return the money but he cannot expunge the other debt and he cannot forgive himself.

Although Judas realizes that he cannot cheat heaven, many vicious persons hope to do just that. In *Nicholas Nickleby*, a novel much concerned with greed and money-getting, Dickens describes the type of scoundrels who "gravely jot down in diaries the events of the day, and keep a regular debtor and creditor account with Heaven, which shall always show a floating balance in their own favour." Whether or not it is designed to cheat Heaven, "such book-keeping," the narrator remarks, "cannot fail to prove serviceable, in the one respect of sparing the recording Angel some time and labour" (ch. 44, 567). Geoffrey Rowell describes Coleridge's dislike for this balance-sheet approach to the rewards and punishments of hell, but to many people it seemed a reasonable analogue from their commercial experience (68). In *Uncle Tom's Cabin* (1851), Harriet Beecher Stowe has a slave trader named Haley explain his attitude toward commerce and salvation.

> "I say," said Haley, and leaning back in his chair and gesturing impressively, "I'll say this now, I al'ays meant to drive my trade so as to make money on't, *fust and foremost*, as much as any man; but, then, trade an't everything, and money an't everything, 'cause we's all got souls. I don't care, now, who hears me say it, — and I think a cussed sight on it, — so I may as well come out with it. I b'lieve in religion, and one of these days, when I've got matters tight and snug, I calculates to tend to my soul and them ar matters; and so what's the use of doin' any more wickedness than's re'lly necessary? — it don't seem to me it's 'tall prudent." (ch. 8, 71)

Tom Loker, a fellow slave trader, is disgusted by Haley's "meanness," and declares, "your 'gettin' religion,' as you call it, arter all, is too p'isin mean for any crittur; — run up a bill with the devil all your life, and then sneak out when pay time comes! Boh!" (ch. 8, 71).

In *Nickleby*, Dickens merely alludes to the moral shell game that some rascals try to play with God, but in *Little Dorrit* a great part of the narrative rests upon a similar kind of moral bookkeeping. When Arthur Clennam returns to England after years devoted to business in the East, he feels an uneasy sense that his family has some reparation to make. When he asks his mother if this is so, she responds with a question of her own: Have I not made reparation in this room these fifteen years? The narrator intrudes to demonstrate the relationship between Mrs. Clennam's secular and spiritual accounting.

> Thus was she always balancing her bargain with the Majesty of heaven, posting up the entries to her credit, strictly keeping her set-off, and claiming her due. She was only remarkable in this, for the force and emphasis with which she did it. Thousands upon thousands do it, according to their varying manner, every day. (Bk. 1, ch. 5, 50)

Mrs. Clennam, like Mr. Bulstrode in *Middlemarch* and other less prominent characters, is a familiar breed of self-punisher in Victorian literature.[1] By punishing herself in this world, Mrs. Clennam expects to expunge the debt she owes for having withheld money that actually belongs to the Dorrits; she has imprisoned herself for moral debt. Hers is the kernel of wrong that generates a great part of the action of the novel. And yet she claims that her manipulating money that was not hers and punishing her husband and his young lover were righteous actions. She feels "that it was appointed to me to lay the hand of punishment upon that creature of perdition" (Bk. 2, ch. 30, 775). And she adds: "If, in this, I punished her here, did I not open to her a way hereafter?" (Bk. 2, ch. 30, 777). Mrs. Clennam exculpates herself in this life by anticipating a moral closure beyond the end-point of earthly existence. With her vision presumably focused on the afterlife, she justifies the plot of her own life. By her misuse of money and of secrets Mrs. Clennam sets going a train of episodes that includes the estrangement of the entire Clennam family one from another and also brings hardship on others. And no small part of Mrs. Clennam's sin is that she masks her vileness in divinity, as the narrator makes clear. "Verily, verily, travellers have seen many monstrous idols in many countries; but no human eyes have ever seen more daring, gross, and shocking images of the Divine nature, than we creatures of the dust make in our own likenesses, of our own bad passions" (Bk. 2, ch. 30, 775). Arthur is correct in his vague sense of obligation. He has innocently inherited the debt of his mother's sin. Arthur, however, is thinking only of a material indebtedness. He has set up no idols to mislead him. It is the accumulating sense of a secret sin requiring expiation that powers much of this intricate narrative. Whereas his mother excuses her actions by anticipating the hereafter, Arthur tries to cleanse his conscience by discovering its injury in the past.

Good plotting locates Amy Dorrit — the beneficiary of the worldly resolution of this problem — at the center of its moral satisfaction as well. Through her Arthur is "redeemed" in more senses than one. Little Dorrit has not felt ashamed of the Marshalsea because she owes no debts. She lives in that confinement out of love for her father, not out of necessity. Her father is legally subject to imprisonment, though the severity of the term seems unjust. Arthur at one point wonders if his mother is not somehow responsible for William Dorrit's incarceration. He is awakened from sleep by his mother's spectral voice saying: "He withers away in his prison; I wither away in mine; inexorable justice is done; what do I owe on this score!" (Bk. 1, ch. 8, 89). Fortunately, his mother's grim Calvinist religion has not sunk into Arthur's heart but has disgusted him, "so the first article in his code of morals was, that he must begin in practical humility, with looking well to his feet on Earth, and that he could never mount on wings of words to Heaven. Duty on Earth, restitution on earth, action on earth; these first, as the first steep steps upward" (Bk. 1, ch. 27, 319).

Ironically, it is this very commitment to duty and restitution that places him in prison. He has tried to profit without labor by speculating in shares. His investment fails and he is imprisoned for debt, but this imprisonment is the beginning of his liberation. Much error must be stripped from him, and only in prison does he learn how much he owes morally to Little Dorrit. "None of us clearly know to whom or to what we are indebted in this wise," the narrator says, but the revelation comes to us in moments of adversity (Bk. 2, ch. 27, 720). Arthur's sickness thus becomes the symbolic expulsion of error, and it calls Little Dorrit to him to heal him with the same traits of love, compassion, and mercy that she has demonstrated throughout. Clennam's refusal of Little Dorrit's offer of financial assistance is more than the stereotype of male pride so frequently employed in Victorian fiction. He is already deeply in her moral and spiritual debt, and he will not have that debt confirmed and compounded in secular terms. He cannot accept money or love from her until he can view himself as worthy of both. Whereas Mr. Dorrit's windfall fortune frees him to the pride and folly of social life and eventually sickness, disclosure, and death, Clennam's imprisonment frees him to spiritual awareness. Amy, who was faithful to her misguided father, is similarly faithful to Arthur. Despite his aversion to the bookkeeping concept of faith, Dickens himself seems to suggest that Amy has laid up a treasure in heaven by her efforts on earth. By contrast, all those who make no deposits on their moral debts on earth face a final reckoning hereafter.

The pattern of Dickens's narrative produces a design of gradual movement through stages of confinement to ultimate freedom. The prisoners and detainees of the first two chapters are individuals confined on suspicion of criminal culpability or physical infection: William Dorrit's case represents a

release from physical into psychological confinement in a world partly private
and partly public; Merdle's enfranchisement through suicide is a wholly public
release that affects a wide spectrum of society at large; and finally Mrs.
Clennam's situation represents the last stage of release from a religion, a
world-view, a philosophy that makes all of existence a punishment. It is as
though we move through a series of cages within cages, the personal release
leaving us still in private-public confinement, release from which leaves us
still restrained by the world of social and institutional structures, which, once
evaded still leaves us metaphysically enclosed until we are freed by the New
Testament's message of love, compassion, and forgiveness. Dickens has thus
structured his narrative to imitate the way the individual soul must work
through the world and find true freedom at last, approaching the Last Judgment with no secret debts to its account.

In *Bleak House* the Day of Judgment is purposely blurred to mean both
the day on which a court decision will be made and the day on which each
and all of us will face eternal judgment. The first Dickens presents as almost
totally capricious, the other as certain. This constant anticipation of a Final
Judgment at trial's end within the text mimics Dickens's own technique of
looking past the conclusion of his story to a decisive act beyond it. Though
Miss Flyte is the symbolic custodian of the irony surrounding the concept of
Final Judgment, releasing her symbolic birds when the "last judgment" in
the case of Jarndyce and Jarndyce comes in, she is one of the least threatened
by the other Last Judgment. Many other characters should be deeply concerned. For example, those who think in terms of retribution may have the
most to fear. Like Mrs. Clennam's, the harsh religion of a Miss Barbary or
Mrs. Pardiggle requires a punitive God. And many in the novel go to face a
potentially fierce reckoning, among them, Captain Hawdon, Jo, Krook, Mr.
Tulkinghorn, Richard Carstone, and Lady Dedlock. But again Dickens means
to suggest that just as we cannot rid ourselves of our debt of sin here on earth,
we may hope for forgiveness by following the lesson of Christ. There are
many illustrations of this lesson, but one of the most direct is the case of Mr.
George Rouncewell, the Prodigal Son.

Elsewhere I have shown how widespread the use of the Prodigal Son
parable was among Victorian writers (Reed, 239–49). Dickens used it often,
but in the case of Mr. George there is a sly irony, for George is one of the
most generous and noble characters in the story. Dickens told his own children
that the parable of the Prodigal Son was "meant to teach that those who have
done wrong and forgotten God, are always welcome to Him and will always
receive His mercy, if they will only return to Him in sorrow for the sin of
which they have been guilty" (*Lord* ch. 7, 74). Mr. George feels he has been
"a thundering bad son," a conviction that keeps him from returning to the
mother he loves (*House*, ch. 20, 296). George feels the weight of a moral

debt that cannot be cancelled and which is ironically symbolized in his financial debt to Mr. Smallweed, where the creditor is morally repugnant and the debtor noble. It is by way of this debt and the threat of imprisonment that Tulkinghorn is able to coerce George into yielding up Captain Hawdon's note. Earthly injustice in the novel is typified by George's arrest on suspicion of murder. But there is a positive element in George's entanglement with Tulkinghorn, for it is at the lawyer's chambers that he sees his mother again without himself being recognized (ch. 34, 482). Later, Mrs. Bagnet brings his mother to George in prison and, in the domain of punishment, his displaced guilt is forgiven. George's overscrupulous sense of guilt has prevented him from returning home, though he has thoroughly repented what he considers his offence. His real economic debt begets a crisis that happily discloses a clean moral account. In a cunning reversal, the good man discovers that his debt of sin has been imaginary. After reconciliation with his mother, the innocent prodigal returns home to a life of quiet contentment that requires no fatted calf and calls up no resentment in his virtuous brother. The lesson of Mr. George is just what Dickens wanted the Prodigal Son to represent for his children — a conviction that we must not pre-condemn ourselves but trust that at the Last Judgment a loving God might willingly forgive what we have freely repented.

Mr. George is a benign example of an individual being his own worst enemy, but he is so out of excess charity. Other characters, such as Richard Carstone, Mr. Tulkinghorn, and Lady Dedlock, create more unfortunate destinies for themselves. Their selfish and inconsiderate acts set in train a course of events that eventually destroys them. Like the disclosing finger of Sergeant Bucket and the pointing finger of the Roman figure on Tulkinghorn's ceiling, the plot moves toward an overdetermined conclusion. The good may suffer in this world, but the wicked have paved their way to a more serious judgment elsewhere. The implied author of this novel uses two contrasting narrative voices to suggest how differently we may interpret the world around us. Esther's voice is hopeful and forgiving, a voice of faith; the other voice is retributive and judgmental. Through the playing off of these two voices by foreshadowing, interlocking metaphors, symbolic scenes, and outright indictments, the implied author points to the outcome of his characters' acts, to the bad conscience we all carry about with us. Some of us are willing, one way or another, to acknowledge our sins and shortcomings, real or imagined; others hide them deep within themselves. But they cannot be hidden from the self. Eventually the pointing finger will oblige the guilty mind to reveal itself. The implied author's is the warning finger of destiny that points to the true terminus for us all — the Day of Judgment when Miss Flite frees her captive birds like liberated souls. Material debt may be removed by payment, but psychological and moral debt can be expunged only through true penitence and human forgiveness. Cancelling such a moral debt on earth permits the heavenly ledger to be balanced. This sense of transgression as an accumulating debt lends a powerful teleological force to Dickens's narrative, a force that drives past human existence to a justice hereafter. As the Schoolmaster says at the scene of Little Nell's death in *The Old Curiosity Shop*: "It is not . . . on earth that Heaven's justice ends" (ch. 71, 539). Human justice resolves little in *Bleak House*, but narrative justice assures us that pardon will await all those who, like Richard Carstone and Lady Dedlock, can close their lives with the talismanic word "Forgive" on their lips.

The narrative of *Bleak House* literally points beyond the judgment of this world to the more profound encounter with justice that may be expected in the next. But it is not unique in this trait. Facing the judgments of an English court for his crime of returning illegally to England from his transportation to Australia, Magwitch, old and dying, has a dramatic moment:

> The sun was striking in at the great windows of the court, through the glittering drops of rain upon the glass, and it made a broad shaft of light between the two-and-thirty and the Judge, linking both together, and perhaps reminding some among the audience, how both were passing on, with absolute equality, to the greater Judgment that knoweth all things and cannot err. Rising for a moment, a distinct speck of face in this way of light, the prisoner said, 'My Lord, I have received my sentence of Death from the Almighty, but I bow to yours,' and sat down again. (*Expectations* ch. 56, 434)

The great significance of this moment may be lost on many modern readers who will recognize in it a fine theatrical effect but not the moral pressure of the scene. *Great Expectations* is a novel obsessed with money and guilt in which the central character, narrating his story from some moment well past the conclusion of its events, recounts his own lapsing from the simple virtues of life in expectation of a wealth that would guarantee leisure, comfort, and high social station. The scene of Magwitch midway between the powers of this earth and the Judgment to come would have reinforced powerfully for a Victorian audience the inevitability of having to leave behind the accumulated treasures of this world and of rendering up an account before the Judgment seat in Heaven. Immediately after Magwitch's death, Pip falls seriously ill, is nursed by Joe, and recovers. Soon after, he asks forgiveness of Joe and Biddy, a clear sign that he has changed his expectations. Now he will work for his living, and, by implication, for his salvation. He will build up his moral account on good works, not on selfish indulgence, so that, beyond whichever ending of the novel you prefer, he will be prepared to open his books before the Recording Angel.

Sometimes Dickens's narrator participates far more directly in guiding readers' attention to an impending judgment. *Dombey and Son* is about the misuses of money and the failure of affection. Good characters in the novel are not much concerned with money but put their faith in affection. Little Paul, who is in communication with the next world for almost the whole of his short life, asks his father, "What's money?" and is not convinced by his father's responses, since money could not save his mother from death (ch. 8, 92). But Mr. Dombey can neither render true affection nor appreciate the danger of founding his self-esteem on money. He makes no pretence of laying up a treasure in heaven, though his behavior on earth rapidly accumulates an enormous moral debt. At one point, the narrator becomes so enraged by Dombey's cruel treatment of his loving daughter that he exclaims: "Let him remember it in that room years to come" (ch. 18, 256). The narrator thus marks the moment but also evokes its corollary moment in a part of the story not yet told but whose shape is forecast by the very nature of his warning.

Chapter 59 is entitled "Retribution." Dombey's business and fortune are lost and his wife dishonored. The narrator reminds us — and Dombey — of his warning. "Let him remember in that room years to come," and adds: "He did remember it," and suffered in that remembering (ch. 59, 838). Having trusted to the riches of this world, Dombey has no other resources and is considering suicide when Florence enters to ask her father's forgiveness. The narrator exclaims in amazement that this paragon comes "[a]sking *his* forgiveness" (ch. 59, 843). Of course, it is Dombey who must seek forgiveness of his daughter, and, in recognizing love as the true wealth in life, begin to even his moral account by loving behavior before he is called to Judgment. By signalling proleptically that Dombey's behavior will bring its own retribution upon him, the narrative voice endorses a diegetic thrust that encourages the pattern of transgression and punishment to be projected into the next world. But the "Retribution" chapter itself enacts the condition of the Last Judgment, where hidden sins are disclosed to view and sinners recognize their liabilities. At the same time, it installs forgiveness as the ever-possible amelioration of that otherwise terrifying last prospect. In effect, Mr. Dombey gets a trial run at Last Judgment and has an opportunity to audit and correct his moral ledgers before the real thing.

On a broader scale, the Last Judgment becomes a touchstone for a whole nation's behavior in *A Tale of Two Cities*. Dickens accepts the notion that the French Revolution was the consequence of sins committed by the aristocracy. He describes the inevitable violent retribution as Fate, but, like his friend Carlyle, he might also have referred to the unquestionable Justice that eventually brings its own punishment to each transgression. Retribution is a lively theme throughout the novel, but midway in the story the narrator sardonically indicates the ultimate standard against which behavior should be tested. At the Monseigneur's reception in Paris where earthly privileges, favors, and rewards are distributed, there is an elegant turn-out of court hangers-on. The narrator observes "that all the company at the grand hotel of Monseigneur were perfectly dressed. If the Day of Judgment had only been ascertained to be a dress day, everybody there would have been eternally correct" (*Cities* Bk. 2, ch. 7, 101).

A day of earthly retribution and judgment comes for these aristocrats who are unprepared for divine judgment. The revolutionaries set up their own court and pass bloody justice upon their oppressors. In doing so, they substitute one tyrannical injustice for another. "Vengenace is mine, sayeth the Lord," and Dickens tried to support that sentiment in his fiction, where most of the characters who arrogate punishment to themselves are also transgressors. Yet Dickens permits his narrator to assign doom because, except in the first-person narratives, he stands outside the world of the characters and may operate as a surrogate of divinity. The narrative of *A Tale of Two Cities* passes judgment while indicating that a further judgment is coming.

Resurrection is one of the obvious themes of *A Tale of Two Cities* that has various resonances. Time and again a character is supposed buried and gone only to reappear. At the metaphorical level, the burying of the truth may be followed by its reappearance in a terrifying manner. The St. Evrémonde brothers, representative of the French aristocracy, bury the truth only to see it resurrected again in the person of Dr. Manette. Embedded narratives of resurrection have a proleptic effect, supporting narrative passages more overtly referring to the future. The whole novel leans forward in time, specifically toward that time when Charles Darnay will be asked to pay the debt incurred by his relatives. But Darnay is redeemed by Sydney Carton's successful counterfeit. Carton's has been a largely useless life — the one unquestioned value in it is Lucie Manette. By substituting himself for Darnay, Carton has increased the value of both, for his act wipes out a poor account and instantly gives him a secure standing before God. His face is peaceful when he faces death. He is confident of his reward and so can say: "It is a far, far better thing that I do, than I have ever done; it is a far, far better rest that I go to than I have ever known" (Bk. 3, ch. 15, 358).

Before making his sacrifice, Carton has brooded on Christ's words: "I am the Resurrection and the life. . . ." In other novels, Dickens had demonstrated the lesson of the Last Judgment chiefly in negative examples. In *A Tale of Two Cities*, human justice is presented as highly fallible, even vicious, as with the revolutionaries. But the narrative shows that beyond this justice is resurrection to true judgment. Carton's concluding monologue foresees a time when "the evil of this time and of the previous time of which this is the natural birth, [is] gradually making expiation for itself and wearing out" (Bk. 3, ch. 15, 356). He also sees himself held in the sanctuary of the Darnays's hearts and Lucie's son, named after him, making that name illustrious as "the foremost of just judges and honored men" who brings his own son to Carton's grave to "tell the child my story . . . " (Bk. 3, ch. 15, 358).

Elsewhere in Dickens's fiction the relationship of the individual soul to Divine Judgment is conspicuously rendered in terms of commercial debt and redemption. Final Judgment was largely an awful prospect for most people in Dickens's time. Unlike contemporaries like Thackeray and Trollope, Dickens's narratives exploit the *difference* between the closures of fiction and the dreaded closure of human existence. His narratives anticipate by their proleptic hints, a life after fiction where each of us must open his or her register to the Great Accountant. But in *A Tale of Two Cities*, though the prospect of Final Judgment remains, Dickens has temporarily abandoned his counting-house metaphor and substituted instead a world in which what is lost may be regained, a world in which one noble act of love, modelled on Christ's Atonement, may erase a life of waste and error and guarantee a triumphant entry into heaven. But more than this, Dickens has embodied in the very strategies of his fiction a way of confirming the need always for weak human beings to keep the standard of the Last Judgment as the guide for how they spend their lives.

Wayne State University

NOTES

1. Elizabeth Jay notes "The effort to maintain a favourable spiritual bank balance by acts of gratuitous self-punishment provides the common denominator in characters otherwise as diverse as Mrs. Clennam, Miss Clack, Mrs. Prime and Mrs Bolton, Christina Pontifex and Mr. Bulstrode" (181–82).

WORKS CITED

Barnes, Albert. *The Atonement, in its Relations to Law and Moral Government.* Philadelphia: Parry & McMillan, 1860.

Dale, R. W. *Christian Doctrine: A Series of Discourses.* New York: A. C. Armstrong, 1895.

Dickens, Charles. *Bleak House.* London: Oxford UP, 1966.

———. *Dombey and Son.* London: Oxford UP, 1960.

———. *Great Expectations.* London: Oxford UP, 1975.

———. *The Life of Our Lord.* New York: Simon and Schuster, 1934.

———. *Little Dorrit.* London: Oxford UP, 1963.

———. *Nicholas Nickleby.* London: Oxford UP, 1960.

———. *The Old Curiosity Shop.* London: Oxford UP, 1967.

———. *A Tale of Two Cities.* London: Oxford UP, 1967.

Greg, William Rathbone. *The Creed of Christendom: Its Foundations Contrasted with Its Superstructure.* Toronto: Rose-Belford Publishing Co., 1878.

Hilton, Boyd. *The Age of Atonement: The Influence of Evangelicalism on Social and Economic Thought, 1795–1865.* Oxford: Clarendon P, 1988.

Jay, Elizabeth. *The Religion of the Heart: Anglican Evangelicalism and the Nineteenth-Century Novel.* Oxford: Clarendon P, 1979.

Matthew, H. C. G. *Gladstone 1809–1874*. Oxford: Clarendon P, 1986.

Maurice, Frederic Denison. *Theological Essays*. Second edition with new preface and other additions. Cambridge: Macmillan, 1853.

Pusey, Edward Bouverie. *Sermons for the Church's Seasons from Advent to Trinity*. New York: E. P. Dutton, 1883.

Reed, John R. *Victorian Conventions*. Athens: Ohio UP, 1975.

Rowell, Geoffrey. *Hell and the Victorians: A Study of the Nineteenth-Century Theological Controversies Concerning Eternal Punishment and the Future Life*. Oxford: Clarendon P, 1974.

Ruskin, John. *The Winnington Letters: John Ruskin's Correspondence with Margaret Alexis Bell and the Children at Winnington Hall*. Ed. Van Akin Burd. Cambridge, Mass.: Belknap–Harvard P, 1969.

Spurgeon, Charles Haddon. *The Cheque Book of the Bank of Faith*. New York: A. C. Armstrong, 1889.

Stowe, Harriet Beecher. *Uncle Tom's Cabin*. New York: Airmont, 1967.

Thackeray, William Makepeace. *Vanity Fair*, Vols. 1–2. *The Works of William Makepeace Thackeray*. 26 vols. London: Smith, Elder; Philadelphia: J. B. Lippincott, 1901.

Thornton, Henry. *Family Prayers: To Which Is Added, A Family Commentary Upon The Sermon On The Mount*. 3rd American Edition. New York: Swords, Stanford, 1837.

Weber, Max. *The Protestant Ethic and the Spirit of Capitalism*. Trans. Talcott Parsons, with foreword by R. H. Tawney. New York: Scribners, 1958.

Wheeler, Michael. *Death and the Future Life in Victorian Literature and Theology*. Cambridge: Cambridge UP, 1990.

JAMES THOMSON AND THE CONTINUUM OF LABOR

By Linda M. Austin

WHEN IN 1876 James Thomson asked readers of the *Secularist*, "Why work, work, work . . . ," he recalled the futile asceticism of Carlyle's biblical command, for to the younger man, the Night (in *Sartor Resartus*) that awaited all laborers seemed "black[,] abyssmal . . . inscrutable, utterly void and silent" (*Essays* 144). Unsupported by doctrinal faith in God or an afterlife, the Carlylean imperative was in fact, Thomson tells his readers in "Indolence," a command to "save yourselves from yourselves; to overwhelm and exhaust the natural . . . man in each of you; to occupy all your hours and make them pass as swiftly as possible, thus distracting yourselves from vain talk and thought and self-consciousness, until you are . . . impotent for further mischief" (144). As William Schaefer observes, Thomson attacked the doctrine of work because as an atheist he thought life meaningless and, as a result, worthless (*Beyond "The City"* 112). But lack of purpose does not necessarily attend atheism. Shelley, one of the poets Thomson admired most, sustained a sense of vocation without faith in God or other conventional allegiances. In the "Hymn to Intellectual Beauty," writing becomes a metaphysical calling; and "Mont Blanc," an exploration of the boundaries of the subject within objective reality, assumes the worth of the individual body and spirit as it questions their perimeters. Indeed, the paean to suicide at the end of "Adonais" is possible because the distinction between the subject and the external world, empirical and noumenal, has remained nebulous. Thomson, however, was a materialist; he had answered for himself his predecessor's ontological questions. And he had no conception of vocation: he viewed labor from the perspective of the working and underclass, as necessary for physical survival. Like Shelley, he felt the allure of suicide, but only as a "much more rapid and easy process than the prolonged galley-slavery or penal servitude enjoined by our austere sage [Carlyle]" (*Essays* 145). For the materialist, death finished the progressive devaluation of the soulless body.

69

Shunted into the peripheral literary world of radical outlets like the *National Reformer* and the *Secularist*, Thomson made a paltry living with his writing from 1866 to his death in 1882. For this reason, perhaps, he attacks the evangelical view of work sanctified in *Sartor Resartus*, and he demystifies the vision of art-labor as an almost sacred vocation. In this sense, Thomson belongs with fellow Victorians Tennyson and Arnold, who often questioned the role and purpose of the poet. However, as many of his essays and poems intimate, Thomson thought of himself as a hack; he associated himself with the community of downtrodden laborers; it was from their perspective that he wrote about work. Generally, the early polemics of Marx and Engels had not reached them; the Chartists had left them no spiritual legacy. Their lives and their ideals were far from the communal felicities of Morris and the Ruskinians. They never expressed their values in the terms of an economic or philosophical discourse, and Thomson never wrote as their polemicist. Rather, he conveyed and shared their hostility toward work as well as their submissiveness to prevailing economic doctrine; in particular, he displayed their materialism, their utilitarian dreams, and their Malthusian unhappiness. A number of his poems bespeak the masses' inability to defy or escape the fundamental values of an economic system that they complained enslaved their bodies and minds.

Thomson's experience, then, confirmed traditional theories of labor as subsistence, which was the germ of the production-based economic systems in Smith and Ricardo. Malthus had contributed the clearest and most frightening formulation of an economy of subsistence at the close of the last century, and his ideas had passed into popular thinking by the 1840s. In the Malthusian economy and the Ricardian theory of labor into which it developed, laws of necessity that enabled nature as a whole to survive ensured misery and vice for individual persons. Human labor, in particular, sacrificed the body and mind in the service of the species. It was both a biological and a social evil. Even after a prosperous midcentury, when economists had dismissed Malthus's apocalyptic theory along with the "Condition of England" debate, the dismal science of economics filtered into the work of Thomson because it explained the grim facts of his own labor and that of many working-class radicals.

Thomson's iconoclastic views of ethics, art, and religion disinherited him from the traditional aesthetic solutions to cultural and personal impotence. He eschewed not only the spiritual but the symbolical elevation of work into a noble asceticism: labor signified nothing invisible, and it brought no unseen reward. In general, he refused to see art-labor as intrinsically valuable, or genius as an estimable quality. The self-imposed limits of his vision result in *The City of Dreadful Night*, in which he focuses on the terrible lives of fruitless work and idleness within a society that esteems only production.

This highly abstract work of the early seventies nonetheless evinces the materialist values Thomson embraced elsewhere, chiefly in his "cockney" poems of 1865–66. These celebrate the body as a locus of asceticism in spiritual, literary, and economic discourses: in dramatic monologues or conversations, workers worn out from their labor utter the joys of rest and excess. In doing so, however, they express the very horror of the self and the physical that Thomson exposes in Carlyle's imperative, most memorably through the restive and enervated wanderers of *The City of Dreadful Night*.

The Poet as Laborer: Wilkinson, Robert Browning, Thomson

THE CIRCUMSTANCES OF HIS WORK led Thomson to generalize and attribute to writing the features of all labor within the conventional discourse. He views writing as mental exertion, which in Mill's redaction of Ricardo is just as debilitating as physical work. No artist, Thomson declares in "Per Contra: The Poet, High Art, Genius," an essay of 1865, regards work as the quiddity of life; rather, it is what one does in order to live. As testimony to this principle, he provides statements or examples of revered writers. Shakespeare "wrote no more when he could afford to live without writing" (*Essays* 134). Sonnet CXI, in which he confesses, "my nature is subdued/To what it works in, like the dyer's hand," suggests to Thomson a prosaic view of genius and explains why the dramatist eventually retired on his fortune "as a jolly burgess" (*Essays* 133). Poetry may be the occupation of choice when one simply is better at it than ploughing, but in Thomson's eyes it often is the resort of thwarted ambitions. "Shelley yearned for the direct action of political life, and was disabled and outcast into the mere life of poetry"; lordosis made Leopardi a scholar; blindness and old age forced Milton into the labor of *Paradise Lost* and other written "consolations" for political and ideological defeats (134). Without denying the greatness of their work, Thomson observes them from a central, material perspective: writers become, in Terry Eagleton's phrase, "commodity producers" who exist "more and more on the margins of a society . . . not inclined to pay high wages to prophets" (20). Thomson's attitude toward genius resembles Arnold's in *Empedocles on Etna* and "Stanzas from the Grande Chartreuse," which also affect a central or mundane position to cast a skeptical eye on the practical effects of poetry's formalized introspection and emotion. Thomson, however, does not worry himself about whether poetry can teach us how to live; he already has set its value, and the debate about art's efficacy is for him over. Art is a trade that serves life. Therefore, writing is subject to the utilitarian valuation of labor within conventional, Ricardian economics.

A great reader, especially of Heine and Leopardi, Thomson was not levelling the quality of all writing in "Per Contra"; he was instead emphasizing that the act of creation was fundamentally labor and therefore subject to the conditions and consequences implicit in the general discourse. He seemed aware that readers might interpret his comments as indictments of writers he esteemed, like Shakespeare and Shelley, and his tone in the essay is playful and half-ironic. But Thomson reinforced his materialistic view of the creative process when some years later he undertook a lengthy analysis of the poet, historian, and physician James John Garth Wilkinson's efforts to compose by "Impression," a form of automatic writing. Called *Improvisations from the Spirit*, the book had been published by the Swedenborg Society in 1857 and was out of print by 1876, the year Thomson's essay was serialized in the *Liberal*.[1] There was no pressing need for Thomson to review the book, but having written "Per Contra," he naturally was interested in Wilkinson's experiment in spontaneous production.

The pieces in *Improvisations from the Spirit* resemble the personal and accidental associations which the eighteenth-century philosopher Archibald Alison traced to the stimulus of particular objects. His account of image trains derived from David Hartley's idea of vibrations, a neurophysiological process in which sensations course through the nerves and trigger adjacent vibrations to produce reasoning, memory, imagination, and will. Alison turned this associationism into a theory of beauty, and it survived through the nineteenth century in various forms: Ruskin's second volume of *Modern Painters* (1846) and Pater's conclusion to *The Renaissance* (1873) treat beauty in part as an associational effect. The automatic writing in *Improvisations from the Spirit* was a doctrinal version of this aesthetic since the associations developed from a list of Swedenborgian correspondences. Wilkinson's poems have very short lines, and this semantic terseness is the chief indication of their associative, improvisational shaping. Short rhyming lines of unadorned phrases suggest what Dante Gabriel Rossetti called "an abnegation of personal effort" in his comparison of Wilkinson's poetry with Blake's. (*Jerusalem* was supposedly the product of automatic writing [*Biographical* 304].)[2] Yet most of the pieces in the volume are rhymed, some are in *ottava rima*, and one is in Old English alliterative verse. Thomson uses these aural regularities to contest Wilkinson's claim that the Impressions differ from other kinds of composed poetry, and he proceeds to argue for the improvisational nature of all writing (confining his examples to poetry). He calls attention to the paradox in *Don Juan*: it appears at once as slapdash invention and as controlled artifice. In the same light, Wilkinson's short, rhymed Impressions exhibit the conventional signals of inspiration that Blake and the Wordsworth of *Lyrical Ballads* popularized.

Thomson did not debunk Wilkinson's claims completely; he believed that a degree of spontaneity separates highly methodical, polished composition from improvisation. However, because he saw even automatic writing as mental exertion — a species of labor — he applied utilitarian measures to the Impressions and thereby demystified Wilkinson's account of their genesis.

In the review, he defines improvisation as a rate of writing, in this case an average of 160 lines per hour. He is brought to this calculation by Wilkinson himself: the writing of the Impressions is described by their author as "recreation, after days not unlaborious" (*Biographical* 333). As the paradox suggests, he does not separate play from work; the first seems a subcategory of the second. Indeed, Wilkinson depicts his experiment as a time-study of labor. He notes spending 50 hours on the entire project; copying, which entailed no correction, took twice as long as writing (332–33). His "production," "attended by no feeling and no fervour," thus follows the economic principle of operation, laissez-faire (333). *Improvisations from the Spirit* represents fanatical conformity to the tenet; its robotic economy of art reflects the era's faith in measurement, evident for example in Francis Galton's quantification of boredom, beauty, and intelligence (the last being a result of brain size).[3] The book's aesthetic also parallels Gradgrind's methods of education in Dickens's *Hard Times*, though Wilkinson predictably infuses it with a vaguely evangelical theism:

> *Laissez-faire* in the present state of the world, is so active a vortex, and so fiery, that few persons dare to see its consequences. All men will see them though, because Providence comes in with marvels wherever self succumbs itself. (299)

The association of a passive creativity with a "fiery" but unresistant economics encouraged Thomson to consider the Impressions as labor. He dismissed the dogmatic spiritualism overlying the mechanistic process and focused on Wilkinson's proclaimed intellectual inertia, his conscious estrangement from his "production," and the valorization of quantity. All reduced *Improvisations from the Spirit* to a "rapidity of writing" without premeditation or revision; it differed from copying only in speed (333). Using Wilkinson's own claims, Thomson the materialist depicted the experiment as a product of a system of laissez-faire in which the individual worker functioned, like the factory-hand or clerk, without will or purpose.

The constraints of journalism undoubtedly encouraged Thomson to view art from this economic perspective, and they demanded from him a prosaic deftness that confirmed his materialism. (His reviews for *Cope's Tobacco Plant,* for instance, had to mention smoking, even within discussions of Ben Jonson and Edmund Burke.) The language of the reviews is commercial; its figures refer mainly to production and exchange and thereby subject literature to the values of the larger utilitarian economy, just as Wilkinson validated his poetic experiment by the principle of laissez-faire. Thomson writes of Tennyson, "Scarcely any other artist in verse of the same rank has ever lived on such scanty revenues of thought." He is "a pensioner on the thought of his age'' (*Biographical* 265–66). The phrases suggest that the economic sphere provided the conceptual referent for the notion of value. And even though the image of individual or cultural intellect as capital operates as little more than a suitable and common display of wit for a commercially-minded, rather iconoclastic reader of the *National Reformer* in 1866, monetary analogies here evoke, and thereby bring to, his literary criticism the ideological apparatus of the economic discourse.

For example, when in "Per Contra" Thomson indicts contemporary novels for their padding — "thoughtless pages of trite reflection, inventory description, and multitudinous insignificant detail" (*Essays* 128) — he condemns one of the conventions of realism by ancient standards of thrift. The latter are linked with wise management, force, and masculinity. The novel is, in his words, a "feminine" genre and realism, by implication, a feminine mode because both involve the pith of narration in a meaningless surplus of conceptual, emotional, and concrete detail (*Essays* 128). He perceives the style of the realistic novel as a violation of a standard of efficiency that appears as early as Aristotle's *Laws* and permeates Ricardian economics. Aristotle's prohibition of usury as valueless multiplication of money or tokens and the eighteenth-century Physiocrats' view of wealth as an annual measure of production and consumption of tangible goods both imply an economy of visible correspondence between signifier and signified.

The link between inefficiency and the feminine is especially visible in the divisions of labor in the middle and lower-class family, as the American economist and proto-sociologist Thorstein Veblen observed at the end of the century. Veblen incorporated gender distinctions in his study of the pecuniary basis of aesthetics and value, *The Theory of the Leisure Class*. In general, he connects waste, his nonpejorative word for vicarious consumption, to the duties of wives and domestic workers. When labor involves excessive spending of money or time and surpasses use, it turns into "nonproductive consumption" and signifies a reputable and aesthetically pleasing waste. Thus the appearance and domestic activities of the middle-class woman seemed to contemporaries both proprietous and appealing because their tastes conformed to an aesthetic that "demands just these evidences of wasted effort," states Veblen (82). In a gradual and unnoticed substitution, the monetary and social significance of waste becomes a sign of beauty.

In linking the feminine with the novel's verbal waste, Thomson does recognize the purposive vacuity of the genre and credits superfluous detail with furnishing a texture of reality.[4] He sees waste, however, not from the sociological perspective of Veblen, who traces the etiology of leisure, but through the lenses of labor theory, which denigrates what is visibly unproductive and nonquantifiable. In Thomson's eyes, waste does not differ from futile effort; it carries a negative aesthetic and pecuniary standard. Whereas Veblen has included a psychological element in the economy and can show the utility of waste, Thomson never strays from his materialistic position, and like Ricardo and the Physiocrats before him he values only productive activity. For him all art, which in some way transgresses the bounds of the merely serviceable, represents an inferior, "feminine" labor within the conventional economic discourse.

In his praise of Robert Browning, Thomson reveals the basis of his aesthetics in orthodox, production-based economies like Ricardo's and the way in which his critical canon subsumes gender distinctions. He thought Browning a genius, but he exempted the famous poet from the physical and mental weakness, as well as the material conditions, which he felt made writing a substitute for life or a poor way to make a living. Browning's poetry embodies the vitality of its creator. In a paper he read at the third meeting of the Browning Society in 1882, Thomson readily identified the poet with his work:

> I look up to Browning as one of the very few men known to me by their works who, with most cordial energy and invincible resolution, have lived thoroughly throughout the whole of their being, to the uttermost verge of all their capacities . . . whereas nearly all of us are really alive in but a small portion of our so much smaller beings, and drag wearily toward the grave our for the most part dead selves, dead from the suicidal poison of misuse and atrophy of disuse. (*Biographical* 456)

The robust Browning defies the conditions of labor; his life and art contrast with the enervated Wilkinson in his *Improvisations* and the pallid and estranged work of almost everyone else. Unlike other writers of genius such as Leopardi and Milton, Browning and his labor are reciprocal expressions of each other; in his paper, Thomson never separates the man from his poetry.

Yet the poet does not transcend the economic measurement Thomson uses on others. Browning is presented as an industrial wizard, an exceptional worker within the continuum of labor. His originality, like Tennyson's staleness, is figured in monetary terms. Thomson states that he "stamps with vigorous clearness his own image and superscription on his word-mint-age . . . instead of issuing the common currency with the common image and superscription half-effaced by multitudinous usage" (*Biographical* 445). Browning has his own currency; it has no connection with the "demonetised, vulgarised vocabulary of the newspapers" (445). Using the common parallel between money and words, Thomson defends Browning's verbal obscurity (a frequent complaint of critics) by scorning the market of poetry; superior artistry keeps Browning's work from wide circulation. In this context, he uses "demonetised" to indicate an over-circulated, hence devalued, object.[5]

Unlike journalism, which Thomson implies has inundated readers with verbiage and in the process lost its currency, Browning's words have retained their worth; they are the real money.

Passing over this indirect slight of his own work and pursuing the analogy with economics, Thomson figures the mind of the poet as a mechanical wonder, quoting Swinburne with approval: "[Browning] never thinks but at full speed; and the rate of his thought is to that of another man's as the speed of a railway to that of a waggon, or the speed of a telegraph to that of a railway" (446). These similes seem "peculiarly felicitous" to Thomson, "inasmuch as the railway train not only runs ten times faster than the waggon, but also carries more than ten times the weight" (446). He goes on to portray the poet's powers of "transcendent analysis" and "synthetic exposition" as "intellectual and moral vivisection, whose subjects grow the more living in their reality the more keenly the scalpel cuts into them" (449). With these comparisons to production, distribution, and finally to manual dexterity, Thomson conveys the subtlety, penetration, and originality of Browning's poetry.

Besides being obscure, Browning's work also was said to be affected, and the remark about its "demonetised" language was supposed to refute this charge with a practical explanation. In the poetic market, "affected" — really "unfamiliar" — was the provincial attribute for what was rare. However, since analogies with railways, telegraphs, and vivisection linked Browning's work with scientific advancement, rarity could be synonymous with invention during its early circulation among readers, and "affected" at this stage could also mean progressive. Thus at first, Thomson's defense of Browning seems contradictory, aimed at two different and opposing audiences: on the one hand, his poetry possesses superior worth because it is not a widely distributed commodity; to the enemies of economic laws of value, it is aloof from and therefore superior to the market. On the other hand, to champions of progress and liberal individualism, the rate of production of the poems and their stylistic novelties evince the mechanistic genius of their producer. Yet perhaps most readers, like Thomson, did not detect a contradiction in his defense: their esteem for rates of production and industrial improvement did not necessarily nullify their appreciation for the rare commodity. For in his remarks, Thomson never intimates that Browning's poetry does not circulate at all. Its scarcity raises its value but in no way elevates that value above economic standards; it merely insinuates the existence of a small group of discriminating consumers.

Attuned to signs of the production-based discourse, Thomson comprehends Browning's masculinity, a quality embedded in economic theory and industrial achievement. By measurable standards, Browning is a fast, efficient worker who distinguishes himself in the poetic market by the novelty of his work and its limited distribution. In this materialistic critique, the rapidity and density of Browning's thought are industrial, not natural, marvels. (The romantic standard, which privileges a spontaneous but naive response to the external world, does not apply to this poet, especially since it signals verbal effusion, or surplus.) Thomson sees in the poet's response to the outside world an energy and a force which he attributes to a "masculine soul for passion, a masculine intellect for thought, and a masculine genius for imagination" (451). This efficiency and power contrast with the results of romantic spontaneity, verbal waste. Implicitly then, Thomson characterizes Browning as a pariah within the still predominant feminine aesthetic, which stresses through verbal excrescence sincerity rather than vigor. The praise of Browning as a super-worker, productive as a machine, arises from the prosaic view of art Thomson stresses in "Per Contra," since within the century's rhetoric of progress, the poet is an exemplary laborer. His work marks the desirable end of the continuum of labor on which Thomson placed all art: it is the most vigorous, the most masculine, the most efficient; but still it is labor. It escapes the hostility Thomson shows toward the Carlylean imperative in "Indolence" only because the poetry is so virile.

Thomson's pedestrian view of art coalesced not only from his own writing habits but from the contemporary view of his poetic virtues. His second volume of poems (in 1881) was praised by George Saintsbury in the *Academy* as "not merely the work of the scholar *der sich übt*," but of one "fully *vollendet*" (*Essays* [2]). He refers to the "long and patient apprenticeship" he detected in poems dating from the sixties. Their workmanlike features include a variety of metrical and rhyming patterns and blatant imitation of the distinctive styles and phraseologies of others. Unlike Wilkinson, Thomson operated consciously within the arena of poetry, creating out of what Ernst Gombrich calls "traditional schemata" (*Art and Illusion* 175); the voices of Shelley, Heine, Leopardi, and, as I will mention, Browning and Swinburne are some of the most audible in his pieces. At times he glosses his passages with similar lines from his models, as if to fend off charges of plagiarism, for many of the allusions echo their originals. There is a mediated, sometimes stuffy quality about much of his work, especially the precursors of *The City of Dreadful Night*, and even in the colloquial "cockney" poems of the midsixties. For the most part, his pieces display what Jeannette Marks has called an "executive" rather than a "creative" faculty (97). *The City*, his best known poem, is filled with personifications and allegorical set-pieces, and the "cockney" productions circulate "a certain 'accepted' use of words . . . a sort of unprivileged Tennysonianism," Marks comments (103). When serious, he is pretentious; he "seeks trophies of the erudite or absolute," she continues (106); when colloquial, he bears "the composite, a little degraded personality, of a whole class of people" (109). At bottom, Thomson himself is a cockney, something for which Marks in 1926 condemned his work. Yet the vulgarity of Thomson's skill — its obvious workmanship, particularly its flagrant copying of colloquial and poetic voices — is not an unfortunate and contemnable feature of his work. Rather, it is the predominant value *in* many of the poems, particularly the carefree cockney pieces of the sixties. For in essence they are representations of and responses to labor within the production-based discourse that pervades the essay on Browning.

In the context of Thomson's materialism and allegiance to labor theory, the detectable presence of other voices in his poems valorizes their recorded rather than their created quality. They are the products of a skilled copyist. The conversations of the working-classes that comprise "Low Life" and "Sunday at Hampstead" (both of 1865) make these poems appear as transcriptions. Less obviously, the first section of "Sunday at Hampstead," which describes a prospect spanning London from a suburban heath, represents the natural world as an already mediated phenomenon. The city lacks delineation for the urban speaker on holiday in Hampstead. St. Paul's and surrounding house-tops look adumbrated; the whole outline of London is flattened and blurred on the horizon. "Under the clouds and the light" (I.6), the city "Seems a low wet beach, half shingle,/With a few sharp rocks upright" (I. 7–8). But Thomson also presents the rustic setting from a cockney viewer's eyes, so it appears distanced and unreal. The speaker of this "idle idyll" (subtitle) sees the heath in verbal clichés, as "green, green" with an "open sky . . . Where the earth's sweet breath is incense/And the lark sings psalms on high" (I. 21–24). Intent on the illusion of far-off London disintegrating into nature, he ignores the landscape surrounding him. To eyes accustomed to urban sights, the country lacks a particularized presence.

The stale depiction of nature in this poem may replicate urban vision, but it also hints at Thomson's workmanlike habits. The scene that opens "Sunday at Hampstead" closely resembles Ford Madox Brown's *An English Autumn Afternoon*. In this painting, a couple rest on a patch of grass and survey the roofs and trees of Kentish Town and Islington, suburbs of the great city that seems so far away. As in the poem, St. Paul's is just visible in the distance, but the city itself vanishes on the line of the horizon. It appears as the "low wet beach" (I. 6) of the poem, the edge of the world. In his catalogue of 1865, Brown called the painting "a literal transcript of the scenery around London, as looked at from Hampstead" (Hilton 148). In fact, he was living at Hampstead when he worked on the picture from 1852 to 1854. The heath, which he could see from his window, was then a "real suburb," remarks Timothy Hilton, "where Middlesex, with its lanes, its farms, met the houses of London" (148). There are other similarities between the poem and the painting. In both, the man sprawls while the woman sits. ("I am sinking," murmurs Thomson's cockney. "It is hard to sit upright!/

Ford Madox Brown. "An English Autumn Afternoon" 1852–54. Reproduced by kind permission of the Birmingham Museums & Art Gallery, Birmingham, England.

Your lap is the softest pillow" [I. 45–47].) The couple are in their Sunday finery; "in an hour they will go home to tea," muses Hilton, gazing at the picture. Thomson's pair also look forward to tea, with friends. In sections that follow, the speaker recounts the "lower-middle-class romance" Hilton sees captured in Brown's painting (147).

Thomson never mentions *An English Autumn Afternoon* as the source of the opening stanzas of or the inspiration for "Sunday at Hampstead," though he certainly could have seen it; Brown entered it in the International Exhibition of 1862 in London and again in his one-man exhibition a month before Thomson, then living nearby, wrote the poem.[6] He may have been influenced by other, earlier pictures as well, for increasingly suburbs had been represented as playgrounds for urban dwellers; in the twenties and thirties, John Constable had painted Hampstead heath with city strollers.[7] By the time Brown was working, observes Ann Bermingham, "the landscape would not work up into a picture not because it had been made 'ugly' by suburbanism but because at some fundamental level it was no longer an inevitable part of experience and therefore became difficult to represent" (178). Thus the fragmented and cursory treatment of the landscape in "Sunday at Hampstead" reflects a general urban estrangement from nature and rustic life discernible in much contemporary art. Thomson's use of Brown's *plein air* painting or similar pictures as the source of description illustrates the cockney experience of nature as it demonstrates the cockney division of labor, in which writing becomes less personal, more like transcription.

The Continuum of Labor in the Cockney Poems

FROM 1864 THROUGH 1868, Thomson composed at least seven light-hearted poems about city workers. All but one eventually appeared in the radical journals to which he also contributed essays and reviews.[8] The cockney poems represent the continuum of labor in two ways: first, their production — which includes some of the formal qualities I have discussed — makes their writer a kind of copyist. Second, they often depict labor or the life of laborers in ways that reinforce the capitalistic values of a production-based economics, as well as the class polarities that arise within such an economy. That these happy poems of the sixties affirm the value of labor for the working classes is surprising in light of Thomson's professed animosity toward the Victorian shibboleths of work and duty. As I have discussed, in "Indolence" Thomson not only questions labor's function as a physical and ideological balm for the horrors of subjectivity, but he doubts the ethics of work, finding much "honest commercial labour" "mischievous" (146); it inculcates the passivity already valorized in the laissez-faire economy that all people support simply by working. England is a nation of Bumbles, he declares in "Bumble, Bumbledom,

Bumbleism,'' an essay of 1865, borrowing from Dickens to give Arnold's Philistine a more suitably English name and character. Like *Oliver Twist*'s beadle, Bumble opposes change; he wants to remain comfortable, even if in his present state he is not able to gratify all his desires. His selfishness does not derive from any sort of Hobbesian or Benthamite conception of the personality; Thomson does not think of human beings as psychological entities. Bumble is intellectually lazy because he is tired, for work saps everyone's energy. No one *can* object to new opinions or practices because no one has the physical or mental strength to survive the stress. It is easier for Bumble "to acquiesce quietly in whatever creed" prevails (*Essays* 121).

"Low Life," a poem written the same year as the essay on Bumble and published ten years later in the *Secularist*, illustrates this insidious effect of work and the Carlylean work-ethic in a laissez-faire economy. In twenty quatrains of fairly regular, rhymed (aabb) tetrameter, the poem repeats a dialogue between a seamstress and a copyist, who begin by recounting the hardships of their jobs. The woman tells how she worked past midnight making Sunday dresses for wealthy ladies. One exhausted worker, Mary Challis, is sent to bed; she dies during the night as she lies beside another sleeping, consumptive woman. Most of the women cannot attend the funeral because they have orders to finish. The man commiserates with his companion: he wrote one night "like an engine" (55) until five in the morning; the words he had to copy were barely readable; they covered the margins and backs of the pages. When finished, his "fingers were dead and the letters alive" (56). Although they complain, both speakers take for granted the toll of work on the body. The woman does attribute some of her misery to the pious ladies who "need" new dresses for church, but she does not dwell on this hint of class antagonism. Instead, both she and the copyist depict themselves in the service of objects rather than of exploitative human agents; dresses and words assume the life that ebbs from their bodies.

The radical journals with which Thomson was associated frequently deplored the low wages paid for the kinds of labor women generally did. Dressmaking was an obvious target, and another, coincidentally, was law-writing, the job of the male speaker in "Low Life." It paid, on the average, 25 shillings a week, according to the *National Reformer*.[9] But the poem is far from a working-class protest or proto-feminist argument. In fact, the speakers go on to support the work-ethic their anecdotes seem to attack. They view the labor that weakens their bodies as their means to a life of ease. The copyist, who expects a promotion, envisions his future as a common-law clerk, a job both remunerative and pleasant:

> Just fancy, each morning a jolly good walk,
> And instead of the copying, bustle and talk!

And if I do well — and well I will do —
A couple of sovs. a week for my screw! (65–68)

His hopes lead him to a proposal of marriage, which he frames in terms of labor *they* control:

We'll use our professional talents, my dear:
You shall make such a wedding-dress, best of the year!
And a wonderful marriage-deed I will draw
With magnificent settlements perfect in law. (73–76)

He concludes, "Thus doing our duties in those states of life/In which it has pleased God to call us, *my wife!*" (77–78). The emphasis in the direct address on "my" signals the causal link, in the speaker's mind, between his labor and the reward of possession, as well as between production and consumption. In the economic discourse, they are complementary terms; but the copyist has misread them as causal forces in his association of labor with marriage "duties." He has also applied his mistaken understanding of economics to his own life; he assumes, in other words, that his dutiful labor will result in his own consumption. Responding to his proposal, the seamstress continues to phrase romance in economic terms and imitates the contractual alliances involved in matches between those of wealth or property. " 'And how much a year will you settle on me?' " she asks. The copyist replies, "My body and soul and — what we shall see" (79–80). Their repartee, so obviously tongue-in-cheek, harbors desires for economic security, control, and gratification that marriage, even among the poor, ritualizes.

The proposal in "Low Life" is, therefore, an economic event in which the victimized couple seize control of their labor and create what Ruskin in *Unto This Last* described as the ideal economic relationship, one of mutually beneficial exchange and verbal contract. They are able to do so through the medium of money. Somehow, the higher salary of the new clerkship represents to them a freedom of expenditure that obscures its original signified, labor. Indeed, in developed industrial economies, money is an empty and hence accommodating symbol. It reverts to labor for its significance, but as Marx emphasized, labor itself can provide the source and standard of value only through the possibility of exchange, also figured in money. Writing a few decades after Marx and Thomson, the philosopher Georg Simmel observed its vast symbolic arena: it had become a means "for the presentation of relations that exist between the most superficial, 'realistic' and fortuitous phenomena and the most idealized powers of existence, the most profound currents of individual life and history" (55). Thus the settlement that expresses the couple's relations functions the way inheritance does at the end of romance: "a social institution, . . . [it can] change . . . general conditions only by changing the relations between individuals'' (162). But in this poem, the copyist's deliverance, like the legatee's of a fairy tale, is just a move from one spot to another on the economic continuum. Thomson's couple do not imagine love outside the present sphere of labor and exchange; perhaps that is why they exemplify for him "low life." Only the title indicates contempt for those who filter what Simmel calls "the most profound currents of individual life" (55) through the illimitable and fathomless vortex of money.

The couple on the train are lighthearted, naive members of a Balzacian world. The ease with which they can cathect their desires onto money blinds them to the exploitative character of their labor. They finally justify their physical hardships with a work ethic that derives from the Christian notion of exchange: the atrophied body will bring spiritual, and in "Low Life" material, rewards. If, writes Simmel, "labour power is the content of every value, it receives its form as value only by entering into a relation of sacrifice and gain" (96). Thomson's couple believe that jobs which subject them to the demands of their social superiors will lead to economic control and marriage. "Low Life" thus dramatizes the way in which the philosophic and economic principles of the state, such as laissez-faire, still fashion the desires of those who knowingly suffer under its policies. In light of the ideology of labor that Thomson attacks in his essays, the cheerfulness of "Low Life" is deceptive; if the poem does not harbor his satiric view of work, it at least illustrates, without his understanding perhaps, the way in which an economy structures and contains its subjects' idealism.

Some of his other poems and essays suggest that Thomson objected to more of the prevailing economic discourse than the laissez-faire principle of (in)action and platitudes about the rewards of labor. The acceleration of exchange disturbed him as well. In his essay on Bumble, he speaks of the benumbing circulation of ideas. Debates over religious, scientific, and social issues flood and reduce the effect of separate ideas. In Thomson's view, purveyors of theories "lead us forth gallantly, round, and round, and round, through interminable dreary tracts, and at last bring us, all bewildered and exhausted, to the old flesh-pots again, to the cucumbers, and the melons, and the leeks, and the onions, and the garlic" (*Essays* 115). All new ideas can be reduced, after incessant circulation, to the same few homely items. Bumble resists new ideas justly, then, because he has had to shop in a frenetic market offering stale goods, and he is bored with the merchandise. An intellectual atmosphere that strikes many of us as vital and dramatic drains Thomson; the controversies that drew Ruskin, Arnold, and others into public exchange do not excite him. At bottom, he has some of the obstinacy of a Bumble, but only because he perceives how a surfeit of ideas will weaken their force and, eventually, their value. In his poem, "Mr. MacCall at Cleveland Hall," the speaker, another copyist, records the speech of a well-known freethinker while he watches a young woman in the audience.[10] Quatrains split in two and woven with alternate rhyming convey his divided attention. Too distracted to produce a coherent redaction, he hears but cannot conceptualize words and catches only bits of the lecture, entitled "The Conflict of Opinions In the Present Day." Meanwhile, he gives private thoughts his attention through a cohesive grammar:

> Herder, Wieland, Lessing;
> Bossuet, Montalembert.
>
> Fine names, but the name worth guessing
> Is the name of the sweet girl there. (38–41)

Running through his head are buzz-words from familiar lectures for members of the Secularist Society and other radicals: "Mammon-worship" suggests Ruskin's and Carlyle's diatribes against the Manchester School; "individuality" evokes the recent definition of the word in the zoology of Darwin, the social philosophy of J.S. Mill, and the cultural criticism of Newman and Arnold. The poem is a mosaic of opinion — about impressionistic technique of painters like Whistler, Degas, and Boudin ("We lay on colour in splashes,/ With a mop, or a broom for brush" [22–23]) and the drab clothes of women ("they cannot dress at all" [31]).[11] The prominence of these arguments has spawned encapsulating terms that free the copyist from much of his labor and allow him to pursue more intriguing thoughts. As a result the poem, half of which is his account of the speech, is a list of evocative names that need no content.

Certainly, the attractions of sex and matters of the heart can obscure any intellectual, social, or religious concern, no matter how pressing, but the poem is not celebrating the smaller world of human emotions; that is the province of the realistic novelists. It is a light-hearted attempt to portray what Thomson called in "Bumble" the "immense burden" of the "commonplace": even in "more elevated intellectual and moral life," ideas that have circulated enough to receive labels become "a very great bother and bore" (*Essays* 108). The poem's humor is anti-intellectual; it presents the private life of the senses at the expense of the public life of ideas. It also can be read as another cheerful cockney poem about labor. Like the couple of "Low Life," the copyist at Cleveland Hall finds a way to gratify personal desires through work. He does not subscribe to the work ethic, however, and include his job in his fantasies, but he executes his task in a disaffected, automatic manner. As a result, he is able to devote at least half of his professional time to leisure.

Fantasies about money and love disengage laborers from their physical selves and the actual situations that bore and bind them. Yet their daydreams always return to the body; it is the vortex of all pleasure and pain, and in other cockney poems it basks in its own elemental functions. Sleeping and eating — rather than visions of marriage, prosperity, or romance — provide escape. In the doleful "Vane's Story" of 1864, the main speaker, in bed at sunset, recounts to a friend a dream in which a now-dead sweetheart of his youth appears to reproach him with his great promise as a writer, as yet unfulfilled. His life demonstrates the implications of labor theory for the individual worker. With "body dwindled, brain outworn" (202) all the while "inwardly consumed with thought" (197), Vane now can only "passively endure" living (207). In the poem's Epilogue, he wishes for a more radical inertia within the economic system, a life of corporeal excess. Like Thomson's other workers, Vane is a materialist. Glory and immortality, the ambitions of the poet, do not nourish his body; women and liquor provide "[b]etter warmth" (11, 15). The pleasures of life and solace for fruitless work lie in "[d]rinking mulled wine, punch, or grog,/ Until helpless as a log" (17–18). Better to live the "poorest drudge" (26), he concludes, than to survive through art as a "bodiless roamer' (29). This final vision hardly celebrates the body; he admits the "grossness" of the life he prefers (1). He chooses it, though, because it reverses his position within the economic discourse. Sensual pleasure and stupefaction are extremes of consumption; they oppose the relentless effort that exhausts the body of an unproductive worker like Vane and the exploited laborers in "Low Life." Such consumption, which Vane announces as a principle of action and which the copyist at Cleveland Hall practices in his imaginative but still subversive way, is the recourse of the rebellious laborer within the contemporary economy. Lethargy counters ambition, indulgence asceticism. But Vane cannot raise the value of the body. He can merely turn it from a casualty of production into one of consumption.

To Thomson, the life of the mind, the quality of thought, had no validated existence in a production-based economy, which reduced even leisure to its materialistic form. For example, during the years in which he contributed to the *Secularist* and the *National Reformer*, freethought societies tried to provide constructive activities for the workers' one holiday a week, and the journals frequently contained notices of lectures, excursions, and concerts available for those who lived on bus lines. Sunday in London could be torturously slow for those whose movements usually were supervised and structured, but these events were intended to do more than merely occupy the "dull London Sunday"; they also were meant to stimulate dormant intellects and, despite populistic announcements, to draw the mass labor force into reigning middle-class intellectual and aesthetic culture.[12] But the cockneys on holiday in "Sunday Up The River" and "Sunday at Hampstead" (which appeared in a periodical advocating these activities) are blissfully unaware of these reformist projects. They cannot shed the sense of themselves as laboring bodies, and their recreation always reflects in some way the work that dominates their lives.

The title, subtitle, and epigraph of "Sunday Up the River," which Thomson wrote in the spring of 1865, establish a social context for a speaker's account, in twenty sections, of an afternoon he spends with a young woman in a rowboat. Their tryst is, according to the subtitle, "An Idyll of Cockaigne," the Londoner's imaginary world of indolence and luxury (*Fraser's* 494). Because the subtitle imposes a distance between the working-class speaker and the pastoral scene he can inhabit on Sundays only, he must release and slake all his impulses for rest and play during his day on the river; sometimes his leisure approaches an inertia so extreme that he actually exerts himself to achieve it. At other times he seems actually to turn rest into labor, perhaps because in an industrial age, according to Veblen, "purposeless leisure has come to be deprecated, especially among that large portion of the leisure class whose plebeian origin acts to set them at variance with the tradition of *otium cum dignitate*" (95). As cockney heaven, Cockaigne incorporates the values of the metropolis. Only labor, the source and magnitude of value, elicits the respect of the worker. Play, therefore, is always a response to weekday life: either a repetition of work, a compensatory and often dissolute consumption, or a kind of scheduled exhaustion.

Cockaigne seems more a state of physical and mental lassitude than an actual place, since this poem, like "Sunday at Hampstead," contains no picturesque descriptions of nature. At times the young man proclaims the vitality of life but more often, especially toward the end of the poem, he seems dazed, almost asleep. Various sections dramatize changes in mood and modulations in energy during a day of rowing and drinking. For instance, the heavy initial stresses of "And I row, and I row . . . And you steer, and you steer" in section five drag out lines that echo the couple's regulated exertion:

> And I row, and I row;
> The blue floats above us as we go:
> And you steer, and you steer,
> Framed in gliding wood and water, O my dear. (V. 13–16)

In the next section, "As I lie, as I lie" repeats the meter and phrasing; it is as if the cockney rower does not feel the difference between exercise and rest. In these lines he invests his play with what Veblen terms an "instinct of workmanship" (15). The impulse for effective work which Ruskin described in "The Nature of Gothic" and on which Morris centered his utopia in *News From Nowhere* confirms the enormous value of labor for Victorians. In these texts, work is idyllic or utopian when the labor-impulse remains unharnessed, a natural expression of each person. Thus Cockaigne is the locus of time and space where Thomson's rower masters what on weekdays others bridle and direct. Indeed he exclaims, "I love this hardy exercise,/This strenuous toil of boating" (VI.1–2). The drudgery of industrial labor, linked elsewhere to lack of control over the body or its productions and, therefore, to plebeian work and effeminacy, becomes a sort of heroic exploit as the rower reappropriates the strength that others regiment during the week.

The idea of rowing as an empowering of the worker probably escaped the readers of *Fraser's*, where this poem appeared in 1869. Thomson portrays cockney pleasures without condescension, but in doing so he gave contemporary readers a picture of the vices that the middle-classes often associated with laborers and the poor. (The extent to which this poem confirms the stereotypes about working-class behavior and feeling may explain why it was the only poem Thomson wrote which gained acceptance in a mainstream periodical.) For by section eight the rower begins drinking, and his perception, as well as his body, now evinces the effects of this depressant. With the first sip of Jameson's Irish Whiskey he begins to see the outside world through the screen of alcohol; from now on, he fluctuates between euphoria and lassitude, losing the control of the laboring body he has simulated through rowing.

The speaker now displays the complement of his manual labor, an equally elemental consumption, especially in light of the cultivated leisure — chiefly concerts and lectures — offered by reformist organizations. Ruskin had recently figured consumption in a similarly primal way in *Unto This Last*: "All *essential* production is for the Mouth; and is finally measured by the mouth," meaning that "consumption is the crown of production" (17:101). In "Sunday Up the River," the cockney spans the economic continuum: he complements his physical labor with an immediate reward for the mouth. Having emulated and mastered labor through rowing, he repeats the physical exhaustion with which he habitually links drudgery, striving for an indolence extreme enough to require artificial inducement. In all his pleasures, the Ricardian drudge must be controlled, lethargic; he must in some way emulate the conditions of his own labor.

After a few alternately dreamy and boisterous stanzas in which he gazes into the eyes of his sweetheart and commands her to "Drink! drink! open your mouth" (XIX.1), the rower sinks into a luxuriant semi-consciousness:

> with a swifter motion
> Out upon the Ocean,
> Heaven above and round us, and you alone with me;
> Heaven around and o'er us,
> The Infinite before us,
> Floating on for ever upon the flowing sea. (XX.19–24)

These lines closely resemble Swinburne's "The Garden of Proserpine" (1866) in which water emptying into the sea evokes the draining of all energy from the body.[13] Yet whereas Swinburne's poem sustains the rhythms of the effete voluptuary, Thomson's displays the ebb and flow of energy that intoxication often induces. Unlike Swinburne's persona, the rower does not use nature to project the condition of his own mind and body; he is much less articulate, a mere series of impulses. In fact, the original ending of the poem leaves the rower hungry and thirsty again. Thus the strong Swinburnian resonance of the published conclusion makes the rower a less vigorous animal. It is a somewhat moralistic end, as though the effects of drinking were irreversible.[14] And the rower in the *Fraser's* version is not aware, as is Swinburne's persona, that his respite from work — his drinking — approximates the wish to die. His actions have no mental or emotional continuity; he cannot tap the hidden current of his emotions or detect their flow through his dreams and desires.

On arriving in the country, the cockney of "Sunday at Hampstead" almost immediately falls asleep in the lap of his sweetheart; her charms, like those of the young woman in "Sunday Up the River," are soporific. This "Very Humble Member of the Great and Noble London Mob," nicknamed Lazy, is more aware of his predicament as a laborer than is the rower: he considers his holiday an opportunity for idleness as radical as his "toil in the murk" (I.13) amidst "a vast machinery roaring" (III.13). However, he is equally unable to elude its consequences. His romancing, for instance, is a pretext for the true pleasure, which he says is to "shut my eyes/To feel eternal rest enfolding me" (II. 11–12). Like the rower, Lazy wants to float on and melt into the sea. While meeting a basic need for sleep, this fantasy mimes the passivity he associates with death.

Lazy's instinct of workmanship, like the couple's of "Low Life," surfaces in storytelling; through it he controls but simultaneously repeats the conditions of his labor. In the fanciful history of civilization he gives his friends, he never strays from the subject of work and consumption; his accounts of prehistoric and submarine life center on divisions of labor and the meals that follow. His first picture, of a predatory culture based on hunting, separates men's work from women's and emphasizes the privileges of the former. Hunting is exploit, a mastery of the hostile energies of the natural world; cooking, in contrast, is a primitive form of industrial drudgery, a reworking of nature's passive elements. Men, therefore, have first rights of consumption and devour the boar they have killed while the women wait for the remains. To tease his female companions, Lazy insists on men's original superiority over women. In doing so, he restores the physical ascendancy that modern conditions of labor have begun to eradicate, for in the first section of the poem we learn that both Lazy and his sweetheart are equals in oppression,

"Tied to a desk and a counter,/A patient stupid pair!" (I.14–15). His playful insistence on the virile occupation of primitive men implies that current conditions are unnatural; they have feminized him (as they have the law-writer of "Low Life"). But the women will not give up their parity, which they have earned through equally degrading employment, and envision the future as a reprisal of predatory culture, this time with the roles reversed. They understand the perceived superiority of exploit and aspire to a masculine ideal of labor, with its authorized unlimited consumption.

In succeeding vignettes, Lazy further retreats in time until all labor disappears and the world becomes a paradise of natural abundance, consumption, and inertia. At the primordial stage, androgynous creatures merely exist in "Silence profound and solitude serene" (VIII.8). Thus the sense of floating he feels earlier while resting in his companion's lap corresponds with the originary state he conjures in his fictional devolution toward Eden. Time brings division, of gender and labor:

> Our tail with which like fishes we can swim
> Shall split into an awkward double-limb,
> And we must waddle on the arid soil,
> And build dirt-huts, and get our food with toil (VIII.19–22)

The biblical explanation of the human plight has been replaced by a material, quasi-scientific one: everyone must work to exhaustion because the body has evolved into a laboring mechanism.

Lazy uses his facetious history to express the frustration and desire his real work engenders. Presumably a clerk or copyist, he becomes an independent producer of words on holiday, but he cannot conceive a world other than the economic one of labor and consumption, and his creativity is a mere reversal or rearrangement of these actual conditions. His is not an individual failure; as Thomson implies in his essay on Bumble and reveals in his discussion of Browning, the material world constrains the imagination of every artist and judges creativity with the same quantitative, utilitarian standards that feminize the body of manual workers.

Work in The City of Dreadful Night

LIKE THE SPEAKERS IN BROWNING'S dramatic monologues, Thomson's cockneys reveal the extent to which prevailing material and ideological conditions structure all ideas, emotions, and actions, even rebellion and escape. As I suggested while discussing "Sunday Up the River," Victorian readers most likely did not view these poems as indictments of labor, but as genre pieces of working-class life. These glib cockney voices, their indifference to the weighty matters of culture, may have confirmed middle-class views of laborers and put off the editors of the mainstream journals. But the cockneys also evince no interest in the reformist projects touted in the radical journals. "Mr. MacCall at Cleveland Hall" is an instance of this aloofness; it claims private territory within a public sphere.

Disaffection from all social and intellectual controversy is traceable to Thomson himself; he aspired to a middle-class readership and circulated his work among magazines such as *Cornhill* and *Macmillan's* before trying the *Secularist* and the *National Reformer*. He felt the freethought periodicals did not provide him with a suitable audience and in his journal of 1880 comments that working for the *National Reformer* is "anything but a recommendation" (Walker 47n). This lack of ideological commitment to the radical papers and to his cockney characters suggests, as I have argued, that he held both subversive and conventional positions within the Ricardian ideology.

This ambivalence is a symptom of his famous pessimism as well. Of his philosophical stance Kenneth Hugh Byron remarks, "Thomson could not make a decision and fell into the existential dilemma that to choose not to decide is in itself a choice" (152). *The City of Dreadful Night*, which appeared in the *National Reformer* in 1874, is an abstract declaration of this compromised position. Compared with the cockney poems, it is an intellectually ambitious work, for it inflates the dissolute repetitions of labor into a philosophy of pessimism. Nonetheless, it does not abrogate the impulse to work. Instead, as in the poems, it sets inertia within the continuum of labor and affirms it as the necessary consequence of work in a universe that holds no other meaning or value.

This allegory, Thomson's one well-known text, has been read as an inversion of the romantic quest, a blending of the boundaries between the real and the imaginary, and an existential manifesto.[15] It accommodates all of these views, but through the screen of philosophical pessimism it presents working-class hostilities toward the kind of leisure and labor available to those in a society that prizes exploit and production. Like the speakers of the cockney poems, the narrator of *The City* bows to the demands of a world that has estranged him. His acquiescence in the end to what he calls Necessity encourages existential or deterministic readings of the poem. The personification of Necessity is misleading, however; it elevates what the poem conveys as an immanent force into a theistic doctrine. *The City* concerns a situation, a place; it illustrates Pater's observation in 1867 that "necessity is not, as of old, a sort of mythological personage without us. . . . It is rather a magic web woven through and through us, like that magnetic system of which modern science speaks, penetrating us with a network, subtler than our subtlest nerves, yet bearing in it the central forces of the world" ("Winckelmann" 185). In *The City* marks of Malthusian and Ricardian assumptions about survival and labor pervade philosophical statements. They become both the cause of despair and the medium of endurance.

Generally, Thomson was not a realistic poet; with the exception of the cockney pieces, he expressed himself in abstractions and allegories. In essays such as "In the Forest of Our Past" (1877) as well as in the poems "The Doom of a City" (1857) and "Vane's Story" (1864), both precursors of *The City*, he disguised the familiar and used the dream-vision to present social ills like infant mortality and poverty; in *The City*, he rarefies the material and sensory elements of London. Yet he conceived of metaphysics as a symptom of our desire for universal laws to fill the void behind disconnected facts, and the poem retains its literal reality; the city, in other words, still possesses a "thingness."[16] Thus, though William Schaefer has shown that the first version of the poem employs the quest, not the city, as the controlling image ("Two Cities" 610), Thomson, by merely naming the city in however shadowy a form, has injected his allegory with the texture of real conditions and modelled it after the course of labor and leisure that structures the lives of his cockneys.

Insomnia and weariness are urban conditions, but they manifest an apocalyptic vision that originates in the socioeconomic prophecies of Malthus. Arguably, in the seventies the noxious elements of industrialization, which included overcrowding in cities, revived the Malthusian spectre. During this decade the *Secularist* favored preserving land just outside London as common space for the "crush" of people in the metropolis (26 February 1876:132–33). When *The City* appeared in 1874 in the *National Reformer*, the inhabitants Thomson described — congenitally deformed, or lame, blind, and starving — looked like victims of this crush. The wanderer notices how the "extreme nudity of bone grins shameless, / The unsexed skeleton mocks shroud and pall" (VII.13–14). The crippled and defiled people he sees are, in this context, physical types as well as images of spiritual deformity. The desert to which the wanderer refers suggests the artificial composition of the city-scape where people with "worn faces that look deaf and blind/Like tragic masks of stone" roam (I.52–53). According to recent historians H. J. Dyos and D. A. Reeder, the population of a nineteenth-century conurbation "reshuffled itself by day and by night" in response to fluctuating markets ("Slums and Suburbs" 359). In this light, the insomniacs of the poem are city drudges whom constant short supplies of goods force into nightly employment and migrations. The setting of the poem is, then, a literal place as well as a metaphor; indeed, its metaphorical success depends upon a general agreement about the city's physical properties. People, squares, houses, pillars, and statues educe the clutter of the metropolis while they sublate that thingness into "the condition of human life."[17]

In essence, *The City of Dreadful Night* is the cockney nightmare of toil that shadows the idyls of the sixties. Like Lazy and the rower, the zombie-like wanderers of London suffer from "deadly weariness of heart all day" (I.10). They have internalized the monotony of imposed labor, complaining of the "dreadful strains / Of thought and consciousness, which never ceases, / Or which some moments' stupor but increases" (I.74–76), and they project this onerous boredom onto their surroundings, the "weary roads" they must travel "without suspense" (II.14). The pilgrim of section two and the frightful crawling man of eighteen are condemned to trace paths of "perpetual recurrence" (II.47), searching for the value and meaning of their lives. The poem straddles the physical and the figurative in this way. The city-dwellers' agony comes from Thomson's association of unremitting labor with the unredeemed life.

The city is the site of the exploited; it blinds its subjects to its massive, mechanized force. Finding himself in a dark space of commerce, the narrator only knows that merchandise rushes past him from the noise of "ponderous wheels," the "clash of heavy ironshod feet" (IX.3–4), and a glimpse of a driver "[t]hree parts asleep beside his fellow-drudges" (IX.13). His sense of urban industry is disjointed; its noise and power bewilder him. He is unable to form a cohesive picture of the purpose and physical place of work. "What merchandise? whence, whither, and for whom?" he asks (IX.15). He answers his own questions by totalizing sensory fragments: the wheels belong to a "Fate-appointed hearse,/Bearing away . . . The joy, the peace, the life-hope . . . Of all things good" (IX.16–20). The wanderer cannot sustain a literal description of any urban scene. Whereas the stupefied drudges are reduced to torpor by the beasts and machinery of frenetic industry, the wanderer, a metaphysician, seems driven to meaningful abstraction by the horror and incomprehensibility of the real. In this way the language of the poem evokes the problem through its solution, as do the daydreams and stories of the cockneys.

The poem's metaphysics deracinates work from its mimetic and its economic referent and turns it into a tired metaphor that has shed the image of the laboring body. We are, then, pushed into reading the poem by Thomson's efficient use of allegory. Abstract diction and the traditional link between sustained figures and set-pieces goad us into systematic abstraction. The material and economic referents are buried; but they exist. Labor in the poem is the Ricardian conception that Marx, Engels, and Morris polemicized for working-class radicals. No one in *The City* can see or enjoy the results of labor; its conditions render him or her powerless, as benighted as the narrator who stands in the dark market square. The situation provokes rebellion and despair, but neither provides an escape from the *idea* of labor, which has structured workers' thinking. Toil, the wanderer generalizes, is "foolish," a waste of time, a "weary undelight" (XIII.24–25). The alternative, however, is an indolence akin to the vice and disease that Engels claimed industrial labor itself engendered. The benign drunkenness and inertia in the cockney poems become in *The City* an atrophy of perception and a mental monotony so intolerable that it impels the narrator and those he sees toward suicide. The rampant insomnia in the city manifests a physical and mental energy that urban toil and idleness cannot absorb:

> The hours are heavy on him and the days;
> The burden of the months he scarce can bear;
> And often in his secret soul he prays
> To sleep through barren periods unaware (XIII.8–11)

In the final sections of the poem, a statue of a militant angel crumbles before the impassive figure of a couchant sphinx. Losing first its wings, then its sword, then its head, the statue devolves from a mythical representation of exploit to a less-than-human figure, whose severed head lies between the sphinx's paws. As "that against which man destroys himself," namely life to Kenneth Hugh Byron, the sphinx embodies and prohibits the epistemological question (109). With her "trance-like look" (XX.18) she means "knowing too much, and she means knowing nothing at all."[18] Throughout the poem, the wanderer too has been both sphinx and drudge: he has raised questions about the course and meaning of his life but has forestalled any significant answer. With abstraction and allegory, he has capitulated to the immanent necessity Pater describes, but in doing so he has only elevated his ignorance and monotonous experience into a seemingly empirical philosophy. In ponderous verse the wanderer states over and over again that there is no God, no meaning, that there is nothing.

Laborers do not believe in God, comments Veblen; they are too constrained by "technological necessities" (331). And on the Christian faith in immortality, Thomson comments, "the preacher forgets that . . . hope [in death] can . . . spring from anticipation of perfect peace and unconsciousness after a storm-troubled life" (*Secularist* 24 Feb. 1877:70). In speaking more generally of the necessity that pervades modern life, Pater asks, "Can art represent men and women in these bewildering toils so as to give the spirit at least an equivalent for the sense of freedom?" ("Winckelmann" 185). The figure of Necessity, which appears at the close of *The City of Dreadful Night* (a verbal picture of Dürer's "MELENCOLIA" [XXI.42]) offers an essentially cockney solution to the pain of urban labor and life, the only one possible within the material and economic continuum that governs all these poems. Gazing at this monument to mindless drudgery, the wanderer philosophizes:

> Baffled and beaten back she works on still,
> Weary and sick of soul she works the more,
> Sustained by her indomitable will:
> The hands shall fashion and the brain shall pore,
> And all her sorrow shall be turned to labour (XXI.50–54)

With her "household bunch of keys" (32) and "instruments of carpentry and science" (19), this "bronze colossus of a wingèd Woman" (6), "all too impotent to lift the regal/Robustness of her earth-born strength" (27–28), embodies for Thomson the paradox of labor. For clerks, factory workers, and the millions of other drudges who inhabited cities, work was not fulfilling, rewarding, or physically or mentally invigorating. But as drudgery, it solved the very problem it created by emptying the mind and exhausting the body until it drained any impulse to ask the larger questions about the purpose of life and its meaning. In a sense neither ethical nor spiritual, this foreclosure of the question was the freedom Pater declared art must offer. It was, like Mill's, a liberty of the most negative kind: it existed, that is, within the continuum of labor's iron limits — the socioeconomic conditions that regulated and conceptualized work and leisure — and it manifested itself as freedom on this continuum only as a release from harnessed energy. Indolence, dissolute consumption, and melancholy were its signs. The cockney poems celebrate, while *The City* offers a dismal symbolics for, this point of liberation.

Oklahoma State University

NOTES

1. J.J. Garth Wilkinson was frequently quoted and praised in the *Secularist* during the midseventies, especially by editor G. W. Foote. With his fellow radicals, Wilkinson opposed natural theology as an explanation of human development; and he objected to vaccination, which he considered a noxious transgression of the body by reigning social forces. He was the author of a pamphlet, "The Human Body and its Connection with Man." See Salt 134, and the *Secularist* 25 November 1876.
2. Rossetti comments on Wilkinson's book in his supplementary chapter to Alexander Gilchrist's *Life of William Blake* (1863), from which Thomson quotes. See also Salt 135.
3. See Gould, 75–77, on Victorian craniology. At the time, Galton's studies were regarded seriously.
4. In "The Reality Effect," Barthes traces realism to a wealth of details which are individually nonreferential but together reflexive — in an undelineated, textured sense. In other words, their number literally furnishes the text and gives it the look and feel of a "real" or lived-in world.
5. In the usual context, a demonetised commodity (money included) has been withdrawn from circulation, not overcirculated. Perhaps Thomson has unknowingly

altered the cause of devaluation; in doing so he links Browning's obscurity with superior value and still maintains commercial standards. The poet's work appears novel, progressive, and marketable all at the same time.

6. Brown's one-man exhibition of 100 pictures opened on March 10, 1865, at 191 Piccadilly and ran to June 10. Thomson was then living with the editor of the *National Reformer*, Charles Bradlaugh, and his family at Tottenham and could have seen *An English Autumn Afternoon*, which the artist retrieved from George Rae to include in the show (Bennett 144, 151). "Sunday at Hampstead" was composed in April.

7. Many of Constable's six-foot paintings, exhibited beginning in 1819 at the Royal Academy, depicted views from Hampstead, including the heath — for example, *Hampstead Heath* (ca. 1821). See also John Ritchie's *Hampstead Heath* (1859) in Bermingham, 173.

8. Thomson wrote almost all of the four cockney poems I discuss during March and April of 1865; the exception is "Mr. MacCall at Cleveland Hall," which is dated April, 1866, in William D. Schaefer's bibliography (*James Thomson (B.V.): Beyond "The City"*). There are other light-hearted poems of the same period, though none refers to work and holidays. See, for example, "Shameless" (*Secularist* 12 August 1876).

9. See Edward H. Guillaume, "A Plea for Women." Thomson wrote "Low Life" in April.

10. William MacCall was a regular contributor to the *National Reformer* in 1865. He wrote poems, essays, and autobiographical sketches modelled on the work of de Maupassant and Heine. Cleveland Hall was a frequent meeting place for free-thought lectures in the sixties. In 1876 G. W. Foote, the editor of the *Secularist*, again reserved it for a series called Sunday Secular Freethought Lectures.

11. Thomson alludes to the early stirs over Impressionism and *pleinairisme*. Both were similar in emphasis; Johnson views the latter as a warmed-over Pre-Raphaelite notion that "the colours and atmospheric effects of the natural world could only be captured in pictures painted on the spot" (261). An example is Eugène Boudin's *Beach at Trouville* (1863), which, according to Rosenblum and Janson, "conveys an instant response" through the "broadest strokes of paint" (298). Degas uses a similar technique in his *A Woman with Chrysanthemums* (1865). Most likely Thomson saw Whistler's *Symphony in White Number II: The Little White Girl* at the Royal Academy exhibition opening in May, 1865, hanging with two pendant stanzas by Swinburne (Rosenblum 291; Wise 47, 438). See note 13.

12. See the *Secularist* 1 January 1876: 1, and *passim*. Some titles of lectures from this month and year include "Mental Epidemics; an Account of some of the Chief Excitements and Delusions of Past Times, and a Consideration of their Philosophy," given by Miss Fenwick Miller, sponsored by the Sunday Lecture Society on 2 January; "Poetry and Politics," given by W. C. Bennett on 30 January, sponsored by Sunday Evenings for the People at South Place Chapel, London. This lecture was followed by selections from the works of Gounod. The first excursion of the Sunday League was to Brighton on 14 May; transportation for adults was four shillings, for children two shillings.

13. Salt (242) observes that Thomson imitated the meter of "Hymn to Proserpine" in "He Heard her Sing" (1882). In general, the resemblance between some of Thomson's poems and selections from Swinburne's *Poems and Ballads* (1866) was noticed by many reviewers at the time. But many of the similar pieces like "Sunday Up the River" had been dated, in Thomson's meticulous records, before

the publication of Swinburne's volume. In its notice of *The City of Dreadful Night and Other Poems* (1880), the *Pall Mall Gazette* remarks that Browning, Morris, Rossetti, and Swinburne were just becoming known to the public when Thomson wrote some of his suspiciously correspondent passages (*Essays and Phantasies* [5]). However, in his bibliography, Schaefer notes that several sections of "Sunday Up the River" were written before 1865 (*Beyond* 190).

Moreover, the refrain "And I row" of section V of "Sunday Up the River" resembles "Past we glide, and past, and past" of Browning's "In a Gondola" from *Dramatic Lyrics* (1842). And in fact, a handful of the poems from Swinburne's first volume had appeared before Thomson wrote his. These include "A Song in Time of Order" (*Spectator* 26 April 1862: 466), which like "Sunday Up the River" describes rowing ("Push hard across the sand" [1]). It most closely resembles the many trimeters and anapests of Thomson's poem, but the similarity is not uncanny. The variation of short and long lines in a stanza in Swinburne's "The Little White Girl," the poem accompanying Whistler's painting at the Royal Academy in May, 1865, was another feature of Thomson's poem, dated March and April of the same year.

14. On the recommendation of Charles Kingsley, *Fraser's,* had demanded that Thomson remove the last two stanzas, which he repeats in a letter of 1872 to W.M. Rossetti; they "had the merit in my eyes of bringing back the piece at last to the sober realities of pleasant Cockaigne," wrote Thomson (Salt 74–75, 203). They were restored in his volume of 1880. In them, the rower's appetite revives in blithe, conversational stanzas.

And may mortal sinners
Care for carnal dinners
In your Heaven of Heavens, New Era Millions three?
Oh, if their boat gets stranding
Upon some Richmond landing,
They're thirsty as the desert and hungry as the sea! (Works I: 116)

No doubt *Fraser's* preferred that the poem close, as Thomson wrote, in "the sentimental infinite" (Salt 75); not only does the second ending conjure images of the sea and the idea of eternity, but its language is not colloquial. Moreover, it emphasizes the effects of dissipation.

15. R. A. Foakes argues that the poem inverts and distorts Romantic vision, which he associates with the motif of the quest; see especially 171–79. Focusing on Dürer's *Melencolia*, Noel-Bentley also reads the poem as ironic and explains that it reflects a shift from Calvinistic to scientific determinism. To McGann, the poem in effect questions the separation between the real and the unreal (496).
16. See Thomson, "On the Worth of Metaphysical Systems."
17. Raymond Williams in *The Country and the City* (1973), quoted in Sharpe (65).
18. Hoxie Neale Fairchild (*Religious Trends in English Literature*, 1957), quoted in Byron 109n.

WORKS CITED

Barthes, Roland. "The Reality Effect." *French Literary Theory Today*. Ed. Tzvetan Todorov. Trans. R. Carter. Cambridge: Cambridge UP, 1982. 11–17.

Bennett, Mary. "The Price of 'Work': the background to its first exhibition, 1865" *Pre-Raphaelite Papers*. Ed. Leslie Parris. London: Tate Gallery, 1984. 143–52.
Bermingham, Ann. *Landscape and Ideology*. Berkeley: U of California P, 1986.
Byron, Kenneth Hugh. *The Pessimism of James Thomson (B.V.) in Relation to His Times*. The Hague: Mouton, 1965.
Dyos, H.J., and D.A. Reeder. "Slums and Suburbs." *The Victorian City: Images and Realities*. Ed. H.J. Dyos and Michael Wolff. 2 vols. London: Routledge, 1973. 1: 359–86.
Eagleton, Terry. *Literary Theory: An Introduction*. Minneapolis: U of Minnesota P, 1983.
Foakes, R.A. *The Romantic Assertion: A Study in the Language of Nineteenth-Century Poetry*. New Haven: Yale UP, 1958.
Gombrich, E.H. *Art and Illusion*. Bollingen XXXV. 5. Princeton: Princeton UP, 1969.
Gould, Stephen Jay. *The Mismeasure of Man*. New York: Norton, 1981.
Guillaume, Edward H. "A Plea for Women." *National Reformer* 29 Jan. 1865: 65–66.
Hilton, Timothy. *The Pre-Raphaelites*. New York: Thames and Hudson, 1970.
Johnson, E. D. H. *Paintings of the British Social Scene from Hogarth to Sickert*. New York: Rizzoli, 1986.
McGann, Jerome J. "James Thomson (B.V.): The Woven Hymns of Night and Day." *SEL* 3 (1963): 493–507.
Marks, Jeannette. *Genius and Disaster*. 1926. Port Washington: Kennikat, 1968.
Noel-Bentley, Peter C. " 'Fronting the Dreadful Mysteries of Time': Dürer's *Melencolia* in Thomson's *City of Dreadful Night*." *Victorian Poetry* 12 (1974):193–203.
Pater, Walter. *The Renaissance: Studies in Art and Poetry*. 1893. Ed. Donald L. Hill. Berkeley: U of California P, 1980.
Rosenblum, Robert, and H.W. Janson. *19th-Century Art*. New York: Abrams, 1984.
Ruskin, John. *Unto This Last. The Works of John Ruskin*. Ed. E.T. Cook and Alexander Wedderburn. 39 vols. London: Allen, 1903–12. 17: 25–114.
Salt, H.S. *The Life of James Thomson ("B.V.")*. London: Reeves, Dobell, 1889.
Schaefer, William David. *James Thomson (B.V.): Beyond "The City."* Berkeley: U of California P, 1965.
———. "The Two Cities of Dreadful Night." *PMLA* 77, Part 1 (1962): 609–16.
Secularist 1 January 1876: 1.
———. 26 February 1876: 132–33.
———. 25 November 1876: 321.
Sharpe, William. "Learning to Read *The City*." *Victorian Poetry* 22 (1984): 65–84.
Simmel, Georg. *The Philosophy of Money*. 1907. Trans. Tom Bottomore and David Frisby. London: Routledge, 1978.
Thomson, James. *Biographical and Critical Studies*. London: Reeves, Dobell, 1896.
———. *Essays and Phantasies*. London: Reeves, 1881.
———. (B.V.). "On the Worth of Metaphysical Systems." *Secularist* 13 May 1876: 306–8.
———. *Poems and Some Letters of James Thomson*. Ed. Anne Ridler. Carbondale: Southern Illinois UP, 1963.
———. *The Poetical Works of James Thomson (B.V.)*. Ed. Bertram Dobell. 2 vols. London: Reeves, Dobell, 1895.
———. Rev. of sermons of Principal Tulloch, 1866–76. *Secularist* 24 February 1877: 70.

———. "Shameless." *Secularist* 12 August 1876: 110.

———. "Sunday Up the River." *Fraser's* 80 (1869): 494–503.

Veblen, Thorstein. *The Theory of the Leisure Class*. New York: Modern Library, 1931.

Walker, Imogene B. *James Thomson (B.V.): A Critical Study*. Ithaca: Cornell UP, 1950.

Wise, Thomas James. *A Bibliography of The Writings in Prose and Verse of Algernon Charles Swinburne*. Vol. 20 of *The Complete Works of Algernon Charles Swinburne*. Bonchurch Edition. 20 vols. London: Heinemann; New York: Gabriel Wells, 1927.

VICTORIAN TRAVEL WRITERS IN ICELAND, 1850–1880

By Frederick Kirchhoff

BY THE EARLY YEARS of the nineteenth century, Iceland, once linked to the economy of England, had become a land of mystery to the British imagination. The Danish monopoly on trade had turned Iceland into a backwater; its people, formerly the ravagers of Europe, were unable to defend themselves against pirates.[1] In the course of the eighteenth century, smallpox, volcanic eruption, and famine brought the country to the low point in its history.[2] Its population shrank to 38,400; its two bishoprics were reduced to one; its legislative assembly, long shorn of power, was abolished altogether.[3] As the other nations of Europe began to assume their modern shape, Iceland regressed to the status of a third-rate colony.

The British travellers who visited Iceland in the first half of the nineteenth century were aware that they were crossing a cultural and economic divide. Yet Iceland, backward as its lifestyle appeared, was not simply another primitive society ripe for Europeanization. Iceland was already European. The primitive/civilized dichotomy, facilely applied elsewhere, did not fit here. Travellers who wrote about Iceland, whether describing its stark landscape and volcanic geology, its unique flora and fauna, its quality of light, or the literary remains of its sagas, seldom escaped the puzzle of Iceland's import for the modern world. It could be read as a lesson in cultural decline, but also as a model of cultural preservation, a repository of sacrosanct tradition and a land ripe for exploitation — alternatives that mirrored the conflict between past and present, continuity and progress, that permeated Victorian thought. And, insofar as it played one or more of these roles, the island assumed a symbolic import that shaped both the expectations and the experience of its visitors.

Several factors explain the unusually large number of books on Iceland that appeared in Great Britain between 1850 and 1880.[4] With the publication of the first reliable survey of the island in 1844, the re-institution of free trade in 1854, and the establishment of regular steamship service between Granton and Reykjavík in 1858,[5] travel both to and within Iceland became less difficult, and the island, in turn, attracted the attention of British publishers. In 1858, John Murray issued *A Handbood for Travelers in Denmark, Norway, Sweden, and Iceland;* two years later Longmans published *Suggestions for the Exploration of Iceland.* At the same time, growing interest in Icelandic literature brought new attention to the island. Samuel Laing's translation of *Heimskringla* (1844) and George Webbe Dasent's translations of *The Younger Edda* (1842) and *The Story of Burnt Njal* (1861) initiated a series of accurate English versions of the major sagas.[6] The travellers who set sail for Reykjavík on the *Arcturus* in the 1860s were not only taking advantage of a new steamship service; they were also responding to a minor literary phenomenon.

The desolation of the Icelandic landscape struck most who wrote books on Iceland. Like other loci that intrigued the Victorian imagination — notably Arabia and Tibet[7] — it dramatized the human encounter with nature in its most elemental terms. Chauncy Loomis has traced the early stages of this fascination with the Arctic from Coleridge's "Rime of the Ancient Mariner" and Mary Shelley's *Frankenstein* to its climax in the disastrous fate of the 1845 Franklin Expedition. The inhuman sublimity of the Icelandic landscape remained a theme in later nineteenth-century travel writing; and a sign of changing attitudes in the 1870s was Richard Burton's effort to challenge the topographic exaggerations of earlier travellers. But even Burton describes Iceland as

> the epitome of a world generated by the upheaval and the eruption; dislocated and distorted by the earthquake, and sorely troubled and tortured by wintry storms, rains, snows, avalanches, fierce débâcles, and furious gales. . . . nowhere, even in the fairest portions, can we expect the dense forest of the Alp, . . . the warbling of birds, the murmurs of innumerable bees, the susurrus of the morning breeze, or the melodious whispering of the "velvet forest: " their places are taken by black rock and glittering ice, by the wild roar of the foss, and by the mist-cloud hung to the rugged hill-side. (1: 75)

The violence and hostility of the Icelandic terrain appealed to a post-Romantic imagination attempting to come to terms with the implications of scientific discovery. Lord Dufferin, whose *Letters from High Latitudes* (1857) became a popular classic, compared the scene to "those awful solitudes which science has unveiled to us amid the untrodden fastnesses of the lunar mountains" (135). Yet Iceland was more than a landscape. It was a landscape with a thousand-year human history characterized by unique political institutions and a significant literary tradition. Moreover, the Icelanders were not picturesque exotics like Arabs or Tibetans. The fantasy of Arctic desolation could not ignore the presence of Europeans enjoying a version of European civilization in the midst of a landscape that seemed to deny the significance of human values.

The simplest solution to this paradox was to treat Iceland as a piece of history, suspended in time like a fly in amber. For Henry Holland, who visited the island with the mineralogist George Steuart Mackenzie in 1810, Iceland allowed one a glimpse both of medieval Europe and of the Icelanders' own attainments:

> Education, literature, and even the refinements of poetical fancy, flourished among them. Like the Aurora Borealis of their native sky, the poets and historians of Iceland not only illuminated their own country, but flashed the lights of their genius through the night which hung over the rest of Europe. (Mackenzie 15)[8]

Holland imagined the medieval Icelanders as men of "genius, taste and acquirements" (16) who created a democratic system of government and a body of literature without equal in Europe. He fancied their society a presage of the Enlightenment; and, in keeping with this view, he emphasized the travel of the Icelandic skalds to various nations. They were men of the world, not poets dwelling in seclusion. And their descendents, insofar as they sustained this tradition, maintained a level of education that enabled them to transcend the insularity of their homeland.

From Holland's Enlightenment bias, the virtues of the Icelanders may have been conditioned by their history, but they were not the expression of nationality, much less of race. Later British travellers, who wrote with diminished confidence in cosmopolitanism and progress and with a growing faith in the importance of national identity, looked for something very different in Iceland. From their perspective, Icelandic culture was less interesting as a prefiguration of modern Europe than as a remnant of the pre-industrial, pre-scientific world they believed they had lost. As such, it became the embodiment of a cluster of values associated with primitivism and racial purity, rather than "genius, taste and acquirements." Travel to Iceland, so conceived, was thus a journey back to the primal energy of England's own earliest history.

This view of the North had a literary provenance. Thomas Gray's plan to write "A History of English Poetry" had resulted in his 1761 "Gothic" translations, "The Fatal Sisters" and "The Descent of Odin." Both Gibbon and Wordsworth had considered Odin the likely subject for an epic poem. But nineteenth-century writers sought more than primitive energy in the literature of the North. Thomas Carlyle makes Odin his "Hero as Divinity," not only because he accepts Mallet's euhemerist account of the god, but also because "the essence of the Scandinavian, as indeed of all Pagan Mythologies," is

> recognition of the divineness of Nature; sincere communion of man with the mysterious invisible Powers visibly seen at work in the world round him. This,

I should say, is more sincerely done in the Scandinavian than in any Mythology
I know. Sincerity is the great characteristic of it. (30)

Carlyle may have been writing about early Scandinavians, but he might just
as well have been describing the poetry of Wordsworth. His praise of Norse
heroism was thus an affirmation, neither of Henry Holland's enlightened
skalds nor of the eighteenth-century image of Vikings drinking from human
skulls,[9] but of a race of proto-Romantic poets. For those who shared Carlyle's
sensibility, Iceland promised an historical basis for the Romantic fusion of
race and creative vision.

Ebenezer Henderson, who spent 1814–15 distributing Bibles and New
Testaments in Icelandic for the British and Foreign Bible Society, established
a version of this myth from the perspective of Evangelicalism. Although
relying on the earlier accounts of Hooker and Mackenzie, his *Iceland* became
a model for later writers. Henderson stressed the historical integrity of the
Icelanders:

> In the persons, habits, and customs of the present inhabitants of Iceland, we
> are furnished with a faithful picture of those exhibited by their Scandinavian
> ancestors. They adhere most rigidly to whatever has once been adopted as a
> national custom, and the few innovations that have been introduced by foreign-
> ers are scarcely visible beyond the immediate vicinity of their factories [i.e.,
> trading stations]. (21)

For him, the districts of Iceland freest from foreign influence exemplified all
that is best in the Icelandic character. "Uncontaminated by intercourse with
polished life, the inhabitants of [an] obscure farm" seemed to "preserve all
the original simplicity of natural habits; . . . ignorant of the cunning and
deceit, the perfidy and intrigue, which too often pervade more populous
societies, they are unsuspecting, liberal, and kind, in the highest degree"
(162–63). Reykjavík, in contrast,

> is unquestionably the worst place to spend the winter in Iceland. The tone of
> society is the lowest that can be well imagined. Being the resort of a number
> of foreigners, few of whom have had any education, and who frequent the
> island solely for purposes of gain, it not only presents a lamentable blank to
> the view of the religious observer, but is totally devoid of every source of
> intellectual gratification. (290)

For the representative of the Bible Society, the hinterlands of Iceland
became pockets of primitive but distinctly Protestant Christianity in the midst
of a corrupt modern world. Listening to a congregation singing "an Icelandic
translation of the early confessions, [he] almost fancied [him]self in some
Christian church of the fourth or fifth century" (343). Henderson was not

only distributing biblical texts to men and women whose general literacy distinguished them from his countrymen; he had entered a world defined by the language and geology of those texts. He likened the versification of Icelandic poetry to Hebrew and used the similarity of an Icelandic pony train to a Middle-Eastern caravan as the basis for a series of comparisons assimilating Iceland with the Holy Land. The lava flows at Reykiahlid he found "a prospect . . . which, perhaps, of all the views in the world, bears the most striking resemblance to that of the *Dead Sea*" (143); and his study of the island's vulcanism encouraged an interpretation of the Sodom and Gomorrah legend in which Lot's wife is unexpectedly surrounded by lava.

For most Victorian visitors, however, it was not the vestiges of Christianity, but those of an older and very different cultural heritage, that defined the historical message of Iceland. Like Henderson — and probably influenced by him — Dufferin finds "something of a patriarchal simplicity" in the lives of Icelanders "among their secluded valleys" (54). But the history of the island's pre-Christian settlement plays a more important role in his attitude toward its contemporary inhabitants:

> Colonized as Iceland had been, — not as is generally the case when a new land is brought into occupation, by the poverty-stricken dregs of a redundant population, nor by a gang of outcasts and ruffians, expelled from the bosom of a society which they contaminated, — but by men who in their own land had been both rich and noble, — with possessions to be taxed, and a spirit too haughty to endure taxation, — already acquainted with whatever of refinement and learning the age they lived in was capable of supplying, — it is not surprising that we should find its inhabitants, even from the first infancy of the republic, endowed with an amount of intellectual energy hardly to be expected in so secluded a community. (61)

The Icelanders are, in other words, akin neither to Americans nor — much less — Australians, but to aristocrats like Dufferin who object to paying taxes. Nevertheless, it is their role in the history of democratic institutions that gives them their chief importance.[10] For Dufferin, "the geysers are certainly wonderful marvels of nature, but more wonderful, more marvellous is Thingvalla" (84):

> To these Things, and to the Norse invasion that implanted them, and not to the Wittenagemotts of the Latinized Saxons, must be referred the existence of those Parliaments which are the boast of Englishmen.
> . . . Over the rest of Europe despotism rose up rank under the tutelage of a corrupt religion; while, year after year, amid the savage scenery of its Scandinavian nursery, that great race was maturing whose genial heartiness was destined to invigorate the sickly civilization of the Saxon with inexhaustible energy, and preserve to the world, even in the nineteenth century, one glorious example of a free European people. (361–62)

From the perspective of Dufferin's subsequent roles as Governor General of Canada and Viceroy of India, his reading of the Icelandic character projects the racial presuppositions underlying British imperialism. By claiming that the Norse were "destined to invigorate" Saxon culture with their "inexhaustible energy," Dufferin affirms their descendants' destiny to rouse even more sickly civilizations by virtue of their exemplary status as "a free European people."

Dufferin ignores the debate over Norman vs. Saxon that Scott's *Ivanhoe* had made central to the English identity question. His Saxons are already decadent and "Latinized," and he dismisses medieval Christianity as "a corrupt religion." Dufferin's views, however, typify "the general Romantic belief that vitality flows from north to south" (Bernal 1: 311). The "great race . . . destined" to re-energize this Latinized culture is the product of "savage scenery." Racial potency is the yield of adversity; its characteristic is the public-school virtue of "genial heartiness" — a phrase that echoes Carlyle's characterization of the "old Northmen" as "most earnest, honest; childlike, and yet manlike; with a great-hearted simplicity and depth and freshness" (30). So endowed, they provide an example of human greatness "even in the nineteenth century," when, one infers, industrialism and an expanded franchise make the individualism Dufferin admires especially difficult. Being "a free European people" is thus not the logical end of enlightened progress but an example all the more "glorious" because it is against the trend of Western civilization.

Dufferin was not alone in his views. Andrew James Symington, who made the *Arcturus* journey in 1859, argues that, of the many elements composing the "British race," the Scandinavian "predominates so largely over the others as to prove by evidence, external and internal, and not to be gainsaid, that the Scandinavians are our true progenitors. . . . To the old Northmen . . . may be traced the germs of all that is most characteristic of the modern Briton, whether personal, social, or national" (293–94). The imperialism implicit in Dufferin's *Letters from High Latitudes* becomes explicit in Symington's view that the Viking love of conquest and skill with ships are antecedents — and justifications — for the British empire:

> The various germs, tendencies, and traits of Scandinavian character, knit together and amalgamated in the British race, go to form the essential elements of greatness and success, and, where sanctified and directed into right channels, are noble materials to work upon.
>   It is Britain's pride to be at once the mistress of the seas, the home of freedom, and the sanctuary of the oppressed. May it also be her high honour, by wisely improving outward privileges, and yet further developing her inborn capabilities, pre-eminently to become the torch-bearer of pure Christianity — with its ever-accompanying freedom and civilization — to the whole world! (308)

But faith in the energy of Icelandic culture was difficult to reconcile with the fact that nineteenth-century Iceland seemed very far from energetic. The "national apathy and want of energy" (Holland 54) were frequently noted by travellers.[11] Like Dufferin, Frederick Metcalfe conjures up a vision of the ancient Icelanders at the Althing — "all the great names, in short, of that Scandinavian breed, to which, and not to the Saxon, England owes her pluck, her dash, and her freedom" (70) — yet he finds Reykjavík "inferior even to a second-rate Norwegian town" (54). However glorious the history of Icelandic institutions, travellers who came looking for medieval Vikings were faced with a modern Iceland that appeared to show little trace of its political history.

If the search for the "genial heartiness" and "inexhaustible energy" of the Norse was not to be satisfied by hanging around Reykjavík or camping on the ruins of Thingvellir, travellers could, of course, test their own mettle by pitting themselves against the Icelandic wilderness.[12] Here, braving the elements, they could get a taste of what it must have been like to have grown up amid the "savage scenery" of a "Scandinavian nursery" and at the same time prove their right of succession to the old Norse heroes. The fact that the Icelanders who accompanied them in these tests of manly endurance preferred to avoid unnecessary danger was interpreted as yet another sign of their pusillanimity. E. T. Holland ridicules his guide Sigurdr, for his repeated declarations "that it was impossible to climb an inch higher." But Sigurdr, it should be noted, has no trouble keeping up with the experienced English mountaineers and in the end rescues Holland from a "predicament" (60–62). Complaints about Icelandic guides — "the greatest difficulty in Icelandic travelling" (Metcalfe 409) — were nearly universal. They were, by various accounts, lazy, ignorant, drunken, utterly undependable. Travellers found the Icelanders surprisingly hospitable and generous, but they also found that they made bad servants. Curiously, the independent spirit admirable in the Vikings became a sign of enervation in the nineteenth century. Even the old Norse love of food and drink was now seen as a flaw in character. One wonders how Victorian travellers would have reacted to reminders of the more violent aspects of medieval Iceland.

A sympathetic interest in the manners of nineteenth-century Iceland might have led to a rethinking of the myth of the Vikings. But British travellers came to affirm their belief in their own energetic origins, not to question them. As a result, the modern Icelanders were usually treated as secondary figures in the quest for Iceland: at best, obliging hosts; at worst, disagreeable necessities.

Yet there was another route to the Nordic spirit. For, if the modern Icelanders showed little of the vitality of their ancestors, they nevertheless spoke the same language. Henderson's belief in the cultural integrity of the rural Icelanders had been grounded on a notion of linguistic integrity. Unlike the Scandinavian peoples of continental Europe, they had maintained a language uninfluenced by German, and so "the grand northern dialect of the Gothic language . . . has been preserved in all its purity in Iceland" (21). For mid-century British travellers, who believed, with Coleridge, that language expressed "the embodied and articulated Spirit of the Race" (460), the "purity" of the Icelandic tongue assumed special significance.

The impulse to define a distinctly English identity, which showed itself first in a renewed interest in Anglo-Saxon history and later in the publication of accurate Old English texts, had led inevitably to the study of Icelandic. As the American philologist George Perkins Marsh explained:

> [The Scandinavian languages] are important, not so much as having largely contributed to the vocabulary, or greatly influenced the grammatical structure of English, but because in the poverty of accessible remains of Anglo-Saxon literature in different and especially in early stages of linguistic development, we do not possess satisfactory means of fully tracing the history of the Gothic portion of our language. . . . I should unhesitatingly place the Icelandic at the head of these subsidiary philologies, because, from its close relationship to Anglo-Saxon, it furnishes more abundant analogies for the illustration of obscure English etymological and syntactical forms than any other of the cognate tongues. It is but recently that the great value of Icelandic philology has become known to the other branches of the Gothic stock, and one familiar with the treasures of that remarkable literature, and the wealth, power, and flexibility of the language which embodies it, sees occasion to regret the want of a thorough knowledge of it in English and American grammatical writers, more frequently than of any other attainment whatever. (93–94)

But Old Norse was not only a resource for understanding the history of the English language. By treating the "wealth, power, and flexibility" of the Icelandic tongue as a part of the Anglo-Saxon linguistic heritage, Marsh's argument suggests that the study of Icelandic is also a means of recovering the original vigor of English-speaking culture. Moreover, in keeping with the precepts of Germanic philology, he treats literature as the characteristic expression of the Icelandic language. Thus in their preservation of literary texts, the Icelanders have preserved the essence of their culture.

Frederick Metcalfe's *The Oxonian in Iceland; or, Notes of Travel in That Island in the Summer of 1860, with a Glance at Icelandic Folk-lore and Sagas* illustrates this mixture of philology and Romantic nationalism. Asked by the Rector of the Reykjavík High School why he has come to Iceland, he replies,

> I want to see with my own eyes some of the places where the scenes of your Sagas and legends are laid. I belong to a nation arrived at a very high state of civilisation, artificial in the extreme; in short, we live and move and have our being in a state of machinery from beginning to end. And somehow this very

modernism begets a desire for reverting to old things, old people, old ballads, old customs — something fresh, and rare, and vigorous. I want to look for a bit at the rock from whence we were hewn, and the hole of the pit whence we were digged. (56–57)

The passage may begin with reference to "*your* sagas," but it ends by identifying Iceland as the source of British civilization. The sagas become — as they became literally in the English versions of William Morris — a piece of British cultural history.

Other British travellers echoed this quest for linguistic origins, with its Carlylean equation of antiquity with freshness, age with vigor. Symington rejoiced in the modern Icelander's ability to understand the ancient writings of his people. "This can be said of no other tongue in western Europe." And "to this — the very language of the Vikings — both the old lowland Scotch, and, at a further remove, our modern English, chiefly owe their directness, expressiveness, and strength" (183). But Iceland holds more than the key to past glory: "The language, history, and literature of our ancestors having been thus preserved in the north, we are thereby enabled to revisit the past, read it in the light of the present, and make both subservient for good in the future" (295).

Metcalfe, too, believed that one of the chief values of his journey was the ability to hear "a people remarkable for intelligence, talking in a tongue almost identical with that in which those bold Vikings expressed their thoughts a thousand years ago" (393). Like others, he observed

the old passion for liberty evaporating in petty mimicry of independence, frittering itself away in newspaper polemics, in tirades against Denmark, and unavailing complaints and regrets over the past; instead of steadily shaping itself into a practical endeavour to promote the material wellbeing of the people. (394)

But, despite these reservations, Metcalfe's faith in the formative influence of Icelandic on British culture was undiminished. In 1876 he printed a pamphlet titled *The Saxon and the Norseman; or, A Plea for the Study of Icelandic Conjointly with Anglo-Saxon*, which he expanded four years later into the book *The Englishman and the Scandinavian; or, A Comparison of Anglo-Saxon and Old Norse Literature*. His own text dramatizes this attitude by freely mixing Icelandic with modern English, thus creating a linguistic medium that demonstrates the interchangeability of the two tongues.

Charles Warnford Lock takes a similar position in his *Home of the Eddas*, which he prefaces with the question:

has not the time arrived when the gods of our northern ancestors should hold as high a place in modern education as the unchaste deities from the Mediterranean, and might not some of the hours so fruitlessly spent in misinterpreting

incomprehensible Horace be more fitly devoted to the classics of Northern
Europe? (1–2)

Claiming to be the second Englishman since Henderson to winter in Iceland
and live to write of the experience, Lock sought to immerse himself in
the language of the "pure blooded bonder and peasant classes" (3). Like
Henderson, he comes to the conclusion that the citizens of Reykjavík are no
better than the inhabitants of any other capital city. But "let the traveller get
out amongst the country folk and his experience will be as mine, that the
simple-minded, hospitable peasants have not degenerated" (25–26). Once
again, purity of language becomes the key to moral virtue.

Sabine Baring-Gould similarly emphasizes the link between English and
Icelandic tongues and uses a series of imaginative etymologies to connect
British with Icelandic and German folklore. Just as Henderson's mission had
resulted in prose colored by the language and imagery of Biblical journeying,
Baring-Gould's scholarly knowledge of Old Norse encouraged him to incorporate elements of the sagas into his own text. But Baring-Gould's uncomfortable pose as a traditional story-teller serves, if anything, as a reminder that
the creative spirit of the skalds is not easily recaptured.

Like Lock and Baring-Gould, William Morris had studied Icelandic and,
like Lock, he believed that the literature of the North had right of place in
the literary tradition of England over the Greek and Roman classics.[13] In that
belief he had begun a series of saga translations with the Icelander Eiríkr
Magnússon.[14] Morris's two trips to Iceland were a result of this venture. But
he undertook them with few illusions about what he would find there. He
described the motivations for visiting Iceland in a letter to Edith Marion
Story:

> . . . there is no art there at all, and there is nothing to interest most people there
> but its strangeness and wildness; yet I have felt for long that I must go there
> and see the background of the stories for wh: I have so much sympathy &
> which must have had something to do with producing & fostering their strange
> imagination: also to such a cockney & stay-at-home as I am there is a certain
> amount of adventure about the journey itself which pleases me. (*Letters* 1: 132)

Morris's quest was not for some living remnant of saga culture, but for
the imaginative experience he attributed to the saga poets. However, unlike
travellers who sought living relics of the heroic past, Morris saw the "poetry"
of Iceland in its separation from its own history — a separation emphasized,
ironically, by the remains of the saga sites and the Icelanders' careful preservation of their literary heritage. The word Morris most often associates with
"poetical" is "melancholy." At Laxdale, the setting of his poem "The
Lovers of Gudrun," where landscape might have been expected to kindle an
imaginative potency akin to that of the saga poet, Morris's spirits fall:

Just think, though, what a mournful place this is — Iceland I mean — setting aside the pleasure of one's animal life there: the fresh air, the riding and rough life, and feeling of adventure — how every place and name marks the death of its short-lived eagerness and glory; and withal so little is the life changed in some ways . . . But Lord! what littleness and helplessness has taken the place of the old passion and violence that had place here once — and all is unforgotten; so that one has no power to pass it by unnoticed: yet that must be something of a reward for the old life of the land, and I don't think their life now is more unworthy than most people's elsewhere, and they are happy enough by seeming. Yet it is an awful place: set aside the hope that the unseen sea gives you here, and the strange threatening change of the blue spiky mountains beyond the firth, and the rest seems emptiness and nothing else: a piece of turf under your feet, and the sky overhead, that's all; whatever solace your life is to have here must come out of yourself or these old stories, not over hopeful themselves. Something of all this I thought; and besides our heads were now fairly turned homeward, and now and again a few times I felt homesick — I hope I may be forgiven. (8: 108)

The passage vacillates between alternatives, but the end of equivocation is Morris's awareness that the lesson of Iceland is a diminished sense of the importance of the individual. Returning to the source of cultural energy turns out to be a confrontation with the littleness of human life and human art. Dufferin and others could sustain the myth of heroic continuity by treating the modern Icelanders as peripheral figures and thereby leaving the relationship between past and present unresolved. Morris, granting the modern Icelanders a sense of memory and therefore of loss, reverses the quest for origins: what one discovers in Iceland is not an access to the past, but a confirmation of its irretrievability.

OF COURSE NOT ALL British travellers were concerned with the heroic elements in Icelandic culture or the transformative potential of the Icelandic experience.[15] Moreover, the life of these concerns was itself limited. By 1878, when Anthony Trollope visited the island, the heroic age of Icelandic travel was clearly over. (The geysers failed to impress a traveller who had visited New Zealand.) But one must turn to non-British writers to find truly alternative views of Iceland. Different as men like Dufferin and Lock, Morris and Baring-Gould may be from one another, they reflect the same concerns with race and nationality, with British institutions and British blood. In contrast, travellers from other nations saw Iceland from very different perspectives. Indeed, their writings do not always seem to be about the same place the British described. The American Pliny Miles, for example, finds Iceland more important as a station in the Viking discovery of America than as a link to heroic culture. He acknowledges that the island is "classic ground" but carefully distinguishes the literary achievement of Iceland from that of Mediterranean culture:

> The hundred different kinds of verse now existing in many volumes of Iceland poetry, the sagas, and other literary productions of the Icelanders, have not been read and re-read, translated and re-translated, like the works of Herodotus, Xenophon, Tacitus, and Cicero, and for very good reasons. The country is not one of such antiquity; it is not a country renowned for arts and arms, and overflowing with a numerous population. As a state, it is nearly destitute of works of art, and its scanty population can only procure the bare necessaries of life. (50)

Miles has great admiration for the Icelanders, who, in his view, "are more contented, moral, and religious, possess greater attachment to country, are less given to crime and altercation, and show greater hospitality and kindness to strangers, than any other people the sun shines upon" and "possess a greater spirit of historical research and literary inquiry, have more scholars, poets, and learned men, than can be found among an equal population on the face of the globe" (52). But these virtues have little to do with the historical roots of Icelandic culture; they are characteristics of the modern Icelanders, a people all the more admirable for the disadvantages of their situation: "Thrown on their own resources, in a cold and dreary climate, the same causes operated in raising up a vigorous, moral, and intellectual people, that were shown in the history of our own Pilgrim Fathers" (42). The final phrase is, of course, the giveaway: Miles sees the Icelanders as examples of a new society, much like his own — not a relic of the Teutonic past, but a modern nation in a new world.

But Miles, like his British counterparts, perceived Iceland from a largely male point of view. The aggressive energy men like Dufferin and Lock attributed to the medieval Icelanders was an idealization of conventional Victorian male virtues; in tracing the strengths of the race to the "pastoral simplicity" (Dufferin 54) of these Nordic forebears, they were affirming the masculine origin of British civilization. Inhospitable, cold, unyielding, the island provided an image of nature at odds with fantasies of the maternal — and a setting for male adventure and male camaraderie. Even the innocence of the Icelandic women — who embarrassed British males by helping them undress for bed — seemed a sign of the insignificance of the female.

Fittingly, the period's least idealized account of travel in Iceland was written by a woman, Ida Pfeiffer, a Viennese who prided herself on being the first woman to undertake a journey "ALONE" to Iceland (in 1845) and followed the feat by undertaking A Woman's Journey round the World (1852). Reacting to the idealizations of Henderson, Pfeiffer comments that "the intercourse of [a rural Icelandic] pastor is wholly confined to the society of peasants; and this constitutes the chief element of that 'patriarchal life' which so many travellers describe as charming. I should like to know which of them would wish to lead such a life!" (83). For Pfeiffer, Thingvellir has no associations with democracy and reminds her rather of the Wolf's Glen Scene in

Weber's *Der Freischütz* (116); she confesses to having "found the character of the Icelanders in every respect below the estimate I had previously formed of it, and still further below the standard given in books" (93).

This negativism may reflect Pfeiffer's failure to receive invitations from the ladies of Reykjavík, but it also suggests that idealization of the North was largely a masculine phenomenon.[16] Pfeiffer's journey, undertaken with limited resources and without the benefit of speaking the native language, was more difficult and certainly more lonely than the journeys recorded by male travellers of the period. If she refused to glamorize Iceland, it may have been because, travelling without the baggage of racial myth, she had experienced the country more directly than her male counterparts. In any case, her *Visit to Iceland* provides a revealing contrast to the Anglocentric vision of the island reiterated by British travellers.

At length, however, Victorian manhood itself found other ways to justify its dominance. By the late 1870s, Iceland was rapidly becoming a nineteenth-century society, and Richard Burton was eager to further those processes. His ridicule of exaggerated accounts of the Icelandic terrain prompted the demythologizing of the island. "The Hekla of our ingenuous childhood," he wrote,

> was a mighty cone, a "pillar of heaven," upon whose dreadful summit white, black, and sanguine red lay in streaks and patches, with volumes of sooty smoke and lurid flames, and a pitchy sky. . . . The Hekla of reality, No. 5 in the island scale, is a commonplace heap, half the height of Hermon, and a mere pigmy compared with the Andine peaks. . . . (2: 161–62)

Equally important, his self-characterization as an anthropologist signals a shift from the philologically oriented travellers who preceded him. No Icelandic travel writer is more concerned with the accuracy of his Norse. But, for Burton, it is one language of many and no special key to a special essence, and he is contemptuous of the notion that Iceland is in some sense a racial home to the British:

> It has been the fashion for travellers to talk of "our Scandinavian ancestors in Iceland," to declare that the northern element is the "backbone of the English race," and to find that Great Britain owes to the hyperborean "her pluck, her go-ahead, and her love of freedom."
>
> That a little of this strong liquor may have done abundant good to the puerile futile Anglo-Kelt, and the flabby and phlegmatic Anglo-Saxon, there is no doubt, but happily we have not had a drop too much of northern blood. (1: 130–31)

Burton notes the preservation of the saga-tradition but finds it, not a sign of cultural strength, but a liability. Icelandic education, he argues, has ignored science and mechanics; "reading . . . was confined to Saga-history and theology, both equally detrimental to mental training and to intellectual progress" (1:155). He acknowledges the historical significance of "the humble wonders of Thingvellir," which he compares to the civilizing influence of Delphi and Jerusalem, but he ridicules the movement to "restore the obsolete practice, and transfer the legislators from their comfortable hall at Reykjavík to this wild and savage spot — why not propose that the barons of England meet in parliament at Runnymede?" (2: 194).[17]

Like Dufferin, Burton attributes the backwardness of modern Iceland to the Danish influence. He sees this influence, however, not in some abstract notion of tyranny but in specific measures forbidding the importation of machinery, and his advice for the future of the Icelanders is not political idealism but practical economics: "His future career is in his own hands, and improvement must be sought in extended stock-breeding, in better use of the fisheries, and in extensive emigration" (1: 144). Only Miles the American and Paijkull the Swede show a similar enthusiasm for the material progress of the island.[18]

THE ECONOMIC AND POLITICAL EVENTS that opened Iceland to foreign travel in the middle years of the nineteenth century soon rendered the islanders less exotic and therefore less attractive to the European imagination. In ceasing to be a backwater, Iceland ceased to hold out the lure of the primitive. The symbolic potential of the island did not disappear, however; it was refocused. Instead of emblemizing aristocratic privilege and male heroism, it came to represent the egalitarianism Morris believed to be his "one lesson" learned from Iceland. (*Letters* 2: 229).

Paikjull had anticipated this view, interpreting the Icelandic emphasis on the rights of the individual as "a Spirit of republicanism":

> This may be seen even in the way in which an Icelander salutes one of his countrymen. "Good day, comrade," he says; thus reminding one of the "citoyen" of modern republics. The title "Herre" is almost unknown in the island. In speaking of each other the peasants naturally make use of the Christian name; but they also employ this confidential style in addressing people of superior rank. (34)

Given Iceland's patronymic name system, what Paijkull took for republicanism may have had less political import than he supposed. However the twentieth-century history of the island bears out his reading of its people. No Victorian travel writer, Morris included, grasped the democratic aspect of Icelandic culture with such clear-sightedness. What was obvious to a Swedish geologist went unregarded by British travellers intent on recapturing the ethos of the primitive.

But the evolution of the Socialist movement altered the British perception of Iceland. The "runic" cross that marks the grave of John Ruskin in Coniston churchyard reflects W. G. Collingwood's sense that the philosophy of his mentor was best represented by a Nordic design.[19] Preparing a new edition of his 1937 *Letters from Iceland*, W. H. Auden revisited Iceland in 1964 and found it

> a joy to discover that, despite everything which had happened to Iceland and myself since my first visit, the feelings it aroused were the same. In my childhood dreams Iceland was holy ground; when, at the age of twenty-nine, I saw it for the first time, the reality verified my dream; at fifty-seven it was holy ground still, with the most magical light of anywhere on earth. . . . [M]odernity does not seem to have changed the character of the inhabitants. They are still the only really classless society I have ever encountered, and they have not — not yet — become vulgar. (8)

Auden's admiration for the Icelanders' classlessness is a far remove from Dufferin's praise of the Icelandic aristocracy. But, like his Victorian predecessors, Auden clung to the myth of a "holy ground" and found in Iceland the counterpart of a childhood dream. No longer mysterious, the island had nevertheless retained its capacity to spark the imagination.

Indiana University-Purdue University at Fort Wayne

NOTES

1. The most notorious raid occurred in 1627, when corsairs carried away 400 Icelanders and sold them into slavery in Algiers. In 1808, a British privateer looted the public treasury in Reykjavík of 35,000 rixdaler.
2. Jesse L. Byock notes that the Danish trade monopoly had become "so unresponsive to Iceland's needs by the middle of the eighteenth century that during the famine year of 1784 the island was required to export food" (42).
3. The Althing was reinstituted in 1843.
4. In chronological order: Robert Chambers, *Tracings of Iceland and the Faröe Islands*, London: W. & R. Chambers, 1856; Lord Dufferin, *Letters from High Latitudes*, London: John Murray, 1857; Charles S. Forbes, *Iceland: Its Volcanoes, Geysers, and Glaciers*, London: Murray, 1860; J.W. Clark, "Journal of a Yacht Voyage to the Faroe Islands and Iceland," in Francis Galton, ed., *Vacation Tourists and Notes of Travel in 1860*, Cambridge: Macmillan, 1861; Frederick Metcalfe, *The Oxonian in Iceland; or, Notes of Travel in That Island in the Summer of 1860, with Glances at Icelandic Folk-lore and Sagas*, London: Longman, Green, Longman, and Roberts, 1861; Andrew James Symington, *Pen and Pencil Sketches of Faröe and Iceland*, London: Longman, Green, Longman, and Roberts, 1862; Edward Thurstan Holland, *A Tour of Iceland in the Summer of 1861*, in Edward Shirley Kennedy, ed., *Peaks, Passes, and Glaciers; Being Excursions by Members of the Alpine Club*, 2nd series, 2 vols., London: Longman, Green, Longman, and Roberts, 1862, 1: 3–128; Sabine Baring-Gould,

Iceland: Its Scenes and Sagas, London: Smith, Elder & Co, 1863; C. W. Shepherd, *The North-West Peninsula of Iceland: Being the Journal of a Tour in Iceland in the Spring and Summer of 1862*, London: Longmans, Green, and Co., 1867; William Morris, *Icelandic Journals, The Collected Works of William Morris*, ed. May Morris, London: Longmans, Green, 1910–1915, vol. 8; Richard F. Burton, *Ultima Thule; or, Summer in Iceland*, 2 vols., London: William P. Nimmo, 1875; Anthony Trollope, *How the "Mastiffs" Went to Iceland*, London: Virtue & Co, 1878; Charles G. Warnford Lock, *The Home of the Eddas*, London: Sampson, Low, Marston, Searle, & Rivington, 1879. To this group one might add M. R. Barnard's translation of the Swedish geologist C. W. Paijkull's *A Summer in Iceland*, London: Chapman and Hall, 1868, and four American works, Pliny Miles, *Northurfari, or Rambles in Iceland*, New York: Charles B. Norton, 1854; J. Ross Browne, *The Land of Thor*, New York: Harper & Brothers, 1867; Bayard Taylor, *Egypt and Iceland in the Year 1874*, New York: G. P. Putnam, 1874 [London: Sampson, Low, Marston, Low & Searle, 1875]; and Samuel Kneeland, *Travels in Iceland: An Account of Its Scenery, People, and History, with a Description of Its Millennial Celebration in August 1874*, New York: A. C. Blunt, 1875.

5. The *Arcturus*, a Scottish steamer under contract with the Danish mail service, made four, then six annual roundtrips, the first in March, the last in October, between Copenhagen and Reykjavík, with stops at Granton and the Orkney, Shetland, and Faroe Islands. In 1870, the *Arcturus* was succeeded by the *Diana*, a converted man-of-war; by 1872, the number of roundtrips had increased to seven.

6. For a bibliography of English translations from the Icelandic, see Litzenberg and also Hermannsson.

7. Peter Bishop's *The Myth of Shangri-La: Tibet, Travel Writing and the Western Creation of Sacred Landscape* is a particularly thorough study of this phenomenon.

8. The sections on Icelandic history and literature in Mackenzie's *Travels* were written by Holland.

9. E. V. Gordon points out that eighteenth-century notions of the Vikings were based on a misread kenning for drinking horns which led to the belief in a race of bloodthirsty warriors who drank their wine from human skulls (lxix–lxx).

10. In fact, the democratic institutions of Iceland should be traced not to Dufferin's "aristocratic" first settlers but to the society of small farmers that soon evolved in their place: "as the original land claims throughout the island were divided up into many farms, there became little to distinguish landholders from one another or to support claims to authority made by leading families" (Byock 56). As a result, the rule of law replaced the rule of semi-feudal authority they had known in Norway.

11. Mackenzie, at the beginning of the century, had complained that "the extreme slowness of the Icelanders . . . occasioned much unlooked-for trouble and delay" (xiv). For E. T. Holland, the mountaineer, these traits "make it unlikely that [the Icelanders] should associate themselves, like the Swiss peasants, with their mountains" (54).

12. Or, in Dufferin's case, by undertaking a dangerous voyage further north to Jan Mayen.

13. Morris maintained that the *Volsunga Saga* "should be to all our race what the Tale of Troy was to the Greeks" (*Works* 7: 286).

14. Morris began his study of Icelandic in 1868. He published his first Icelandic translations, *The Saga of Gunnlaug Wormtongue* and *The Story of Grettir the Strong*, in the following year.
15. For example, J. W. Clark and C. W. Shepherd, who visited Iceland in 1861 and 1862, respectively, show little inclination to idealize the island's past.
16. Another reason Trollope's voyage signals the passing of an age of Icelandic travel is the presence of women. The first book on Iceland by a British woman was Ethel Brilliana Tweedie's *A Girl's Ride in Iceland*, (1889).
17. Thomas J. Assad suggests that this tension between romance and realism, "coarseness and tenderness," is characteristic of Burton's work (11).
18. Paikjull cites statistics to evidence the growth in commerce since 1854 and finds Iceland "in a good way to enhance her material prosperity, so far as a country which has been so scantily endowed by nature, as is the case with her, can expect; and it will, therefore, be a matter of great regret if her progress be retarded by political complications and petty quarrels" (312).
19. Collingwood himself, with Jón Stefánsson, had published *A Pilgrimage to the Saga-Steads of Iceland* (1899) a year before Ruskin's death.

WORKS CITED

Assad, Thomas J. *Three Victorian Travellers: Burton, Blunt, Doughty*. London: Routledge and Kegan Paul, 1964.

Auden, W. H., and Louis MacNeice. *Letters from Iceland*. New York: Random House, 1969.

Baring-Gould, Sabine. *Iceland: Its Scenes and Sagas*. London: Smith, Elder, 1863.

Bernal, Martin. *Black Athena: The Afroasiatic Roots of Classical Civilization*. Vol. 1. New Brunswick: Rutgers UP, 1987.

Bishop, Peter. *The Myth of Shangri-La: Tibet, Travel Writing and the Western Creation of Sacred Landscape*. Berkeley: U of California P, 1989.

Burton, Richard F. *Ultima Thule; or, A Summer in Iceland*. 2 vols. London: William P. Nimmo, 1875.

Byock, Jesse L. *Medieval Iceland: Society, Sagas, and Power*. Berkeley: U of California P, 1988.

Carlyle, Thomas. *On Heroes, Hero-Worship, and the Heroic in History*. Ed. Carl Niemeyer. Lincoln: U of Nebraska P, 1966.

Clark, J. W. "Journal of a Yacht Voyage to the Faroe Islands and Iceland." In Francis Galton, ed., *Vacation Tourists and Notes of Travel in 1860*. Cambridge: Macmillan, 1861.

Coleridge, Samuel Taylor. *Selected Poetry and Prose*. Ed. Stephen Potter. London: Nonesuch Press, 1950. 460.

Collingwood, W. G. and Jón Stefánsson. *A Pilgrimage to the Saga-Steads of Iceland*. Ulverston: W. Holmes, 1899.

Dufferin and Ava, Frederick Temple Blackwood, Marquis of. *Letters from High Latitudes: Being Some Acount of a Voyage in the Schooner Yacht "Foam," 85 O.M., to Iceland, Jan Mayen, & Spitzbergen, in 1856*. Boston: Ticknor and Fields, 1859.

Gordon, E. V. *An Introduction to Old Norse*. 2nd ed. Rev. A.R. Taylor. Oxford: Clarendon P, 1957.

Henderson, Ebenezer. *Iceland*. 1818; 2nd ed., Edinburgh: Waugh and Innes, 1819.

Hermannsson, Halldór. "Bibliography of the Icelandic Sagas and Minor Tales." *Islandica* 1 (1908): 1–94.

Holland, Edward Thurstan. *A Tour of Iceland in the Summer of 1861.* In Edward Shirley Kennedy, ed., *Peaks, Passes, and Glaciers; Being Excursions by Members of the Alpine Club.* 2nd series. 2 vols. London: Longman, Green, Longman, and Roberts, 1862. 1: 3–128.

Hooker, William Jackson. *Journal of a Tour in Iceland in the Summer of 1809.* 2 vols. London: Longmans and Murray, 1811.

Litzenberg, Karl. "The Victorians and the Vikings: A Bibliographical Essay on Anglo-Norse Literary Relations." *University of Michigan Contributions to Modern Philology* 3 (1947): 1–27.

Lock, Charles G. Warnford. *The Home of the Eddas.* London: Sampson, Low, Marston, Searle, & Rivington, 1879.

Loomis, Chauncey C. "The Arctic Sublime." In U.C. Knoepflmacher and G.B. Tennyson, eds., *Nature and the Victorian Imagination.* Berkeley: U of California P, 1977. 95–112.

Mackenzie, George Steuart. *Travels in the Island of Iceland during the Summer of the Year of 1810.* Edinburgh: Thomas Allan, 1811.

Marsh, George P. *Lectures on the English Language.* First Series. New York: Charles Scribner, 1863.

Metcalfe, Frederick. *The Englishman and the Scandinavian; or, A Comparison of Anglo-Saxon and Old Norse Literature.* London: Trübner, 1880.

———. *The Oxonian in Iceland; or, Notes of Travel in That Island in the Summer of 1860, with Glances at Icelandic Folk-lore and Sagas.* London: Longman, Green, Longman, and Roberts, 1861.

Miles, Pliny. *Northurfari, or Rambles in Iceland.* New York: Charles B. Norton, 1854.

Morris, William. *The Collected Letters of William Morris.* Ed. Norman Kelvin. 2 vols. Princeton: Princeton UP, 1984–87.

———. *The Collected Works of William Morris.* Ed. May Morris. 24 vols. London: Longmans, Green, 1910–15.

Paijkull, C.W. *A Summer in Iceland.* Tr. M.R. Barnard. London: Chapman and Hall, 1868.

Pfeiffer, Ida. *Visit to Iceland and the Scandinavian North.* 1852; 2nd ed. London: Ingram, Cooke, 1853.

Shepherd, C.W. *The North-West Peninsula of Iceland: Being the Journal of a Tour in Iceland in the Spring and Summer of 1862.* London: Longmans, Green, 1867.

Symington, Andrew James. *Pen and Pencil Sketches of Faröe and Iceland.* London: Longman, Green, Longman, and Roberts, 1862.

Tweedie, Ethel Brilliana. *A Girl's Ride in Iceland.* London: Griffith, Farrar, 1889.

"WORK OF NOBLE NOTE": TENNYSON'S "ULYSSES" AND VICTORIAN HEROIC IDEALS

By Edward Dramin

TENNYSON'S ULYSSES IS A uniquely Victorian character who personifies a specific Victorian concept of heroism and derives his main energies and values from a distinctly Victorian type of hero. A prominent heroic paradigm of the Victorian era possessed Ulysses' salient characteristics: great courage before physical danger; delight in combat and dangerous voyages; an unconquerable will demonstrated by dogged perseverance through enormous difficulties and unwillingness to acknowledge defeat; obsession with attaining glory; passion for travel to distant lands, inexorable roaming with a hungry heart for knowledge of foreign peoples, manners, and climates; experience in governance, making mild a rugged people and subduing them to the useful and the good, a duty for which this kind of hero is temperamentally unsuited and which he ultimately discards.

Ulysses' traits of temperament were prominent characteristics of the notable adventurers and military leaders of Tennyson's era:

> Vigorous, self-confident, prideful, determined, . . . [they possessed] a violent, restless energy which drove them away from the narrow confines of their islands to every part of the civilized world and deep into the vast areas of the unexplored, uncivilized world. Carrying with them their own unbending attitudes, manners, customs and beliefs, they were continually getting into trouble or creating trouble by being in places where they need not have been. (Farwell, *Wars* xvii, 2)

Ulysses is a poetic analogue of such Victorian empire builders as Cecil Rhodes, Chinese Gordon, and Lord Kitchener, as well as African explorers like Henry Stanley, John Hanning Speke, Sir Samuel White Baker, David Livingstone (whose *Missionary Travels and Researches in South Africa* Tennyson read; *Letters* 2: 191), and Sir Richard Burton.[1] Flourishing by the time

117

"Ulysses" was written, this type of hero is exemplified by early Victorians like Lt. Francis Farewell, General George Pollock, Sir Robert Sale, Eldred Pottinger, and Sir Thomas Monro.

Ulysses has been interpreted as a Romantic hero with transcendental aspirations and metaphysical depth. Dwight Culler, for example, believes that Ulysses descends from "high Romantic heroes" like Childe Harold and Alastor. A "Romantic wanderer," Ulysses searches for the "dark and mysterious in the human consciousness" and seeks to "bridge the gulf between the human and the divine." "Ulysses" is thus a "Romantic poem" (Culler 94–99).[2] Culler notes that "the distinctive thing about Ulysses is that his whole life is conducted upon the heroic plane" (98), and Culler acknowledges the presence of Victorian virtues: "the Victorian addition of 'not yielding' "; the "emphasis upon doing 'some work of noble note.' There is more about 'toil' " (97). The connection, though, could be developed more emphatically: Ulysses has a decisive, unambiguous relationship with Victorian interests and goals.

Tennyson's greatest poetry contemplates and seeks to provoke dialogue about prevailing conditions and ideals of the Victorian Era. *In Memoriam* refers to Victorian social problems and scientific developments. *Idylls of the King* is an allegory about the moral and spiritual needs of Victorian society. "The Lotus-Eaters" has been read as a parable of the decadence of the Victorian aristocracy, an exposé of the excesses of Utilitarianism, and a dramatization of a state of "Everlasting No." *Maud* begins with contemporary references to the suffering of the urban poor and concludes with allusions to the Crimean War. Tennyson himself stated that his poetry of the early 1830s was based on "the broad common interests of the time" (H. Tennyson 1: 123). Because the Victorians were obsessed with heroes, because Tennyson's poetry is involved with his own time, and because Ulysses is cast in heroic dimensions, a relationship between Ulysses' type of heroism and Victorian heroes is likely. Like Tennyson's other poetry of the 1830s, "Ulysses" reflects the "broad common interests of the time" in that it presents a hero who is based on the Victorian heroic paradigm cited above, a hero having all that type's salient characteristics, including the Victorian virtues of "work" and "not yielding" which readings like Culler's notice but do not explain. In this essay I shall show how Tennyson's "Ulysses" resonates with echoes of the personalities and careers of real-life heroes of Tennyson's own time; however, Tennyson's poem offers a critical perspective toward them.

Ranking after the Duke of Wellington as Britain's most famous warriors between Waterloo and 1833, Viscount Hugh Gough (1779–1869) and Sir Charles Napier (1782–1853) cherished glory and were peripatetic, tough-spirited warriors. Napier called his own career "a wayward life of adventure." After the Peninsular War and coastal raiding operations against Southern states during the War of 1812, he sailed for the Ionian Islands in 1821.

As military governor of the Greek island of Cephalonia, he governed a population of 60,000 on the rocky island. Visiting Cephalonia in 1823, Lord Byron tried to enlist him in the Greek war for independence, which Napier saw as providing a chance for personal glory (Farwell, *Soldiers* 76). Abandoning this post, Napier resumed his restless wandering, moving from Canada to Normandy to the northern counties of England.

Just as Ulysses resumes his adventures in old age, in his 60s Napier went to India for a second career and augmented his fame. He enjoyed having "become a name" and being "honored of them all." Even in his 60s Napier responded to new honors and victories with the elated egotism of Ulysses: "This is glory! Nine princes have surrendered their swords to me on fields of battle, and their kingdoms have been conquered by me. I have received the government of the conquered provinces and all the honors are paid to me!" (Farwell, *Soldiers* 92). Like Ulysses, Napier was impatient with the common duty of governing with slow prudence and soft degrees, a task which, he feels, is more appropriate for the younger generation:

Substituting Acts of Parliament for the Articles of War! Some whipper-snapper boy, as judge advocate, takes the whole proceedings into his hands and lays down the law. My formula is this: Punish the government servants first! The great recipe for quieting a country is a good thrashing: the wildest chaps are thus tamed. (Farwell, *Soldiers* 92–93)

Beginning his career in hand-to-hand combat at the Cape of Good Hope, Gough fought against pirates in Trinidad, the Spanish in Puerto Rico, and the Dutch in Surinam. Recognized for bravery in the Peninsular War, he was knighted in 1815 and returned to his native Ireland. For eleven years he was magistrate for Cork, Limerick, and Tipperary, whose natives he described as "misguided and infatuated" (Farwell, *Soldiers* 26) when he left the labor of subduing them to the useful and the good to resume his military career in 1827.

At 61 Gough went to the Far East where, Ulysses-like, he won important victories in his 70s and showed the enormous self-confidence and imperviousness to danger that characterize Victorian heroes and Ulysses. At Ferozeshah, Gough launched a suicidal frontal bayonet charge against concentrated Sikh artillery, then rashly continued attacking in the night, causing heavy casualties among British troops who mistakenly fired at each other. Undaunted, Gough commented, "I saw nothing to make me despond. I had not a doubt in my mind as to our success" (Farwell, *Soldiers* 44). Asked to retreat, he exclaimed, "What! Withdraw the troops after the action has commenced and when I feel confident of success? Indeed I will not!" (Farwell, *Soldiers* 47). Such confident rhetoric had the same intentions as Ulysses': to communicate an inflexible will never to yield and thus inspire men to face danger. Feeling indefatigable themselves, heroes like Gough derived a literal delight from battle with their peers. Combat induced an emotional high akin to intoxication:

> What a supremely delightful moment it was! No one can imagine how intense is the pleasure. . . . There is nothing else in the world like it, or that can approach its inspiration, its intense sense of pride. You are for the first time lifted up out of all petty thoughts of self, and for the moment your whole existence, soul and body, seems to revel in a true sense of glory. . . . The unalloyed and elevating satisfaction, the joy I felt as I ran for the enemy's stockades at the head of a small mob of soldiers. (Farwell, *Soldiers* 68)

Tennyson must have known of Napier and Gough while writing "Ulysses," since they had achieved widespread fame by 1833. At this time of Tennyson's growing awareness of his contemporary world, military heroes competed for headlines with explorers, among whom Sir Thomas Stamford Raffles (1781–1826) and Sir John Franklin (1786–1847) were preeminent. The founder of Singapore, Raffles's fame was enhanced by the publication of his memoirs in 1830. Sharing Ulysses' unrelenting thirst for newer worlds of attainment, Raffles also shares Ulysses' confident rhetoric and bold vision of greater future achievement: "I am enabled to do wonders; if time is only given to persevere in the same course for a few years, I think I shall be able to lay the foundation of a new order of things. I promise glorious results" (Coupland 109).

Franklin published narratives of his Arctic voyages in 1823 and 1828 and was described with language appropriate for Ulysses: "doggedly determined and cheerfully buoyant . . . a man of unrivaled fortitude and unsurpassed leadership in the face of unexemplified sufferings" (Trail 104). He saw action in naval battles at Copenhagen, Trafalgar, and New Orleans, and he participated in expeditions to the uncharted coast of western Australia and across the Arctic Ocean from northern Norway to the Bering Strait to search for the Northwest Passage.[3] Hoping to trace the northernmost coast of North America, Franklin led an overland expedition into unknown regions of northern Canada in June, 1821. For two months Franklin skirted the northern Canadian coast, often penetrating northward into the icy Arctic Ocean in fragile birchbark canoes. Sustaining the expedition's morale with "great charm" (Stefansson 39), Franklin eagerly sought danger:

> The return [from the Arctic] did not begin until August 23, which was too late. He had tarried too long. With signs of impending winter, these desperate men made a daring traverse of 25 miles of ocean before a raging north wind, in canoes that were falling apart. The waves were so high that sight of the mast of the adjacent canoe was intermittently hidden. (Houston 208–9)

Like all Victorian heroes, Franklin "suffered greatly" ("Ulysses" 8): during the subsequent cross-country trek through a fierce northern Canadian winter, Franklin endured a nightmarish cycle of debilitating cold, near starvation, and consequent fatigue which made the search for food almost impossible.[4] Half of Franklin's French Canadian voyageurs died of starvation or exposure, and the entire expedition would have perished had not friendly Indians provided food and shelter at the last moment. But rivalling Ulysses' undaunted spirit, Franklin in his journals repeatedly describes being in a cheerful frame of mind despite appalling adversities (see for example, 404, 414, 438, 445, 449). Returning home to a hero's welcome, Franklin was promoted to captain and elected to the Royal Society. Driven by an eagerness for another Arctic expedition, in 1826 Franklin traveled westward along the northern Canadian coast, this time in sturdier oak longboats. Penetrating to Alaska's Bering Strait despite adverse weather (in effect, finding *a* northwest passage), his expedition was considered a triumph and he was knighted in 1828.

Franklin was later governor of Van Diemen's Island, a penal colony near Australia, where he experienced "the unhappiest period of his life." Resenting governing an island of convicts, Franklin also resented his duty to "mete and dole unequal laws" ("Ulysses" 3–4), one set for the convicts, another for the island's non-penal settlers (Delpar 158). After suffering as administrator for six years, he resigned and returned to England. Franklin then undertook his final search for the Northwest Passage to revitalize himself from the depressing effects of governing a rugged people on a barren island (Delpar 158). At 60, an age considered dangerously advanced for Polar exploration, Franklin sailed for the Arctic with the battleships *Erebus* and *Terror*, only to perish with all 129 members of his expedition in one of the great tragedies of world exploration.

Tennyson was connected with Franklin in several ways. He was Franklin's nephew and wrote the epitaph for Franklin's monument in Westminster Abbey ("Not here: the white North hath thy bones, and thou/ Heroic Sailor Soul/ Art passing on thy happier voyage now/ Toward no earthly pole," 1–4). Tennyson's wife, Emily, was Franklin's niece. During the search for the missing Franklin, Emily's journal bears the entry, "Painful tidings of the Arctic Expedition" (*Journal* 39). Anne Sellwood, Emily's sister, married Charles Weld, who assisted Franklin in organizing his Arctic explorations (*Letters* 2: 13n). Franklin's widow financed Captain Francis McClintock's expedition to search for her husband. McClintock's account of his search (*Voyage of the "Fox" in the Arctic Seas: A Narrative of the Discovery of Sir John Franklin and His Companions*) was inscribed by Lady Franklin to Emily Sellwood Tennyson (*Letters* 2: 251n).

Rather than referring to any one hero, Tennyson's Ulysses is a composite, an imaginative synthesis of the age's heroes: I regard him as a social archetype representative of a broad class within the Victorian age. He exemplifies a character type pervasive in a particular era, much as Browning's Bishop exemplifies the worldly Renaissance churchman and Dickens's Bounderby exemplifies the Philistine Victorian industrialist. As a participant in the Victorian popular consciousness and spokesman for his society's values, Tennyson respects his character's positive qualities. Ulysses' exhilarating language, however, conceals shortcomings, and his monologue dramatizes his limitations.[5] By suggesting Ulysses' deficiencies, the poem tacitly questions the personality and goals of egotistical, reckless heroes of Tennyson's era.[6]

Knowledge of this type of hero enhances understanding of "Ulysses": it provides awareness of the social and historical origins of his heroic temperament and shows how Ulysses' personality is related to an aggressive, imperialistic age. Though parallels are undeniable, we may ask how Ulysses' resemblance to these heroes came about in the creative process. Indeed, Ulysses may be a deliberate analogue, consciously based on specific contemporary heroes. Tennyson likely knew of Gough and Franklin in 1833, and he may have consciously derived Ulysses from men like them. Such heroes are not mentioned in Tennyson's collected letters, but this non-reference does not disqualify the connection. Tennyson seldom mentions and never criticizes famous non-literary contemporaries in his correspondence. The absence of such reference is not significant also because of circumstances acknowledged by the editors: "[the letters] conduct no inquiry into the sources of inspiration, they offer no observations or insights that we recognize . . . as the germ of a poem" (1: xxvii). Moreover, these heroes may have exerted a subconscious influence. Since they were a prominent part of the age, their traits may have been involuntarily assimilated within Tennyson's imagination and associated with the concept of Ulysses, ultimately emanating in a character who is a subconscious reflection of a contemporary heroic type.

We know that while writing "Ulysses," Tennyson expressed his admiration for Cervantes's *Don Quixote* (H. Tennyson 1: 79), an interest which suggests a predisposition to criticize the folly of heroism. We also know that Tennyson did not value military heroism since it is attained in warfare, and Tennyson believed that the only justifiable wars were in defense of liberty and country. While acknowledging the need to praise the bravery of those fighting to preserve freedom and national independence, Tennyson condemned war and those who find battle exhilarating:

> You praise when you should blame
> The barbarism of wars. . . .

> I would that wars should cease,
> I would the globe from end to end
> Might sow and reap in peace.
> And some new Spirit o'erbear the old,
> Or trade refrain the Powers
> From war with kindly links of gold,
> Or Love with wreaths of flowers. . . .
> And who loves War for War's own sake
> Is fool, or crazed, or worse.
> ("The Charge of the Heavy Brigade" 69–70, 76–82, 94–95)

Tennyson also does not celebrate intrepid explorers. He admired other kinds of valor, particularly selfless courage before danger in order to save human life. According to Hallam Tennyson, Tennyson declared that the following event, a brave action done out of concern for human life, "contained a noble theme" and was to be "laid aside for future use":

> The American ship "Cleopatra" was descried by Captain Hughes of the Liverpool steamer "Lord Gough," with her colors at half-mast and evidently sinking. The gale and the sea were so terrible that it seemed madness to help her; but volunteers came forward and a boat was manned, when suddenly the colors were hauled down. Captain Hughes, however, persevered, the desperate adventure succeeded, and the "Cleopatra" was saved.

> The United States government forwarded thanks and rewards to Captain Hughes and his men; but noble as their conduct was, Captain Pendleton of the "Cleopatra" had done a nobler thing. Asked why his colors were hauled down, he replied, "Because we thought it wrong to imperil other lives in a hopeless attempt." Captain Pendleton and his men faced the certainty of death by drowning rather than tempt others into danger. (H. Tennyson 2: 373)

The episode moved Tennyson to declare, "Honor to the name of the brave! These deeds should live in song" (H. Tennyson 2: 373).

BECAUSE HE HAS BEEN COMPARED to Werther and Alastor, we may forget that Ulysses is a warrior. Proudly exhibiting a pugilistic spirit, Ulysses is always fighting. Imagery of battle recurs throughout his monologue. He seems to fight against everything — men, gods, nature, and death. He sees life as a continuing battle. He sees himself as a warrior, always fighting and forever marching onward to new victories. He thrives on such continual competition. If he has encountered defeat, he is unhumbled by it: possessing a proud self-confidence, Ulysses assumes he can conquer all obstacles. He is beyond mere aggressiveness, though. He asks his men not simply to "row" against the ocean but to "*smite* / The sounding furrows." The choice of verbs suggests a macho swagger, a flaunting of martial prowess. At the same time, the verb indicates a needless antagonism, a redundant zeal to hurt nature while subduing it.

Ulysses subsequently declares that he has "drunk delight of battle with my peers, / Far on the ringing plains of windy Troy" (16–17). The pun immanent in "drunk delight" evokes a questioning of the legitimacy of both the pleasure and the activity which induced it. Like all Victorian heroes, Ulysses is intoxicated by adventure. Moreover, "drunk delight of battle" indicates what the rest of the poem suggests, his addiction to danger: battle and risky voyages produce an emotional high which he is compelled to seek out repeatedly.

If Ulysses' delight in battle suggests military heroes like Gough, his passion to seek newer worlds connects him with explorers like Franklin. Like them he cannot rest from travel, constantly roaming with a hungry heart toward that untraveled world whose margin forever fades (like Franklin, Ulysses' specific impulsion is toward the west — "to sail beyond the sunset, / And the baths of all the western stars" 60–61). He shares Burton's exhilaration at escaping mundane life in his homeland and renewing movement into the unknown:

> Of the gladdest moments in human life, methinks, is the departure upon a distant journey into unknown lands. Shaking off with one mighty effort the fetters of Habit, the leaden weight of Routine, the cloak of many Cares and and the slavery of Home, man feels at once more happy. . . . Afresh dawns the morn of life. (Burton Journals, cited in Brodie 141)

Although Ulysses' eagerness to escape his homeland and relinquish direction of his people connects him with Victorian explorers and military heroes, this impulse dissociates him from an earlier heroic line and implicitly casts doubt on the ultimate value of his kind of heroism. The great tradition of religious epic literature comprising the Old and New Testaments, the works of Homer and Virgil, and the epics of Spenser and Milton presents an heroic ideal different from Gough and Franklin's: the hero is the One for the Many, the exceptional individual who selflessly serves his people, advancing their well-being and bringing them a new dispensation of divine truth. The hero of this tradition follows the model of Moses, Christ, or Aeneas.

The name Ulysses evokes the earlier heroic line, but Tennyson's version of Ulysses repudiates ideals of that tradition. Contrasting with previous epic heroes, Tennyson's Ulysses seeks personal satisfaction and personal fulfillment, not the advancement of his society. There is no indication that he intends to perform any service to mankind at large, nor does he provide the slightest suggestion that he has ever done so. Ulysses' lack of reference to traditional heroic purposes implies the primacy of his self-interest, while his remarks about Telemachus convey an explicit repudiation of service to society. By leaving "the sceptre and the isle" to his son, Ulysses quietly underscores his dissociation from the older heroic tradition of Western civilization.

Ulysses' polished rhetoric nevertheless strives to conceal his self-centeredness. After 31 lines, his super-ego finally finds a grandiose justification for his new voyage into the unknown: "To follow knowledge like a sinking star, / Beyond the utmost bound of human thought."[7] Long before, however, in his opening statement Ulysses reveals primary motives for leaving his people: their boorishness and their failure to give him the recognition he needs — "a savage race, / That hoard and sleep and feed, and know not me." While not cruel, he is not kind. While not stupid, he can be ingenuous. He naively reveals his vanity and insecurity. He has proven his greatness repeatedly in the past, but he needs continual reassurance of it in the present; he has "become a name," but he rebukes his people because they "know not me." Along with adventure, he is also addicted to fame: like Victorian adventurers, he needs repeated infusions of glory and honor.

Ulysses admits another motive for wandering, his need to be free of "an aged wife," as he perfunctorily dismisses the faithful woman who had preserved his kingdom. Misogyny and male chauvinism are common in Victorian heroes: some fear or loathe women; some need occasional distance from them; others see women as a threat to mobility and personal liberty. Gough was averse to women in general. For Napier, "Marriage is a drag upon military ambitions. I have done pretty well, but not half of what I could have done as a bachelor" (Farwell, *Soldiers* 77). Kitchener and Gordon were notorious for avoiding and deprecating women (Farwell, *Soldiers* 294). Garnet Wolseley commented, "Ninety-nine women out of a hundred are simply fools" (Farwell, *Soldiers* 205). Burton repeatedly deserted his devoted, attractive wife in favor of adventure.

Thus spurred by several motives, Ulysses is constantly in motion. His preference for perpetual movement suggests Victorian heroes like Raffles who, while governor of Malaysia and Java, repeatedly indulged an insatiable appetite for exploration and continual brisk motion:

> The rapidity with which he travelled exceeded anything ever known on the island before. Several were sufferers from the very long journeys he made, riding sometimes sixty and seventy miles in one day. . . . On one memorable day he made his way for fifty miles through forest hitherto unexplored by any European. (Coupland 67)

Always in motion like Franklin and Raffles, Ulysses cannot dwell in one place for any length of time. Nor can he be committed to one purpose for very long. Considered in a broad context, Ulysses' mobility reflects the Victorian fascination with motion in the era of the railroad and steamship. But Ulysses' perpetual movement also suggests a man who is inwardly afraid and running away. His incessant travels are his means of working off underlying anxieties. In fact, he suffers from several kinds of anxiety. He fears commitment. He fears growing old. His continual onward movement is especially founded on his fear of dying. Wanting to experience renewed self-assertion and personal fulfillment before death overtakes him, he is impelled to move across the world continually in an almost naive effort to out-run death.

Typical of Tennyson's great short lyrics, the verse reflects the speaker's character. Ulysses' short statements and unpretentious monosyllabic diction underscore his role as decisive leader and his freedom from debilitating conscious doubt. Reinforcing Ulysses' statement, "How dull it is to pause, to make an end," enjambment emphasizes his conscious, publicly stated will for constant forward movement to new realms and his drive onward into the future:

> I cannot rest from travel; I will drink Life to the lees.
> All times I have enjoy'd
> Greatly, have suffer'd greatly, both with those
> That loved me, and alone; on shore, and when
> Thro' scudding drifts the rainy Hyades
> Vext the dim sea. (6–11)

Ulysses, though, has no fixed destination. His large ego produces a will toward high achievement, but he cannot define a specific goal for which to strive. His unfocussed desires not to be "idle," to grasp "*something* more" (27) and "new *things*" (28), to have "*something* ere the end" (51) and "*some* work of noble note" (52), and not to "pause," suggest a desperation to keep busy at any cost. "To seek a newer world" (57), he drives onward into the future because he must escape from the present, whatever it is. His drive onward to yet another voyage reflects something other than the Victorian desire for concrete, meaningful "work" that Culler sees: though his rhetoric contrives to suggest the Victorian impulse for substantive work and constant progress, Ulysses' life has become a compulsion for movement for its own sake without real progress.[8]

Ulysses' bold language conflicts with reality in other ways. He alleges to have led a rich, rewarding life. In some ways, though, he has led a surprisingly empty life. He strives for an unending succession of new experiences, but he cannot find any one experience entirely satisfying. He finds no delight in any activities except battle and wandering. He has formed no meaningful human relationships. He has little feeling for humanity or for individuals. Like Gough he is impervious to the hardship and feelings of those he leads: he asks his men to venture forth on difficult seas, without any thought about the difficulties they will endure, without thinking that they might not share his enthusiasm for yet another voyage.

The psychological concept of the narcissistic personality subsumes many of Ulysses' traits and further connects him with Victorian heroes like Napier and Gough, since the concept is almost a unifying metaphor for their temperaments. As Otto Kernberg has observed, the narcissist has an inflated concept of self, believes himself superior to others, yet needs to be admired by others. Cold and aloof, yet he needs to be the center of attention. The type is emotionally shallow: he makes no emotional commitments and lacks empathy. His relationships are exploitive: he uses people to achieve his goals, "temporarily idealizing them as potential sources of narcissistic supply" (for example, Ulysses' remarks to his men in order to bind them to his will — "My mariners / Souls . . . / That ever with a frolic welcome took / The thunder and the sunshine, and opposed, / Free hearts, free foreheads. / . . . men that strove with Gods" 45–49, 53). Disregarding others, the narcissist shows contempt ("an agèd wife," "a savage race" 3, 4) and devaluation ("Most blameless is he, centered in the sphere / Of common duties" 39–40). He enjoys life only when worshipped by others and praised for his achievements. Charming on the surface, in reality the narcissist is selfish and self-centered. The narcissist also has an abnormal fear of growing old and dying.

D. F. Masterson's definition of the narcissistic personality is almost an abstract of Ulysses and the Gough-Napier hero syndrome:

> The main clinical characteristics of the narcissistic personality disorder are grandiosity, extreme self-involvement and lack of interest in and empathy for others, in spite of the pursuit of others to obtain admiration and approval. The patient manifesting a narcissistic personality disorder seems to be endlessly motivated to seek perfection in all he or she does, to pursue [lofty goals,] and to find others who will mirror and admire his/her grandiosity. Underneath this defensive façade is a feeling state of emptiness and rage. . . . (Masterson 7)

Like Ulysses, the narcissist can be "stimulating and charming when he [chooses] to be" (9). There is a "continuous activation of the grandiose self" (57). He places an emphasis "upon honor and duty" (10). Always searching "for continuous stroking from his friends" (61), the narcissistic personality is "a sucker" for flattery and expects and responds "very positively to it." When he does not receive flattery and honor, the narcissist becomes "depressed and distraught"(9). He also has "an obsessive fear of and preoccupation with loneliness and death" (9). Masterson observes, "Unable to be close to anyone," the narcissist "pursue[s] his own interests in a selfish manner, ignoring the needs of others, including his wife and children" (11). A patient of Masterson states, "I have a need to be loved but cannot love; I am selfish; there is something horrible inside of me" (11).

If it seems I have been truculent regarding Ulysses, Tennyson invites a critical orientation toward his character by associating him with Dante's creation. In fact, the two Ulysses share two major defects, deception and destructiveness. Both deceive themselves and others, perpetrating their deceit with polished rhetoric which articulates noble purposes. In Canto XXVI of *The Inferno*, Ulysses is condemned for having given "Fraudulent Counsel." He misleads, not only in his calculated deceit of Achilles, the Trojans, and Circe, but more in his self-deception, which includes his deluded ethos. Dante's Ulysses first seems a noble pre-Faustian overreacher aspiring beyond the limits of human intellectual attainment (100–9, 112–20). His obligations to human beings are overshadowed by his desire for "knowledge," which turns out to be not philosophic wisdom but encyclopedic knowledge of humanity and the material world (91–99). But Ulysses is "fraudulent" mainly in his compelling, sophistic advocacy of a voyage of discovery which ultimately proves destructive:

> There before us rose a mountain, dark
> because of distance, and it seemed to me
> the highest mountain I had ever seen.
> And we were glad, but this soon turned to sorrow,
> for out of that new land a whirlwind rose
> and hammered at our ship, against her bow.
> Three times it turned her round with all the waters;
> and at the fourth, it lifted up the stern
> so that our prow plunged deep, as pleased an Other,
> until the sea again closed — over us." (133–142)

Though Tennyson does not describe Ulysses' destruction, Dante's description looms in the background of Tennyson's poem ("It may be that gulfs shall wash us down"), underscoring the delusion of Ulysses' ethos of adventure, the deceptiveness of his attractive rhetoric, and the destructiveness of his course of action. Combining delusions of grandeur with self-destruction is a narcissistic symptom: Masterson observes "the destructiveness of [the narcissist's] grandiose behavior to his best interest" (57).

In turn, Ulysses' destructiveness and his deception connect him with Victorian heroes. Wolseley described the deceitfulness of hero-general Evelyn Wood:

> He is as cunning as a first-class diplomatist. . . . He has a depth of cunning that I could not have believed it possible for any brave man to possess. . . . His intrigues with newspaper correspondents and his popularity-hunting propensities must be kept in check. (Farwell, *Soldiers* 256)

On a more important and complex level of deception, Victorian heroes believed themselves motivated by allegedly higher principles like the White

Man's burden and Duty to Queen and Country. Napier claimed that his victories in India would let the poor "have fairer play under our sceptre," allow a more "humane" way (Farwell, *Soldiers* 85), and permit him to "to do good, to create, to improve, to end destruction, and rise up order" as victor of the conquered (Farwell, *Soldiers* 93). Chinese Gordon campaigned in Africa to "do a great deal to ameliorate the lot of the people" (Farwell, *Soldiers* 118). A fervent reader of Isaiah, Gordon saw himself as God's warrior: "I come . . . with God on my side to redress the evils of the Sudan. I will not fight with any weapons but justice" (Farwell, *Soldiers* 138).

That is, Victorian heroes habitually practiced a reflexive gesture: citing high-minded ideals in confident rhetoric to sanctify their actions. They claimed to be doing "work of noble note." A favorite hero-general of Queen Victoria, Redvers Buller vehemently justified the Zulu War: "I am certain that . . . nobody will doubt that it was a righteous war. It was a war of civilization against barbarity." Battles fought by British armies bring "law and order . . . peace, trade, Christian virtues and good government" as well as British rule, which "was indisputably the best rule for everyone" (Farwell, *Wars* 220). While many Victorian heroes were sincere and shared their society's super ego, such noble pretexts served to rationalize and consecrate primary impelling motives — craving for personal glory; escape from commitment, women, and governance; love of conquest, wandering, and battle. Ulysses deceives his followers, some readers, and perhaps himself by ostensibly subordinating these primal motives to noble purposes conveyed in dignified rhetoric — "to follow knowledge like a sinking star, / Beyond the utmost bound of human thought" (31–32), "work of noble note (52)".[9]

Like Ulysses, Victorian heroes were driven by strong destructive impulses. Fawn Brodie has convincingly shown the self-destructive element in Burton, while one can see powerful self-destructive tendencies in Franklin,[10] Gordon, and Napier.[11] Victorian heroes who did not destroy themselves in their passion for danger and glory certainly brought destruction to some of their followers. Gough was notorious for winning personal glory with reckless tactics that ignored the well-being of his men. As Chilianwala he sent 12,000 against a Sikh army of 40,000 hidden in thick jungle. Failing to utilize his cavalry or attack the enemy's flanks, he directed a frontal infantry charge at the enemy's center. Regiments attacking Sikh cannon were ordered to use only bayonets and not fire their rifles. With one in five casualties, Chilianwala was the bloodiest battle ever fought in India: military historians consider it the infantry equivalent of the charge of the Light Brigade.

While revealing such faults, "Ulysses" is not a one-sided arraignment, as is indicated when Tennyson relates the poem to Hallam:

> "Ulysses" was written soon after Arthur Hallam's death, and gave my feeling about the need of going forward, and braving the struggle of life perhaps more simply than anything in "In Memoriam." (H. Tennyson 1: 196)

Tennyson decisively delineates one of Ulysses' strengths, the ability to carry on in adversity, a capacity which Ulysses exemplifies in transcending paralysis by fear, in exhibiting dignified equipoise, and in persevering in the pursuit of his purposes despite the prospect of death ("to strive, to seek, to find, and not to yield" 70, "Death closes all, but something ere the end, . . . may yet be done" 51–52, "To sail beyond the sunset . . . until I die" 60–61).

Victorian adventurers and military heroes showed strength in coping with the awareness of death, continually transcending fear of it, confronting it with sangfroid, and carrying on with the achievement of larger goals. Gravely wounded and apparently dying at the battle of Busaco, Napier cried out at the appearance of the Duke of Wellington, "I could not die at a better moment." When leading his troops in combat Gough always wore a long white coat, thus drawing enemy fire which he faced unperturbed (Farwell, *Soldiers* 39, 43–44). Lord Wolseley observed Chinese Gordon's "indifference to danger of all sorts" (Farwell, *Soldiers* 197). Forced to sit at a distance from the murderous Abyssinian King Johannis during an audience, Gordon violated decorum by moving close to the throne. When Johannis declared, "I may kill you for this," Gordon coolly replied, "I do not fear death" (Farwell, *Soldiers* 126). Later facing certain death when surrounded at Khartoum, Gordon seemed "to enjoy his predicament . . . and delight in the drama of the situation" (Farwell, *Soldiers* (141). "Ulysses" pays tribute to courageous perseverance, particularly before the reality of death.[12]

Such fearlessness is, paradoxically, psychological compensation for the fear of death. The primal narcissistic need of these heroes to be esteemed, combining with strong compulsions like the will for adventure, generates a compensatory courage which enables the hero to achieve brave deeds bringing recognition and to overcome the narcissistic fear of dying. Furthermore, fear of death is diminished by the prospect of the hero being revered as the result of dying: since a noble death in itself will bring the veneration he requires and since he will be esteemed because of a heroic death, the hero transcends his fear of death. Because death may ultimately satisfy strong narcissistic needs, Ulysses and Victorian heroes can be fearless before it and even seek it eagerly.

ALTHOUGH HE CAN BE related to the Romantic tradition, Ulysses is distant from Romanticism in some basic ways. Compared to emotionally complex Romantic heroes like Werther and Childe Harold, his introspection is perfunctory and relatively shallow ("that which we are, we are" 67, "Death closes all" 51). He communicates no really trenchant truths about himself. His self-examination is at the same level of profundity as that of Napier or Gough. And like them he admits to no faults. His staunch self-righteousness exists without the Romantic capacity for sustained, critical analysis of personal deficiencies (compare with Canto III of Byron's *Childe Harold,* Book I of Wordsworth's *Prelude,* Coleridge in "Dejection," or legitimate Victorian Romantics like Fra Lippo Lippi).

Despite his assurances to the contrary, Ulysses actually seems to fear self-knowledge. Each time he is on the verge of self-revelation, he quickly changes the subject. Just as he is about to achieve an interesting insight into his position in life, he diverts the focus away from himself by offering an impersonal, sententious maxim:

> I am a part of all that I have met —
> Yet all experience is an arch wherethro'
> Gleams that untraveled world. . . .
> . . . You and I are old —
> Old age hath yet his honor (18–20, 49–50)

He also avoids self-analysis by quickly switching his focus from incipient perceptions about his character to mundane external objects:

> He works his works, I mine —
> There lies the port; the vessel puffs her sail. . . .
> [We are] men that strove with Gods —
> The lights begin to twinkle from the rocks. (43–44, 54–55)

Ulysses' incessant travels are those of a man escaping self-awareness. His constant geographical movement allows him to avoid self-analysis and the discovery that he lacks the intellectual qualities which he claims to respect. Like Victorian adventurers, Ulysses' principal focus is outward, away from himself, on deeds and places.

The shallowness of Ulysses' Romanticism is also indicated by his obliviousness to nature and beauty. In his entire monologue, only two images acknowledge the loveliness of the external world. Both images are vague and suggest Ulysses' limitations. "Gleams that untraveled world whose margin fades forever and forever when I move" (20–21) indicates a speaker attracted to objects that may not be attained or even seen.[13] "The lights begin to twinkle from the rocks" suggests an external glitter which covers something ultimately hard and barren. Describing locales he has seen or seeks, his typical images of nature are bleak: "barren crags" (2), "the dim sea" (11), "gloom the dark broad seas" (45), "the rainy Hyades" (10), and "the deep/moans round" (55–56). Dramatizing the speaker's concealed state of mind, such images reflect a latent morbidity and turmoil, rudimentary depressive impulses against which he fights.[14] Moreover, these images indicate that Ulysses fears nature: like Gough or Franklin, he has too great a sense of the danger of nature to love it. Ulysses' Romantic spirit is, in fact, more like Gough's than it is like Alastor's or Childe Harold's (or Fra Lippo's): he desires to see the world, but he has relatively little appreciation of its magnificence; Ulysses mainly appreciates the magnificence of his own unrelenting voyage.

Comparison with other versions of Ulysses shows the deficient Romanticism of Tennyson's character. Ulysses of C. P. Cavafy's "Ithaca" deliberately refutes his Tennysonian namesake. While striving to transcend his homeland, Cavafy's Ulysses appreciates Ithaca's humble, commonplace worth rather than scorning it (24–36). An open, southern Mediterranean temperament who is unafraid of pleasure, Cavafy's Ulysses is more receptive to impending sensuous enjoyment than is Tennyson's Victorian, Anglo-Saxon character. Resembling the Ulysses of Dante and Tennyson in paying lip service to higher knowledge and in using such knowledge as a legitimatizing pretext for his quest (23 and 35), Cavafy's Ulysses more readily acknowledges the material purposes of his voyage (15–21). But the major difference is the emotional maturity of Cavafy's character. Whereas Tennyson's Ulysses is unaware of his own demons and cannot experience delight because of the hostility and anxiety he carries within his psyche, Cavafy's Ulysses knows that his greatest dangers are his own negative emotions, especially irrational fears which must be subdued before his voyage can be profitable:

> Do not fear the Lestrygonians
> And the Cyclopes and the angry Poseidon.
> You will never meet such as these on your path,
> If your thoughts remain lofty, if a fine
> Emotion touches your body and your spirit.
> You will never meet the Lestrygonians,
> The Cyclopes and the fierce Poseidon,
> If you do not carry them within your soul,
> If your soul does not raise them up before you. (4–12)

THE POPULARITY OF MEN like Gough and Franklin, when considered with Tennyson's frequent celebration of Victorian ideals, causes us to ask why Tennyson would have reservations about Ulysses and his type of heroism. Tennyson's own personality suggests one answer. Tennyson admired personalities different from his and shared Ulysses' courageous perseverance. But reticent and self-effacing, humble and introspective, Tennyson is the antithesis of his creation: "It goes somewhat against my grain to give any account of myself or mine to the public. . . . I have no life to give — for mine has been one of feelings not of actions" (*Letters* 1: 155). Emerson refers to him as "unaffected. — Quiet and sluggish" (*Letters* 1: 284). Other contemporaries describe a reclusive man passionately craving placid domesticity, not adventure. Aubrey de Vere observed Tennyson's desperation to "marry and find love and peace or die," adding that he "cared nothing for fame" (*Letters* 1:

239 . A travelling companion describes Tennyson as "soft and unmuscular, . . . [a] man of study, rather than . . . a sporting country squire. . . . He assumed no airs either of superiority, or affectation; but, on the contrary, spoke blandly, and . . . conducted himself with an unostentatious and gentlemanly manner" (*Letters* 1:301).

Tennyson's poetry suggests the principal reasons for his skepticism about Ulysses and shows that character's distance from Tennyson's concept of true heroism. The type of hero represented by Ulysses is detached from the traditional Christian beliefs and values expressed by Tennyson as his personal creed in *In Memoriam*. Contemplating heroism in another of his favorite poems, "Ode on the Death of the Duke of Wellington," Tennyson reaffirms the larger purposes of the hero. Minimizing Wellington's victories in Spain and at Waterloo, Tennyson finds the Duke to be a true hero, the one legitimate hero of his age, because his heroism consisted in selfless efforts to protect the welfare of his people and advance the interests of his nation. Wellington is now revered by "those he wrought for" and "those he fought for" (10–11). He is praised for working for "a common good" (27) in a life of "long self-sacrifice" (41). Without ambition for personal glory, the Duke was "one that sought but Duty's iron crown" (122). He was a colossal figure who showed his age that "The path of duty was the way to glory" (210). Wellington's greatest triumph for his nation and Europe was not a military victory but the preservation of liberty ("He kept us free," 91). The Duke's most admirable personal quality was his humility, his lack of egotism and boastfulness: he was "Our greatest yet with least pretence" (29). Wellington deserves fortune's favor because he was one who:

> . . . cares not to be great
> But as he saves or serves the state;
> . . . only thirsting
> For the right, and learns to deaden
> Love of self. (199–205)

To be true to the Duke's spirit, those praising him must follow Wellington's example and:

> . . . refrain
> From talk of battles loud and vain,
> And brawling memories all too free
> For such a wise humility. (246–49)

Along with its declared purposes, Tennyson's Wellington ode tacitly criticizes contemporary Victorian heroes of the Gough-Napier mould.

Ulysses is also the antithesis of the concept of heroism delineated in *Idylls of the King*. He and his real-life counterparts lack the qualities of King

Arthur, including dedication to spirit and intellect, compassion and humility. Unlike Ulysses, the true heroes of Camelot show an all-consuming commitment to advancing social, moral, and religious purposes external to the selfhood:

> Man am I grown, a man's work must I do
> Follow the deer? Follow the Christ, the King —
> Live pure, speak true; right wrong, follow the King —
> Else, wherefore born? ("Gareth and Lynette" 115–18)

Men like Ulysses and Gough pursued their own agendas with varying degrees of self-centeredness, a quality which eventually undermines Camelot. Abnegating the labor of making mild a rugged people to quest instead for "that untraveled world whose margin fades forever," Ulysses and Victorian heroes recall those deluded knights of the Round Table who search for the unattainable Holy Grail, instead of preserving order within society and working for human welfare in concrete, immediate ways. In fact, throughout *Idylls of the King* warriors with values, impulses, and temperaments like Ulysses' are at the lower levels of Camelot's moral and intellectual hierarchy:

> They be of foolish fashion, O Sir King,
> The fashion of that old knight-errantry
> Who ride abroad, and do but what they will. ("Gareth and Lynette" 613–15)

> "Fair Sirs," said Arthur, "Wherefore sit ye here?"
> Balin and Balan answered, "For the sake
> Of glory; we be mightier men than all
> In Arthur's court; that also have we proved;
> For whatsoever knight against us came
> Or I or he have easily overthrown." ("Balin and Balan" 29–34)

Characterized by braggadocio, a thirst for glory, and an egotistical quest for self-fulfillment,[15] Balin and Balan illustrate Tennyson's belief that true heroism requires more than courage, military prowess, and readiness for adventure: the true hero possesses "courtesy," by which Tennyson means the obligation to behave with selflessness, humility, and gentleness.

"ULYSSES" IS THUS one expression of Tennyson's overall skepticism about Victorian heroes and heroic ideals. While creating a compelling character in Ulysses, almost deifying the legendary King Arthur, and revering the Duke of Wellington, Tennyson extends no such celebration to any of the many significant, larger-than-life heroes of his age. His silence is itself suggestive. And it reenforces the quiet strategies of specific poems: in the Wellington ode, while presenting his model of the true hero, Tennyson repeatedly invites comparison between the Duke and the age's other heroes, thus continually implying their deficiencies; in "Ulysses" the speaker, almost a metaphor for contemporary heroes, dramatizes his own failings, thus allowing the reader to acknowledge the shortcomings of the contemporary heroic archetype. Tennyson's understated skepticism about Ulysses and Victorian heroes has a two-fold implication: Tennyson does not wish to oppose directly his society's enthusiasm for this type of hero — because at that moment in the Victorian era this heroic type was seen as necessary for the preservation of Empire, because these heroes promoted public morale and a sense of national unity, and because that heroic paradigm exhibited an ideal of courageous perseverance necessary for humanity in its mundane struggles in daily life; at the same time, because of that type's defects of ethos and temperament, Tennyson cannot unqualifiedly celebrate that heroic paradigm as an appropriate model for the moral and spiritual progress of his society.

"Ulysses," in turn, marks the beginning of ambivalence about Victorian heroes in Victorian culture. After "Ulysses," alongside Victorian hero-worship there arises a countertradition of hero-criticism, even hero-caricature. Lord Larrian of *Diana of the Crossways*, for example, is George Meredith's satiric portrait of Gough. As the Victorian period progresses, the reticence of Meredith and Tennyson evolves into direct assaults, reflecting public disillusionment at such failures of the Victorian heroic ethos as Gordon's defeat at Khartoum and the annihilation of an entire column of Lord Chelmsford's army at Isandhlwana. Gilbert and Sullivan's frontal attack on Victorian heroic ideals includes the "modern major-general" of *The Pirates of Penzance,* a caricature of Lord Garnet Wolseley, who in earlier decades would have been immune to satire and seen as a legitimate hero — Commander-in-Chief of the British Army, ardent reformer of the purchase system, and would-be rescuer of Gordon at Khartoum. The culminating statement of this countertradition of heroic irreverence, Lytton Strachey's portrait of General Gordon in *Eminent Victorians,* is a response to a war and a precursor of modern attitudes which themselves have made hero worship an act of heroic faith.

New Rochelle, New York

NOTES

1. Interesting in himself, Burton also merits attention because, taking shape after publication of Tennyson's well-known poem, his life almost seems an instance of reality imitating art. His continual wanderings, motives, and rhetoric almost seem based on Ulysses'. In part Burton's wanderlust was due to an aversion to his homeland: "Of all the various countries I know, I hate England most" (Pakenham 60). For Burton, as for Ulysses, the urge to travel was itself a primal, uncontrollable obsession: "The man wants to wander, and he must do so or he

shall die" (Burton's *Pilgrimage*, cited in Brodie 89). Becoming the first European to see Lake Tanganyika, Burton shared Ulysses' passion to excel: "To be first in such matters is everything, to be second nothing" (Brodie 204). He had an insatiable love of honor: "At Benin . . . they crucified a fellow in honour of my coming — here nothing!" (Brodie 212). Exhibiting Ulysses' restlessness and grandiosity of metaphor, Burton called himself "a caged hawk," "a Prometheus with the Demon Despair gnawing at my heart" when inactive (Brodie 204).

2. H. F. Tucker in *Tennyson and the Doom of Romanticism* shares Culler's viewpoint. Ulysses' quest is one which "Romantic precursors have chartered." He progresses to a final "transfiguration of context" which ultimately "effaces the self in favor of a Romantic desire . . . that cancels altogether the work of knowing and being known" (214). Ulysses thus becomes a "vanishing, finally vanished self." His "otherworldly Romantic quest" finally "dissipates the self's old anxieties as to time, place, and destination" (238).

3. Several heroic Royal Navy officers won fame in the 1820s while searching for the Northwest Passage. Sir John Ross (1777–1856) led the Admiralty's first expedition in 1818. Commanding another expedition in 1829, Ross spent four winters trapped by ice in the Gulf of Bootha, in one of the era's most harrowing Arctic adventures. At 74 Ross led his own search for the missing Franklin. Sir William Parry (1790–1855) sailed through Lancaster Sound in 1819–20, becoming the first to discover this entrance to the Northwest Passage. After searching for the Passage in 1821–23 and 1824–25, Parry tried to reach the North Pole by sled from northern Norway in 1827, achieving a latitude of 82° 45'N, the record for fifty years. Made commander in 1820 and post captain in 1821, he was knighted in 1829 and later served as commissioner in Australia.

4. Franklin describes his ordeal in telling detail:

In clearing the snow to pitch the tents we found a quantity of Iceland moss, which was boiled for supper. This weed . . . proved so bitter, that few of the party could eat more than a few spoonfuls of it.
    Our blankets did not suffice this evening to keep us in tolerable warmth; the slightest breeze seeming to pierce through our debilitated frames. . . . On many nights we had not even the luxury of going to bed in dry clothes, for when the fire was insufficient to dry our shoes, we durst not venture to pull them off, lest they should freeze so hard as to be unfit to put on in the morning. . . . Having no food to prepare, we crept under our blankets. . . . [The next day] we were gratified by the sight of a large herd of rein-deer on the side of the hill near the track, but our only hunter, Adam, was too feeble to pursue them. Our shoes and garments were stiffened by the frost, and we walked on in great pain. . . . (Franklin 414, 438)

5. Tennyson's detachment from Ulysses has been noted. For Robert Langbaum, Tennyson rebukes Ulysses's "too vigorous presumption in daring to sail beyond the limit assigned to man" (91). J.H. Buckley states that Tennyson shows a hero "absorbed exclusively in his own inability to pause, to make an end" and lacking "the conviction that 'Though much is taken, much abides' " (Buckley 60–61).

6. Tennyson was generally averse to egotistical, strident, overbearing personalities: [Trench is] . . . always strung to the highest pitch, and the earnestness which burns within him so flashes through all his words and actions, that . . . it is difficult to prevent a sense of one's own inferiority . . . yet have I no faith in any one of his opinions. (*Letters* 1: 71)

Conversely, Tennyson's heroes avoid magniloquent recitations of achievement and the flaunting of self-confidence. One of Tennyson's heroes was the Italian freedom fighter Garibaldi, whom Tennyson respected for bringing liberty to his nation while preserving a quiet, gentle demeanor like Chaucer's Knight:

> What a noble human being! I expected to see a hero and I was not disappointed. . . . His manners had a certain divine simplicity in them such as I have never witnessed in a native of these islands . . . and they are gentler than those of most young maidens I know. (*Letters* 2: 364)

7. Tennyson condemned the impulse of contemporary Englishmen to repudiate immediate duty to country and cross the seas for adventure:

> Britons, Guard your own.
> Call home your ships across Biscayan tides,
> To blow the battle from their oaken sides.
> Why waste they yonder
> Their idle thunder?
> Why stay they there to guard a foreign throne?
> ("Britons, Guard Your Own" 36–41)

8. Citing the "amoral purpose" of Ulysses' voyage, Walter Houghton states that Ulysses forgets his work of noble note because it is "undefined." Houghton thus sees a similarity between Ulysses and Arnold's Scholar-Gypsy who "has no aim" but is "busy drifting": both are without specific goals; their respective voyages are ends in themselves. Ulysses' travels illustrate an age where the "need for ideals" has been lost and replaced by "the grandeur of aspiration itself and/ or the sheer excitement of vivid experience" (Houghton 296–97).

9. Victorian military leaders believed that their work of noble note included fighting to uphold the principles of Lord Palmerston: British armed forces would fight "Wherever British subjects are placed in danger. . . . and a military presence may be required for the protection of British interests" (Farwell, *Wars* 21); "the watchful eye and the strong arm of England will protect" a British subject "against injustice and wrong . . . wherever he might be" (Farwell, *Wars* 167). The Palmerston doctrine was applied frequently. The murder of British envoys was twice the pretext for British conquest of Afghanistan. Colonel G. J. Younghusband asserted that the second Afghan War showed how "the strong resistless power of British bayonets" brings "justice" and supports "the law of nations" (Farwell, *Wars* 210). Victorian military heroes also fought because it was their "responsibility" to protect "some weak and friendly tribe" and to prevent "the triumph of anarchy among the natives" (Farwell, *Wars* 223).

10. For an example, see the account of Franklin's first Arctic expedition, above, page 120, bottom.

11. Granted that death was an occupational hazard in their chosen fields, Victorian explorers and military heroes are inordinately self-defeating, if not self-destructive, in courting severe, life-threatening wounds. Napier is typical. In one Peninsular skirmish, after a rifle ball broke his leg, he was bayoneted in the side and

back, sabered on the head, had his ribs broken by another gunshot, and received several concussions when hammered on the head by a musket butt. Bouncing back for additional punishment at the battle of Coa, Napier needlessly exposed himself to death. Serving on Wellington's staff (which should have kept him relatively out of harm's way), Napier was the only officer who refused to wear a less conspicuous blue cloak, preferring to expose himself in a bright red jacket which made an excellent target. Obligingly, a musket ball smashed into the side of Napier's nose and lodged in his jaw, shattering the bone and permanently damaging his palate and nasal passages. The wound resulted in an acute feeling of suffocation which persisted for the rest of his life (Farwell, *Soldiers* 68–70).

12. When Ashanti warriors broke through British lines to attack headquarters, which was defended only by staff officers, newspaper reporters, and physicians, Henry Stanley saw Lord Wolseley conducting himself with "a calm, proud air" (Farwell, *Wars* 197). Showing another type of courageous perseverance before death, when informed of the death of his son in the Boer War, British commander Lord Roberts "pulled himself together . . . [and] refused to allow this disaster to turn him aside from his duty" (Farwell, *Soldiers* 185). Lord Kitchener, noted for coolness under pressure, fit the description which Gibbon applied to the emperor Septimus Severus: "He was never diverted from his steady course by . . . apprehension of danger" (Farwell, *Soldiers* 323).

13. These lines may be what J. H. Buckley has in mind when he acutely observes that Ulysses resembles Faustus in pursuing "endlessly unsatisfied desire as a good in itself" (60).

14. Langbaum hears in Ulysses a "cry of pain" and a "longing for oblivion." His thirst for life is, in reality, only "an old man's appetite exceeding potency." Langbaum thus regards his final voyage as "a decline, a sinking . . . [a death] deliberately sought for. . . . [Death is] the inevitable goal of the journey." Ulysses has endured life "only because it leads to death" (90–91).

15. Such flaws are endemic in the breed. Defending Lord Wolseley from detractors, Disraeli told Queen Victoria, "It is quite true that Wolseley is an egotist and a braggart. So was Nelson" (Farwell, *Wars* 228).

WORKS CITED

Alighieri, Dante. *The Inferno*. Trans. Allen Mandelbaum. New York: Bantam, 1982.

Buckley, Jerome Hamilton. *Tennyson: The Growth of a Poet*. Boston: Houghton Mifflin, 1960.

Burton, Sir Richard. *A Mission to Gelele*. C. W. Newbury, ed. London: Routledge & Kegan Paul, 1966.

— — — . *Pilgrimage to Mecca and Medina*. London: Herbert Joseph, 1937.

Brodie, Fawn M. *The Devil Drives: A Life of Sir Richard Burton*. New York: W. W. Norton, 1967.

Cavafy, C. P. *Complete Poems*. Trans. Rae Dalven. New York: Harcourt Brace, Harvest paperback edn., 1976.

Coupland, Sir Reginald. *Raffles of Singapore*. London: Collins, 1946.

Culler, A. Dwight. *The Poetry of Tennyson*. New Haven: Yale UP, 1977.

Delpar, Helen, ed. *The Discoverers: An Encyclopedia of Explorers and Exploration*. New York: McGraw-Hill, 1980.

Farwell, Byron. *Eminent Victorian Soldiers*. New York: W. W. Norton, 1985.

————. *Queen Victoria's Little Wars*. New York: W. W. Norton, 1972.

Franklin, Captain John. *Narrative of a Journey to the Shores of the Polar Sea, in the years 1819–22*. London: John Murray, 1823. Rpt. New York: Greenwood P, 1969.

Houghton, Walter E. *The Victorian Frame of Mind, 1830–1870*. New Haven: Yale UP, 1957.

Houston, C. Stuart, ed. *Arctic Ordeal: the Journal of John Richardson, Surgeon-Naturalist with Franklin, 1820–22*. Montreal: McGill-Queen's UP, 1984.

Kernberg, Otto. *Borderline Conditions and Pathological Narcissism* New York: Jason Arson, 1975.

Langbaum, Robert. *The Poetry of Experience*. New York: Random House, 1957.

Masterson, James F. *Narcissistic and Borderline Disorders: An Integrated Developmental Approach*. New York: Brunner-Mazel, 1981.

Pakenham, Achmed Abdullah T. Compton. *Dreamers of Empire*. New York: Stokes, 1929.

Tennyson, Alfred Lord. *Idylls of the King*. J. M. Gray editor. New Haven: Yale UP, 1983.

————. *The Letters of Alfred Lord Tennyson*. 2 vols. Ed. Cecil Y. Land and Edgar F. Shannon, Jr. Cambridge, Mass.: Harvard UP, 1981.

————. *Poems*. Ed. Jerome Hamilton Buckley. Boston: Houghton Mifflin, 1958.

[Tennyson, Emily Sellwood.] *Lady Tennyson's Journal*. Ed. James O. Hoge. Charlottesville: UP of Virginia, 1981.

Tennyson, Hallam. *Alfred Lord Tennyson: A Memoir by his Son*. 2 vols. New York: MacMillan, 1897.

Stefansson, Vilhjalmur. *Unsolved Mysteries of the Arctic*. New York: MacMillan, 1939.

Trail, Henry D. *The Life of Sir John Franklin*. London: John Murray, 1896.

Tucker, Herbert F. *Tennyson and the Doom of Romanticism*. Cambridge, Mass.: Harvard UP, 1988.

FROM ROMANTIC TO VICTORIAN: THE GERMANO-COLERIDGIAN NOVELS OF JOHN STERLING AND F. D. MAURICE

By Robert O. Preyer

I

THOUGH MOST VICTORIAN NOVEL COURSES begin with the great novelists who were coming into prominence in the decade of the 1840s — a period brilliantly explicated by Professor Kathleen Tillotson — recent scholarship has begun to turn attention to the very confusing generic scene in earlier decades. Eiger and Worth argue in their introduction to *Victorian Criticism of the Novel* that significant Victorian criticism of the novel as a literary kind began as a response to the deaths in 1832 of both Scott and Goethe and the public acknowledgement of necessary change occasioned by passage of the Reform Bill. This fortuitous conjunction of events provided the journals with an obvious occasion for reflection on the roles of Scott and Goethe in transforming a despised genre into the most profitable art form in the nineteenth century. This essay takes a closer look at two forgotten works of fiction, *Arthur Coningsby* (1833) by John Sterling (1806–44), and *Eustace Conway* (1834) by Frederick Denison Maurice (1805–72).[1]

These works are resurrected not simply as exempla of stylistic and generic contradictions and complexities associated with the writing of fiction in the decade of the thirties, an uneasy cultural moment when the expectations of readers and writers were uncomfortable and often misunderstood by both parties to the transaction. There is an additional interest having to do with the two authors' intimate acquaintance with the writings of Coleridge and Wordsworth and their involvement at Cambridge with leading proponents of the new historical and comparative philology imported from the continent. Their closest friends among the tutors and undergraduates at Trinity and Trinity Hall, Cambridge, were precisely the group singled out by Hans Aarsleff in his classic account *The Study of Language in England 1780 — 1860* as the leading spirits who instigated and supported the Oxford English Dictionary, perhaps the most remarkable monument to Victorian scholarship in a century when historical philology reached its peak.

Many of their teachers were men who had been undergraduates during the period of political and intellectual repression associated with the struggle with France which did not conclude until the defeat of Napolean in 1815. These young tutors and dons were vitally interested in continental developments which had taken place during the interregnum. They travelled widely; made contact with European scholars, writers, artists, and natural philosophers; translated many of their works; or incorporated continental approaches in new textbooks. Julius Hare, in his second year as classical lecturer at Trinity (1823), introduced Maurice — who had been reading Coleridge's prose and poetry before coming up to Trinity — to Schlegel on *Dramatic Literature* (Frederick Maurice 1: 48). Hare had taught Connop Thirlwall German in 1817, and they introduced German methods of studying language and culture through a close scrutiny of syntax and the subtle shifts in the meaning of words in varying contexts. Maurice was later to write, "To his lectures on Sophocles and Plato I can trace the most permanent effect on my character, and on all my modes of contemplating subjects, human and divine" (Frederick Maurice 1: 55). Many years later (1855) another student, Richard Trench, reprinted and endorsed Julius Hare's words on the significance of the diachronic method: "A history of the language . . . would throw more light on the development of the human mind than all the brainspun systems of metaphysics" (*English* 4). The prophet of historicism was not without honor in his old college. Hare's favorite pupil (and subsequently his curate at Herstmonceux Rectory) was John Sterling, whose *Essays and Tales* he collected and edited in two volumes (1848) prefaced by a book-length "memoir" which so annoyed Carlyle that he wrote his own life of Sterling (1851).[2] The challenge, passed down from teachers to undergraduates, was to end the years of complacency and stagnation within the Anglican church and its two great universities and to inaugurate a spiritual and intellectual renewal. The ideas and attitudes of the dons, suggestively sketched out in such works as *Guesses At Truth By Two Brothers* (1827), Julius at Trinity and Augustus who taught at Oxford, were eagerly canvassed by a band of elite undergraduates, many of whom were members of the famous Apostles Society in the decade 1825–35 and of Gladstone's *Essay Club* at Oxford which was founded, at Arthur Hallam's suggestion, as a counterpart to the Apostles.

Many undergraduate Apostles were subsequently associated with their former faculty mentors (Hare, Thirlwall, William Whewell, Hugh James Rose) in the proceedings of *The Cambridge Etymological Society* (1830) and of the significant journal, *The Philological Museum* (1832–33), the direct precursors for the *Philological Society of London*, which was inaugurated in

1842 with Thirlwall, now Bishop of St. David's, in the chair — the sponsoring organization for the O.E.D. Trench's first ecclesiastical appointment was as Rose's curate; his subsequent rise in the Church — Professor of Divinity, King's College, London (1846–58), Dean of Westminster (1856–63), and Bishop of Dublin (1863–86) — was closely related to his immense popular success as author of *On The Study of Words* (1851, 19 editions) and *English Past and Present* (1854, 15 editions). John Mitchell Kemble, brother of the actress Fanny Kemble, with Trench, Hallam, Tennyson, and Maurice had played a leading role in the Sterling-instigated attempt to reinstate constitutional government in Spain by supporting the revolutionary rising of General Torrijos. When that doomed attempt was about to end, Kemble left Gibraltar in May 1831 and continued his studies in Germany where he was to become an intimate of the Grimm brothers. He returned to become sole editor of *The British and Foreign Review* (1835–44) and a distinguished Anglo-Saxon scholar, the first native-born "professional" philologist in England. (It is worth noting that the impulsive Kemble had his Cambridge degree "deferred" in 1829, apparently for daring to write exam papers which sneered at Locke's "loathesome infidelity" and termed Paley "a miserable sophist" (Aarsleff, 191). In this he faithfully echoed the ideological line of the new conservatives — Coleridge, Hare, Whewell, Maurice, Hallam, Tennyson, and Sterling. (See, in this regard, Tennyson's several verse rebukes to old-style dons and his warm poetic tribute to Maurice.)

It was a crucial moment of linguistic excitement. The new historical and comparative philology hinted strongly that the time was ripe for an idealist replacement for the received rationalist accounts of how language signified. As early as 22 September 1800 Coleridge had written to William Godwin urging that eminent theorist to undertake a treatise "on the power of words and the processes by which human feelings form affinities with them — in short I wish you to philosophize Horne Tooke's System, and to solve the great questions . . . [such as] is thinking impossible without arbitrary signs?" (Coleridge, 155). The Wordsworthian process of reconstituting psychic health through the recovery and re-experiencing of once pristine and pure feelings associated with childhood responses bore a tantalizing analogy to the recovery and enrichment of word meanings through the methods of historical philology. (Thus we find Honoria, in *Eustace Conway*, announcing that "any object that comes back to us from the years of infancy" is significant: "O! What a happiness it is not to have our view bounded by the little speck of ground on which we stand, to see a world of living beings behind us, and to feel that we are part of it"; (1: 107).

Hare's *Guesses At Truth* explored the possibility, first broached by Wilhelm von Humboldt, that ideas were created by language. He was also intrigued by Herder's notion that one could, through language study, re-experience feelings and attitudes known to our ancestors but unavailable in contemporary modes of prehension.

> A man should love and venerate his native language as the first of his benefactors, as the awakener and stirrer of all his thoughts, the frame and mould (sic) and rule of his spiritual being, as the great bond and medium of intercourse with his fellows, as the mirror in which he sees his own nature, and without which he could not even commune with himself, as the image in which the wisdom of God has chosen to reveal itself to him. (*Guesses At Truth* 235)

This is a far cry from the attitude of post-Saussurean linguists to the "always already existing" *structure* of language which, we are to believe, precedes rational reflection and thought. In sharp contrast, the generations in the early decades of the nineteenth century affirmed that a lost wisdom could be retrieved from what Emerson called the "fossil poetry" of language (Emerson, "The Poet" 457). Emerson's remark alludes to paleontology and geology where new knowledge had definitely been created by application of the diachronic method — an acknowledgement of the potency not the poverty of historicism. As these references indicate, the fictions of Sterling and Maurice were composed in a period which is the reverse of our present Derridean and Foucaultian moment, with its skeptical evacuation of faith in the possibility that any certain knowledge can emerge from the discovery of "codes" for combining and deciphering the *différance* between simultaneously existing sets of representational signs. When the young Apostles turned from revolutionary politics to the study of language as the most significant cultural and political action available to English intellectuals in the romantic, religious, and pre-Darwinian epoch, it was with no sense that life had become, in Frost's phrase, "a diminished thing" ("The Oven Bird"). Dean Farrar, a Trinity pupil of Whewell, a disciple of Coleridge, and a representative "amateur" popularizer of linguistics took it for granted that "A language is a noble and powerful instrument of thought in proportion as it keeps in view the motives and principles which originated the words of which it is composed" (Farrar 20).

Maurice's novel *Eustace Conway* seeks to dramatize the process by which a contemporary protagonist can make his way through the minefield of competing ideologies by developing a vivid responsiveness to the expressive potential inherent in language. Great intellects deploy the full range of meaning that can be quarried from language use; they provide touchstones by which one can register a fraudulent or debased use of the language. The key to Eustace Conway's spiritual salvation is his final recognition that "language is a barrier against the encroachments of falsehood which will never give way, unless through our negligence in failing to replace its bricks, when any of them are fallen down, or our wilfulness in substituting others in their place'' (1: 275). Sterling's *Arthur Coningsby* is similarly preoccupied throughout with the moral centrality of a full aesthetic response if we are not to be deceived by insincere, indeed, inauthentic modes of utterance. The alluring speech of those who would wean us to another paradigm of belief is dramatized — indeed melodramatized — and entire chapters are taken up with conversations analyzing levels of style, sincere or otherwise, in the discourse of third parties. It is the only sure grounds of defense available to a callow youth who is unable to detect sophistical logic in some plausible system of thought. Conway's life is blasted, his hopes for happiness blighted, by his inability to resist false systems. Eustace succeeds because he is a close observer and user of language. Scattered throughout the text are these sorts of linguistic notation: "there are states of mind, in which we feel that we have no right to profit from the hidden virtues of words" (1: 167); "he could never revolutionize his vocabulary" (1: 276); "I cannot separate matter and style; I never could, I never shall learn to do it (1: 85); "I thought the words which I used were any thing but vague, because they immediately recalled a physical operation, which expounded them" (1: 91). Much of the *texture* of the novel is provided by these reiterated reflections on speech.

II

MAURICE HAD GONE UP to Trinity in 1823 at age 18. "The more brilliant but less profound" John Sterling sought him out and brought him into the Apostles by 1825 (Brookfield 203). In 1825–26 the earliest known publications of the undergraduates Maurice, Sterling, and John Kemble appeared in the four issues of a short-lived *Metropolitan Quarterly Magazine*, a student venture edited by Maurice and published in London. The nucleus of contributors was made up of Apostles, with an occasional contribution by Cambridge men of a slightly earlier vintage, among them, Derwent Coleridge (St. John's, 1824), who wrote two able expositions of the poetry of his father and of Wordsworth. Derwent Coleridge offered a bridge of sorts to the Praed, Bulwer, Macaulay set who had provided most of the material for a similar but professionally-edited London journal, *Knight's Quarterly Magazine* (1823–24). Subsequently Maurice and Sterling became editors of the London *Athenaeum* (1828–29), which became the successor vehicle for their generation of Apostles and which also published pieces by their tutor Julius Hare and other Cambridge intellectual mentors. As undergraduates, many of the Apostles had been attracted by the Philosophic Radical position developed from Bentham's teaching by James and John Mill and others. References abound: Richard Monckton-Milnes writes his mother that he has joined the the Union Debating

Society "where 'a Mr. Sterling told us we were going to have a revolution, and he didn't care if his hand should be the first to lead the way' " (Brookfield 229). This unnerving and potent negative critique of the traditional order of things was eventually overcome, but it made Sterling and Maurice sharply aware of the necessity for new intellectual foundations if the traditional structures of church and state and society were to be affirmed in post-Napoleonic and industrializing times. The intellectual salvation they wished to propound came to the attention of John Mill

> in 1828 and 1829, when the Coleridgians, in the persons of Maurice and Sterling, made their appearance in the [London Debating] Society as a second Liberal and even Radical party, on totally different grounds from Benthamism and vehemently opposed to it; bringing into these discussions the general doctrines and modes of thought of the European reaction against the philosophy of the eighteenth century. (90)

Mill subsequently coined the useful term "Germano-Coleridgian" as a shorthand reference to this Apostolic point of view.

Mill read Sterling's *Arthur Coningsby* and sent his copy along to Thomas Carlyle in May 1833. Two well-known passages in Carlyle's *Life of Sterling* show his reaction:

> The hero an ardent youth, representing Sterling himself, plunges into life such as we now have it in these anarchic times, with the radical, utilitarian, or mutinous heathen theory, which is the readiest for inquiring souls; finds, by various courses of adventure, utter shipwreck in this; lies broken, very wretched: that is the tragic nodus, or apogee of his life-course. (91)

> It is in the history of such vehement, trenchant, far-shining and yet intrinsically light and volatile souls, missioned into this epoch to seek their way there, that we best see what a confused epoch it is. (101)

0   This is a fair description. Kemble was in London when, as he recalled, Maurice and Sterling decided each to write a "psychological novel . . . studiously weighing and analyzing, — confuting or agreeing with — every theory and opinion which presented itself to the mind of its hero" (Brookfield 211). He went on to note that Maurice, unlike Sterling, wrote himself out of his difficulties, rediscovered a vocation for the church, and subsequently made his way to Exeter College, Oxford, to complete the necessary requirements for taking Orders in the Church of England.

Both novels can be read as early English versions of the "novel of ideas" — a form well known in Germany and France but rarely practised in England. The nearest models to hand were produced by Disraeli and Bulwer, clever authors who had learned from Scott that it was possible, in times of

Figure 1. "John Sterling in 1830." From the painting by B. Delacour.

Figure 2. "F. D. Maurice." Line drawing by Samuel Laurence, 1846. Reproduced by kind permission of the National Portrait Gallery, London.

rapid change, to dramatize in a fictional present the historical conflict between simultaneously existing representatives of a past and present order of social relationships. In what follows, I will first make a few obserations on the structural and stylistic awkwardness of these nascent novels of ideas and then go on to suggest why so many intellectuals — Emerson, Carlyle, Gladstone, Trench, Kemble, Hare, Thirlwall, James Spedding, Coleridge — cherished a fondness for these fictions which suggested to them the possibility of an as yet unwritten Victorian mode, the novel of spiritual search and renewal. They saw in these works both the seedbed of the Victorian sensibility and perhaps a kind of deathbed for a number of rhetorical and formal procedures associated with pre-Victorian authors like Byron and Henry Mackenzie and the writers of Gothic melodrama and even silver-fork fiction.

Carlyle in 1827 had struggled without success to complete *Wooton Reinfred* a novel structured to combine elements of Scott and Byron with a heavy admixture of procedures derived from his reading and translation of Goethe's *Wilhelm Meister's Apprenticeship.* By 1831 he finally found a way of fusing this maze of fictional procedures in *Sartor Resartus*, perhaps his nearest approach to the novel form.[3] Mired in an analogous generic confusion, Sterling and Maurice experiment with multiple conventions of storytelling. Picaresque adventure, myth, allegory, sermon, even science fiction and verse (not to mention letters and diary entries and disquisitions on sculpture and painting) jostle one another in dizzying juxtaposition. There are operatic variations of a "standard" eighteenth-century expository diction and syntax, reminding one of the blank verse arias and elevated diction to be found in Disraeli's *Vivian Grey*, composed in 1826 in his twenty-second year.[4] Echoes abound, as well, in both plot and characterization. A fictional model for Arthur Coningsby is surely George Staunton in *Heart of Midlothian*, described by Jane Milgate as "a travelling Englishman eager for excitement and the indulgence of his romantic appetites" who becomes "an anarchic and destructive force, incapable of reassimilation into the fabric of society" (152). Like Staunton's son, Coningsby ends his days with Native Americans, another borrowing from Scott.

It was an histrionic decade, and writers indulged in lurid devices of romance to provide readers with thrilling enactments, textured like dream experiences, which project the noblest apirations and most fearful collapses that can afflict the psyche. No doubt Sterling and Maurice made use of the modalities of romance and melodrama to provide direct access to the fantasy life of their audience and thus, as Peter Brooks suggests, "perhaps with greater effect than was ever achieved by more sober works . . . [to] open up the social concerns, make them imaginatively believable" (Brooks 168). Confusingly, however, these lurid modes are juxtaposed in seemingly random fashion, with passages of social satire reminiscent of the style of Jane Austen.

(In mitigation one should remember that these were "first novels," after all.) These multiple conventions of storytelling make for unstable and, on occasion, risible compounds. Though Sterling and Maurice disliked the aristocratic Whig liberalism of the most popular Trinity novelist of their era, Edward Bulwer (later Bulwer-Lytton), one suspects they read and borrowed from the six novels he composed between *Falkland* (1827) and *The Last Days of Pompeii* (1834). Bulwer breezily ran through most of the generic possibilities available and seemed determined, at least theoretically, to obviate the stale critical dichotomy between realism and romance. Today his critical pronouncements (notably, "On Art in Fiction," 1838, reprinted in Eiger and Worth) make better reading than his fiction. Finally, it should be noted that there are moments in both novels when one senses an indebtedness to the tone of a mode or kind, the psychodrama of ideological possession, first popularised by Schiller's *Die Raüber*, and given an English Protestant twist in William Godwin's *Caleb Williams*, Wordsworth's *The Borderers*, and Coleridge's drama, *Remorse*.

    With all these voices sounding in the echo chamber of the novel, it is no wonder that readers had difficulty following the narrative. What holds these novels together, gives some coherence to this fictional melange, is, I will be arguing, the *leitmotif* of linguistic salvation. *Arthur Coningsby* and *Eustace Conway* dramatize the experience of being overwhelmed by the exciting possibilities present at the dawn of a new historical paradigm, one which seemed to throw a blinding new light on a variety of cultural preoccupations — religious, social, political, as well as intellectual. Here was a potent counter to the attractions of the French revolution and attendant philosophical and radical ways of structuring experience. They had first-hand knowledge of the way in which William Whewell was already forging a linkage between historical philology and natural sciences (minerology and geology in particular). Whewell defined as "palaetiological" any investigations ". . . which refer to actual past events, and attempt to explain them by laws of causation." (637) The way is open to the historical study of animals and human beings — evolution, in brief. This rearrangement of fields of study in the light of the new historicism seemed to open possibilities in every direction. The initial and operative concept remained, however, the historical development of language, the tool of thought.[5] Richard Chenevix Trench, Whewell's former student, concluded the Fourth Lecture in his immensely popular *On The Study of Words* (1851) by quoting a passage from Whewell's *The Philosophy of the Inductive Sciences* (1840) which expressed "with a rare eloquence all which I have been labouring to utter" (92):

> Language is often called an instrument of thought, but it is also the nutriment of thought; or rather, it is the atmosphere in which thought lives; a medium

essential to the activity of our speculative powers, although invisible and imperceptible in its operation; and an element modifying, by its qualities and changes, the growth and complexion of the faculties which it feeds. In this way the influence of preceding discoveries upon subsequent ones, of the past upon the present, is most penetrating and universal, although most subtle and difficult to trace.[6]

Thus the Master of Trinity College, William Whewell, the Kantian "natural philosopher" who provided Faraday and others with much of their nomenclature and, in that connection, coined the words "physicist" and "scientist." One should note also that Hensleigh Wedgwood (Trinity, 1827), a cousin to Charles Darwin and the chief source for his theories of language and expression, came out of this same excited milieu. Some of the implications of these speculations are worked out thematically in the fictions of Maurice and Sterling and make us aware of the momentum and power of a new intellectual paradigm, deeply conservative in its application, to be sure, but radical in its power for transfroming private lives and giving new energy and direction to social and political attitudes. There is nothing quite like it until one ponders the prestige and aura enveloping the pronouncements on language by Nietzsche, Saussure, and Heidegger in more recent times.

III

STERLING AND MAURICE offer as protagonists young men of "sensibility" who have woken up to the inadequacies and injustices of the paternalistic, authoritarian organization of society in which they are privileged elite by birth, gender, and education. They wish to reform or restructure this organization of power and in a hurry, yet their model for a good social order remains that of the eighteenth century Virgilian idyl — idealized gentry and clergy presiding over a grateful tenantry. The problem of course is the present degraded state of that utopian vision of social harmony: how can one hope to reconstitute such an ideal in some future re-ordering of cultural and social arrangements?

The plot of Sterling's novel defines experience as both an apprenticeship and a journey, one that ends not with discovery but with a pilgrimage into despair more redolent of Byron's *Cain* and Goethe's *Werther* (rather than the more upbeat *Wilhelm Meister*). Arthur Coningsby, just down from Oxford, wakes in a turret room at Deerhill, the Barrington country estate where he had been brought up by his uncle after the death of both parents. He has just graduated from Oxford. Here, after a long interval away with tutors and then at college, he renews an intimacy with Isabel Barrington, a cousin with whom he had shared his childhood. She is secretly in love with him and increasingly disturbed as it becomes apparent that Arthur, initially overwhelmed by "one constant irresistible feeling of reverence . . . lost and overpowered in the solemn spiritual being of my mother university' (1: 78) had reversed direction and become "intimate with a few individuals of larger views and stronger intellects than the mass. Among them I first obtained what became the keystone of my mind, and learned to look on everything from the one vantage place of a belief in the Rights of Man as the foundation of society and government" (1: 83). Aware of "a rude discordance between the thoughts which I most desired to cultivate, and the spirit of the place," he is nevertheless proud that " . . . my public views appeared to separate me from my former self" (1: 83). Isabel, of course, knows better. "But it seemed to her that speculations and pursuits which broke the continuity of the mind, and made it regard its earlier years as portions of another being than itself, could scarcely be so natural and salutary as Arthur represented them" (1: 84). Betrayed by his Oxford friend, he finds himself a political outlaw and escapes to France. At Paris he meets Madame de Valence and is introduced by her to the revolutionary intelligentsia of the days shortly before the September massacres. An interesting combination of passionate heroine and *schöne Seele* ("beautiful soul"), Victoria de Valence, born into the Spanish aristocracy and presently the widow of a great French noble, is able on several occasions to preserve Arthur from death at the hands of revolutionary tribunals, and together they watch, appalled, as their millennial dreams gutter out in carnage and atrocities. Self-absorbed, Arthur is unable to return her love under the impression that she is not "pure" in the English sense. He only realizes what damage he has done, how he has wronged the generous heart of this beloved widow, after he peruses Victoria's interminable autobiographical narrative, thoughtfully handed to him shortly before her decline and death. Though filled with remorse, he nevertheless returns to seek out his English Isabel, but she will not have him. The third volume trails off in a series of letters in which we learn that a despairing Arthur has been putting in time as a sort of professional soldier, fighting with the Mamelukes in Egypt and the Middle East and, when not occupied as a Byronic corsair, climbing the most inaccessible mountain peaks and otherwise carrying his bleeding heart about the fringes of Europe. Like Werther, he has neurotically manipulated his affairs of the heart so that salvation through the love of a good woman — willingly offered by both his English Isabel and the dark, passionate Victoria de Valence — will not provide a solution for his self-pity and political and social nihilism. His final act will be to bury himself in the American wilderness, "that stage on which man walks in individual freedom" and where, safe from societal corruption, he will "know not any brother but the Indian, its primeval inhabitant" (3: 396). Thus ends Sterling's cautionary tale of a world-weary Byronic rebel, all passions spent.

The search for an alternative to the existing order of things has failed. Even The Reverend Dr. Wilmot, just such a reformed cleric as Coleridge yearned for as member of an imagined clerisy capable of sustaining in futurity the values of the old system, is portrayed as often reduced to despair by the debility and obtuseness of contemporaneous institutions of church and state. Tensions and contradictions in both the domestic and public spheres point to the illegitimate exercise of power by authority figures, whether fathers or magistrates; if rulers did not play their part adequately, how could dependents respond so that loyal and affectionate ties continued to exist? That is the kind of question — the Condition of England question *par excellence* — which troubled Apostles like Maurice and Sterling and their friends. The dream of renewal of a benevolent social paternalism binding in harmony people of unequal status or power, whether in personal family life or in the civic and public sphere, was recognized, painfully, as fantasy, unrelated to present circumstances. With no avenues open to a brighter future, the attitudes and behaviour of *Childe Harold* and *Werther* offered an obvious solution to the problem of behaviour. Arthur Coningsby maintains a Byronic posture of defiance and brackets the awkward question of how to reform existing institutions. The plot slides away from scenes of carnage and bloodletting on the streets of Paris and into the lassitude and intricacies of illness, depression, and a suffocatingly private relationship with the tormented Victoria. One feels that Sterling, like Goethe before him, had deliberately contrived a hopeless private love as a means of evading recognition of the fact that he had destroyed all his chances for action in the public realm.

Ignoring the contradictions of the French Revolution altogether, Maurice places his protagonist squarely in the intellectual milieu Maurice had known at Cambridge and subsequently in London in the 1820s and '30s. This contemporaneous setting solves a number of narrative problems and provides *Eustace Conway* with considerably more psychological depth and intellectual bite. The plot is straightforward. Eustace, a young hero with a mind seemingly permeable by any and all ideologies on offer, is attracted, while still an undergraduate, by a band of youthful Benthamites. In London he is taken by a worldly and ironic friend to attend several parties given by convinced Philosophic Radicals, a very depressing experience. The same mentor leads him to the mysterious Rumbold, a daemonic necessitarian who has freed himself from all ethical concerns and lives by the exercise of selfish will. German pantheistic "Spiritualists" appear as well. Slowly Eustace begins to sort out and register the import of these encounters. The inauthenticity of the languages of false consciousness shocks him into an awareness of the magnitude of his spiritual loss, and he returns to a proper Anglican position.

The full title of the novel, *Eustace Conway, Or The Brother and Sister*, is significant. In his own life, it had been the example of a much loved dying sister which led Maurice to a realization, amounting to a conversion experience, of the necessity of revelation if one were to accept Anglicanism.

In fiction, as well as in his life, Maurice relied on women to bring their brothers and lovers into a right relation to actuality. If we bracket, for the moment, those female characters who are morally depraved or consumed by a religious vocation and if we ignore several wronged stage heroines who revenge themselves by criminal acts, there still remain a core of intelligent, observant young women who would not be out of place in a Jane Austen novel. Depicted initially as novelistic sterotypes — the true English lily or the exotic, raven-haired passion queen of foreign extraction — these female characters soon transcend received clichés of representation and try to talk political sense to their rash young men, to wean them from excited rhetoric and futile dreams of societal transformations. They are prudent, not through lack of imagination, but precisely because they imaginatively grasp, as their male counterparts do not, the full cost of *open* defiance and public rebellion, not to mention the improbability of its success. Dependents within a paternalist and patriarchal order, its true nature often veiled by good manners and domestic affections, they nevertheless have learned to recognize and cope with the day-by-day manifestations of social injuries and unfairness and are, in consequence, less shocked than the naive young men by the unexpected realization — the shock of discovery — that all was not well in the traditional order of things. Characteristically, the female concern is not to diminish or replace the prerogatives of those who wield authoritarian power but rather to insist that they exercise these powers in a responsible way.[7] They impart this conservative lesson to the young idealists who have impulsively sought to abolish the system. As they see the matter — and the novel dramatizes this vision — the danger to social order comes not from the working class but from flighty and erratic fathers who forget the responsibilities of their inherited leadership role and in so doing endanger vulnerable family members and injure their neighbors. Political agitation for some alternative structure of power as offering a better model for class, gender, and social relations is suspect to them. One must begin by rectifying feelings, with a change of heart.

Eustace Conway is especially concerned with signs of concealed infidelity and character weakness in the class of hereditary leaders like Mr. Vyvyan of Vyvyan Hall, who very nearly succumbs to the plans of a land surveyor who would destroy all that was picturesque and beautiful in the ancestral country estate, cutting down trees planted by great-grandfathers to make a road useful to commercial travellers. Egged on by the scorn of his daughter, he eventually dismisses pecuniary considerations urged by the disciple of progress (a civil engineer with the Dickensian name Knatchbull) and retreats into the role of defiant Tory squire: "I will try to be nothing worse — and I can think of nothing better — than an English country-gentleman" (1: 6).

The reader, however, has been alerted to something factitious: "Mr. Vy-vyan's dress, which was rustic even to extravagance" is the first clue. Trained as a polished diplomat, Vyvyan had spent many years on the continent, and as Mrs. Hartman insinuates, 'he is the most thorough squire you ever met; and, you know, he adopted the character from choice" (1: 155). Honoria Conway, his teenage adopted daughter takes the point and is alerted to an inauthentic acting out of a role. Eustace is oblivious to all this female shrewd-ness. As the plot unfolds Mr. Vyvyan betrays all his family and marries a villainess who has concealed the fact that she is the actual mother of Fannie Rumbold, a monstrous rationalistic child, ostensibly the sister of Rumbold, the most depraved nihilist in the book. Indeed the plot contains a sequence of betrayals of ties of the heart extending over two generations and the heroic efforts to mend matters by two generations of sisters. Maurice is at his best in recounting the secret psychic histories of networks of women, operating unbeknownst to their menfolk. He retained all his life a deep concern for their predicament as powerless members of thoughtless paternalistic family structures in which crossed loyalties and secret divisions between siblings and parents were more the rule than the exception. It was more than his startling good looks which made him such a popular and sought-after minister among women parishioners.

Both novels have much to say about childhood ties and impressions of place and the failures of traditional educational methods to take these seriously into account. Eustace, in disguise, becomes a tutor, and entire chapters are given over to diary entries describing his experiences as a teacher and his theories of education. Eustace subsequently attributes many of his bad charac-ter traits to being sent away at age eleven from the childhood Eden he shared with his cousin Honoria Conway and into the hands of an easy-going tutor who allowed him to indulge his pernicious taste for romantic escapist literature:

> Dr. Wilmot's mode of education did not make it necessary to endure any severe or long-continued labour. . . . This system encouraged in us a volatile kind of intelligence. . . . he left as little room as possible for any other than voluntary exertion. . . . to all that is deeper, stronger, and more dogmatic in Christianity Dr. Wilmot was naturally disinclined. (1: 71)

When Eustace Conway, on the other hand, meets an enlightened clergyman with impeccable literary taste (an admirer of both Wordsworth and Shelley) and, additionally, a scorner of Paley's moral philosophy, he accepts guidance. Here is an entirely unexpected version of Christianity, one that Eustace will ultimately assent to.

In the interim, he listens to the siren voice of Herr Kreutzer who is as spiritual and transcendental as Emerson and perhaps a better psychologist. Kreutzer shrewdly notes that Eustace is uncomfortable with the "rational" analysis of the affective life by Hartley and Hume as a matter of vibrations and attractions. Do you need an abstract theory to explain your own feelings, he inquires:

> Why not let your feelings be their own interpreters? And what do they tell you . . . how do they account for the delight they draw from Nature? Do they not proclaim . . . that there is in you a spirit, a higher self? — that in the subjection of the lower self to it, consists the true freedom of a man? — that this same spirit lives through the whole of creation? (2: 172)

Eustace eventually sees through this enthusiastic rhetoric, which did not account for ". . . a constraint, a compulsion upon me somewhere" — in short Christianity and notions of duty implanted by God: ". . . revelation, not reason and expediency dictate a belief in Christianity." Kreutzer's "system of benevolence" is seen as a dreamy pantheism with no relation to moral decision-making (3: 50). In another crucial encounter with the atheist Marmaduke Rumbold, Eustace learns that "a belief in conscience, if severed from a belief in God, was simply a recognition and assertion of our will power and independence" (1: 274). The doctrine of Will has attractions for Eustace, who desires above all to be a free spirit. But Rumbold himself has no imagination and assumes as a matter of course that the stale counters "good" and "evil" retain no remnant of their momentous ethical content for men more sensitive to language than he. Eustace is shocked by the essential vulgarity and paucity of significance in Rumbold's manipulation of language. The recollection of what these words had meant in childhood and could mean again returns to defeat the casuist. Maurice daringly speculates that an innate power in words can migrate from one conceptual scheme to another: "A principle which we have ceased to recognize may yet impregnate another we hold, and thus keep alive a seed of itself for future generation" (1: 274). In this fashion Eustace slowly works his way deeper into the wisdom which is encased by language.

Carlyle thought that Sterling's novel demonstrated the impossibility of a return to the Church; Julius Hare had a different opinion. Certainly Maurice's fiction demonstrated how such a return might be orchestrated. Whatever interpretation the reader settles on, it remains evident that memory and childhood relationships, fixated in early word use and associations, are presented as the surest stay against insidious ideologies and nihilistic despair — and that the path back to this pristine and saving awareness is through the recollection of the anterior significance embedded in words. When one considers the impact of our mentors on language — Nietzsche, Saussure, and Heidegger — the strength of this counter-faith in the performative power of language does not seem unfathomable.

The novel of the 1830s was indeed an evolving and indeterminate form, and the genre experiments of Maurice and Sterling deserve a closer scrutiny in their own right. They were more than casual missteps in the career patterns of Anglican divines who subsequently found themselves embroiled in most of the great theological, educational, and social conflicts of their era. But their real interest is as harbingers of the historicist tide which came into its own in the mid-century with Ruskin's "Lamp of Memory" and the historical novels of Dickens, Reade, and George Eliot. As late as 1874 one finds F. D. Maurice maintaining ". . . it is almost impossible to conjecture how much light would be thrown upon our national history, upon the history of our wars, arts, and manufactures, above all upon the history of our mental and spiritual progress, by an examination of the senses which words have borne in different times . . . words do indeed bear witness to man's connection with that which is earthy and material . . . but they also testify . . . of man as a spiritual being . . . nay it is impossible to meditate upon the history of any single word without carrying away the conviction that he is so, which all the materialism of the world cannot set aside" (*Friendship of Books* 51, 55). Maurice to the end of his life remained true to the Coleridgian theory of "desynonymy" as it is explicated in Paul Hamilton's *Coleridge's Poetics*:

> Desynonymy for Coleridge means increasing the vocabulary of a language by showing how words which were thought to be synonyms in fact mean different things. The original thinker adds to the number of meanings in the language we use. He does this by coining new words, and showing that we need them. Or he can desynonymize existing words by showing that we are putting words which we mistakenly think are synonyms to quite different uses. (65)

When one recalls the many distinctions made by Coleridge — between fancy and imagination, abstractions and generalization, between pleasure, gladness, happiness, bliss, and joy, even between "for" and "because" — we can see why he so impressed young men of the 1830s. The fictions we have been considering convey the excitement of experimenters with a new paradigm which links the progress of knowledge to a progressive articulation of false analogies. There is more here than period whimsy or antiquarianism, much more than bits of local color to amuse the social historian.

Cambridge, Massachusetts

NOTES

1. The Houghton Library at Harvard University contains several inscribed copies of works by Sterling which belonged to R. W. Emerson, Sarah Orne Jewett, Jane Carlyle, Thomas Carlyle, and the author's father, Edward. The Houghton copy

of *Essays and Tales by John Sterling* is inscribed "T. Carlyle/Chelsea 1848" and contains many significant and characteristic marginalia lamenting the influence of Coleridge and Maurice and attacking Hare's Memoir. One example: Hare speaks of young Sterling's eager perusal of the *Edinburgh Review* as "unwholesome food for a young mind." Carlyle responds in the margin, "Nonsense, Sir! It was the best, indeed the only Picture of the actual world he had been born into, that was available to him, — or to anyone" (ix).

2. Carlyle was a member of the Anonymous Club — subsequently renamed the Sterling Club — founded by Sterling in 1838, with James Spedding as secretary and including in its membership at least twelve other Apostles (among them, Tennyson, Trench, Maurice, Milnes, and William Donne) as well as Thirlwall, Hare, George Cornwall Lewis, Sir Frances Palgrave, Lord Lyttelton, and the painter Charles Eastlake. Carlyle was aware that these quite diverse friends of Sterling would not be happy if he did not veil, to some extent, his private and hostile opinions of Coleridge, Hare, and Maurice which can be gleaned from the marginalia scrawled in his copy of *Essays and Tales by John Sterling*. John Mill's careful and balanced account of Maurice (*Autobiography* 107) reads in part:

> But I have always thought that there was more intellectual power wasted in Maurice than in any other of my contemporaries. Few of them certainly have had so much to waste. . . . The nearest parallel to him, in a moral point of view, is Coleridge, to whom in merely intellectual power, apart from poetical genius, I think him decidely superior."

In the same place Mill notes, "With Sterling I soon became very intimate, and was more attached to him than I have ever been to any other man."

3. In his *Life of Sterling* (134–45), Carlyle reprinted only parts of a massive letter-response by Sterling to his reading of *Sartor Resartus* (which had appeared in magazine parts before book publication). Sterling identifies with precision the components of Carlyle's mannered style, complains that a complex and strange world view should be couched in lucid and common language, and uses the epithet "alienation" in discussing Teufelsdrockh's inability to believe in "one Living *Personal* God. . . . " The letter was written from Herstmonceux Rectory during his time as Curate to Julius Hare. Sterling presided at the marriage there of his wife's sister to Maurice.

4. Disraeli disliked Maurice's introspective and tortuous processes of reasoning, describing him as one of "the nebulous professors, who seem in their style to have revived chaos, and who, if they could only succeed in obtaining a perpetual study of their writings, could go so far as to realize that eternal punishment to which they object" (Vidler, 31–32).

5. A typical passage illustrating the use of historical etymology occurs in *Eustace Conway*:

> Thanks to the disgust with which the carping trivialities of the Benthamites had inspired him, he could never bring himself to revolutionize his vocabulary. . . . The words walked about, with a new cloak thrown upon them, yet clad in their stout old garments underneath. But for this remnant of his former self, he never could have recoiled as he did, at the notion of adopting a prudential view of life . . . of gratifying the animal instinct on principle, and yielding to his passions on calculation. (1: 176)

6. I am indebted to Dennis Taylor for this reference. Linda Dowling observes that Trench was "fond of quoting Grimm's opinion that English was a world language destined to prevail all over the globe." Dowling also quotes from *English Past and Present*, in which Trench refers to "Schlegel's view that "a nation whose language becomes rude and barbarous must be on the brink of barbarism in regard to everything else. A nation which allows her language to go to ruin, is parting with the last half of her intellectual independence and testifies her willingness to cease to exist" (162).

7. I wish to express a general indebtedness to arguments developed in Rosemarie Bodenheimer's brilliant *The Politics of Story in Victorian Fiction* (1990).

WORKS CITED

Aarsleff, Hans. *The Study of Language in England, 1780–1860*. Princeton: Princeton UP, 1967.

Bodenheimer, Rosemarie. *The Politics of Story in Victorian Social Fiction*. Ithaca: Cornell UP, 1988.

Brookfield, Frances M. *The Cambridge "Apostles."* New York: Scribner's, 1907.

Brooks, Peter. *Reading for the Plot*. Oxford: Clarendon P, 1984.

Coleridge, Samuel Taylor. *Unpublished Letters of Samuel Taylor Coleridge*. Ed. Earl L. Griggs. New Haven: Yale UP, 1933, Vol. 1.

Dowling, Linda. "Victorian Oxford and the Science of Language." *PMLA* 97.2 (1982): 160–78.

Eigner, Edwin M., and George J. Worth. *Victorian Criticism of the Novel*. Cambridge: Cambridge UP, 1985.

Emerson, Ralph Waldo. *Essays and Lectures*. New York: The Library of America, 1983.

Farrar, Frederic. *An Essay on the Origin of Language*. London: Longmans, Green, 1865.

Frost, Robert. *The Poems of Robert Frost*. New York: The Modern Library, 1946.

Hamilton, Paul. *Coleridge's Poetics*. Oxford: Basil Blackwell, 1983.

Hare, Julius C., and Augustus W. Hare. *Guesses at Truth by Two Brothers*. 1827. 3rd ed. London: Macmillan, 1874.

Hare, Julius C., ed. *Essays and Tales by John Sterling*. 2 vols. London: J.W. Parker, 1848.

Maurice, Frederick, ed. *The Life of Frederick Denison Maurice, Chiefly Told in His Own Letters*. 4th ed. 2 vols. London: Macmillan, 1885.

Maurice, Frederick Denison. *Eustace Conway, Or The Brother and Sister*. 3 vols. London: Richard Bentley, 1834.

———. *The Friendship of Books and Other Lectures*. London: Macmillan, 1874.

Mill, John Stuart. *Autobiography of John Stuart Mill*. Ed. John J. Coss. New York: Columbia UP, 1924.

Millgate, Jane. *Walter Scott: The Making of the Novelist*. Toronto: U of Toronto P, 1984.

Sterling, John. *Arthur Coningsby*. 3 vols. London: Effingham Wilson, 1833.

Tillotson, Kathleen. *Novels of the Eighteen-Forties*. Oxford: Oxford UP, 1954.

Trench, Richard C. *On the Study of Words*. London: Macmillan, 1852.

— — — . *English Past and Present*. London: Macmillan, 1855.

Vidler, Alex R. *F. D. Maurice and Company.* London: SCM Press, 1966.
Whewell, William. *On the Philosophy of Discovery. Chapters Historical and Critical Including the Completion of the Third Edition of the Philosophy of the Inductive Sciences.* 1860. New York: Burt Franklin, 1971.

"THE PLAGUE SPREADING AND ATTACKING OUR VITALS": OPIUM SMOKING AND THE ORIENTAL INFECTION OF THE BRITISH DOMESTIC SCENE

By Barry Milligan

BY THE BEGINNING OF the nineteenth century, opium was inextricably associated in the British imagination with the Orient.[1] The association was reinforced both by travel narratives, which repeatedly portrayed opium eaters and smokers in exotic Oriental settings, and by the common knowledge that opium was becoming increasingly important in the Oriental colonies as the East India Company solidified its monopoly over Indian poppy crops (Collis 74–76). But, while opium was surrounded by this Oriental aura, it was also becoming the chief analgesic for everyday applications in England in the early 1800s, and the ease with which the English people were adopting this exotic Oriental commodity was soon to be taken up as cause for some alarm. The opium visions of Coleridge and De Quincey, for instance, associated opium with a threatening Oriental contagion. Coleridge claimed that the almost palpable images of a seethingly violent and seductive Orient he described in "Kubla Khan" (first published in 1816) "rose up before him as *things*" (*Poetical Works* 1: 296) during "a sort of Reverie brought on by two grains of opium" (Crewe 185), and his tale differs only in degree of hysteria from De Quincey's accounts in his *Confessions of an English Opium-Eater* (1821) of torturous opium dreams in which he was plagued by a violent Malay who "ran 'a-muck' " at him, and "every night . . . transported [him] into Asiatic scenes" (92, 108). Both authors painted tableaux in which an intimidating Orient was somehow distilled in the Oriental substance of opium, enabling it invisibly to enter the British body that ingests the drug and to reconstitute itself with threatening vividness in the British consciousness.[2]

This literary paradigm is readable as a metaphor for a concurrent historical phenomenon: the growing colonial commerce with the Orient was plying
the domestic market with ever greater quantities and kinds of exotic commodities, "pestilent Luxuries" which some Britons feared were infiltrating and
deteriorating British culture and identity, "leav[ing] an indelible stain on our
national character" (Coleridge, *Collected Works* 1:226) by irreversibly making it more Oriental and less British. In other words, just as Coleridge and
De Quincey had drunk laudanum and thus allowed the Orient to invade their
bodies, so had the body of Britain "drunk up, demure as at a grace, /
Pollutions from the brimming cup of wealth ("Fears in Solitude" lines
59–60), in effect enabling an Oriental invasion of the British Isles. Such
fears were not necessarily widely shared by Coleridge and De Quincey's
contemporaries — indeed the beginning of the nineteenth century in England
saw a growing rage for Persian rugs, paintings of harem scenes, and "Chinoi-
serie" in fashionable decor, Chinese gardens on the best estates, and the
Oriental tales of Byron, Southey, and Moore in any well-stocked library. But
for those who did share Coleridge and De Quincey's fears, this increasing
ubiquitousness of Oriental cultural traces was all too easily interpretable as a
silent but significant threat: the English had "offended very grievously, / And
been most tyrannous" in the Orient ("Fears in Solitude" 42–43), and they
were making themselves vulnerable to reprisals by allowing unlimited entrée
to the very culture they had so grievously offended. Such fears combined with
what Edward Said calls "the nineteenth-century academic and imaginative
demonology of 'the mysterious Orient' " (26) to form a mythologized enemy:
the pernicious, demonic, sometimes invisible Oriental, who could be expected
to use subtle and evil means to avenge England's grievous offenses, and to
bide his time and endure privations in doing so.
   Although these fears may have been somewhat anomalous early in the
century, they gained a broader base by mid-century, when many English
voices rose against the policies behind the "opium wars" of 1839–42 and
1856–58, in which England militarily forced the Chinese imperial government
to lift its ban on British-controlled Indian opium. And as the number of
Oriental immigrants appearing on English shores increased dramatically in
the 1860s, some Britons saw a peculiarly appropriate retribution for the opium
wars taking shape in a practice these immigrants brought with them: opium
smoking, which one British critic of the Indo-Chinese opium trade called
"the reflex action and retributive consequence of . . . the opium traffic at the
hands of our government . . . the plague spreading and attacking our vitals"
(Piercy 240).
   This impression of opium smoking as at once infectious epidemic and
hostile invasion informed a new literary genre that grew and thrived late in
the century: narratives about mysterious and evil opium dens in the East End

of London — a region itself repeatedly figured as an Orient in miniature within the capitol of the empire.[3] These narratives portray Orientalism as a transmittable disease, and opium smoke as the means of transmission. Thus, when the aforementioned critic of the opium trade speaks of "the plague spreading and attacking our vitals," he does not necessarily mean only or even primarily an increased incidence of addiction to smoking opium in East End dens; more fundamentally, he seems to fear a comprehensive infectious Chineseness that is not limited to the opium den, and is eating away at the very identity of the British people.[4]

I

FROM THE BEGINNING, opium den narratives are informed by the idea that the dens are insidiously orientalizing British people who breathe their smoke. The opium den's absorption of poor dockside Englishwomen in particular is an obsession of the early narratives. The only purportedly English person to appear in one early account is an ironically labelled "London lady," an impoverished opium smoker who lives next door to an East End opium den and is gradually acquiring an Oriental identity. "I've lived here these dozen year, and naturally have got into many of their ways," she says, and indeed she has so fully "got into many of their ways" that she is now known only by the quasi-Oriental name of "Mother Abdallah." This contagious Orientalism is apparently inevitable, for a similar fate has befallen her cohorts, "Cheeny (China) Emma" and "Lascar Sal" ("Lazarus, Lotus-Eating" 423–24). Other reporters dwell on the fact that many Chinese "opium masters" have British wives who are being menacingly Orientalized by the insidious influence of opium smoke. The English wife of one such opium master is portrayed as undergoing a macabre metamorphosis into a mystical Oriental living-dead: "Poor English Mrs. Chi Ki looks as though she is being gradually smoke-dried, and by and by will present the appearance of an Egyptian mummy" ("East London" 72).[5] Another opium master's wife is so extensively transformed that

> it was only by her speech that her nationality could be so readily decided. A small lean women, with such a marvellous grafting of Chinese about her, that her cotton gown of English cut seemed to hang awkwardly on her sharp shoulders. Her skin was dusky yellow, and tightly drawn at the nostrils and the cheekbones; and evidently she had, since her marriage, taken such a thoroughly Chinese view of life, that her organs of vision were fast losing their European shape, and assuming that which coincided with her adopted nature. She was very ill, poor woman. It was killing her, she said, this constant breathing of the fumes of the subtle drug her husband dealt in. (Greenwood 233)

The recurrence of the pattern is indicative at one level of the classic fears surrounding exogamy (women of one ethnic, national, or cultural group marrying into another group). By permitting intermarriage, so the anxiety goes, a group allows elements of other groups to mix with its own, thus diluting and dispersing its own special identity. This ancient patriarchal anxiety, at least as old as the Hebrew Bible, was exacerbated in late nineteenth-century Britain by the heightened stakes of separating "us" (England) from "them" (Eastern colonies) entailed in the imperial project, which was approaching its zenith in the latter half of the century.[6] But the Oriental infection of Englishwomen also betrays another fear even closer to "home." As Judith Rowbotham says, "The tradition of *Home* and *Woman* as the *Angel* in it was one of the earliest 'inventions' of the rising middle classes" (9). This totemized woman who maintained the home and raised the children was seen as the foundation of British life and identity in a very real sense. In such a scenario, an Orientalized Englishwoman ultimately implies an Orientalized society at large.

Dickens explores this next stage in *The Mystery of Edwin Drood* (1870), in which another Englishwoman "has opium-smoked herself into a strange likeness of the Chinaman. His form of cheek, eye, and temple, and his color, are repeated in her" (38). But in Dickens's narrative we also see, for the first time, an English *man* in the den;[7] and he is in turn being infected by the Orientalized English woman: "As he watches the spasmodic shoots and darts that break out of her face and limbs . . . some contagion in them seizes upon him: insomuch that he has to withdraw himself . . . until he has got the better of this unclean spirit of imitation" (39).[8] The fact that it is a woman's influence that overtakes him is not merely incidental; she is the proprietor of the den rather than just a victimized customer, and she presides over her den as a middle-class woman would presumably preside over her household, perceiving her relationship to her customers as that of a mother to her children: "Well, there's land customers and there's water customers. I'm a mother to both," she says; and it is this domestic angle that gives her the edge in her business, making her "Different from Jack Chinaman t'other side the court. He ain't a father to neither. It ain't in him" (266). The Oriental opium master is unable to secure a foothold beyond the East End because he has no access to the domestic infrastructure. It takes a woman to gain such influence with the middle classes.

And the middle-class Englishman who breathes her smoke is the ideal transmitter, for although he lacks the domestic influence she weilds, he enjoys the mobility exclusive to his class and gender and is able to carry the Oriental influence from her sequestered East End to his middle-class domestic environs. The fact that all of the opium smokers in the previous narratives were either Oriental men or poor English women from the dock districts left open an escape clause for the infection anxiety: if the practice of opium smoking was spreading to English people, perhaps it was limited to only the most

Figure 1. "The Lascar's Room from *Edwin Drood*," Gustave Doré and Blanchard Jerrold, *London: A Pilgrimage* (London: Grant & Co., 1872).

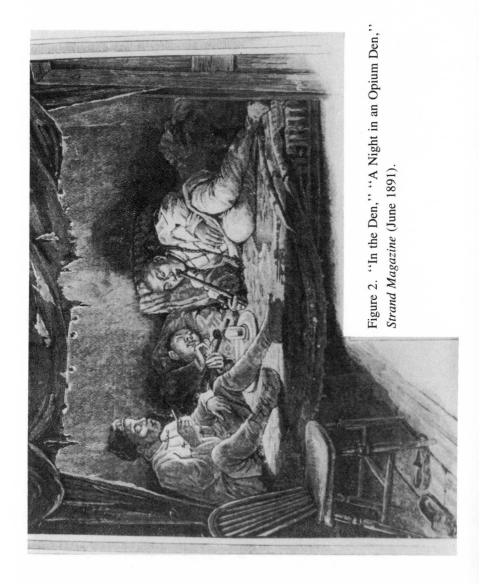

Figure 2. "In the Den," "A Night in an Opium Den," *Strand Magazine* (June 1891).

marginal groups. But this infected Englishman, John Jasper, could hardly be less marginal: he is neither Oriental nor female nor one of the poor of the London docks; he is instead white, English, male, middle-class, and — of all things — a choirmaster in an English cathedral town. We are presented with an outwardly upright, bourgeois Englishman who leads a second, hidden life centered on, and enabled by, the Oriental influence of opium. John Jasper represents an important new twist on the opium den narrative: the portrayal of the Orient's infection of a more mainstream English domestic scene outside the East End opium den.

This opium-induced merging of threatening Orient and English domestic scene is foreshadowed in the novel's first paragraph. The reader views the den through Jasper's opium hallucinations as a corroded and corrosive agent piercing the boundary between the quaint English cathedral town and the teeming, violent Orient. In his opium stupor Jasper sees "The well-known massive grey square tower of [his town's] old Cathedral," but it appears behind an unfamiliar "spike of rusty iron." He drowsily decides that the mysterious spike is a tool of Oriental violence, "set up by the Sultan's orders for the impaling of a horde of Turkish robbers, one by one." This exotic and threatening Oriental imagery then dominates his vision in an intimidating show of destructive potential: "cymbals clash, and the Sultan goes by to his palace in long procession" as "Ten thousand scimitars flash in the sunlight" (37). The metal spike turns out to be a much more mundane object than a device for impaling Turks: it is actually the top of a broken bedpost in the dilapidated East End den. This piece of rusty iron, which comes to be a sort of emblem for the opium den in the novel, is the only actual physical presence to be incorporated into Jasper's vision, where the corroding metal spike punctures the boundary between the English domestic scene and the violent Orient, allowing one to enter the open wound in the other.

Once the opium den has punctured the figurative membrane between East and West the infection spreads as Jasper carries his opium and its attendant contagious influence from his secret East End existence to his respectable cathedral town life. Back in Cloisterham, he smokes opium in his own home, polluting it too with "the Spectres it invokes at midnight" (77), spectres which we know from the novel's first paragraph take the shape of violent Oriental hordes. Like twentieth-century American cold war fictions such as *Invasion of the Body Snatchers, Edwin Drood* draws a scenario in which a malignant alien influence has already infected the seemingly upright citizen next door, thus working its way outward from the otherwise isolated landing site (London's East End docks) into the fundamental fabric of the culture (the small-town, middle-class domestic environment).

II

THE IDEA THAT THE Orient is contaminating the English domestic scene is further developed in the growing number of popular opium den narratives of the following decades. The character of the middle-class Englishman whose secret life in the East End opium den seeps into his domestic existence is picked up and elaborated notably in Oscar Wilde's *The Picture of Dorian Gray* and Sir Arthur Conan Doyle's Sherlock Holmes adventure "The Man With the Twisted Lip" (both 1891). In each story the opium den and its trappings initially appear to be the opposite of the quintessential middle-class English domestic existence, but ultimately they prove to be merely a more visible manifestation of domesticated Oriental elements that are otherwise so thoroughly interwoven with English culture as to be invisible.

Like John Jasper, Wilde's Dorian Gray outwardly appears to be a morally upright citizen, but he leads a secret second life that runs radically counter to conventional Victorian middle-class morality. Also like Jasper, his decadent indulgences tellingly reach their climax amidst "the heavy odour of opium" in an East End den populated by the stock menagerie of stereotypical animalistic and menacing Orientals: "some Malays . . . crouching by a little charcoal stove playing with bone counters, and showing their white teeth as they [chatter]," and "A half-caste, in a ragged turban and a shabby ulster, [who grins] a hideous greeting" (223–24). But the strange influence that drives Dorian to the den originates in his middle-class surroundings. Before he leaves his home to visit the den, he becomes transfixed by a cabinet at the other end of his study, "as though it were a thing that could fascinate and make afraid, as though it held something that he longed for and yet almost loathed." As "a mad craving [comes] over him" (218), he unlocks the cabinet and accesses a secret drawer, where he finds "a small Chinese box of black and gold-dust lacquer, elaborately wrought, the sides patterned with curved waves, and the silken cords hung with round crystals and tasselled inplaited metal threads. He open[s] it. Inside [is] a green paste, waxy in lustre, the odour curiously heavy and persistent" (219). He hesitates for a moment, smiling enigmatically and shivering over the mysterious substance until he finally dresses "commonly," hails a cab, and orders the cabman to "drive fast . . . towards the river" (that is, eastward), where he visits the opium den (219).

The aromatic green paste is almost certainly meant to be opium,[9] which we see resides not only in the East End dens but also in a West End private library, where it exerts a strange and corruptive influence that draws an upper-middle-class Englishman irresistibly to the East End.[10] It even effectively alters his identity, causing him to dress like an East Ender himself.[11] This identity-altering influence is exercised *outside* the opium den; opium is inextricably woven into the details of this gentleman's daily life. Indeed both opium

Figure 3. "A Malay," "A Night in an Opium Den." *Strand Magazine* (June 1891).

and Orientalism are central to Dorian's pursuit of guilty pleasures from that pursuit's roots in the influence of his friend Lord Henry Wotton. Wotton, who appears in many ways to be defensively occidental, with his declared allegiance to "the Hellenic ideal" and his laments of the decay of "our race" (41), is nonetheless steeped in a subtle Orientalism, as evidenced in the decor of his study, the "long-fringed Persian rugs" and "large blue china jars" that Dorian admires and emulates (69). Dorian's programmatic indulgences are likewise largely inspired by Wotton's pithy credo "To cure the soul by means of the senses, and the senses by means of the soul" (220); but the peer's seductive influence over the young man is more tellingly figured in their first encounter by "thin blue wreaths of smoke that [curl] up in such fanciful whorls from his heavy opium-tainted cigarette" (24).[12]

In Conan Doyle's "The Man With the Twisted Lip," the double identity of the middle-class man explodes into a surprising duplicity of all the trappings of middle-class existence, including home, occupation, and financial base. The slippery, too-permeable boundary between the pairs of identities is again the opium den, which also serves as a point of reference and renders visible the Oriental influence beneath a number of otherwise innocuous conventions previously taken for granted as middle-class and English. The adventure itself is initiated by a series of disruptions of proper domestic order which ultimately originate in what Holmes calls "the vilest murder-trap on the whole riverside," an East End opium den run by a "rascally Lascar" and a "sallow Malay" (626, 624). First, Watson is shaken from an easy chair beside his wife with her sewing to answer another young wife's request that he retrieve her husband from a dockside opium den and restore him to his empty hearthside. When he arrives at the den, Watson finds Holmes there investigating the disappearance of yet another young husband who was last seen peering anxiously from a window upstairs. Within only the first few pages, the den draws three young middle-class husbands from their homes, leaving fretting wives next to empty easy chairs.

Once these men are within the den they assume alternative identities appropriate to their haunts. Like the women in the dens of earlier narratives, the man for whom Watson searches becomes quasi-Oriental, "with yellow, pasty face, drooping lids and pin-point pupils" (623). Similarly, like the costumed slummers in other accounts, Holmes is at first unrecognizable in his disguise as a hardened opium smoker, "very thin, very wrinkled, . . . an opium pipe dangling down from between his knees" (625). And, as Holmes discovers in the end, the man for whom he has been searching, Neville St. Clair, also has a second, opium den identity and has been leading two lives with the opium den as gateway between them. It turns out that St. Clair has been earning a fortune as a beggar in the City, then spending it as a husband

and father in the suburbs. As he tells Holmes in the end, the passage between these two poles of his existence was the "low [opium] den in which I used to lodge in Swandam lane, where I could every morning emerge as a squalid beggar, and in the evenings transform myself into a well-dressed man about town" (637).

But while the opium den seems at first to act as a closable valve between St. Clair's two existences, opening twice a day to allow only the squalid beggar into the City and only the well-dressed man about town out of it, it becomes increasingly evident that assorted detritus accompanies both gentleman and beggar in each passage until the two existences are in many ways indistinguishable from one another. In the most fundamental instance of their merging, the St. Clair family's suburban existence ironically is financed by Neville's begging. But the two realms mesh in other, more subtle ways as well. When the pseudo-beggar wants to hide his dual identity from the police, for instance, his secret is nearly revealed by the presence of his expensive clothes and some children's building bricks in his room at the opium den. The two existences mix with one another until it is impossible to say whether St. Clair is a suburban family man impersonating a beggar or a beggar impersonating a suburban family man.

At first glance, it appears as if class is more the contagious factor than Orientalism — St. Clair becomes a beggar rather than a Lascar or Malay — and that the Orient is more or less safely contained in the vile murder trap on the river-side.[13] But a closer look reveals that the Orient is initially unapparent elsewhere only because it has so fully integrated with what at first seems to be unexceptionably English. The story opens with Dr. Watson's description of Isa Whitney, who appears to be the paradigmatic respectable member of one of the English middle classes. He is introduced as the "brother of the late Elias Whitney, D.D., Principal of the Theological College of St. George's" (623); we are then also told that he is "much addicted to opium" and now even physically resembles the Oriental smokers described in previous opium den accounts, "with yellow, pasty face, drooping lids and pin-point pupils" (623). Whitney's habit at first appears to have an English rather than an Oriental source as it ostensibly originates with De Quincey: Watson claims that "The habit grew upon him . . . from some foolish freak when he was at college, for having read De Quincey's description of his dreams and sensations, he had drenched his tobacco with laudanum in an attempt to produce the same effects" (623). But even this tenuous Englishness drops away. For apart from the fact that De Quincey himself associated his own habit with Oriental contagion, he also never *smoked* opium, but only *drank* it in the form of laudanum. Smoking opium was an exotic Oriental practice essentially unheard of in England in De Quincey's time, and it was still thought of as a peculiarly Oriental vice even in Dickens's day half a century later. The fact that Whitney's habit was acquired not from a bamboo pipe in an East End den but from an English brier or meerschaum smoked in rooms at Oxford or Cambridge suggests that the Englishness and Orientalness of the habit have become inseparable — that what was once peculiarly Oriental is now unexceptionably English, and vice versa.[14]

If Whitney's laudanum-laced tobacco smoking *suggests* that English and Oriental are not differentiable, Holmes's peculiar tobacco-smoking practices *insist* that they are merged. Watson describes Holmes's ritual as he prepares to spend the night in a guest bedroom in the St. Clairs' house:

> He . . . wandered about the room collecting pillows from his bed, and cushions from the sofa and arm-chairs. With these he constructed a sort of Eastern divan, upon which he perched himself cross-legged, with an ounce of shag tobacco and a box of matches laid out in front of him. In the dim light of the lamp I saw him sitting there, an old brier pipe between his lips, his eyes fixed vacantly upon the corner of the ceiling, the blue smoke curling up from him, silent, motionless, with the light shining upon his strong set aquiline features. (633)

Holmes's tobacco-smoking posture of course echoes that of the opium smoker, but with a strange amalgam of incongruous English elements. He sits on an "Eastern divan," but it is composed of arm-chair and sofa cushions; with "pipe between his lips, his eyes fixed vacantly upon the corner of the ceiling, the blue smoke curling up from him, silent, motionless," he resembles the Oriental smokers in the den, but he is nonetheless clearly occidental, with "strong set aquiline features"; the room in which he smokes, "full of a dense tobacco haze," looks much like the "room, thick and heavy with the brown opium smoke" Watson described earlier in the East End den (624), but Holmes's den is a bedroom in a suburban villa, and the smoke is from shag tobacco rather than opium.

This last incongruity is particularly significant: the critic of Anglo-Oriental opium policies who warned against Oriental contagion attributed it to the spread of opium dens, but "The Man With the Twisted lip" gradually takes that assumption apart. At the beginning, we found Isa Whitney smoking opium from a regular tobacco pipe at an English college; in the midst of the adventure, we see St. Clair's passage through the opium den blending the East End with the suburban domestic scene, even though he never smokes opium; and by the end of the story, the influence of the opium den is discernible in English domestic elements that are disconnected, in any physical sense, from either opium, the Orient, or the East End. Objects and practices are simultaneously characteristic of both the opium den and the English domestic scene: the sofa cushions are also an Eastern divan, the shag tobacco is also opium, and the suburban bedroom is also an opium den.

This nineteenth-century Oriental contagion interestingly has much in common with late twentieth-century theories about viral diseases. Unlike bacterial infections, which besiege the body for a time and either kill it or are killed themselves, viruses are currently believed to enter the cells of the organism, sometimes even becoming a part of its very genetic structure. The viruses thus invisibly reproduce themselves with each reproduction of the host cell, of which they are now a permanent part, and may go on replicating and integrating with the host cells for years without manifesting noticeable symptoms, only to cause unpredictable complications in the later life of the organism.[15] A similar process is at work in Conan Doyle's undifferentiable Anglo-Oriental domestic scene, in which Oriental elements enter British culture by way of the opium den and become permanent but almost invisible components of the culture, integrating and reproducing along with the host culture, and perhaps causing unexpected complications later on.[16] Just as the opium smoke enters the smoker's body, permanently altering the cells and restructuring the smoker's identity,[17] so do foreign elements introduced into a culture become part of that culture, restructuring the national identity until what were previously perceived as rigidly divided cultures are now inseparable, as in Conan Doyle's subtly Orientalized suburban bedroom. This cultural blending is both enticing and frightening — enticing perhaps because it brings the often romanticized, adventurous frontiers of colonialism to the English doorstep, but frightening because those frontiers themselves are often frightening, and bringing them home gives a seemingly hostile culture a foothold, perhaps ultimately enabling the replacement of a national identity which at least *seemed* predictable with an unpredictable changeling. The late nineteenth-century English wariness of opium smoke, then, is inseparable from simultaneous anxieties about the imperial process: a growing awareness that the British Empire cannot appropriately be viewed as an entity in which the home culture of England overwrites the Oriental culture of the colonies, nor can "English culture" be pointed to as a stable entity. The British Empire must instead be viewed as a volatile multinational identity at every level from nations to individuals, and from the outposts in the colonies to the hearthsides in London.

Duke University

NOTES

An earlier version of this essay was presented as part of the Literature and Addiction conference at the University of Sheffield, April 1991. I would like to thank the other participants for their helpful questions and comments.
1. I use the terms "Orient" and "Oriental" in the sense in which they were used in England and Europe throughout much of the nineteenth century, when Britons and Europeans saw the alien "Orient" as including roughly all of Asia, what

Americans now refer to as the Middle East (including Turkey) and parts of Northern Africa. See, for instance, Edward Said, *Orientalism*, and Rana Kabbani, *Europe's Myths of Orient*.

2. For a rich discussion of De Quincey's fears of Oriental infection and their intersection with imperialist anxieties, see Barrell.

3. In one account of a slumming expedition, for instance, "the horse's head is turned — east" as "we leave familiar London" to enter "savage London." The East Enders are equated with East globers: "the natives of which will look upon us as the Japanese looked upon the first European travellers in the streets of Jeddo" (Doré and Jerrold 142, 144).

4. Virginia Berridge also discusses "the belief that opium smoking was spreading among the white middle-class population, that the establishment of such a practice was an illustration of the degeneracy of the race which had such widespread contemporary implications," but the emphasis of her discussion does not fall on those contemporary implications or their manifestations in the popular accounts (15).

5. The Oriental nature of the mummy is overdetermined in opium den narratives, for, apart from its Egyptian roots, it is also associated with the appearance of the Chinese opium master. The narrator of "Lazarus, Lotus-Eating," for instance, says of the Chinese opium master in the den he visits that "His sunken eyes, fallen cheeks, cadaverous parchment-like skin, and deathly whiteness, make him resemble a hideous and long-forgotten mummy" (424).

   The miscegenative, contagiously opium-smoking Oriental men are not always Chinese. The narrator of another article meets an opium-smoking Englishwoman who "had married an Indian and from him had learned the Hindustani language and the practice of the luxury which had cost her so much" ("Opium Smoking in Bluegate Fields" 261).

6. As one would expect, this fear is manifest in other narratives of late century as well. See especially John Allen Stevenson's fascinating discussion of *Dracula* as playing out a characteristic imperialist anxiety he calls the fear of "excessive exogamy" (139).

7. Of course there is no way of knowing whether Englishmen smoked opium before Dickens's novel was published, but only after it do other narratives portray Englishmen drawing on the opium pipe. Eve Kosofsky Sedgwick suggests that the already multilayered fear of contagion also takes on a homophobic aspect when it involves men.

8. Jasper ultimately becomes so like the woman that his nephew, the eponymous Edwin Drood, later meets her in the street and "looks down at her in a dread amazement; for he seems to know her. 'Good Heavens!' he thinks, next moment. 'Like Jack . . . ' " (178).

9. It is possible that Wilde meant to evoke another stereotypically Oriental consciousness-altering substance: hashish, which appears in the Orientalist prose of his beloved Nerval as "a box full of a greenish paste" (*Journey to the Orient* 87). "Waxy," however, is an adjective consistently associated with opium and never explicitly with hashish. But even if Dorian's box is filled with hashish rather than opium, the implications of Oriental infringement upon middle-class environments beyond the East End are much the same.

10. Opium was the most common home remedy for a number of ailments for much of the century, and it would not have been unusual to find it in a middle-class home. But it would almost certainly have been in the form of laudanum (a

relatively small concentration of opium dissolved in alcohol), and it would not likely have been found in the library, nor would it have been guiltily hidden. The pasty-waxy raw opium Wilde describes would have been a clandestine substance, however, as it was sold exclusively to pharmacists and other licensed medical professionals, having been forbidden to others by the Pharmacy Act of 1868 (see Berridge and Edwards).

11. Dressing up as an East Ender is an essential part of the slumming expedition in several other opium den narratives as well (see, for instance, "Opium Smoking in Bluegate Fields" 259; Doré and Jerrold 142; Greenwood 229). The pattern echoes that of typical imperialist exploration narratives such as Sir Richard Burton's *A Pilgrimage to El-Medinah and Mecca* and Charles Doughty's *Travels in Arabia Deserta*, which, as Daniel Bivona says, "reveal their authors' almost 'childish' delight in exploration, disguise, and the penetration of mysteries that lurk behind the veil of cultural boundaries" (35).

12. In this particular habit, as in other traits, Lord Henry appears to be modelled after his author. As one observer said of Wilde during the year he composed *Dorian Gray*, "he never stopped smoking opium-tainted Egyptian cigarettes" (qtd. in Ellmann 346). Opium-tainted cigarettes in particular had already been targeted by the anti-opium press as one of the more insidious ways to disseminate the destructive influence of opium smoke beyond the opium den: "The last device for secretly supplying the slaves of opium in San Francisco is said to be a tiny cigar made from tobacco which has been impregnated with the fumes of the burning drug. The poison is more effectually administered in this manner than when the smoke is inhaled directly from the burning paste" ("Opium Cigarettes" 208).

13. Audrey Jaffe explores a sort of contagion anxiety around class identity in "The Man With the Twisted Lip," claiming that both the beggar and the capitalist "man who does something in the City" are anathema to a nineteenth-century work ethic because both are able to earn a living without apparently putting in an honest day's work. She argues that it is this invisible mode of production, both liberating and anxiety-inducing, that dissolves the distinction between St. Clair and Hugh Boone: neither identity has a visible basis, both being paradoxically grounded in exchange.

14. The anti-opium *Friend of China* reprinted or reviewed a number of accounts of such instances of opium smoking seeping into middle-class contexts beyond the opium den, always to detrimental effect. In one account, two young medical students mix opium with their tobacco and are later found lying almost dead in the street ("The Danger"). Another piece recounts with horror a report in the *Pall Mall Gazette* that one can buy packages of cigarettes like Lord Henry Wotton's, "impregnated with the fumes of the burning drug" ("Opium Cigarettes" 208).

15. The HIV virus is a notable and all too familiar example of this phenomenon. For an accessible and informative overview of contemporary theory and research on viruses, see Hapgood.

16. Such later complications of ostensible Oriental infection were indeed perceived in subsequent British culture. In the first part of the twentieth century the popular press, fiction, and movies were flooded with xenophobic images of extensive Oriental criminal undergrounds, only occasionally and slightly visible to the casual observer, but nonetheless supposedly controlling and degrading British culture primarily by means of addictive drugs (opiates and cocaine). For an

overview of these phenomena see Terry M. Parssinen's chapter "Agents of Corruption" in *Secret Passions, Secret Remedies* (115–28).

17. The notion that opiates permanently alter and take control of the user's cells becomes a standard trope in the literature of opiate addiction. William S. Burroughs is a representative example: "I think the use of junk causes permanent cellular alteration. Once a junky, always a junky. You can stop using junk, but you are never off after the first habit" (117).

WORKS CITED

Barrell, John. *The Infection of Thomas De Quincey: A Psychopathology of Imperialism*. New Haven: Yale UP, 1991.

Berridge, Virginia. "East End Opium Dens and Narcotic Use in Britain." *London Journal* 4 (1978): 3–28.

Berridge, Virginia, and Griffith Edwards. *Opium and the People: Opiate Use in Nineteenth-Century England*. New Haven: Yale UP, 1987.

Bivona, Daniel. *Desire and Contradiction: Imperial Visions and Domestic Debates in Victorian Literature*. Manchester: Manchester UP, 1990.

Burroughs, William S. *Junky*. Harmondsworth: Penguin, 1977.

Coleridge, Samuel Taylor. *The Collected Works of Samuel Taylor Coleridge*. 16 vols. London: Routledge and Kegan Paul, 1969–73.

———. *Complete Poetical Works of Samuel Taylor Coleridge*. Ed. Ernest Hartley Coleridge. 2 vols. Oxford: Oxford UP, 1912. 1: 257–63, 295–98.

———. Crewe MS of "Kubla Khan." *William Wordsworth and the Age of English Romanticism*. Ed. Jonathan Wordsworth, Michael C. Jaye, and Robert Woof. New Brunswick: Rutgers UP, 1987. 184–85.

Collis, Maurice. *Foreign Mud: being an account of the Opium Imbroglio at Canton in the 1830's and the Anglo–Chinese War that followed*. London: Faber and Faber, 1946.

Conan Doyle, Arthur. "The Man With the Twisted Lip." *Strand Magazine* (1891): 623–37.

"The Danger of Experimenting in Opium-Smoking." *Friend of China* 6 (1883): 95–96.

De Quincey, Thomas. *Confessions of an English Opium Eater*. Ed. Alethea Hayter. Harmondsworth: Penguin, 1971.

Dickens, Charles. *The Mystery of Edwin Drood*. Harmondsworth: Penguin, 1974.

Doré, Gustave, and Blanchard Jerrold. *London: a Pilgrimage*. New York: Benjamin Blom, 1968 (facsimile of London: Grant and Co., 1872).

"East London Opium Smokers." *London Society* 14 (1868): 68–72.

Ellmann, Richard. *Oscar Wilde*. New York: Knopf, 1988.

Greenwood, James. "An Opium Smoke in Tiger Bay." *In Strange Company: Being the Experiences of a Roving Correspondent*. London: Henry S. King, 1873. 229–38.

Hapgood, Fred. "Viruses Emerge as a New Key for Unlocking Life's Mysteries." *Smithsonian* (November 1987): 116–27.

Jaffe, Audrey. "Detecting the Beggar: Arthur Conon Doyle, Henry Mayhew, and 'The Man With the Twisted Lip.' " *Representations* 31 (Summer 1990): 96–117.

Kabbani, Rana. *Europe's Myths of Orient*. Bloomington: Indiana UP, 1986.

"Lazarus, Lotus-Eating." *All the Year Round* 15 (1866): 421–25.

de Nerval, Gérard. *Journey to the Orient*. Trans. Norman Glass. New York: New York UP, 1972.

"Opium Cigarettes." *Friend of China* 6 (1883): 208.

"Opium Smoking in Bluegate Fields." *Chemist and Druggist* 11 (1870): 259–61.

Parssinen, Terry M. *Secret Passions, Secret Remedies: Narcotic Drugs in British Society 1820–1930*. Philadelphia: Institute for the Study of Human Issues, 1983.

Piercy, George. "Opium Smoking in London." *Friend of China* 6 (1883): 239–40.

Rowbotham, Judith. *Good Girls Make Good Wives: Guidance for Girls in Victorian Fiction*. Oxford: Blackwell, 1989.

Said, Edward. *Orientalism*. New York: Random House, 1978.

Sedgwick, Eve Kosofsky. "Up the Postern Stair: *Edwin Drood* and the Homophobia of Empire." *Between Men: English Literature and Male Homosocial Desire*. New York: Columbia UP, 1985. 180–200.

Stevenson, John Allen. "A Vampire in the Mirror: The Sexuality of *Dracula*." *PMLA* 103 (March 1988): 139–49.

Wilde, Oscar. *The Picture of Dorian Gray*. Harmondsworth: Penguin, 1985.

DEAF-MUTES AND HEROINES IN THE VICTORIAN ERA

By Elisabeth Gitter

DURING THE LATE VICTORIAN period, the sign language of the deaf, earlier praised for its naturalness and sincerity and widely used in deaf schools and asylums, came under increasingly acrimonious and effective attack.[1] Although linguists have now come to understand that Sign is a complete language with its own syntax and grammar and with the capacity to generate an infinite number of propositions, late Victorian educators scorned it as primitive pantomine, barbaric, emotive, "inadequate for abstraction," and inimical to "the entire and harmonious development of mind and character."[2] Like despised pidgin and African languages, which were often characterized as inferior in the evolutionary theories of language popular in the nineteenth century, Sign was ridiculed as a "low" language; by the 1880s it was banned in most schools for the deaf in the United States, England, and much of Europe. Despite the arguments of Sign's advocates, who protested that Sign was the preferred language of the preverbally deaf and that deaf children who were not allowed to sign did not acquire language competence, "oralism" — the philosophy of teaching speech to the deaf — prevailed from the last quarter of the nineteenth century through the 1950s.

The similarities between late Victorian criticisms of Sign and of African languages suggest that the conflict over Sign was stimulated in part by contemporary theories linking hierarchies of language to hierarchies of race or culture. Less obvious than this connection to hierarchical linguistic theory, but also helpful in understanding the rise and fall of Sign as the predominant and socially approved language of the deaf, is the role that gender imagery and values have played. During the nineteenth century, deaf-mutism in general and gestural language in particular were feminized in a variety of ways. While deaf men, much discussed in the late eighteenth and early nineteenth centuries, faded from public notice, deafness during the Victorian period was almost exclusively personified in a number of popular deaf-mute women, who were widely celebrated in inspirational biographies and religious tracts.[3] Sign

179

language, too, was discussed in gender-laden terms. Because gestures do not name things as words do, Sign was despised as a primeval or debased form of "fathered" oral language. This Victorian feminizing of both deafness and sign language may have contributed to a striking cultural coincidence: the changes in attitude toward Sign in the nineteenth century paralleled changing attitudes toward silent women, both fictional and real. Sign flourished at a time — the mid-century period — when silent heroines were celebrated in art and in life; Sign was attacked at a time — the end of the century — when the mute woman was more often depicted as unbalanced, menacing, or duplicitous, and when the most popular deaf woman, Helen Keller, was able to speak.

In the eighteenth century, the best known deaf people were male. Philosophers interested in the origin of language and the status of innate ideas examined and wrote not only about mute wild boys but also about accomplished deaf men like Azy d'Etavigny, Saboureux de Fontenay, Jean Massieu, and Laurent Clerc. After the 1820s, however, deaf women attracted the greatest public attention. In poetry, biography, popular magazine articles, and on the stage, deafness was personified and even eroticized in a variety of adorable or inspirational gesturing women. Lovely blue-eyed Alice Cogswell, who inspired the work of Thomas Gallaudet, was the subject of sentimental poetry by the "Sweet Singer of Hartford," Lydia Sigourney, and of a statue by Daniel Chester French (Lane 175, 180). Marianne Willis was "as beautiful a human being as imagination ever drew. Brow, cheek, lips, just such as poet would like to describe, and burn to kiss"; Phebe Hammond was "an uncommonly beautiful and interesting child" who like, Willis, succumbed to an early and picturesque death (Mann 275, 295). Blind-deaf girls like Julia Brace, Eliza Cooter, and Willie Elizabeth Robin, were the subjects of inspirational biographies in England and America (Poulsson; Greeley; *Light in Darkness*; Mann). More celebrated even than these young women, who were moderately well known in their time, were two internationally publicized blind-deaf heroines, Laura Bridgman, who was made famous by Charles Dickens in his *American Notes*, and, of course, the much-loved Helen Keller.

The feminizing of deaf-muteness is also suggested by the imagery of Sign's critics, who feared that Sign challenged the Adamic "paternity" of naming. Failing to understand that Sign, despite its many iconic characteristics, is neither deictic nor pantomimic, and that signs, like words, are conventionally fixed, complex, arbitrary symbols, Victorian linguists saw Sign as primitive, emotive, or debased.[4] They imagined that the origins of Sign, like those of the archaic languages used by the primordial goddesses who appear in Victorian fantasy literature, were "still more primeval than those which philologists seek to determine" (Arnold 9; Hall 244).[5] Like the irrational babble of women, Sign was imagined as disorderly, passionate, and retrogressive; only fathered, verbal language, language based on naming, not gesture, could foster "mental development, precision of thought, and progress in knowledge (Arnold 9). Just as tonal West African languages were thought to be symptomatic or expressive of racial or cultural primitiveness, so Sign was imagined as the barbaric pantomime of the deaf and female discourse was ridiculed as childish and emotive (Adas 14, 304–305). As described in late Victorian philology, Sign, tonal West African languages, and female discourse were alike in their primitiveness, childishness, and concreteness.

The implication of gender values in the Victorian history of Sign is suggested not only by the prominence of deaf women and by the imagery of Sign's critics, but also by parallels between changing public attitudes toward Sign and changing cultural representations of silent heroines, both fictional and, like Laura Bridgman and Helen Keller, real. Signing schools and asylums predominated during the time that the conventional speechless heroine, revived and popularized in the fairy tales of the Grimm brothers and other folklorists, was reanimated and elaborated by many mid-century Victorian writers and artists. At this prosperous time in Sign's history, the silent Laura Bridgman achieved celebrity as a redemptive heroine who had herself been redeemed from darkness. Near the end of the century, however, when Sign was attacked for its barbarism and proscribed in most schools, the mute heroine became a more ambiguous figure, associated in some fiction and medical literature with disease or malevolence. To late Victorian observers, Laura Bridgman, too, now seemed ambiguous, strange, and unappealing. Thus, the destruction of Sign and signing institutions coincided with the devaluation both of the traditional literary figure, the silent redemptive heroine, and the living embodiment of that figure, Laura Bridgman.

The history of Sign in England and America is, broadly speaking, one of gradual rise and dramatic fall. The brief period of Sign's ascendancy began in the middle of the eighteenth century in France, in signing schools founded by the Abbé de l'Epée, who employed a systematized language of signs based on the gestural language of the uneducated deaf people he had observed on the streets of Paris. Although the French signing system was attacked by German and English oralists who were also establishing schools at this time, their refusal to divulge their methods or train important teachers like Thomas Gallaudet inevitably limited their influence and credibility. Gallaudet himself further enhanced the prestige of the French method both by his spirited advocacy of Sign and by his success at the Hartford School (later called the American Asylum for the Deaf), which was regarded, even in England, as a model school (Love 252). Indeed, the mid-century period became for the signing asylum — as for the insane asylum — a kind of golden age: sign language was refined and expanded, deaf-mutes were trained as teachers of the deaf, and signing schools, cultural activities, and communities flourished.

In the 1870s and '80s, however, an intense and successful campaign against Sign was mounted by a new generation of wealthy and politically active oralists, many of whom also subscribed to eugenicist theories: Benjamin St. John Ackers, an influential barrister and member of Parliament; Samuel Gridley Howe, the head of the Perkins Institution for the Blind and celebrated teacher of Laura Bridgman; Horace Mann; and, most important, Alexander Graham Bell, who used his $200,000 profit from the sale of his rights to the gramophone to establish an oralist lobbying organization, the Volta Bureau. Although none of these oralists knew Sign, they condemned it not only for what they saw as its irrationality and primitiveness, but also for its social and eugenic dangers. They feared that, gravitating to signing communities, the deaf would become, like other members of minority groups, "foreigners in their own country," breeding as "a race apart." Using only their own primitive language, the signing deaf would inevitably sink to the "lowest stratum of barbarism" (Bell and Gillett 1; Lane 312; Arnold 15).

Led by Bell, the "oral revival" was a political success. Persuaded that "pure" oralism would allow the deaf to assimilate fully — in effect, to disappear — into the hearing community, many European governments in the 1870s and 1880s became willing to educate the deaf in oralist schools at public expense. In this period, in the United States and western Europe, and even in France, oralism displaced Sign in existing schools, new oralist schools and normal schools for hearing teachers of articulation opened, and deaf teachers were dismissed. In the more doctrinaire oralist schools, rules against signing were strictly enforced: students were not allowed to go home for holidays for the first six years of instruction to prevent their regression to Sign, and if they were caught signing their hands were slapped or they were made to wear gloves or pay fines (Turnbull 10–11). Although, by the turn of the century, it was clear to many educators that prelingually deaf students in doctrinaire oralist schools were lagging in intellectual development and failing to master articulation, oralism remained the dominant philosophy in deaf education until the 1950s, when it was modified by the introduction of manual forms of oral languages, sometimes with limited use of Sign.

The late Victorians who thought that Sign, because it was gestural, was debased and barbaric were in a sense questioning earlier celebrations of inarticulateness by Romantic writers. In the first quarter of the century, when signing schools were first being established in most of Europe and America, the Romantics were also implicitly questioning the primacy of speech. Both Wordsworth and Coleridge, for example, suggest that accession to language is a fall, a loss as much as a gain. Words fail because they are inescapably imitative; they foster solipsism because their noise deafens the speaker to the nonverbal "gentle sounds" of God's "eternal language" (Coleridge 240–42, 264–67). The poet must struggle against verbal language, regress past the "imperfect sound" of words, in order to recapture the prelingual "infant sensibility" that allows him to imbibe images, "drink in" feelings, swallow and be swallowed up by unmediated sensation (Wordsworth 504, 593). Unspoiled by the accomplishment of expressive language, a natural poet like Wordsworth's Wanderer can retain the power of receiving impressions, of reading the "silent faces" of the clouds:

> . . . Sound needed none,
> Nor any voice of joy; his spirit drank
> The spectacle; sensation, soul, and form,
> All melted into him; they swallowed up
> His animal being; in them did he live,
> And by them did he live; they were his life. (205–10)

Like the mute — or the child in Wordworth's *Ode* — the inarticulate Wanderer is peculiarly and, for the poet, enviably, receptive to images, while the rest of us, imprisoned in "a world constructed in words," are blinded by speech (Bewell 225).

By mid-century, as literary enthusiasm for inarticulate rustics, savages, and infants waned, and as writers and artists became increasingly interested in the theme of women in love, the Romantic celebration of speechlessness narrowed into a more limited glorification of the inarticulate heroine and into an identification of silence with a spiritualized femininity. In this early Victorian period, when signing schools and communities most vigorously flourished, beautiful young women were also characteristically silenced in popular genre paintings in which they are shown dozing, reading, or lost in reverie, their eyes downcast and their hands idly plucking the petals of a flower, the pages of a book or letter, or the strings of an instrument. With titles like "The Novel Reader" (Edward Matthew Ward, 1851), "Home Dreams" (Charles West Cope, 1869), "Thoughts of the Past" (John Roddham Spencer Stanhope, 1859), "Convent Thoughts" (Charles Allston Collins, 1851), "Old Letters" (Alfred Holst Tourrier, 1869) and "The Poor Teacher" (Richard Redgrave, 1844; Fig. 1), these paintings invite the viewer to discover a narrative not only in the welter of significant background details typical of the period, but most importantly in the physiognomy and attitude of silent women.

In literature, the mute princesses of fairy tales were recreated in the familiar Victorian type of the redemptive heroine too fragile, unworldly, or innocent to use her tongue. Unlike the many spirited and articulate heroines who were also popular at the time — heroines like Catherine Earnshaw, Lucy Snowe, Margaret Hale, Maggie Tulliver, and Lily Dale — the silent

Figure 1. Richard Redgrave. "The Poor Teacher" or "The Governess" (1844). By kind permission of the Board of Trustees of the Victoria and Albert Museum, London.

Beatrices, Madonnas, and Cinderellas idealized by Dickens, Wilkie Collins, Tennyson, and Ruskin often cannot speak: at crucial moments they are choked with tears, tongue-tied by emotion or shyness, too ill or faint to find their voices. Dickens's Little Nell, for example, faced with her grandfather's betrayal, is struck "dumb — quite dumb," with "no voice to cry for help" (*OCS* 301–302); the voice of Tennyson's Gardener's Daughter is shattered into "silver fragments" (71; 1. 229); in Wilkie Collins's *The Woman in White*, the androgynous Marian Halcombe takes "the business of talking" easily and readily "into her own hands," while the lovely Laura Fairlie hesitates in her trembling and childish speech, unable to defend or explain herself (43).

Speechless, though often able to sing pleasingly, heroines of this type communicate through a synecdochal code of blushes, dimples, tears, and glances; their eyes are eloquent and their fingers, busy with needlework, tremble with meaning. In *A Tale of Two Cities*, Lucie Manette, one of Dickens's most gestural — and thus aptly named — heroines, communicates almost all of her strong feelings in pantomime: when she first encounters her lost father, for example, she looks at him

> with hands which at first had been only raised in frightened compassion, if not even to keep him off and shut out the sight of him, but which were now extending towards him, trembling with eagerness to lay the spectral face upon her warm young breast, and love it back to life and hope. . . . With the tears streaming down her face, she put her two hands to her lips, and kissed them to him; then clasped them on her breast, as if she laid his ruined head there. (73–74)

Mute, angelic heroines like Lucie were also popular on the stage in Auber's opera *La Muette de Portici* or *Masaniello* (1828) and in melodramas like John Farrell's *The Dumb Girl of Genoa* (1827), both of which were performed throughout the mid-century period. So popular was the figure of the saintly dumb girl that the idea was lampooned in Bernard Bayle's 1841 farce, *The Dumb Belle*. The heroine of that play sets out to win the hero by pretending to be his ideal woman: a mute. Without the least wagging of her "little red rag," she tricks him into modifying his fantasy that women be born able to speak only with their eyes to a wish that, like Solitary Reapers, they be instead "comparatively dumb, that they might sing, but not speak." (3, 14).

If, as Nina Auerbach argues, in the Victorian period "the vocation of the real woman was to become that corporate creation, a work of fiction" (*Ellen Terry* 17), then Laura Bridgman was the real woman who most perfectly and publicly enacted the role of speechless heroine. Internationally celebrated as the first blind deaf-mute to be formally educated, Laura Bridgman helped forge the link between the ideal of feminine silence and the actual speechlessness of the deaf. A seven-year-old *tabula rasa* — a newly discovered wild child — when she entered the Perkins Institution for the Blind in Boston in 1837, Bridgman became a kind of artifact, the sole creation of her Pygmalion, Samuel Gridley Howe, who directed and then wrote about every aspect of her life (Fig. 2).

As a real girl, Bridgman became a living laboratory for research into the existence of innate ideas: she was studied, poked, prodded, and discussed not only by Howe, but by an array of scientists and pseudoscientists that included the psychologists G. Stanley Hall and Wilhelm Wündt; the philosopher, Francis Lieber; the phrenologist, George Combe; and prominent oculists and aurists; even Charles Darwin was interested in her (266, 273). At the same time, however, she was mythologized in the writings of Howe and other admirers as a redemptive angel, whose sufferings would touch the most hardened hearts, whose instinctive "innocence and purity" were exemplary, and whose rescue by Howe from spiritual darkness movingly reenacted the Christian drama (Combe 2:205; Hall 264). Dickens, using lengthy excerpts from Howe's reports in his chapter on Bridgman in *American Notes*, discovered in Laura an incarnation of his own recent creation, Little Nell: "gentle, tender, guileless, grateful-hearted" (81). In a metaphor that recalls Nell on her deathbed in her vaulted chamber, her lips moving soundlessly while her hand — "the hand that had led him on through all their wanderings" — stretched out to her grandfather, Dickens imagined Laura "in a marble cell, impervious to any ray of light, or particle of sound; with her poor white hand peeping through a chink in the wall, beckoning to some good man for help, that an Immortal soul might be awakened" (OCS 654, AN 81). For Carlyle, too, Laura was a spiritualized heroine brought to life: "The good little girl: one loves her to the very heart. No Goethe's Mignon, in most poetic fiction, comes closer to one than this poor Laura in prose reality and fact. A true angel-soul and breath of Heaven, imprisoned as none such ever was before" (Courtesy of the Houghton Library).

Laura as spiritualized heroine was also a popular subject for articles and poems in Christian tracts and women's magazines. The Bridgman imagined in the sentimental and religious writing of this period lives in "blessed silence," hearing "angelic symphonies" and seeing "visions of beauty" in her "inmost soul"; like Dickens's Nell, she is "a candidate for immortal glory . . . a being that, deaf, dumb and blind as she was, could be made to sing, and hear the angels sing, in heaven; and see and taste all the beatitudes enjoyed there by spirits that never were pent in clayey tabernacles as windowless as hers on earth" (Burritt 45; *Echoes* 23–25).

This sort of spiritualizing and idealizing of Laura Bridgman depended, of course, upon her silence. In fact, however, like many deaf people, she

DR. HOWE AND LAURA BRIDGMAN.

Figure 2. "Dr. Howe and Laura Bridgman." Reprinted from *The Fifty-Sixth Annual Report of the Trustees of the Perkins Institute and Massachusetts Asylum for the Blind* (1887), Boston.

made, sometimes unconsciously and sometimes for her own pleasure, a variety of noises which were characterized both by her teachers and by psychologists who studied her as "repulsive," "disagreeable," "uncouth," "rude," and "unladylike" (Hall 266; Lamson 80–81, 133; Lieber 10, 24). Her education at the Perkins Institute included not only training in finger-spelling, reading, and writing, but also the systematic repression of these intolerable sounds. Although the psychologist G. Stanley Hall testified that, unless she put her hand on her throat to feel the vibrations, she was "utterly unconscious" of many of her noises, her teachers complained repeatedly of what they saw as her willful refusal "to grow still and gentle" (Hall 265–66; Lamson 281). As a child, Laura sometimes acquiesced to her own silencing; her teacher, Mary Swift Lamson, reports, for example, that after half an hour's talking-to, Laura "promised to *try* to remember to be quiet, and during the rest of the day she did remember very well. In the latter part of the day she made a noise in a whisper, and said, 'That was with my tongue, I made your smooth noise' " (135). Ultimately, however, she rebelled against silence, protesting that " 'God gave me much voice,' " and in 1845 Howe agreed that at set times she could go into a closet, shut the door, and then "indulge" herself "in a surfeit of sounds" (27).

Howe's insistence on hiding away Laura's noisy, recalcitrant, and unladylike other self is illuminated by her contemporary, Emily Dickinson, in a complaint against her own silencing:

> They shut me up in Prose –
> As when a little Girl
> They put me in the Closet –
> Because they liked me "still" – (302)

The shutting up of unladylike sounds is also, of course, reenacted in the confinement of the growling Bertha Mason of Brontë's *Jane Eyre*. Just as the frighteningly androgynous, deep-voiced Bertha Mason interferes with the metamorphosis of her more submissive alter ego, Jane Eyre, into a conventional bride, so the noisy, rebellious Laura Bridgman threatened the existence of the spiritualized heroine of Howe's creation. The defiant Laura, like Bertha hidden and locked in the attic, had to be contained, suppressed, and silenced.

The necessity of silencing the real Laura Bridgman in order to protect her idealized image can also be understood when she is compared to her more perfectly mute fictional offspring, Madonna, the deaf heroine of Wilkie Collins's *Hide and Seek* (1854). Although Collins claims to have used the autobiographical writings of the deaf Biblical scholar John Kitto as his "authority for most of those traits in Madonna's character which are especially and immediately connected with the deprivation from which she is represented as suffering'' (355), he was also well acquainted with Laura Bridgman's story, both from the chapter devoted to her in Kitto's book, *The Lost Senses* (1847), and from Dickens's account. In his descriptions of Madonna's purity, silence, innocence, and redemptive power, Collins seems far more likely to have had Bridgman in mind than the scholarly and accomplished Kitto, who could speak.

Naturally silent even before the accident that deafened her, Madonna is beatified by speechlessness. Against the doctor's advice, she instinctively refuses to talk in the deep, gruff, masculine voice of the deaf, and, unlike both Kitto and Bridgman, joyfully embraces mutism: "Oh how happy she was the first day I wrote down on her slate that I wouldn't worry her about speaking any more!'' her nurse recalls (76). Whereas in his autobiography, Kitto, Collins's authority, describes in poignant detail his feelings of isolation and loneliness and recounts his successful struggle to regain the power of articulation, in contrast Madonna rejoices in her release from speech, gladly exchanging her unnatural male's voice — "the strangest, shockingest voice to come from a child'' — for a pretty little slate framed in red and gold on which her words can be written and erased (71). This choice of feminized silence — the speechlessness of the angelic type of mid-century heroine — over masculine sound provides a fictional corrective to the stubborn noisiness of the real Laura Bridgman. Unlike the occasionally rebellious and unladylike Bridgman, who never fully acquiesced in the identity Howe constructed for her, Madonna, the fictional mute heroine, could joyously embrace the role of voiceless and self-denying heroine.

By 1880, however, at the same time that oralism increasingly prevailed in the political sphere, the silent heroine whom Howe's Laura Bridgman had personified was beginning to be represented and analyzed as a more complex and ambiguous figure. In this late Victorian period, when growing medical interest in female hysteria coincided with intensified artistic preoccupation with the conventional figure of the Fatal Woman, the association between mute, gestural language and the feminine became more problematic. In paintng and literature, Ruskin's rhetorical question, "If she be mute, is she not pure?'' (348) was answered equivocally by the Pre-Raphaelites and Symbolists who embellished and sensationalized the conventional figure of the Fatal Woman. Their numerous Lamaias, Salomes, Liliths, mermaids, and Circes use silent gesture or mysterious, ancient languages to express — or conceal — madness or malevolence; the silence of these dangerous females is explicitly implicated in descriptions of narcissism, murderousness, vampirism, and madness.[6] Embodied and popularized in sinister characters like Le Fanu's Carmilla, Swinburne's Ladies of Pain, and Pater's "La Gioconda,'' the Fatal Woman of the Decadent era was mythologized as a silent predator, whose muteness expressed or disguised her bestiality, self-absorption, or primitiveness.

Just as an angelic female face could be seen by late Victorians like Pater, Braddon, and Stoker as concealing the demonic aspect of the Fatal Woman,[7] so also female silence might be revealed as deceptive or ambiguous. Even Hardy's inarticulate Tess, an innocent victim like Little Nell, has, in her silence, an occasionally vampirish aspect: her "peony" mouth is transformed, when she yawns, so that its "red interior" is revealed "as if it had been a snake's"; her baby sickens and dies after she "devour[s]" it with kisses; and she appears to Angel Clare, speechless, with blood on her lips, after inflicting on her seducer a small but deadly wound that bleeds him dry (144, 231).

While silent or enigmatic witches and female vampires were being exorcised in many late Victorian novels, poems, and paintings, the female hysterics under the care of Jean Martin Charcot, Pierre Janet, Breuer, and Freud were being treated for the wordlessness that revealed their pathology. Beginning in the 1870s with Charcot, psychologists connected silence with repression and gesture with the symptomatic body language of hysteria, which was viewed symbolically, if not always medically, as a woman's disease (Showalter 148). Charcot's pupil, Pierre Janet, saw in hysterical mutism, with its signing and *attitudes passionnelles*, not only disease but also ugliness: "Yes, ugliness; these subjects, whose mind retrogrades . . . lose the delicacy, the perfection, of certain functions, and you can very well notice their return to animality from the vulgarity of certain delicate movements" (214). In the 1880s, through the analysis of aphasic female hysterics, most notably Anna O., Freud and Breuer theorized that hysterical muteness, disordered speech, and somatic symptoms were precipitated by and often symbolized psychic disturbances which had found no verbal outlet (3–17). They speculated, for example, that Anna O.'s intermittent disorganization of speech, difficulty finding words, deafness, aphasia, and loss of German represented her inarticulate rebellion against her monotonous and stifling role as dutiful daughter and nurse to an adored — and resented — father, and that the constriction of Fräulein Rosalia H.'s throat came from her suppressed rage at an oppressive and brutal uncle (40–41; 169–71).

In this late-century period the speechless Laura Bridgman, once apotheosized, ceased to be a popular heroine. Middle-aged, forgotten by the public, silently plying her needle at the Perkins Institution until her death in 1889, she was no longer even completely to be trusted: her exquisite sense of touch, praised in 1841 as a sign of her "innate craving for knowledge" and heightened appreciation of "qualities and appearances, unappreciable by others" (Combe 2: 394) was diagnosed in 1881 by Stanley Hall as resembling, "save in degree," the sensitiveness "described by Charcot and Westphal as one of the characteristic symptoms of incipient mania" (259). By 1888 — the year that Helen Keller, hailed as the "new Laura Bridgman," met the obsolete original at Perkins — Bridgman, then almost sixty, struck some observers as grotesquely childish, unable to cope with the world, "rigid," "like a statue," "jealous," and "eccentric" (Brooks 22; Sanford 34). The young Helen Keller, who could talk, seemed, near the turn of the century, far healthier and more appealing.

It is not surprising that Keller, born in 1880 into a world in which female silence was often portrayed as symptomatic of mental disease, anger, or malevolence, would, when she was only ten years old, spell into Sarah Fuller's hand the words, "I must speak" (Lash 114). Keller was the creation of others, a living fiction as much as Laura Bridgman had been: indeed, her mother got the idea of educating her from reading Dickens's *American Notes*. Her mentor, Alexander Graham Bell, echoing Howe on the subject of his Galatea, Laura Bridgman, said of Keller, "I feel that in this child I have seen more of the Divine than has been manifest in anyone I ever met before" (Lash 172). Bell collaborated with Anne Sullivan and Keller herself in shaping her into a new, improved kind of redemptive heroine. Unlike the pale, ethereal Bridgman, isolated with her needlework at Perkins, Keller would be trained for a life of active service in the world. Speech would be a blessing to her and allow her to be a blessing to others: "It brings me," she wrote, "into closer and tenderer relationship with those I love, and makes it possible for me to enjoy the sweet companionship of a great many persons from whom I should be entirely cut off if I could not talk" (Keller 248). She believed that, whatever the difficulties, her mutism had to be remedied, as if it were a mistake or a defect: "Sometime, somewhere, somehow we shall find that which we seek. We shall speak, yes, and sing, too, as God intended we should speak and sing" (Keller 248–49).

Keller's mastery of speech, reenacted in the vaudeville act that she and Anne Sullivan performed between 1919 and 1922, helped to define her publicly as a modern improvement over Laura Bridgman, a New Woman, a Joan of Arc. Her writings, however, reveal the extent to which she hid from her public the agony of her struggle to speak. Although she was presented to the world as a dazzling success, a mute who, almost magically, could talk, her speech was always to her a source of great frustration, anguish, and disappointment. Indeed, her struggle to master articulation — her prolonged and painful talking cure — lasted for much of the rest of her life. Encouraged by Bell, Keller studied with a variety of voice teachers who employed the newest methods in an effort to teach her to speak "normally" and even to sing. Anne Sullivan's efforts to improve her pupil's speech were apparently so relentless that Sullivan's husband, John Macy, cited Sullivan's "unintelligent nagging" of Keller as one of the irritations that drove him away from the household that the three of them shared (Lach 398, 404). Keller's own frustration at the difficulty of her quest for speech is documented in her letters:

> "In voice-training I have still the same old difficulties to contend against; and fulfillment of my wish to speak well seems O, so far away! Sometimes I feel sure that I catch a faint glimpse of the goal I am striving for; but in another minute a bend in the road hides it from my view, and I am again left wandering in the dark!" (Keller, 133–34)

Her sense of herself as wounded by her own silence and as struggling to find a voice reverberates in the literature — and of course the feminist politics — of Keller's day. Her often desperate frustration with the muteness that made her feel maimed recalls, for example, Mary Elizabeth Coleridge's view of the silenced woman in "The Other Side of a Mirror":

> Her lips were open — not a sound
> Came through the parted lines of red.
> Whate'er it was, the hideous wound
> In silence and in secret bled.
> No sigh relieved her speechless woe,
> She had no voice to speak her dread. (88)

Similarly, Virginia Woolf's appeal in A Room of One's Own for the resurrection of the stifled and buried voice of Shakespeare's sister (117–18) echoes Keller's, "I must speak." Keller's determination to heal the "hideous wound" of her own silence by talking incomprehensibly until she could master speech also resembles Anna O.'s "great efforts" to talk herself back to health (Breuer and Freud 30, 37). Only by talking could Anna hope, in Keller's phrase, to "speak like other people": both women thought they could be healed by speech. Keller's effort to find a voice most obviously parallels the suffragist struggle of her time — a struggle in which she was an active participant — while her attempt to refashion herself as a more complete person recalls the feminist "dream" of creating a new woman.[8]

Helen Keller's rejection of her own muteness and her determination to speak did not, however, guarantee ultimate success. With her astonishing persistence, considerable financial resources, and extraordinary intellectual ability, she made far more progress in articulation than most deaf people can, but attaining the full power of speech proved for her, as it did for some of Freud's patients, an elusive goal. After years of constant study and struggle, Keller still complained of her own inadequacy in speech, and in 1915 she admitted to her voice teacher that her speech training was hopelessly stalled: "We still meet people on tours who say that my voice is improving, and I find it easier to talk with strangers. . . . But, I need hardly tell you, my voice has not brought me the happiness that I anticipated" (Lash 421). Keller tied her fingers up in papers when she "sinned" by finger-spelling, and she spoke frequently in public, both in vaudeville and on the lecture circuit, but she never cured herself of differentness or bridged her isolation with speech. Her voice remained, as Maude Howe Elliott, the daughter of Samuel Gridley Howe, testified, "the loneliest sound I have ever heard, like waves breaking on the coast of some lonely desert island" (Lash 117).

Keller's androgynous voice, desolate and frightening, "like that of a Pythoness," (Lash 117) still resonates in our own discussions of female speech and silence. On the one hand, Keller's broken speech can be heard as a defiant repudiation of feminized silence, a triumphant revision of the Philomela story, a deep-voiced rejection of the confined, unworldly existence of Laura Bridgman. At her college graduation Keller embraced this active, feminist identity, proclaiming "The doors of the bright world are flung open before me and a light shines upon me, the light kindled by the thought that there is something for me to do beyond the threshold" (Lash 315). On the other hand, however, her voice, in its loneliness, has a cautionary echo: her inability, after a lifetime of struggle, to "cure" her muteness with "normal" speech argues the utter futility of the oralist enterprise and the pointlessness of privileging word over gesture. Constrained and frustrated by the inefficiency of finger-spelling, ignorant of Sign, and unable to function fully in speech, Keller felt like an outsider in the world of the deaf as well as that of the hearing. Her attempt to be what the current jargon calls "mainstreamed" left her without a communal language: wishing to speak like others, she ended by speaking like no one.

Although she was a suffragist, a pacifist, a Swedenborgian, and a socialist, Keller was, in her desire to talk in the voice of a hearing woman, deeply conventional, profoundly eager to please. The discomfort that her androgynous voice awakened in others pained her as well. The valiant pretense of her life — the pretense that she was not different and not suffering — made her an adored celebrity.[9] Her struggle to preserve the comfortable illusions of her public — and perhaps her own illusions as well — prevented her, however, from coming to terms with the disturbing differentness of her own voice.

Dependent on others for nearly all their knowledge of the world, virtual *tabulae rasae*, both Bridgman and Keller were, at least in theory, the most malleable of women. Each of them was shaped not only by the educational philosophies of her generation, but also by tangled beliefs and imaginings about language, muteness, gesture, and femininty. Bridgman was molded by Howe to conform to a popular literary type — the silent angel. Keller, more energetic and astute, collaborated with Bell and Sullivan in her own construction as a New Woman, a political activist and reformer, a militant women's suffragist, a breaker of pathological silences. Howe's need to keep Bridgman silent, like Sullivan and Bell's to help Keller talk normally, reflected a changing, but persistent, Victorian impulse to impose cultural and gender values upon unconventional modes of expression. This impulse, still not wholly vanished, has long confused and obstructed efforts to understand and educate the deaf; it persists, even today, in the ongoing conflict over the status and value of Sign. [10]

John Jay College of Criminal Justice

NOTES

1. I will use the term "Sign" to refer to natural gestural languages like American Sign Language and French Sign Language, as distinct from manual forms of spoken languages like Signing Exact English and Seeing Essential English, which were developed for pedagogical purposes and are often used by the deaf to communicate with hearing people. For extended nontechnical descriptions of Sign see Higgins and Nash; Padden and Humphries; and Sacks.
2. Lane provides a complete history of late Victorian attacks on sign language.
3. John Kitto, an English Biblical scholar who lost his hearing when he was twelve years old, was the one deaf man who was well known in England and the United States during the nineteenth century. His partly autobiographical book, *The Lost Senses*, offers a particularly poignant description of the experience of deafness. Kitto, who struggled to retain his ability to speak, disliked Sign, but recognized it as the natural language of the prelingually deaf, who, he observed, can be taught to speak only "as a bear can be taught to dance" (18).
4. Unlike languages with words, Sign is performance-based: meaning is communicated by movements of the hands and body combined with facial expression. For that reason, Sign cannot be translated "word for word" into oral language.
5. Gilbert and Gubar discuss atavistic languages in Victorian literature (7–10).
6. Turn-of-the-century misogynistic themes have been discussed by many scholars, including Dijkstra, Pierrot, and Praz.
7. See Auerbach (*Woman and the Demon* 88–108) for a fuller discussion of this idea.
8. See Smith-Rosenberg (245–96) for a useful history of the "New Woman." Helen Keller was active in many of the reformist causes that Smith-Rosenberg describes.
9. Bettelheim (85–90) discusses Keller's comforting "pretense" of a complete and happy life.
10. For their help with this essay I thank Robert Crozier, Max Gitter, Jacqueline Jaffe, Shirley Schnitzer, and Anya Taylor. I am especially indebted to Patricia Licklider and to Kenneth Stuckey, curator of the Perkins Institution archives.

WORKS CITED

Adas, Michael. *Machines as the Measure of Men*. Ithaca: Cornell UP, 1989.
Arnold, Thomas. *Language of the Senses*. Margate: Keble's Gazette, 1894.
Auerbach, Nina. *Ellen Terry: Player in her Time*. New York: Norton, 1987.
———. *Woman and the Demon: The Life of a Victorian Myth*. Cambridge: Harvard UP, 1982.

Bayle, Bernard. *The Dumb Belle, A Farce in One Act*. Chicago: Dramatic Publishing, 1841.
Bell, Alexander Graham, and J.L. Gilbert. *Deaf Classes in Connection with the Public Schools*. Washington, D.C.: Volta Bureau, 1895.
Bettelheim, Bruno. "Miracles." *The New Yorker* 4 Aug. 1980: 85–90.
Bewell, Alan. *Wordsworth and the Enlightenment*. New Haven: Yale UP, 1989.
Breuer, Josef, and Sigmund Freud. *Studies on Hysteria*. Trans. James Strachey. 1955. New York: Basic, 1988.
Brooks, Van Wyck. *Helen Keller: Sketch for a Portrait*. New York: Dutton, 1956.
Burritt, Elihu. *Miscellaneous Writings*. Worcester, MA: Thomas Drew, 1850.
Carlyle, Thomas. Letter to Samuel Gridley Howe. 23 Oct. 1842. Howe Papers. Houghton Library, Harvard University.
Coleridge, Mary Elizabeth. *The Collected Poems of Mary Coleridge*. Ed. Theresa Whistler. London: Rupert Hart-Davis, 1954.
Coleridge, Samuel Taylor. *Poetical Works*. Ed. Ernest Hartley Coleridge. 1912. New York: Oxford UP, 1967.
Collins, Wilkie. *Hide and Seek*. 1854. New York: Dover, 1981.
———. *The Woman in White*. 1860. New York: Oxford UP, 1973.
Combe, George. *Notes on the United States During a Phrenological Visit in 1838-9-40*. 2 vols. Philadelphia: Carey and Hart, 1841.
Darwin, Charles. *The Expression of the Emotions in Man and Animals*. 1872. New York: Philosophical Library, 1872.
Dickens, Charles. *American Notes*. 1842. New York: Penguin, 1972.
———. *The Old Curiosity Shop*. 1841. New York: Penguin, 1972.
———. *A Tale of Two Cities*. 1859. New York: Penguin, 1970.
Dickinson, Emily. *The Complete Poems of Emily Dickinson*. Ed. Thomas Johnson. Boston: Little Brown, 1951.
Dijkstra, Bram. *Idols of Perversity*. New York: Oxford UP, 1986.
Echoes in Nature. Philadelphia: Biddle, 1845.
Gilbert, Sandra, and Susan Gubar. *No Man's Land 2: Sexchanges* New Haven: Yale UP, 1989.
Greeley, I. "Willie Elizabeth Robin." *Mentor* 1 (1891): 201–05.
Hall, G. Stanley. *Aspects of German Culture*. Boston: James Osgood, 1881.
Hardy, Thomas. *Tess of the D'Urbervilles*. 1891. New York: Penguin, 1978.
Higgins, Paul, and Jeffrey Nash, eds. *Understanding Deafness Socially*. Springfield, IL: Charles C. Thomas, 1987.
Howe, Samuel Gridley. *Thirteenth Annual Report of the Trustees of the Perkins Institution and Massachusetts Asylum for the Blind*. Boston: 1845.
Janet, Pierre. *The Major Symptoms of Hysteria*. New York: Macmillan, 1913.
Keller, Helen. *The Story of My Life*. Ed. John Macy. 1903. New York: Airmont, 1965.
Kitto, John. *The Lost Senses*. Edinburgh: Oliphant, 1848.
Lamson, Mary Swift. *Life and Education of Laura Dewey Bridgman, The Deaf, Dumb, and Blind Girl*. 1881. New York: Arno, 1975.
Lane, Harlan. *When the Mind Hears: A History of the Deaf*. New York: Random House, 1984.
Lash, Joseph. *Helen and Teacher*. New York: Delacorte, 1980.
Lieber, Francis. "The Vocal Sounds of Laura Bridgman." *Smithsonian Contributions to Knowledge* 2: 1851.
Light in Darkness. Brighton: W. Moon, 1859.

Love, James Kerr. *Deaf Mutism*. Glasgow: MacLehose, 1895.

Mann, Edwin. *Deaf and Dumb*. Boston: Hitchcock, 1836.

Padden, Carol, and Tom Humphries. *Deaf in America: Voices from a Culture*. Cambridge: Harvard UP, 1988.

Pierrot, Jean. *The Decadent Imagination: 1880–1900*. Trans. Derek Coltman. Chicago: U of Chicago P, 1981.

Poulsson, Laura. "Willie Elizabeth Robin." *Kindergarten News* 10 (1897): 758–74.

Praz, Mario. *The Romantic Agony*. Trans. Angus Davidson. 2nd ed. New York: Oxford UP, 1956.

Ruskin, John. "Trust Thou Thy Love." *The Oxford Book of Victorian Verse*. Ed. Arthur Quiller-Couch. Oxford: Oxford UP, 1912.

Sacks, Oliver. *Seeing Voices*. Berkeley: U of California P, 1989.

Sanford, E.C. *The Writings of Laura Bridgman*. San Francisco: Overland Monthly Publishing, 1887.

Showalter, Elaine. *The Female Malady: Women, Madness, and English Culture, 1830–1980*. New York: Penguin, 1985.

Smith-Rosenberg, Carroll. *Disorderly Conduct: Visions of Gender in Victorian America*. New York: Knopf, 1985.

Tennyson, Alfred. *The Complete Poetical Works of Tennyson*. Ed. W. J. Rolfe. Cambridge: Riverside Press, 1898.

Turnbull, Charles Smith. "A Consideration of the Welfare of Deaf Children and the Duty of the Medical Profession." *Proceedings of the First International Conference in America on the Welfare of the Child* 1908: 10–11.

Woolf, Virginia. *A Room of One's Own*. New York: Harcourt, Brace, 1929.

Wordsworth, William. *The Poetical Works of Wordsworth*. Ed. Thomas Hutchinson. 1904. New York: Oxford UP, 1964.

WILKIE COLLINS AND SURPLUS WOMEN: THE CASE OF MARIAN HALCOMBE

By Susan Balée

Can you look at Miss Halcombe and not see that she has the foresight and resolution of a man?

Count Fosco in *The Woman in White*

. . . The very dust of literature is precious, and its dross may be of more worth to the historian than its beaten gold.

E. S. Dallas, *Blackwood's*, 1859

Fiction forsooth! It is at the core of all the truths of this world; for it is the truth of life itself.

Dinah Mulock (Craik), *Macmillan's*, 1861

WILKIE COLLINS'S BEST-SELLING novel, *The Woman in White*, first appeared in the 26 November 1859 edition of Charles Dickens's popular periodical, *All the Year Round*. For the space of a page — page 95 — Dickens's latest novel, *A Tale of Two Cities*, and Collins's new one were juxtaposed. Sydney Carton spoke his famous last words in column 1, and Walter Hartright inaugurated the genre of sensation fiction in column 2 with this prophetic sentence: "This is the story of what a Woman's patience can endure, and what a Man's resolution can achieve."[1]

Dickens's tale of the French Revolution had been a steady seller, but *The Woman in White* soon eclipsed it, generating enormous sales for the magazine and becoming one of the most popular novels of nineteenth-century England.[2] Collins had initiated a genre of fiction that intrigued Victorian readers for nearly ten years before its power subsided with its decade — the Sensational Sixties faded into the unsentimental 1870s.

In its own time, *The Woman in White* elicited both praise and moral indignation from a wide variety of reviewers. Margaret Oliphant, writing in *Blackwood's* in 1862, praised Collins for not using any supernatural effects

197

to produce his sensations ("Sensation Novels" 566), but she lamented that his elevation of crime to an art form would inspire less-talented followers and that these "disciples will exaggerate the faults of their leader, and choose his least pleasant peculiarities for special study" (567).

Nevertheless, Mrs. Oliphant admitted that Collins did what he did well, and that Dickens — usually considered to be Collins's tutor — could not compete with his student as a sensation novelist.[3]

Comparing *Great Expectations* to *The Woman in White*, Oliphant put the dunce's cap on Dickens.

> Mr Dickens is the careless, clever boy who could do it twice as well, but won't take pains. Mr Wilkie Collins is the steady fellow, who pegs at his lesson like a hero, and wins the prize over the other's head. ("Sensation Novels" 580)

In later reviews of sensation fiction, Oliphant noted that the new-fashioned heroines of these novels were the real sources of their immorality, that such fiction "has reinstated the injured creature Man in something like his natural character, but unfortunately it has gone to extremes, and moulded its women on the model of men . . ." ("Novels" 258).

H. L. Mansel, whose celebrated "Bampton Lectures" on religious thought were the table talk of 1859, came to the same conclusion in his review of sensation fiction in the *Quarterly Review* in 1863. He vilified the genre for its dependency on the subversion of female morality to achieve its shocking effects. The point of Mansel's review was the same as that of his Bampton Lectures: he insisted that there are only two roads that the mind is capable of taking, one that "leads up to light and hope," and another that perceives only a "dark atheistic view which detects nothing in the universe but unconscious forces breaking out" (Smith 49). Clearly, Mansel felt that sensation novels led readers along the darker path. E. S. Dallas, a brilliant mid-century British critic, also perceived the unusual power of sensation-novel heroines, but rather than denigrating heroines who did not fit the angel in the house ideal, he applauded them.

> . . . If the heroines have the first place, it will scarcely do to represent them as passive and quite angelic, or insipid — which heroines usually are. They have to be pictured as high-strung women, full of passion, purpose, and movement. . . . ("Lady Audley's Secret" 4)

Nancy Armstrong in *Desire and Domestic Fiction* argues that conduct books of the late eighteenth century helped to create the domestic woman of the nineteenth.[4] Words created this dainty maternal creature, and words maintained her. As Davidoff and Hall detail in *Family Fortunes*, this ideal of the domestic woman was promoted in the 1830s and '40s by "church and chapel" which "were central to the articulation and diffusion of new beliefs and practices related to manliness and femininity" (149). Further, "if a man's ability to support and order his family and household lay at the heart of masculinity, then a woman's femininity was best expressed in her dependence" (114). Therefore, it is not surprising that until the advent of the sensation novel, "the young, dependent, almost child-like wife was portrayed as the ideal in fiction. . . . Such an image of fragility and helplessness enhanced the potency of the man who was to support and protect her" (323).

Women characters who did not fit this ideal of femininity were treated as abnormal, even evil. Dickens, for example, in *Little Dorrit* (1855–57) presents in a minor role an androgynous, powerful female character — Miss Wade. But Miss Wade is portrayed as a dark force, a probable lesbian who seeks to lead the rebellious young Tattycoram to her doom.

Wilkie Collins, whose novel appeared two years after his friend and advisor's, recreated in *The Woman in White* the androgynous heroine not as an evil force, but as a wonderful alternative version of womankind. Further, he would bring this character — Marian Halcombe — to center stage. She, with Count Fosco, would number among the most compelling characters of her day and after. Even Dickens praised her in a letter written to Collins on 7 January 1860: "I have read this book with great care and attention. There can be no doubt that it is a very great advance on all your former writing. . . . In character it is excellent." The depiction of Marian, Dickens added, is particularly "meritorious" (*Letters* 89). Years later, in an interview with Edmund Yates, Collins recalled the many letters he had received from English bachelors who wanted to marry the original for Marian Halcombe (4–6). Clearly, the moment for a new ideal of woman had come, and Collins began to fashion her in words and to promulgate her in fiction.

The Woman in White began its literary devaluation of the angel in the house in 1859 by contrasting her with the strong-minded old maid, Marian Halcombe, as a new ideal of womanhood.[5] Sensation fiction, and Marian's creation, had everything to do with a social dilemma that had begun in England in the 1850s. This dilemma centered on a proliferation of single women who, as men emigrated to the colonies or were killed in the Crimea, would never find mates, would never have the chance to become those maternal angels beloved by Victorian iconography. Something had to be done for and about England's "surplus women," and Collins began to do it in the medium most likely to influence the millions — the serial novel.

FITZJAMES STEPHEN, WRITING in the *Edinburgh Review* in July 1857, commented on the new role of authors as the boom in periodical literature brought their words into more households than ever before. There is, he said, "one class of writers who are, perhaps, the most influential of all indirect moral teachers — we mean contemporary novelists" (125). Crime reportage, which had increased enormously in the 1850s, soon filtered its facts into fiction; crime and its detection became one of the distinguishing features of the 1860s sensation novels.[6] Stephen, as early as 1857, feared that "novelists will become a pest to literature, and they will degrade, as some of them have already degraded, their talents to the service of malignant passions, calumny, and falsehood" (155).

Stephen's words in this instance were aimed specifically at Charles Dickens and Charles Reade. Stephen felt that Dickens unfairly represented English bureaucracy with his portrayal of the Circumlocution Office in *Little Dorrit*, and that Reade was guilty of base falsehoods in his novel of prison reform, *It is Never Too Late to Mend* (1856–57).

Stephen was by no means the last to comment on the extraordinary turn that literature was taking as periodicals flooded the market. E. S. Dallas, in an essay entitled "Popular Literature — the Periodical Press" published in *Blackwood's* in January 1859, noted that "literature . . . is not only the expression of public opinion and the index of contemporary history, it is itself a great force that reacts on the life which it represents, half creating what it professes only to reflect" (97). Further, and this is a point that carried much weight with all the serially-published novelists,

> A periodical differs from a book in being calculated for rapid sale and for immediate effect. . . . It is necessary, therefore, to the success of a periodical, that it should attain an instant popularity — in other words, that it should be calculated for the appreciation, not of a few, but of the many. (101)

Two years later, W.H. Ainsworth, the former editor of *Bentley's Miscellany*, discoursed on the problems inherent in the rapid production of serial literature — it lacked research, he admitted, and thus could only amuse rather than instruct.

> Every month sees the birth of some new periodical . . . [and] the writer who has in any way gained the ear of the public is sure to obtain work, not only profitable but tolerably regular in its nature. At the same time, however, it cannot be denied that the character of our literature has degenerated. (215)

Ainsworth, despite his acknowledgment that the demands of serial publication forced writers to sacrifice quality to meet weekly or monthly deadlines, did little to rectify the situation. He himself was the successful author of several serial novels, including the very popular *Jack Sheppard* (1839). As an editor, he fostered the talents of numerous popular writers. The sensation novel that was destined to become *the* best-selling book of nineteenth-century England, Mrs. Henry Wood's *East Lynne* (1860–61), was written under his guidance and initially published in another of the magazines he edited, *The New Monthly Magazine*.

Ainsworth, like Dickens and Thackeray, both wrote for and edited the publications under his management. He noted that this, too, was new in the history of literature. "All of our great writers," he wrote, "bestow their energies on the serials they have under their management, and the result is such as has never been seen before in literature" (218). Ainsworth's protégée, Mrs. Henry Wood, would go on to manage her own magazine as would Mary Elizabeth Braddon,[7] another tremendously successful sensation novelist, and the author of *Lady Audley's Secret* (1861–62).

The changes in the production and publication of literature in the 1850s and '60s cannot be extricated from the changes that were happening concurrently in women's roles. That Mrs. Henry Wood and Mary Elizabeth Braddon could make the transition from contributing to popular magazines to being their proprietors is yet another indication of the way that the role and social status of women underwent dramatic change in the 1860s. That these changes were linked to the influence of popular literature seems undeniable. For it is certainly true that scores of writers in the late 1850s and early 1860s were commenting on the way that periodical literature together with increased literacy had revolutionized public knowledge. Perhaps Dinah Mulock (Craik), writing for *Macmillan's* in the spring of 1861, put it best:

> The amount of new thoughts scattered broadcast over society within one month of the appearance of a really popular novel, the innumerable discussions it creates, and the general influence which it exercises in the public mind, form one of the most remarkable facts of our day. (442)

THE WOMAN IN WHITE IS a novel that plays on the theme of sex-role reversals. D. A. Miller first explicated the ways "sensations" — which the sensation novel produces internally (on its characters) and externally (on its readers) — are gendered. Miller interprets the novel as an elaborate play on the Victorian readers' desire for and fear of homosexuality:

> no less than that of the woman-in-the-man, the motif of the the the man-in-the-woman is a function of the novel's anxious male imperatives (*"cherchez, cachez, couchez la femme"*) that, even as a configuration of resistance, it rationalizes, flatters, positively encourages. (114)

Miller reads the novel — breathlessly — as an elaborate pathology of male homosocial bonds and "free-floating homoerotics" (122). I read it rather differently, as a subversion of Victorian sexual stereotypes (the angel in the house, the manly man) in order to promote new icons. *The Woman in White* actively works to dismantle old myths of sexuality in order to construct new ones that would be of greater use to an economically-altered society. It is no surprise that the angel-in-the-house icon rose to prominence with the industrial revolution and market capitalism, the phenomena that put men to work outside the home and confined women within it. Wives and mothers were idealized, even as they were robbed of economic power (see Christ).

By the late 1850s, single women outnumbered single men significantly: in 1851 in Great Britain there were 2,765,000 single women aged fifteen and over; by 1861, the figure was 2,956,000; by 1871, it would reach 3,228,700 — an increase of nearly seventeen percent in twenty years (Banks 27).[8] This imbalance meant that large numbers of women would never be able to get married, would never live the role of angel in the house — a role that had been presented to them for decades as not only the ideal, but virtually the only part they could play. Cultural ideology and economic necessity, which had reinforced each other for so long, were suddenly in conflict. Women required an alternative ideal of femininity that was not maternal as more and more of their numbers remained unmarried.

When we first see Marian Halcombe through Walter Hartright's eyes, she is shockingly androgynous. Walter, at this point in the novel, perceives Marian through the filter of conventional ideals of female beauty.

> The easy elegance of every movement of her limbs and body as soon as she began to advance from the far end of the room, set me in a flutter of expectation to see her face clearly. She left the window — and I said to myself, The lady is dark. She moved forward a few steps — and I said to myself, The lady is young. She approached nearer — and I said to myself (with a sense of surprise that words fail me to express), The lady is ugly! (58)

What makes Marian ugly to Walter is her distinctly masculine face set upon a perfectly feminine figure. Marian's complexion is dark, and she has an incipient moustache (58). A page later, in direct contrast to Marian, we hear our first words of Laura Fairlie, the blonde angel with whom Walter Hartright will fall in love. She is classically feminine, right down to her nerves. ''My sister is in her own room,'' Marian informs Hartright, ''nursing that essentially feminine malady, a slight headache'' (59).

As the novel progresses, Marian's masculine strength of mind is continually juxtaposed with Laura's weakness; readers are left to form their own opinion as to which character is the more admirable of this novel's two heroines. Or perhaps I should say *three* heroines, for as Barbara Fass Leavy points out, ''the woman in white'' of the title — Anne Catherick — represents a third and very important heroine (91). Anne Catherick, Laura's half-sister on the father's side, continually figures as a paler version of Laura herself. Both are blonde, physically fragile, and mentally weak. The physically and mentally durable Marian, Laura's half-sister on her mother's side, stands out in dark contrast to these two fluttering angels.[9]

Marian despises her own sex in general, her affection for Laura excepted. What she feels for Laura seems to be a chivalrous, brotherly love[10] that deepens as Laura comes to rely on her more and more. Marian, as the novel progresses — particularly after she experiences a jolt of mutual sexual attraction to Count Fosco — begins to display more classically feminine characteristics. It might be said that Fosco literally makes a woman of her when he reads her diary. His invasion of her room (a private sanctuary that, in psychoanalytic terms, may be read as her "womb") and his taking possession of her innermost thoughts constitutes a kind of psychic rape (358–60).

Before she meets Fosco, Marian responds to strong emotions with manly reticence. When Laura tells her that she must honor her engagement to a man she does not love, Marian manages her feelings like a man. "I only answered by drawing her close to me again. I was afraid of crying if I spoke. My tears do not flow so easily as they ought — they come almost like men's tears, with sobs that seem to tear me in pieces, and that frighten everyone about me" (187). However, after she comes under the spell of Fosco, Laura's troubled marriage causes Marian to weep like a woman. "Crying generally does me harm; but it was not so last night — I think it relieved me" (289).

Fosco, it should be mentioned, is also described in the most androgynous terms. Although he has a face like Napoleon, he is also fat and feminine in manner. He resembles "a fat St. Cecilia masquerading in male attire" (250). He is tenderly maternal to his pet birds and mice, and is described by Marian as a "Man of Sentiment" (308). Manly reticence is not one of his virtues, yet his charm for Marian is his honeyed tongue. She says,

Women can resist a man's love, a man's fame, a man's personal appearance, and a man's money, but they cannot resist a man's tongue when he knows how to talk to them. (278)

One may extend this compliment to Wilkie Collins, who put the words in Fosco's mouth.

If Marian is an androgynous character who becomes somewhat more feminized towards the close of the novel, Walter Hartright is described as a eunuch who becomes more manly through his association with Laura and Marian. Hartright first describes himself as safely emasculated.

I had long since learnt to understand, composedly and as a matter of course, that my situation in life was considered a guarantee against any of my female pupils feeling more than the most ordinary interest in me, and that I was admitted among beautiful and captivating women much as a harmless domestic animal is admitted among them. (89)

He is irresolute and tearful when he realizes that he must leave Laura; Marian exhibits more manly composure than himself. "She caught me by both hands — she pressed them with the strong steady grasp of a man" (148). Nevertheless, as Walter is called into service as Laura's protector and becomes the detective who will unravel the crime that has robbed her of her identity, he behaves increasingly like the Victorian ideal of manhood. Ann Cvetkovich draws a connection between Hartright's accession to patriarchal power and property (when he becomes the accepted suitor, and later the husband of Laura) and his deepening masculinity.

Nevertheless, Collins inverts traditional stereotypes of manliness and femininity in order to alter them. Laura Fairlie, who retains her role as angel in the house throughout, is a pathetic character. When Walter sets up house together with Marian and Laura (in a *ménage à trois* that must have delighted Collins as he penned it[11], he and Marian play mother and father to Laura, whose brief incarceration in a lunatic asylum has rendered her childlike. Even Laura recognizes her own helplessness.

> "I am so useless — I am such a burden on both of you," she answered, with a weary, hopeless sigh. "You work and get money, Walter, and Marian helps you. Why is there nothing I can do! You will end in liking Marian better than you like me — you will because I am so helpless!" (498–99)

Walter and Marian play a friendly deception on Laura — they tell her that Walter is selling her drawings as he sells his own:

> Her drawings, as she finished them, or tried to finish them, were placed in my hands. Marian took them from me and hid them carefully, and I set aside a little weekly tribute from my earnings, to be offered her as the price paid by strangers for the poor, faint, valueless sketches, of which I was the only purchaser. (499–500)

Laura's childlike dependency on her artist lover reminds one of David Copperfield's Dora who held his pens and believed she was helping him to compose.[12]

Laura's inability to compete economically — she has no marketable skills and several liabilities — reiterates the unfeasibility of the angel-in-the-house role for women who would be forced to earn their own living. When *The Woman in White* appeared in late 1859 with its positive protrayal of an old maid and its negative portrayal of the Victorian ideal of womanhood, it entered a fiery discussion on the condition of English women that had been heating up the pages of popular periodicals since the mid-1850s. Ideologically-opposed essayists argued about the economic and legal rights of women, examining work opportunities for "the fairer sex" as well as new legislation that affected women. Again and again the question was asked: What could England do about its growing population of impoverished, middle-class spinsters?

> An Old Maid, eh? The phrase is quite enough: you have only to mention it, and of course everybody begins to snigger, simper, or sneer.
>
> Francis Jacox, *Bentley's Miscellany*, March 1859

THE CRIMEAN WAR (1853–56) was a crucial event for English women insofar as one of the heroes it created was a heroine: Florence Nightingale. Nightingale was a single woman possessed of ambition and abilities worthy of any man of her time. Her life, fortunately, coincided with a historical moment that enabled her to develop her talents. Martha Vicinus asserts that Florence Nightingale was the most important role model for single women that the century would produce (19). Vicinus adds:

> Nightingale was exceptional in many ways — her class connections, iron determination, and brilliant analytic skills would have placed her in the forefront in any age — but her highly publicized work in military camps gave her an incomparable public image. (20)

Even contemporary commentators were quick to note that men who admired Florence Nightingale — for it was not only single women whom her deeds had impressed — were more likely to extend their esteem to other single women. An anonymous reviewer writing in the *Edinburgh Review* in January 1856 intuited that the nurse reformer's important work in the Crimea would reflect well not only on herself, but on all English women.

> From the high and the low, from the most noble among the subscribers to the Nightingale Fund to the humblest ballad singers who are singing Miss Nightingale's praises in our streets, we learn lessons of faith in the readiness with which man's esteem is given where it is earned by woman. Her whole sex will profit by the reflection of the light her example has shed upon us; and it is to be hoped that many a woman will feel it both a responsibility and an encouragement that she has lived at the same time with Florence Nightingale. ("Lectures to Ladies" 153)

By now it should be evident that the web of causes and effects that ultimately produced a significant change in the role and status of women is both dense and subtle. Nevertheless, certain events and individuals do stand out in this complex weave, and Florence Nightingale is one of them. It was soon after her exploits in the Crimea that a new series of articles on the legal and social status of women began to appear in all of the important magazines.

Margaret Oliphant, who later wrote scathing reviews of sensation novels, first took up the cudgels against women's rights in the April 1856 edition of *Blackwood's*, in a book review entitled "The Laws Concerning Women." Oliphant, reviewing a pamphlet that detailed the ways women had been wronged by marriage and property laws, attacked the writer with the rhetoric that would soon become the trademark of those opposed to more lenient legislation for women. The catchwords of this rhetoric were "natural," "pre-ordained," and "self-evident." That man should rule woman, that a husband should dominate his wife, Oliphant insists is "natural," and that the existing laws that confer on him his power to do so are also "natural." Oliphant declares that "Nature confers this official character upon the head of a household, the law has no choice but to confirm it, and all honest expediency and suitableness justifies this ordination of God and of man" (386). Oliphant concludes this piece by throwing the traditional bone to the angel in the house. Women, she declares, actually have more power than men because — although they have no economic or legal rights — they rule the house, the moral center of society (387).

As Michel Foucault's archeological digs into various fields of knowledge and history have shown us, wherever there is power, there is resistance. I would add that this is particularly evident when a long-standing balance of power is about to make a heterostatic shift in favor of the resistance. This shift happened as the 1850s wore on and surplus women became more numerous while, at the same time, mistreated wives became more vocal about the rapacity of husbands who had full legal rights to their wives' property, and even to their children in the event of divorce (which became an option for the first time in 1857).

The Matrimonial Causes Act of 1857, it should be noted, is one of the first legal inklings that there was trouble in the paradise of Victorian matrimony, that heretofore hallowed state that was so closely bound to the cult of wife and motherhood, the safe haven of home, the bliss of family life. All of the myths, interconnected as they were, began to suffer together. But this Act, which permitted certain unhappy — and very rich — spouses to get free of one another, did little to advance the rights of women. Men could petition for divorce on the basis of adultery, but women had to prove desertion, cruelty, rape, bestiality, or incest as well.[13]

T. E. Perry, reviewing the divorce bill for the *Edinburgh Review* in 1857, vehemently advocated married women's property rights. (The Married Women's Property Bill of 1857, which would have protected them, was dropped in order to pass the divorce act. It resurfaced in Parliament ten years later — just as sensation fiction was beginning its decline — and finally became law in 1870.) "The time is past," he wrote, "when the law could annihilate, by a fiction, the rights of one half of society, and repudiate the claims of that portion which stands most in need of legal protection'' (183). Perry, unlike Oliphant, found nothing natural about the law. Instead, he cites numerous instances of the unnatural ways it deprived specific women — such as Caroline Norton — of their personal inheritances and their children. Perry insists that no law can be natural when so much public sentiment is against it.

> It appears that during the last Session upwards of seventy petitions with 24,000 signatures have been presented to Parliament, complaining of the law of property as it affects married women; and if such petitions are to be weighed *pondere non numero*, it will be found that the names attached comprise some of the most eminent thinkers of our day, and nearly all the distinguished women who have made the present such a remarkable epoch of female literature. (191)

The unhappy state of marriage, particularly for women, would begin to make the spinster's lot look better than it ever had. Frances Power Cobbe, one of the feminists who stands out in this period, reprinted one of her essays in *Fraser's* in 1862 entitled ''Celibacy v. Marriage.'' Cobbe concludes, '' 'the old maid's life may be as rich, as blessed, as that of the proudest of mothers with her crown of clustering babes'' (233). Furthermore, Cobbe reasoned, ''while the utility, freedom, and happiness of a single woman's life have become greater, the knowledge of the risks of an unhappy marriage (if not the risks themselves) has become more public'' (234). Single women, for one thing, enjoyed exactly the same property rights as men.

What single women did not enjoy — and which commentators now began to discuss at great length — were equal employment rights. Mrs. Oliphant, writing in *Blackwood's* in 1858, challenged the notion that single women were any worse off than they had ever been historically.[14] Oliphant, ever opposed to change, once again made the plight of women seem ''natural.''

> There were single ladies as there were single gentlemen as long as anybody can remember, yet it is only within a very short time that writers and critics have begun to call the attention of the public to the prevalence and multiplicity of the same. (''Condition'' 141)

Oliphant argues that the statistically large numbers of surplus women cited by the author of *Women's Thoughts About Women* (the book that Oliphant is here reviewing) cannot possibly be correct; Oliphant is sure that old maids number a mere handful, that they are simply individuals ''drop[ped] . . . out of the current'' (141). Oliphant concludes

> It is, however, an unfortunate feature in the special literature which professes to concern itself with women, that it is in great part limited to personal ''cases''

and individual details, and those incidents of domestic life which it is so easy, by the slightest shade of mistaken colouring, to change the real character. (153)

Before she reaches this resounding closure to her argument, however, Mrs. Oliphant has herself indulged in a personal "case" to make her argument. The case is literary; Mrs. Oliphant discusses how Charlotte Brontë's *Jane Eyre* "bears with no small force upon the present subject" since it treats of the abysmal life of governesses (142). However, Oliphant declares, the Brontë sisters, though they suffered wretchedly as governesses, were no worse off than their brother Branwell, who had a miserable position as a tutor. Oliphant triumphantly concludes that "so far as this example goes, the theory of undue limitation and unjust restraint in respect to women certainly does not hold" (143).

Mrs. Oliphant had probably recently read Elizabeth Gaskell's *Life of Charlotte Brontë* (1857) from which she culled her facts; what is interesting is that she should have suppressed so many equally valid pieces of information about Branwell's life that were detailed in Gaskell's book. Long before Branwell was a tutor he was sent to art school — where his sisters could not follow even if they wished to — and after he failed as a painter, he became an assistant clerk to a railway company (another job not open to women in the 1840s); it was only after he was fired from this job for intemperate negligence that he took up full-time employment as a tutor. All along, Branwell had had educational and work opportunities that were denied to his sisters, but Oliphant does not choose to mention these facts.

Harriet Martineau, Charlotte Brontë's former close friend, in an anonymous essay entitled "Female Industry," published in the *Edinburgh Review* in April 1859, argued directly against thinkers like Oliphant. Martineau immediately acknowledges the problem of surplus women, and argues for broadened work opportunities for women as well as pay equal to men's.

> In a community where a larger proportion of women remain unmarried than at any known period; where a greater number of women depend on their own industry for subsistence . . . how can there be a doubt that the women will work more and more, and in aggregate ways . . . ? (322)

Martineau cites the greatest obstruction to women's education and employment as "the jealousy of men in regard to the industrial independence of women" (329).

Nevertheless, there were still plenty of people — particularly men — who agreed with Mrs. Oliphant in 1859. An anonymous article entitled "A Fear for the Future that Women Will Cease to be Womanly," published in *Fraser's* in February, lamented the damage done to that cherished myth of Victorian iconography — the angel in the house. It was hard to let her go, and the author of this piece bemoans the way that "young ladies" have changed: "the pretty ignorance, the fascinating helplessness, the charming unconsciousness that enslaved us bachelors of long ago — where are they all gone to?" (245)

The battle would rage back and forth throughout the 1860s, with feminists like Frances Power Cobbe, Harriet Martineau, and John Stuart Mill on the one side, and advocates of the old ideology about women, such as W. R. Greg, W. E. Aytoun, and John Ruskin[15] on the other. The familiar rhetoric invoking nature, God, and historical precedent would be employed again and again, just as it is in this piece by Aytoun:

> . . . by the common consent of mankind in all ages, certain vocations have been assigned to each of the sexes, as their proper and legitimate sphere of action and utility — and that any attempted readjustment of these could lead to nothing save hopeless error and confusion. (198)

What was particularly frightening to men like Aytoun was the notion that the entry of women into the working world of men would deprive women of their femininity and men of their masculinity. When males and females transgress the gender rules of work, he wrote, the result is to "make men effeminate and women masculine by tempting them to unsuitable occupations" (199).

It was exactly these gender rules that Collins broke in *The Woman in White*; further, the novel's allegiance (and by extension, the readers') is given to the masculine woman and the sensitive man.

D. A. Miller NOTES that Marian Halcombe is outside the sexual system of the novel (and, presumably, of Victorian society) because she is neither male nor female. She cannot do what males do because she lacks a penis, and she cannot be the recipient of male desire because she lacks the ability to attract men (116). Without realizing it, Miller has offered another definition of the phrase "surplus woman." At the novel's close, Marian also seems to be the extra or "surplus" woman in the household with Walter and Laura and their child, because she is not a member of this nuclear cluster. Collins, however, skews this perception of Marian's redundancy in the family by having Marian — not Laura — holding the baby (645). And the very last line of the novel is a tribute to the manly spinster as the real heroine of the story: "The long happy labour of many months is over. Marian was the good angel of our lives — let Marian end our story" (646).

Many critics of this novel, such as U. C. Knoepflmacher, D. A. Miller, and Sue Lonoff note that Collins undermines the order of the Victorian world only to restore it with a traditional happy ending. Lonoff thinks that Collins, although "his rendering of women seems enlightened from a twentieth-century perspective," is really ambivalent about the strong heroines he creates because they "ultimately set their independence aside" (138). I would counter this by saying that Collins knew his audience; he wanted to portray women as he really saw them — strong and capable — but he did not want to alienate his readers. Furthermore, the happy endings tacked on his novels do not eradicate what came before; the subversiveness is still there, and still lingers in the minds of the readers.

I would further argue that the happy ending helped Collins to disguise his real aim, social reform. In Collins's later novels, this reformatory zeal — to redress the wrongs of prostitutes, governesses, illegitimate children — became less and less disguised and, as a result, his reputation sharply declined. Swinburne is reputed to have created this cruel little couplet to describe the once-great novelist's fate: "What brought good Wilkie's genius nigh perdition? Some demon whispered — 'Wilkie! Have a mission'." Because *The Woman in White* appears to have no political bias, it offers readers ideology in its most influential form.[16] As Dinah Mulock Craik and countless of her contemporaries were aware, there was no influence on public opinion more powerful than a really popular novel.

The Woman in White was such a novel, and it does not seem too much to say that by its laudatory portrayal of an androgynous old maid, Wilkie Collins helped the movement towards broadened opportunities for single women. It is certainly true that after his novel appeared and throughout the 1860s, work opportunities for women increased and legislation, such as the 1870 Married Women's Property Act, was passed in their favor. Frances Power Cobbe noted in 1862 that the "popular prejudice against well-educated women is dying away" ("What Shall We Do with Our Old Maids?" 606), as the first ladies' colleges were instituted in England. New ones were opened throughout the 1860s. The widening sphere of education for women resulted in a widening sphere of career opportunities, a movement that would continue throughout the nineteenth century and up until our own day.

The line that began Wilkie Collins's *The Woman in White* and that inaugurated the genre of sensation fiction is often misread as a reaffirmation of Victorian sex role stereotypes. When Walter Hartright says, "This is the story of what a Woman's patience can endure, and what a Man's resolution can achieve," the reader assumes that Walter is the resolute man and that Marian or Laura is the patient woman. I beg to differ. Throughout the novel, by virtually every male character who encounters her, from Walter to Mr. Gilmore the solicitor to Fosco the wily villain, Marian is described as "resolute." Walter, who leaves Laura to go on an expedition to Central America, with no hope that he can ever win her love, is patient. Despite every hardship and the deaths of almost all of his companions, he makes his way back to England and finds her again. Throughout the period when he is tracking Fosco and solving the mystery of Laura's identity, he is patient. He holds his temper, waits for his chances, and takes them when they come. Because he is patient, he solves the case, marries Laura, and becomes the proprietor of her estate. The first line of *The Woman in White*, then, presages what the novel is really about: the subversion of sexual stereotypes. Because this is the story of what a man *with a woman's patience* can endure, and what a woman *with the resolution of a man* can achieve.

Columbia University

NOTES

1. Further references to *The Woman in White* are from the 1974 Penguin edition, edited by Julian Symons.
2. Kathleen Tillotson cites the unprecedented reader response to Collins's novel. See also Elwin. For an overview of the Sensational Sixties and the four most prominent sensation novelists — Collins, Wood, Braddon, and Reade — see Winifred Hughes. Another account of the critical reaction to sensation novels, particularly as they pertained to women and women's roles, may be found in the third volume of Helsinger, Sheets, and Veeder.
3. A number of mainstream Victorian novelists added sensational effects to their productions in this period. Dickens, in fact, had employed them much earlier; in *Bleak House* (1852–53), the "chancellor" of the rag and bone shop, Krook, dies of spontaneous combustion, which Dickens had read about in a periodical. In similar fashion, sensation novelists would later read the detailed newspaper accounts of lurid murder trials of the late 1850s and '60s and incorporate spouse poisoning, bigamy, and insanity into their titillating tales.
4. "Conduct books imply the presence of a unified middle class at a time when other representations of the social world suggest that no such class yet existed" (Armstrong 63). The industrial revolution and the changes it produced in the middle-class family required a new kind of woman. "Sexuality," Armstrong asserts, "has a history that is inseparable from the political history of England" (15).
5. Anti-angel heroines were not new to fiction — one has only to think of Thackerary's Becky Sharp in *Vanity Fair* (1847–48) — but Collins's extremely *positive* portrayal of an unwomanly woman was new. Other sensation novelists would devalue the angel in the house by showing her to be a demon in disguise (as M.E. Braddon did in *Lady Audley's Secret*), but Collins went further — he not only debased the old icon, he minted a new one: the androgynous heroine.
6. Altick treats this phenomenon in *Victorian Studies in Scarlet*. He tentatively draws a connection between the sensational murders of the 1850s and '60s and the birth of sensation fiction; in *Deadly Encounters* he sees a direct cause and effect relationship between two sensational murders in the summer of 1861 and subsequent sensation fiction. Thomas Boyle argues for a subtler connection between real crime and its literary manifestations; he emphasizes the complex weave of cause and effect surrounding sensation fiction, asserting that there is not "any really extended pattern of imitation of real-life crime from the newspapers. So these are not 'non-fiction novels' or 'true fiction'" (146). However, Boyle acknowledges that "almost all the writers used newspapers as sources of information in one way or another" (146).

7. Braddon founded *Belgravia* in 1866 and Ellen Price Wood acquired *The Argosy* in 1867.

8. Vicinus points out that most surplus women during this period were from the working class, because the middle class comprised only fifteen percent of the total population. Nevertheless, most contemporary discussions of surplus women focused on the plight of middle-class spinsters. "The conviction shared by all middle-class commentators that the number of unmarried middle-class women was steadily increasing was due to their increase in absolute numbers and their increased visibility, brought about in part by their acceptance of paid work and in part by the public discussion of their plight" (27).

9. Laura Fairlie is the legitimate and Anne Catherick is the illegimate daughter of a dissolute aristocratic father. Besides passing on his looks, one can infer that Philip Fairlie also passed on his mental instability, the other trait that Laura and Anne share. That the Fairlies represent a kind of physical, mental, and moral degeneration of the upper class may be further seen in the still-living Mr. Frederick Fairlie (Laura's uncle) whose nervous disorder, intensely fey mannerisms, and cruelty to servants are persistently pointed up by Collins. The other representative of English aristocracy in this novel, Sir Percival Glyde, is, of course, an out-and-out villain: a coarse, brutal drunkard who does not stick at the notion of killing his wife to claim her inheritance, nor of confining Anne Catherick to an insane asylum to keep her from revealing his life's guilty secret.

10. Lambert suggests that Marian has lesbian designs on her half-sister (13). The evidence does not seem to support this, especially in light of what we know about the strong bonds of Victorian sisterhood and the effusive expressions of love permissible between sisters (and brothers) during this period. (The relationship between Florence and Paul Dombey in Dickens's *Dombey and Son* (1847–48) had been similarly misread by late twentieth-century critics.) For more about the relationships of Victorian female siblings, see Helena Michie.

11. Collins never married, but he supported two mistresses, Caroline Graves credited by Davis as the original "woman in white") and, later, Martha Rudd. Collins formed a liaison with Rudd after Graves left him to marry a plumber. When she returned, disenchanted with her marriage, Collins supported both his mistresses *au même temps*. The untenable legal status of illegitimate children — Collins had several — is a minor theme in *The Woman in White* (Sir Percival Glyde's terrible secret is that he's a bastard) and a major one in *No Name* (1862).

12. Laura's inability to compose — to tell her own story — is underscored by the structure of the novel itself. Marian writes two of the narratives, but Laura does not write any. Laura can never, therefore, be the author of herself, but is dependent upon the way other narrators represent her.

13. Nor did the divorce act provide for spouses who wanted to get divorced for reasons other than adultery. Charles Dickens, one of the Victorian era's greatest spokesmen for the sacred bonds of marriage and family life, found himself in an uncomfortable position in the same year that Parliament ratified the Matrimonial Causes Act. Desperately unhappy with his wife of twenty-two years, Catherine Hogarth Dickens, the novelist longed to break out of his marriage. But according to the new act, he would have to prove Catherine's adultery to divorce her legally, and Catherine had committed no such crime. Her crimes were that she was fat, fortyish, complacent, and no intellectual match for her brilliant husband. In 1858, Dickens separated from Catherine. He gave her a house and settled 600 pounds a year on her for maintenance. For the rest of his life he also maintained Ellen Ternan, the mistress whom the law did not permit him to marry.

14. Besides the other logical problems with Mrs. Oliphant's argument, it begs the initial question. By invoking historical precedent, Oliphant avoids the grievance itself: the limited employment opportunities for single women who had to support themselves.

15. Ruskin's *Sesame and Lilies* appeared in 1865, and included the essay entitled "Of Queens' Gardens." This essay is one of the most persuasive pieces of writing celebrating the angel-in-the-house myth and its attendant fantasies of the idyllic family and happy home that one can find in the Victorian period; as such, it is frequently cited by scholars studying the stereotypes and realities of Victorian family life. What renders it additionally fascinating, however, is that Ruskin should have been the man to write it. Ruskin's own wife, Effie Gray, succeeded in annuling their marriage in 1854 on the grounds that it had never been consummated. Ruskin, who admitted that he found his wife's adult body "disgusting," later fell in love with the young girl he tutored, Rose La Touche — a passion that was unrequited. At no point did Ruskin's real life resemble the familial fantasy he sketched so poignantly in "Of Queens' Gardens."

16. To those who would argue that Marian Halcombe cannot really represent the impoverished surplus women of the 1850s and '60s because she does not need a job, let me say this: Collins in this novel was not striking at the issue directly — as did Cobbe, Martineau, Oliphant, and many other commentators — but obliquely. What Collins was doing was reducing the power of a potent icon — the angel in the house — by contrasting her with a strong lovable, laudable new version of womanhood: the androgynous spinster. In his next novel, *No Name* (1862), Collins treated the issue of single women's employment more overtly but less successfully. Magdalen Vanstone and her sister, Norah, the heroines of *No Name*, lose their inheritance and are forced to work — one as a servant, the other as a governess. But *No Name* did not capture the imagination of the public as its predecessor had done; its lessons were not disguised *enough*.

WORKS CITED

[Ainsworth, W.H.] "The Present State of Literature." *Bentley's Miscellany* 49 (February 1861): 215–19.

Altick, Richard D. *Deadly Encounters: Two Victorian Sensations*. Philadelphia: U of Pennsylvania P, 1986.

———. *Victorian Studies in Scarlet*. New York: W.W. Norton, 1970.

Armstrong, Nancy. *Desire and Domestic Fiction: A Political History of the Novel*. Oxford: Oxford U P, 1987.

[Aytoun, W.E.] "The Rights of Woman." *Blackwood's Edinburgh Magazine* 92 (August 1862): 183–201.

Banks, J.A., and Olive Banks. *Feminism and Family Planning in Victorian England*. New York: Schocken Books, 1964.

Boyle, Thomas. *Black Swine in the Sewers of Hampstead: Beneath the Surface of Victorian Sensationalism*. New York: Viking, 1989.

Braddon, Mary Elizabeth. *Lady Audley's Secret*. 1862. Ed. Jennifer Uglow. London: Virago P, 1985.

Christ, Carol [T.] "Victorian Masculinity and the Angel in the House." *A Widening Sphere: Changing Roles of Victorian Women*. Ed. Martha Vicinus. Bloomington: Indiana U P, 1977. 146–62.

Cobbe, Frances Power. "Celibacy v. Marriage." *Fraser's* 65 (February 1862): 228–35.
———. "What Shall We Do With Our Old Maids?" *Fraser's* 66 (November 1862): 594–610.
Collins, Wilkie. *No Name.* 1862. New York: Stein and Day, 1967.
———. "The Woman in White," first installment. *All the Year Round* 2 (26 November 1859): 95–104.
———. *The Woman in White.* 1861. New York: Penguin, 1974.
Cvetkovich, Ann. "Ghostlier Determinations: The Economy of Sensation and *The Woman in White.*" *Novel* 23 (Fall 1989): 24–43.
[Dallas, E.S.] "Lady Audley's Secret." *The Times* (18 November 1862): 4.
[———.] "Popular Literature — the Periodical Press." *Blackwood's* 85 (January 1859):96–112.
Davidoff, Leonore, and Catherine Hall. *Family Fortunes: Men and Women of the English Middle Class, 1780–1850.* Chicago: U of Chicago P, 1987.
Davis, Nuel Pharr. *The Life of Wilkie Collins.* Urbana: U of Illinois P, 1956.
Dickens, Charles. *Letters of Charles Dickens to Wilkie Collins.* Ed. Laurence Hutton. New York: Harper & Brothers, 1892.
———. *A Tale of Two Cities*, final installment. *All the Year Round* 2 (26 Nov. 1859).
Elwin, Malcolm. *Victorian Wallflowers.* London: J. Cape, 1934.
"A Fear for the Future that Women Will Cease to be Womanly." *Fraser's* 59 (February 1859): 243–48.
Foucault, Michel. *The History of Sexuality.* Trans. Robert Hurley. New York: Pantheon, 1978.
[Greg, W.R.] "Why Are Women Redundant?" *National Review* 15 (1862): 434–60.
Helsinger, Elizabeth K., Robin Lauterbach Sheets, and William Veeder. *The Woman Question: Society and Literature in Britain and America, 1837–1883.* Volume 3. Chicago: U of Chicago P, 1983.
Hughes, Winifred. *The Maniac in the Cellar: Sensation Novels of the 1860s.* Princeton: Princeton U P, 1980.
[Jacox, Francis.] "Old Maids." *Bentley's Miscellany* 45 (1859): 345–55.
Knoepflmacher, U.C. "The Counterworld of Victorian Fiction and *The Woman in White.*" *The Worlds of Victorian Fiction.* Ed. Jerome H. Buckley. Cambridge, Mass.: Harvard U P, 1975. 351–70.
Lambert, Gavin. *The Dangerous Edge.* London: Barrie and Jenkins, 1975.
Leavy, Barbara Fass. "Wilkie Collins's Cinderella: The History of Psychology and *The Woman in White.*" *Dickens Studies Annual* 10 (1982): 91–141.
"Lectures to Ladies on Practical Subjects." *Edinburgh Review* 103 (January 1856): 146–53.
Lonoff, Sue. *Wilkie Collins and His Victorian Readers.* New York: AMS P, 1982.
[Mansel, H.L.] "Sensation Novels." *The Quarterly Review* 113 (April 1863): 481–514.
[Martineau, Harriet]. "Female Industry." *Edinburgh Review* 109 (April 1859):293–336.
Michie, Helena. " 'There Is No Friend Like a Sister': Sisterhood as Sexual Difference." *ELH* 56. 2 (Summer 1989): 401–21.
Mill, John Stuart. *The Subjection of Women.* 1869. Cambridge, Mass.: MIT P, 1970.
Miller, D.A. "*Cage aux Folles:* Sensation and Gender in Wilkie Collins's *The Woman in White.*" *The Nineteenth-Century British Novel.* Ed. Jeremy Hawthorn. London: Edward Arnold, 1986. 95–126.

[Mulock, Dinah.] "To Novelists — and a Novelist." *Macmillan's* 3 (April 1861): 441–48.

[Oliphant, Margaret.] "The Condition of Women." *Blackwood's* 83 (February 1858): 139–54.

[————.] "The Laws Concerning Women." *Blackwood's* 79 (April 1856): 379–87.

[————.] "Novels." *Blackwood's* 102 (Sept. 1867): 257–280.

[————.] "Sensation Novels." *Blackwood's* 91 (May 1862): 564–84.

[Perry, T.E.] "Rights and Liabilities of Husband and Wife." *Edinburgh Review* 105 (January 1857): 181–205.

[Smith, William Henry.] "Dr Mansel's Bampton Lectures." *Blackwood's* 86 (July 1859): 48–66.

[Stephen, Fitzjames.] "The License of Modern Novelists." *Edinburgh Review* 106 (July 1857): 124–56.

Tillotson, Kathleen. "The Lighter Reading of the Eighteen-Sixties. *The Woman in White*. Boston: Houghton Mifflin, 1969.

Vicinus, Martha. *Independent Women: Work and Community for Single Women, 1850–1920*. Chicago: U of Chicago P, 1985.

Wood, Ellen Price (Mrs. Henry). *East Lynne*. 1861. New Brunswick, N.J.: Rutgers U P, 1984.

Yates, Edmund. "Interview with Wilkie Collins." *The World* (26 December 1877): 4–6.

THAT ARNOLDIAN WRAGG:
ANARCHY AS MENSTROSITY IN
VICTORIAN SOCIAL CRITICISM

By Susan Walsh

JUST BEYOND THE CONTRACTING GORGE of the "Mad Maid's Bellows-pipe" and the "Black Notch," sequestered within a "purple, hopper-shaped hollow" irrigated by a "redly and demoniacally" boiling river, lies the industrial purgatory of Melville's "The Paradise of Bachelors and The Tartarus of Maids" (215, 219). Inside the "whited sepulchre" of a New England paper mill, the blanched bodies of "blank" female laborers move like "mere cogs to the wheels" of a great iron gearwork (216, 220, 221). Scores of these anemic women attend merciless engines whose overwhelming, piston-like thrum converts factory workers into mute and obeisant slaves. The systolic pump or heart of the mill is a massive water-wheel turned by the valley's "Blood River," a "turbid brick-colored stream" that emblematizes both the human circulatory and the female menstrual system (215). In Melville's telling, it is as if the blood from the stooped, probably amenorrheaic women has been redirected into the roiling industrial current. And, in fact, in a "rag-room" swimming with poisonous lint, the factory's "maids" shred heaps of rags that eventually join with and absorb water from the red stream. Upon this chamber of death depends the "albuminous" mixture of rags and water that makes the beginning of foolscap. Slowly and steadily, the pulp flows from two vats into the "abdominal heat" of the rolling room. There, human and "metallic necessity" meet as the giant apparatus, like a woman's body, shapes spider-threads of matter into warm quires of tabula rasa (224, 227). The clockwork precision of the mill's involuntary gestation and expulsion of paper, every nine minutes "to a second," is both magnificent and terrible to behold (226).

In the above exposé of industrial working conditions, Melville assumes that women are biologically determined, that they inexorably bend to the will of the mysterious uterine engine with its one immutable purpose. Whereas the three men in his story — "Old Bach," the mill owner; Cupid, his agent; and the unnamed "seedsman"/narrator — move about the premises freely, exercising proprietary interest and control, in contrast, the maids illustrate the "unbudging fatality" of biological reproduction that leads all women a "blank, raggy life" (227, 223). Melville's narrator pities the tartarean workers. At the same time, however, they offer a symbolic solution to an ideological problem increasingly apparent within nineteenth-century economic thought.[1]

Laissez-faire capitalism, with its competing interests of management and labor, represented economic man as both autonomous actor and industrial cog, as both captain and worker. Amidst growing fears that men were trapped within the depersonalizing processes of production and exchange, the disturbing differences between the free master and the subordinate man were displaced, relocated within the biological differences between men and women. As Sally Shuttleworth has noted, manhood came to be "articulated against and defined by its opposite: while the attributes of self-control and self-help were aligned with masculinity, woman was increasingly viewed as an automaton at the mercy of her body" (64). Women's bodies provided analogues for the exploitation of human labor because women themselves were thought to engage in a "natural" form of debilitating production. Melville can use the female body as a metaphor for factory oppression precisely because his readers would have perceived the female reproductive system as inherently mechanistic and killing.

And indeed, nineteenth-century advertising and medical writing abounds in images of women at the mercy of a menstrual process which, save for the ministrations of intervening doctors, could cause nervousness, hysteria, or insanity.[2] In much of this literature, as in "The Tartarus of Maids," writers typically speak of the female body as an organic machine, with the uterus as its seat or center of circulation. It is not surprising, then, that the mechanizing and pathologizing of the menstrual process, along with the workings of the uterine economy in general, became a resource for displacing other social problems — the increasing antagonism between the classes, for instance, or the disturbing implications of mechanistic models of political economy. As Shuttleworth reminds us, we cannot comprehend Victorian preoccupation with "regulating the circulation of the female uterine economy" apart from "the wider social and economic ideologies of circulation that underpinned the emergent social division of labor within industrial England" (48).

My argument is that the opposite is equally true: we cannot fully grasp Victorian anxieties about the downward slide into socioeconomic anarchy without understanding how those fears were sometimes articulated through embedded metaphors of the female body. In this essay, I shall be looking at several works by Ruskin and Arnold in which the image of the menarchic woman becomes an index of national socioeconomic health. Both of these self-appointed social critics employ a two-part strategy of diagnosis and recuperation in order to accomplish part of their ideological work. First, in symbolically charged images of female debasement, they locate *within women's bodies* the anarchistic threat posed by laissez-faire economics, the very system that both guaranteed and threatened to end bourgeois prosperity. Second, as they move from symptomatology to projected cure, they set against the model of woman-as-disordered-machine the well-known forms and functions of pure domestic womanhood, one of the cornerstones of economic paternalism. Ruskin's and Arnold's appeals to domestic ideology, however, end up emphasizing what they wish to suppress: the middle-class woman, the woman whose refined spirituality should steer England towards reform, nevertheless lives in a body. And that body makes her prone to the very disorders she is supposed to correct.

I

BY MID-CENTURY it was visibly apparent that laissez-faire economics did not really work to everyone's benefit; that wealth was not distributed "as by an invisible hand"; that the impoverished and disease-stricken industrial worker would not settle for political as well as economic disenfranchisement; that the industrial waste accumulating around manufacturing centers would one day convert England's green and pleasant land into a dust heap. In order to highlight the disequilibrium and horror of "Do Nothing" economics, Arnold and Ruskin turn to the image of the menstruous female laborer tyrannized by internal and external forces of pollution. In so doing, they assume, but do not formally articulate, several functional equivalencies between laissez-faire economy and woman's uterine economy. Oversimplified, and without much attention to the variety of medical opinion on the subject, those correspondences might be sketched in the following way: women's bodies are inefficient reproducers of society. Every kind of uterine process, from menses to pregnancy to birth, constitutes a falling away from health. Women's periodic illnesses are systemic, endangering physical, intellectual, and emotional well-being.[3] The menstrual discharge in particular is a recurring sign of women's "natural" dysfunction insofar as it is understood as impure, "unnatural" waste and as the announcement of the non-child, the absence of conception.

Likewise, laissez-faire economics is an inefficient, ecologically and morally sick system wherein the production of goods is inevitably attended by foul excretions. Blackened skies, cholera epidemics, slag mounds, sickness and unrest among the poor were among its unintended results — though it should be noted that Herbert Spencer argued that Nature had providentially arranged to slough off the indigent poor by attaching "penalties" of disease to their "ignorance and imbecility" (qtd. in Wiltshire 142). But not everyone was so sanguine about the ethics of such models of economic evacuation. In pointing out the diseased, anarchic potential of the laissez-faire system, Arnold and Ruskin, like Spencer, draw upon the long-standing homology between the social organism and the human body. Ruskin and Arnold modify it, however, by making that human body female, a body already known to be undermined by pollution and disorder. When the economy of the body politic is imaged in terms of the uterine economy of the female body, they seem to ask, what is revealed? What does a re-gendered representation of the body politic — *femina economicus* — make visible?

In "The Function of Criticism at the Present Time," it makes visible the anarchic threat posed by Elizabeth Wragg, the infamous subject of Arnold's celebrated "Wragg is in custody" passage. Horrible and pathetic, she embodies the destructive potential not only of the underclass, but also of the diseased processes of the female body. Hers is the biological model of womanhood Arnold has in mind in *Culture and Anarchy* and *Friendship's Garland* when he works so hard to rescue the middle-class woman from the Deceased Wife's Sister Bill. Wragg's example suggests that all women, including middle-class daughters and wives, are contaminated by their bodies and liable to fall, economically as well as ethically. If woman is morally, socially, and physically disabled, however, she cannot fulfill her proper function as the moral "guarantor" of laissez-faire (Poovey, "Speaking" 36). In light of what Wragg represents, then, the self-congratulatory "dithyrambs" of Arnold's favorite whipping boys, Sir Charles Adderley and John Arthur Roebuck, seem ridiculous indeed.

"The old Anglo-Saxon race," Adderley had effused to the Warwickshire farmers, according to Arnold, "are the best breed in the whole world." "I ask you," Roebuck had seconded to the Sheffield cutlers, "whether, the world over or in past history, there is anything like it?" (3: 272). Against Roebuck's enthusiastic embrace of laissez-faire, Arnold dramatically juxtaposes the celebrated newspaper report:

> A shocking child murder has just been committed at Nottingham. A girl named Wragg left the workhouse there on Saturday morning with her young illegitimate child. The child was soon afterwards found dead on Mapperly [sic] Hills, having been strangled. Wragg is in custody. (3: 273)

Curiously, Arnold's famous dilation upon her case focuses not so much upon the crime itself as upon its metonymic representative, the surname Wragg. That is because, like "Ernest" in *The Importance of Being Earnest*, it is a name sufficient to produce "vibrations." Arnold repeats, italicizes, even exclaims it — "*Wragg!*" — as if each iteration produces in writer and reader alike a shudder of perverse recognition. But of what?

I think it is Wragg's menstrosity, closely linked to the post-partum madness that makes a desperate mother turn her infant back into lifeless matter, to discharge it as detritus upon the Mapperley Hills.[4] Wragg's sickness, acted upon if not catalyzed by the wretchedness of the workhouse, leads to a kind of abortion after the fact. Certainly the depravity of this young murderesss, as Arnold describes it, embodies the corporeal "grossness" of her sex and class. She both bears the trace of woman's "original shortcoming" and bequeaths to her illegitimate offspring a crushing legacy of squalor and death. Indeed, that barbarous surname — Wragg — is the ultimate female marker (3: 273). The adjectives with which Arnold surrounds her case — grossness, hideousness, grimness, inhumanness — suggest that as a "breeder" of "our old Anglo-Saxon breed" she herself emblematizes the dark tenements teeming with life and infanticide, the polluted drains of the female body, and the diseased recesses of the industrial slums. As the depraved thing that destroys its own issue, she embodies (literally) the genocidal potential of the laissez-faire economic machine.

Wragg's menstruousness is displayed so prominently that we miss it, like Poe's purloined letter — or, more precisely, we misidentify it, mistaking our act of recognition for an aesthetic recoil against the "harsh," "ill-favoured" vulgarities of a common English name. And just as Wragg encodes a female sort of wastage, her sterility is amplified by three other double-g names that point to a male version of non-reproduction. In this case, another sort of body fluid is spilled, or rather, improperly and improvidently deposited. "Has any one reflected," Arnold asks, "what a touch of grossness in our race, what an original shortcoming in the more delicate spiritual perceptions, is shown by the natural growth amongst us of such hideous names — Higginbottom, Stiggins, Bugg! In Ionia and Attica they were luckier in this respect than 'the best race in the world' " (3: 273). These three surnames imply a violation of the male spermatic economy, yet another "original shortcoming" enjoying a "natural" growth on England's shores. In fact, they pretty much form a complete sentence. "By the Ilissus," Arnold proclaims, "there was no Wragg, poor thing" (3: 273). By the Ilissus, however, or in Ionia or Attica, there may well have been Higginbottoms, Stigginses, and Buggs, for by that selfsame Ilissus, Socrates and Phaedrus had discoursed upon homosexual *Eros*, the kindred love that impels philosophers towards Truth. When Higginbottom, Stiggins, and Bugg are placed in the context of the *Phaedrus* and its homosexual discourse, they, like Wragg, suggest a kind of sterility and death. Higginbottom, Stiggins, and Bugg were, as R. H. Super informs us, names of "great antiquity" in England (3: 479). So much the worse: between the "Wraggishness" of Wragg and the "Buggery" of Bugg — the name that dares to speak its love — Adderley's "old Anglo-Saxon breed" is in a sad reproductive way.

For Arnold, the "final touch" of the newspaper report is the blunt omission of Wragg's first name, the "sex lost," "the superfluous Christian name lopped off" (3: 274). In a sense, however, this unceremonious amputation is little different from Arnold's own semiotic practice in "The Function of Criticism at the Present Time," where he extends the process of objectification that the newspaper had begun. Once Wragg's given name, her individual distinctness, has been "lopped off," she is free to be used as a cultural sign within a widening field of reference. The reporter's terse recitation of details already places her within the catalogues of misery familiar from Martineau, Gaskell, Mrs. Tonna, Parliamentary Papers, the ubiquitous sensationalism of crime reports. Nottingham, a lace and hosiery center, more specifically associates her with the ranks of distressed needlewomen and factory workers profiled by the above literatures.[5] The "shocking child-murder" further locates her within public debates about the New Poor Law of 1834, which had made it virtually impossible for unwed mothers like Wragg to escape the workhouse without murdering or "throwing away" their children in baby farms.[6] As Ann Higginbotham has argued, stereotypes of the irrational mother's wild response to unwanted pregnancy eventually led to the Infanticide Act of 1922, which "declared all mothers to be potentially insane for the first few months after giving birth" (337).

But it is Arnold who completes the transformation of Wragg into a thing, a tattered cast-off of a commodity culture. Insofar as her own uterine economy provides an analogue for the laissez-faire system, Wragg's reproductive dysfunction raises doubts about whether the "cash nexus" is moral enough or stable enough to confer anything more than a provisional prosperity. As the antithesis of "our old Anglo-Saxon breed" and the epitome of laissez-faire, Elizabeth Wragg comes to stand, not for herself, but for an anarchic social and political economy whose factories spawn abominations. "Mr. Roebuck," Arnold concludes, "will have a poor opinion of an adversary who replies to his defiant songs of triumph only by murmuring under his breath, *Wragg is in custody*; but in no other way will these songs of triumph be induced . . . to fall into a softer and truer key" (3: 274). While it may appear as if Arnold means to liberate the working class from Roebuck and Adderley's sentimentalized portrait of the happy nonexploited laborer, he actually works to reestablish Victorian classism with his ugly, jarring portrait of Wragg. She becomes a corrective, unsentimental refrain to Roebuck and Adderley's urban-pastoral hymn.

When the defects of laissez faire are thus "naturalized" as being like a woman's chronic disability, however, they begin to seem irremediable, just as the woman's body, despite constant medical intervention, finally eludes total health. To posit some sort of solution, then, in *Culture and Anarchy* and *Friendship's Garland* Arnold locates woman outside the marketplace red in tooth and claw, depathologizing her and implicitly restoring the original masculine form to the homology between the economic and the human body. In "Our Liberal Practitioners," the final essay of *Culture and Anarchy*, Arnold extolls the refining virtues of a woman whose admirable delicacy throws the savage proclivities of Elizabeth Wragg into sharp relief: the Philistine wife. If Wragg, as lower-class worker, embodies the dysfunctional machinery of laissez-faire economics, the Philistine wife serves as that system's guarantor of cultural health, economic stability, and social harmony. Where Wragg, as child-murderer, enacts the anarchic potential of industrial capitalism through the menstruous madness her surname connotes, in *Culture and Anarchy* the Philistine wife remains cordoned off from the tainted processes of free-trade and the female uterine economy. Safely harbored within an essentialized, desexualized domestic space, she tacitly invites the Philistine husband to operate within her cleansed ethical field, to govern the "arbitrary range of his personal action" according to "the subtle instinctive propensions and repugnances of the person with whose life his own life is bound up" (5: 207).[7] But the liberty-loving Philistine is too caught up in his fetish-worship of radical individualism, his desire to "do as he likes," to benefit from his wife's "finer shades of feeling" (5: 205, 207). Were he not so "insensible," Arnold implies, he would see the women of his class standing ready to help usher in the triumph of Culture under the blazon of "feminine nature," the "subtle instinctive propensions" of the "feminine ideal" (5: 207–8).

But, Arnold argues, the Philistine husband will not harken to his wife. Instead, he pursues the fool's paradise offered by the Deceased Wife's Sister Bill, that "very interesting operation" aimed at enabling "a man to marry his deceased wife's sister" (5: 205).[8] In Arnold's estimation, as one biographer has put it, the bill threatened to undercut the partial victory of culture already discernible in current marriage practices, practices "which had been won, painfully and with effort, from the unbridled promiscuity of primitive life" (G. W. S. Russell, qtd. in Anderson 79).[9] According to the bill's critics, the "unbridled promiscuity of primitive life" was precisely the atavistic condition to which the measure would return the sexual relations of English men and women. To convey what this reckless endangerment would mean, Arnold borrows a favorite rhetorical gambit from the Parliamentary and newspaper debates surrounding the controversy. For over twenty years, and with undiminished verve, proponents and opponents of the bill had spun out mini-melodramas about who the bill would protect and who it would destroy. As Margaret Morganroth Gullette has remarked, these debates often read like fiction-writing contests featuring a "second-chance plot," and pitting heroes against scoundrels, victims against opportunists, portraits of innocence against profiles of guilt (153).

Who, the bill's supporters sentimentally asked, is more naturally suited to take the motherless child to her bosom than its aunt? Especially if the dying wife requests it? That child's grandmother, or paternal aunt, or "active, cleverly, good-tempered neighbour," its critics retorted (Hansard 195: 1310 [21 April 1869]). For surely, the detractors claimed, any widower and sister-in-law who chafed within a platonic cohabitation must be motivated by shameful carnality, not by a "principle of prudence" (Hansard 195: 1294 [21 April 1869] directed solely towards the welfare of bereft children, as the proponents argued. Surely those profligates who acted upon illicit desire were traffickers in a "free trade in fornication" (*The Saturday Review*, 16 June 1883, 754), if not violators of the "one-flesh" doctrine promulgated by St. Paul and Gladstone, his latter-day spokesman.[10] Surely the very possibility of marriage with a deceased wife's sister would inject jealousy and suspicion into the beautiful love between sister and wife and sully the "stainless intercourse" between husband and sister-in-law. And who could doubt, as *The Saturday Review* dolefully suggested, that once sisters-in-law became "extinct," wives deprived of their resident "sheet anchor of daily life" would be unable to resist forming "other associations" (*The Saturday Review*, 16 June 1883, 755; 24 April 1869, 548).

When Arnold comes to offer his version of the Deceased Wife's Sister plot in *Culture and Anarchy* and *Friendship's Garland*, then, he is not alone in challenging the pious narrative of the sober second marriage advanced by the bill's supporters. Characteristically, he enters the thick of the fray, scripting narratives in which the bill all but lurks in the middle-class doorway twirling its mustachio, eager to drag the women of the house back down into the barbaric regions of "unbridled promiscuity," down, in short, into the world of Mapperley Hills. His hue and cry in *Culture and Anarchy* against "the great sexual insurrection of our Anglo-Teutonic race" is in many respects but a louder refrain of "Wragg is in custody," now clamorous rather than muttered under the breath (5: 207).

The Deceased Wife's Sister drama in "Our Liberal Practitioners" offers a wide spectrum of characters, from the infamous to the seemingly innocuous, who stand in for widowers desirous of wedding their deceased wives' sisters. Through allusions and brief scenarios, Arnold offers several kinds of matrimonial extravagence either perpetrated by a liberty-loving profligate, or endorsed by an apostle of "doing as one likes," or both. Collectively, these illustrations are meant to give the impression that the Liberals' notorious "nostrum," as sponsored by Thomas Chambers, was based upon, connected with, or otherwise compromised by the dubious morality of the precedents Arnold rounds up. Through their scandalous examples, ranging from hypocritic legalism to righteous polygamy to adultery to just plain conjugal excess, they give the lie to cultural narratives interested in presenting bereaved widowers and deceased wives' sisters as being "as good, as moral, as religious" as anybody else

(Hansard 183: 299 [2 May 1866]). The names of the libertines are diverse, if not legion: Henry VIII, whose gluttonous "craving for forbidden fruit" was matched only by his "craving for legality"[11]; Mr. Hepworth Dixon, proselytizer for the Mormons, and the "Colenso of love and marriage"[12]; John Humphrey Noyes, bellwether of the Oneida free-love collective in America[13]; and lastly, King Solomon, Israel's "wisest king," most remarkable in this context for his full complement of "seven hundred wives and three hundred concubines" (5: 206, 208).

"Concubines," Arnold's concluding word on the subject in "Our Liberal Practitioners," neatly, if balefully, encapsulates what is at stake here. It is "the feminine nature, the feminine ideal" personified by the Philistine wife, the moral instructress identified as playing such an important role in the struggle towards Culture. Arnold protects her from her body in "Our Liberal Practitioners" by etherealizing her into "instinctive propensions and repugnances." But because he needs to show how she is imperilled, he reduces her unmarried sister to *corpus* entirely, representing her as a body fit for a king's seraglio, a body for the begetting of Henrican heirs, a body to be circulated, harem-scarum, in an American free-love commune. When he continues his ridicule of the Deceased Wife's Sister Bill in *Friendship's Garland*, he presents the unmarried middle-class woman, like Elizabeth Wragg, as both social victim and social threat. For by mid-century, Victorians had begun to perceive the swelling ranks of "odd" women as a cause for alarm. The sheer numbers of "supernumerary" spinsters, in fact, were greeted by William R. Greg as "positively and relatively . . . indicative of an unwholesome social state" (qtd. in Showalter, *Sexual Anarchy* 19). They were yet another unintended, accumulating side-effect of nineteenth-century economics.

In *Friendship's Garland*, Arnold assigns the role of the "redundant" woman to Miss Hannah, sister to the dying Mrs. Bottles. For even though the last words of *Culture and Anarchy* are, quite literally, "deceased wife's sister," (5: 229), as if the thought of marriage to her constitutes the height of absurdity and the anarchy of anarchies, the final curtain does not drop upon the Deceased Wife's Sister drama until the bathetic death of Mrs. Bottles in *Friendship's Garland* (1871). This collection of sardonic letters written to the *Pall Mall Gazette* is dense with humorous caricatures, including Baron Arminius Von Thunder-ten-Tronckh, a cantankerous Prussian Carlyle who loves to fulminate against the British, especially its middle-class representative, Mr. Bottles, a rich Reigate manufacturer "something in the bottle way" (5: 38). In Letter 8 (8 June 1869), these adversaries are joined by "Adolescens Leo," a young turk reporter for *The Daily Telegraph*, and a meek, retiring, Gulliveresque character named Matthew Arnold. Here, Arnold as satirist does a fair imitation of Edmund Burke's "return . . . upon himself." Specifically, he is moved in the case of the Deceased Wife's Sister Bill to speak, like Burke and Balaam, from "the opposite side of the question" — to consider how women might be surprisingly empowered by the bill (3: 267).

As recorded by Leo's "sparkling pen," the scene opens upon the "melancholy occasion" of Mrs. Bottles's demise (5: 313). Congregated at the Bottles mansion in a spirit more resembling the smoking room of a men's club than a deathbed vigil are young Leo; his friend "Nick," the Paris correspondent for *The Daily Telegraph*; that "offensive young Prussian," Arminius; Arminius's new young man (obviously Frederic Harrison) for whom he has thrown over Arnold; a Baptist minister married to his deceased wife's sister (a relic from the old days before the Bottleses had prospered their way into the Anglican Church); Job Bottles, Mr. Bottles's Stock Exchange brother; Bottles himself; Hannah, Mrs. Bottles's no-longer-youthful sister; Mary Jane, Mrs. Bottles's attractive niece, and Matthew Arnold: the only one of the company to be found "snivelling and crying in a corner" — unmanned and distraught, it would appear, from the double derelictions of Arminius and Mrs. B. (5: 314).

Addressing himself to "Nick" of the diabolically salty wit, Leo turns speculative:

> "They say," I began, "that if Mr. T. Chambers's excellent bill, which the Liberal party are carrying with such decisive majorities, becomes law, the place of poor Mrs. Bottles will be taken by her sister Hannah, whom you have just seen. Nothing could be more proper; Mrs. Bottles wishes it, Miss Hannah wishes it, this reverend friend of the family, who has himself made a marriage of the same kind, wishes it, everybody wishes it." "Everybody but old Bottles himself, I should think," retorted my friend: "don't envy him at all! — shouldn't so much mind if it were the younger one, though." (5: 315)

Excited by Nick's off-the-cuff hypothetical, Leo makes extrapolative leaps of his own. " 'And why not the younger one, Nick?' said I, gently: 'why not? Either as a successor to Miss Hannah or in lieu of Miss Hannah, why not?' " What follows is an inspired parody of John Bright's speech to the House of Commons on 21 April 1869 in which Arnold travesties the supporters' best adoptive mother argument. "Let us apply John Bright's crucial tests," Leo begins. "Is [Mary Jane] his first cousin? Could there be a more natural companion for Selina and the other Bottles girls? . . . If they got married . . . and if you were to meet them on the boulevard at Paris during their wedding tour, should you go up to Bottles and say: Mr. Bottles, you are a profligate man?" "Oh dear, no," returns Nick, with a "slight rapid droop of one eyelid"; "I should never dream of it" (5: 315).

Leo's loopy enthusiasm makes for great comedy, but Arnold devotes most of his energy to seconding the critics' "where will it stop?" argument (if marriage with the deceased wife's sister now, can marriage with the deceased wife's niece — or mother, or daughter — be far behind?). In wilder and wilder permutations, Leo inflects that argument with the inexorability of Greek tragedy — or of French farce:

> You noticed Mr. Job Bottles. You must have seen his gaze resting on Mary Jane. But what with his cigars, his claret, his camellias, and the state of the money-market, Mr. Job Bottles is not a marrying man just at this moment. His brother is; but his brother cannot last for ever. . . . We have heard of the patience of Job; how natural, if his brother marries Mary Jane now, that Job . . . may wish, when she is a widow some five years hence, to marry her himself. And we have arrangements which make this illegal! (5: 317)

Utterly vanquished in this spousal relay is the contention that widowers and relatives-in-law who wish to marry are driven by a "principle of prudence." The deceased wife's sister marriage is not about selflessness, Arnold indicates, but about allure and amour.

Moreover, as Miss Hannah the stock Old Maid stands in the wings anticipating her matrimonial windfall, it is as if what the critics predicted about the Deceased Wife's Sister Bill has finally come true. Mr. Bottles the widower-to-be is obliged to affiance himself to his deceased wife's sister even before his wife is properly deceased.[14] The source of the humor, however, lies not so much in the new power that wives might exert over their husbands, as in the spectacle of calculating spinsters eager to exercise, as one Parliamentarian put it, a "reversionary interest in the pillow" (Hansard, 183: 315 [2 May 1866]). For under the Deceased Wife's Sister Bill, the middle-class spinster's sexuality would be activated and licensed by her sister's deathbed altruism. More disturbingly, the middle-aged woman's sexuality would be publically legitimated by the very fact that the deceased wife's sister marriage, along with second marriages in general, openly acknowledged midlife sexuality to be alive and well in over-the-threshold bedrooms throughout England.

The Deceased Wife's Sister Bill would seem to foreground what social critics like Arnold needed to obscure in order to invoke the "female principle" as a corrective check upon "Do Nothing" commerce: the active sexuality, the obvious physicality, of the Philistine woman. In *Friendship's Garland*, Arnold denies this physicality by making it laughable. Miss Hannah's body is unappealing, her marital designs unseemly and mildly predatory; Arnold sets her faded graces against the comeliness of Mary Jane so that the very idea of her as a sexual partner seems ludicrous. Mary Jane's body — the body the Philistine woman is not supposed to have — serves her little better, since through it she appears to have sunk in class rank and respectability. For "Mary Jane," as Arnold's readers would have known, was the name of the "hypothetical female domestic" who starred in newspaper debates about "the servant problem" in the mid-1860s (5: 468). Ogled by Job Bottles and his co-conspirators Nick and Leo ("*Mary Jane!*" Leo exclaims; "I never pronounce the name without emotion"; 5: 314), she seems less like a cherished niece of the Bottles family than a pretty little parlor maid whose serving-class body is sexually available. Clearly, she arouses the amorous desires of the men who survey her, rather than elevating their higher moral selves. And, in fact, before Mrs. Bottles is cold in the sod, Leo imagines Mary Jane passing from brother to brother like material goods, waxing in market value even as she wanes in intrinsic purity.

Friendship's Garland comically portrays middle-class women as bodies that are evaluated as sexual commodities, fair and foul. And when Arnold portrays these bodies as subject to the inequities of supply and demand (Mary Janes are scarce, Miss Hannahs are abundant), the Philistine woman becomes implicated by the system her recuperative ethics are imagined to reform. In *Friendship's Garland*, then, the Philistine woman is not so far from her lower-class counterpart as she might at first appear. Arnold presents Elizabeth Wragg as a horrible byproduct of laissez-faire commerce; she commits infanticide because that system has used her as an economic and sexual instrument. Similarly, he presents the deceased wife's sister as both victim (in *Culture and Anarchy*) and potential victimizer (in *Friendship's Garland*). As Arnold's argument proceeds, it becomes clear that "sexual insurrection" is also sexual anarchy, registered also as class slippage, or class anarchy. It becomes clear, too, that the middle-class woman is well-suited for making these connections, since popular wisdom held that she could not suffer a sexual fall without suffering an immediate and irreversible class fall as well. Arnold's hyper-mockery of the Deceased Wife's Sister Bill is, in effect, an effort to patrol the borders between upper and lower classes. Above all, Arnold intends to protect the "feminine ideal" necessary to ensure the health of a bourgeois social economy. But in humorously showing how the "feminine nature" may fail, he suggests that it is far from dependable or unassailable.

III

BY THE TIME ARNOLD finishes with Elizabeth Wragg in "The Function of Criticism at the Present Time," we can almost hear the door of the jail cell clang shut in his muttered refrain, "Wragg is in custody." Ruskin as well as Arnold knew, however, that in the most important respects, Wragg was still at large. In *The Ethics of the Dust*, published two years after "The Function of Criticism," Ruskin, like Arnold, invokes the image of the menstruous woman to convey the economic disasters of industrial pollution, laissez-faire competition, dehumanizing factory work, and the influx of women into the labor force. In his "Ten Lectures to Little Housewives," based upon frequent visits to a progressive girls' academy in Cheshire, Ruskin fabricates a series of Socratic dialogues in which he cavorts with and instructs a veritable aviary of girl-"birdies."[15] Enclosed within the green world of Winnington School, the Carlylean prophet lies down with the lambs as an avuncular "Old Lecturer" of "incalculable age" (18: 207). In typical Ruskin fashion, however, the dream-lessons meant to tutor his readers in the principles of crystallography, political economy, and Queenship inevitably venture into unpeaceable kingdoms blotted by the uncontrolled generation and accumulation of capital.

Like Charles Dodgson, Ruskin was fascinated and appalled by the girl-child's nightmarish potential for metamorphosis. "How one feels the *current* of human life" at Winnington School, he wrote to Sir John Murray Naesmyth; "the child of last year is the woman of this; and the faces seem to change almost from day to day — it is like a dream" (36: 362). The *dramatis personae* of *The Ethics of the Dust* are all between 9 and 20 years old, situated at or near what the medical books labelled the perilous "epoch" of 14–20, the make-or-break age of menarche.[16] As if charting the growth (or fall) of the Winnington girls' own bodies, the Old Lecturer inserts himself into their play-making and quickly launches a covert investigation into the corruptions inherent in the adult woman's uterine economy. The *Ethics* begins with young Isabel and Florrie's imaginary excursion into Sinbad's Valley of Diamonds. But before long, strains of Dante, Spenser, and Bunyan convert their Arabian Nights story into a chilling urban allegory. Within its fantastic landscape, women's overactive menstrual systems have reached a critical mass, despoiling England's economic life-sources by turning her industrial waterways into bloody streams.

What, 11-year-old Isabel enquires, does the river beside the valley road look like?

> L. It ought to be very beautiful, because it flows over diamond sand — only the water is thick and red.
> ISABEL. Red water?
> L. It isn't all water. (18: 212)

This ominous note is followed by a description of bejewelled serpents who sing in the contorted branches of great mulberry trees, their siren songs accompanied by hordes of silkworms whose munching is "so loud that it is like mills at work." The mulberries are "the blackest you ever saw; and, wherever they fall, they stain a deep red"; their juices soak the grass, permeate the river, and dye everything so indelibly red that "nothing ever washes it out again." Nice girls who sojourn there, the Old Lecturer warns, may "spot" their smocks with the dark berries and even transform into serpents themselves (18: 213).

This barely disguised description of gaily decorated prostitutes hawking their wares as their sisters labor in the textile factories is a startling vision of "capital" being spun out of the female body. Ruskin's ostensible purpose, as he later explained it, was to critique the mindless getting and spending of common "traffickers," and to show, through the serpents, the true condition of human souls "who had lived carelessly and wantonly in their riches" (18: 367). He counts on the Medusan images, however, to evoke an immediate, visceral reaction to female sexuality so that he need not explain too explicitly (or too restrictively) the debased physical and spiritual realities to which these images are "felt" to correspond. As repulsive objects, the singing serpents themselves, like Arnold's "lopped off" Wragg, effectively convey a general revulsion at woman's physicality. Ruskin insures this reaction by associating his seven-headed sirens with the Whore of Babylon, "the mother of harlots and abominations" (Rev. 17.5), thus connecting the middle-class woman's vanity with prostitution — an equation that would be made more explicitly and controversially by Eliza Lynn Linton in "The Girl of the Period" (1868). Like Linton's artificial, pleasure-loving girl, Ruskin's middle-class superconsumer wears upon her back and head the fruit of her sister-worms' labor, arrayed like a street-walker for conspicuous display. Both prostitute and over-adorned bourgeois woman are public spectacles of immorality, the prostitute because she has abandoned her proper role as cottage spinner, weaver, or baker in favor of finery and independence, and the middle-class woman because self-aggrandizement prevents her from serving as the cottager's redeemer, patron, and friend.

But the horrible unnaturalness of the worms' birth-spinning, counterpointed by the serpents' song-weaving, does more than expose the degenerative power of mechanized labor, the excesses of middle-class consumerism, and the perverse ethics of a system based upon exchange value. By collapsing woman's processes of biological reproduction into the factory system's operations of material production — by showing capital being generated from the female body, a body not devoted to the production of children — Ruskin suggests that women who toil outside the household economy are not just miscreants but miscreators. The bleeding millworkers and preening prostitutes are the same self-victimized urban workers Ruskin denounces in *Fors Clavigera* as "neglected and distracted creatures." They are madwomen who "hold it for an honour to be independent of [their husbands], and shriek for some hold of the mattock for themselves" (27: 80). As *The Ethics of the Dust* makes clear, the price these shrieking mattock-wielders pay for an enlarged sphere of material production is a reduced capacity for biological reproduction. Subjected to the moral and bodily pressures of industrial manufacture, women's already unstrung uterine economies become sources of barren discharge rather than sites of pregnancy and birth.

In effect, Ruskin gives the homology between the laissez-faire system and the woman's body yet another twist. Laissez-faire is not only *like* the woman's anarchic body, its potential for producing waste is made *worse* when women's *actual* bodies are incorporated within its machinery of commodity production. It is therefore, according to Ruskin's conservative economic vision, doubly pathologized. His solution, like Arnold's, is to vaunt the middle-class woman's capacity to blunt the antagonisms and cruelties of an amoral marketplace. "Of Queens' Gardens" (1865), with its paeans to the women of Coventry Patmore, Tennyson, Wordsworth, and Shakespeare, is his most notorious celebration of the feminine ideal. Like *Culture and Anarchy*, "Of Queens' Gardens" combines domestic ideology and economic paternalism, but with an important difference. Whereas Arnold imagines his wifely guides as already being in place, however their husbands and sons might ignore them, Ruskin admits that his Queens do not as yet exist as a potent cultural force. Indeed, in bitter moments fueled by despair over his thwarted courtship of Rose La Touche, he sees women as vindictive and degraded, as Medeas and Salomes; in 1871 he almost rescinds his earlier praise of womanhood, saying that he had spoken "in faith only" (18: 46).[17] Nevertheless, from the 1860s onward Ruskin dedicates himself to outlining the education and spheres of public and private duty suitable for the ideal Lady, or "loaf-giver" (18: 138). Always, the figure of the bountiful woman stands at the center of his perfect commonwealth, like the maternal cottager baking bread in *Sartor Resartus*, as a powerful symbol of national health.[18]

Like Arnold's Philistine wife with her "instinctive propensions and repugnances," Ruskin's noble guarantor senses rather than thinks deeply, sympathises widely rather than moves freely. As outlined in "Of Queens' Gardens," she is just enough versed in "the work of men" to aid and understand; just capable enough to experience knowledge not as "an object to know," but as a thing "to feel, and to judge." Guarded from "peril and trial" by the man hardened by "rough work," her home knows "no danger, no temptation," no error or wrong-doing, "*unless she herself has sought it*" (18: 125, 122; emphasis mine). Like Browning's Pippa, she ventures philanthropically into "the darkness of the terrible streets," gathering and replanting the drooping flowers of a wayward humanity (18: 142), including, as Kate Millett has observed, the "feeble florets" of fallen womanhood (Ruskin, qtd. in Millett 80). Ruskin argues that the true queen's incapability of doing wrong — "as far as one can use such terms of a human creature" — will sheathe her against the infectiousness of public strife (18: 123). But just as Arnold cannot help but picture the middle-class woman as both protected and fallen, as both Philistine wife and deceased wife's sister, Ruskin inevitably qualifies, if not overturns, his already provisional claims for womanly "incapability."

In part, the contradictions within Ruskin's portraits of womanhood spring from differences between typological and mythological modes of thinking. Typology, which sets ideal type against incomplete, sometimes corrupted antitype, assumes a center of perfected reference beyond time (Christ) and yet also exhibits the movement towards apocalypse, judgement, and New Jerusalem. By contrast, mythology, while also wise in "things which are for all ages true," lacks progressivist *telos* (19: 310). For Ruskin, its deities are necessarily and eternally manichean, exhibiting always the "curious reversal or recoil" of meaning which makes Athena, his obsession and alter ego in the late 1860s, both maid and war-wager, both the quickening wind of inspiration and creative reform, and the "Dies Irae" of punitive, obliterating wrath (19: 317, 399). As Paul Sawyer describes her, Ruskin's Athena is *natura naturans*, "the objectivized form of moral virtue inscribed in the physical order," but also the Medusan symbol of woman's castrating force, "her power to condemn, to cast off, to darken, never to forgive" ("Matriarchal Logos" 139, 140). Her multiple aspects in *The Queen of the Air* (1869), though separable for the sake of discussion, are nevertheless interwoven like "threads through figures on a silken damask," not detachable into types and antitypes (19: 315). Ruskin's typologically conceived women have the ultimate power to decide, like the *Ethics* children eventually must, whether to devolve into antitype (devil-serpents, "dust"), or to evolve into ideal type (angel-birds, "something better than dust"; 18: 222). But his mythological women cannot choose to be either birds or worms; for better and for worse they are both, immutably, at once.

In *Time and Tide by Weare and Tyne*, or, "Twenty-Five Letters to a Working Man of Sunderland on the Laws of Work" (1867), *typos* and *mythos* collide in an arresting image of vitiated girlhood. Written on the eve of the Second Reform Bill, the letters are ostensibly addressed to Thomas Dixon, a respected master cork-cutter and a real-life, perfected type of Mr. Bottles. Characteristic of Ruskin's last decades, they combine the admonitory declamations of Jeremiad with the apostolic guidance of pastoral missives. As Ruskin reads the signs of his times typologically, all the evidence, from sensationalist sex murders to the "charnel-house" engravings of Gustave Dore, points to cultural dissolution as England readies for the "Niagara Leap" into universal enfranchisement (17: 401). Disintegration is represented, as in *The Ethics of the Dust*, in terms of a degenerate female sexuality. Letters V-VII of *Time and Tide*, for example, are filled with Ruskin's eyewitness reports of nascent little women performing for the voyeuristic delight of Covent Garden pleasure-seekers, among them John Ruskin. In *The Ethics of the Dust*, the Old Lecturer had asserted that dance is "the first of girls' virtues" (18: 293). In Letter VII of *Time and Tide*, Ruskin shows that virtue degraded in the rhythmic contortions of a young, dancing girl. And this girl "of twelve or fourteen," like the *Ethics*' mill-worms and Melville's bloodless, tartarean maids, seems driven by oppressive inner mechanisms that suggest and are suggested by the factory machine.

Ruskin had watched one evening in aghast fascination as the Covent Garden girl executed her movements. Her dance consisted

> only in a series of short, sharp contractions and jerks of the body and limbs, resulting in attitudes of distorted and quaint ugliness, such as might be produced in a puppet by sharp twitching of strings at its joints: these movements being made to the sound of two instruments, which between them accomplished only a quick vibratory beating and strumming . . . reminding one of various other insect and reptile cries or warnings: partly of the cicala's hiss . . . and partly of the deadened quivering and intense continuousness of the alarm of the rattle-snake. (17: 343)

Like a sentient marionette, the dancer performs a repertoire of motions to harsh, monotonous strokes, as would a slave rowing in a galley ship or a worker serving an engine. Clearly she has rehearsed her contortions, yet they wrench her body like involuntary reflexes or movements imposed from without. Ruskin appears to find her routine disturbing not only because it replicates the body-twisting repetitions of industrial clockwork, but also because that routine mimics the internal operations of the female uterine economy pictured in *The Ethics of the Dust*. For this girl is "twelve or fourteen" years old, just entered upon the perilous "epoch" of menarche in which women's bodies are overtaken by biological necessity. What Ruskin sees in her "distorted and quaint ugliness" is the fearful choreography of female adolescence in which the dancer is controlled by the dance. On the threshold of adult sexuality, her body is snakey, shuddering, terrible yet pitiable. For Ruskin, the serpent is the divine hieroglyph of "dissolution," "dislocation," and "the grasp and sting of death" (19: 362, 363). In *Time and Time* the dancing girl exhibits "the strength of the base [serpentine] element" (19: 362), and is linked iconographically to the reptilian seducers and robotic worms ensnared within the dystopic industrial landscape of *The Ethics of the Dust*.

Against this girl's spasmodic movements Ruskin sets the true type of rejoicing: "And Miriam the prophetess, the sister of Aaron, took a timbrel in her hand, and all the women went out after her with timbrels and with dances" [Exodus, 15.20] (17: 344). Ruskin finds the grace of Miriam only once in the evening's festivities, within the pantomine of Ali Baba and the Forty Thieves. This extraordinary drama featured forty thieves, their thievish companions, assorted Oxford and Cambridge men engaged in a boat race, forest flowers, "four hundred and forty fairies," and a chandelier — all ably played by English girls (17: 336). Amidst these "novel" elements of pantomime, a beautiful little daughter of Ali Baba, eight or nine years old, danced a pas de deux with a donkey. No "infant prodigy," she moved "simply, as a child ought to dance":

> She caricatured no older person, — attempted no curious or fantastic skill. She was dressed decently, — and she danced her joyful dance with perfect grace, spirit, sweetness, and self-forgetfulness. And through all the vast theatre, full of English fathers and mothers and children, there was not one hand lifted to give her sign of praise but mine. (17: 337–38)

The plain little maid fulfills most of the requirements of perfect girlhood outlined in "Of Queens' Gardens," moving as instinctively and trustworthily as flowers grow (she is "self-forgetful"). But this prepubescent daughter of Ali Baba is but a child, and if she survives her incubation in Nature's bosom, as Wordsworth's exemplary Lucy did not, she must one day transform into her twitching, serpentine, adolescent sister.

And, in dream language released from the direct pressures of his public argument yet saturated with visual details from *Sesame and Lilies, The Ethics of the Dust,* and *Time and Tide,* Ruskin captured the painful moment of that awful transmutation. On August 8, 1867, in one of the frequent erotic nightmares he recorded in his diary during the late 1860s, Ruskin dreamed that a child "half like a monkey" had brought him an "exquisite" bunch of ivory and silver keys. All at once,

> I was in a theatre, and a girl of some far-away nation — half like Japanese, but prettier — was dancing, and she had never been used to show her face or neck, and was ashamed; and behind there was a small gallery full of children of the same foreign type, singing, and the one who brought me the keys was one of them, and my father was there with me. And then it came back — the dream — to the keys, and I was talking about them with some one who said they were the keys of a great old Arabian fortress; and suddenly we were at the gate of it, and we could not agree about the keys; and at last the person who held them said: "Would it not be better no one should have them?" and I said, "Yes"; and he took a stone, and crushed them to pieces, and I thought no one could now ever get into the fortress for its treasures, and it would all moulder into ruin; and I was sorry, and woke. (*Diaries* 2: 628)

Mythos most vividly triumphs over *typos* as the quaint charm of Ali Baba's daughter and the grotesque sexuality of the marionette girl merge in the humiliated blushes of Ruskin's dream child. The monkey-like vendor of the keys specifically recalls the Japanese children who also appear in the Covent Garden section of *Time and Tide.* Those simian children had performed in a juggling act by encouraging their father's dexterity with "short sharp cries, like those of animals." To Ruskin, they seemed to exhibit the prehensile agility of a primitive, "partially inferior race" (17: 341). His dream girl resembles the foreign children but is only half Japanese, and therefore only half-simian (half-foreign, half-sexual); her performance, by the same token, is therefore but half-English (half-domestic, half-free of sex).

What Ruskin implicitly wants of her he explicitly covets from her architectural correlative, the mysterious and erotically-provocative ("Arabian") stronghold. Two contradictory visions of the locked female interior emerge from this part of the fantasy. The female "fortress" houses riches to be examined, valued, hoarded, objectified, aestheticized, and above all possessed, as Ruskin longed to possess Rose La Touche and, after her death, what he read of her in the visage and history of Carpaccio's *St. Ursula*. In his dream, women do not dwell apart untouched by the marketplace; they are accumulated objects of great price. Their domestic enclaves, in fact, become the treasuries in which female "wealth" is stored. But such "treasure" is also perishable, despoiled by ignoble handling, perhaps even by ownership itself, caught in the organic circuit of birth, "mouldering," and death. It is indeed a thing to yearn after and to feel "sorry" about. As if aware of this, the girl herself feels distressed, her embarrassment exacerbated, if not called forth, by Ruskin's intrusive spectatorship and his wish to penetrate the forbidden places, to use the keys he knows "no one" should have. Again, inherently, it is all of one coin: the reverse of Ali Baba's daughter is the rattlesnake girl; the obverse of Ruskin's own rapturous praise of perfect girlhood and womanhood, as typified in Miriam's dance and song, is the voyeur's gaze upon the reluctant, invaded, self-conscious dream child. In Ruskin's mythological gardens, young Queens and old Queens are always also Monarchs of the Dust.

IV

WHEN ARNOLD MOCKS the Deceased Wife's Sister Bill in "Our Liberal Practitioners" and *Friendship's Garland*, and Ruskin criticizes female greed and self-display in "Of Queens' Gardens," *The Ethics of the Dust,* and *Time and Tide*, they labor hard to erect rhetorical barricades around "the feminine nature, the feminine ideal." Woman, they agree, is most properly empowered by her economic *in*utility. Mothers, wives, and daughters can remedy social unrest, poverty, and corruption only if they can radiate good influence over the individual men embroiled in cutthroat competition. When Arnold and Ruskin invoke the middle-class woman as an ameliorative force standing outside the sphere of material production, however, they must erase her body. To do so, they rely upon what Nancy Armstrong has termed the post-Renaissance notion of "deep self" domesticity, that is, an interiority invented for the domestic woman in conduct manuals from *The Whole Duty of Women* (1695) to Sarah Stickney Ellis's *The Women of England* (1839). In these instructional works, the ideal woman is evaluated according to privatized qualities of mind and temperament (she is self-disciplined, frugal, orderly, maternal, subordinate — except within her own household) and defined against an earlier tradition of opulent aristocratic display. Ostentation, sartorial excess, the self as public spectacle, now become indications of inferiority or corruption, so that women's material bodies, once the place where value was exhibited, are deemphasized in favor of internal character. This location of female virtue inside a modestly dressed body, Armstrong argues, "provided people from diverse social groups with a basis for imagining economic interests in common" (59). The idea of the domestic woman not only helped make possible the economic man posited by classic economic theory but also seemed the means by which economic harmony and social accord might be achieved.

But competing with the "deep self" of domesticity is another essentialist model of womanhood that focuses on the uterine disorders of the female reproductive system. Through images of tyrannized women, Ruskin and Arnold invoke this second, medical representation as a metaphoric equivalent of the polluted and polluting laissez-faire system they wish to critique. Shocking child murders in Nottingham and debauched entertainments in Covent Garden begin to enfigure not just moral laxity and the disease of industrialism, but also the repellent processes of the woman's reproductive economy. Those processes reduce the female laborer to body; so, Ruskin and Arnold fear, do they weaken the improving powers of the middle-class guarantor. As Paul Sawyer has observed, drawing upon the insights of Armstrong and Catherine Gallagher, "there is no such thing in the Victorian period as a Woman Question that is not also a question about bourgeois hegemony" ("Ruskin" 131). Judging from the role the menstruous woman plays in Ruskin and Arnold's social criticism, it likewise appears to be the case that there is no such thing as a Woman Question that is not also a question about Victorian periods. For if medical writing suggests that the "feminine ideal" of bourgeois hegemony is housed in a corrupt temple, then how can it perform the good offices believed to regenerate capitalist masters and men? To some, it seemed little short of miraculous that women ever transcended the flesh; to many, the martyr's battle fought by the middle-class woman was, like the Christian hero's, a struggle never fully won. For us, it remains as one of the great ironies of nineteenth-century economic conservatism that the argument-from-biology used to keep women out of the marketplace worked against, if it did not exactly subvert, the "deep-self" virtue at the very heart of domestic ideology.

University of New Hampshire at Manchester

NOTES

1. Wiegman likewise reads "The Paradise of Bachelors and The Tartarus of Maids" as propping up the myth of the egalitarian male bond. According to Wiegman, Melville juxtaposes the "metaphoric homosexuality" of "Bachelors" against the "mechanized heterosexuality" of "Maids" and thereby locates within women what is oppressive and unequal in economics as well as in human reproduction (737). In this way, Melville can preserve the male bond "for masculine wholeness and democratic possibility itself" (742), though, I would argue, this is far from unproblematically achieved.
2. Showalter in *The Female Malady* discusses women's "disorders," especially chapters 5 and 6. See also Lander, Duffin, and Poovey, *Uneven Developments*.
3. In 1869, for example, J. McGrigor Allan ("On the Real Differences in the Minds of Men and Women") argued that menstruating women "suffer under a languor and depression which disqualify them for thought or action, and render it extremely doubtful how far they can be considered responsible beings while the crisis lasts." In 1862, Edward Tilt maintained in *The Lancet* that women are never free from crisis, for the uterus and ovaries throw them into "a state of haemorrhagic and other orgasm every month" (qtd. in Duffin 32).
4. It is difficult to determine which populations of Victorians joked about menstrual rags, or how widespread such joking was, since this kind of taboo humor rarely survived in recorded form. Pearsall provides the following quote from an 1870 parody of Kingsley's "The Three Fishers": "They longed for a prick, but they thought of the flowers, And the clap-rag they rolled it up, ragged and brown" (271). Having "the flowers" was a relatively well-known euphemism for having a menstrual period. In what may be another example, Henry Mayhew records that one of his costermonger informants, having been an ear-witness to the price haggling between household servants and street-buyers of old rags, reported that "a little joking not of the most delicate kind" often accompanied these transactions (275).
5. According to Briggs, for instance, Thomas Hood's pathetic portrait of the red-eyed seamstress, "Song of the Shirt," had passed into "literature" by the 1860s (207). For a history of nineteenth-century needlewomen and female factory workers, see Neff.
6. According to the evidence presented at her trial on March 13, 1865, Elizabeth Wragg, already the mother of a young infant, had left the Nottingham Union workhouse with her two-week-old son on September 10, 1864. That afternoon the child was found naked and dead upon Mapperley hills. Though the piece of cotton framework around the baby's neck indicated that his mother might have strangled him, Wragg claimed that she had thrown him upon the grass and run away. While she was in custody, Wragg asked a female warden, "Do you think I shall be hanged? I should never have done it if I had had a home for him. My mother said she would never have me at home again with another child." The jury convicted her of manslaughter rather than murder, considering that in her "weak and enfeebled" post-partum state she was incapable of malice aforethought. The judge, noting that "the case was as near murder as it well could be," sentenced Wragg to twenty years of penal servitude ("Spring Assizes").
7. The Philistine wife illustrates Arnold's idea of the trans-class "best self" — an idea crucially important to *Culture and Anarchy*, for without it Arnold cannot really explain how the agents and processes of Culture would work. His categories

of Philistine, Barbarian, and Populace reflect a need to order an increasingly fluid, inchoate social ground; his "best self" fraternity, composed of men from all walks of life, would affirm "sameness" without dismantling class difference. The Philistine wife who exhibits the domestic self already imagined to cut across class lines is a "best-self" success story at work. She embodies qualities available to all women, although these qualities are somehow most fully and naturally found within the middle class.

8. The Parliamentary history of the Deceased Wife's Sister Bill spanned almost Victoria's entire reign. It aimed at overturning "Lord Lyndhurst's Act" in which all unions formed between widowers and deceased wives' sisters before August 31, 1835 were declared legal; all marriages within the prohibited degrees of affinity after that date were declared null and void, *ab initio*. Ironically, Lord Lyndhurst had not wished to legislate for the ages or to pronounce upon the validity of Levitical or ecclesiastical law, but only to secure the legitimacy of the seventh Duke of Beaufort's son. The "futurity clause" was added as an eleventh-hour compromise intended to conciliate Anglican objectors. The bill had been so altered and revised that its original sponsor, Lord Lyndhurst, "distinctly and specifically disavowed" it (Hansard 183: 288 [2 May 1866]). For an overview of the bill's history, see Behrman; see also Anderson.

9. Although Arnold later surrendered his opposition to the bill, largely because resistance to its inevitable passage seemed to divert attention from more serious concerns such as improving the industrial slums and forestalling the disestablishment of the Anglican Church, he protested the measure most strenuously in the 1860s and '70s.

10. Leviticus 18 forbade unions between fathers and daughters-in-law or between brothers and sisters, but left others unspecified. Proponents of the Deceased Wife's Sister Bill maintained that because marriage with a deceased wife's sister was not expressly forbidden, it must not violate God's law and therefore should not be legally proscribed. Opponents countered that "Moses, acting under Divine authority, had, in drawing up the code . . . in each case brought up one only of two alternative cases, leaving the other prohibited by implication" (Hansard 195: 1307 [21 April 1869]). Gladstone was very much of the "one flesh" persuasion, announcing to the House of Commons on 20 June 1849 that "A man and his wife were one. He did not . . . wait to declare whether it was mystical, or social, or civil" (Hansard 106: 622).

11. Henry the VIII was frequently invoked by the bill's opponents: he had annulled his first marriage on the grounds that he had committed incest with his brother's wife; annulled his second on the grounds that he committed incest with his mistress's sister; and, no incestuous grounds being available in the case of his fifth marriage, had annulled his union with Anne of Cleves because she was ugly.

12. Hepworth Dixon's book, *Spiritual Wives*, had spoken approvingly of Noyes, the Mormons, and the new "mystic sense of a higher sexual affinity" that authorized each man to pursue "the bride of his soul" — even if pursuer or pursued were already married to somebody else (qtd. in *Arnold* 5: 442, and Kirby 1: 345). As one American reviewer observed, Arnold could not resist piggybacking Dixon's thesis onto the arguments of Thomas Chambers, the bill's major spokesman, so that "Mr. Chambers' proposition [appeared] as though it had been based on Mr. Dixon's book" (Oakeshott 171).

13. Thomas Chambers had cited the moral probity of Massachusetts as indisputable evidence that marriage with a deceased wife's sister creates no national "laxity

of moral sentiment'' (Hansard, 183: 291 [2 May 1866]); see also John Bright's speech for 21 April 1869 (Hansard, 195: 1317). Despite Arnold's well-known dissatisfaction with many of Gladstone's policies, he echoes the Prime Minister's disapproval of America's "formidable relaxations" in marriage law (Hansard, 106: 626).

14. Under the bill, critics argued, the wife would indeed enjoy new rights as a *de facto* legator, though she could exercise those rights only in a kind of Pythian deathbed shot. The idea that she would have the prerogative of "willing" her husband to her sister filled at least one letter-writer to the *Times* with undisguised dread. "Are men to be haunted," he asked, "with the presence of a sister-in-law offensive to them, but useful to their wives, most kind to their children; such haunting consisting in the prospective phantom of having her at the last made a legacy to their children in the shape of a second wife to themselves?" (S. G. O.).

15. In his letters Ruskin addressed the Winnington girls as his "dear birds," "birdies," or "babies." See Burd, *Winnington Letters*.

16. Dr. Edward H. Clarke, in *Sex in Education, or, A Fair Chance for the Girls* (1873), argued that if the young woman's "epoch of development" were delayed or seemed otherwise abnormal, the resulting "legacy of evil" might include anemia, amenorrhea, painful or excessive menstruation, hysteria, perhaps even sterility (qtd. in Lander 35). Bullough and Frisch offer useful historical overviews of the onset of menstruation in young women of varying ages and social class. For surveys of Victorian attitudes towards menarche, see Gorham: see also Hellerstein, Hume, and Offen.

17. As Rosenberg has noted, *Time and Tide* is haunted by the presence of Rose La Touche, the child-woman with whom Ruskin was torturously in love from the 1860s until his death. Ruskin had proposed to Rose in 1866 shortly after her eighteenth birthday; she postponed her answer for three years. Many of the letters in *Time and Tide* poignantly echo Ruskin's personal struggles to rescue Rose from what he perceived to be the serpentine coils of her protective mother. For particularly acute accounts of what Rose meant to Ruskin, see Burd (*John Ruskin and Rose La Touche*), Spear (*Dreams of an English Eden*) and Sawyer (*Ruskin's Poetic Argument*).

18. The antitype of the loaf-giving lady is the half-crazed Medusan virago, like the insurrectionist women of Carlyle's *The French Revolution*. As an emblem of revolt she is never very far from Ruskin's mind. See Spear's "Filaments, Females, Families and Social Fabric" for a study of these figures in Carlyle.

WORKS CITED

Anderson, Nancy F. "The 'Marriage with a Deceased Wife's Sister Bill' Controversy: Incest Anxiety and the Defense of Family Purity in Victorian England." *Journal of British Studies* 21 (Spring 1982): 67–86.

Armstrong, Nancy. *Desire and Domestic Fiction: A Political History of the Novel.* New York: Oxford UP, 1987.

Arnold, Matthew. *The Complete Prose Works of Matthew Arnold.* Ed. R. H. Super. 11 vols. Ann Arbor: U of Michigan P, 1960–77.

Behrman, Cynthia Fansler. "The Annual Blister: A Sidelight on Victorian Social and Parliamentary History." *Victorian Studies* 11 (June 1968): 483–502.

Briggs, Asa. *Victorian Things*. London: B. T. Batsford, 1988.

Bullough, Vern L. "Menarche and Teenage Pregnancy: A Misuse of Historical Data." *Menarche: The Transition from Girl to Woman*. Ed. Sharon Golub. Lexington, MA: D. C. Heath, 1983. 187–93.

Burd, Van, Akin ed. *John Ruskin and Rose La Touche: Her Unpublished Diaries of 1861 and 1867*. Oxford: Clarendon P, 1979.

———, ed. *The Winnington Letters: John Ruskin's Correspondence with Margaret Alexis Bell and the Children of Winnington Hall*. Cambridge, MA: Harvard UP, 1969.

"Deceased Wife's Sister." *Saturday Review* 24 April 1869: 548–49.

"The Deceased Wife's Sister," *Saturday Review* 16 June 1883: 754–55.

Duffin, Lorna. "The Conspicuous Consumptive: Woman as an Invalid." *The Nineteenth-Century Woman*. Ed. Sara Delamont and Lorna Duffin. New York: Barnes & Noble, 1978. 26–56.

Frisch, Rose E. "Fatness, Menarche, and Fertility." *Menarche: The Transition from Girl to Woman*. Ed. Sharon Golub. Lexington, MA: D.C. Heath, 1983. 5–20.

Gallagher, Catherine. *The Industrial Reformation of English Fiction: Social Discourse and Narrative Form, 1832–1867*. Chicago: U of Chicago P, 1985.

Gorham, Deborah. *The Victorian Girl and the Feminine Ideal*. Bloomington: Indiana UP, 1982.

Gullette, Margaret Morganroth. "The Puzzling Case of the Deceased Wife's Sister: Nineteenth-Century England Deals with a Second-Chance Plot." *Representations* 31 (Summer 1990): 142–66.

Hansard's Parliamentary Debates. 3rd series. 356 vols. Vol. 106. London: G. Woodfall, 1849. Vols. 183 & 185. London: Cornelius Buck, 1866 & 1869.

Hellerstein, Erna Olafson, Leslie Parker Hume, and Karen M. Offen, eds. *Victorian Women: A Documentary Account of Women's Lives in Nineteenth-Century England, France, and the United States*. Stanford: Stanford UP, 1981.

Higginbotham, Ann R. " 'Sin of the Age': Infanticide and Illegitimacy in Victorian London." *Victorian Studies* 32 (Spring 1989): 319–37.

Kirby, John P. "Matthew Arnold's 'Friendship's Garland,' Edited, with an Introductory Essay." 2 vols. Diss. Yale U, 1937.

Lander, Louise. *Images of Bleeding: Menstruation as Ideology*. New York: Orlando P, 1988.

Mayhew, Henry. *Mayhew's London*. Ed. Peter Quennell. London: Bracken Books, 1984.

Melville, Herman. "The Paradise of Bachelors and the Tartarus of Maids." *Selected Tales and Poems by Herman Melville*. Ed. Richard Chase. New York: Rinehart, 1950. 206–29.

Millett, Kate. "The Debate over Women: Ruskin Versus Mill." *Victorian Studies* 14 (1970): 63–82.

Neff, Wanda F. *Victorian Working Women: An Historical and Literary Study of Women in British Industries and Professions, 1832–1850*. Holland: Frank Cass, 1966.

O., S. G. Letter. *Times* 8 May 1849.

Oakeshott, B. N. "Matthew Arnold as a Political and Social Critic." *The Westminster Review* 149 (February 1898): 161–76.

Pearsall, Ronald. *The Worm in the Bud: The World of Victorian Sexuality*. Toronto: Macmillan, 1969.

Poovey, Mary. "Speaking of the Body: Mid-Victorian Constructions of Female Desire." *Body/Politics: Women and the Discourses of Science*. Ed. Mary Jacobus, Evelyn Fox Keller, and Sally Shuttleworth. New York: Routledge, 1990. 29–46.

———. *Uneven Developments: The Ideological Work of Gender in Mid-Victorian England*. Chicago: U of Chicago P, 1988.

Rosenberg, John D. *The Darkening Glass: A Portrait of Ruskin's Genius*. London: New York: Columbia UP, 1961.

Ruskin, John. *The Diaries of John Ruskin*. Ed. Joan Evans and John Howard Whitehouse. 3 vols. Oxford: Clarendon P, 1956–59.

———. *The Works of John Ruskin*. Library Edition. Ed. E. T. Cook and Alexander Wedderburn. 39 vols. London: George Allen, 1903–12.

Sawyer, Paul. "Ruskin and the Matriarchal Logos." *Victorian Sages & Cultural Discourse: Renegotiating Gender and Power*. Ed. Thaïs E. Morgan. New Brunswick: Rutgers UP, 1990. 129–41.

———. *Ruskin's Poetic Argument: The Design of the Major Works*. Ithaca: Cornell UP, 1985.

Showalter, Elaine. *The Female Malady: Women, Madness, and English Culture, 1830–1980*. New York: Pantheon, 1985.

———. *Sexual Anarchy: Gender and Culture at the Fin de Siècle*. New York: Penguin, 1990.

Shuttleworth, Sally. "Female Circulation: Medical Discourse and Popular Advertising in the Mid-Victorian Era." *Body/Politics: Women and the Discourses of Science*. Ed. Mary Jacobus, Evelyn Fox Keller, and Sally Shuttleworth. New York: Routledge, 1990. 47–68.

Spear, Jeffrey L. *Dreams of an English Eden: Ruskin and His Tradition in Social Criticism*. New York: Columbia UP, 1984.

———. "Filaments, Females, Families and Social Fabric: Carlyle's Extension of a Biological Analogy." *Victorian Science and Victorian Values: Literary Perspectives*. Ed. James Paradis and Thomas Postlewait. New Brunswick: Rutgers UP, 1985. 69–84.

"Spring Assizes." *Times* 15 March 1865.

Wiegman, Robyn. "Melville's Geography of Gender." *American Literary History* 1 (Winter 1989):735–53.

Wiltshire, David. *The Social and Political Thought of Herbert Spencer*. New York: Oxford UP, 1978.

WORKS IN PROGRESS

Robert Langbaum's "Hardy: Versions of Pastoral" is from a forthcoming book, *Thomas Hardy in Our Time*

George Levine's "Objectivity and Death: Victorian Scientific Autobiography" is from a current project on objectivity, science, and narrative

Patricia O'Neill's "*Paracelsus* and the Authority of Science in Browning's Career" is from a book in progress on Tennyson, Browning, and Hardy

Simon Petch's "Law, Narrative, and Anonymity in Browning's *The Ring and the Book*" is from a current project on legal aspects of the poem

HARDY: VERSIONS OF PASTORAL

By Robert Langbaum

THE RETURN OF THE NATIVE is Hardy's greatest nature poem. Hardy achieves the imaginative freedom and intensity of great poetry by daring to make the heath the novel's central character, the all-encompassing identity from which the human characters derive the individualities that emerge from the pass back into the heath. Hardy ties his characters to the heath by means of a device which is most conspicuous in *Far from the Madding Crowd* and *The Return of the Native*: characters appear for the first time as distant shapes on the heath, mysterious archetypes, taking on individualizing lineaments as they approach the observer. Hardy sometimes renews a character's identity by *re*introducing him or her in this manner, making the observer (the technique requires an observer) *re*recognize the character as if for the first time.

Thus Eustacia, after the opening chapter's powerful description of the heath at nightfall, appears to the observer as a landscape object. The reddle-man watches the "form" of an old man (Eustacia's grandfather) "as it diminished to a speck on the road and became absorbed in the thickening films of night." He then looks upward toward a distant hill with a barrow (a prehistoric burial mound) upon it, and becomes aware that the barrow's summit

> was surmounted by something higher. It rose from the semi-globular mound like a spike from a helmet. . . . There the form stood, motionless as the hill beneath. . . . The form was so much like an organic part of the entire motionless structure that to see it move would have impressed the mind as a strange phenomenon.[1]

"Strange" in the manner of Wordsworth's old leech-gatherer (probably in Hardy's mind) who, in his stillness breaks upon the observer as a huge stone that can only have moved there supernaturally. Only when Hardy's "form" moves can it be distinguished from the heath as a woman's figure, which turns out many pages later to be Eustacia. Instead of just evolving from the landscape, as in Wordsworth, Eustacia evolves from the heath through association with a primitive artifact and Guy Fawkes bonfires both of which

245

descend from ancient Celtic culture. Hardy adds to Wordsworth an anthropological view of man's relation to landscape through organically evolved culture.

In *The Return of the Native* Hardy goes beyond Wordsworth in attempting to portray the heath as totally objective, beyond human categories of understanding. Insofar as the heath is comprehensible at all, it is comprehensible through contradictory aspects both deriving from and not deriving from human observation. This despite Hardy's usual practice as described in his journal entry of 23 August 1865: "The poetry of a scene varies with the minds of the perceivers. Indeed, it does not lie in the scene at all."[2] Hardy's art is not so far as is generally thought from that of his contemporary, Henry James; the difference is that Hardy employs many points of view instead of one — almost all his important actions are carefully framed by observers, sometimes animal observers. The heath is unusual because not presented through points of view. Yet in this exceptional instance and others there remains the sense that the landscape or animals (the animals in the dicing scene, for example) are objectively there whether observed or not and that the full intensity of their being exceeds human observation.

For Hardy the objective is that which remains inscrutable. He admired Swinburne's ability to project the inscrutability of things, an inscrutability merging with oblivion of consciousness.[3] Hardy's contribution to nature poetry, as I have suggested, is his portrayal of nature in its inscrutably nonanthropomorphic otherness; whereas in Wordsworth nature's mysteries are the mysteries of imaginative projection — they are sublimities.

Because his presentation is exceptional, Hardy's opening description of the heath at twilight exemplifies the aesthetic of the sublime, given the heath's affinity to night and its slightly threatening aspect:

> [T]he heath wore the appearance of an instalment of night which had taken up its place before its astronomical hour was come. . . . [A]t this transitional point of its nightly roll into darkness the great and particular glory of the Egdon waste began. . . . It could best be felt when it could not clearly be seen.

Hardy goes on to distinguish between the sublime and the beautiful in the manner of Burke's *The Sublime and the Beautiful* (1756). Its nocturnal and threatening qualities, says Hardy, "lent to this heath a sublimity in which spots renowned for beauty of the accepted kind are utterly wanting" (I,i,2–3). The difference is that Burke treats the sublime as an alternative aesthetic; whereas Hardy treats it as antiaesthetic, as emphatically the taste for the nonbeautiful of modern reflective men who through science know the bleak truth about nature. These modern men, we learn when Clym is described, cannot themselves be beautiful because their faces are ravaged by thought and unpalatable knowledge. The modern taste for the antiaesthetic sublime becomes the post-Darwinian way of relating to nature. "I feel that Nature is played out as a Beauty, but not as a Mystery," Hardy wrote in his diary for January 1887 (*Life*, 185). With the current revival of interest in the sublime, Hardy's revision of Burke should be especially relevant.

The heath is presented as a particular place but also as the whole earth in "its nightly roll into darkness." In *The Return of the Native*, Hardy goes beyond Wordsworth in portraying the landscape as a total environment. The characters move on the heath as fish swim through the sea; the characters are brushed by the grasses they push through, they are observed uncomprehendingly by animals. "Tall ferns buried [Eustacia] in their leafage whenever her path lay through them, which now formed miniature forests, though not one stem of them would remain to bud the next year" — the last clause will apply also to Eustacia (IV,iii,202). And of Clym we are told:

> The ferns, among which he had lain in comfort yesterday, were dripping moisture from every frond, wetting his legs through as he brushed past; and the fur of the rabbits leaping before him was clotted into dark locks by the same watery surrounding. (III,vi,165–66)

As other examples of animal observation we read: "Clym as he walked forward, eyed by every rabbit and fieldfare [thrush] around" (III,iii,143); and "[a]t each brushing of Clym's feet white miller-moths flew into the air just high enough to catch upon their dusty wings the mellowed light from the west" (IV,vii,228). Such passages (the verse contains nothing more poetic) belie Hardy's stated aim to present the heath as nonbeautiful, but there are other passages in which nature is presented as locked in the Darwinian struggle for existence.

The characters' total immersion in nature suggests pastoralism, and indeed *The Return of the Native* brings to a climax the series of pastoral novels beginning with *Under the Greenwood Tree* (1872). But *Return of the Native* is also the first of the great tragic novels constituting Hardy's major period. In making the transition to tragedy, *Return of the Native* seriously modifies pastoral which does not traditionally mix with tragedy. Hardy makes them mix by deepening the psychology to a point usually inappropriate to pastoral, and by taking a Darwinian view so that the nature which totally embraces the characters does not know them. The lovely sentence about miller-moths just precedes Clym's discovery of his mother dying on the heath of a snake bite.

If we begin with the obvious definition of "pastoral" as an idealizing picture of country life implying its superiority to city life,[4] we must ask whether the word aptly describes Hardy's novels after *Greenwood Tree*. In *The Country and the City*, Raymond Williams argues that we misread if we impose on Hardy's novels "a neo-pastoral convention of the countryman as an age-old figure, or a vision of a prospering countryside being disintegrated by Corn Law repeal or the railways or agricultural machinery." Corn Law repeal made little difference in Dorset, Williams explains, and "the coming of the railway gave a direct commercial advantage in the supply of milk to London," as we see in Tess's reflection on the Talbothays milk that will appear on London breakfast tables the next morning. Douglas Brown, instead, powerfully describes the agricultural depression that hit Britain after 1870, causing catastrophic depopulation of the countryside.[5] There is certainly evidence in the novels that this catastrophe was very much on Hardy's mind. To approximate the truth we probably have to combine the views of Williams and Brown.

Certainly Williams's argument that Hardy's sympathy does not rest entirely with the country is supported by Hardy's almost Marxist essay, "The Dorsetshire Labourer," in which he shows how farm laborers have become as itinerant, free-market oriented and alienated as industrial workers, while arguing that this transposition has brought both gains and losses. In this essay Hardy projects both the nostalgically backward-looking pastoral view and the forward-looking realistic view.

The conjunction of the two views is expressed when Hardy, after speaking of all that has been lost by the new generation of Dorsetshire laborers, says in Darwin's manner that "new varieties of happiness evolve themselves like new varieties of plants."

> Thus, while their pecuniary condition in the prime of life is bettered, and their freedom enlarged, they have lost touch with their environment, and that sense of long local participancy which is one of the pleasures of age.

The feudal obligation to maintain the aged laborer is lessened now that the laborer's youthful strength

> has often been expended elsewhere. The sojourning existence of the town masses is more and more the existence of the rural masses, with its corresponding benefits and disadvantages. With uncertainty of residence often comes a laxer morality, and more cynical views of the duties of life. Domestic stability is a factor in conduct which nothing else can equal. On the other hand, new varieties of happiness evolve themselves like new varieties of plants, and new charms may have arisen among the classes who have been driven to adopt the remedy of locomotion for the evils of oppression and poverty — charms which compensate in some measure for the lost sense of home.[6]

Hardy's novels might be ranged along a continuum, with at one end the relative stability of *Under the Greenwood Tree* and at the other the increasing locomotion in *Mayor of Casterbridge, Tess*, and most notably *Jude*.

To understand Hardy's achievement in *The Return of the Native*, we must now turn back to the two more purely pastoral novels that preceded it — *Under the Greenwood Tree* (1872) and *Far from the Madding Crowd* (1874). In these earlier novels nature is always beautiful and in harmony with the characters, though nature can be dangerous in *Madding Crowd*. The problems that turn up in a small way in *Greenwood Tree* and in a much bigger way in *Madding Crowd* (which contains much violence) can still be resolved to promote the happy endings of pastoral comedy. The problems in *Return of the Native*, instead, lead to tragedy in the main plot with the happy ending reserved problematically for Thomasin and Venn. After *Greenwood Tree*, Hardy always exceeds the limits of pastoral; so that pastoral becomes a useful taking-off point rather than a determining principle of my discussion.

Hardy's first published novel, *Desperate Remedies* (1871), is not pastoral; it is a curiously sophisticated even decadent work, involving suggestions of lesbianism — hardly the debut to be expected from a young man of humble country origins. Between the pastoral novels *Under the Greenwood Tree* and *Far from the Madding Crowd* Hardy published *A Pair of Blue Eyes* (1873), which is not pastoral though it takes place mainly in the country with some high-society scenes in London. *A Pair of Blue Eyes* is a powerful novel of manners in which the principal characters, except for the socially rising hero, are upper-class and in which class distinctions take on an importance (in this novel a bitterly tragic importance) they do not have in the more pastoral novels. The novel is so successful (it was Tennyson's favorite) that if it does not count as major, it is probably because of overplotting. The novel shows how Hardy's dexterity at plot-making will be both a strength and a danger.

I cite these two nonpastoral novels to emphasize that Hardy was not a country bumpkin who had inevitably to write pastoral, but that he wrote or did not write pastoral as a deliberate literary choice. In the August 1871 letter to Macmillan accompanying the manuscript of *Greenwood Tree*, Hardy wrote that he turned to rural life because in his previous novel *Desperate Remedies* "the rustic characters & scenery had very little part yet to my surprise they were made very much of by the reviews."[7] Nevertheless he did approximately alternate between the novels that are pastoral or allude to pastoralism and other kinds of novels; the alternation approximately corresponds to the alternation between major and minor novels. Like much of the verse the minor novels tend to be obviously intellectual, and as highly intelligent novels of ideas have an enduring interest of their own.[8]

Hardy's next major novel, *The Mayor of Casterbridge* (1886), alludes to pastoralism, but takes place in a market town rather than the country, and deals with trading, indeed speculating, in wheat rather than with its production. In *The Woodlanders* the following year, Hardy returns directly to pastoral in order to subvert it. Hardy alludes again to pastoral in *Tess of the d'Urbervilles* (1891), especially in his portrayal of the idyllic Talbothays dairy farm where Tess and Angel meet and fall in love. But the pastoral experience proves illusory and destructive; the couple do not, to quote *Madding Crowd*, know "the rougher sides of each other's character" before marrying. The antipastoral Flintcomb Ash farm, with its devilish harvesting machine and cash-nexus relation to labor, seems truer than Talbothays to modern reality. In Hardy's last novel *Jude the Obscure* (1896), nature hardly appears at all, appearing when it does in its cruelest aspects. *Jude* takes place in towns through which the by now rootless characters wander. Yet the pastoral tradition is indirectly recalled in this novel as a measure of all that has been lost.

UNDER THE GREENWOOD TREE, Hardy's third but first artistically successful novel, is a masterpiece of pastoral comedy. The fragility and deftness of its art ("the work is so delicate as not to hit every taste," wrote the publisher's reader) gives evidence enough to refute those who consider Hardy a clumsy bucolic genius with little craft. There has been an invidious mixture of social and literary condescension in the judgment of Hardy — as in Henry James's "The good little Thomas Hardy has scored a great success with *Tess of the d'Urbervilles*, which is chock-full of faults and falsity and yet has a singular beauty and charm." Some reviewers, however, linked Hardy to George Eliot for "philosophic thought," to Meredith for "serious . . . thought and intention," and to Thackeray for having "raised the standard of workmanship."[9]

What is so impressive artistically about *Under the Greenwood Tree* is Hardy's attention to the requirements of his chosen genre. His original title *The Mellstock Quire* refers to the novel's account of the village's old-fashioned instrumental choir and its dissolution. The insertion of the phrase from a song in Shakespeare's pastoral comedy *Much Ado About Nothing* — making the title *Under the Greenwood Tree or The Mellstock Quire* — calls attention to the *artfulness* of pastoral, as does the subtitle *A Rural Painting of the Dutch School*.

The first sentence establishes a criterion for judging character which will inform all the pastoral novels. "To dwellers in a wood almost every species of tree has its voice as well as its feature."[10] The most worthy characters are sufficiently steeped in nature to detect the subtle variety of its signals. In *The Return of the Native*, Thomasin trusts "for guidance to her general knowledge of the [heath's] contours, which was scarcely surpassed by Clym's or by that of the heath-croppers themselves" (V,viii,283). And in *The Woodlanders* Grace says that Marty and Giles, the book's two noblest characters, " 'could speak in . . . the tongue of the trees and fruits and flowers themselves.' "[11] Even in *Greenwood Tree*, where harmony with nature is taken for granted, the hero Dick Dewy stands out by being late for his wedding because his bees "swarmed" and had to be tended to. His instinct is right since "swarming" bees on a wedding day are a good omen, clearly an omen of fertility.

The opening of *Greenwood Tree* continues:

> At the passing of the breeze the fir-trees sob and moan no less distinctly than they rock; the holly whistles as it battles with itself. . . . And winter, which modifies the note of such trees as shed their leaves, does not destroy its individuality. (I,i,39)

This lovely passage on the individuality of tree species throws light on Hardy's principles of characterization in the pastoral novels. We are told of Grandfather William Dewy, the book's model character, that "to his neighbours he had no character in particular" (I,iii,50), that they see him as changing according to their own changing perceptions — as, in other words, the way they see a natural object. We are told the same thing about Gabriel Oak in *Far from the Madding Crowd*: "when his friends and critics were in tantrums, he was considered rather a bad man; when they were pleased, he was rather a good man; when they were neither, he was a man whose moral colour was a kind of pepper-and-salt mixture."[12] Character, we are to understand, should not derive from the eccentricity so much prized in modern literature, but rather from the individuality of the species, from a deep rootedness that unfolds through fundamental situations. In *The Return of the Native* Thomasin, in a sentence Lawrence might have written, is characterized organically: "An ingenuous, transparent life was disclosed; as if the flow of her existence could be seen passing within her" (I,iv,30). Yet this natural characterization, which works well for Grandfather Dewy and Gabriel Oak, makes Thomasin mainly uninteresting, perhaps because she has to compete with Eustacia and Clym who are vividly individualized and psychologized in the modern manner.

In the purely pastoral *Under the Greenwood Tree*, there is surprisingly little description of nature after the beautiful opening paragraph. Nature is taken for granted as a background, gorgeous when described:

> It was a morning of the latter summer-time; a morning of lingering dews. . . . Fuchsias and dahlias were laden till eleven o'clock with small drops and dashes of water, changing the colour of their sparkle at every movement of the air . . . (III,iii,156)

and the novel is divided according to the four seasons, which correspond to the burgeoning of love and marriage between Fancy Day and Dick Dewy. Nevertheless the main subject of *Under the Greenwood Tree* is not nature but community — the organic community resulting from the pastoral vision of organic connection between man and nature. The community dealt with is not that of farmers and shepherds, as in the later *Far from the Madding Crowd*, but the village community of artisans and trandesmen, the community of Hardy's family. The main story, about the replacement of the Mellstock choir by what Hardy significantly calls the "isolated organ," is a fable of organic community and its inevitable dissolution. The choir of village instrumentalists, to which Hardy's father and grandfather belonged, came to an end the year Hardy was born, but he grew up in the ambience of its memory. The family remained musical; Hardy himself played the fiddle at country dances, often in the company of his father as first violinist and his uncle as cellist.

In the novel the choir is a communal enterprise involving not only the musicians but also their relatives and friends, so that there is no division between community and church affairs. "The displacement of these ecclesiastical bandsmen by an isolated organist," says Hardy in the Preface, "has tended to stultify the professed aims of the clergy, its direct result being to curtail and extinguish the interest of parishioners in church doings" (33). The novel gives us the sense of an outside world for which the village life portrayed is already anomalous in the 1830s. The regional novel characteristically assures the modern urban reader that in so remotely rural a place as Dorset such a village choir could still have existed so late in time.

In "The Dorsetshire Labourer," Hardy writes that an urban visitor to backward Dorset would learn that

> wherever a mode of supporting life is neither noxious nor absolutely inadequate, there springs up happiness, and will spring up happiness, of some sort or other. Indeed, it is among such communities as these that happiness will find her last refuge on earth, since it is among them that a perfect insight into the conditions of existence will be longest postponed. (*Personal Writings*, 169)

If we understand the "perfect insight" to be scientific insight, we understand why regionalism, coinciding in this respect with pastoralism, is indirectly a comment on modern life. (Regionalism coincides some of the way but not always all of the way with pastoralism, in that the regional writer is more absorbed than the pastoralist in the particularity of the locale and takes a more "historical — or even archaeological" interest in its "customs and survivals."[13] Hardy occupies and exceeds both categories.) Hardy's statement that "perfect insight into the conditions of existence" can only be postponed suggests the inevitable dissolution of happy organic communities, an inevitability confirmed in *Under the Greenwood Tree* by the choir's curious acquiescence in its own demise.

The references in this novel are less to nature than to music, dance and the other arts, the arts being symbols of community. In the first chapter the members of the Mellstock choir appear — in a manner conspicuous in the later novels — as figures emerging from the landscape. But nature soon gives way to art as we meet a man singing a folk song that sets the pastoral tone: "The lads and the lasses a-sheep-shearing go." Dick Dewy is presented as a kind of archetypal figure against the light sky, "his profile appearing . . . like the portrait of a gentleman in black cardboard." The other members of the choir advance "against the sky in flat outlines, which suggested some processional design on Greek or Etruscan pottery" (I,i,41,40).

When we meet these men again at the cottage of Dick's father Reuben, a "tranter" or carrier, the emphasis is still on artifacts. Each choir member wears the costume or carries the tools of his craft. Mr. Penny, the shoemaker, draws forth his last; while William Dewy, a mason, "wore a long linen apron." "His stooping figure formed a well-illuminated picture as he passed towards the fire-place" (I,iii,51). The lighting recalls the Dutch genre painting alluded to in the novel's subtitle. And indeed such Ruskinian idealization of craftsmen becomes another version of pastoral, given the typing and innocence of these characters. We are surprised by the quaint spirituality of their conversation about music. " 'Strings be safe soul-lifters,' " says Mr. Spinks. Mr. Penny agrees, " 'Clar'nets were not made for the service of the Lard.' " The tranter objects that " 'angels be supposed to play clar'nets in heaven' " (I,iv,58–59), and he says later of his father, " 'he'd starve to death for music's sake" (I,viii,86). This highmindedness of simple craftsmen recalls the opening carpenter shop scene in *Adam Bede*, where George Eliot also uses Dutch painting as a visual model. *Under the Greenwood Tree* might be considered Hardy's smaller, lighter *Adam Bede*; though it was the anonymous serialization of *Far From the Madding Crowd* that was attributed by a reviewer to George Eliot.

It is Christmas Eve and the choir circulates in the village singing carols in a rural manner no longer heard, "embodying a quaint Christianity in words orally transmitted from father to son through several generations" (I,iv,60). We see signs that the tradition is ending when we see the cool reception given the carolers by three of the community's most highly placed citizens — the schoolmistress Fancy Day, the rich farmer Shiner, and the newly arrived vicar Mr. Maybold: the three who will replace the choir by the "isolated organ." It is because the traditional community is dissolving that it can be idealized through nostalgia as it could not be while flourishing.

In the pastoral novels the social range is narrow. In *Under the Greenwood Tree* the farm and village laborers occupy the bottom position; near the top stand the farmers and village tradesmen; while the gentry enter only by way of the vicar. Class distinctions are easily bridged; Fancy Day, the daughter of a head gamekeeper and timber-steward on an estate, could have married the vicar. What matters in the pastoral novels is education — whether a character has been educated outside the community and thus alienated from it by a selfconsciously critical turn of mind. The educated Fancy, Clym and Grace are deferred to by the friends and relatives with whom they grew up. After Dick Dewy's request for Fancy's hand has been haughtily refused by her father, Dick modestly "turned away wondering at his presumption in asking for a woman whom he had seen from the beginning to be so superior to him" (IV,ii,182) — superior only in education.

It is a sign of a new social mobility that the fathers of Fancy and Grace, having risen above their peers financially, invest in their daughter's education in order to advance them socially through opportune marriages. In *Greenwood Tree* Mr. Penny, the shoemaker, argues against social mobility when he speaks of an inherited stability of foot: even if the boots differ in looks and price, " ' 'tis father's voot and daughter's voot to me, as plain as houses' " (I,iii,54). Social ambition connected with a desire to modernize cause the problems in *Under the Greenwood Tree* and *The Woodlanders*.

Problems which become serious in the later novel are, in a pastoral comedy like *Greenwood Tree*, introduced lightly in order to be quickly resolved. Fancy is only a little separated from the community by her education, which leads her no higher than job of village schoolmistress. Her education does not prevent her from falling in love with Dick and never shows up in her conversations with him. If she keeps him dangling a while, it is because of the social ambition her father has put into her head but mainly because of female vanity. Vanity, Eve's weakness, is the complication Fancy brings into the Edenic innocence of Dick's world.

This recalls Bruce Johnson's definition of pastoral based on "the old pastoral opposition of otium [i.e., Dick's contentment] and the aspiring mind [i.e., Fancy's vanity and social ambition]," with pastoral on the side of otium. Johnson contrasts Gabriel Oak's contentment in *Madding Crowd* with Bathsheba's vanity and aspiration "to an identity achieved apart from conventional love and marriage"; though Hardy "rather admires," says Johnson, "the peculiar nature of her aspiring."[14]

Despite Fancy's vanity and social ambition, she resists her father's insistence that she marry the rich farmer Shiner, whose claim to superior social status is not accepted because he lacks education. She takes to bed with lovesickness until her frightened father agrees to her engagement to Dick. Mere men are no match for Fancy. Besides this is a benevolent pastoral world in which no one can for long thwart the desires of young lovers.

Hardy's masterly light touch is evident in his portrayal of Fancy's charm and Dick's ardently innocent lovemaking. Dick falls into a love swoon, disappearing afterwards from the group of carolers when Fancy, to thank them, appears as a framed illuminated vision in her window. The courtship is carried on through the elaborately described country dances at the Dewys' Christmas party. Dick makes the most of his turns with Fancy, "her breath curling round his neck like a summer zephyr that had strayed from its proper date" (I,viii,83). Never again will Hardy portray a love so sweetly innocent.[15]

Remarkably the choir harbors no resentment against Fancy for playing the instrument that replaces them. Fancy herself does not seek to play the organ in church, but is pushed into it by the vicar Mr. Maybold acting at the suggestion of Farmer Shiner because both men are smitten by her charms. The newly arrived Mr. Maybold wants also to modernize the church.

Fancy dresses for her debut "with an audacity unparalleled in the whole history of village-schoolmistress at this date." When poor Dick, who has to attend a friend's funeral, complains about such dazzling dress for an occasion from which he will be absent, she pouts, " 'I do take a little delight in my life, I suppose' " (IV,v,193–94). Clothes are a continuing issue between them, an issue showing his moral superiority. In three other major novels a man — Oak, Venn and Jude — is the morally superior character, in two others a woman — Elizabeth-Jane and Tess — is morally superior, while in *The Woodlanders* both Giles and Marty are morally superior; all this shows Hardy's evenhandedness in moral evaluation of men and women.

So overwhelmed is Mr. Maybold by the proximity to his pulpit of this organ-playing divinity that he resolves to commit the most imprudent act of his life by proposing marriage to one so inferior to himself in station. We have been prepared to expect that Fancy, despite her engagement to Dick, will be unable to resist this temptation to climb socially, especially after Maybold has said, " 'your natural talents, and the refinement they have brought into your nature . . . are equal to anything ever required of the mistress of a quiet parsonage-house' " (IV,vi,199). Nevertheless they will move to Yorkshire to obscure her humble origins. In *The Woodlanders*, where social distinctions are taken more seriously, Fitzpiers will suggest a similar move to Grace for the same reason.

Just before Maybold's proposal that evening, Fancy observes a contrast in clothing between Dick, who returned with his black mourning suit dripping wet because he gave away his umbrella to the ladies at the funeral, and Maybold who after Dick's departure appears in the distance as a "form," dressed elegantly in black and carrying an umbrella. Even before discerning the man, Fancy is attracted to the elegant clothing; whereas in pastoral it is usually the rough appearance that suggests goodheartedness.

Fancy's treachery, however, is only momentary. She no sooner accepts Maybold than she begins to reject him when he reaches out to embrace her:

"No no, not now!" she said in an agitated whisper. "There are things; — but the temptation is, O, too strong, and I can't resist it; I can't tell you now, but I must tell you! Don't, please, don't come near me now!" (IV,vi,200)

As befits pastoral comedy, which repeats the ritual of spring, the spirit of winter, the threat to the lovers' happiness, is introduced so it can be quickly defeated. In the benevolent world of this novel, Maybold himself withdraws when the next day he meets Dick who announces his engagement to Fancy. Maybold's letter to Fancy chiding her for not telling him of the engagement crosses hers saying she had no right to accept him. Cannily she describes as aesthetic virtues her moral defects, if indeed they are defects: " 'It is my nature — perhaps all women's — to love refinement of mind and manners' " and " 'elegant' " surroundings. " 'Ambition and vanity they would be called; perhaps they are so.' " She begs him to keep forever secret what passed between them. The vicar sends an unsigned note, " 'Tell him everything; it is best. He will forgive you' " (IV,vii,204–05). Fancy has too much commonsense to follow such advice; as a character in comedy, she does not make Tess's tragic error. The same situation with a different turn becomes dark comedy in *The Woodlanders* (where Fitzpiers tries to keep secret his affairs with other women) and tragedy in *Tess*.

The wedding of Dick and Fancy takes place as spring returns. The novel is organized according to the cycle of the seasons, beginning two winters back. The second winter is significantly omitted, perhaps because the spirit of winter was defeated with Maybold's withdrawal at the end of the "Autumn" section. In the wedding ceremonies nature blends with community. The couple are married in church, a symbol of community, but the wedding procession threads its way "among dark perpendicular firs, like the shafted columns of a cathedral" (V,i,219). The wedding festivities, full of song and dance, symbols of community, take place in the shade of "an ancient tree," symbol of a fertility that makes natural communities:

> Many *hundreds* of birds had been born amidst the boughs of this single tree; *tribes* to rabbits and hares had nibbled at its bark from year to year; quaint tufts of fungi had sprung from the cavities of its forks; and countless *families* of moles and earthworms had crept about its roots. (V,ii,221; my italics)

Almost as ancient as the tree is the communalizing country custom requiring the wedding party to walk in couples around the parish. The educated Fancy balks at the prospect of such an exhibition; but she accedes to tradition, showing her ability to make realistic compromises. Her vanity, however, remains evident. " 'I wonder,' " says one grandfather to the other, " 'which she thinks most about, Dick or her wedding raiment!' 'Well, 'tis their nature,' " the other replies (V,i,219). The humor, one might protest, is at the woman's expense; except that Fancy triumphs by understanding, with Sancho Panza's realistic comic wisdom, that a little female vanity is necessary to make the world of love go round — so also is a little deceptiveness necessary. ". . . 'what was goodness beside love!' " thought Fancy when she set about deceiving her father to make him approve her engagement to Dick (IV,iii,185).

Now in the novel's final passage, Dick in his happiness bursts out quixotically:

> "We'll have no secrets from each other, darling, will we ever? — no secret at all."
>
> None from today," said Fancy. "Hark! what's that?"
> From a neighboring thicket was suddenly heard to issue in a loud, musical, and liquid voice — "Tippiwit! swe-e-et! ki-ki-ki! Come hither, come hither, come hither!"
> "O, 'tis the nightingale," murmured she, and thought of a secret she would never tell. (V,ii,225–26)

The nightingale is both twitting her deceptiveness and, as the bird of lovers, telling her (the message she hears) to be deceptive for the sake of love.

Fancy's education makes no important difference in her behavior, which springs ultimately from the laws of biology and of pastoral. (Here she differs from Grace, who is always tied up in educated selfconsciousness.) In the Eden where *Under the Greenwood Tree* essentially takes place, Fancy remains an Eve who, as a character in pastoral comedy, never goes so far as to bring on the Fall through too much moral scrupulousness.

FAR FROM THE MADDING CROWD (published two years later in 1874) does not deal with exactly the same problems as *Under the Greenwood Tree, The Return of the Native*, and *The Woodlanders*. Education and the impact of modern ideas are not issues. The returned native of *Madding Crowd* is Sergeant Troy, whose alienation from the community comes not from modern education (though we hear he is educated) but from the traditionally rootless, irresponsible life of the soldier. When early in the novel Gabriel proposes to Bathsheba and is refused, she says, " 'You are better off than I. I have hardly a penny,' " but " 'I am better educated than you.' " There is, however, no evidence that her education has been modernizing, or that her education rather than her nature has made her a bold, independent, almost feminist woman. It is probably her education that makes her say, conservatively, " 'I want somebody to tame me; I am too independent; and you would never be able to, I know' " (IV,29). To some extent the novel tells a traditionally comic "taming of the shrew" story. Of all the pastoral novels, *Far From the Madding Crowd*, which is set retrospectively in an unspecified near past, is the most protected from the modern world.

Michael Millgate discusses the social unrest, from the 1830s to the early 1870s, in Dorset, a county "notorious" for its "social and economic backwardness'' (*Hardy: Career as Novelist*, 98–100). But the novel ignores social problems, portraying a timeless rural existence with its natural hardships. This novel, which introduces the regionalist motif by first using the name Wessex, is so steeped in pastoralism that Hardy, who composed it within and outside his father's house amid the sites he was portraying, later recalled that when he ran out of paper he would continue writing on ''large dead leaves'' (*Life*, 96).

Far from the Madding Crowd is like *Greenwood Tree* (but unlike *Woodlanders*) in making little of class distinctions. At the beginning Farmer Oak is socially superior to the penniless Bathsheba; later, after he has lost his land and she has become a landowner, she is superior. But at no point is their social difference a bar to their marrying. Nor does Farmer Boldwood's slightly superior station exert much force as a reason for Bathsheba to marry him. As an itinerant soldier and seducer of Bathsheba's servant, Troy is an outsider; so that his marriage to Bathsheba seems socially and sexually outrageous (Hardy makes their relation seem illicit though they are technically married). But even here the class distinction between sergeant and landowner is minimized by the rumor that Troy is the illegitimate son of a nobleman. Class distinctions are bridged by the strong sense of community.

We see this vividly in two episodes. In the first, Bathsheba, in taking over the farm she has inherited, announces at a meeting of the farm labourers that she has dismissed the bailiff and will manage the farm herself. Having amazed every one by asserting her authority in a man's world, Bathsheba calls the payroll, inquiring considerately of each man his name and occupation and adding to his wages a ten-shilling gift, thereby winning the men's loyalty and strengthening their sense of community. Gabriel instead, who is employed as her shepherd, she distinctly puts in his place: '' '[Y]ou quite understand your duties? — you I mean, Gabriel Oak?' '' Gabriel was ''staggered by the remarkable coolness of her manner.'' Nobody would have dreamt that they ''had ever been other than strangers'' (X,67). But Gabriel keeps shifting rank in her regard, depending on her need for his support; so that her pretense of distance enhances their unspoken acknowledgment of the tie between them.

The second episode is the sheep-shearing supper, where all the farm community sit at the same table with one end extended over the sill into Bathsheba's parlow window. They could all sit at the same table just because differences of rank were recognized and absorbed in the sense of community. Bathsheba elevates Gabriel by asking him to officiate at the bottom of the table; but when the gentleman farmer Boldwood arrives, she asks Gabriel to yield him the place. Throughout she expresses her sexual interest in Gabriel by teasing him with their difference in rank, while he bears with dignity the necessary torments of the romance hero at the hands of his cruel lady. I employ the model of the long-suffering romance hero to demonstrate Gabriel's strong sexuality throughout, a point often disputed by critics. The model is established by Gabriel's passionate words at the beginning, after Bathsheba has refused his marriage proposal: " 'I shall do one thing in this life — one thing certain — that is, love you, and long for you, and *keep wanting you till I die* ' " (IV,29).[16]

The supper is idyllic. All ranks join in communal song, recalling, as Empson points out, "the essential trick of the old pastoral, which was felt to imply a beautiful relation between rich and poor" (*Some Versions of Pastoral*, 11). In a particularly harmonious moment Bathsheba sings accompanied by Gabriel's flute and Boldwood's bass voice. "The shearers reclined against each other as at suppers in the early ages of the world" (XXIII,123). The idyl emerges from the nineteenth-century-long argument for feudal community as opposed to the equality that produces isolation. But the argument is only implied. There is not even so much overt concern with historical change as we find in the yielding of the communal choir in *Greenwood Tree* to the "isolated organ."

Yet *Far from the Madding Crowd* is more complex, though less perfect (the Fanny Robin subplot is sentimental melodrama), than *Greenwood Tree* because in *Madding* Hardy gives us, as Ian Gregor says, "a pastoral world shot through with passion and violence which just manages to contain and subdue these disruptive forces."[17] When we consider that the novel contains two deaths, one the result of seduction, the other of a murder which sends the murderer to lifetime confinement as insane, we must marvel at the artfulness which makes the novel regain its pastoral composure, though it also contains elements of romance, melodrama, tragedy and modern realism. The final serenity is achieved not only by the happy ending in the long awaited union of the two lovers, but also because Hardy has minimized our sympathy for Troy and even for Boldwood so that we do not mind seeing them eliminate each other, thus clearing the path for Gabriel and salvaging the novel's main genre, pastoral comedy, in the ritual of which Troy and Boldwood are obstructing spirits of winter for opposite reasons — Troy through a too-sensuous relation to Bathsheba, Boldwood through excessive idealization of her.

The practical Gabriel comes to represent the golden mean between these extremes. We can see that Hardy has overmanipulated the plot in order to achieve the mutual elimination of Gabriel's rivals, but we suspend judgment because Hardy is fulfilling the purpose of pastoral and romance by fulfilling our desire and the lovers'. Even the death of the mawkishly good Fanny Robin might be understood as a death of winter since her main scenes are played out in the snow, and since her death brings on the crisis that makes Bathsheba a better woman, preparing her for marriage in the spring. The penultimate chapter begins: "Bathsheba revived with the spring" (LVI,297).

Another reason for the reestablishment of pastoral over turbulence is the retrospective view which bathes the novel in an aura of timelessness within which temporary eruptions of passion drop back into the pervading stillness. Timelessness is most clearly evoked in the passage on the Gothic barn where the sheep-shearing takes place, the barn becoming still another emblem of organic community. Echoing Ruskin, Hardy shows that in Gothic there is no distinction between practical and aesthetic-spiritual considerations. Thus the barn has the same groundplan as the contemporaneous Gothic church nearby, with the advantage over Gothic church and castle that "the purpose which had dictated its original erection was the same with that to which it was still applied." The mind dwelt upon the barn's

> history, with a satisfied sense of functional continuity. . . . [F]our centuries had neither proved it to be founded on a mistake [like the church] . . . nor given rise to any reaction that had battered it down [like the castle]. . . . The defence and salvation of the body by daily bread is still a study, a religion, and a desire. (XXII,113–14)

We see here that exaltation of practicality which is the novel's leading moral idea, again reminiscent of George Eliot.[18]

As pointed out by J. Hillis Miller in *Hardy: Distance and Desire*, the barn is simultaneously presented both in its cinematic immediacy and its permanence. Hardy's double portrayal leads to his explicit statement of the novel's time-sense. "Weatherbury was immutable." The city-dweller's

> *Then* is the rustic's *Now*. In London, twenty or thirty years ago are old times . . . in Weatherbury three or four score years were included in the mere present, and nothing less than a century set a mark on its face or tone.

Hardy also sums up the novel's sense that organic community is as "natural" as nature: "So the barn was natural to the shearers, and the shearers were in harmony with the barn" (XXII,114). No other Hardy novel, not even *Greenwood Tree*, is so deliberately "immutable" as this one.

Yet *Far from the Madding Crowd* is more complex than *Under the Greenwood Tree* because turbulence and also psychology intrude into the "immutable" pastoral scene. In *Greenwood Tree* there is hardly any psychology at all, perhaps a little in Fancy's conflict between father and lover. But the portrayals of Bathsheba and Boldwood are Hardy's first excursions into the sexual psychology for which he is distinguished. The treatments of Gabriel and Troy, instead, are moral rather than psychological.

Hardy hints at sexual problems in earlier novels — Miss Aldclyffe's possible lesbianism in *Desperate Remedies*, Henry Knight's frigidity in *A Pair of Blue Eyes* — but he does not develop these problems, perhaps because he feared censorship or was mainly interested in plot. Bathsheba and Boldwood, instead, are portrayed in depth as two people who think themselves invulnerable to sex, and are taken by storm; they have no defenses when sexual desire breaks upon them. We are told of Boldwood that "[t]he insulation of his heart by reserve during these many years, without a channel of any kind for disposable emotion, had worked its effect. . . . the causes of love are chiefly subjective" (XVIII,97). His love for Bathsheba becomes as pathologically obsessive as his previous aloofness from women. We are told of the bold Bathsheba, after Troy has stirred up in her a mood of masochistic capitulation she was not prepared to recognize in herself, we are told, "Capitulation — that was the purport of [her] simple reply, guarded as it was — capitulation, unknown to herself" (XXVI,135).

> Bathsheba loved Troy in the way that only self-reliant women love when they abandon their self-reliance. When a strong woman recklessly throws away her strength she is worse than a weak woman who has never had any strength to throw away. (XXIX,147)

Bathsheba is not armed with the strength in passivity of so-called "weak" women, who in the engagements of love prove stronger than she.

Bathsheba's boldness may seem mannish. But Hardy is pro-feminist in not stereotyping the sexes as masculine-aggressive, feminine-passive. I can cite as examples the dominating Miss Aldclyffe in *Desperate Remedies*, the expert horsewoman Elfride in *A Pair of Blue Eyes*, who heroically rescues Henry Knight, the significantly named Paula Power in *A Laodicean* and also Ethelberta in *The Hand of Ethelberta*: both Paula and Ethelberta give the orders and pay.

Bathsheba can be most fetchingly feminine in her apparently masculine moments, when at the beginning she does acrobatics on horseback unaware that Gabriel is erotically peeping through a loophole of his hut, or later when she trades successfully at the Corn Exchange while the other traders, all men, are smitten with her charms. Her defiant bargaining increases her feminine attractiveness, suggesting "that there was potentiality enough in that lithe slip of humanity for alarming exploits of sex" (XII,74). When later her maid Liddy says, " 'You would be a match for any man,' " Bathsheba asks anxiously, " 'I hope I am not a bold sort of maid — mannish?' . . . 'O no, not mannish; but so almighty womanish that 'tis getting on that way sometimes' " (XXX,155).

It is because Hardy deals here with the problem of the modern independent woman's femininity that some male critics — notably Henry James, who bridled at her "wilful . . . *womanishness*"[19] — have disliked Bathsheba and left us wondering whether Hardy intended us to like her. I think he did intend us to like her, but critically. On the whole Hardy is not a feminist even though he makes Bathsheba say, " 'I *hate* to be thought men's property'" (IV,27) and " 'It is difficult for a woman to define her feelings in language which is chiefly made by men to express theirs' " (LI,270).

Bathsheba exhibits what Lawrence disapproving calls "female self-sufficiency," in her case enhanced by economic self-sufficiency. After she has begun to regret her marriage to Troy, we are told:

> [S]he had felt herself sufficient to herself, and had in the independence of her girlish heart fancied there was a certain degradation in renouncing the simplicity of a maiden existence to become the humbler half of an indifferent matrimonial whole. (XLI,212)

The feeling is not incompatible with her flirtatiousness where she holds the upper hand, while marriage is in her view submission.

Her early remark to Gabriel, " 'I want somebody to tame me,' " shows a mistaken understanding of love as a power relationship, which explains her attraction to Troy. For a while it looks as though Troy has "tamed" her, through his spectacular competence at sword-play, suggesting competence in sex. But Troy loses his dominance when, after their marriage, he proves incompetent at running the farm. Gabriel, who begins as passive compared to Bathsheba (she even rescues him from suffocation), asserts his reliable supportiveness through unfailing competence at work. His name Oak suggests supportiveness, not mastery, and also phallic strength. His first name recalls the angel who in *Paradise Lost* guards Adam and Eve. Bathsheba learns what other Hardy heroines will have to learn, that the cruel man is not necessarily the sexiest. Her marriage to Gabriel is not, as some critics think, a defeat or submission but an equal partnership in the work of running the farm. Unlike other lovers, they will "associate . . . in their labours" (LVI,303).

In *Far from the Madding Crowd* competence at work first emerges as a criterion for judging character, a criterion probably derived from George Eliot. When in the erotic atmosphere of the sheep-shearing Bathsheba impulsively fires Gabriel for not admitting he still loves her, his unique ability to save the sheeps' lives makes her swallow her pride to summon him back by irresistibly feminine means: " '*Do not desert me, Gabriel!*' " she writes (XXI,111).

We see the erotic emotions deriving from their working together the night Bathsheba turns against Troy and toward Gabriel on the issue of competence. Troy has just gotten the farmhands drunk, so that he and they are lying in a stupor, when the thunder storm Gabriel has been predicting breaks out, threatening Bathsheba's ricks (wheat stacks). Singlehandedly Gabriel tries to save them by thatching, laboring like a hero of romance to serve "that wilful and fascinating mistress whom the faithful man even now felt within him as the embodiment of all that was sweet and bright and hopeless'' (XXXVI,190). (Bathsheba as modern independent woman merges with the romance figure of the cruel superior lady; Gabriel is both romance hero and hero of modern realistic fiction.) Also worried, Bathsheba appears in the dark rickyard carrying a lantern which lights up a recognition scene between them — the first of a series suggesting their increasingly profound discovery of each other. They work together with the repetitive movements that may have influenced Lawrence's ritualized stackyard scene in *The Rainbow*. Almost blinded by a flash of lightning, Gabriel "could feel Bathsheba's warm arm tremble in his hand — a sensation novel and thrilling'' (XXXVII,194). One recalls the lightning that finally breaks down the inhibitions of Dorothea and Will in *Middlemarch*. Their erotic excitement increases as they peep *together* through a chink into the barn where Troy and the farmhands lie snoring. Feeling constrained to account for her marriage, to assure Gabriel that she drove to Bath intending to break off her engagement to Troy, she thanks him for his devotion with new warmth. Her gratitude for his usefulness is undistinguishable from her love, but this does not matter since the reader has been sure of her love and has been waiting for her to discover it. Bathsheba belongs to the line of Jane Austen's Emma and George Eliot's Maggie and Dorothea — headstrong women who have to discover what they really desire.

It is because her emotional life is at the beginning so shallow that Bathsheba can toy with men's emotions without foreseeing the consequences. She is vain like Fancy, but more dangerous because more intelligent and wilful. When Gabriel first beholds her, she is gazing into a hand-mirror, blushing, just as Eve in *Paradise Lost* falls in love with her own reflection in a pond. One might conclude from her narcissism that Bathsheba is developmentally behind Gabriel; but in these early chapters she functions more effectively than he.

In the first four chapters the birth of erotic feeling between Gabriel and Bathsheba is evoked through a remarkable series of lookings and peepings. In their first meeting, Gabriel is aroused by *looking* at the unknown girl *looking* at herself. He recognizes her again when, "putting his eye close to a hole" in a barn, he sees her inside with cows the way "Milton's Satan first saw Paradise'' (II,15–16). Bathsheba first appears in the guises of Eve and a pastoral milkmaid. When after her peeped-at acrobatics on horseback she emerges from milking, "It was with some surprise that she saw Gabriel's face rising like the moon behind the hedge." All this voyeurism is summed up in Bathsheba's feeling that "without eyes there is no indecorum . . . that Gabriel's espial had made her an indecorous woman'' (III,18,20).[20] Having run after Gabriel in such a way as to elicit his proposal of marriage, she rejects him, and Gabriel, after vowing eternal love, adopts the romance hero's strategy of patient selfless service, even to the point of promoting Boldwood's suit in the hope of saving Bathsheba from Troy.

Bathsheba's toying with Boldwood has more serious consequences. Piqued because he refused to look at her in the Corn Exchange, she jestingly sends him a valentine, affixing to it a large red seal before she realizes with a laugh that the seal bears the words " 'Marry Me' " (XIII,79). Boldwood's stormy reaction is implausible unless we apply Freudian concepts of repression and understand in his reaction Hardy's criticism of Shelleyan idealism. For Boldwood falls in love with an idea in his own head, *seeing* Bathsheba only a little better now than in the Corn Exchange. When after having sent the valentine Bathsheba again enters the Exchange, we are told of Boldwood: "Adam had awakened from his deep sleep, and behold! there was Eve" (XVII,93). Boldwood beholds an image. We are told of his courting: "The great aids to idealization in love were present here: occasional observation of her from a distance, and the absence of social intercourse with her" (XIX,98).

Neither does Troy *see* her the night they meet in her garden (recalling Satan in the Garden) by getting entangled in each other's clothes — she is too sensuously close for visual observation. Only Gabriel comes to see her as she really is, and continues loving her: he "was ever regardful of [her face's] faintest changes" (XVIII,97). As the mean between extremes Gabriel, as I have suggested, is portrayed morally rather than psychologically. Troy, too, is portrayed morally because he is given no mitigating inner life — he is simply the sensualist living in the present with no thought of consequences. His one trace of inner life, his remorse for the deaths of Fanny and their baby, is soon wiped out ironically when the rain, running all night through the mocking jaws of a gargoyle while he sleeps by Fanny's grave, washes away the flowers he just planted there. That ends his remorse. He makes for Budmouth where, leaving his clothes on the beach, he takes the swim in the ocean from which he does not return, unintentionally giving the impression he has drowned.

In Bathsheba's portrayal, instead, psychological understanding mitigates moral judgment, as we can see by the narrator's comment after she has "unreflectingly" sent the valentine: "Of love as a spectacle Bathsheba had a fair knowledge; but of love subjectively she knew nothing" (XII,79). Only after Bathsheba, in the effectively melodramatic scene over Fanny's coffin, suffers rejection by Troy does she come to understand love subjectively by suffering the pain she has so casually inflicted on others.

In the confrontation with Troy over the coffin, Bathsheba "suffered in an absolute sense" more than Fanny in all her sufferings. When Troy sinking upon his knees kisses the dead Fanny, Bathsheba flings her arms round his neck, "exclaiming wildly from the deepest deep of her heart," a depth she only now discovers in herself, begging him to kiss her too.

There was something so abnormal and startling in the childlike pain and simplicity of this appeal from a woman of Bathsheba's calibre and independence, that Troy, loosening her tightly closed arms from his neck, looked at her in bewilderment. . . . Troy could hardly seem to believe her to be his proud wife Bathsheba.

Bathsheba is brought still lower when Troy, refusing to kiss her, calls Fanny his true wife. " 'If she's — that, — what — am I?' " Bathsheba sobs, recalling to our minds the illicit quality of their marriage. She emits "a wail of anguish" (XLIII,230–31) that brings back all the wailings in the literature of the past. The moment makes us wonder how much weight we should give to the historical reverberations of the names Troy and Bathsheba. Both names recall cases of illegitimate sexual attraction leading to violence — with in Troy's case the characteristically Greek tragic conclusion; and in Bathsheba's case the characteristically Hebrew providential conclusion, for the Biblical Bathsheba became the mother of Solomon and thus of King David's legitimate successors.

Bathsheba descends even lower when she flees to pass the night in a ferny hollow like the hollow where Troy first seduced her with his swordplay. Only this hollow is swampy, exhaling "the essences of evil things in the earth, and in the waters under the earth" (XLIV,233). The going under, the passage through evil, is widely recognized as a necessary stage in the experience of rebirth into a less egocentric selfhood.

The rebirth symbolism continues as Bathsheba, after her infernal night, becomes aware the next morning of two saving figures. The first is a passing schoolboy who chants the prayer for "grace" which applies to her condition. The second, an apparition in the mist, turns out to be Liddy. It is a sign of Bathsheba's spiritual isolation that she warns Liddy not to try crossing the swamp. Nevertheless Liddy, like Jesus walking on the water, crosses to her, creating as she trod, "[i]ridescent bubbles of dank subterranean breath" that "burst and expanded away to join the vapoury firmament above" (XLIV,234). The movement from "dank subterranean breath" to "vapoury firmament" signifies rebirth, as does Bathsheba's discovery that she has after the night's exposure lost her voice. Hardy's poems contain no texture of imagery denser than the imagery of this episode. The recollection of the earlier hollow suggests that if Bathsheba has finally matured from girl to woman, it is Troy who began the process by bringing her to life sexually, that Troy paved the way for Gabriel.

Bathsheba goes to the opposite extreme symbolically by ascending from the hollow to her attic, where she imprisons herself in order to hide from Troy. Bathsheba's penitential self-imprisonment corresponds to what Hardy calls Troy's "romanticism" in hoping to compensate for his crime against

Fanny by giving her an expensive tombstone. Troy soon abandons his remorse; whereas Bathsheba continues her moral development, though her rebirth yields at first a listless woman, lacking the sparkle of the bold, self-
centered girl. Thus out of guilt over Boldwood and fear for his sanity, she
reluctantly submits to a six-year engagement to him — six years to see
whether Troy returns.

With Gabriel receded into the background, the novel becomes perfunctory — kept going by dazzling tricks of plot, like Troy's return as performer
in a circus show attended by Bathsheba and Boldwood who do not recognize
him. Hardy even makes Bathsheba lean so far back against a circus tent that
Troy, on the other side, can slip a hand beneath the tent to lift from her
fingers a note informing her of his return. Hardy's virtuosity with plot is, as
I have said, both a strength and a danger.

The virtuosity and the danger are illustrated by Troy's disguised entrance
and unmasking at Boldwood's Christmas party. He has come, he announces,
to claim his wife. In a momentary display of subtle psychology amidst the
melodrama, Hardy makes Boldwood say, in an unrecognizable voice masking
his frustration, " 'Bathsheba, go with your husband!' " "Sudden despair
had transformed him" (LIII,289). It is Bathsheba's scream when Troy touches
her that causes Boldwood to shoot and kill him, then rush to the police to give
himself up. As I have suggested, we accept the manipulation that eliminates
Gabriel's rivals because, as in all good melodramatic romance, this highly
theatrical scene brings to fulfillment our desire to see the two lovers married.

There is a return to psychological validity in Bathsheba's suffering over
her responsibility for so much disaster. She shows a new generosity of spirit
in having Troy buried with Fanny. Outside a church within which children
are singing, she weeps copiously, allowing as never before a release of
emotion. She becomes aware of a waiting presence. It is Gabriel who, having
been made farm manager, tells her he must resign, that he is leaving England.
Reverting to her earlier feminine appeals, she cries out, " '[N]ow that I am
more helpless than ever you go away!' " (LVI,299). Gabriel gives " 'that
very helplessness' " as his reason for departing. By laying down this rough
ultimatum, Gabriel becomes both the model for and the agent of Bathsheba's
renewal of self-confidence — a renewal which would not take place were
he overgentle with her, as Giles is with Grace in *Woodlanders*. Earlier Bathsheba had recognized that Oak's superiority lay in his patience and objectivity:
:

> What a way Oak had, she thought, of enduring things. Boldwood, who seemed
> so much deeper and higher and stronger in feeling than Gabriel, had not yet
> learnt, any more than she herself, the simple lesson which Oak showed a

mastery of . . . that among the multitude of interests by which he was surrounded, those which affected his personal well-being were not the most absorbing and important in his eyes. (XLIII,226)

In envying Oak's adjustment to objective reality, she is advancing the novel's
main moral idea.

Now after Gabriel's ultimatum, Bathsheba

was aggrieved and wounded that the possession of hopeless love from Gabriel,
which she had grown to regard as her inalienable right for life, should have
been withdrawn just at his own pleasure in this way. She was bewildered too
by the prospect of having to rely on her own resources again: it seemed to
herself that she never could again acquire energy sufficient to go to market,
barter, and sell. (LVI,300–301)

Such a passage would seem to confirm Peter Casagrande's argument that
Bathsheba makes no moral improvement, that Hardy's aim is to show
" 'Woman's prescriptive infirmity' '': "Her [egocentric] irrationality is
curbed, not transformed, by the end of the novel."[21] If Casagrande is right,
the novel mainly tells a traditionally misogynistic "taming of the shrew"
story — an unlikely stand for a progressive late-Victorian writer. Penny
Boumelha is more accurate in saying, in *Hardy and Women*, that "the radicalism of Hardy's representation of women resides . . . in their resistance to
reduction to a single and uniform ideological position."[22] Hence Hardy's
shifting between apparently feminist and apparently antifeminist positions.
Irving Howe cuts through the argument with this fundamental insight: "As a
writer of novels Thomas Hardy was endowed with a precious gift: he liked
women."[23]

Let us look carefully at the end of *Madding Crowd*. As earlier, Bathsheba
pursues Gabriel, this time to his cottage, to elicit his proposal of marriage.
Picking up her signal Gabriel, "tenderly and in surprise" (words that argue
against the "taming of the shrew" reading) says:

"If I only knew one thing — whether you would allow me to love you and
win you, and marry you after all — If I only knew that!"
"But you never will know," she murmured.
"Why?"
"Because you never ask." (LVI,303)

Accompanying her home happily, Gabriel talks not about love but about his
forthcoming tenure of the farm Boldwood left him — an inheritance that
equalizes them, giving their marriage the social appropriateness required by
traditional comic endings.

Many critics consider the marriage of Gabriel and Bathsheba a settling
for less, a tragedy of reduced expectations. But the text suggests, instead, a

fulfillment of Hardy's advanced ideas about marriage. Hardy's approval of Gabriel's omission of love talk ("pretty phrases and warm expressions being probably unnecessary between such tried friends") suggests a realistic new statement about love and marriage. Hardy concludes with marriage, the required happy ending, but gives us also a critique of traditional marriage. According to Hardy's revision of the old idealizing view, it is an advantage that Bathsheba's love of Gabriel is buttressed by self-interest while self-interest is justified by love. In the important view of marriage proposed in the chapter's last paragraph, a view toward which the whole novel has been leading, there is no talk of female submission but rather of "good-fellowship — *camaraderie*" between the partners in a working and a love relationship, "romance growing up in the interstices of a mass of hard prosaic reality."

> Theirs was that substantial affection which arises (if any arises at all) when the two who are thrown together begin first by knowing the rougher sides of each other's character, and not the best till further on, the romance growing up in the interstices of a mass of hard prosaic reality. This good-fellowship — *camaraderie* — usually occurring through similarity of pursuits, is unfortunately seldom superadded to love between the sexes, because men and women associate, not in their labours, but in their pleasures merely. Where, however, happy circumstance permits its development, the compounded feeling proves itself to be the only love which is strong as death . . . beside which the passion usually called by the name is evanescent as steam. (LVI,330–04)

Paradoxically this genuine romantic love, "the only love which is strong as death," endures because the lovers began by knowing the worst about each other. Thus Bathsheba does not in the end need to be morally perfect in order to be loved and become capable of loving. With the self-confidence that comes from being loved, her competence, it is implied, will return and she will participate with Gabriel in the management of the farm.

FINALLY WE MUST NOTICE Gabriel's moral development; for of all Hardy's heroes Gabriel comes closest to perfection, and serves therefore as a model by which the others are to be judged. Gabriel combines, as I have suggested, three modes of heroism: he is a hero of pastoral and romance and, as he evolves, a hero also of the new realistic mode.

Gabriel is first presented as a pastoral, flute-playing shepherd, who has through past competence worked himself up from shepherd to farmer by leasing a small sheep farm at Norcombe. We see right away a combination of pastoral and realist virtues — a combination reinforced when we are told that Gabriel reads the stars both for their beauty and for practical information, and that he is only middling in looks and goodness and is "Laodicean" (I,7) or lukewarm in religious conviction (for Hardy an advantage despite the contrary judgments of Revelation 3.14–16 and Dante). Gabriel's general attractiveness increases as we see him in *action* in real circumstances over a long period of time.

When the story begins Gabriel seems lacking in competence, for he falls asleep on two crucial occasions. On the first he falls asleep with the windows of his shepherd's hut closed, so that he would have suffocated were it not that Bathsheba — whom he has seen only once, long enough to have fallen in love with her — exhibits her competence by saving his life. He awakes to find "his head was upon her lap, his face and neck were disagreeably wet, and her fingers were unbuttoning his collar," a physical intimacy suggesting that they will be lovers (III,21). On the second occasion he is sleeping so soundly that he does not hear his young, inexperienced sheep dog driving his sheep over a precipice, killing them all. He is financially ruined.

His total defeat at Norcombe works a great change in Gabriel, giving him that serene attunement to reality which Bathsheba will spend the rest of the novel catching up with.

> He had passed through an ordeal of wretchedness which had given him more than it had taken away. He had sunk from his modest elevation as pastoral king into the very slime-pits of Siddim; but there was left to him a dignified calm he had never before known, and that indifference to fate which, though it often makes a villain of a man, is the basis of his sublimity when it does not. And thus the abasement had been exaltation, and the loss gain. (IV,34)

The "slime-pits of Siddim" (Gen. 14.10) parallel the swampy hollow in which Bathsheba will experience a similar rebirth.

The romance theme continues when Gabriel falls asleep for the third time, this time beneficially; for the wagon in which he falls asleep deposits him on Bathsheba's newly inherited farm at Weatherbury, just as her ricks are burning, so he can take charge and save them. Falling asleep is clearly the means by which Gabriel follows his destiny, fulfilling his deepest desires. Falling asleep will work the same way for Tess.

Gabriel's heroic skill leads to an almost magical recognition scene in which the farmer, a lady on a pony, veiled against the fire, "lifted the wool veil tied round her face, and looked all astonishment," when Gabriel asks, " 'Do you happen to want a shepherd, ma'am?' " "Gabriel and his cold-hearted darling, Bathsheba Everdene, were face to face" (VI,41).

As Bathsheba's shepherd Gabriel behaves with manly dignity, braving her wrath by telling her the truth about objective circumstances and by refusing to make the declarations of love that would expose him to further rebuffs. Even as he labors alone in the night, like a romance hero, to save Bathsheba's ricks, he calculates, like a hero of realism, the impending loss to her in pounds and shillings. Nor does his serviceableness make him uncritically subservient to Bathsheba as Giles is to Grace. Gabriel learns to treat Bathsheba with loving roughness.

In contrast to Boldwood who because of his hopeless love lets his farm fall into ruin, Gabriel's hopelessness does not interfere with his efficiency. Bathsheba, who for most of the book understands love only in terms of power (either she dominates as with Boldwood, or is dominated as with Troy) mistakes Gabriel's gentleness for lack of masculine strength. Having told him he was not the one who could "tame" her, she is constantly surprised and angered that so faithful a servant can successfully resist her domination. Gabriel finally "tames" her, to use her inappropriate word, by making himself so quietly supportive that she finally realizes she wants to lean on him. Gabriel's is the true masculine strength because it reinforces her feminine strength, suggesting the only kind of sexual competence that can be combined with enduring love and mutual respect.

Because there is no conflict between Gabriel's piety and his competence, he can without loss of integrity win in the end his long sought goal, Bathsheba's hand in marriage, along with unsought for material benefits — Boldwood's farm and Bathsheba's. His combination of country skills with reading and spiritual wisdom contrasts with Clym's regressive pastoralism in renouncing his intellectual ambitions to become a furze cutter, the least skilled of country occupations.

Giles in *The Woodlanders* excels in country skills, and is like Gabriel a hero of pastoral and romance; but he cannot take care of himself in the struggle that would advance him economically and socially. Nor can he compete sexually; his courtship of Grace is inept. It is true that Giles is threatened, as Gabriel is not, by characters from the outside modern world (the world of the late 1870s) — by Mrs. Charmond who takes his houses and Fitzpiers who takes Grace. This outside world renders the novel's pastoral setting anomalous and Giles's country virtues obsolete. But Gabriel, with his realist virtues, could one feels adapt to modern conditions. He has the ability to survive and that, as we see over and over again, is an ability respected by the Darwinian Hardy.

For all his altruism Gabriel is not an "idealist," for in him there is no dissociation between the ideal and the real. He stands as a criterion of judgment for Hardy's subsequent studies of failed idealists, beginning with Clym Yeobright. Gabriel is Hardy's model for what Yeats was to call Unity of Being.

University of Virginia

NOTES

1. Thomas Hardy, *The Return of the Native*, ed. James Gindin (New York: Norton, 1969), Bk. I, ch. ii, pp. 8–9.

2. Florence Emily Hardy, *The Life of Thomas Hardy 1840–1928* (London: Macmillan, 1982), p. 50.
3. In writing to Swinburne, for example, Hardy praises his translation of Sappho's line in "Anactoria": " 'Thee, too, the years shall cover,' " saying "Those few words present, I think, the finest *drama* of Death and Oblivion, so to speak, in our tongue" (*Life*, p. 287).
4. See, for example, W. W. Greg in his classic *Pastoral Poetry and Pastoral Drama*: "What does appear to be a constant element in the pastoral as known to literature is the recognition of a contrast . . . between pastoral life and some more complex type of civilization" (London: A. H. Bullen, 1906), p. 4. William Empson was revisionist in discovering also nonrural versions of pastoral (*Some Versions of Pastoral*, 1935, rpt. Norfolk, Conn.: New Directions, 1950). Michael Squires regards "the pastoral novel as a variation . . . of traditional pastoral" in combining "realism with the pastoral impulse" (*The Pastoral Novel: Studies in George Eliot, Thomas Hardy, and D. H. Lawrence*, Charlottesville: UP of Virginia, 1974, p. 2). Also relevant to Hardy is Annabel Patterson's demonstration of the extent to which pastorals since Virgil have been used for political and social criticism (*Pastoral and Ideology: Virgil to Valéry*, Berkeley: U of California P, 1987).
5. Raymond Williams, *The Country and the City* (New York: Oxford University Press, 1973), p. 208. Douglas Brown, "The Agricultural Theme," *Thomas Hardy* (London: Longmans Green, 1961). For a comprehensive survey of the economic, social and literary aspects of the country background, see Merryn Williams, *Thomas Hardy and Rural England* (London: Macmillan, 1972).
6. Thomas Hardy, "The Dorsetshire Labourer," *Personal Writings*, ed. Harold Orel (Lawrence: U of Kansas P, 1966), p. 182.
7. Thomas Hardy, *The Collected Letters*, 7 vols. eds. R. L. Purdy and M. Millgate (Oxford: Clarendon P, 1978), I: 11.
8. For detailed discussions of the minor novels, see Norman Page, *Thomas Hardy* (London and Boston: Routledge & Kegan Paul, 1977) and Michael Millgate, *Thomas Hardy: His Career as a Novelist* (New York: Random House, 1971).
9. *Thomas Hardy and His Readers: A Selection of Contemporary Reviews*, ed. Laurence Lerner and John Holmstrom (New York: Barnes and Noble, 1968), pp. 17, 85, 162–63.
10. Thomas Hardy, *Under the Greenwood Tree or The Mellstock Quire: A Rural Painting of the Dutch School*, ed. David Wright (Harmondsworth: Penguin, 1978), p. 39.
11. Thomas Hardy, *The Woodlanders*, ed. James Gibson (Harmondsworth: Penguin, 1981), ch. XLIV, p. 399.
12. Thomas Hardy, *Far from the Madding Crowd*, ed. Robert C. Schweik (New York: Norton, 1986), ch. I, p. 7.
13. See W. J. Keith, "A Regional Approach to Hardy's Fiction," in *Critical Approaches to the Fiction of Thomas Hardy*, ed. Dale Kramer (New York: Barnes and Noble, 1979), p. 36. See also David Havird, *Thomas Hardy and the Aesthetics of Regionalism* (Unpub. diss., Charlottesville: University of Virginia, 1986). Carl J. Weber dates the action of Hardy's novels in *Hardy of Wessex: His Life and Literary Career* (New York: Columbia University P, 1965), p. 224.
14. Bruce Johnson, *True Correspondence: A Phenomenology of Thomas Hardy's Novels* (Tallahassee: U Presses of Florida, 1983), pp. 10–11, 43.
15. In *Anatomy of Criticism*, Northrop Frye characterizes pastoral and romance through "*the analogy of innocence*" (Princeton: Princeton UP, 1957), p. 151.

My ideas about genre have inevitably been influenced by this seminal work. See also Alastair Fowler, *Kinds of Literature: An Introduction to the Theory of Genres and Modes* (Oxford: Clarendon P, 1982).

16. See Susan Beegel's persuasive argument for Gabriel's "potent, life-affirming sexuality" in "Bathsheba's Lovers: Male Sexuality in *Far from the Madding Crowd*," in *Sexuality and Victorian Literature, Tennessee Studies in Literature*, vol. 27, ed. Don R. Cox (Knoxville: U of Tennessee P, 1984), p. 116.

17. Ian Gregor, *The Great Web: The Form of Hardy's Major Fiction* (London: Faber and Faber, 1982), p. 34.

18. In *Adam Bede*, for example, where Adam replies to his pious brother Seth by saying that the man who " 'scrats at his bit o' garden and makes two potatoes grow istead o' one, he's doing more good, and he's just as near to God, as if he was running after some preacher and a-praying and a-groaning' " (George Eliot, *Adam Bede*, ed. John Patterson, Boston: Houghton Mifflin, 1968, p. 10).

19. "[W]e cannot say that we either understand or like Bathsheba. She is a young lady of the inconsequential, wilful, mettlesome type . . . the type which aims at giving one a very intimate sense of a young lady's *womanishness* (Henry James's review in *The Nation*, 24 December 1874; reprinted in *Hardy and His Readers*, p. 33.) James's hostility to Hardy here and elsewhere suggests competitiveness.

20. Freud writes that "in scopophilia [erotic looking] . . . the eye corresponds to an erotogenic zone." "The eye is perhaps the zone most remote from the sexual object, but it is . . . liable to be the most frequently stimulated by the particular quality of excitation whose cause, when it occurs in a sexual object, we describe as beauty" (Sigmund Freud, *The Standard Edition of the Complete Psychological Works*, 24 vols., tr. James Strachey with Anna Freud, London: Hogarth Press and Institute of Psycho-Analysis, vol. VII, pp. 169, 209). In *Thomas Hardy: Distance and Desire*, J. Hillis Miller skillfully treats *watching* in Hardy as an epistemological stance, a "detachment of consciousness" (p. 9), without noting the erotic quality of watching (Cambridge: Harvard UP, 1970, especially ch. I, "The Refusal of Involvement").

21. Peter J. Casagrande, "A New View of Bathsheba Everdene," in *Critical Approaches to Fiction of Hardy*, ed. Kramer, pp. 69, 57.

22. Penny Boumelha, *Thomas Hardy and Women: Sexual Ideology and Narrative Form* (Madison: University of Wisconsin Press, 1982), p. 7. Boumelha sounds ideological, however, in saying later that "the only freedom granted" Bathsheba and Paula Power, despite inherited wealth and absent fathers, "is the freedom to choose a man" and so resubject themselves "to the patriarchal structures" (p. 40). Hardy became increasingly critical of marriage as an outmoded burden upon both men and women.

23. Irving Howe, *Thomas Hardy* (New York: Macmillan, Collier-Macmillan, 1967), p.108.

OBJECTIVITY AND DEATH: VICTORIAN SCIENTIFIC AUTOBIOGRAPHY

By George Levine

THE IDEAL OF KNOWLEDGE canonized in the nineteenth century and still dominant today entails, metaphorically at least, death for both subject and object. And that metaphor has often had all too literal incarnations. One form of the metaphor is worked out in science fiction movies characteristic in particular of 1950s and '60s: the scientist/protagonist becomes "inhuman," obsessed with knowing at the risk of allowing the monstrous mutant to doom the world. This knowledge-obsessed figure, a descendant of Victor Frankenstein, no doubt, will be destroyed by what he wants to know as, it is possible to believe, Western civilization is doomed to be destroyed by the consequences of its own science.

If the figure of Frankenstein has often been taken as a perfect metaphor for modern Western science, the story of that science — starting with Adam and Eve — is also a story of conflicts over how much it is legitimate to know. In the fundamental narrative of Western culture, knowledge is made contemporaneous with, and equal to, death: Adam and Eve were quite literally dying to know. And in their story the linking of moral, religious, and epistemological elements is most obvious. For Bacon and Descartes, perhaps the founding theorists of modern science, the impulse to clear away the errors of the past was explicitly moral, and the conditions they prescribed for discovering the truth are both moral and epistemological. Questions of knowledge are always questions of morality; implicitly they are questions of religion, too. Was it right to attempt to understand atomic energy? Is it right to continue to study the nature of genetic materials and even to make literal Frankenstein's fictional effort to create new forms of life?

My larger argument is that these popular questions and interpretations of the activities of science are consistent with the ostensibly innocuous modern ideal of knowledge — the view that knowledge can only be authoritative

273

when it is uninfluenced by the feelings, desires, or personal ambitions of the investigator, when, that is, it is objective and disinterested. Objectivity entails the denial of subjectivity; disinterest requires denial of normal human relations with the thing to be known. To know requires self-denial, the renunciation of normal human claims and desires. That is surely one of the reasons that scientific journals are written as they are. But the degree to which the potentialities for violence of this ideal are embedded in the most rational and casual discourse can be inferred from some of the most attractive and canonical examples of Victorian prose. There is, of course, the transformation of Arnold's ideal of the best self, unswayed by desire or political party, into the justification of what looks very much like an authoritarian state. Less extravagantly, there is the odd similarity in such strikingly different documents as the autobiographies of Charles Darwin, John Stuart Mill, and Anthony Trollope.

I read these works in the context of the ideals of science I have been describing, and of some of its complications. To begin with, I need to elaborate my opening argument.[1] The special authority of the ideal of knowledge is derived from its similarity to Western ideals of art, morality, and religion. All these have also traditionally insisted that salvation, virtue, or success depend upon the rejection of the self: the great artist speaks not personally but universally, not with his or her own voice but with the inspiration of a muse. Morality specifically rejects demands for the self, requires that we imagine ourselves as others, doing unto others as we would have others do unto us. Religion requires the imitation of God, and in Christianity in particular that means that one can only be saved by dying to the world. The ideal of Christianity is the imitation of Christ, death to the world. "Thou fool," says St. Paul, "that which thou sowest is not quickened, except it die" (1 Cor. 15.36). And one can only know clearly *after* one dies: "Now we see through a glass darkly, But then face to face" (1 Cor. 13.12). The nineteenth-century ideal of knowledge requires, similarly, a renunciation of self if one is to know the other as in itself it really is.

Here are a few nineteenth-century examples, in which the ideal of knowledge blends with the ideal of these other great human values. An obvious example is Carlyle's *Sartor Resartus*. At the center of that strange book, Diogenes Teufelsdröckh undergoes a spiritual conversion in the experience of what he calls the "Everlasting Yea." But the Everlasting Yea is more "no," than "yea." It requires not the courageous affirmation of self against the material bleakness of the universe (which was what Teufelsdröckh had called the "Everlasting No") but a denial of the self. In a language parodically but, I believe, significantly "scientific," he affirms:

> So true is it . . . that *the Fraction of Life can be increased in value not so much by increasing your Numerator as by lessening your Denominator*. Nay, unless

my Algebra deceive me, *Unity* itself divided by *Zero* will give *Infinity*. Make thy claim of wages a zero, then; thou hast the world under thy feet. Well did the Wisest of our time write: "It is only with Renunciation (*Entsagen*) that Life, properly speaking, can be said to begin." (191)

This is a dressed up version of a Christian truism — that true moral being requires self-sacrifice. But it is important to note that Teufelsdröckh's statement affirms the necessity for renunciation of life, the obliteration of self, as a means to empowering the self. It mixes the language and forms of religion and science, but like science, it is fundamentally secular.

Later in the "Everlasting Yea" chapter, Teufelsdröckh proclaims,

May we not say . . . that the hour of Spiritual Enfranchisement is even this: When your Ideal World, wherein the whole man has been dimly struggling and inexpressibly languishing to work, becomes revealed, and thrown open; and you discover, with amazement enough, like the Lothario in *Wilhelm Meister*, that your "America is here or nowhere". . . . Yes here, in this poor, miserable, hampered, despicable Actual." (196)

The language of the spirit is there, but the world is illuminated at the moment that one discovers that the ideal is the actual. In effect, Carlyle, who was notoriously evasive about religion, invokes the religious pattern to affirm the secular. Like the ideal of knowledge that I have been discussing, Carlyle is trying to endow the material present with the authority of the ideal and spiritual. Unrelentingly secular and anti-metaphysical, the new ideal of knowledge carries with it the aura of moral and spiritual authority that had belonged to traditional religion.

Carlyle's work makes a major document in Victorian literary and cultural history in part because it attempts to find a language to authorize the secular. And that, of course, was the project of science as well. In his work epistemology is inextricably linked with religion and morality. But Carlyle is not as peculiar in this respect as his extravagant language might make it appear. The connections among epistemology, religion and morality are still being made, and in the conduct of everyday life as well as in philosophy and science. Here is an argument made by Rom Harré, a distinguished Oxford philosopher of science. "In my view," he says,

science is not just an epistemological but also a moral achievement. In defending the scientific community's just claims to knowledge I am also defending the moral superiority of that community relative to any other human association.

I believe that the scientific community exhibits a model or ideal of rational co-operation set within a strict moral order, the whole having no parallel in any other human activity. And this despite the all-too-human characteristics of the actual members of that community seen as just another social order. Notoriously the rewards of place, power and prestige are often not commensurate with the quality of individual scientific achievements when these are looked at from a historical perspective. Yet that very community enforces standards of honesty, trustworthiness and good work against which the moral quality of Christian civilization stands condemned. (5)

For Harré, then, the scientific community is more moral than the Christian. And by this, he means in part that scientists qua scientists transcend the human, are, precisely, "inhuman," as they adhere rigorously to agreed upon methods and procedures that get beyond the merely personal. The scientific community is characterized by "trust" that in scientific matters concerns about personal interest will not enter. To be a true scientist one must, for the time being at least, be personally dead.

The pervasiveness of this epistemological/moral ideal in nineteenth-century thought is evident even in Keats's famous formulation of the ideal of negative capability: "the poet has . . . no identity," he wrote; "when I am in a room with People," he goes on, "the identity of every one in the room begins to . . . press upon me that, I am in a very little time an[ni]hilated" (279–80).

Or consider Matthew Arnold's famous case of criticism and culture. For Arnold, of course, such violent language as Carlyle's or even Keats's "annihilation" would be a symptom of the emotional affirmation of self that true knowledge needs to negate. For him, criticism, the attempt "simply to know the best that is known and thought in the world" (270), was only possible through a rejection of the practical — a rejection, that is, of utilitarian satisfaction of personal needs. In its place is required "disinterestedness": the absence of personal interest, bias, desire. Any sort of partisan position interferes with the possibility of attaining the truth. So criticism must be understood as "a disinterested endeavour to learn and propagate the best that is known and thought in the world," and salvation comes when the "ordinary self" is rejected. To be sure, Arnold believes in what he calls a "best self," but this self is defined as impersonal and is characterized by its universality. Rejection of the ordinary self in pursuit of truth can lead to an ultimate affirmation of something like a transcendent self — and the parallel to Christian salvation becomes almost exact.

The positivist model of knowledge is programatically self-alienating. For Feuerbach, for example, the distinctively human begins with self-consciousness; and self-consciousness is self-fragmentation, the power of the self to make itself an object. The life of man, says Feuerbach, is "twofold," for the "inner life of man is the life which has relation to his species, to his general, as distinguished from his individual, nature" (2). While Feuerbach's project is to integrate the two, he demonstrates how Christianity builds on the dual nature of the human to require the annihilation of the human.

Feuerbach's analysis of consciousness as consciousness of self and species, and thus of the infinite (as opposed to brute knowledge of the particular) perfectly represents my point. That is to say, the quest for particular knowledge is death because it exposes one's own finiteness and finiteness equals nothingness; the quest for full consciousness (knowledge) is recognition of one's "essential" self, that is, one's self as an expression of the species. Thus, the true infinite knowledge is a knowledge that denies one's individual being.

Similarly, when Comte, the true author of official positivism, attempts to establish his "social physics," the scientific study of humanity by humanity, he disentangles the self observing from the self observed:

> there can be nothing like scientific observation of the passions, except from without, as the stir of the emotions disturbs the observing faculties more or less. It is yet more out of the question to make an intellectual observation of intellectual processes. The observing and observed organ are here the same, and its action cannot be pure and natural. In order to observe, your intellect must pause from activity; yet it is this very activity that you want to observe. (80)

This crisis of objectivity is the crucial obstacle to Comte's new science (which is one of the reasons, I believe, that he rejected psychology as a science) as it has remained the crisis of the social sciences, and there is no more obvious point at which the ideal of knowledge demands the death of observer and observed; they must hold still in order to know and be known.

Positivism had far other intentions, of course. Comte's late prose implicitly takes Comte as infallible prophet of the new religion. His project was to affirm human power, not to destroy it; and I want to insist that the language we use in our inheritance of the ideal of science is inevitably paradoxical in this way. Both Bacon and Descartes rhetorically minimize the self and effectually celebrate it. The positivist ideal contains both the model of death and the implication of ultimate self-affirmation, or resurrection. Positivism was, in any case, a movement with revolutionary implications (even while its forms in Comteanism were conservative replications of medieval ideals). While it was anti-metaphysical, it also attempted to establish a ground of epistemological certainty in place of the religious, metaphysical and a priori authorities it had dismissed. Comte's positive method derived from feeling, yet required objectivity and disinterest. It insisted that all knowledge is grounded in experience, yet it denied the status of knowledge to any experience that could not be verified and replicated.

Comte's positivism in effect codified the ideal of knowledge I have been discussing and, in the name of love and feeling, rejected any intrusion of the subjective — which included any intrusion of that which could not be "experienced" universally, like such things, even, as "cause and effect." Comte believed it was possible to extend scientific method to the study of humanity, and was thus instrumental in the creation of the "human sciences," where the paradoxes implicit in the ideal of knowledge were most exaggeratedly evident. Darwin, of course, made humanity the subject of science; and Claude Bernard made the human body such a subject. Throughout the nineteenth century, science intruded on the subject of humanity — in biology, sociology, anthropology, psychology. And those human sciences, as they adopt scientific method, entail the methods of self-alienation. In objectifying humanity they became precisely the knowledge of self-alienation, the transformation of self into object. Comte's work helped convince John Stuart Mill, among others, that the project was a credible one, and many Victorians more or less self-consciously came to accept the view that as the physical sciences were making the natural world comprehensible and bringing them under control, so the social sciences could make human experience comprehensible hence controllable and predictable.

One example of the way the late nineteenth-century scientific naturalists responded to this extension of science to the realm of human life should suffice to suggest how the metaphorical equivalence of the pursuit of knowledge and the surrender to death might be justified. John Tyndall in the notorious, Belfast Address, pursues life to its material base. At one point he says,

> We can trace the development of a nervous system, and correlate with it the parallel phenomena of sensation and thought. We see with undoubting certainty that they go hand in hand. But we try to soar in a vacuum the moment we seek to comprehend the connection between them. An Archimedean fulcrum is here required which the human mind cannot command; and the effort to solve the problem . . . is like that of a man trying to lift himself by his own waistband. All that has been said in this discourse is to be taken in connection with this fundamental truth. When "nascent senses" are spoken of, and when these possessions and processes are associated with "the modification of an organism by its environment," the same parallelism without contact, or even approach to contact, is implied. Man the *object* is separated by an impassable gulf from man the *subject*. There is no motor energy in the human intellect to carry it, without biological rupture, from the one to the other. (II,195)

Tyndall is trying to recuperate the spiritual by locating a point at which science can no longer provide explanation. But he can only save the spirit by positing a radical alienation between body and spirit, and by creating a model like Huxley's automata — a machine that runs by itself.

Positivism, in later forms, continues to thrive in the practice of science and the language of the social sciences, and more surreptitiously, in the rather looser standards that govern argument and knowledge among ordinary people. It is the way the culture thinks about knowing, and it is endorsed by spokesmen for aspirin who don white coats for television commercials, by the almost universal insistence on objectivity, disinterest (as opposed to uninterest), and selflessness, by science's faith in the possibility of achieving knowledge without recourse to divine intervention or mere institutional authority. Positivism entailed a self-conscious shift, initiated by Bacon long before, from reliance on "authority," specifically a religious and metaphysical authority, to reliance on the secular. Its relation to religion is clearly enough suggested by Comte's attempt to create out of Positivism a religion of humanity, a secular version of the Roman Catholicism he had abandoned. And its function was to replace that authority and to offer a pragmatic and unquestionably grounded mode of explanation of the natural and the human worlds that would answer the fundamental question of the romantics and Carlyle — what is it possible to believe in a post-revolutionary world from which God has been largely banished?

Knowledge, then, in the tradition of Western positivism becomes an odd process of alienation and possession. All attempts to know within this tradition entail both the creation of an "other" and possession of it. To know oneself one must stand outside oneself. The act of knowing becomes an act of repossession. So to know is both to kill and to possess; and while this may seem an excessive metaphorization of the process, it would be possible to trace out the realization of these metaphors in the West's relation to nature and the "other." Of course, in the more strictly scientific formulations, the extreme demands of self-annihilation and self-alienation are not explicitly made. But notice how in that deeply influential early discussion of scientific method, John Herschel extends the Baconian proscription of "idols":

> [T]here is one preliminary step to make, which depends wholly on ourselves: it is the absolute dismissal and clearing the mind of all prejudice, from whatever source arising, and the determination to stand and fall by the result of a direct appeal to facts in the first instance, and of strict logical deduction from them afterwards. (80)

Certainly, in the autobiographies I will be looking at, it is possible to see the metaphors realized in the way the writers dramatize themselves.

Arnold implies again the paradox that underlies this subject: denial of self becomes a means to knowledge which in turn empowers the self that has been denied. Denying the self is understood to be a virtue — and virtue means "power." Denying the self is a means to salvation and the ultimate survival of self. And in the nineteenth century, this ideal was particularly embodied in the positivist attempt to equate all knowledge with science.

In summary, then, positivism as a faith is deeply paradoxical, and the paradoxes I am most interested in foregrounding are these: first, that positivism implies both a strong reliance on the self and individual experience and a radical distrust of the self; second, that despite its resistance to metaphysics and to the a priori authority asserted by religion and church, positivism draws much of its power from the way it echoes, even shares, the culture's deepest assumptions about religion, morality, and art; and third, that the ideal ultimately requires the obliteration of selfhood, and death. If you really want to know, you will have to die (although if you die you can't know), and along the way, you will probably have to kill the thing you want to know. The final irony of this story, however, is that the obliteration of self required in positivist knowledge often derives from and can easily become a strong affirmation of the self.

The attempt to equate scientific knowledge with knowledge has been largely successful. In 1866 T. H. Huxley notoriously announced that he believed the world would discover that "there is but one kind of knowledge and but one method of acquiring it" (41). Hubristic and professionally self-serving as the assertion was, it articulated an already dominant view, one that had pervaded the culture and was shaping the forms of cultural expression even as it gave to science and its new professional formations peculiar authority. And if Huxley's view had any historical validity at all, reflections of the positivist ideal of knowledge should be evident even in discourse not directly scientific. I seek those reflections in the autobiographies of a scientist, Charles Darwin, of a spokesman for science, John Stuart Mill, and of the most unscientific of novelists, Anthony Trollope. The point of connection that fits them neatly to my argument thus far was their use of a typical strategy of Victorian genius, the refusal both of genius and of the self-dramatizing stance of genius, the denial indeed of their own importance. While the shadow of Rousseau hangs over these autobiographies, they resist conventional literary categories through a persistent strategy of self-minimizing or self-deprecation and through a stylistic and formal looseness that seems to deny all literary ambition — and in these very qualities they echo the ideal of objective knowledge connected so tightly to Victorian science.

The science connection here has first to do with the question of authority. When Arnold, the advocate of humanistic over scientific education, announced, in his turn to poetry to provide the compensations of religion, that the fact has failed us, he revealed how completely he ascribed authority to science over religion, even in his attempt to construct a new kind of religion. This unselfconscious endorsement is characteristic. The authority of science in matters of knowledge manifested itself in everything from the condition of the church and religion, to social programs, to narrative, to the textures of these three not terribly inspiring autobiographies. The very qualities that mark these works as unliterary, their casual and ostensibly unrhetorical styles, their tendency to formlessness, the registering of apparently unimportant details and, particularly, their persistent self-deprecation can be read as reflections

of the implications of a pervasive scientific vision which give the documents
the authority the rhetoric seems to be disclaiming. Denial of specialness —
of genius, of heroism — is a mark of much ninteenth-century narrative, and
a further gesture in the intellectual imperialism of nineteenth-century science.

It is also part of that other epistemological ambition — the determination to tell the truth. To do that, all three autobiographies implicitly agree, it
is necessary to write according to the rules of science, the most highly developed form of truth-telling. Thus, even as it offers itself as a respite from
science, a piece of family indulgence, Darwin's *Autobiography* can be seen
as James Olney, for example, sees it, as yet another part of Darwin's case
for evolutionary theory.[2] And Linda Peterson places it as a kind of fountain-
head of scientific autobiographies, governed by what she calls a scientific
hermeneutic. But what is striking here is the unscientific voice through which
the scientific project is inferred to emerge: "I have thought the attempt would
amuse me," Darwin says, with self-deprecating charm, "and might possibly
interest my children or their children" (*Autobiography* 21).

There is a parallel self-dismissal in Trollope's autobiography. "The
garrulity of old age, and the aptitude of a man's mind to recur to the passages
of his own life, will, I know, tempt me to say something of myself," Trollope
apologetically notes — as though an autobiography ought to contain anything *but* a discussion of the self writing it. Discussions of the self will,
however, be unsystematic and rambling, mere self-indulgences. Or to look
at my other example: while Mill's narrative does make some gestures at
pedagogical system, in emulation of his harrowing education, it produces no
coherent design and merely ticks off his intellectual activities so that the last
29 years before the writing can be put in only very small compass — all,
Mill claims, that "is worth relating of my life" (132).

The authority of the scientific model that I believe underlies these curiously self-abnegating expressions was built on a faith in the possibility of
disinterest and in the uniformity of nature. Charles Lyell's uniformitarian
geology, which was so important to Darwin's intellectual development and
so crucial for his theory, affirmed certain unprovable assumptions that accorded to science ultimate authority in matters of secular knowledge. For
Lyell, and indeed for most working scientists in the nineteenth century, natural laws were constant through space and time, and all phenomena could be
accounted for by causes now in operation. The insistence that they could be
so accounted for was obviously part of a concentrated quasi-professional
attempt to exclude any religious or spiritual intervention from the consideration of secondary causes, that is, of the natural world. The assumptions were
heuristic. As Stephen Jay Gould has recently put it, "to proceed as a scientist,
you assume that nature's laws are invariant and you decide to exhaust the
range of familiar causes before inventing any unknown mechanisms" (120).

The move did not entail the denial of religion and religious learning, only its irrelevance to the understanding of nature. Lots of scientists were religious and uniformitarian at the same time. But removing dependence on the world of spirit to explain nature clearly eroded religious belief because gradually it became less necessary to invoke God to account for anything that science could account for. Enter Huxley and the claim of science to dominion over the whole world.

As is well known, Lyell's uniformitarianism smuggled in other meanings, meanings that were not universally accepted by other scientists and that, according to Gould, were not legitimately inferable from the basic ones I have mentioned or from the empirical evidence. In particular, Lyell, like Darwin after him, insisted that nature does not make leaps: it moves gradually and at constant pace. This assumption, like the preceding ones, excludes miracles, but excludes also any radical or abrupt changes. Uniformitarianism establishes the authority of science by excluding divine intervention, but also by implication excluding romantic or heroic narratives. Great voluntary changes are not possible in such a world. The mechanisms of change are ineluctable and inhuman.

I want to suggest that uniformitarianism belongs to the same cultural cluster that evokes in narrative a realism intent on the minutiae of domestic life and on the possibility of detached and therefore disinterested registration of phenomena, and in politics a movement towards democracy, or at least meritocracy. The authority of uniformitarian science entailed — if it were to be consistent — a fundamental denial of genius and heroism, the traditional models for virtue and knowledge. With the death of the authority of God and the authority of the text, science asserted its power through a nature doggedly uniform, persistent, hard-working, the new moral exemplar; and its most effective mediators were the keenly trained hard-working scientific observers, who, like the nature they studied, were products of gradual and persistent development.

Although these uniformitarian assumptions were not at all universally held by Victorians, their pervasiveness was remarkable — especially given the power of alternative and popular non- or anti-scientific positions like those of Carlyle. And even Carlyle, partly because of his demand for self-denial, became a kind of moral and even intellectual model and inspiration for later scientific believers in the uniformity of nature, like John Tyndall and T. H. Huxley.

Nevertheless, when uniformitarianism appears blatantly, amidst the various pyrotechnics of Victorian rhetoric, it seems odd, flat, and banal, seems to be lacking precisely that quality it was invented to assert — intellectual authority. The genius of the realists and of the autobiographers I discuss here can be understood in the context of this new assertion of secular authority through uniformitarianism.

Trollope, Darwin, and Mill all minimize the specialness of their own powers within the only literary form they adopt in their long and productive careers that requires attention to themselves. Of course, they write within the context of decorum appropriate to the Victorian gentleman, and from that perspective there is something intrinsically ungentlemanly about autobiography — as Rousseau's notorious example manifested to the Victorian reading public. Thus their self-deprecation might easily be taken as a rhetorical device meant to imply the specialness it literally denies. In fact, the modesty *is* a means to authority, but not in the same way as, for example, in Newman, who frequently reminds his readers of how awkward and embarrassing it is to have to talk about himself but who never for a clause or a phrase gives evidence of self-doubt and never shows himself in the past as uncertain of his own powers or actions. His claims to reluctance to speak about himself are part of the strategy by which Newman evokes sympathy for his having been pressed to such unmanly activity by the even unmanlier poisoning of the wells of Kingsley and his anti-catholic fellow citizens. Newman is consistently strengthened by a deep intuition of self and creator that allows him to speak with stunning confidence at brilliantly interspersed moments. Characteristically, right near the start, he claims in a sentence of declarative briefness about the slanders against him: "They will fall to the ground in their season" (7). Arguments against him he will "easily crumble into dust." These pronouncements, like many others that follow them, have a visionary intensity in their very simplicity that is altogether absent from the unliterary autobiographies.

The differences of the *Apologia pro vita sua* in intention and design obviously account for many of the differences in manner. But while Newman elaborates the trope of modesty, there is nothing in his style equivalent to Trollope's mentioning casually in the first sentence of his autobiography "so insignificant a person as myself," and feeling the need to justify his book by suggesting it is not about him, as such, but about what he "and perhaps others round me, have done in literature" (1). Nor is there anything like Mill's touching second sentence: "I do not for a moment imagine that any part of what I have to relate, can be interesting to the public as a narrative, or as being connected with myself" (3). Notice, too, that Trollope's book is called *An Autobiography*, the indefinite article suggesting no significant identity at all, just one thing among many.

The kind of relation between Trollope and Darwin that I mean can be suggested by a comment Darwin makes in a letter of 1877: "Trollope in one of his novels [*The Last Chronicle of Barset*] gives as a maxim of constant use by a brickmaker — 'It is dogged as does it' — and I have often and often thought that this is the motto for every scientific worker'' (I, 370–71). Odd though it may appear at first to find Trollope providing a maxim to guide all scientists, it makes sense within the uniformitarian context and might help suggest why, with all their overwhelming differences, Darwin and Trollope produce autobiographies rhetorically akin in many ways. Hard work, that is, a certain kind of willed and hence moral commitment, is the key to what is thought of as genius. Genius is available to anyone who puts his or her mind to it. Such strategy is most notorious in Mill's *Autobiography*. Darwin certainly indulges it, calling himself a poor critic with a weak memory and ''no great quickness of apprehension or wit'' (*Autobiography* 140).

Indeed, a central principle of all the books, and for Mill and Trollope the ostensible justification for their inception (and hence their thematic center) is an insistence that the writer, despite extraordinary achievements, is not specially gifted: anyone could have done it. Most famously, there is that painful sequence in Mill's autobiography in which after discussing his terrifying and dehumanizing education, he comments about his early achievements:

> What I could do, could assuredly be done by any boy or girl of average capacity and healthy physical constitution: and if I have accomplished anything, I owe it, among other fortunate circumstances, to the fact that through the early training bestowed on me by my father, I started, I may fairly say, with an advantage of a quarter of a century over my cotemporaries. (20)

The governing moral assumption of Mill's education thus became part of his belief about himself and is reflected in the bathetic impersonality of the whole book.

The assumptions that govern Mill's rhetorical strategies, and Darwin's as well, are exposed in another letter Darwin wrote, this to Francis Galton, whose book *Hereditary Genius* was to argue for the *inheritance* of the qualities necessary for success. ''I have always maintained,'' Darwin says, ''that, excepting fools, men did not differ much in intellect, only in zeal and hard work'' (*More Letters* II,41). ''It is dogged as does it.'' To be fair, Darwin was impressed with Galton's book, after all, and his own theory of natural selection entailed an argument that genealogical differences could, over time, become extreme. But what is importantly missing from both Mill and Darwin's consideration of the powers of the self is any Newmanian or Carlylean deep intuition of the self or of divine connection. Darwin's uniformitarianism would allow for differences, but it would tend to emphasize minute rather than large ones. Intuiting no genius in himself, he maintains that he belongs to the large mass of essentially undifferentiated members of the species.

Trollope and Darwin share this sense of themselves but they agree too on what constitute their most important activities, as scientist and novelist. Here too the new kind of authority is being asserted, through empirical hard work and not through imaginative design or verbal brilliance. For Trollope, "the portion of a novelist's work which is of all the most essential to success" is "observation." Without the work of "observation and reception," his "power cannot be continued, — which work should be going on not only when he is at his desk, but in all his walks abroad, in all his movements through the world, in all his intercourse with his fellow-creatures" (198). This emphasis on observation is an essential theme of science, and Darwin makes his one claim of superiority here: "I am superior to the common run of men in noticing things which easily escape attention, and in observing them carefully. My industry has been nearly as great as it could have been in the observation and collection of facts" (*Autobiography* 140–41). The two writers converge in the shared Victorian view that the common basis of authority was to be empirical evidence — the record of what is available to the senses. The apparent coincidence of the triumph of realism (whose duplicities the twentieth century is busy exposing) and of empirical science (whose basis in language and fictions is being asserted with equal energy and complexity) was no accident. Trollope and Darwin (despite Darwin's own deviousness on the possibility of objective perception) are very much brothers in their almost obsessive commitment to observation and their belief that their work gathers its authority from observation, an activity that at best requires training and hard work, but certainly not genius.

In refusing the "extraordinary" as a name for their obviously extraordinary achievements, and in indicating that they resulted from the mere accumulation of ordinary qualities, Trollope and Darwin apply their gradualism and uniformitarianism to their own identities. Personal modesty in these cases implies the positivist episteme. The apparently extraordinary must be understood as the product of everyday experience, as the great geological phenomena of the world are the product of causes now in operation. This kind of explanation deromanticizes the self and the natural world. Not miracle nor catastrophe nor genius needs to be invoked to explain the way things and people are. At the same time, deromanticizing the world requires reimagining and revaluing and observing freshly with heightened intensity the particulars of every day. The world then becomes explicable to anyone who tries hard enough, and is not the domain of the mystic hierarchies of pre-scientific culture. But the plain and modest style as a cultural norm and value depends on a faith in the universal availability through observation and hard work of the facts and of their meanings. Trollope's realism is very much a product of a new scientific culture.[3]

Trollope prided himself on Hawthorne's famous comment that his novels were "just as real as if some giant had hewn a great lump out of the earth and put it under a glass case, with all its inhabitants going about their daily business'' (Trollope 125). Christopher Herbert suggests that seeing ''Trollope's characters as specimens lifted unknowingly out of their daily lives and placed under glass for purposes of observation'' implies the techniques of scientific experiment (114). Herbert claims, moreover, that

> It is the scientist's voracious appetite for data that underlies the amazing volume of Trollope's fiction; and it is exactly the impulse of scientific study that governs his passionate insistence on fidelity to nature as well as his studiously flat, unpoetic, ''objective'' writing style. (114)

The rhetorical strategies of the two autobiographies reflect a mutual determination to get at the real akin to that of the novels and scientific studies. The manner reflects the dominant empiricist ideal: all mere literary ornateness, all obstructions from myth or metaphor, must be dismissed, as the Royal Society dismissed them two centuries before, for the plain style that makes possible an unmediated apprehension of the world.

In an alienated and dispassionate way, Darwin notoriously characterizes himself, his powers, his emotional inadequacies, and sees himself as a ''machine for grinding general laws out of large collections of facts'' (Autobiography 139). The particular disrupts easy generalizations, and the power to handle the particular — especially in the construction of a large encompassing theory — is a mark of genius. In his *Autobiography*, Darwin seems content simply to lay down the facts, to avoid introspection and theorizing, and he creates what we might call a small, loose baggy monster, as, in the *The Origin of Species,* he created a large one. But apparent looseness disguises a new kind of structure built from an obsessive cultural need to examine empirically the myriad of particulars that would, in the Platonic scheme of things, be thought of as mere ''accidents.'' The autobiographies understate and evade their tendencies toward speculation and symbolizing, just as they minimize the genius of their authors. The narratives they unfold celebrate the virtues of doggedness and application, talk about their authors as ''other,'' with a kind of scientific detachment, and enact dramatically the alienation of self described in Feuerbach and Comte. Making minimal claims for the self, they protect themselves and their work from attack; at the same time, in their insistence that no fuss is to be made, they stick with iron determination to their achievements.

Trollope's autobiography provides considerable evidence of this way of perceiving: ''I can tell the story, though it be the story of my own father and mother, of my own brother and sister, almost as coldly as I have often done some scene of intended pathos in fiction'' (29) — that is, almost as coolly as if they were not human at all. Contemporary critics complained of this dispassion, but for Trollope, the effect of reality depended upon it. Darwin's parallel comment is even more disquieting: "I have attempted to write the following account of myself, as if I were a dead man in another world looking back at my own life. Nor have I found this difficult, for life is nearly over with me. I have taken no pains about my style of writing" (*Autobiography* 21).

THE PRICE OF SCIENTIFIC DISINTEREST is indeed death, at least death of the self. The scientific ethos of the nineteenth century entailed that ultimate Victorian virtue — self-annihilation. These autobiographies draw their authority precisely from this ethos. Each writer aspires to a style which is no style (an aspiration as unachievable as disinterest). The self-descriptions are authenticated by the absence of a self writing.

Yet anyone who has read these books must be aware that in my insistence on their self-deprecation I have lost the paradoxical aspect of the ideal of knowledge I have been discussing. There is, even in Mill's autobiography, where the neurotic self-distrust is unquestionably authentic and not merely rhetorical or polite, a steely confidence. And this manifests itself in the quietly or, in Trollope's case, not so quietly proud frankness of its rhetoric. Here the voice of Rousseau can still be heard dimly, affirming the supreme value of the individual, precisely in his individuality.

The other side of this almost self-destructive self-deprecation, then, is a style that insists without stating it that the author has courage superior to most others. And the courage consists in a dogged commitment to speak truthfully even where the self is alienated in the process. Even Mill concludes his introductory passage by saying, "The reader whom these things do not interest, has only himself to blame if he reads farther, and I do not desire any more indulgence from him than that of bearing in mind, that for him these pages were not written" (3). This is a characteristic note, in which self-deprecation almost slips over into arrogance. And it is the dominant tone of Trollope's autobiography (which read from another perspective is a brilliantly contrived defense against his own miserable childhood and painful vulnerability). In Darwin, of course, the tone is never arrogant. He takes the middle road, but the note is clear in, for example, a brief passage about his Cambridge life when he says, "Looking back, I infer that there must have been something in me a little superior to the common run of youths, otherwise the above-mentioned men, so much older than me and higher in academical position, would never have allowed me to associate with them" (*Autobiography* 67).

The genuine self-effacements in these texts are the instruments of empowerment. And here, too, they run parallel to the self-effacement required in the scientific ideal of objectivity. All of these writers, strong men who achieved celebrity because of extraordinary work, can share a self-confidence that is inextricably part of their self-deprecation. The patterns in any case are similar, and the autobiographies all exploit the ultimate authority of disinterested observation of particulars. Together they help dramatize the extraordinary connections between the scientific uniformitarian ideal, which is the new condition for authority, and an ideal of self-annihilation. Nevertheless, they also imply not only a latent self-contradiction in the scientific ethos that persists into our time, but an imperial assertion of a new secular authority. Self-deprecation lapses over into arrogance; the plain style becomes rhetorical after all. The implicit hubris of scientific intellectual imperialism shyly reasserts itself.

Many readers will have noticed that I am talking here about autobiographies by men, and it is important to recognize that the ethos that these texts evoke is powerfully, distinctively male. Women — even mothers and wives — emerge only shadowily in these books. There were few woman scientists, and fewer who wrote autobiographies. In those who did — Mary Somerville being the most obvious example — some of the same tropes and strategies are evident. But in Somerville's autobiography and, for example, Harriet Martineau's, the tropes work differently, and the extravagances of self-effacement that one finds in Mill and Darwin simply are not there. The reasons for this are complex.[4] Without opening another extended argument that would double the size of this study, I would simply argue that most women connected with Victorian science internalized the cultural demand for self-abnegation, but that for them the very act of self-abnegation in work required strong self-assertion. Florence Nightingale talks of how women "are accompanied by a phantom — the phantom of sympathy, guiding, lighting the way — even if they do not marry. Some few sacrifice marriage, because they must sacrifice all other life if they accept that . . . if she has any destiny, any vocation of her own, she must renounce" marriage (40). In a sense then, for women intellectuals, the man's pattern is reversed. Darwin makes his way through self-abnegation and self-effacement, and through these achieves extraordinary authority. Harriet Martineau, Mary Somerville, and Nightingale begin by making claims for the self that require a renunciation of "normal" women's satisfactions in order even to *do* the work to which they aspired. Self-affirmation and self-denial are entangled in ways more complicated even than they are for men. And in their work, women are responsible to readapt that ideal of self-renunciation that, in a way, they had renounced in order to work at all.

As a postscript to this argument, it seems appropriate to turn to the work of a woman intellectual — George Eliot — who was in the center of the Victorian scientific ethos, and most of whose work explicitly affirms it. But in her last novel — *Daniel Deronda* — there are some curious reversals that challenge, or modify, the deadly scientific ideal of objective knowledge.

Obviously, the book fights many more battles than can be subsumed under the theme of epistemology. But while that novel has often been regarded as a partial retreat from the brilliant and tough engagements with the harsh, unaccommodating actual that characterize much of the early work, and a wish-fulfilling fantasy of a father-like hero who can achieve elsewhere what George Eliot had given up on in England, it is also and centrally a reconsideration of her own epistemology. George Eliot was deeply aware of the difficulties and contradictions latent in the positivist ideal of objectivity, and she had already found in *Middlemarch* that acquiescence in it seems inevitably to end by closing off all possibility for change, for the new. Her novels are studded with martyrs to reality — Maggie Tulliver, Felix Holt, Romola — and occasionally marred by her attempts to transform defeat into victory. The pursuit of knowledge in George Eliot, while ostensibly teaching her characters to act with "patient obedience" to the teaching of nature, requires the most strenuous refusals to countenance their own desires. The literal consequence of knowing in George Eliot, as extravagantly enacted by Latimer in "The Lifted Veil," is dying.

But in allowing Mordecai to "will" Daniel Deronda into Jewishness, she explicitly argues for a new epistemology, a rigorous extension of the old that allows for passion, will, human desire. George Eliot seeks what Michael Polanyi was later to call "Personal Knowledge," a knowledge compatible with the rigors of science that yet reflects the intensity of human personal engagement with its subject. Like Polanyi, George Eliot continues to believe in science and argue for it, but she has, by the end of her career, found that the ideal of scientific objectivity feels too much like "dying to know." Mordecai, too, dies, perhaps from the excess of energy required to "know." Yet his story attempts a conciliation between the epistemological necessity of self-annihilation and the all too human energies of desire. His story challenges the lesson of Carlyle's Everlasting Yea, and in Daniel's questioning of Mordecai, the challenge becomes explicit:

Was such a temper of mind likely to accompany that wise estimate of consequences which is the only safeguard from fatal error, even to ennobling motive? But it remained to be seen whether that rare conjunction existed or not in Mordecai: perhaps his might be one of the natures where a wise estimate of consequences is fused in the fires of that passionate belief which determines the consequences it believes in. The inspirations of the world have come in that way too: even strictly measuring science could hardly have got on without that forecasting ardour which feels the agitations of discovery beforehand, and has a faith in its preconception that surmounts many failures of experiment. And in relation to human motives and actions, passionate belief has a fuller efficacy. Here enthusiasm may have the validity of proof, and, happening in one soul, give the type of what will one day be general. (571–72, ch. 41)

The questions here imply a more active model of science, one in which the self engages, desires, transforms; and it is, I believe, much closer to what scientists like Darwin really did than the "Baconian model" that they officially endorsed. The scientist is no passive observer of the world, allowing it, simply *there* outside the perceiving self, to shape him. Rather, the scientist is, as Claude Bernard had helped teach George Eliot and George Lewes, always an experimenter, a shaper, an imaginer. The prophetic Mordecai is also the persistent, hard-working, desiring scientist, whose intuition, shaped by desire, tested constantly against the constraints of harsh unaccommodating reality, turns out to be true because the pressure of his investigations helps make it true.

It is no accident, I believe, that it is a woman who imagines this new narrative of a life-affirming science. The project of many of the best contemporary feminist philosophers of science — Evelyn Keller, Donna Haraway, Helen Longino, Sandra Harding — is not to trash science but to imagine a genuinely human one, a science satisfied to forego the universal and the transcendent, a science implicated in the give and take of laboratory life and its social and moral contexts, a science driven explicitly not by an abstract ideal of epistemological purity and truth, but by a commitment to make knowledge and science instruments of humans for humans. Mordecai's kind of self-abnegation justifies the intensity of vocation and transforms humility before the pressures of the world into a liberation. Here is George Eliot's dream of a positivism beyond positivism, a mode of knowledge that grants authority, at last, to passion and desire, to the human and the living, rather than to disinterest and objectivity, the transcendent and the dead.

Rutgers University Center for the Critical Analysis of Contemporary Culture

NOTES

1. For a brief summary of the position, see Levine, "Dying to Know." Since that essay grows out of the same project as my present study, there will be some overlap in argument and examples.
2. Olney captures well the parallels between Darwin's scientific commitments to objectivity and the way he writes the autobiography, but, I believe, takes without sufficient irony and the possibility of disingenuity, Darwin's claim to be a mere collector of facts, a "machine" for grinding them out.
3. I have made this argument in a different and more elaborate way in *Darwin and the Novelists*.
4. I try to address them in a work in progress that pursues the lines laid out in this paper. One point is surely crucial: for women, the self-abnegations required by science, and in which they acquiesced, were felt to be liberations from a more oppressive, culturally required self-abnegation.

WORKS CITED

Arnold, Matthew. *Lectures and Essays in Criticism*. Ed. R. H. Super. Ann Arbor: U of Michigan P, 1980.

Carlyle, Thomas. *Sartor Resartus*. Ed. C. F. Harrold. New York: Odyssey, 1937.

Comte, Auguste. *Auguste Comte and Positivism: The Essential Writings*. Ed. Gertrud Lenzer. Chicago: U of Chicago P, 1975.

Darwin, Charles. *The Autobiography of Charles Darwin, 1809–1882*. Ed. Nora Barlow. New York: Norton, 1958.

Darwin, Francis and A. C. Seward, eds. *More Letters of Charles Darwin*, 2 vols. New York: Appleton, 1903.

Eliot, George. *Daniel Deronda*. Ed. Barbara Hardy. Harmondsworth: Penguin, 1967.

Feuerbach, Ludwig. *The Essence of Christianity*. Trans. George Eliot. New York: Harper, 1957.

Gould, Stephen Jay. *Time's Arrow, Time's Cycle: Myth and Metaphor in the Discovery of Geological Time*. Cambridge: Harvard UP, 1987.

Harré, Rom. *Varieties of Realism: A Rationale for the Natural Sciences*. New York: Blackwell, 1986.

Herbert, Christopher. *Trollope and Comic Pleasure*. Chicago: U of Chicago P, 1987.

Herschel, John. *Preliminary Discourse on the Study of Natural Philosophy*. 1831; Chicago: U of Chicago P, 1987.

Huxley, T. H. "On the Advisableness of Improving Natural Knowledge." *Methods and Results*. London: MacMillan, 1893.

Keats, John. Letter to Richard Woodhouse, 27 October 1818, in *Selected Poems and Letters*. Boston: Riverside, 1959. 279–80.

Levine, George. "Dying to Know." *The Victorian Newsletter*, No. 79 (1991): 1–4.

———. *Darwin and the Novelists*. Cambridge: Harvard UP, 1988; rpt. U of Chicago P, 1991.

Mill, John Stuart. *Autobiography and other Writings*. Ed. Jack Stillinger. Boston: Houghton Mifflin, 1969.

Newman, John Henry. *Apologia pro vita sua*. Ed. David J. DeLaura. New York: Norton, 1968.

Nightingale, Florence. *Cassandra*. Old Westbury: Feminist Press, 1979.

Olney, James. *Metaphors of Self: The Meaning of Autobiography*. Princeton: Princeton UP, 1972.

Peterson, Linda. *Victorian Autobiography: The Tradition of Self-Interpretation*. New Haven: Yale UP, 1986.

Trollope, Anthony. *An Autobiography*. London: Oxford UP, 1961.

Tyndall, John. "The Belfast Address." *Fragments of Science*. 2 vols. New York: Appleton, n.d. II, 135–201.

PARACELSUS AND THE AUTHORITY OF SCIENCE IN BROWNING'S CAREER

By Patricia O'Neill

DEPENDING ON THEIR ATTITUDES towards Browning's predecessors, the early reviewers of *Paracelsus* either decried its evocation of the mysticism of Shelley, or they saluted Browning as the newest member in the Romantic tradition of Shelley, Coleridge, and Wordsworth (Kelley and Hudson 3: 347–86). As a young, aspiring poet of the "Faustian" school, Browning's choice of character and manner of presentation in *Paracelsus* equals that of any high Romantic quester. Like the poet in *Alastor* or like Manfred, Browning's medieval alchemist dies recognizing the high cost of his self-alienating obsession with learning the secrets of nature. In retracing the rise and fall of the quest for knowledge beyond and in spite of social conventions, however, Browning's poem initiates what might be called a post-Romantic approach to the quest for knowledge.

In his final speech Paracelsus justifies his life's work in the context of natural history and social development. Recognizing that his quest for knowledge has lacked a complementary understanding of love, he reaches to clasp hands with Aprile, the poet who has also failed and died because he loved without knowledge. Paracelsus's evocation of the origins of the earth and the unfolding of creation then supports a hope for the reconciliation of their quests in the future perfection of humankind:

> Let men
> Regard me, and the poet dead long ago
> Who loved too rashly; and shape forth a third
> And better-tempered spirit, warned by both:
> As from the over-radiant star too mad
> To drink the life-springs, beamless thence itself —
> And the dark orb which borders the abyss,
> Ingulfed in icy night, — might have its course

293

A temperate and equidistant world.[1] (5.885–93)

The conciliatory tone of Paracelsus's prophecy establishes him as a different kind of figure of cultural authority than his Romantic precursors. For Paracelsus places the quest for knowledge and love in the context of the evolutionary processes of nature.[2] The same operations which cosmologically have shaped forth that "equidistant world," the earth, predict the evolution of "better-tempered" spirits, successors to Paracelsus, whose quests also will benefit from a more "temperate" social climate. The consequences of this moderating approach to the Romantic quest appear immediately in the responses of Browning's first reader, his friend Monclar.

At the time of its publication, 1835, André Victor Amédée de Ripert-Monclar summarized the poem's tantalizing significance for its audience. In *Paracelsus*, the alienated genius of Romantic apocalyptic visions is replaced by Browning's conception of the "superior man," working in submission to divine will for the benefit of the human race: "Continuous advancement is the law of mankind. The mission of the superior man is to hasten that progress. To achieve that goal, two things are necessary for him, *to know and to love*."[3] Monclar ends his account of the poem by contrasting the "doubt," "chaos," and "despair" of Manfred and Faust to the "consolation," "hope," and "faith" of Browning's Paracelsus (Kelley and Hudson 3: 416, 424).

In response to Monclar, Browning tellingly insists that what Paracelsus misunderstands is that "*to Love* is as much a science as *to Know*. . . . He proceeds at once to Basil, promulgates some few of his discoveries, is received with enthusiastic applause — but for the want of the *science of Love*, above mentioned, is still unhappy — he cannot love Men — nor see any worth in the sort of love they bear to himself." Thus Browning underlines the authority of science, "how to discover the *elements of love* in the hatred, envy and uncharitableness he is about to provoke" (Kelley and Hudson 3: 420; emphases are Browning's). Unlike the failed questers of his Romantic precursors, Browning's Paracelsus sees behind and beyond the opposition between knowledge and love a unifying principle — "progress is / The law of life" (5.742–43) — which not only justifies the alchemist's own endeavors, but also suggests the gradual and general process of human understanding, the "elements" of love, that will eventually embrace both the naturalist's and the poet's discoveries.[4] Thus Browning appreciates the importance of science as a cognitive and communal process rather than as a body of knowledge produced from a fixed or exclusive standpoint. The consequences of Browning's insights remained unacknowledged and unproblematic, however, until the authority of science in Victorian society cast Browning's subject and methods in a new light.

What follows is an account of the unfolding cultural significance of this pre-Darwinian poem. Reviewers and critics of *Paracelsus* have always emphasized its importance in Browning's intellectual and poetical development. Its allusions to Shelley have led modern critics to reflect upon the productive, and often revisionary, apprenticeship of its author to his most important Romantic precursor.[5] But my concern is somewhat different. I am less interested in Shelley's influence on Browning than in the way *Paracelsus* participates in a nineteenth-century debate about poetry's relationship to science. For Browning's poem demonstrates in an exemplary way how a literary work can mediate ideological conflicts and become in turn the object of ideological constructions. As a cultural artifact *Paracelsus* can tell us about some of the ways in which poetry may be related to social and intellectual concerns beyond the purview of the literary tradition. The history of *Paracelsus* shows how Victorian interpretations of Browning's work mutated in a changing intellectual environment.[6]

FROM THE TIME OF ITS PUBLICATION, reviews of *Paracelsus* focused on the subject of Browning's poem and its poetic style. But the merits of Browning's choice of spokesperson and his discursive manner can be understood more fully if we notice the context and the language with which the critics appraised the poem. In 1835 Browning's alchemist was a controversial choice of hero. Although a reviewer for the *New Monthly Magazine* could applaud Goethe's choice of Faust to represent in poetical terms human desire and intellectual ambition (44: 371), Browning's choice of an historical alchemist was unacceptable. "Quack" is the favorite word of early reviewers of the poem. And how could a quack and an imposter be a subject for poetry? In 1847, George Lewes claimed that the problem with Browning is his "love rather of the extraordinary than of the true" (Litzinger and Smalley 121). The criterion of "the true" is obviously more problematic in its application to an historical rather than an imaginary character. By choosing a quack, Browning seems to undermine Lewes's critical preference for moral prototypes. Nevertheless, Browning's love of the extraordinary eventually made his work fashionable in an age of invention, for the poet's argumentative misfits point out the inadequacies of Lewes's generalizing view. In the struggle between appearances and feelings, between history and individual choices, between the empirical and the transcendental, his characters mediate the discourses of science and poetry.

A similar contradiction in critical expectations informs discussions of the properly transcendent and the improperly obscure quality of Browning's language. While the visionary manner of *Paracelsus* reminded early reviewers of the Romantic quests of Shelley, the difficulty of Browning's "unpoetical" language separated him from the poetic tradition of his lyrical precursors. The reviewer for the *Athenaeum* uses Browning's poem to warn writers that "though it is not difficult to imitate the mysticism and vagueness of Shelley, we love him and have taken him to our hearts as a poet, not *because* of these characteristics — but *in spite* of them'' (Kelley and Hudson 3: 350). More often the obscurity of *Paracelsus* is attributed not to his affinities with Shelley but to Browning's own harsh and difficult style. Even the generally favorable review given in *Leigh Hunt's Journal* includes cautionary words against poetic affectation. If in the initial reviews of *Paracelsus* the awkwardness of Browning's language is excused in deference to its originality and the poet's immaturity, by 1845 (and undoubtedly in response to the impenetrability of *Sordello*) the obscurity of *Paracelsus* is linked to the arcane quality of Browning's erudition. According to one reviewer, ''the author will often persist in supposing that we know what he means so well, that there is no necessity for him to inform us on the matter'' (Litzinger and Smalley 110). In 1849, Thomas Powell's survey of Browning's work includes this observation: ''if Mr. Browning wishes to make a simile, and illustrate redness, he will not take the rose, but select some out of the way flower equally red, but of whose name not one in a thousand has ever heard'' (Litzinger and Smalley 134–35). Browning may be said to fulfill Wordsworth's prophecy in the Preface to the *Lyrical Ballads* that the discoveries of scientists may become proper objects of the poet's art, but for these reviewers, Browning's poetry was certainly not written from the Wordsworthian viewpoint of ''a man speaking to men.'' For years, Browning's verse was condemned by friends and foes for its difficulty. Yet in *Victorian Scrutinies*, Isobel Armstrong notes that by the 1860s the harsh, complicated style of Browning's poetry was increasingly recognized as valuable and praised for its complexity, in contrast to the precious quality of Tennyson's work (50–59). The new criteria for judging Browning's poetry developed in part because critics began to appreciate the power of analysis in other fields. Like Browning's choice of an historical rather than a literary or mythic figure, his language seemed to require of a reader the mental effort of a specialist or at least an ability to approach poetry with as much intellectual energy as the poet himself. With a growing readership attuned to the demands of scientific approaches to knowledge, the difficulty of Browning's poetry became a sign of his modernity.

The need to write poetry that would provoke the same respect as scientific inquiry was apparent to Browning early on from the influential reviews by his mentor and literary godfather, William J. Fox. As reviewer and editor respectively for the *Westminster Review* and *The Monthly Repository*, Fox encouraged Browning and other young poets to write poetry that would promote the larger scientific and progressive movements of the day. In his 1830 review of Tennyson, Fox notes:

> The great principle of human improvement is at work in poetry as well as every where else. What is it that is reforming our criminal jurisprudence? What is

shedding its lights over legislation? What purifies religions? What makes all arts and sciences more available for human comfort and enjoyment? Even that which will secure a succession of creations out of the unbounded and everlasting materials of poetry, our ever-growing acquaintance with the philosophy of mind and of man, and the increasing facility with which that philosophy is applied. . . . Now whatever theories may have come into fashion, and gone out of fashion, the real science of mind advances with the progress of society like all other sciences. The poetry of the last forty years already shows symptoms of life in exact proportion as it is imbued with this science. (Jump 23–24)

If none of Browning's reviewers noticed the topicality of his vision of natural history in part five of the poem, Fox quotes it at length and praises the poem as a whole for its "intense poetical sense which the author combines with strong powers of thought" (Kelley and Hudson 3: 357). Connections between the quest for knowledge through a "real science of mind" and the poem's interest in a particular theory of evolution, or transmutation, as it was then called, remained in the background — until the shifting cultural concerns of Browning's audience brought his subject under new scrutiny. By mid-century Paracelsus's quest and his progressive views reflect with renewed intensity a specifically modern attitude toward "evolutionary" development. Finally, after the controversies generated by Darwin's *Origin of Species*, Browning's choice of character, his discursive style of poetry, and especially the juxtaposition of the quest for knowledge and the quest for love in *Paracelsus* find new appreciation in a society enmeshed in the problem of "two cultures."

IN 1834 BROWNING could hardly have predicted his place in one of the great intellectual movements of the Victorian age. For the 23-year-old Browning the assumption of authority before his public was still tenuous. Yet in retrospect the finale of *Paracelsus* resonates with an appropriate sense of destiny: "Yes, it was in me; I was born for it — / I, Paracelsus: it was mine by right." (5.600–601) Paracelsus, the medieval alchemist who burned the books of his rivals, was credited by his contemporaries with restoring life. Yet despite his early fame and modern reputation as one of the founders of modern chemistry, Browning's character speaks these brave words from his deathbed to the only friend he has left, the loyal Festus. According to Browning's nearly exhausted Paracelsus, his predecessors had searched and longed for and seized bits of knowledge and rapture from Nature,

> But this was born in me; I was made so;
> Thus much time saved: the feverish appetites,
> The tumult of unproved desire, the unaimed
> Uncertain yearnings, aspirations blind,
> Distrust, mistake, and all that ends in tears

> Were saved me; thus I entered on my course.
>
> .   .   .   .
>
> I stood at first where all aspire at last
> To stand: the secret of the world was mine.
> (5.622–27, 636–37)

A madman might speak so, and Browning gave voice to two fanatics in his "Madhouse Cells," published the following year. But his Paracelsus is different. His claim to greatness is contradicted by his own recognition of his isolation and impending death. As he pours forth his vision of the origins of life and human consciousness, the eloquence of his insights justifies the retrospective prophecy of his place in history. Although he has failed to understand or convince his own community, Paracelsus predicts his importance as the precursor for a new stage in human development:

> If I stoop
> Into a dark tremendous sea of cloud,
> It is but for a time; I press God's lamp
> Close to my breast; its splendour, soon or late,
> Will pierce the gloom: I shall emerge one day.
> (5.899–903)

To err greatly is itself a sign of greatness. Paracelsus recognizes the rightness of his course despite his failure to attain the "better-tempered spirit" he himself portends.

Browning's character speaks with the passionate authority of an old man and establishes his young author as a poet of consequence. Paracelsus, not the poet in *Pauline* or Sordello, becomes the imaginative and ideological forecaster of Browning's newly unfolding career. For many years afterwards Browning showed his own partiality by advertising his volumes of poetry as "by the author of *Paracelsus*." For nineteenth-century readers and reviewers of Browning, *Paracelsus* remained the poem from which they measured his subsequent development as a poet for a modern age.

Given the importance of *Paracelsus* to Browning's bid for poetic authority, it is not surprising that modern critics have looked at the juxtaposition of Paracelsus and Aprile in order to explore Browning's relationship with Shelley. The figure of the poet who would "supply all chasms with music, breathing / Mysterious motions of the soul" (2.477–78) embodies Browning's tribute to Shelley, a tribute that also suggests the already anachronistic position of Browning's precursor in this new treatment of the quest for knowledge. Paracelsus's naturalistic survey of the progressive tendencies of natural history and of social development in part five insists on the importance of a general increase of knowledge to the social or moral perfection of humankind. If, for Browning, to love is as much a science as to know, his characterization of

Aprile underlines the failure of an unscientific approach. If we compare *Paracelsus* to its most important literary precursor, Browning's scientific bias may be seen as a revision of the mythopoeic optimism in Shelley's *Prometheus Unbound*.

In his revelatory deathbed speech, Paracelsus's vision of the history of life — beginning with "the centre-fire" (5.653), followed by an age of volcanic eruption, an era of winter and a spring that brings natural and supernatural joy — echoes the cosmic transformations that accompany the reunion of Prometheus and Asia in Act 4 of *Prometheus Unbound* (4.319 ff). Shelley's and Browning's cosmogonies — unlike Goethe's and Carlyle's Neptunist visions of the earth's origins by the slow receding of a vast, ancient ocean — invoke the so-called Vulcanist theory of high temperature and pressure within the earth and the elevation of land by earthquakes and volcanoes. But in *Paracelsus* the dynamic processes of nature humanize without anthropomorphizing the landscape:

> The centre-fire heaves underneath the earth,
> And the earth changes like a human face;
> The molten ore bursts up among the rocks,
> Winds into the stone's heart, outbranches bright
> In hidden mines, spots barren river-beds,
> Crumbles into fine sand where sunbeams bask —
> God joys therein. (5.653–59)

Using poetical terms to describe ages of volcanic activity and of ice, Paracelsus also characterizes the beginning of organic life as the springtime of creation, without the linearity of Pope's eighteenth-century view of a chain of being:

> The grass grows bright, the boughs are swoln with blooms
> Like chrysalids impatient for the air,
> The shining dorrs are busy, beetles run
> Along the furrows, ants make their ado;
> Above, birds fly in merry flocks, the lark
> Soars up and up, shivering for very joy;
> Afar the ocean sleeps; white fishing-gulls
> Flit where the strand is purple with its tribe
> Of nested limpets; savage creatures seek
> Their loves in wood and plain — and God renews
> His ancient rapture. Thus he dwells in all,
> From life's minute beginnings, up at last
> To man — (5.671–83)

The natural dynamism conveyed by Browning's verbs in this passage reflects the interactivity and plenitude of organic life. Although the perspective is terrestrial rather than cosmic, the creative joy that informs Browning's version of natural supernaturalism recalls the ecstatic finale to Shelley's *Prometheus Unbound*. There the overthrow of the tyrannical Jupiter transforms both the matter and the spirit of the new world, revealing earth's inner core and its "cancelled cycles" (4.289). A love duet between the Earth and the Moon celebrates the renewal of "this true fair world of things — a Sea reflecting Love" (4.384). If Paracelsus looks forward to a time "When all mankind alike is perfected, / Equal in full-blown powers" (5.750), Shelley's utopian moment envisions a new humanity to whom nature willingly submits her power:

> The Lightning is his slave; Heaven's utmost deep
> Gives up her stars, and like a flock of sheep
> They pass before his eyes, are numbered, and roll on!
> The Tempest is his steed, — he strides the air;
> And the abyss shouts from her depth laid bare,
> "Heaven, hast thou secrets? Man unveils me, I have none." (4.418–23)

Like Prometheus, Paracelsus has special knowledge and follows a destiny that is god-like; but, more vulnerable than Prometheus, he fails to understand or to work with others, making his knowledge and power useless. By his failure as well as by his accomplishments, however, Paracelsus claims authority for his insights into the laws of nature and the will of God. He sees that God's joy has included "existence in its lowest form" (5.647), and that every stage in human development has been marked by what appear as obstacles but which lead to a higher and better understanding of possibilities: Power, "controlled / Calmly by perfect knowledge" (5.693–94); Knowledge, "Strengthened by love" (5.698); and Love, "A half-enlightened, often-chequered trust" (5.705). Nature itself has left traces of this view of history in fossils which record the slow convergence of faculties,

> Anticipations, hints of these and more
> Are strewn confusedly everywhere — all seek
> An object to possess and stamp their own;
> The inferior natures, and all lead up higher,
> All shape out dimly the forthcoming race,
> The heir of hopes too fair to turn out false,
> And man appears at last. So far the seal
> Is put on life. (5.706–13)

In both *Prometheus Unbound* and *Paracelsus* the poets project a collective rather than an individual heroic response to changes in the natural or social order. In Shelley, humanity becomes a harmonious whole in order that "Man, oh, not men!" may become "a chain of linked thought, / Of love and might to be divided not'' (4.394–95). In *Paracelsus* power, knowledge, and love are interwoven in a process that will ''tend still upward, progress is / The law of life, man is not man as yet'' (5.742–43).

But while many of the particulars of the poems are similar, Browning defers to a retrospective and gradual view of change rather than predict a futuristic or revolutionary transformation. The evolutionary vision presented in *Paracelsus* replaces both Paracelsian cosmology and Shelley's view of cataclysmic change by proposing a temporal process of increasing complexity leading up to the emergence of humankind.[7] If we compare Browning's work to his literary precursor further, we will see that the poets' contrasting attitudes to social change are related to their differing views of science. For *Paracelsus* and *Prometheus Unbound* represent cosmologies based on ideological considerations as much as empirical study or interest, especially in Paracelsus's claim that ''progress is law'' rather than a Promethean myth. The quest for ''laws'' distinguishes Browning's approach from Shelley's and underlies a post-Romantic approach to knowledge not only in poetry but in every intellectual endeavor in the nineteenth century.

From the earliest debates about evolutionary processes, scientific theories were related to social theories of progress. John Bury identifies two that are relevant to early nineteenth-century thought. One theory of progress, associated with the early socialists and supporters of the French Revolution like Shelley's father-in-law, William Godwin, viewed humanity as a closed system, capable of complete transformation under the influence of ideas alone. Shelley's interest in chemistry was well-suited to his view that social systems were capable, with the right catalyst, of spontaneous upheaval, and that change itself resulted from the natural volatility of elements not in harmony.[8]

A second theory of progress, to which Browning clearly subscribes, reviewed the gradual ascent of increasingly complex species in the fossil record and contended that by an interplay of indefinite forces, humankind itself would move slowly toward increasing social harmony (Bury 236). Browning's references to paleontological phenomena — ''attributes had here and there / Been scattered o'er the visible world'' (5.685–86) — support this view of change. According to Peter Bowler, responsible geologists of both catastrophist and uniformitarian persuasions accepted the ''purpose of the whole creation as the gradual preparation of the earth for the appearance of man. . . . Natural theology thus tied in with directionalism to give an explanation of the progressive steps observed in the fossil record'' (*Fossils and Progress* 29). In geology as well as in social theory, then, Victorians could view progress as an indefinite but lawful unfolding of a divine plan.

Bowler and Francis C. Haber also point out the importance of fossils to concepts of time and process in the early nineteenth century.[9] An awareness of the greatly increased time-span of terrestrial history was a necessary first step for the discourse of gradualism that informs Browning's poetry. In *Paracelsus*, the appearance of humankind shows "the consummation of this scheme / Of being, the completion of this sphere / Of life," which retrospectively "Illustrates all the inferior grades, explains / Each back step in the circle" (5.683–85; 715–16). Such a view of natural history — one that uses the present to illustrate continuity with the past — suggests the uniformitarian scheme of Charles Lyell, whose *Principles of Geology* (1830–33) was widely reviewed. Lyell's work effectively secured the idea of a steady, continuous operation of natural forces over time. As reported in the *New Monthly Magazine*, a journal Browning read and contributed to, Lyell's thesis shows that "the disposition of the seas, continents, and islands, and the climates have varied: so it appears that the species have been changed, and yet they have all been so modelled, as types analogous to those existing plants and animals, as to indicate throughout a perfect harmony of design and unity of purpose" (40: 378). Lyell's reported view of harmonious and gradual changes consistent with a divine purpose finds a parallel expression in this part of Paracelsus's vision:

> Thus he dwells in all,
> From life's minute beginnings, up at last
> To man — the consummation of this scheme
> Of being, the completion of this sphere
> Of life: whose attributes had here and there
> Been scattered o'er the visible world before,
> Asking to be combined, dim fragments meant
> To be united in some wondrous whole,
> Imperfect qualities throughout creation,
> Suggesting some one creature yet to make,
> (So would a spirit deem, intent on watching
> The purpose of the world from its faint rise
> To its mature development) — some point
> Whereto those wandering rays should all converge. (5.681–92)

Similar to the views of geologists like Lyell, the imagery Browning uses suggests that the processes of nature have remained the same: those we see now are analogous to those of the past, because, in part, the "purpose" remains the same.

The progressive view of changes in the earth's surface and the development of life in *Paracelsus* coincide with the directional thinking of Shelley's revolutionary interpretation of transmutations in natural history. But because Browning thinks of evolutionary time in cyclical terms, encompassed from the beginning by God's love and joy, there are no discontinuities and no special or divine interventions necessary to establish a harmony between the past and the present. Closer to Lyell's uniformitarianism, than to Shelley's catastrophism, Browning's vision finds behind the empirical record of change the continuous presence of the unitary will of God.

Natural history, as represented by Lyell and Browning, gives a coherent form to the obvious diversity of organic life by the application of a transcendental principle. What Browning later called the "everlasting moment of creation" (*Luria*, 5.233) allows for a scientific view of natural law operating continuously on otherwise multifarious objects, while insisting on its social and ethical significance as an expression of divine love as well as power. This understanding of the ideological complementarity between natural law, divinely sanctioned, and gradual social development was seriously challenged by Charles Darwin's theory of natural selection.[10] But in the early nineteenth century what Susan Cannon has termed the "truth complex" allowed a happy synthesis of the fossil record, natural theology, and early Victorian liberalism. In *Paracelsus* we can see how much Browning had absorbed the quest for knowledge as a quest for the "law" of progress, wherein scientific truth was as yet undifferentiated from poetic truth.

AS SCIENTIFIC APPROACHES TO KNOWLEDGE and to social progress assumed greater authority, Browning's audience redefined the value and significance of Browning's work in general and of *Paracelsus* in particular. Historians have long recognized the importance of Darwin's publication of *Origin of Species* in 1859 for Victorian culture as well as for the history of science (see Heyck, 1982). One of the implications of Darwin's theory of natural selection was that the study of nature would no longer lead directly to an understanding of God's beneficence or to a moral law of life. Consequently, scientific endeavor became a professional matter with its own priorities, and the authority of science was increasingly viewed as encroaching on or in conflict with the authority of the church. Such changes in the social context for poetry stimulated new appreciation of Browning's theme and poetic style. The dichotomization of knowledge and love in *Paracelsus* seemed prophetic of the kind of opposition between science and culture that fueled post-Darwinian intellectual debate. In the second half of the nineteenth century, Browning and his interpreters reconstruct the poem's significance in light of changing views about evolutionary theory and the importance of scientific knowledge to other areas of human endeavor.

Although Browning had insisted in *Paracelsus* on the importance of the quest for knowledge and for what we might call social science — the "elements of love" necessary for the acceptance and dissemination of knowledge — he became increasingly ambivalent about the authority of science to govern all forms of understanding. One clue to Browning's own changing views about the relationship of science to other ways of knowing appears in his revision of the lines "progress is / The law of life, man is not man as yet" (5.742–43). Between 1849 and 1863 Browning revised the line to "man's self is not yet Man." This change suggests Browning's awareness that the soul's progress might be a moral rather than a social prospect; and certainly Browning's politics in these years moved further away from any Shelleyan radicalism or scientific positivism. The switch in 1863 back to his original wording with a slight change, "man is not Man as yet," returns to the evolutionary theme; but after the explosion of controversy over Darwin's theories, it reads ironically. Capitalizing "Man" celebrates transmutation without any commitment to natural selection as the mechanism of change. By 1863 Browning's confidence in the gradual advancement of humankind subordinates the contingencies of natural history to the general tendency of each individual to God, just as Browning's use of scientific allusions in his later poetry subordinates the solutions of scientific materialism to the moral calculus of his Christian metaphysics. Browning's revision of this important line suggests the ideological pressures of Victorian science to identify knowledge with scientific reasoning and social progress with natural law. If at the time of publication Browning had to contend that "to love is as much a science as to know," by mid-century he was increasingly concerned to show that moral law and self-knowledge were as important to human progress as natural law and laboratory experience. Meanwhile Browning's critics and reviewers began to identify the poet with a scientific approach to art, and his poetics with the fragmented circumstances of modern life.

In 1864, William Stigand of the *Edinburgh Review* points out a new moral in *Paracelsus* and a new way of characterizing Browning's dialectic of knowledge and love: "the culture of science must, in order to bear salutary and lasting benefits for humanity, be allied with the culture of beauty, — a truth which the present generation have especial need to lay to heart" (Litzinger and Smalley 237). But the "present" generation represented by Stigand is one in which the quest for knowledge has led to a unpoetical use of language. Although Stigand applauds the message he finds in *Paracelsus*, he complains in his extensive review of Browning's poetics that the poet's work exemplifies the "mysterious fascination in obscure half-expressed thoughts" of a "practical and mechanical age" (260). Once Browning's poem is recognized in these terms, however, as a representation not only of an historical alchemist but of the ascendency of science, critics find it easier to explain Browning's difficult use of language and his importance to Victorian culture.

By 1868, the connection between Browning's language and the demands of a scientific age is prominently touted as one of the chief characteristics of his work. According to the *Saturday Review*, "it is nearly as hard work to get through *Paracelsus* as to get through Dr. Salmon's *Analytical Conics*. Both of these excellent works are in the highest degree repaying; but we speak merely of the difficulty'' (Litzinger and Smalley 297). In 1869, with the Darwinian controversy at its height, Browning's most virulent critic, Alfred Austin — whose defense of the poetical must have been his chief claim to the laureateship in 1896 — criticizes his fellow poet by putting him in the camp of science altogether:

> What is our account of him? A subtle, profound, conscious psychologist, who scientifically gets inside souls, and, having scrutinised their thoughts and motives in a prose and methodical fashion, then makes them give the result, as if they had been scrutinising themselves, in verse. . . . It is, in reality, nothing more than the analysis completed and stated, and is no more synthesis than a lecture by Professor Huxley on the *vertebrata* is an animal. (Litzinger and Smalley 343)

Austin's attack shows that Victorian intellectuals were concerned not only with scientific discovery and the implications of the theory of evolution, but also with the methods of scientific reasoning. For no one questions the discourse or practices of professionals inside their own areas of expertise. The need to demarcate spheres of influence and authority, however, made Browning's analytical and discursive poetry controversial. To the degree that Browning's practice was judged scientific, he was given intellectual authority; but inasmuch as his language was the language of analysis, his works were often judged unpoetical. Yet as literary critics themselves imbibed the perspective of scientific discourse, criticism of Browning's diction and style slowly metamorphosed into grudging praise of his intellectual vigor. By the 1870s, the characteristic phrases of critics describing Browning's work actually echo the language of scientific endeavor. Browning is said to have ''the skill of a practised soul-anatomist,'' ''the unique and incomparable genius of analysis''; ''He deals with human character as a chemist with his acids and alkalies'' (Litzinger and Smalley 368, 394, 416).

Even when Browning openly criticizes or parodies the arrogance of scientistic opinion, his poetics continue to challenge his readers. For despite the metaphysical themes of Browning's late works, his discursive style cultivates, as *Paracelsus* had, an attitude of empirical and intellectual labor that resonates with the positivistic tenor of the age. Reactions against the growing authority of science do affect appraisals of Browning's work. Edward Dowden, for instance, praised Browning in 1877 for his ''militant transcendentalism . . . at odds with the scientific'' (Litzinger and Smalley 428). On the other hand, Walter Theodore Watts criticized *La Saisiaz* for its ''vigorous and eloquent protest against the scientific materialism of the day'' because, for him, there was no necessary conflict between religious faith and evolutionary theory (Litzinger and Smalley 450). Another reviewer, writing for *The Saturday Review*, avoided discussion of the argument for immortality in *La*

Saisiaz and instead criticized it for its obscure style, consisting "not in some odd and recondite fragment of knowledge, but in a complicated process of thought which might perhaps be approximately understood by an equally subtle intellect" (Litzinger and Smalley 453–54). Richard Hutton called *Jocoseria* "more evidence of protest against science," but he too complained that Browning's argument relies on "successive shocks of thought or feeling": "even the spirit of perfect love and harmony is perpetually startling this dull world by galvanising it with vivid spasms of thought and feeling, such as he himself has the skill to administer" (Litzinger and Smalley 477, 479). In other words, even though Browning himself was becoming more critical of science, his poetic style retained the experimental and intellectual rigors associated with the procedures of a natural philosopher, metaphysician, or Frankenstein, and not the conventional melodies of poets in the literary tradition.

By the 1880s Browning's ambiguous position between the authority of science and the discourse of poetry could be summed up this way: Mr. Browning's poetry supplies "a sort of poetic anthropology. There had always been a somewhat scientific bias in his view of life; but it was empirical, wanting in method, and continually swayed this way or that by a desire for purely poetic expression" (George Parsons Lathrop in Litzinger and Smalley 484). Given this comment and many others over the 50 years of Browning's career, Edward Berdoe's often criticized contributions to the Browning Society, especially his celebration of Browning as a "scientific poet," gain more credibility (Peterson 62). Victorian readers and admirers were simply attributing to Browning's work the same analytic approach to knowledge that they respected in scientific investigations.

In his 1881 letter to the ever curious president of the London Browning Society, Frederick Furnivall, Browning himself quickly dismissed the accusation that he was "strongly against Darwin, rejecting the truths of science and regretting its advance" (Hood 199). Instead he assumes that Darwin's theory is an extension of the theories of organic evolution he had embraced from the time of *Paracelsus*:

> all that seems *proved* in Darwin's scheme was a conception familiar to me from the beginning: see in *Paracelsus* the progressive development from senseless matter to organized, until man's appearance (*Part* v.) . . . for how can one look at Nature as a whole and doubt that, wherever there is a gap, a "link" must be "missing" — through the limited power and opportunity of the looker? (Hood 199)

Browning repeats here the assumptions of many nineteenth-century evolutionists, not only with reference to progressive development but also with regard to the problem of an incomplete fossil record. Browning goes on in the same letter to disassociate himself from religious fundamentalists, those who interpreted discontinuities in the fossil record as evidence of global catastrophies and successive divine acts of creation. Instead he maintains a belief in a first cause and imputes to Darwin a rather Lamarckian view of changes "brought about by desire and will in the creature" (Hood 200). But so did many scientists, even those who otherwise accepted Darwin's views. Most striking in this letter are the number of references to evolutionary theory Browning finds in his poetry and the confidence in his own empirical observations of nature — "tortoises never saw their own shells" (Hood 200) — which support his skepticism about proposed mechanisms of transmutation. Browning's detailed response assumes the importance of science to his position as a Victorian sage. As the only living poet with literary societies dedicated to deciphering his works, Browning seems impelled to address the demands of his scientifically-attuned audience from his own point of view and experience.

In "Parleyings with Francis Furini" (1887), Browning returns explicitly to the themes of science and art raised in *Paracelsus*. This time the quest for knowledge is represented by an artist. Furini, a painter-priest of the late Renaissance, becomes the spokesman for Browning's own arguments with his nineteenth-century audience whom he has Furini address as "Evolutionists." In comparing the work of a painter of the nude to that of the natural scientist, Browning contends that

> One and all
> We lend an ear — nay, Science takes thereto —
> Encourages the meanest who has racked
> Nature until he gains from her some fact,
> To state what truth is from his point of view,
> Mere pin-point though it be: since many such
> Conduce to make a whole, she bids our friend
> Come forward unabashed and haply lend
> His little life-experience to our much
> Of modern knowledge. Since she so insists,
> Up stands Furini. (255–65)

Browning thus reduces scientific method to finding "what truth is from his point of view," an approach to the quest for knowledge that parallels rather than excludes the procedures of the artist. But the juxtaposition of the scientist's and the artist's quests has a different purpose here than it had in *Paracelsus*. This time Browning emphasizes the problem not of the potentially overreaching of genius, but of the failure of reception. Furini criticizes the "evolutionists," the "cultured, therefore sceptical" (252) public, who have rejected the authority of art as a means for both knowledge and social well-being because of their narrowly scientistic views.

In his evolutionary fervor, Paracelsus had defined the ideological imperative of both science and poetry by his assertion that "progress is law." The
history of Browning's reception shows how much the authority of science
came to define "progress" and how much Browning's presumed "scientific
bias" helped shape evaluation of his work. While Browning's own confidence
in science to discern the soul's progress amidst its discoveries about human
origins waned, his discursive and analytical style made it possible for him to
assert the intellectual power of modern poetry. In a culture whose knowledge
of evolutionary theory was often less than its belief in the authority of scientific explanation, Browning's provocative choice of subject in *Paracelsus* and
his sustained commitment to a poetic exploration of, in Fox's terms, "the
real science of mind" created an audience for a new kind of poetics as difficult
and challenging as the modern science it somewhat ironically helped to establish.

Hamilton College

NOTES

1. All quotations of *Paracelsus* are from the 1835 version as noted in Pettigrew and
   Collins (I: 1028–1039).
2. Korg notes Browning's allusion to Herschel's theory of stellar evolution in this
   passage.
3. Monclar's summary of *Paracelsus* and a translation of it, plus Browning's annotations are printed in Kelley and Hudson (3: 416–25).
4. See Dale for Browning's optimistic approach to the problem of the unavailability
   of truth or perfect knowledge.
5. See Pottle, Maynard, and Tucker.
6. Because I am more interested here in Browning's reception by his contemporaries
   than in Browning's actual knowledge of science, I have interpreted Browning's
   relationship to science in a different way than other critics whose work precedes
   mine. See Maynard, Stevenson, Roppen, Dean, and Ross.
7. In *A Browning Handbook*, DeVane has claimed that Browning's evocation of
   evolution "owes much to Milton and Pope and little to the historical Paracelsus"
   (55). But unlike his eighteenth century predecessors, Browning temporalizes
   the chain of being. Roppen places Browning's conception of evolution halfway
   between science and metaphysics: "the process of Nature is to him cumulative
   and organic, and man emerges as the last fruit of its slow purposive growth.
   Underlying this intuition there is throughout a neo-Platonic belief in God the
   maker of the world, whose joy and goodness permeates all being with an urge
   or nisus to perfection" (125). For my purposes the significance of these passages
   in *Paracelsus* is in their relationship to early nineteenth-century conceptions of
   natural history and in the way the pressure of Darwin's theory of evolution
   made *Paracelsus* appear more prophetic and inevitable than it had to its earlier
   interpreters, including Browning himself.
8. See also Grabo and Dowden.

9. Haber describes the history of compromise between paleontologists and Mosaic geologists as the fossil record revealed the extent of prehistoric life.
10. See Gould's analysis of the ideological considerations underlying Lyell's revisions of *Principles of Geology* (99–179).

WORKS CITED

Armstrong, Isobel. *Victorian Scrutinies: Reviews of Poetry 1830–1870*. London: Athlone P, 1972.

Bowler, Peter J. *Fossils and Progress*. New York: Science History Publications, 1976.

———. *The Non-Darwinian Revolution: Reinterpreting a Historical Myth*. Baltimore: Johns Hopkins UP, 1988.

Browning, Robert. *The Poems*. Ed. John Pettigrew and Thomas J. Collins. 2 vols. Harmondsworth, England, and New Haven: Penguin Books and Yale UP, 1981.

Bury, John Bagnell. *The Idea of Progress: An Inquiry into its Origin and Growth*. 1932. London: Macmillan, 1955.

Cannon, Susan F. *Science in Culture: The Early Victorian Period*. New York: Science History Publications, 1978.

Dale, Peter Allan. "*Paracelsus* and *Sordello*: Trying the Stuff of Language." *Victorian Poetry* 18.4 (1980): 359–69.

Dean, Dennis. " 'Through Science to Despair': Geology and the Victorians." *Victorian Science and Victorian Values*, ed. James Paradis and Thomas Postlewait. New Brunswick: Rutgers University P, 1985. 111–36.

DeVane, William C. *A Browning Handbook*. 2nd ed. New York: Appleton, 1955.

Dowden, Edward. *The Life of Percy Bysshe Shelley*. London: Kegan Paul, Trench & Co., 1886.

Gould, Stephen Jay. *Times' Arrow, Time's Cycle: Myth and Metaphor in the Discovery of Geological Time*. Cambridge, Mass: Harvard UP, 1987.

Grabo, Carl. *A Newton Among Poets: Shelley's Use of Science in Prometheus Unbound*. Chapel Hill: U of North Carolina P, 1930.

Haber, Francis C. "Fossils and the Idea of a Process of Time in Natural History." *Forerunners of Darwin: 1745–1859*. Ed. Bentley Glass, Owsei Temkin, and William L. Strauss, Jr. 1959; Baltimore: Johns Hopkins UP, 1968.

Heyck, Thomas W. *The Transformation of Intellectual Life in England*. New York: St. Martin's P, 1982.

Hood, Thurman L., ed. *Letters of Robert Browning Collected by Thomas J. Wise*. New Haven: Yale UP, 1933.

Jump, John D., ed. *Tennyson: The Critical Heritage*. London: Routledge, 1967.

Kelley, Philip, and Ronald Hudson, eds. *The Brownings' Correspondence*. Vol. 3. Winfield, Kansas: Wedgestone P, 1985.

Korg, Jacob. "Astronomical Imagery in Victorian Poetry." *Victorian Science and Victorian Values: Literary Perspectives*, eds. James Paradis and Thomas Postlewait. New Brunswick: Rutgers University Press, 1985. 137–58.

Litzinger, Boyd, and Donald Smalley, eds. *Browning: The Critical Heritage*. London: Bell & Sons, 1970.

Maynard, John. *Browning's Youth*. Cambridge, Mass.: Harvard UP, 1977.

New Monthly Magazine and Literary Journal "Critical Notices" 40 (1834, part I); 377–18; 44 (1835, part II); 369–72.

Peterson, William S. *Interrogating the Oracle: A History of the London Browning Society*. Athens: Ohio UP, 1969.

Pottle, Frederick Albert. *Shelley and Browning: A Myth and Some Facts.* Hamden, Conn.: Archon Books, 1965.

Roppen, Georg. *Evolution and Poetic Belief.* Oslo: Univeritetsforlaget, 1956.

Ross, Blair. "Magic and the Magus in Browning's *Paracelsus* and 'Fust and his Friends.' " *Studies in Browning and His Circle* 16 (1988): 86–104.

Shelley, Percy Bysshe. *Shelley's Poetry and Prose.* Eds. Donald H. Reiman and Sharon B. Powers. New York: Norton, 1977.

Stevenson, Lionel. *Darwin Among the Poets.* Chicago: U of Chicago P, 1932.

Tucker, Herbert F., Jr. *Browning's Beginnings: The Art of Disclosure.* Minneapolis: U of Minnesota P, 1980.

LAW, NARRATIVE, AND ANONYMITY IN BROWNING'S *THE RING AND THE BOOK*

By Simon Petch

NOBODY HAS EVER HAD MUCH TO SAY for the anonymous voices who speak in books II–IV of *The Ring and the Book*. "Half-Rome," "The Other Half-Rome," and "Tertium Quid" have consistently attracted less attention than other parts of the poem.[1] In critical studies of the poem they invariably get lumped together or ignored. Even their main advocate, Louise Snitslaar, offers her case only as "a vindication of these minor characters" (28), and a lonely attempt to shift attention in commentary on *The Ring and the Book* from character to plot, which involves some detailed consideration of these books, has isolated Bruce McElderry as a voice in the wilderness. In *Narrative Discourse*, Gérard Genette offers *The Ring and the Book* as a canonical example of multiple narrative, but in spite of suggestive hints long ago from Charles W. Hodell and A. K. Cook, the narrative methodology of the poem has had little detailed attention.[2] This is presumably because its proliferation of stories causes the poem to work against conventional notions of narrative structure, for however many times the story of the Franceschini case gets told, it can never be told definitively, and can exist only in variant forms. Such proliferation and variation are the essence of legal story-telling, and are borrowed by the poem from the legal documents which constitute its main source. Drawing attention to "the immense and often distorting role of language — of narrative — in law," Richard Weisberg has said that "story-tellers find in law a precise duplication of their own narrative techniques" (1612–13). *The Ring and the Book* goes beyond such duplication, however, using the law to test the constraints of narrative, and using narrative to explore the possibilities of legal discourse in relation to other uses of language.

This paper addresses itself to the poem's narrative methodology. It does so primarily through analysis of the various constructions of plot in the three anonymous books that constitute the first major movement of the poem, and in the two anonymous pamphlets in the source on which these books are based. Criticism has understandably focussed on the great characters of *The Ring and the Book* — Guido, Pompilia, and Caponsacchi — but those characters are themselves the agents of the plot, which they create and recreate in their monologues. If the speakers at the beginning of the poem do not have the appeal of the three principals, that is because books II–IV of *The Ring and the Book* are concerned less with character than with the dynamics of narrative. In these books, stories are plotted, and re-plotted, in the context of social and cultural pressures. "Plotting" here means the shaping activity defined by Peter Brooks as "the logic of narrative discourse, the organizing dynamic of a specific mode of human understanding" (7). The structures produced by such an activity are intentional as well as organizing, and the poem's speakers simultaneously fabricate and disguise them by writing the plot under the pretence of reading it:

> And, after all, we have the main o' the fact:
> Case could not well be simpler, — mapped, as it were,
> We follow the murder's maze from source to sea,
> By the red line, past mistake: one sees indeed
> Not only how all was and must have been,
> But cannot other than be to the end of time. (II.182–87)

This designation of plot has a narrative structure of its own: a maze becomes a map, a plot is revealed as a chart. By translating sequence into simultaneity, the map figure seems to write out the dimension of temporality that is so crucial to story-telling, while promising that plot alone can deliver that "anticipation of retrospection" which Brooks rightly calls "the master trope" of narrative logic (23). In legal narrative especially, this trope gives coherence to the story it controls; yet such coherence is always provisional, for all legal plots contain stress-points at which they will be challenged by competing, adversarial plots. (Thus, the substantive certainty of the final line of verse quoted above is subverted by the metrical stress-point occasioned by a twelve-syllable line. To read the line rhythmically, to maintain the plot of the iambic pentameter, involves hurrying over some distracting syllabic detail.) In *The Ring and the Book*, the variant plots of "Half-Rome," "The Other Half-Rome," and "Tertium Quid," conflict and compete with each other, but their plots are made in similar ways. Their speakers use a semi-official discourse on the fringes of the law, and like lay-lawyers, they draw on a fund of stock stories — stories which embody human, social, and political values, and which do not simply describe social relationship but constitute it.[3] This discourse and these stories give them a language with which to plot the Franceschini case.

The anonymous pamphlets on which these books are based have a special status in the Old Yellow Book. They are in the vernacular Italian rather than the law Latin of the pleadings; they provide the coherent narratives that are missing from the fragmentary pleadings; and, as documents that "were probably distributed throughout Rome," they took the case beyond the court and the tribunal and before the "bar of public opinion" (Hodell 240). In these pamphlets, and in the parts of the poem based on them, a legal code speaks to a social world. The anonymous pamphlets at once elide and establish the relationships between law and ordinary life. They also offered Browning narrative principles which his poem could use to order the dispersed nature of the legal pleadings, and the anonymous books in the poem redeploy the narrative coherences of the anonymous pamphlets into the complex poetic universe of *The Ring and the Book*. James Boyd White's words about Aeschylus are wonderfully appropriate to Browning's legal epic: "The poet sees that the law is at its heart a species of narrative and dramatic poetry" (180).

The poem's creative interest in legal narrative can be seen in its development and expansion of legal citation. In the ninth pamphlet of the Old Yellow Book, Spreti defends Guido against the aggravating circumstances of the case, and makes a series of citations in support of his point. Each citation works as a compressed narrative, but a narrative that subordinates the story *in* the trial to the story *of* the trial,[4] for the actions which prompted the case are processed in a discourse which privileges decision, reasoning, and sentence over "what happened." For example, Spreti refers to a case cited by Marius Muta, a Judge of the Supreme Court of Sicily, in which one Leonardus, using his son, or her son, or their son (the Latin text says only "*per filium*") as an intermediary, lured his unfaithful wife outside the city walls, and there killed her and left her body to be eaten by dogs:

> "A report of the case therefore having been made in the General Visitation in March 1617, before his Excellency, because there appeared the wicked method of killing her, she having been thus called by his son and afterwards her corpse was discovered just as though the dogs had devoured it outside the walls, Leonardus himself was sentenced to the royal galleys for seven years." (Gest 430)[5]

When the case is rewritten by the poem, the citation of legal authorities moves closer to narrative fiction. Thus, Browning's Archangeli:

> For pregnant instance, let us contemplate
> The luck of Leonardus, — see at large
> Of Sicily's Decisions sixty-first.
> This Leonard finds his wife is false: what then?
> He makes her own son snare her, and entice
> Out of the town-walls to a private walk,

> Wherein he slays her with commodity.
> They find her body half-devoured by dogs:
> Leonard is tried, convicted, punished, sent
> To labour in the galleys seven years long:
> Why? For the murder? Nay, but for the mode!
> (VIII.809–19)

The poem makes the trial part of the story. It foregrounds the story *in* the trial, by avoiding the institutional passive, by using the present tense, and by changing the sequence. (Archangeli's extra-legal play with language — ''pregnant'' — also leers at a pre-legal story.) The accounts in both source and poem begin with the decision, but whereas Spreti moves from the decision through the reasons behind it to the actions informing it, Browning's Archangeli goes from the decision, to the actions, to the sentence, and concludes with the reason for the decision. The sequence in the poem changes the order of priority, placing the narrative of events prior to both the sentence and the reasons for it. The coherences of Spreti's account, on the other hand, are not those of chronological sequence; his story is shaped by the way the judgment constructs the circumstances of the case, and a language of judgment writes out a language of description (James Boyd White 65). The rewriting of this precedent in the poem draws out the descriptive structures which the judgmental language of the law suppresses, but on which it depends. Stanley Fish has pointed out that precedent is itself a means to authority and coherence, ''the process by which the past gets produced by the present so that it can then be cited as the producer of the present'' (514). Legal citation, that is to say, not only takes a narrative form; it also locates its primary case within larger configurations of social meaning to which it does not, explicitly, refer. Thus Browning translates ''per filium'' as ''her son,'' which Gest seems to have thought incorrect; but this turning against his wife of her own son intensifies the betrayal on which the judgment turns and which the (poetic) lawyer wishes to stress, and also heightens the poem's strong sense of a patriarchal plot against all women.

Precedent is a form of analogy. ''This Leonard finds his wife is false'' asks us to look for similarities between the situation of Leonard and that of Guido, and the search for an apt analogy tempts Archangeli to exercise his narrative skill. As he defends Guido's killing of the Comparini, he leaps from the arguments of his prototype in the Old Yellow Book into a world of legal parable:

> Do you blame us that we turn law's instruments
> Not mere self-seekers — mind the public weal,
> Nor make the private good our sole concern?
> That having — shall I say — secured a thief,

> Not simply we recover from his pouch
> The stolen article our property,
> But also pounce upon our neighbour's purse
> We opportunely find reposing there,
> And do him justice while we right ourselves?
> He owes us, for our part, a drubbing say,
> But owes our neighbour just a dance i' the air
> Under the gallows: so we throttle him.
> The neighbour's Law, the couple are the Thief,
> We are the over-ready to help Law . . . (VIII.880–93)

In place of the citations which occur in the Old Yellow Book at the equivalent point to this (879, *Everyman* 20), Archangeli here justifies his client's action by an analogy that does not quite fit: "the couple are the Thief"; and the lack of fit in the analogy questions the representational or referential claims of legal discourse. "Analogy is not a logical operation, nor can analogies be proved" (Goodrich 77): the reworking by Browning's Archangeli of these devices of analogy and precedent suggests the unacknowledged reliance, by the law, on the tropes of narrative to construct the apparently logical coherences of its own rhetoric.

Like Archangeli in book VIII, the anonymous speakers in books II–IV of *The Ring and the Book* show us legal narrative being made. The substantial narrative movement of this part of the poem occurs at a crucial stage in the development of the legal plot: after the *processus fugae* and the other suits, some of which were pending on appeal at the time of the murders, but before the murder trial itself (IV.1306–30). Conscious of legal stories that have not yet come to closure, these speakers create the arguments of which Guido, Pompilia and Caponsacchi are the creatures. The anonymity of Half Rome, Other Half-Rome, and Tertium Quid confers on these speakers an identity that is discursive and social, and their stories focus the cultural forces that are shaping the legal plot. For all their divergent opinions and with all their distinguishing variations in style and argument, they speak the same language and share a common cultural syntax; their narratives locate and give meaning to several sets of legal institutions and prescriptions; and, as situated speakers embedded in a context of practice, they are merely doing what comes naturally.[6]

In this context of practice, levels of narrative enter discursive competition and collaboration. Perhaps the most dramatic moment in *The Ring and the Book*, repeated and reworked throughout the poem, is when Guido enters the room in the inn at Castelnuovo where Pompilia is asleep. This is described in the poem for the first time by Half-Rome, who stresses the compromising circumstances of the situation for Pompilia:

> Her defence? This. She woke, saw, sprang upright
> I' the midst and stood as terrible as truth,
> Sprang to her husband's side, caught at the sword
> That hung there useless, since they held each hand
> O' the lover, had disarmed him properly,
> And in a moment out flew the bright thing
> Full in the face of Guido, — but for help
> O' the guards who held her back and pinioned her
> With pains enough, she had finished you my tale (II.1029–37)

"Defence" here focuses Pompilia's story, in both senses of that phrase: what did she say in court, and what is she said to have done at the inn? The word rushes us from the court to Castelnuovo, conflating the documents with the deeds they record. "Defence" glibly if uneasily mediates levels of narrative, and integrates one institutionally-produced discourse (the evidence of eyewitnesses) with another (the testimony of the principal witness). As a legalism, the word suppresses Pompilia's spontaneous self-assertion by redefining it. Actions may speak louder than words, but they are accessible only through language, and the speaker concludes his account of the episode by drawing attention to yet another narrative dimension: "she had finished you my tale" betrays his self-conscious awareness of the discursive continuity between Pompilia's story and his own.

The complex interweaving of levels of discourse is also focused on the poem's discussions of torture. Here, Browning went behind the Old Yellow Book to one of its most frequently cited authorities, Sanfelicius Farinacci, and even made his own Archangeli quote the jurist (Cook 167). Farinacci's sober tone — at least in Hodell's translation (Hodell 335–36) — his injunction that the torment be tempered, and his awesome sense of the cruelty of the procedures, are all absent from Archangeli's jocular account:

> "Of all the tools at Law's disposal, sure
> That named *Vigiliarum* is the best —
> That is, the worst — to whoso has to bear . . .
> Out of each hundred cases, by my count,
> Never I knew of patients beyond four
> Withstand its taste, or less than ninety-six
> End by succumbing: only martyrs four,
> Of obstinate silence, guilty or no, — against
> Ninety-six full confessors, innocent
> Or otherwise, — so shrewd a tool have we!" (VIII.330–44)

The terms *martyres* and *confessores* are Farinacci's, but Archangeli adds the qualities of "guilt" and "innocence." These words cross-reference each other in evident misalignment, and in the sudden switch from "best" to "worst" to describe the "tool" of the *tormentum vigiliae* the language translates itself into contradiction. The disturbances in Archangeli's own language dramatise the legal stress-point at which torture becomes talk, and pain, procedure. In the legal process torture is equated with argument; it is a form of discourse that is instrumental in producing further discourse.[7]

The stress-points in the anonymous monologues are frequently those at which talking becomes telling, where chat hardens into directed story, and where the shifting levels between talking and story-telling bring speaker and listener together in a context that is linguistically pressured. Behind Half-Rome's description of Guido returning to Arezzo after the *processus fugae* lurks a threat, which the listener must pass on to his cousin, but the threat is disguised in the "chorus of inquiry" confronting Guido on his return home:

> "And did the little lady menace you,
> Make at your breast with your own harmless sword?
> The spitfire! Well, thank God you're safe and sound,
> Have kept the sixth commandment whether or no
> The lady broke the seventh: I only wish
> I were as saint-like, could contain me so.
> I am a sinner, I fear I should have left
> Sir Priest no nose-tip to turn up at me!"
> You, Sir, who listen but interpose no word,
> Ask yourself, had you borne a baiting thus?
> Was it enough to make a wise man mad?
> Oh, but I'll have your verdict at the end! (II.1252–63)

The anticipated "verdict" signals the speaker's awareness of his quasi-legal context, but this context is disturbed by more personal revelations. The interpolated "I" directs the speaker's sexual insecurity, and the ironic approval of Guido in "another" voice becomes an indirect threat. The threat is disguised by the complication of voices and situations, but gets its patriarchal authority from the appeal to the commandments. The conventions of the monologue are doubled to create a layered, and pressing, impersonality. And the end of this paragraph looks ahead to the end of the monologue, where the power of the patriarchy, and the threat, re-emerge in an explicit context of insecurity and misogyny.

Other Half-Rome has no wife, but his sentimental predisposition towards Pompilia barely disguises a similarly patriarchal bias, and his indirect address to Guido in the following passage sees him similarly using Guido as a stand-in for his auditor. Other Half-Rome's direct relationship with his listener is one of agreement, however, and at the end of the monologue the Comparini-Franceschini wrangle is displaced by his approval of the power of the legal institution to determine inheritance disputes:

> I who have no wife,
> Being yet sensitive in my degree
> As Guido, — must discover hurt elsewhere
> Which, half compounded-for in days gone by,
> May profitably break out now afresh,
> Need cure from my own expeditious hands.
> The lie that was, as it were, imputed me
> When you objected to my contract's clause, —
> The theft as good as, one may say, alleged,
> When you, co-heir in a will, excepted, Sir,
> To my administration of effects,
> — Aha, do you think law disposed of these?
> My honour's touched and shall deal death around!
> Count, that were too commodious, I repeat! (III.1678–91)

The speaker and his listener are united by the law. They solved their disagreement in court, and, as co-heirs, were regarded in law as a single unit (Finley 135; Maine 150, 188). This fiction dissolves the speaker's individuality, and redefines his identity in terms of the institutional processes of the law. An argument about law and property has detached itself from the story of Pompilia which it was the speaker's ostensible purpose to tell.[8] Pompilia is abandoned, and the speaker's sentimental reverence for her is replaced by a very unsentimental appreciation of property and inheritance, these being the main instruments of the Patria Potestas in Roman law.[9] His most substantial argument about the Franceschini case turns on property and inheritance; it is that Guido waited for the birth of his child before carrying out the murders, for then all the money in dispute would come to him:

> By an heir's birth he was assured at once
> O' the main prize, all the money in dispute:
> Pompilia's dowry might revert to her
> Or stay with him as law's caprice should point, —
> But now — now — what was Pietro's shall be hers,
> What was hers shall remain her own, — if hers,
> Why then, — oh, not her husband's but — her heir's!
> That heir being his too, all grew his at last. (III.1546–53)

The legal inheritance works here through linguistic lineage, as female yields to male in the assonantal progression from "hers" through "heirs" to "his." The argument used here is one of the strongest in the Old Yellow Book, where it is put forward by Bottini (*Everyman* 189–90; Gest 394–95; Cook 69), but in its transposition to the poem the legal strength of the argument is over-ridden by its use to indicate the patriarchal prejudices of this speaker. A formally powerful argument is weakened by its contextualisation, and the disjunction here between Other Half-Rome's story and his argument exposes a fault-line in his narrative.

At such moments, the stress-points in the complex interplay of past and present dramatically make themselves apparent in narrative discourse. The main stress-point in the Old Yellow Book itself is the decree or sentence handed down in the *processus fugae*. Caponsacchi was "relegated" to Civita Vecchia for three years "pro complicitate in fuga, & deviatione Franciscae Comparinae, & deviatione Franciscae Comparinae, & cognitione carnali eiusdem" (Hodell xcix); as Gest translates, "for complicity in the elopement or flight, and for the seduction of Francesca Comparini and for carnal knowledge of her" (11; *Everyman* 106). The story told in this decree was constructed differently by each of the anonymous writers (*Everyman* 149, 222–23). In *The Ring and the Book*, Caponsacchi maintains that this sentence is no more than a provisional contrivance, a form of words that has given rise to unwarranted inference, "a simple penman's error" (VI.2007–22). Any error that may have been involved was far from simple. It is apparent from the Old Yellow Book that, at the instigation of Lamparelli, this decree was to have been changed in some of its particulars (this was to strengthen Pompilia's position in the suit brought by the Convertites against her estate), and was to have been made less specific; but the change was not actually recorded in the documents as having been carried out (Cook 136–37; Gest 259–64). This incomplete story *of* the decree necessarily complicates the story *in* the decree, suggesting alternative versions of the latter; and in the poem Bottini uses the anti-Guido writer's figure of a sign outside the door of an inn to focus the discrepant or incomplete relationship between sign and referent suggested by the decree (IX.1543–50; *Everyman* 223).

Bottini's "word for word" translation alters the decree distinctly:

> "Decreed: the priest, for his complicity
> I' the flight and deviation of the dame,
> As well as for unlawful intercourse,
> Is banished three years" . . . (IX.1516–19)

"For unlawful intercourse" is a curious translation of "pro cognitione carnali." "Carnal" is contained by and submerged in "unlawful," although it possibly surfaces in "intercourse." (Previously Bottini has used "intercourse" and "conversation" in ways that both suppress and suggest their sexual meaning [1274, 1278], language again enacting the intercourse or conversation of ambiguous narrative levels.) In a bizarre development in the textual history of the poem (and indirectly in the history of the case), Hodell made his own corrections to the decree. Taking the hint from Lamparelli in the Old Yellow Book, Hodell follows the Bottini of the poem, although his "deviation" lacks the deviousness of Browning's lawyer. Hodell renders the pro-Guido writer's "carnalmente" as "carnally" (cxlv, 120), but in the anti-Guido pamphlet translates "pro cognitione carnale" as "criminal knowledge" (ccxxi, 180), thus filtering his own pro-Pompilia bias through the poem's prosecutor.[10]

The interdependence of the poem and the translation of the source of the poem, and the presence of the poem's precedent "deviations" in the translation of its source, are arbitrarily decreed by the law's imprecise and haphazard sentences. The sentence or decree in the *processus fugae* is not a legal fiction in the formal sense of the term, but the advocates' attempts to renegotiate meanings behind verbal formulations themselves signify the instability of language as institutionalized in the legal fiction. At about the same time that Browning found his Old Yellow Book, Henry Maine was eulogizing legal fictions as agents of reform. Maine uses the term " 'Legal Fiction' to signify any assumption which conceals, or affects to conceal, the fact that a rule of law has undergone alteration, its letter remaining unchanged, its operation being modified" (21–22).[11] Maine regards the legal fiction as a valuable expedient for overcoming the rigidity of law, and such expedience is entirely predicated on a legitimate instability in the relationship of word and referent. The fictions of the poem's speakers, of the writers of its source, and of the translator of that source, are all authorised by the unstable and nonreferential quality of language as acknowledged and institutionalized in legal procedure.

The decree in the *processus fugae* thus yielded variant meanings, which were inevitably construed as competitive by the adversarial procedures of the law. The *processus fugae* itself produced different legal verdicts: the judgment of the court at Arezzo, which condemned Pompilia to imprisonment in the Stinche for life, and the judgment of the court at Rome, which took effect as Pompilia was then under Roman jurisdiction (*Everyman* 5–7, IV.1501–20). Furthermore, Guido may have told "two tales to suit the separate courts" (VI.2043), just as Violante told two stories about Pompilia (II.585–87), and just as Pompilia herself was reputed to have made two confessions (IV.1477–80). Competing confessions, competing verdicts, competing tales in different courts: all these features of the legal discourse in the Old Yellow Book are at the basis of the poem's profound sense of the inadequacy of human discourse to capture any final version of truth. The method of *The Ring and the Book*, as Langbaum pointed out in a seminal essay on the poem's relativism, makes clear "that no point of view is identifiable with the truth" (130), for truth exists only as a set of variants.

Legal narrative claims authority by presenting itself as history, but history, like law, produces only as a range of variant narratives (Hayden White 20). Even Tertium Quid is baffled by this, as he says after a brief survey of the case: "It makes a man despair of history, / Eusebius and the established fact — fig's end!" (IV.41–42). Although the anonymous pamphlets in the

Old Yellow Book discuss and indeed discover the facts of the Franceschini case through their competing narratives, an "established fact" may still be the occasion of dispute. For example, it is agreed that after the Comparini moved to Arezzo (one of the conditions of the marriage contract) there were disagreements in the Franceschini household. To the pro-Guido writer, these proceeded from "the bitter tongue of Pietro and the haughtiness of Violante, his wife" (*Everyman* 147), whereas the anti-Guido writer places these disagreements within the larger network of family affairs. By harassing the Comparini to an early grave, the Franceschini would have full advantage of the property they stood to inherit under the terms of the marriage contract (*Everyman* 212). This is the rhetorically superior argument, for it creates a more plausible "order of meaning" (Hayden White 5). It develops the domestic discord as a consequence of the marriage contract, and also as a consequence of the Comparini's discovery that they had been tricked by Guido's statement of his income, a statement designed to lure them into the contract in the first place.

Guido stated his income as 1700 scudi, and the falseness of this figure is admitted by both writers as a fact (*Everyman* 146, 213; Cook 99). A document which contains lies and is possibly forged is given a firm place in the narratives by the conflicting interpretations which it sustains. According to the anti-Guido writer, this document was used to tempt Violante; whereas the pro-Guido writer argues that the statement of income was produced, not for the sake of tricking the Comparini, but at the instigation of Violante to get Pietro to agree to the marriage (*Everyman* 212, 146). In this version, Guido's statement is virtually re-authorised to Violante, and in each account the document is plotted differently, as it becomes evidence, not of Guido's income, but of the competing chains of motivation by which the document itself was produced. The writers agree that the problem for both Guido and Violante was to persuade Pietro to agree to the marriage, but in each case the solution to the problem is plotted differently.

Any legal document, such as the title of the Old Yellow Book (I.121–31), or the decree in the *processus fugae*, may contain submerged narrative structures without taking on a specifically narrative form. Even a contract — here, the marriage contract — may be construed as a plot, for it tells a story, or rather two stories. The opposing writers of the anonymous pamphlets agree on how much Pietro was worth, they confirm the amount of Pompilia's dowry, and they agree on the terms of the Comparini's maintenance (*Everyman* 145–46, 211). Louise Snitslaar rightly points out that "a contract and a money transaction can only be a contract and a money transaction" (41), but her language locks itself into meaningless stasis. The terms of the marriage contract (the document itself has not survived) are only activated by the structures of cause and motivation which give the contract legal meaning and social signficance, and of course the writers plot their respective narratives quite differently. The "facts" can exist only through "the mediate word" (XII.857), and in the poem as in these pamphlets the language of contract comes alive only in the force-field of narrative.

Tertium Quid pauses to reflect on who cheated whom:

> There was a bargain mentally proposed
> On each side, straight and plain and fair enough;
> Mind knew its own mind: but when mind must speak,
> The bargain have expression in plain terms,
> There was the blunder incident to words,
> And in the clumsy process, fair turned foul. (IV.508–13)

In the movement from mind to speech, not even the "plain terms" of contract can prevent the bargain, in the legal sense of "compact," from translating itself into a blunder. Social pressures require that the cynical nature of the bargain be packaged in decent language, and under the influence of those pressures the language of the law writes a story in which no-one's intention gets clearly expressed:

> According to the words, each cheated each;
> But in the inexpressive barter of thoughts,
> Each did give and did take the thing designed,
> The rank on this side and the cash on that —
> Attained the object of the traffic, so. (IV.527–31)

At the very instant of its creation, the contract falsifies itself, for its conception in language brings alive the narrative potential of variability. "Incident to words," the bargain is simultaneously incident to "the shifting and variable effects produced by stories powerfully — that is, forcefully — told"; and in this "contest of persuasive styles," the notion of the "plain effect" of the language of contract, of "an agreement sealed by its verbal representation," cannot hold (Fish 507; and see 4). In the poem, as in the pamphlets, legal documents exist only as interpreted, and the interpretive contexts can only be competitive. The plain language of the contract is dispersed in different stories, and its plain effect is conflict: "According to the words, each cheated each."

One writer's conflict may be the means to the other's coherence. Yet another established fact to which different meaning is assigned by the pamphleteers is the departure of Guido's brother Paolo from Rome when Pompilia was released from prison into house-arrest. Faced with the need to explain this, the pro-Guido writer slips into indirect discourse to focalise Paolo's inner life, and map his feelings through metaphor: "for although it was indirectly that he was offended, that is, in the person and honour of his brother, nevertheless it seemed to him that every man's face had become a looking-glass, in which was mirrored the image of the ridicule of his house" (*Everyman* 151). Such narratorial sophistication amounts to no more than special pleading to explain away a difficult problem, and the opposing writer takes full advantage of this difficulty: "[Paolo] left Rome to take part in the planning of that notorious murder, which followed a little while later" (*Everyman* 219). Paolo's mysterious absence, which the pro-Guido writer could explain only by moving outside the conventions of legal discourse, is here deftly turned into his hidden presence in the murder plot. His departure is continuous with the murder, and the smoothness of the rhetorical move is best gauged by its easy establishment of plausible narrative coherence.

Bernard Jackson maintains that the plausibility of a story told in a legal context is "a matter of the internal coherence of the narrative" rather than a question of "correspondence" or representation (58; see also 41).[12] The legal narratives in both the Old Yellow Book and *The Ring and the Book* can only be evaluated in terms of "coherence" rather than "correspondence," for such coherences as the narratives possess are discursive and rhetorical rather than referential. The norms to which law appeals, the events of which it speaks, and the rules of closure which structure its operations, are effects of its discourse: "they are constructed within those forms of discourse, and form part of the system of signification which makes such discourse meaningful" (Jackson 140). Coherence is conspicuous primarily through its absence. The writers of the pamphlets and the speakers of the poems occasionally fail in their attempts to achieve the coherence that is necessary to a powerfully unified narrative. To the writers of both pamphlets, Caponsacchi is something of a wild card in the legal game they are playing. In both narratives he is denied volition, and subpoenaed occasionally to whatever role the argument requires him to play. His character, that is to say, is strictly a function of plot. To the anti-Guido writer, Caponsacchi is both Pompilia's rescuer and her dupe, writing risqué poems and observing the limits of due modesty, but firmly detained at Civita after the *processus fugae* lest he disturb the plot. The pro-Guido writer, on the other hand, requires Caponsacchi to exert a needling pressure on Guido after the *processus fugae*, so in this narrative Caponsacchi returns from Civita, less for the purpose of visiting Pompilia than for joining the plot against Guido. Figuratively defrocked, Caponsacchi returns cloaked in predatory metaphors: "For like a vulture, Caponsacchi wheeled round and round those walls, that he might put beak and talons into the desired flesh for the increase of Guido's disgrace" (*Everyman* 152).

In the poem, the presence of Caponsacchi as a disruptive threat to narrative coherence is realised most fully in "The Other Half-Rome." McElderry points out that this is the only monologue which gives a "closely chronological account of the action" (197), but the speaker's attempt to tell a chronological story is interrupted by Caponsacchi; after the first mention of his name,

"Now begins / The tenebrific passage of the tale" (III.788–89). Coherence is impossible to maintain, and the story needs yet another beginning: "There was a certain young bold handsome priest" (839); but each new beginning only leads the speaker to a point at which he has to loop back and begin again: "Will you go somewhat back to understand?" (964). The problem is that the testimony of Caponsacchi keeps interfering with what Pompilia has said, and Other Half-Rome finds that he can no longer tell the story because there is no longer any one story to tell. The conflicting stories of Pompilia and Caponsacchi turn Other Half-Rome's own narrative into a story of difference, and its interpretation slides out of his grasp: "Here be facts, charactery; what they spell / Determine, and thence pick what sense you may!" (837–38).

The insistent contradictions between the stories told by Pompilia and Caponsacchi ensure that conflict displaces coherence in the speaker's own narrative. He gives Pompilia a quasi-legal authority as she thrice "avers" her story about the letters (908, 919, 923), but the more committed Other Half-Rome is to Pompilia's credibility, the harder Caponsacchi is to explain away. The speaker tries to intensify the suasive power of his discourse, and the monologue signals its stress-point, as once again the presence of the auditor dramatises the problem the speaker is trying to resolve. The problem is still Pompilia's story that she and Caponsacchi met and came to agreement without communicating by letter:

> Is that credible?
> Well, yes: as she avers this with calm mouth
> Dying, I do think "Credible!" you'd cry —
> Did not the priest's voice come to break the spell . . . (922–25)

The coercive syntax depends on a crucial, and momentarily disguised identification between speaker and auditor, as the "I" magically transforms itself into "you" through shared credibility. But Caponsacchi again breaks the spell; his contradictory assertion "damns the story credible otherwise" (931), and this leads the speaker to total *impasse*: "why should the man tell truth just here / When graceful lying meets such ready shrift?" (938–39).[13]

As Other Half-Rome moves to his account of the flight, pursuit, and capture, he abandons any pretence at coherence. Pompilia gives her account (1121–70), Caponsacchi his (1171–1202), then "Guido's tale begins" (1203), and later concludes with his discovery of the letters at the inn. As if in reflection of the speaker's own problem, Guido is continually confronted by situations that test *his* narrative ingenuity. Each crisis poses a double problem: what is he to do, and what is he to say? What story would he tell to explain the different shapes taken by the past? (1293–94, 1307). There is a partial resolution for both speaker and Guido in the discovery of the letters at the inn, which provides Guido with a new story, and which offers a backward loop to Other Half-Rome's plotting of the narrative, allowing him to regroup his stories and regain some degree of narrative coherence. This monologue puts stories into dialogue with each other; it is a story about stories. But the stories do not agree, and the meta-narrative is subject to the same instabilities as the stories it is trying to control.

Even at stress-points, when we are aware of the speaker, we are aware of him less as a character than as a would-be controller of his own discourse. In the anonymous books, as in the pamphlets, the question of characterisation is always subordinate to the question of coherence: "Focus in such a text is on one side of a dispute, not on the people who are involved" (Kurzon 478). The anonymous pamphlets are more conscious than the pleadings themselves of character, although it is very clear that the only character who matters is Guido. Neither writer has the slightest interest in the subjective lives of either Caponsacchi or Pompilia, whose maternal instinct, which is so significant in the poem, is not mentioned in the source. Guido's instinct is important to the writer defending him, but is carefully contextualised within the discursive practices of the law. The writer describes Guido's mental response to the decree in the *processus fugae*:

> Let any one who has the sense of honour consider in what straits and perturba-
> tions of mind poor Guido found himself, since even the very reasonless animals
> detest and abominate the contamination of their conjugal tie, with all the ferocity
> that natural instinct can suggest. They not only avenge the immodesty of their
> companions by the death of the adulterer, but they also avenge the outrages and
> injuries done to the reputation of their masters. For Elian in his Natural History
> tells of an elephant which avenged adultery for its master by the death of the
> wife and the adulterer found together in the act of adultery. (*Everyman* 149)[14]

Instinct springs to life as the direct consequence of a legal verdict, and is scrupulously situated in discourse; a legal sentence produces instinctive behaviour which is then ratified by legal citation. Instinct is placed firmly within the structures of the legal discourse which validate its operations, and Guido's physical actions and mental processes are united in verification of the theoretical propositions which justify and explain them. His subjective life is rendered at the level of social discourse, ensuring that the issues raised in the trial are ideological and political rather than individual and subjective. The pamphlets agree that their plotting should be on this level, for in both of them the narrative is a testing-ground for social principles and attitudes rather than a story about individuals.

Robert M. Cover has said that any legal tradition is "part and parcel of a complex normative world. The tradition includes not only a corpus juris, but also a language and a mythos — narratives in which the corpus juris is located by those whose wills act upon it'' (9). Such myths establish paradigms of normative behaviour, and the legal narratives of the pamphlets constantly appeal to the social and cultural norms by which they are constituted, and which their institutional authority sustains. While the various roles among the principal figures in the Old Yellow Book are distributed according to the needs of legal argument, the roles themselves play out a drama of family, property, and patriarchy. Even in the most technical of legal matters, the ''content of the law'' is always ''some social, moral, political, or religious vision'' (Fish 131; and see 226), and the vision in these texts is that of the Patria Potestas; its guiding concept is that of the family. Although a product of ancient society, this distinctively Roman institution of patriarchal power was basic to the codes, social and cultural as well as specifically legal, that effectively wrote the Franceschini trial in the Old Yellow Book, and it determines the plotting of the narratives in the anonymous pamphlets.

The starting-point for the pro-Guido writer is money. His narrative begins with details of Pietro's financial affairs, and then moves into an account of the relations between the Franceschini and the Comparini. Guido is above all the representative of the Franceschini line and the guardian of its honour, and he only enters the narrative as an independent agent when he wakes up one morning to find his wife gone (*Everyman* 148). In response to this, the anti-Guido writer begins Guido's story much earlier, and introduces him as an idle loafer in Rome looking about for a wife, although this comes after a long preamble which attempts to shift the ground of the murder plot from *causa honoris* to greed and *causa litis* (*Everyman* 210). This writer places Paolo behind Guido as surely as the pro-Guido writer places Violante behind him. Guido's behaviour and motivation are conditioned by family and inter-family politics, which in turn are determined by the social power of marriage, money, inheritance, and the place of women in the social economy.

In each narrative, the plotting is meticulous. The pro-Guido writer places Violante's confession in narrative sequence *after* Pietro's declaration by judicial notice that Pompilia is not his daughter (*Everyman* 147), a plotting strategy which locates Violante as the prime mover in the Comparini's own plot against Guido. And, through a series of similar delaying tactics, this writer presents Guido as enmeshed in the need to restore the family honour, which has been betrayed by feminine wiles. (This writer is eager to discredit all women — Violante in particular, but also Angelica and of course Pompilia, whose behaviour is explained in good part by her ''most vile parentage'' [*Everyman* 147].) The main problem for Pompilia is that she is a woman, as the anti-Guido writer acknowledges by his unwillingness to do better for her than ''the unfortunate child'' or ''the poor wife'' (*Everyman* 223, 225). At worst, Pompilia betrays the institutional expectations of the feminine; at best she cannot live up to them. The behaviour of the principals is constantly referred to social forces and values by the writers, who agree in their high valuation of honour, but disagree as to whether or not honour motivated the murder. To the anti-Guido writer, Pompilia kept her wifely honour intact, thereby guarding this valuable institutional commodity (*Everyman* 216). In the pro-Guido writer's presentation of Pompilia, honour is besmirched by "immodesty" (*Everyman* 156), which, along with "modesty" and "impudence" constitute a complex of terms in the Old Yellow Book that is put to complex use in the poem.[15] However the writers plot the relationship of Guido and Pompilia, they appeal constantly to the same social principles, and for both of them characters exist only on a socially-defined level.

In stories told by the speakers of the anonymous books in *The Ring and the Book*, the poem's great characters are no more than counters in a game of social narrative. Half-Rome's misogyny extends the pro-Guido writer's bias into the aggressive contempt for "the weaker sex" that pervades the corpus juris as found in the Old Yellow Book (*Everyman* 211, IX. 225). This speaker believes that the law failed Guido as husband and father (1388–89), leaving him with no choice other than to "take the old way trod when men were men!" (II. 1524; see III. 880, and VIII. 419). And Half-Rome sees Guido's appeal to the four co-killers as sons, husbands, brothers, and fathers as a justifiablle patriarchal fundamentalism that goes beyond law and gospel (1395–98).

The patriarchal worldliness of Other Half-Rome is more elusive than this fundamentalism because it masquerades as spirituality. This speaker adumbrates the Pope by opening up the central religious themes of the poem (Finley 143), but he can only see Pompilia as helpless and victimised. To him, Pompilia is "the most lamentable of things" (224), diminutive and dehumanised, "little Pompilia," a child, a plant, a bird, an egg, — anything but a woman. His superstition — "Thus saintship is effected probably" (111) — and his insistence on Pompilia's survival as miraculous (7, 34, 54, 241, 1641) are as expressive of patriarchal attitudes as is his reverence for property and the law of inheritance:

It seems that, when her husband struck her first,
She prayed Madonna just that she might live
So long as to confess and be absolved . . .
to speak and right herself from first to last,
Right the friend also, lamb-pure, lion-brave,
Care for the boy's concerns, to save the son
From the sire, her two-weeks' infant orphaned thus,
And — with best smile of all reserved for him —
Pardon that sire and husband from the heart. (8–33)

Such patriarchal altruism is miraculous indeed. Her prayer to Madonna, mentioned in the Secondary Source but not in the Old Yellow Book itself (Cook

55, *Everyman* 263), is a conspiracy between women to make things easier for the men involved in the situation.

This monologue introduces Fra Celestino into *The Ring and the Book*. He is ridiculed by Other Half-Rome, whose proprietorial attitude to Pompilia makes him envious of Fra Celestino's privileged position as her confessor. To this speaker, "the Augustinian Brother" (18) is as much in love as anyone else with Pompilia, and Other Half-Rome defines himself against the authority of the church by his impatience with Fra Celestino's orthodox doctrine of original sin (98–104). In his desire to see Pompilia as a special case, this speaker appropriates religious discourse as a form of special pleading, dissociating it from its institutional authority and putting it instead in the service of his patriarchal reverence for property and inheritance. He expresses what he calls the "fatal germ" in the story, the Comparini's craving for an heir, as a spiritual desire on their part (143–54); and by giving the desire for an heir precedence over the usufruct, he reverses the order of priority given by Half-Rome (II.209ff). The official representatives of religion in this monologue are either villainous (Paolo), stupid (Fra Celestino), or problematic (Caponsacchi), but Other Half-Rome's own sentimental Christianity is no more than a mask for the commitment, which he shares with Half-Rome, to the patriarchal institution of the law.

Tertium Quid lives in a world of gossip, and he too speaks the language of the law. The Old Yellow Book gives no specific authority for this voice, but "Tertium Quid" brings legal discourse alive in the social world to which he clings. The merging of the society world and the linguistic world of the law is the most significant feature of this monologue, in which gossip does the work that is done by legal citation in the pleadings. Taking his illustrations from the world around him, Tertium Quid joins the conspiratorial male plot against Pompilia. His search for an appropriate figure to illustrate Pompilia's own justification of her choice of Caponsacchi, leads him from Pompilia herself, to Eve, to Eve's daughters, his point being that women blame men for their own misdemeanours: " 'Adam so starved me I was fain accept / The apple any serpent pushed my way' " (V.858–59); and then he uses a generalisation masked as a question — "How could a married lady go astray?" (867) to link Pompilia with a recent instance of aberrant social behaviour:

> Look now, — last week, the lady we all love, —
> Daughter o' the couple we all venerate,
> Wife of the husband we all cap before,
> Mother o' the babes we all breathe blessings on —
> Was caught in converse with a negro page. (872–76)

This incident is made to work strongly against all women by condemning them to a pattern of behaviour that the subsequent story establishes as normal or even inevitable — a stock story:

We must not want all this elaborate work
To solve the problem why young fancy–and–flesh
Slips from the dull side of a spouse in years,
Betakes it to the breast of brisk–and–bold
Whose love–scrapes furnish talk for all the town! (898–902)

Yet the words of the accused daughter, wife and mother, which constitute the majority of this long paragraph (878–97) struggle free of this context and reveal a woman reacting against imposed roles. The ''citation'' contains two narratives, and the story contains its own sub-text, in a way that is typical both of Tertium Quid's duplicitous detachment and of the radical instability of the narrative method of *The Ring and the Book*. In one story, the moral is that women should be harshly treated because that is what they truly want; in the other, the moral is that women react against the roles which society forces on them. The latter rewrites Pompilia's beahviour as authentic rebellion, but the important precondition of both narratives is the implicit existence of a social centre conferring authority and meaning (Hayden White 11, 19).

Tertium Quid dissolves any barriers between the social world of his audience and the legal world of the case by expanding a legal issue until it fits the audience's structure of assumptions. For example, he draws an analogy between the Comparini robbing the heirs by the appropriation of Pompilia, and the recent discovery of a sapphire by one of his listeners:

The story is, stooping to pick a stone
From the pathway through a vineyard — no–man's–land —
To pelt a sparrow with, you chanced on this (261–63)

The analogy depends on legal right over property, or ''occupancy.'' In Roman law, jewels disinterred for the first time fell into the category of *res nullius*, ''things which have not or never had an owner'' (Maine 203). Again, the analogy tells two stories. Superficially, it justifies Pietro and Violante; but it also dehumanises Pompilia by turning her into a precious stone, and defines her as masculine property, ''no man's goods'' (Maine 208) in ''no–man's–land.''

Such use of legal tropes and language in ordinary speech is an exceptionally powerful way of talking, and Tertium Quid is the great contextualiser of the power of legal discourse in *The Ring and the Book*. This power does not serve Tertium Quid's purpose of ingratiating himself with his audience, and the aside with which his monologue ends at once exposes his failure and contextualises his unwitting self: ("You'll see, I have not so advanced my-self, / After my teaching the two idiots here!'') (1639–40) This ending is a strong example of the speakers' unknowing contextualisation of each other. The "two idiots" are, for Tertium Quid, "Her Excellency" and "Her High-ness," but for the reader they must also be the two speakers who have preceded Tertium Quid, Half-Rome and Other Half-Rome. Unconsciously enmeshed in the same narrative network, the speakers contextualise them-selves, and each other, without being aware of it. In the Old Yellow Book, the second anonymous pamphlet was formulated in response to the first; their relationship was avowedly adversarial. In *The Ring and the Book*, the speakers are placed in relation to each other by the language and discourse that consti-tute the world they inhabit.

They inhabit a world of legal narrative, a world of plotting and fiction which is also a social world of relationship and interpretation. "Narrative locates us in a network of connections that makes our world intelligible and gives our actions a context" (Clayton 45). The law is just such a system of narrative contextualisation, for the form of the story is the bridge between legal and lay discourse, linking the narratives of the law with those of ordinary life (Jackson 64, James Boyd White 175). Narrative is a poetic principle of legal discourse which the law leases, in perpetuity, from the more general world of social discourse and communication. Law and society meet in narra-tive, and talk to each other through it. "The virtue of literary stories about law," according to Weisberg, "is that they force us to grapple with the unique elements that often come to the fore when law acts on people" (1612); but this general formulation does less than justice to Browning's great poem. *The Ring and the Book* forces us to grapple with the complicated nexus of individual story-telling and institutional authority — indeed, with the gen-eral question of discursive legitimacy — that *always* comes to the fore when law acts on language. Half-Rome, Other Half-Rome, and Tertium Quid, are situated at the noisy limit of the legal world, where social pressures translate the language of the law into prejudice; their constructions of social reality through language are powerful manifestations of the invisible discourse of the law (James Boyd White 63). The anonymity of these speakers signifies that they are the effects of an institutional discourse to which they give an affective shape. Contextualised as they are in this way, they bear witness to the continuity of "literature" with other forms of discourse. Their stories are inadequate, partial, and biased; but they also are evidence of a vital cultural relationship between law, language, and living.

University of Sydney

NOTES

This paper was read in draft by Bruce Gardiner, Roslyn Jolly, Jennifer McDonell, Warwick Slinn, and James Boyd White. I am grateful to all these people for their suggestions, all of which have strengthened this paper. I owe a special debt to Frances Muecke, of the Latin Department at the University of Sydney, who has given generously of her time and expertise in response to my many queries about the Latin in the Old Yellow Book, and in *The Ring and the Book* itself.

This paper is for Roslyn Jolly.

1. The most recent book on the poem, by Ann P. Brady, barely mentions these speakers. William E. Buckler puts all three in a single chapter, as does Mary Rose Sullivan. Richard D. Altick and James F. Loucks give these books appropriate emphasis in their integrated discussion of the poem, but their perspectives differ from my own.
2. Some recent critics who discuss the function of narrative in the poem are David D. Bedell, Susan Blalock, Sue Lonoff, and Vivienne J. Rundle. The plot is discussed by Boyd Litzinger.
3. For official language, see Frank Burton and Pat Carlen; for lay-lawyers and stock stories, see Gerald P. Lopez; and for legal discourse in *The Ring and the Book*, see Simon Petch.
4. This distinction is made in relation to legal narrative by Bernard S. Jackson 35. Jackson also points out that the "casuistic" form of ancient law "is in fact a mini-narrative," and he contrasts this narrative model with the more abstract model of the modern legal rule:98–99.
5. Spreti cites the case twice: see Gest 430, 322; *Everyman* 140, 29.
6. For "cultural syntax," see James Boyd White 63; for narrative as the location of legal institutions and prescriptions, see Robert M. Cover 4–11; and for "doing what comes naturally," see Fish ix.
7. For legal attitudes to torture at the time of the trial, see Cook Appendix VI, Gest ch. 4, and Hodell 335.
8. For a fruitful distinction between "story" and "argument," see Lopez 32–35.
9. For the Patria Potestas, see Maine *passim*, and ch. 44 of Gibbon's *History of the Decline and Fall of the Roman Empire*.
10. See *Everyman* 175, where Hodell again uses "criminal"; and compare Gest 270, who uses "carnal" rather than "criminal" in his translation of the same passage. Gest's general remarks (11) on the sentence are also relevant.
11. See also 107, 281. The standard work on Legal Fictions is by Lon L. Fuller. This is critically evaluated by Kenneth Campbell, who regards Maine's definition as "laconic," but acknowledges that it is "not wrong":365 n.47. On Legal Fictions as legitimated metaphor, see Owen Barfield. For a recent theoretical discussion, see Scheppele.
12. Guido would agree (XI.849–73), as would Hayden White:2, 21.
13. For a lucid and comprehensive account of the vexing discrepancies between the depositions of Pompilia and Caponsacchi in the *processus fugae*, the discrepancies between their monologues, and the discrepancies between their monologues and their respective depositions, see Cook Appendix V.
14. This citation of Elian occurs more frequently in the poem than it does in the Old Yellow Book: see Cook 11, and 1.232ff.
15. *Everyman* 149; see also Fra Celestino's affidavit (*Everyman* 57–58), and Bottini, IX.793, 803.

332   VICTORIAN LITERATURE AND CULTURE

WORKS CITED

Altick, Richard D., and Loucks, James F. *Browning's Roman Murder Story: A Reading of* The Ring and the Book. Chicago: U of Chicago P, 1968.

Barfield, Owen. "Poetic Diction and Legal Fiction." *Essays Presented to Charles Williams*. London: Oxford UP, 1947. 106–27.

Bedell, David D. "Paring *The Ring and the Book*: A Note on the Poem's Narrative Organization." *SBHC* 11 (1983): 63–65.

Blalock, Susan. "Browning's *The Ring and the Book*: 'A Novel Country.' " *BIS* 11 (1983): 39–50.

Brady, Ann P. *Pompilia: A Feminist Reading of Robert Browning's* The Ring and the Book. Athens Ohio: Ohio UP, 1988.

Brooks, Peter. *Reading for the Plot: Design and Intention in Narrative*. Oxford: Clarendon P, 1984.

Browning, Robert. *The Ring and the Book*. Ed. Richard D. Altick. Penguin English Poets. Harmondsworth: Penguin, 1971.

Buckler, William E. *Poetry and Truth in Robert Browning's* The Ring and the Book. New York: New York UP, 1985.

Burton, Frank, and Carlen, Pat. *Official Discourse: On Discourse Analysis, Government Publications, Ideology and the State*. London: Routledge and Kegan Paul, 1979.

Campbell, Kenneth. "Fuller on Legal Fictions." *Law and Philosophy* 2 (1983): 339–70.

Clayton, Jay. "Narrative and Theories of Desire." *Critical Inquiry* 16 (1989): 33–53.

Cook, A. K. *A Commentary Upon Browning's* The Ring and the Book. London: Oxford UP, 1920.

Cover, Robert M. "*Nomos* and Narrative." *Harvard Law Review* 97 (1983): 4–68.

Everyman. The Old Yellow Book. London: Dent, n.d. [1911]. See Hodell below.

Finley, C. Stephen. "Robert Browning's 'The Other Half-Rome': A 'Fancy-fit or Not?' *BIS* 11 (1983): 127–48.

Fish, Stanley. *Doing What Comes Naturally: Change, Rhetoric, and the Practice of Theory in Literary and Legal Studies*. Durham, NC: Duke UP, 1989.

Fuller, Lon L. *Legal Fictions*. 1930–31. Stanford: Stanford UP, 1967.

Genette, Gérard. *Narrative Discourse*. Trans. Jane E. Lewin. Oxford: Blackwell, 1980. First published 1972.

Gest, J. M. *The Old Yellow Book. Source of Browning's* The Ring and the Book. A New Translation with Explanatory Notes and Critical Chapters upon the Poem and Its Source. 1927. New York: Haskell House, 1970.

Goodrich, Peter. *Reading the Law: A Critical Introduction to Legal Method and Techniques*. Oxford: Blackwell, 1986.

Hodell, Charles W. *The Old Yellow Book*. Carnegie Institute Publication No. 89. Washington DC: Carnegie Institute, 1908. Rpt. *Everyman* (see above).

Jackson, Bernard S. *Law, Fact and Narrative Coherence*. Legal Semiotics Monographs 1. Merseyside: Deborah Charles Publications, 1988.

Kurzon, Dennis. "How Lawyers Tell Their Tales: Narrative Aspects of a Lawyer's Brief." *Poetics* 4 (1985): 467–81.

Langbaum, Robert. *The Poetry of Experience: The Dramatic Monologue in Modern Literary Tradition*. London: Chatto and Windus, 1957.

Litzinger, Boyd. "The Structural Logic of *The Ring and the Book*." *Nineteenth-Century Literary Perspectives: Essays in Honor of Lionel Stevenson*. Ed. Clyde de L. Ryals. Durham NC: Duke UP, 1974. 105–14.

Lonoff, Sue. "Multiple Narratives and Relative Truths: A Study of *The Ring and the Book, The Woman in White*, and *The Moonstone.*" *BIS* 10 (1982): 143–61.

Lopez, Gerald P. "Lay Lawyering." *UCLA Law Review* 32 (1984): 1–60.

Maine, Henry. *Ancient Law: Its Connection with the Early History of Society, and Its Relation to Modern Ideas*. 1861. New York: Dorset Press, 1986.

McElderry, B. R. "The Narrative Structure of Browning's *The Ring and the Book.*" *Research Studies of the State College of Washington* XI (1943): 193–233.

Petch, Simon. "Browning's Roman Lawyers." *Browning Centenary Essays: Special Edition of AUMLA*. Ed. Simon Petch and Warwick Slinn. *AUMLA* 71 (1989): 109–38.

Rundle, Vivienne J. " 'Will you let them murder me?': Guido and the Reader in *The Ring and the Book.*" *VP* 27 (1989): 99–114.

Scheppele, Kim Lane. "Facing Facts in Legal Interpretation." *Law and the Order of Culture: Special Issue of Representations*. Ed. Robert Post. *Representations* 30 (1990): 42–77.

Snitslaar, Louise. *Sidelights on Robert Browning's* The Ring and the Book. Amsterdam: Swets and Zeitlinger, 1934.

Sullivan, Mary Rose. *Browning's Voices in* The Ring and the Book: *A Study of Method and Meaning*. Toronto: U of Toronto P, 1969.

Weisberg, Richard H. "Entering With a Vengeance: Posner on Law and Literature." *Stanford Law Review* 41 (1989): 1597–1626. Review of Richard A. Posner, *Law and Literature: A Misunderstood Relation* (Cambridge: Harvard UP, 1988).

White, Hayden. *The Content of the Form: Narrative Discourse and Historical Representation*. Baltimore: The Johns Hopkins UP, 1987.

White, James Boyd. *Heracles' Bow: Essays on the Rhetoric and Poetics of the Law*. Madison: U of Wisconsin P, 1985.

REVIEW ESSAYS

WOMEN AND THE THEATRE: ECONOMICS, MYTH, AND METAPHOR

By Martha Vicinus

IN SPITE OF THE VALIANT EFFORTS of such respected critics as David Mayer, Michael Booth, Margot Peters, Martin Meisel, Peter Brooks, John Stokes, and Nina Auerbach, Victorian drama remains the poor step-sister of the Victorian arts. We all know that we should like it better — after all, it was the most popular form of entertainment of the century, outside of drinking and betting. And Carlyle, Dickens, the Brontës, even Tennyson, drew inspiration from the theatre. We Victorianists are accustomed to defending long, sentimental novels, wordy poems on high subjects, and stentorious advice-giving by bearded sages. But somehow nineteenth-century drama remains in the realm of bad taste; or as my graduate students primly point out when I try to convert them, melodrama, in the words of the OED, "is characterized by sensationalism and spurious pathos." Do we disapprove of Victorian emotional excess because it seems dishonest, like bad television? Or are we so cowed by the principles of modernism that an anti-realistic acting style seems too stilted, too unnatural? I want to argue that we may avoid the Victorian theatre because it contains within it the powerful contradictions and dangers of a step-mother, rather than a forlorn step-sister.

The Victorian theatre makes us uncomfortable, I believe, for two major reasons. First, it demands a new set of criteria: we must suspend our traditional expectations about the purpose of art, or even its form — plot is all, character immediately visible to anyone in the audience (even if those on stage are fooled), and action pre-determined rather than chosen. Second, live performance by its very nature is ephemeral — we cannot recreate those lost moments, and in spite of the many detailed descriptions of such stars as Edmund Kean, Madame Vestris, Henry Irving, or Mrs. Patrick Campbell, we can never fullly recreate the experience, and why it was so important to contemporaries.

What matters most in Victorian drama is its extraordinary visual effects. As the century evolved, technical advances enabled stage managers to stage more and more complicated scenarios, sacrificing speed of movement for historically accurate backdrops, intricate special effects and luxurious costumes. By the end of the century, drama seemed trapped in its own conventions, but reforming playwrights, directors and actresses successfully transformed it into what we now define as modern drama. This change may have revitalized one form of the theatre, but it also insured the division between the popular and the serious that lasts to this day. Already by mid-century, audiences were flocking to the music hall, circus and burlesque. These too depended upon visuals for their effect — precise costuming and timing combined with short, fast "turns" (in the music hall no performer had more than twenty minutes) to create an evening of unsurpassed variety. We cannot reproduce the extraordinary color, vitality and energy of these productions, whether on stage or in a circus rotunda (photographs reduce the cast to smudged dots and backdrops to towering, obvious fakes); only through an act of imagination can we know this world dominated by the visual over the spoken, the seen over the heard.

Under these circumstances, it is not surprising that many theatre critics have chosen to concentrate on the historical context, or analyses of why particular stars were important, or why an author is now unduly neglected. Russell Jackson's *Victorian Theatre: The Theatre in its Time* (New York: New Amsterdam Books, 1989), an excellent anthology of excerpts from memoirs, diaries, autobiographies and reviews, is characteristic of this recuperative effort. The collection is divided into five sections, covering the audience, the actors' lives (with a very few excerpts on or by actresses), behind the scenes, the pitfalls and windfalls of the management, and the erstwhile careers of playwrights anxious to rise in literary status. Throughout, the twin themes of pleasure and money intertwine. For the audience, and sometimes for the performer, the stage means excitement and escape into a grand imaginative world. But always in the background is money — the theatre is a speculative business, with high risks and rare high profits. Those alluring figures who strutted across the provincial stage worked long hours, purchased their own stage clothing, met all their travelling expenses, and yet often went unpaid when the till was empty.

It is this aspect — the grimy, workaday world of the typical actress — that Tracy C. Davis writes about in *Actresses as Working Women: Their Social Identity in Victorian Culture* (London and New York: Routledge, 1991), an ambitious study of the economic and social conditions of the Victorian actress. She argues convincingly that theatre historians have concentrated for too long on the atypical stars, neglecting the lives of the invisible hundreds who earned a modest living through hard work, and occasionally, a little help from a gentleman friend. Davis effectively uses census returns to prove that the income of most was little better than that of a factory worker, and sometimes much worse. Few could make the transition in middle age into "heavy parts," that is, the minor roles of doting mother, village shrew or spinster aunt. Old age for the unmarried or widowed could be a nightmare. The first half of the book provides the kind of documentation we need for every occupation with large numbers of women — here, in capsule, is where an actress generally lived, how much she earned, what kind of career she could expect to have, and from what social class she generally came.

During the nineteenth century the theatre changed from a closed occupation dominated by a few families who toured together and trained their own children to an open occupation with few controls over entry. For the stage-struck aspirant it embodied the possibility of economic and sexual freedom, no matter how many warnings were published against launching into a career without training or contacts. By the end of the century contemporaries were insisting that the stage had become almost respectable because so many members of the middle class had entered its ranks. But Davis questions this easy generalization, based upon a few well-documented examples. While the absolute number of middle-class women taking up the profession may have increased, their percentage remained small. She sees little evidence that middle-class women stuck it out unless driven by necessity or success. For Davis, acting is a hard-working profession with little room for idealism, art or glamour.

Davis also reminds us that the theatre was big business in London, a city of specialized employment, with few major industries and virtually none that employed as many as the 900 that Drury Lane took on for its Christmas pantomimes. All the special effects demanded not only hundreds of supernumeraries, but also hundreds of men back stage to shift the sets, man the lights, and insure that the props and different costumes were on hand. She is not the first to point out that the London theatres provided important supplemental income for working-class families, and indeed, often the first paid work undertaken by girls. But Davis provides the necessary statistics — how much children were paid, and who might expect what job when. Such vast enterprises drew the attention of both those looking for lucrative investments and suspicious moral reformers. As Davis acutely observes, reformers were far more successful at closing theatres in working-class districts than in the West End. Indeed, most efforts met a brick wall of judicial timidity (collusion?), press laughter, and political vacillation. After the Empire was forced in 1895 to remodel its pavilion, a notorious hangout for high-class prostitutes, shareholders' dividends dropped from 75% to 30–40% on old stock (157). The 35% earned by Crofts and Mrs. Warren in Shaw's *Mrs. Warren's Profession* (1894) on their set of international brothels seems only just in comparison.

Davis vigorously exonerates her heroines from any connection with either Mrs. Warren or her girls. While this may be literally true, much of the second half of her book documents the numerous sexual temptations to which an actress in the growing world of popular entertainment was subjected. For Davis, the audience is predominantly composed of men on the prowl, who revelled in verbal double entendres, plenty of female flesh and visual excitement of any sort. As she explains, by the 1870s, "This convention of 'clothed nudity' in ballet was adopted wholesale into extravaganza, pantomime, opera bouffe, burlesque, and music hall acrobats. The female leg, naked in tights, became synonymous with the female performer, with enjoyment, and with the theatre itself" (135). However much talent, daring or training had won the acrobat, dancer or singer her job, her success depended upon the audience's being able to see the female body encased in flesh-colored tights. And sexual titillation led naturally to the expectation that those who earned little — the young girls at the back of the chorus or corps de ballet — were available after hours.

Davis's strengths are also her weaknesses. She is sometimes surprisingly censorious. And she accepts too literally fulminations against the stage. Surely the sheer volume of protest for and against the theatre indicates its extraordinary importance in the nineteenth century. Obviously some Evangelical families, however much they might have enjoyed a Sunday morning outing to hear a famous preacher, detested the stage as the work of the devil. But many, many Victorians played charades and home theatricals, always took their children to the Christmas pantomime, and made every effort to see such touring superstars as Henry Irving and Ellen Terry should they pass through town. And families filled the suburban music halls and travelling circuses. They wanted a purified theatre, not one that specialized in leg acts. Moreover, as Auerbach argues, a good many Victorians knew that they needed the theatre as part of their imaginative world. While I do not want to minimize anti-theatrical feeling in England, I think that we have too simplistically accepted comments about the theatre's dangerous lack of respectability. What is disreputable, yet alluring, needs reform, not expunging. Could not the errant middle-class daughter take on symbolic as well as literal meaning for the pater familias? Any analysis of the theatre must include not only its gritty economics but also its magic.

This magic is inevitably intertwined with the demonic powers of sexuality — which, as we well know, is always already female. Even so determinedly scientific and neutral a man as the sexologist Havelock Ellis could not see the actress as simply a hard-working girl. As he laboriously explained in 1894:

> There is at least one art in which women may be said not merely to rival but naturally to excel men: this is the art of acting. . . . It is not difficult to find

the organic basis of women's success in acting. In women mental processes are usually more rapid than in men; they have also an emotional explosiveness much more marked than men possess, and more easily within call. At the same time the circumstances of women's social life have usually favoured a high degree of flexibility and adaptability as regards behaviour; and they are, again, more trained in the vocal expression of both those emotions which they feel and those emotions which it is considered their study to feel. (Quoted in Stokes, Booth and Bassnett 7)

Such essentialism both confirms Davis's contention that the actress was by definition "the female leg" but also implicitly encompasses the mythic elements of Woman into the actress and vice-versa. Those ogling "swells" at the Empire and the many other West End theatres exposed their own need, even as they reified the actresses. Men looked to the actress to fulfill their sexual fantasies; women looked to her to fulfill their power fantasies.

While Davis attempts to undermine the myth of the commanding, well-paid actress, in *Bernhardt, Terry, Duse: The Actress in her Time* (New York: Cambridge UP, 1988), John Stokes, Michael R. Booth and Susan Bassnett seek to explore the realities of this larger-than-life figure through three studies of the most famous international stars of the late nineteenth century. In their introduction they remind us of the difficulties in recreating the performance styles of the past, especially when such phrases as "psychological realism" and "naturalistic" had such different implications then. By our standards none of these actresses was "realistic," though each diverged from earlier acting traditions. Rather, they combine the magnificent visual effects of the nineteenth century and the emerging emphasis upon character delineation. Bernhardt, Terry and Duse were not universally admired, but aroused anxiety, hostility and veneration among their fellow professionals, critics and members of the audience. Each tried to use her power as a sex object to shape her own career and the future of the theatre. Their successes and failures are emblematic of the major cultural shift drama was undergoing at the end of the nineteenth century.

Stokes is the best of the three in presenting a new perspective on Bernhardt, who must surely be one of the best documented actresses of all time. Countless pictures and memoirs recall her to mind, whether in her coffin (she claimed to have slept in it every night), or as a travesti Hamlet, or as the vengeful lover Theodora. In all of these photos, what we first notice is how *posed* she seems — frozen in an extreme emotion, gesture or stance. Stokes shrewdly places Bernhardt on the side of modernism, but against modernity. For him, she belongs to the Symbolists, those aristocrats of the art world, who despised modernization, even as they promulgated their anti-realist avant-garde art. Her decorative style epitomized their goal of raising theatrical art above its demotic origins and creating an enlightened art for the few. Is it any wonder that Wilde sought her out for the lead in his most unconventional play, *Salome*?

Booth, unfortunately, seems unwilling or unable to place Ellen Terry in the wider context of changing cultural fashions. For him, she remains the quintessential Victorian actress, combining seductiveness and sweetness — excessively nice, and altogether too charming. He defines her as a minor artist made great by the genius of her long-time acting partner, Sir Henry Irving. Much of Booth's essay is a discussion of the many portraits of Terry, but significantly he does not mention *Choosing*, by her first husband, G. F. Watts. It shows the young Terry crushing dying violets in one hand, whilst smelling the scentless camellia, held in the other. Most contemporaries read the painting as an allegory of renunciation in favor of the humble violet, but the painting is far more ambiguous. Nina Auerbach's revisionary biography, *Ellen Terry: A Player in Her Time* (1987), which probably appeared too late for Booth to consider, shows greater insight into Terry's alleged charm. While she may not have had the range of Duse or Bernhardt, Auerbach argues that "She dominates by seeming to disappear; her boundaryless submergence in her surroundings is her power" (*Ellen Terry* 19). Terry had the power to encompass both the violet and the camellia — a dangerous dissimulation that could attract and repulse.

Susan Bassnett, charged with introducing the least known of the three actresses to an English audience, makes many good points, but her essay is marred by repetitiousness. A shorter, tighter essay would have brought home more fully why modernists preferred the self-controlled minimalism of Eleanora Duse over the excesses of her great rival, Bernhardt. Duse was brought up in the old system of small stock companies playing a style of theatre still akin to Renaissance *commedia del' arte*, with its narrow range of stereotyped characters. Its star-system earned her the money that she then used to wrench Italian theatre out of its moribund traditions. Contemporaries saw her as utterly dedicated to her art, coolly disregarding critical opinion to follow her vocation. Among her most successful roles were Ibsen's controversial Nora and Hedda, according to Bassnett, for she could bring to them her characteristic capacity for presenting a strong inner life in contradiction with a seemingly happy outer life.

Bassnett is especially good at demonstrating the difficulties faced by a brilliant artist dissatisfied with existing roles and theatre traditions, but unable to imagine or create a viable alternative, financially or artistically. She could, however, have teased out the similarities between Duse and Bernhardt here. Both Duse and Bernhardt harbored notions of creating a serious, national drama. Both distrusted the new enthusiasm for realism but were bored with such warhorse money-makers as Dumas's melodrama, *La Dame aux camellias*. They, like Terry, had been made by the elaborate visual effects of the late nineteenth century; it was inconceivable to drop them wholly. Historical tragedy seemed the only genre that could revivify serious theatre. In 1901 Duse funded the enormously expensive *Francesca da Rimini*, written by her young lover, Gabriele D'Annunzio. Symbolic lighting, a nationalistic theme, and historically accurate sets could not save the excessively long and dull play. In the same year Bernhardt played the hero of *L'Aiglon*, an historical play she had commissioned from her faithful collaborator, Edmond Rostand. Its shameless patriotism appealed to Parisians, if no one else, more than her other effort at travesti high art, Musset's closet drama, *Lorenzaccio* (1897). These plays did not travel well — the sets were too elaborate, the cast of characters too large, and foreigners found the historical references opaque or distasteful. Yet audiences did respond to the hyperbolic qualities of these dramas; they wanted their heroines to be super-stars, clad in expensive gowns and striking unfamiliar poses. The visuals were wonderful. But where was the action?

Simply put, the action had migrated to the music hall and extravaganzas, while intellectual experimenters focused upon character and language. Plot, the backbone of Victorian melodrama, seemed less important than either skillful performance on the popular stage or character development on the serious stage. In either case, we must ask, what role was available for women? If even such powerful actresses as these three were unable to alter the course of drama, could those less trapped by their fame do so?

Part of the answer to this question lies with now-forgotten women who pioneered as directors, managers and playwrights during the same years that Bernhardt and Duse struggled to find fresh vehicles for their talents. The contributors to *The New Woman and Her Sisters: Feminism and the Theatre, 1850–1914*, edited by Vivien Gardner and Susan Rutherford (Ann Arbor: U of Michigan P, 1992), look neither to the famous nor the average, but instead to the forgotten margins of the profession. There they have discovered some fascinating women, well worth further study. Cecily Hamilton is best remembered as the author of *Marriage as a Trade* (1911), a powerful indictment of bourgeois marriage, and *How the Vote Was Won* and *Pageant of Great Women*, two popular fund-raising plays for the suffragists. But she appears here as the author of an unconventional (and long-playing) farce, *Diana of Dobson's* (1908). In an excellent essay Sheila Stowell shows Hamilton's effective use of traditional forms as a vehicle for new messages — a format her more famous contemporary, George Bernard Shaw, based his career upon. Linda Fitzsimmons retrieves an even more obscure drama, a realist play about a lower-middle class couple, *Chains* (1909) by the once-praised Elizabeth Baker. Neither Hamilton nor Baker made any pretence of writing avant-garde drama, but their "truth-telling" plays sound more worthy of revival than the pompous, self-aggrandizing works Duse and Bernhardt threw themselves into.

The essays in this volume come from a conference sponsored by Manchester University's fine drama department. Like any group of conference papers, they are uneven. Some contributors appear to have just discovered the historical context within which drama exists; like Dickens's proverbial streaky bacon, their discussions alternate slabs of history with close analyses of plays. The best essays, however, provide insight into forgotten plays and freshly illuminate familiar material. Elaine Aston captures the excitement of Manchester's Gaity Theatre under the management of Annie Horniman, where young, enthusiastic reformers, local working-class couples, and budding socialists all rubbed shoulders. Geraldine Harris explores the *café concert* world of raffish satire and elegant slumming created by the French chanteuse, Yvette Guilbert. She is very good on why cabaret became the dominant musical idiom of the continent, but less sure when she postulates why it never succeeded in Britain. British music-hall audiences may not have been ready for *la Femme Moderne*, but plenty of British intellectuals crossed the sea to follow Guilbert and the German Margo Lion (and somewhat later, the better-known Marlene Dietrich). Guilbert, like Duse, created an art that broke with its demotic roots and could only be sustained as a specialist act, appealing to the politically knowing or the Bohemian intelligentsia.

Considering how important cross-dressing was for the Victorian actress, these five books say remarkably little about it. In particular, no one has tackled the principal boys (fleshy women in tights) and dames (comic actors in voluminous skirts) of pantomime, the most resilient and long-lasting dramatic genre from the nineteenth century. I long for a good study that takes this form from 1836, when David Mayer concludes *Harlequin in His Element: English Pantomime, 1806–36* (1969), to the First World War. Stokes has other fish to fry in his study of Bernhardt, or perhaps he feels that too much has been said about her "thought-wracked heroes." Jill Edmonds usefully gathers together a good deal of information on the minor forerunners to Bernhardt who played Hamlet, but she has little to say about why audiences were so accepting of women as Hamlet, Romeo and other tragic heroes. Auerbach mentions in passing that Peter Pan, the boy who will not grow up, is always played by a woman; she also notes that vulnerable children, waifs and strays were always played by young women.

Only J. S. Bratton, in one of the best essays in *The New Woman and Her Sisters*, eloquently defends the importance of minor music-hall male impersonators. She sees such famous performers as tuxedo-clad Vesta Tilley or Ella Shields as atypical; the lesser-known performers whose stage personae were more polymorphous are crucial to understanding the power invested in the transvestite. Like Terry Castle, who has written on eighteenth-century masquerades, Bratton concludes, "I think it is reasonable and helpful, when one considers the full range of distorted, mocking, exaggerated images of masculinity projected by these women from the music-hall stage, to read male impersonation as carnivalesque, and to interpret it as transgressive, provocative, an act of clowning that is a subversive manipulation of the masks of stereotype. It might be called feminist, but it is quite profoundly at odds, in its dark suggestiveness and anarchy, with the rationality of the New Woman" (89).

It is an attractive conclusion, but perhaps too dichotomized. Male playwrights, like their peer Havelock Ellis, were utterly unable to see the New Woman as rational. Sidney Grundy, Arthur Wing Pinero, Henry Arthur Jones, and even George Bernard Shaw, slotted the New Woman into the pre-existing stereotype of the heavy or comic woman; her rationality and education are always seen as a thin veneer covering suppressed sexuality. Whatever her political claims, their New Woman characters invariably succumb to hysteria, or flagrantly contradict their beliefs or drop everything to catch a man. As both Vivien Gardner and Jill Davis point out in their essays, strong, politically active women often found themselves playing demeaning roles in anti-feminist plays; even Shaw's Vivie Warren seems to personify male resistance to the New Woman rather than the New Woman herself.

Bratton's allusion to suggestiveness and anarchy, however, points to one of the limitations of Davis's approach. Davis's actresses work to a script written by the men in the audience; they never speak their own lines. Both Bratton and Helen Day, in her article on "Female Daredevils," provide evidence for the ways actresses seized the scripts with which they were provided and changed them for their own ends. However limited such actions might — could — have been, Emmaline Ethardo, the contortionist who dressed both in male attire and in pink tights as part of her act, or Zazel thrown from her cannon, or the massive Mrs. Boardman-Palmer, who, as manager of her own touring company, insisted upon playing Hamlet when 57 and over 200 pounds, had a control over their destiny that many of their viewers, male or female, must have envied.

Both the dark anarchy and the comic irrationality of drama are used by Nina Auerbach in *Private Theatricals: The Lives of the Victorians* (Cambridge: Harvard UP, 1990), her study not of the theatre itself, but of its impact upon major Victorian writers. "Private theatricals" is a metaphoric, not literal title, although I am sure that Auerbach shares my enthusiasm for accounts of that very Victorian family activity. Auerbach is especially good at describing authors as varied as Carlyle, Arnold, Charlotte Brontë, Dickens, and Wilde, who were both enchanted with and distrustful of masks, poses, disguises and acting. In their search for a humanistic alternative to religion, these great Victorians turned to the theatre as an explanatory model for the meaning of life. For Auerbach, "Theatricality was not only a spirit of Victorian culture; it was a cultural fact. The idea of the theater troubled the attempts of writers to create, in the absence of orthodox faith, a humanist religion, but most Victorian writers would not have written the works we know without the theater to inspire them" (12–13).

We have come to expect from Auerbach an original perspective on the Victorian age; she has a marvelous ability to turn familiar figures upside down and reveal new, or forgotten, aspects of them. This book, based upon a series of lectures given at the University of Washington, does just this, but it also builds on many familiar Auerbach themes. For example, one chapter elaborates upon an article published in 1975 on the Victorian orphan's combination of glass and steel. He/she returns to haunt this book as the child actor, showing us how to die, as if that were the essential moment in which our real selves come to the fore. Even those characters who reject death, such as Jane Eyre and Pip, are "[s]teeped, despite themselves, in theatrical modes of breathtaking visual transformation . . . they realize themselves when they *see* themselves theatrically translated. . . . The self is a spectacle; the child is not its priest, but its audience and one of its masks" (34–35). While I am not always convinced by Auerbach's arguments, her connections are always exhilarating, and often illuminating.

The final chapter of *Private Theatricals* is a tour de force on death scenes, real and fictional, demonstrating their constructed, dramatic nature. It is as if, argues Auerbach, the Victorians could not imagine a stable self, even though all their art moved toward this goal, unless it were caught in the moment of death. Since "Victorian iconography suggests that in the midst of death we are also in life" (93), she concludes with an analysis of several famous Victorian ghost stories. Ironically, even as the Victorians believed in the superior integrity of the dead, they created ghosts who partook in the instability of the living.

In one of Auerbach's final examples, Vernon Lee's unjustly neglected "The Phantom Lover" (1886), the spectral Alice Oke participates in a private theatrical, played by the bored Okes and their friend, the narrator. Mrs. Oke's dramatization — self-creation — as the flamboyant, murderous seventeenth-century Alice Oke, virtually summarizes the themes I have been discussing. A seemingly ordinary upper-middle-class woman becomes obsessed by a dead person; she proceeds to become that character through historical costuming, for the visual delectation of her husband and the narrator; both are sexually aroused and horrified at the transformation. The masquerade permits the expression of suppressed emotions, which then envelop not only Mrs. Oke, but also her husband. The beautiful, passive Mrs. Oke becomes the demonic Woman; in a maddened fit, her husband retaliates against female power by murdering Alice/his wife. No wonder the Victorians both feared and adored their actresses — perhaps they knew something about the theatre that we have forgotten or denied.

University of Michigan

CONTEMPORARY BIOGRAPHERS OF NINETEENTH-CENTURY NOVELISTS

By Frederick R. Karl

WHEN I WROTE an earlier article-review of contemporary biographers of nine-teenth-century novelists (*Dickens Studies Annual* 17), I found that one of the hopeful signs in the genre came in what I called hybrid biographies, those like John Maynard's study of sexuality in Charlotte Brontë and Ian Watt's study of Joseph Conrad in the nineteenth century. In these books, biography, criticism, and interpretation are intermixed; whereas in some of the other examples I wrote about — John Halperin's *Austen* and *Gissing*, James Pope Hennessy's *Trollope*, even Michael Millgate's far more successful *Hardy* — there was little display of the biographer's craft. One can report that in some instances biography has indeed improved; but even so we must be cautious, for, withal that improvement, there are still few instances of a fully-fashioned life that captures all the essential elements of biography. Too many of our writers are penning lives without being biographers; too few understand that to "catch" a life, it is not enough merely to lay the subject out on a dissecting table and then pound along chronologically.

With Peter Ackroyd's *Dickens* as a notable exception, biographers have not learned how to use the subject's own works as biographical data. We do not speak of the work as synonymous with the subject's life; but recommend that the biographer find in the novels, stories, or poems some psychological or even philosophical interworking between subject and his or her literary expression. In a recent biography of George Eliot, Ina Taylor proudly an-nounces in her section "What's New About George Eliot" the following: "a reappraisal of the second half of her life, unhindered by the plots of her novels, revealed a woman with a keen appetite for sex and money." The biographer's assumptions here are mind-boggling. "Unhindered" suggests the novels would interfere with our understanding Eliot, whereas without the novels, she would have been merely another interesting nineteenth-century woman who went professionally unfulfilled. The remark also suggests that

348

sex and money were somehow negative goals. An even more appalling suggestion is that sex and money were the sole engines which drove her, rather than extremely complicated motives.

The desire to sensationalize major figures — here Eliot, also Jeffrey Meyers's Conrad — seems a carryover from those mud-slinging biographies we associate with celebrities. But there is more, and that is the effort to carve out some new territory when the biographer is not prepared to do the real work or is unable to find anything new to say. Biography has changed rapidly in the last twenty or thirty years, and yet many of the examples we cite here — the two Dickens biographies are exceptions — proceed as though nothing has changed. Strict chronological sequencing, forgoing of psychological patterning in the subject, lack of prolepsis, inability to incorporate critical analyses of the subject's work into biographical data, the lack of any overriding thesis that explains the artistry or creativity of the subject, failure to aquire a critical vocabulary suitable for biography, contempt, indeed, for newer forms of criticism: all or some of these are apparent. Biography is no longer an easy enterprise.

In commenting on Jeffrey Meyers's *Joseph Conrad* (New York: Scribner's, 1991), I want to isolate one significant portion of the biography rather than discuss the entire study. One reason for avoiding the book as a whole is that with his major fiction coming in the twentieth century, Conrad falls beyond this review. But at the same time, because Meyers's use of certain materials has resonances in biography as a genre, it is suitable for inclusion here. I am referring to his conclusion that Conrad, then almost sixty, had a love affair — the sole one apparently outside his marriage — with Jane Anderson, an American journalist and, then, wife of the composer Deems Taylor. Meyers marshalls a fearsome array of circumstantial material that would support his claim, but then he takes the leap from circumstantial evidence and speculation into certainty, a declaration that such an affair actually occurred.

Apart from turning speculation into statement, the problem with this is that such material takes up a disproportionate amount of space in his biography — an entire chapter of 18 pages, then 14 pages of an Appendix, finally another four pages of Anderson bibliography, for a total of 36 pages, or a little less than one-tenth of the total length of the book. *Nostromo*, on the other hand, Conrad's masterpiece, gains eight consecutive pages, plus other random remarks, adding up at most to half of the Conrad-Taylor affair. Similar disproportionate page counts can be made of *Heart of Darkness, Lord Jim*, and other major works. Clearly, the Taylor matter figures large, perhaps because it becomes for Meyers his main effort to contribute to Conrad biography. I must add that in my own biography of Conrad, I spend two pages (perhaps 1200 words) on the affair, find it full of flirtation, even desire, but with no proof of a conclusion. I am not defending my own assessment, as I hope these remarks make clear, but trying to probe the limits of what is biographically possible.

But before arriving at Meyers's major "find," we should assess how he hoped to validate his biography. The problem of writing biography when there is little left to say is one which Meyers attempts to remedy with strange prefatorial remarks listing what is new. Meyers cites Conrad's suicide attempt, but rides on all previous explanations. He speaks of Conrad's "positive attitude toward the Jews," which only came late in his life, as everyone agrees, whereas earlier he had many of the attitudes derived from his background and class. Meyers writes of his close friendships with Perceval Gibbon and Sir Robert Jones — friendships cited in previous studies and of almost no significance in his life or art. His Polish background, another matter cited by Meyers as "new," has been scoured and re-scoured — nothing novel here. Clearly, the sole item that remains of interest is "his love affair," as Meyers describes it, "with the wild and beautiful American journalist Jane Anderson, who became a traitor in World War Two." The language here is not reassuring; "wild and beautiful," then traitor twenty years after Conrad's death — these sound like blurbs for celebrity biographies. No more reassuring are Meyers's opening lines of Chapter 16: "He fell in love with her, met her secretly and — seizing the last chance for sexual romance — wrote her passionate letters. She became his mistress in the summer of 1916 and was the only woman, apart from Jessie [his now fat and crippled wife], whom we know he slept with." Meyers goes on to say Jane Anderson inspired him in his war effort, stimulated his interest in films and in America, and underlay the character of Rita de Lastaola in *The Arrow of Gold*.

Meyers then attempts to find backing for his claim. He cites Jane as "probably" having been the lover of Northcliffe, the press lord. He mentions she "may have been" the lover of the "hot-blooded" Sir Leo Chiozza Money, then private secretary to Lloyd George. This is to establish that Jane was wild and uninhibited — but we note, by now, the "probably" and the "may have been." When Jane visited Conrad and Jessie, she rolled on the floor with their nine-year-old son John, and Conrad "perhaps" desired to join in the rolling. Conrad's letters to his friends and to his wife "suggest" he fell in love with Jane; and when he went to her flat for tea, they "possibly" consummated their affair. In the same passage, her relationship with Northcliffe has passed from "probably" to their being lovers.

The affair with Conrad reached a crisis on September 18, 1916, because Jane had "perhaps" boasted of Conrad's love letters (none of which has survived). Jessie claimed to have discovered a love letter (not extant) which "would have proved" all that Jane had said about the relationship; but Meyers has not seen the letter, and Jessie was evening scores when she wrote — a more unreliable witness hardly existed. Meyers uses material gathered by Ian Watt and John Halverson, but their claims are more modest, and they do not turn the affair into a harlequin type of romance. As Meyers puts it: "Conrad tried to live up to the gallant role Jane offered him, but knew he had no future with her." Halfway through Chapter 16, he treats the "perhaps" and "probably" and "maybe" as certainty; so that the affair "illuminates the most obscure aspect" of Conrad's character. "Jane was Conrad's last (and perhaps first) chance to sleep with a beautiful, well-born woman. He knew this and seized the opportunity." The rest of the chapter reverts to "may have," the qualification which subverts certainty. Meyers then moves to Borys, Conrad's older son, and suggests an affair there, as well as one with Retinger, which seems more firmly based on fact. Finally, he sees the affair as central to *The Arrow of Gold* — for which there is no evidence — while reaffirming all the relationships now as "liaisons."

Biographically, we observe a breakdown of language, which is a breakdown of the genre itself. The biographer is so intent on establishing the new — and validating his own study — he misuses language. He moves from uncertainty to certainty as if words had no meaning. This is not the way to do it, obviously, and Meyers has written well on other figures, Wyndham Lewis, for example, D. H. Lawrence, Ernest Hemingway, and Katherine Mansfield. Yet here we observe such an insistence on topping previous biographers of Conrad that he constructs traps for himself and falls in. The ambitious preface about what is new gives way to a sequence of uncertainties. The genre becomes an endangered species. We must ask why publishers continue to permit the proliferation of biographies which serve no function. We must assume that when a potential biographer makes a claim for his subject and his treatment of it, the publisher — especially a commercial publisher like Scribners in this instance — has no means of verification, no editing process, no resident expert, and no interest in weeding out what is meaningful from what are merely fanciful claims.

The three biographies of George Eliot under consideration are extremely brief; and this in itself creates a problem. One of the issues in writing biography, it seems obvious, is what kind to write, given the era, given previous work, given the need. After Gordon Haight's detailed, scholarly study of Eliot and Ruby Redinger's biographical-critical study, a brief biography can only justify itself in a few areas: inclusion of new material, presentation of new points of view, special insights into the subject missed by previous writers, or else, as in two of these instances, an effort to relate the subject to a new discipline, here feminist studies. Ina Taylor's book, *The Life of George Eliot: A Woman of Contradictions* (New York: Morrow, 1989), fits into none of these. There is, perhaps, a fifth area which Taylor does try to fulfill:

offering a readable, opinionated, not too detailed biography for those who find the Haight and the Redinger too heavy; a kind of lighter touch on a solemn author. Gillian Beer's *George Eliot* (Bloomington: Indiana UP, 1986) and Jennifer Uglow's *George Eliot* (New York: Pantheon, 1987), however, are informed more by critical analyses than by efforts to dig out new biographical facts, or to penetrate into Eliot's character more psychologically.

These books are determined, largely, by the need to expand our sense of Eliot as a female writer; to demonstrate the curve of her achievement as, somehow, overcoming the hesitation and traditionalism of many of her stated views about women and the so-called woman question. On the whole, they succeed in helping to "re-create" Eliot; that is, to move away from Haight's once influential point that Eliot was tethered to certain conventions she could not break from; and to reinterpret her — rightfully, I think — as a profound feminist in her fictional thinking, if not in her public statements or activities. As Uglow states it, her purpose is not to try to assimilate Eliot into feminist writing, or to seek any "l'écriture feminine." Rather, it is "simply to trace the double curve of her life and her fiction, seeing where the arcs cross and intersect" (9). The faults we can find are the brevity of the effort, the lack of sustained analysis of the work precisely to reveal this "double curve" of life and work, the paucity of deeper psychological analysis which would derive from Eliot's works.

Uglow is especially strong in her chapter "George Eliot and the Woman Question in the 1850s." Here she validates her study by demonstrating how the would-be novelist met a succession of women who were pioneers in feminist interests, Barbara Leigh Smith (later Bodichon), Bessie Parkes, Anna Jameson, Clementia Taylor, Hilary Bonham Carter, Florence Nightingale, Mrs. Samuel Smith. Comparably, Eliot's essays for John Chapman's *Westminster Review*, where she was more than sub-editor but less than editor, helped organize her thoughts on feminist issues, especially her reviews of Margaret Fuller and Mary Wollstonecraft. She revealed her disagreement with some of George Henry Lewes's remarks on "The Lady Novelists." Uglow runs through Lewes's comments before he met Eliot — he located female creative energy in biological difference, thought Brontë's *Shirley* would have been stronger if she had had children, asserted that men are better at structure, plot, and character, women at passion and sentiment — and we observe how the latter fought against some of these views in her fiction, but especially in her life.

Uglow concludes that Eliot was partially formed by the preoccupations of the fifties, in and around the *Westminster Review*:

The nature of womanhood; the fear of change; the exclusion of women from the realm of the intellect and from effective power; the alliance in oppression of women, workers and slaves which gives them a shared rhetoric of freedom and resistance; the conflict between the new drive for autonomy and the older ethic of self-sacrifice; the difficulty of achieving independence without losing the possibility of sexual passion and family life — all these provide structures for the inner drama of her fiction. (80)

Uglow is also compelling in her discussion of *Romola*, a problematic novel for readers because it often seems more cultural history than novel. She observes the terrible tensions existing in the novel which lead back to Eliot — daughter and father in particular — but also the sexual dilemmas. Eliot saw that sexual passion created entrapment for both parties when they were unequal, whether socially, intelletually, or otherwise. One argument she makes for gender equality is based on how it affects sexual energies, causing great harm when their focus is between unequals. This imbalance is further revealed when a given subject, here Romola, is torn between desire for sexual fulfillment and her need for self-denial: the classic triangle of father-daughter-male intruder. In such a scenario, Romola is locked out of fulfillment, and this becomes, for Eliot certainly, a key way in which women must suffer. Romola seeks surcease, then, not in sexual or passionate fulfillment, but in service; not through Savonarola, who calls for martyrdom, but in the sacredness of helping others more in need than she. None of this, Uglow observes, is carried out easily; at every stage, Eliot recognizes how women must pick up the pieces left behind by careless, deceptive, or obsessive men.

Author of an influential study, *Darwin's Plots: Evolutionary Narrative in Darwin, George Eliot and Nineteenth-Century Fiction* (1983), Gillian Beer for her part attempts to assimilate Eliot into feminist criticism, even while recognizing that the English author does not easily fit into any categories. While pursuing many of the leads suggested by Sandra Gilbert and Susan Gubar in *The Madwoman in the Attic* — although hardly agreeing with all of their conclusions — Beer rightfully sees Eliot's feminist ideas reflected in her fiction, while often denied in her life. This is not an ordinary biographical study, but a kind of mutant form in which a critical procedure overlays a biographical base. Eliot's life is led along by commentary rather than by the detail we associate with traditional biography. Beer strongly disputes the Gilbert and Gubar position that intellectual malnourishment meant for Eliot a compensatory emotional strength. On the contrary, Beer argues — correctly, I believe — that Eliot's view of educational opportunity for women was separate from her very controversial views on women's emotional lives: her belief that the emotions gave women a higher ground than men, especially in their ability to sustain pain and suffering.

One problem with Beer, as with many critics promoting a thesis, is that in their brilliant pursuit of consistency in Eliot, they fail to recognize, if not inconsistency, then doubt and uncertainty. On occasion they fall into the trap of believing that she was above it all, a kind of god-like or sybilline figure, rather than recognizing there were sides to her character and situation which remained unresolved. She was not the Delphic Oracle, but a deeply conflicted and on several occasions despondent woman whose inner and outer lives did not always mesh. Her very artistry lay in the fact that her presentation of female characters was part of an inner battle: to be honest to her artistic creation and yet not to deceive herself personally. Beer certainly recognizes this. "Alongside George Eliot's respect for organicism, and her passionate need for interdependence, went an indefatigable awareness of misunderstanding and, equally, of the impossibility of writing within a single discourse" (43).

Most of Beer's biographical-critical study (heavier on the latter) is concerned with revealing Eliot's qualities as a female writer: what her femaleness was, how it affected what she wrote, how it distinguished her from her male contemporaries, how it influenced her observations, her type of realism, her ability to undercut that very realism. She is especially convincing in discussing someone like Mrs.Transome in *Felix Holt*, unfortunately one of Eliot's more important neglected novels. As Beer points out, Mrs. Transome reflects nearly every role a woman in the nineteenth century could play; and from Beer's discussion, one is almost convinced that the novel — as Eliot's notebook at Yale suggests — was first and foremost to be the Transome story, not that of Felix. With her marriage to a man now senile, her having had a vile, psychologically disoriented son by her husband, then her giving birth out of wedlock, her ability to run the estate and its properties (although she is being defrauded by the man with whom she had her youthful affair) — with all of these elements ongoing, she has assimilated into herself the total Victorian range of female activity and possibility. As a wife, she is embittered; as a mother — with one son dead after an evil life, and another son returning who dismisses her as a meddlesome female — she has failed; as a woman fully capable of handling affairs, but shunted aside, she is being positioned for marginality and eventual death. Her life has come to nothing, although at nearly every stage she has had expectations. Beer's strength is in emphasizing these points.

The purpose of Ina Taylor's biography of Eliot, we must assume, was to liven things up. Her idea was to present a woman unencumbered by the shadow of John Cross, Eliot's husband and "biographer," and Haight, both of whom she accuses of whitewashing a more interesting life than the one they present. Inadvertently, perhaps, she creates several biographical problems. In her desire to be different, Taylor tries to sensationalize a life by misportraying its highs. "There is the woman," she writes, "who found herself the object of lesbian affections, yet loved men and experienced several love affairs before she finally married; the woman whose 'immoral' behaviour meant she was cast out of society, yet was fêted by intellectuals, aristocrats and even royalty; the woman who flouted the rules, yet was desperately concerned to be respectable; the woman who claimed her writing as an art form, yet approached it from a mercenary angle'' (xv). These introductory remarks seem more suitable for a *Vanity Fair* magazine article about some third-rank hack, not George Eliot.

Nearly every claim is either false or the result of overreach. There is the intimation of lesbianism, then withdrawn, when there is no evidence of any; the ''several love affairs'' cannot be proved, however much Eliot hung on to Charles Bray, Dr. Brabant, and John Chapman at one time or another. Her ''immoral'' behavior did not mean she was ''cast out'' of society — not only intellectuals continued to see her, but so did feminists, female friends, and others on the fringes of the artistic world; she was shunned by some, but not ''cast out,'' which implies pariah status. It is true she wished to be considered respectable, but she did not ''flout the rules,'' except in the eyes of those who had narrowed the rules to exclude someone extraordinary like Eliot. She ran away with Lewes once his marriage was sundered; she was not a husband-stealer except in the judgment of those for whom marriage was perpetual bondage. She was hardly mercenary, and she did not approach writing purely from a monetary angle. With *Romola*, for example, she refused to make chapter divisions that would have brought her an additional £3000. But Taylor is not through. She says that Eliot proposed to John Cross, when the question is unclear; that it never crossed Eliot's mind that Cara Bray might resent her husband's attention to this much brighter, more accomplished woman; that Robert W. Mackay, a friend of Eliot's and a one-time possible suitor, was the model for Edward Casaubon in *Middlemarch*; that Eliot recognized she had to her ''horror'' struck a ''blow to feminism'' by running off with Lewes; that Lewes at first expected the ''elopement'' to Europe in 1854 to be little more than a quick affair and then Eliot would ''become someone else's mistress''; that Eliot played the ''part of the fragile genius'' in permitting Lewes to protect her against adverse criticism; that Eliot yearned for the ''comfortable rituals'' of her youth and in later life would have returned to the Church if Lewes had not been so negative about religion. None of these claims can be supported.

Biography has no place for assertions which sensationalize the subject, no less a person of such supernal dignity as Eliot. Taylor's book, and Meyers's in part, suggest a critical point in contemporary biography: that under the influence of more popular biography, especially of lesser subjects, there is a certain dressing up to make a solemn figure seem more sensational. The more popular and commercial biographical enterprises have slanted into the more serious kind; and figures who should be treated with great deliberation are being infiltrated by biographers who, while trying to justify still another study, become merely unreliable witnesses themselves.

To write a biography of Jane Austen is a daunting task. The life was so lacking in overt activities, and yet the fiction is so tuned to the fine points of human behavior, that the biographer must somehow account for what he or she must assume Austen saw. A good deal of Austen biography must take place in the seams of her life, where her day-to-day perceptions and observations became the stuff of her fiction; or, conversely, whereby her fiction took over what she had trained herself to see. Recent Austen biography until Park Honan's *Jane Austen: Her Life* (New York: Ballantine, 1987) has revealed severe deficiencies, whether through lack of critical judgment, failure to explore the larger literary scene around Austen, inaccuracies because of insufficient scholarship, or else through claims made which are not supported by analysis of her work. The biography by Honan shows meticulous research and the constructive use of new materials focussed on family archives. This study is the first to satisfy all requirements of scholarship, critical acumen, taste, and discretion. Honan is particularly good at showing how Austen's life, thin stuff that it externally seems to be, served as the engine of her novels; how, in fact, she conjured up fictions from the finest threads of experience, as Henry James was later to advise the beginning writer to do.

Yet Honan is curiously deficient in one salient area. While he makes excellent use of Austen's life and observations as they became transformed into her fiction, he is curiously remiss in failing to utilize the fiction as a way of reflecting certain ideas and patterns in Austen. His analysis goes one way, from life to fiction, but fails to make the necessary linkage in the other direction. Lacking any real psychological analysis, he does not perceive in Austen's fiction several areas that require interpretation as part of her biography. He makes little, for example, of the profusion of inadequate parents in her novels, parents who are either foolish or so enraptured with their own needs they fail to provide guidance or understanding for their children. He does not get deeply into novelistic meanings of such a family as the Bertrams in *Mansfield Park*: the father autocratic or away (on the slave trade, among other things), the mother otiose to the point of anomie, the children morally directionless except in what they can glean from their own needs. Fanny Price's family in Portsmouth is dysfunctional; in *Pride and Prejudice*, the father is a cynic and blind to the divisions he has helped create in his children, the mother a fool in most matters. In *Emma*, the titular character lacks direction, until a potential suitor, Mr. Knightley — more a father-figure than Emma's own father — can help bring her back to discretion. The "parentless child" is only one such strategy in Austen which calls out for biographical meaning, since on the surface Honan can find little in her own relationships to the Reverend Austen and her mother for this kind of caustic, cynical view. Austen is almost Dickensian in her sense of parental remissness.

We catch some of Honan's wariness with critical procedures, whether psychological analysis, or the new forms which he himself cites somewhat suspiciously. He announces that *Pride and Prejudice* has had an abiding value for us, so that now "it appeals to critics in an era of feminism and semiotic theories, post-structuralism and Derrida's deconstruction" (320). Late in the biography, Honan does cite feminism as a valid forum for Austen, where he states, rightly it seems to me, that "Austen was a woman's advocate — and yet unlike others she had presented the real thing, real men as viewed by believable women and views of real female consciousness" (403). But even here he is chary, seemingly suspicious of any extended critical theorizing.

Our focus here is not on criticism, but on biography; but both seem wedded. Reader-response, semiotics, deconstruction: these might help us with Austen biography, although we must be careful they do not overwhelm it. Honan is so strong on plain biographical detail, however, that his book would appear to be in little danger of being overtaken by more penetrating analysis which could, in turn, lead to deeper levels of biographical interpretation.

In another area, Honan displays some mannerisms which one can either accept or see as intrusive, even subversive. Like Ackroyd in his *Dickens*, Honan inserts remarks into the biography which are purely subjective. What function they serve is unclear. One example: "Her [Austen's] conscience was *not* of the kind that adjusts quickly to error. Blank days advanced. Grieved, vexed, we [not the reader, but Austen] finally tire of our own wretchedness" (198). Examples abound: "Few of our unhappy trials last as long as we imagine they may" (227) or "She [Austen in 1806] might have been a person landing on her feet after jumping from a gaoler's wall, or a girl leaving a horrid seminary for the very last time" (228). All seem to emanate from within Austen, but in reality derive from the biographer. There can be no possible source, only a kind of Trollopian-like interruption to remind the reader of man's common fate.

The reader of this biography, then, must make several decisions. In terms of Austen studies, Honan's book is clearly superior to any other biography of the writer, surely superior to Halperin's 1984 *Life of Jane Austen*, which Honan himself cites as showing "little fresh research" and as being "very inaccurate." Other previous biographies fare better, including Marghanita Laski's in 1969 and Jane Aiken Hodges's in 1972. But none has the reach of Honan's in his ability to follow up material, to flesh out the Austen family, and to locate the author herself in the middle of the world she re-created fictionally. What remains after this is less effective: the above-mentioned lack of a critical apparatus, chiefly psychological, which would have permitted a greater utilization of Austen's own fiction for biographical purposes; and the question of certain mannerisms which put words into Austen's mouth. Honan's is old-fashioned biography in several respects; he does not lead biographical studies into any new areas. But he does reveal how a thorough, meticulous researcher can create a sense of Austen in her time and place.

It may be in the nature of Anthony Trollope biography that deep probing is impossible. In most respects, N. John Hall's *Trollope: A Biography* (New York: Oxford, 1991) is ideal. He is well acquainted with all the material so that it is well digested; he has worked out all the necessary chronologies; he has done considerable research into Trollope's extra-literary activities, particularly his establishment of the Irish Post Office system; he introduces us well to his subject's contemporaries; and he catches much of the era's important history. But a persistent problem exists; and that is that Hall uses the novels as plot outlines, not as a massive design by which one could read Trollope. As a consequence, the conception of the biography is mechanical: some life, then a work (once Trollope began to write with the three-decker *The Macdermots of Ballycloran* in 1847), then another segment of the life, then another work, and so on to the end.

This is the kind of study most reviewers love to read; they know at every point where they are, they do not have to struggle with loops or involuted narrative, they can settle back and feel they have a hold on their subject, and they can, as they wish, skip around, since there will be no surprises. Hall supplies precisely what they want, and he even smooths over little difficulties when they might arise and create a larger ripple. This Trollope fits together. But there could be problems. For example, the novelist's long association with Kate Reid, an American woman who knew most of the American and English writers contemporaneous with Trollope, is handled neatly, when the relationship for the latter might have been emotionally messy. She was a spellbinder, apparently, and Trollope — he was 45, she 22 — was no exception to those who felt her charm. He kept in touch with her for almost the remainder of his life, and she seemed to invade his imagination in several ways, but mainly as the romance he never experienced. Hall writes of Trollope as "happily married" and "therefore unthreatening" to Reid; but he fails to examine how threatening Reid might have been to him. Trollope may never have even vaguely considered breaking up his marriage, but his use of Kate Reid in his formulation of female characters, of all types, is of considerable interest.

The lack of analysis of this extended episode is symptomatic of Hall's lack of interest in pursuing elements back and forth between Trollope's emotional life and his novels. Hovering over all is the writer's own autobiography; but there is no reason to accept that document as a reliable witness. Hall appears tied to his documents, and while that is in one respect obviously a good thing, it also hampers him. There are linkages here, but no sense that documents are subversive, no awareness that facts depend on perception; and that a psychological probe, while somewhat speculative, is no less compelling than a hewing to documentation, and often, with a literary subject, far more rewarding. If Meyers with Conrad and Taylor with Eliot went too far from evidence, Hall sticks too close.

He falls into the pattern of Trollope's other biographers — although his is by far the superior of them all to date (Victoria Glendinning's is yet to come) — and that is to take the novelist at his word. The result is that he was indeed, as he claimed, a writing machine. But Trollope was a tempestuous man, one filled with wounds — Hall is good at showing how the writer often blustered to compensate for such hurts. He was also a man of terrible contradictions in his energies, establishing a postal system while authoring books which made him rich and famous, riding to the hounds at every opportunity, full of masculine ardor; and yet, withal, a man capable of considerable satire, mockery, even burlesque in his fiction. These are not, perhaps, contradictions so much as they are forces which must be addressed.

Other areas call out for further analysis, mainly the large question of how serial publication affected the kind of novel Trollope wrote, how it shaped his imagination, how it perhaps hobbled or abetted him. Hall mentions that after *Framley Parsonage*, Trollope published another thirty-nine novels, of which only four were released originally in book form; and of these four, two had been intended for serial publication, and one other was also so intended had Trollope lived. We can say that of the thirty-nine, thirty-eight were planned for serialization (*Miss Mackenzie*, 1865, was the exception). Yet Hall's explanation of what this meant to Trollope fills only one paragraph (205); failing to take us into the novels themselves, he relies on Trollope's own comments, which were self-serving and mechanical.

This does not suggest that the "key" to the novelist lies in the detailing of how serial publication interworked with his imagination; but it does indicate that areas which would have linked the novel-maker with the person could have been enhanced. Similarly, Hall is quite candid in taking up Trollope's anti-Semitism, but he hardly carries it sufficiently into the imaginative process itself, into certain contradictions in the writer, to areas he could not resolve, to the question whether his prejudices were merely those of his contemporaries or peculiar to himself. His anti-Semitism is not in itself overly important, since it was a given of Victorian England and not virulent. But it, like so many other elements, could have provided a way into Trollope's conceptualization of his fiction, and in some manner into himself.

Another area, not entirely unrelated to the above, was Trollope's recognition he was overcrowding the market, so that he often published anonymously. This, too, has large implications which Hall does not adequately pursue. As a consequence of the above "lacks," Trollope does not quite emerge. In several earlier biographies of major Victorian figures, such as Haight's magisterial work on Eliot, this quality of emergence is also missing; although Haight knows everything about her, there is still little sense of Eliot herself. Edgar Johnson's *Dickens* is the opposite; he catches Dickens (in his two-volume, not one-volume abbreviated, study) but loses the battle when it comes to linking Dickens's dark sides to his work.

Trollope was not Dickens, nor was he Eliot or even Thackeray; and very possibly Hall's reticence about the inner person is connected to his realization that his subject cannot be measured against the highest levels of literary achievement. But even with a writer such as Trollope, we expect the subject to stride forth, and yet Trollope in Hall's meticulous and scrupulous treatment remains an enigma. New strategies are called for, those that break with pure chronology and that probe the fiction more tellingly; but when that is said, it is hard to see how Glendinning or anyone else can improve on what Hall, flaws and all, has finally given us. We only wish it were more.

One of the several virtues of Peter Ackroyd's *Dickens* (London: Sinclair-Stevenson, 1990; New York: HarperCollins, 1991) is his concern with biography itself. Instead of merely plowing ahead, as many of our other biographers have done, he periodically stops to assess what he is doing, why he is doing it, even whether it is worth doing. These are inset segments, or brief chapters, which interrupt the flow of the biography proper; but also within the main text itself, Ackroyd makes us fully aware of what an artifact biography is, how it deceives by providing false continuity, how it gives chronology to a life which is in fact all bits and pieces.

A certain awe persists in his very approach to Dickens: his wonder that someone like himself would be sufficiently audacious to attempt a biography of such a secretive, complex, many-layered individual. He recognizes that Dickens is all labyrinths, dead ends, circuits which seem to lead nowhere and everywhere; and yet he, Peter Ackroyd, is going to penetrate into the inner sanctum, into the sacred heart of it all. He writes the biography as though he were undertaking a tremendous quest, almost something extraterrestrial, a Parsifal or Jason ready to encounter the unexpected. We also sense that writing this biography will not only make a mark on Dickens scholarship, but in the best respect alter Ackroyd's way of perceiving fictional as well as factual materials. He will come away changed, so intense is the experience, so overwhelming is the pressure of Dickens on his imagination.

In the interpolated segment VI, within 200 pages of the end of the biography, Ackroyd asks whether there are "particular virtues to this biography"; whether his book is "too academic"; whether his method of "trying to relate specific passages of his [Dickens's] fiction to events of his own life" is worth doing, especially since "sometimes this really doesn't work." He worries about other aspects of the book, especially the opening chapters about family ties and early childhood, which "are the two most boring elements in anyone's life." He asks if he admires other biographies of Dickens, and says he does not care for John Forster's and finds Edgar Johnson's "awfully wrong-headed." He admits *he* may seem wrong-headed in future decades and has reconciled himself to the fact that "biography is a prisoner of its time." He worries that he has made too much of the fact "that Dickens *saw* reality as a reflection of his own fiction." Did he overdo it that "his novels dominated his understanding of people and even of himself"? He indicates why he wrote the book — he was attracted to the "idea" of Dickens; and he cites how he organized his material. He asks if he was fond of the writer by the end of his labors and admits he has no firm answer; in fact, all he wanted to do was to understand Dickens, not to like or dislike him. He wonders if biographies are in some sense like novels and concludes that they are "in the need to make the narrative coherent. To impose a pattern upon the world."

This is the most significant of the interpolations or interludes, and it establishes that Ackroyd's other career as a novelist has infiltrated into his sense of biography. He is eager, as novelist, to establish rapport with his readers; and as a fictionalist, he is aware of how much all gathered material is an artifact. His interludes argue for the artificiality of even the most carefully researched and organized biography; suggesting that, in the long run, it is a kind of fiction under the guise of something else — history, psychology, sociology, whatever.

Apart from its self-reflexiveness and monumental research, Ackroyd's biography, as he well knows, depends critically on one main line of interpretation. It is his view that Dickens, as he developed as a novelist, speaker, and public figure, began to blur the edges between who or what he was and what he was writing. In this view, Dickens was carried to the edge of his life, where it encountered his fictional self, and he was incapable of disentangling the two. From this flowed several possibilities: Dickens gained an unshakable belief in his own rightness in all things, since his fiction had proven so successful; the view also bolstered him in taking public positions, often conservative, even when these seemed to clash with his fictional positions; it gave him a kind of hero's posture, since his life flowed into his work, and then his work flowed back into his life — his was a seamless existence where no flaws surfaced. In purely literary terms, this seamlessness afforded Dickens a kind of organic presence in the mid-nineteenth century; in the readers' minds, the man and the work became identified as a living unit. From this, Dickens's life was perceived as mythical, both in its own right and in his interpretation of himself; his secrets became the legendary fare of the age, as it became impossible to dissociate his personal posture from what the age itself offered.

This interpretation recurs in Ackroyd's biography, almost ad nauseam, as he is well aware. It is the hinge on which everything in this immensely long book depends. His Dickens becomes a oneness with the age; and while the life unfolds in more or less chronological fashion, Ackroyd is able to loop around by way of this and other interpretive matter. That looping is dependent on the biographer's adept use of the subject's fiction as a lodestar in understanding Dickens. Without making the life and work congruent or synonymous in any vulgar way, Ackroyd reveals how Dickens played with his deepest secrets, his labyrinthine experiences, his greatest forms of shame and anger in almost infinite ways in his fiction. And by understanding the constructs of these fictions, we as readers can see how Dickens found the fictional means to tell his story; but more than that, in biographical terms, we can perceive how certain things obsessed him throughout his life by way of their recurrence in his fiction. Ackroyd is masterly in handling this circuitry; so that his Dickens achieves a biographical stature we associate with Ellmann's *Joyce* or Painter's *Proust*, in their ability to work back and forth between life and fictions.

Ackroyd's novelistic sense also gives him a way of measuring Dickens's language, his narrative skills, his use of detail; he shows how Dickens's point of view can be exhibited in a seeming trifle, how an obsessive personal factor can be interwoven into story line or plot. "Many of Dickens's characters," he writes, "have in the past been described as copies of real originals, with Harold Skimpole as Leigh Hunt, Lawrence Boythorn as Walter Savage Landor, and so forth. There is truth to this, but it is only a partial one. Dickens might begin with the appearance or behaviour of a certain individual but, as he writes, the character takes on the novelist's own feeling and expression far more than it copies the eccentricities of any presumed original. The novelist, not the external model, infuses himself into the creation" (401). From this premise follow compelling psychological insights. Ackroyd stresses how private a man Dickens was despite his need for public acclaim: "The isolated child was also the isolated man and he needed that isolation, however temporary it was; he hugged it to him as if in its enclosure he might remain true to himself. But here he had obtained no rest and no privacy; 'everything public, and nothing private,' he exclaimed" (354).

As a psychologically-oriented biographer, Ackroyd uses prolepsis — that anticipation of future events — with great skill. Well ahead of time, he can characterize 1856 as the year before something "irrevocable" would occur in Dickens's life, his meeting with Ellen Ternan: a year of restlessness, which suggests that despite his enormous success Dickens experienced an emptiness and a dissatisfaction that went beyond his disintegrating marriage.

The restlessness was the bane of his existence, but also the engine that drove him to frantic achievement. Through anticipation, patterning, even considerable repetition, Ackroyd captures these various cycles of destruction as they took over Dickens's later years, and made him seem like an actor in his own life at the time that he, the fictionalist, played the actor in so many amateur productions.

Yet even as Ackroyd focusses on the many selves Dickens experienced and presented, he does not scant on historical and cultural backgrounds. He is always there with descriptions of London, of the larger English scene, of social developments which helped shape Dickens's vision as much as had his earlier childhood experiences. This is a complete biography and, in its way, a handbook on how biography at the end of the twentieth century can be done.

Fred Kaplan's *Dickens* (New York: Morrow, 1988) is an effective biographical study of Dickens which displays no doubts about what biography should be. Unlike Ackroyd, Kaplan works in the main chronologically, although he does begin his book with a dramatic moment in Dickens's life, when the writer burned nearly all of his correspondence. In 1860, at a time of considerable personal despondency, Dickens made a bonfire of letters from Carlyle, Tennyson, Wilkie Collins, Browning, Thackeray, from his immediate family, even from Ellen Ternan. This is a brilliant touch for a biographer, although Kaplan chooses not to pursue here the self-destructiveness, the hopelessness, the gesture of suicide in this act. Instead, he views Dickens's burning of letters as consistent with his hatred of private matters becoming public; or, conversely, of the private, such as letters and their like, taking over from his books or his other public utterances.

Yet the destruction of these letters also involved, we can assume, the effacement of others, the banishment of their presence from his life; and, as such, their ashes indicate that only Dickens remains. The act is one of acute psychological and emotional balance: between a terrible depression that seeks to wipe out the past and an act of ego which diminishes all of one's famous contemporaries so that only the receiver of the letters survives. It is, in another respect, an act of murder: burning the letters means through some magical act doing away with the writers of them. Yet even while it assures Dickens's immortality by removing the competition, we must not dismiss the self-destructiveness implied in the burning.

After this start, Kaplan moves basically along into the details of Dickens's life, using a chronological-historical approach with some literary interludes. He emphasizes, as does Ackroyd, the "bad mother" against whom Dickens reacted through most of his adult life, in his personal decisions as well as in his fictive representations of maternal or near-maternal figures. Kaplan is particularly strong in his recognition that Dickens had to create a

Dickens myth: in *Pickwick*, his first novel, he "created the purest myth, touched by a manageable darkness, of his own and his culture's recovery from economic and emotional deprivation. In the *Pickwick* world, the recovery occupies the present of an optimistic consciousness without ever denying the past or promising that the future will be undeviatingly bright and inclusive. It is a novel of personal myth, not history, of the brightness of his own first triumphant self-assertion" (82).

One wishes for some discussion of how this making of a myth fits with the nine tales interpolated into the novel — those tales which caught the eye of Edgar Allan Poe, among others. The most salient is the one called "A Madman's Manuscript," and it tells of how a lunatic is able to negotiate in respectable society because of his money, a tale of bizarre horror, murderous plans, and self-destruction. This is clearly the other side of Pickwick and the Pickwickians, and it provides Dickens with that psychological duality which both supports his myth and helps to subvert it. Several of the tales are of the Abraham and Isaac variety, whereby the child becomes a sacrifice to the father or mother, a theme that possessed Dickens for his entire life after the blacking factory episode at twelve.

Such lines of interest would turn Kaplan's into more of a psychological — even pathological — study than he intends; his pursuit is of a different kind, without his forgoing certain areas of psychological analysis. In a sense, his Dickens is a more manageable, empirical figure — one whose life can be caught in a still-lengthy 550 pages, but does not require the enormity of Ackroyd's 750,000 words, or Edgar Johnson's two fat volumes, not to speak of Forster's own several volumes. This is hardly a pared-down Dickens, but it drops away a lot of the excess baggage. It is clean and efficient, whereas Ackroyd's is intentionally messy and convoluted. Kaplan, for example, needs only 49 pages to take Dickens to eighteen; after 100 more closely-printed pages, Ackroyd has him at twelve.

While the latter is obsessed with the idea of how someone unfathomable like Dickens can be managed between pages, Kaplan has no doubts he can identify what is significant in the writer's life and bring it forth in words; and in this he succeeds. In Ackroyd, the reader lives a somewhat precarious life, since there is always the possibility the biographer will break down at some point, so preoccupied is he with the nature of his undertaking; whereas with Kaplan, one is comfortable. The two biographies could not be more different, even though they clearly overlap. Common to both is how tortured Dickens was in his private life, even while he carried on such a varied public life; how words were his means of survival even when his emotional stability was precarious. As the self-conscious, reflexive observer trying to enter so fully into Dickens's life that he must periodically examine his own motives, Ackroyd plumbs and probes to get to the bottom of an enigma. His book is also, as mentioned, a meditation on the biographical process itself, involving all the players — biographer, subject, lesser characters — in a terrible emotional and psychological drama. Kaplan stands off, although he is particularly concerned with the dissolution of Dickens's marriage and what it meant to the novelist, the egomaniacal way in which he treated poor Catherine, mother of his ten children, how he demanded their loyalty and how he manipulated them to the degree that they had little choice but to disappoint him as his father had earlier. Behind the façade, but barely, was a dysfunctional family of several generations, and Kaplan hammers away at this point, revealing a disintegrating Dickens in his private life even as fame rewarded the public. What he suffered after 1860, when he was still only 48, was his inability to generate long novels, with only *Our Mutual Friend* completed in the final ten years of his life. It was not so much that he was exhausted as that he had exhausted the personal capital which had been his material; he was mined or quarried out. Even Dickens ran down, a complex machine subject to entropy.

In purely biographical terms, it does seem that the discipline can energize itself when two such different Dickenses emerge. We wonder: does this end Dickens biography for a long time? Obviously, there will be future Dickens biographical studies, especially when all the letters (over 20,000) are assembled and edited; but for the time being Kaplan's on one hand, Ackroyd's on the other will stand for the next decade or more.

New York University

THE STUDY OF VICTORIAN
MASCULINITIES

By Herbert Sussman

SEVERAL YEARS AGO, I went to Wordsworth, a state of the art academic bookstore in Harvard Square, to buy Barbara Ehrenreich's *The Hearts of Men* (New York: Anchor, 1983), an account of the relocation of manliness from suburban split-level to Playboy pad in 1950s America. Unsure of where such a book would be shelved, I asked the clerk, whose computer told us that it was to be found in Women's Studies. When I suggested that it might be less than appropriate to set a book about men in a section devoted to women, I was told, "That's the way we do it."

That might have been the way Wordsworth did it only a few years ago, but when I went back this past summer to buy David Leverenz's *Manhood and the American Renaissance* (Ithaca: Cornell UP, 1989), a superb study of the conflicted self-fashionings of manhood in such nineteenth-century American figures as Emerson, Thoreau, Douglass, and Hawthorne, I found that Wordsworth had added between Women's Studies and Gay and Lesbian Studies three shelves devoted to what was now called "Men's Issues," a section containing not only Robert Bly's *Iron John* (New York: Vintage, 1990), but Leverenz's study as well as Ehrenreich's *The Hearts of Men*.

This anecdote of re-shelving illustrates, in brief, the history, the current condition, and the problematics of a field of study that I will, provisionally, call the study of masculinities. Shelving scholarly works about men to follow Women's Studies suggests the theoretical source of such studies of masculinity in the feminist scholarship of our time, particularly in the awareness of gender as a social construction, multiform and historically specific. That studies of masculinity now have a shelf of their own suggests that the examination of the social construction of the masculine now constitutes a demarcated field of study, while the position between Women's Studies and Gay and Lesbian Studies indicates the inextricable connection of such inquiry with the study of other gender constructions. And that these studies of masculinity in history take up only three shelves, as opposed to many times that number for books about women and about gay and lesbian life, indicates the relatively small scale of this project at the moment. Finally, that in these few shelves devoted to Men's Issues the highly theorized psychoanalytic writing of Leverenz and the politically astute high popularization of Ehrenreich rub book jackets with the cult of Bly indicates the connection of intellectualized and historicized study of the formations of masculinity to the "Issues" or tensions in the lives of Wordsworth's customers.

For this field of study, I would suggest, rather than Men's Issues, the term "study of masculinities," a name that foregrounds the major concerns of this new project. If all gender constructions are self-conscious, some are more self-conscious than others; using "masculinities," as opposed to Men's Issues or even Men's Studies, emphasizes not the biological but the social construction of what we consider the masculine. Furthermore, employing the plural, "masculinities" stresses the multiple possibilities of such social formations, the variability of the gendering of the biological male, and the range of such constructions over time and at any specific historical moment. To my mind, this emphasis on the multiplicity, the plurality of male gender formations is crucial not only to counter the still pervasive essentialist view of maleness, but also to deconstruct the monolithic view of masculinity, the unitary vision of the "masculine" that, with seeming disregard of the success of feminism in exploding such essentialist and monolithic thinking about women, still pervades and even structures discussion of men, particularly in the nineteenth century. Only a sense of the plurality of formations of the masculine among the Victorians can productively open the discussion of masculinity in the nineteenth century to the issue of competition among multiple formations of masculinity during the period, to the instability in the configuration of male identity shaped from among these competing formations by specific individuals and specific groups of men, and to the ways in which such tensions are inscribed in the literature and the art of the period.

Yet the study of masculinities as a scholarly project faces several crucial issues that must be discussed at the outset. One of the chief difficulties lies, quite simply, in the issue of power. If Women's Studies as well as Gay and Lesbian Studies derives its energy and purpose from engaging a history of oppression and liberating the self from that oppression, the study of masculinities explores the history of the oppressors, of the hegemonic discourse, of the patriarchy. This justifiable anxiety about the study of the "masculine" must be acknowledged, and may be engaged in several ways. For one, the emphasis on the constructed rather than the innate, and on the multiple rather than the unitary view of the "masculine," calls attention to the historical contingency of such masculine formations and of male power itself, thus questioning male dominance and supporting the possibility of change within qualities marked as masculine. But for the writer on masculinities, particularly on Victorian

masculinities, the problem of power and patriarchy calls for a double awareness, registered in the best works on the subject, such as Adrienne Munich's
*Andromeda's Chains: Gender and Interpretation in Victorian Art and Litera-
ture* (New York: Columbia UP, 1989) and Elaine Showalter's *Sexual Anarchy: Gender and Culture at the Fin de Siècle* (New York: Viking, 1990) —
a sensitivity both to the ways in which these masculine social formations
create conflict, anxiety, tension in men while acknowledging that, in spite of
the stress, men accept these formations as a form of self-policing or discipline
that is crucial to patriarchal domination. As Munich notes at the beginning
of her study, "Men used the Andromeda myth not only to celebrate the
rewards of a patriarchal system, but also to record their discomforts with it"
(2).

A second major problematic for the study of masculinities in the Victorian period lies in the relation of this enterprise to the field of gender study
currently so important to Victorian studies — Gay Studies. Here, as with
the issue of power, a doubleness of vision is needed, a sensitive negotiation
that acknowledges the interconnection of these approaches to nineteenth-
century male identity, while recognizing differences in emphasis. I would
suggest that a study of masculinities would acknowledge male-male desire as
crucial to the construction of and the problematics of male identity in the
nineteenth century, but would not privilege such desire as the primary consti-
tutive force in the formation of and conflicts within Victorian masculinities.
Rather, the study of the social construction of Victorian manliness would
consider the homoerotic as one among the many psychological and social
forces — including industrialization, class conflict, the development of
bourgeois hegemony, the feminization of culture — that troubled Victorian
manhood. As I have argued in another context ("'Robert Browning's 'Fra
Lippo Lippi' and the Problematic of a Male Poetic," *VS* 35: 185–200), in
the example of Browning the chief problematic in his sense of himself as poet
lay not in negotiating the troubled boundary between the homosocial and the
homosexual, although the term homosocial illuminates his ideal of a poetic
shared only by other men — figured in "Fra Lippo Lippi" by the conversation with the night watch — but in reconciling the function of the male poet
with the hegemonic ideal of entrepreneurial manhood.

A study of Victorian masculinities that acknowledges but decenters male-
male desire in the formation of male identity need not absorb, co-opt, nor
diffuse the project of Gay Studies. The enormous importance of Gay Studies
for Victorianists lies in its emphasis on such crucial matters as the development of a gay or homosexual discourse in the period, exemplified in the path-
breaking work of Richard Dellamora, *Masculine Desire: The Sexual Politics
of Victorian Aestheticism* (Chapel Hill: U of North Carolina P, 1990); in its
illuminating the conflict between male-male desire and its social interdiction

as an important reason for the instability of male identity in Victorian male writers, as described by Eve Kosofsky Sedgwick in *Between Men: English Literature and Male Homosocial Desire* (New York: Columbia UP, 1985), one of the most important and influential contributions to the study of Victorian masculinities.

Indeed, Sedgwick's model describing male-male relationships along the spectrum of the homosocial/homophobic/homosexual, as opposed to a simple binary of straight/gay, suggests that exciting work is to be done at the boundaries between the emerging gay discourse and the hegemonic forms of masculinity. If students of masculinities must be attentive to the conflicts between male-male desire and the normative formation of Victorian masculinity, gay studies must be as attentive to the complex appropriation, transformation and even acceptance of such normative forms of heterosexual masculinity within the development of gay discourse. As recent critics have demonstrated, an awareness of the reciprocity of varied forms of manliness has energized work on specific figures, especially Pater. The awareness of the complexity of this interchange is exemplified in Dellamora's work, as in his account of "male love" as "androgynous in character" (153) in *The Renaissance*, and by the recent work of James Adams on the re-creation of normative forms of Victorian masculinity in Pater. In "Gentleman, Dandy, Priest: Manliness and Social Authority in Pater's Aestheticism (*ELH*, 59: 441–466) Adams, sensitive to "the volatile and perpetually contested character of [Victorian] 'manliness' " (442), persuasively demonstrates the ways that in *Marius the Epicurean* Pater attempts to "reinscribe norms of masculinity within the ethos of aestheticism" (442).

These studies, like any examination of the construction of Victorian masculinities, are, of course, grounded in the work of Michel Foucault, most specifically his *The History of Sexuality. Volume I: An Introduction* (New York: Pantheon, 1978), devoted to the Victorians and most compellingly to the overthrow of what he terms the "Repressive Hypothesis." The second volume, *The Use of Pleasure* (New York: Pantheon, 1985), in deploying the model of the "aesthetics of existence and . . . technologies of the self" (11) provides a crucial theoretical paradigm for examining the complex alignments of energy and control within Victorian masculinities as "a history of ethical problematizations based on practices of the self" (2: 13). Indeed, seeing the history of Victorian masculinity along the lines of a Foucauldian history of sexuality is particularly relevant since the Victorians themselves wrote the history of art as the history of male sexuality.

Another theoretical model that students of Victorian masculinities might well draw upon is Klaus Theweleit's *Male Fantasies: Volume 1. Women, Floods, Bodies, History* and *Male Fantasies: Volume 2. Male Bodies: Psychoanalyzing the White Terror* (Minneapolis: U of Minnesota P, 1987, 1989).

In these fascinating volumes, Theweleit uses published materials such as novels and letters to present the configuration of the psychic life of men in the fascist para-military Freikorps in Germany between the wars. In rather horrific detail, he shows in these "soldier males" the interconnected fantasies of bodily dissolution, the threats of women to bodily integrity, the pleasure of violence as "flood," and so on. What is theoretically interesting is that he does not posit a hidden explanatory ground, such as male-male desire or even a Freudian unconscious or libido, which these fantasies express, and does not theorize the shared fantasies of this specific group of males about the body, about women, about violence and about the structure of society at a specific historical moment within a specific culture as signs of something else. As he states, "Most centrally, we will look at . . . the language of the soldier males. The question here is not so much what such language 'expresses' or 'signifies,' as how it functions, its role in the man's relation to external reality, and its bodily location. The relationship of human bodies to the larger world of objective reality grows out of one's relationship to one's own body and to other human bodies. The relationship to the larger world in turn determines the way in which these bodies speak of themselves, of objects, and of relationships to objects" (1: 24). In its historical specificity and focus on a clearly defined group, in using sources beyond the high literary, and in its concern with the shape of male consciousness with special attention to the image of the body, Theweleit's study provides a model for describing the psychic lives of Victorian men.

As Foucault and Theweleit demonstrate, the construction of male consciousness must be seen as historically specific, and as specific to individuals and to groups or classes at any given historical moment. Any study of the inscriptions of the masculine must, then, be grounded in the history of these social formations, in their variousness, their contradictions, their instabilities, and their transformations over time. Until recently, histories of masculinities have been remarkably rare, but there has recently been, if not a flood, a fruitful stream of studies of particular value to Victorianists. The oldest, and still the best general study of "manhood as an evolving social construct reflecting some continuities but many more changes" (3) from the beginnings to the present moment is Peter N. Stearns's *Be a Man!: Males in Modern Society* (2nd Ed. New York: Holmes & Meier, 1990). Stearns's discussion of the nineteenth century in Europe and America is particularly useful for its concern with the effects of industrialism on the shape of manhood, and the inflection of industrial manhood by class. His distinction between working-class and middle-class manhood in the nineteenth century provides a valuable corrective to the continuing tendency of Victorianists to conflate bourgeois forms of manliness with Victorian manliness in general. Norman Vance's

The Sinews of the Spirit: The Ideal of Christian Manliness in Victorian Literature and Religious Thought (Cambridge: Cambridge UP, 1985), although it provides a useful account of muscular Christianity, exemplifies this tendency to generalize Christian manliness into Victorian manliness. Indeed, most accounts of Victorian masculinities, albeit self-consciously, focus on the bourgeoisie. These valuable works include Leonore Davidoff and Catherine Hall's *Family Fortunes: Men and Women of the English Middle Class, 1780–1850* (Chicago: U of Chicago P, 1987); Peter Gay's *The Bourgeois Experience: Victoria to Freud: Volume I. Education of the Senses* (New York: Oxford UP, 1984); and Carol Christ's "Victorian Masculinity and the Angel in the House," in *A Widening Sphere: Changing Roles of Victorian Women*, ed. Martha Vicinus (Bloomington: Indiana UP, 1977), 146–162. Although its primary focus is on France, Richard Sennett's *The Fall of Public Man* (New York: Vintage, 1978), in describing the retreat from public theatricality for a style of reserve grounded in fear of revealing inner impulse, provides a challenging model of the transformations in the public culture and private lives of Victorian men.

My own favorite among the recent histories of nineteenth-century masculinities is Mark C. Carnes's *Secret Ritual and Manhood in Victorian America* (New Haven: Yale UP, 1989). Carnes argues that in the nineteenth century with the separation of home and workplace, the increase in class mobility, and the feminization of child rearing, the need for men to differentiate themselves from the female was simultaneously intensified and made more difficult. This new crisis in achieving manhood, according to Carnes, explains the efflorescence of male secret societies such as the Masons and Oddfellows, whose sole purpose appears to have been the invention of traditions or secret rituals, described in fascinating detail, for initiating new members of the society into manhood. Carnes also suggests that, like so much else in the nineteenth century, this psychological and social need to achieve manhood was also displaced from the public space into private rituals of reading (124) — a suggestion that opens the view that the popular Victorian tales of male initiation may be seen as surrogates for a felt loss of public rites of passage, a vicarious experience that satisfied the newly intensified emotional need for stable male identity.

One effect of reading such histories of male initiation as Carnes's or the quite fascinating cross-cultural anthropological survey of male initiation rites by David D. Gilmore, *Manhood in the Making: Cultural Concepts of Masculinity* (New Haven: Yale UP, 1990) is to see that our theorizing of masculinity as well as our critical language must foreground not only the constructed nature of technologies of the male self, but also the instability of such formations. It seems to me useful, then, to reserve a term such as "maleness" for the fantasies about the essential nature of men, that which a society such as the Victorians think of as innate in the biological male, and to employ "masculinity" and "manliness" for those various social constructions of the male current within the society. Such a distinction is especially important for the Victorians, for whom the hegemonic bourgeois view defined "manliness" as control and discipline of an essential "maleness" fantasized as a dangerous energy manifested in sexuality and aggressiveness. Furthermore, as Carnes and Gilmore suggest, the term "manhood" may best be applied to the condition of an achieved masculinity or manliness, an achievement gained often through public or private ritual. Manhood as achieved manliness must be seen not only as the end of a process of masculinization, but a condition once reached that is, particularly for the Victorians, exceedingly difficult to maintain; for nineteenth century men, manhood may best be seen as an unstable equilibrium of barely controlled energy. In other words, for the Victorians manhood is not an essence but a plot, a narrative over time, and a narrative that structures Victorian writing from *Past and Present*, through *Tom Brown's Schooldays* to *Marius the Epicurean*.

This cross-cultural, historicist approach opens up such terms as Victorian manliness, masculinity, manhood — so often identified with a single formation such as muscular Christianity or bourgeois paternalism — so that they may be seen as encompassing a variety of competing formations of the masculine. Stearns sees emerging in the nineteenth century an "industrial manhood," a category that he subdivides into "working-class" and "aggressive middle-class" masculinity and that he sees as co-existing with the type of the "professional man." Davidoff and Hall speak of the opposition of "gentry" style to "the construction of a new subject — the Christian middle-class man" (110).

Such typologies of Victorian manliness productively complicate the pervasive academic model of nineteenth-century conflict *between* masculine and feminine by raising the issue of conflict *within* the masculine. From the varied constructions of manliness available in the culture, men had to fashion a personal configuration of masculinity, and these individual formations internalized and often failed to resolve the contradictions of male identity within the culture. The theoretical model of conflict among styles of manhood as registered in the psychic lives of individuals and in their writing is employed to stunning effect in Leverenz's study of male writers of the American Renaissance, where he points to tensions in these figures in terms of an effort to reconcile what he sees as the "patrician," the "artisan" and the "entrepreneurial" paradigms of manhood. Consideration of British Victorians might add to Leverenz's categories such styles of artistic manhood as the gentleman, the professional, as well as the prophet-sage and the Bohemian.

The best recent studies of masculinities in Victorian literature and culture, then, share the qualities seen in the recent theorizing and historicizing of masculinities. They see masculinity as an historical construction rather than an essentialist given; they consider Victorian masculinity not as monolithic but as varied, an interplay within each male figure of the cultural possibilities, and are thus attentive to the specific configuration of masculinity within each figure. These studies assume male identity within the individual not as a stable achievement but as problematic so that the governing terms become contradiction, conflict, anxiety. They see the homoerotic not necessarily as the primary determining quality of masculine identity, but as inseparable from other problematics of masculinity, and conversely see the construction of Victorian homosexuality as inseparable from normative constructions of manliness. Finally, they are attentive to the complex ways that these unstable and conflicted forms of manhood both subvert and maintain patriarchal power.

Among such studies the broadest in scope and most exemplary in method is Munich's *Andromeda's Chains*. By focusing on a single subject, the Andromeda myth — the very open subject of the bound maiden rescued from a monster by the heroic male — Munich powerfully demonstrates the variousness of Victorian masculinities as well as the range of, in Theweleit's terms, Victorian male fantasies, from Robert Browning's identification with the chained maiden, to the attraction/repulsion toward female sexuality in the Pre-Raphaelites, to G. M. Hopkins's transformation of the monster into uncontrolled female sexuality and feminist political activism. The book also shows a nuanced sense of the deep unease within the psyches of these Victorian men, of "the problematics rather than the fixities of [Victorian men's] apparently rigid gender economy" (179). Munich sees the varied representations of the myth as manifesting an anxiety focused not only on female sexuality, but also on men's own sexual desire, an anxiety increased by the need to maintain a show of unflappable reserve and a position of gendered power. In Foucauldian fashion, Munich is occupied with such power, but sees this masculine power as itself unstable. As she notes, the Victorian obsession with the story of Andromeda, with the bound female, her rescue and marriage, suggests that the myth "polices a boundary of social behavior, but its very repetitions indicate that the boundary has not been safely secured" (185).

Munich acknowledges that her work emerges from the methods of feminist criticism, and indeed much of the best recent work on Victorian masculinities has been produced by feminist critics who have turned their methods to the study of men's art and men's psyches. Among the most useful for Victorian scholars is Griselda Pollock's discussion of D. G. Rossetti in *Vision and Difference: Femininity, Feminism and Histories of Art* (London: Routledge, 1988). More polemical than Munich, Pollock sets Rossetti within the gender discourse of the mid-nineteenth century in order to deconstruct or perhaps explode the masculinist writing of art history as the equation of male creativity with male sexual potency. The discussion of "Woman as Sign in Pre-Raphaelite Literature: The Representation of Elizabeth Siddall" (ch. 4) examines the ways in which these visual works "negotiated and articulated emerging bourgeois definitions of masculine sexuality through representations of 'femininity'" (92). "Woman as Sign: Psychoanalytic Readings" (ch. 6) links such readings to the formal qualities of Rossetti's late paintings, specifically the rejection of narrative, and shows the connection of such formal innovation to mid-Victorian male anxiety about uncontrolled erotic desire.

For all its power in debunking the masculinist critical tradition that praises Rossetti's artistic power as signified by his love of female beauty, Pollock's use of an historicized gaze theory still assumes the power of the patriarchal artist implied in such theory and thus neglects the other side of Rossetti's problematic as a Victorian male artist — the effects of his self-distancing from the hegemonic bourgeois construction of manliness, particularly in his later years. A valuable balance to Pollock, and an exemplary analysis that foregrounds the internal stress rather than the patriarchal power of the male Victorian artist, is Barbara Charlesworth Gelpi's "The Feminization of D. G. Rossetti," in *The Victorian Experience: The Poets*, ed. Richard A. Levine (Athens: Ohio UP, 1982, 94–114). Gelpi compellingly argues that the price paid for Rossetti's self-exclusion from the bourgeois male sphere led in his later life to a set of psychic and psychosomatic symptoms marked by the age as "feminine," to what must be called a form of male hysteria.

As the case of Rossetti indicates, one of the crucial subjects in the study of Victorian masculinities is the complex ways in which artists and writers negotiated the disjunction between the normative bourgeois model of manliness and the role of male artist. But work on the problematic, the oxymoron, of Victorian "masculine artist" must be attentive to several matters. As Munich and Pollock demonstrate, discussion of the issue must be responsive to the complex mix of stress and of power in the work of these writers and artists. Furthermore, such studies must unpack the term "masculine" to recognize the varied possibilities of self-fashioning, the diverse styles of literary and artistic manhood available to the male poet, novelist, painter. The recent historical study by Paula Gillett, *The Worlds of Art: Painters in Victorian Society* (New Brunswick: Rutgers UP, 1990), provides a useful account of the changing spectrum of roles available and especially of the drive of male Victorian artists to achieve respectability within the hegemonic formation of manliness by shifting the role of the painter from that of artisan to the realm of the gentlemanly and the professional.

Yet the scholarly study of the artistic and poetic careers of Victorian men has tended to remain within the simple binary of masculine/feminine, and within that binary critics have tended to privilege the "feminine," particularly in Victorian poets, as in the perceptive and influential article by Elliot

L. Gilbert, "The Female King: Tennyson's Arthurian Apocalypse" (*PMLA* 98: 863–78), and in U. C. Knoepflmacher's "Projection and the Female Other: Romanticism, Browning, and the Victorian Dramatic Monologue" (*VP* 22: 139–59). As attractive as it may be to rescue Victorian male poets for feminism, such an emphasis diverts attention from what was for the Victorians and continues to be in our day an enormously powerful strategy for resolving the basic opposition between hegemonic Victorian manhood and artistic or poetic manhood. I am speaking of the poetic strategy that locates the source of poetry not in those qualities of isolation and inwardness associated then and now with the feminine and the female sphere, but, as in the example of Browning, as grounded in those qualities such as commercial engagement, warfare, male bonding, phallic sexuality, and imperialism marked by the Victorians as "masculine." An exemplary work in acknowledging and engaging the zeal of Victorian poets for masculinization is Linda Shires's "*Maud*, Masculinity and Poetic Identity" (*Criticism* 29: 269–90), which addresses Tennyson's effort to free himself from the associations with the feminine in the work of his middle period. As a compelling and methodologically exemplary study of this same drive toward masculinization in our own time, I would recommend Susan Jeffords's *The Remasculinization of America: Gender and the Vietnam War* (Bloomington: Indiana UP, 1989).

In drawing parallels between our own time and the late Victorian period, Showalter in *Sexual Anarchy* also recognizes the drive toward masculinization as a strategy of men faced with what they perceive to be threats to stable masculine identity. Here, Showalter employs not only the model of a battle between the sexes, the single descriptive paradigm employed by Sandra M. Gilbert and Susan Gubar in *No Man's Land. Volume 1: The War of the Words* (New Haven: Yale UP, 1988), but also that of "a battle *within* the sexes. Men, too, faced changes in their lives and sexual identities" (9), changes she contextualizes not merely as a "response to female literary dominance," but more broadly in terms of the effects of "British imperialism and fears of manly decline" (83). Within this historically specific context, the study calls attention to the emergence of literary forms marked as masculine, particularly to the creation of what she terms "the male quest romance," the search for "a mythologized place elsewhere where men can be freed from the constraints of Victorian morality" (81). Although this form can be seen earlier in the nineteenth century, in Browning's "Childe Roland" and Tennyson's "Locksley Hall," Showalter is acute in pointing to the particularly "masculine" qualities of the quest romances of Rider Haggard, Kipling and Conrad — the themes of "the male muse, male bonding, and the exclusion of women" (83), the ideal of the circulation of wisdom among men, and the male fantasy of self-engendering. Her sympathetic sense of the stress and tension within male identity in this period, exemplified in her reading of Haggard's *She*, contrasts sharply with the harsh, dismissive treatment of Haggard and of masculine gender anxieties at that same historical moment in Gilbert and Gubar's *No Man's Land. Volume 2: Sexchanges* (New Haven: Yale UP, 1989, 10–28).

Showalter's discussion of the masculinization of literary forms in the later nineteenth century points to the possibility of rewriting literary history throughout the century as contestation in the gender classification of literary forms, as a struggle to conquer and maintain discursive territory for male and for female. This model of an ongoing struggle to gender and thus claim literary forms is persuasively applied to the early Victorians by Carol Christ in " 'The Hero as Man of Letters': Masculinity and Victorian Nonfiction Prose,'' an article in *Victorian Sages and Cultural Discourse: Renegotiating Gender and Power*, ed. Thaîs E. Morgan (New Brunswick: Rutgers UP, 1990, 19–31). Here Christ focuses on Carlyle's influential essay to examine the contested masculinization of the position of sage.

To understand not only this masculinizing of literary forms, but also the thoroughly gendered quality of Victorian cultural discourse, it is necessary to recapture the contemporary meanings of the gendered vocabulary employed within that discourse. Cracking the code of gendered Victorian critical terminology is a crucial project for understanding not only Victorian masculinities, but also the structure of Victorian literary and cultural life. In this enterprise, the recent work of Linda Dowling, in "Ruskin's Pied Beauty and the Constitution of a 'Homosexual' Code" (*VNL* 75: 1–8), and Thaîs E. Morgan provides a methodological model. In "Mixed Metaphor, Mixed Gender: Swinburne and the Victorian Critics" (*VNL* 73: 16–19), Morgan examines the contemporary charges against Swinburne, in particular such use of gendered criteria as the judgment that his poetry is "not virile or even feminine, but epicene . . . far from being chaste or noble in the masculine or any other sense" (17). By focusing on this critical language within the Victorian context rather than applying our own gendered criteria, Morgan can not only recuperate the contemporary force of such judgments, but also point to the ties of such criteria to a Victorian understanding of the classical critical tradition and, more generally, to the connection of this gendered vocabulary to an ideology that is "determinedly heterosexual and masculinist: [that] believes that social control depends on control of the body and on control of language as a representation of the body" (17).

For the Victorian critic the terms "virile," "feminine," "epicene" flow together in a desperate if vain endeavor to achieve sharp gender classification. An awareness that the Victorians sought but never achieved this clear demarcation of gender might remind us that any study of Victorian masculinities must be embedded within the larger field of Victorian gender construction. Perhaps, in the future, Wordsworth will re-shelve once again, combining the sections on Women's Studies, Men's Issues and Gay and Lesbian Studies into one vast section called simply Gender Studies.

Northeastern University

RECENT WORK IN VICTORIAN POETRY

By Dorothy Mermin

THE FIRST THING I DISCOVERED in surveying books on Victorian poetry from the last few years is that while just about every approach now operative in the academy has been applied to one writer or another, interest centers mostly on cultural context and — more surprisingly — on "mystery." The second is that Tennyson is still the poet laureate of Victorian England and *In Memoriam* still the quintessential Victorian poem. More is written about Tennyson, on more subjects, than about any other poet, and almost invariably with approbation. Browning also enjoys high regard, mostly as a deconstructor of authoritarian views on language and gender. In both poets, what was once dismissed as garrulity, conventionality, and absence of thought (Auden's jibe about Tennyson's stupidity still rankles) has increasingly opened up to reveal cunning structures, significant meaning, and subversive intent. Arnold, on the other hand — with his apparently elitist "culture" and relatively sparse output — has fallen on hard times. His poems receive little attention, much of it negative. Hopkins and Hardy (as a poet), unlike Arnold, have recent books to themselves; but while Hopkins seems second only to Tennyson in the amount that is written about him, he appears relatively seldom (and Hardy hardly at all) in books that deal with several authors, and critics of these two poets seem less engaged with contemporary critical issues. Morris, Swinburne, and Clough get sensitive and sympathetic attention. But criticism of women poets is disappointing.

Tennyson provides grist for almost every mill: religion, the family, gender, sexuality, class, politics, science, myth — and, of course, the mysteries of poetic power and the uses of language. Garrett Stewart's *Reading Voices: Literature and the Phonotext* (Berkeley: U of California P, 1990), in which even "the poets of high Victorian sonorities" (85) are allowed a small place in the historical survey, begins with the "silent-speaking words" of *In Memoriam* 95 — which in Stewart's "phonemic reading" becomes "silence speaking" (6): "that *speaking silence* which is textuality itself" (6). Donald

378

S. Hair's *Tennyson's Language* (Toronto: U of Toronto P, 1991) also starts with *In Memoriam* 95: "how hard to frame / In matter-moulded forms of speech." Hair elucidates "matter-moulded forms" as a combination of Lockean and Coleridgean ideas about language (the primacy of sense data versus the shaping power of the mind) and then traces Tennyson's close but critical engagement with the new philology, which saw language as a kind of quasi-natural phenomenon, with its own organization and laws, but also, in the view of Tennyson and others, as part of the providentially guided development of history. The book ends with a reading of *Idylls of the King* that traces the decline of language from the divine Logos into explicitness and externality, duplicity and evil. One learns a great deal from this book both about Tennyson and about Victorian theories of language.

Gerhard Joseph's *Tennyson and the Text: The Weaver's Shuttle* (Cambridge: Cambridge UP, 1992) takes its main subject and its model from the Lady of Shalott's art of weaving and unweaving, which Joseph associates with both Pater and Penelope. The book self-reflexively reweaves many of Joseph's own past meditations on Tennyson, deftly drawing together strands of modern criticism — deconstructive, psychoanalytic (especially Freud on mourning and melancholia), cultural, feminist — in genial and thoughtful opposition to the critical tradition represented at its best by Christopher Ricks. Like several critics, Joseph is drawn to the dark and mysterious aspects of poetry — what Tennyson has in common with Poe, who figures largely in the discussion. He considers particularity and vagueness as aesthetic ideals and draws on ideas about eyesight, optics, perspective, frames, photography, windows, mirrors, and *mises en abyme*: themes, like weaving, that lend themselves to feminist analysis. There is also a fine discussion of swords, including a wonderful early story by Tennyson. This book, with its musings on critical roads not taken, evokes Tennyson's poetic power and locates his poetry in a variety of perspectives.

Joseph Bristow's *Robert Browning* (New York: St. Martin's, 1991) is a short general introduction to Browning's poetry that provides, with less elegance and originality than Joseph but with more doggedly catholic range, a kind of compendium of current approaches. Bristow provides information about Wordsworth, Fox, Bentham, and Mill, politics and society, gender issues, and so on. He gives many readings of poems, sometimes quite long and often with a mildly deconstructionist cast, beginning with an excellent use of "Transcendentalism" to illustrate the disjunction between statement and meaning in dramatic monologue. He devotes a good deal of space to *Sordello*, read as a poem about poetic authority, "designed to contest the linear compulsions of narrative" (85). But he also goes dutifully through "My Last Duchess," apparently because the design of the book demands it, as well as other poems that students will find on their syllabuses. This is a useful book for students who want a reliable, up-to-date guide to Browning. A more localized scholarly contribution to the general tendency to refute condescending attitudes towards Browning is offered by a musicologist, Nachum Schoffman, in a short monologue, *There Is No Truer Truth: The Musical Aspect of Browning's Poetry* (New York: Greenwood, 1991). Demonstrating that Browning was expert in music history, in harmony, and as a performer, Schoffman compares his well-informed musical imagery with the Aeolian harps and dulcimers of his Romantic predecessors, noting that his musical imagery often evokes "not so much the sound of music as the feel of playing an instrument" (57).

Post-structuralist criticism is peculiarly suited to the analysis of Victorian poetry, which inherited a poetics of presence, transcendence, and plenitude in which it could no longer believe and worried obsessively about the status of language (as Hair demonstrates) and the construction of the self. E. Warwick Slinn, one of several critics who have set themselves in recent years to dismantle the picture of Victorian poets as garrulous, vague, unintellectual upholders of the social and literary status quo, argues in *The Discourse of Self in Victorian Poetry* (Charlottesville: UP of Virginia, 1991) that "the supposed prolixity of nineteenth-century poetry is related to sophisticated conceptions of mind" and that "the poetry of the time is fundamentally subversive" (6). This short, tightly argued book moves in two introductory chapters from Hegel to Derrida, analyzing several poems along the way, and following up with chapters on *Maud, Amours de Voyage*, and *The Ring and the Book* that show how everything in those poems is seen to be textualized and founded in contradiction.

Slinn draws from the Pope's monologue in *The Ring and the Book* the moral that "No judgement (including this one) escapes the conditions and processes of its own enactment" (146). In *Victorians and Mystery: Crises of Representation* (Ithaca: Cornell UP, 1990), W. David Shaw, who also draws extensively on (*inter alia*) Hegel and Derrida, concludes with a tour-de force reading of *The Ring and the Book* as implying a similar moral — "that interpretive purity of any kind breeds self-destruction" — and advocating "immersion in a text and in its history" (315). Such immersion is part of Shaw's own critical practice. *Victorians and Mystery* treats fiction, non-fictional prose, and poetry, with particular attention to *In Memoriam*, "The Wreck of the Deutschland," *Amours de Voyage*, Christina Rossetti's religious poetry, some Arnold, and a lot of Browning: listening for "the words never uttered that are nevertheless meant to be heard or overheard by an attentive reader" (197). Shaw's elaborated categories of mystery are less useful than his stylistic and rhetorical analyses, his demonstrations of the close fit between contemporary critical practice and Victorian ideas, and above all his ability to sound the mysterious depths of poetry. He urges us to revel in mystery, not try to analyze it away.

One would have hoped it was no longer necessary to demonstrate that Victorian poetry is not flatly unmysterious and foolishly single-minded, but such hope is clearly premature. Clyde de L. Ryals argues in simpler terms than Slinn and Shaw in *A World of Possibilities: Romantic Irony in Victorian Literature* (Columbus: Ohio State UP, 1990) against "either/or" readings of Browning's "Christmas-Eve," Arnold's poems, and *Idylls of the King* as well as four prose texts. What appear to be contradictions in the *Idylls*, for instance — conflicting accounts of Arthur's origins and the cause of the city's downfall, shifts in symbolism, style, authorial authority, and narrative technique — are, Ryals rightly says, signs not of waffling or confusion but of significant complexity. Ryals defines Romantic irony as an awareness of the duplicitousness of language and of meaning as always provisional and in process of becoming, accompanied by self-reflexiveness on the part of the artist, distrust of the idea of determinacy, and avoidance of closure. This has a rather deconstructive ring, but Ryals includes in his attack on "either/or" readings those in which the impossibility of meaning is itself the single fixed meaning always to be found.

Another sign that we are catching up with the times is Antony H. Harrison's *Victorian Poets and Romantic Poems: Intertexuality and Ideology* (Charlottesville: UP of Virginia, 1990), which combines intertextual and new historicist approaches to several poets: an excellent if perhaps overambitious project. Harrison shows us how important, and how tricky, it is to examine the ways in which the Victorian poets read their predecessors and contemporaries. He is especially good on the irritatingly successful Spasmodics, and he usefully reminds us that to read *Maud* in light of *Hamlet* one has to think about how the Victorians read Shakespeare. Still, his intertexual threads are sometimes tenuous. The project of reading Arnold's Empedocles as an aging Keatsian poet is more persuasive than one might have expected, but the link between "The Triumph of Time" and the "Immortality" Ode is rather flimsy. (Other chapters deal with "Cleon," D. G. Rossetti, Christina Rossetti and Barrett Browning, and Morris.) The "intertextual" argument, furthermore, tends to have it both ways: likeness demonstrates connection, unlikeness is "ironic" or "subversive."

John Lucas's *England and Englishness: Ideas of Nationhood in English Poetry 1688–1900* (Iowa City: U of Iowa P, 1990) evaluates the major Victorian poets by an anti-Arnoldian, anti-authoritarian, anti-elitist standard, defining their connection to "a myth of Englishness which becomes increasingly troubling as the century progresses because it is increasingly xenophobic and eventually racist" (173). Lucas sets poets against each other in familiar pairings: Browning against Tennyson, Arnold against Clough, Browning against

Arnold. The Browning of *Men and Women* comes out best, because he doubts accepted notions of English masculinity and encourages a diversity of voices, whereas Arnold attempts to arrogate an unchallenged authority to his own voice and silence opposing ones. Tennyson both acquiesces in and resists his role as Laureate, the voice of a conservative, privileged, patriarchal, xenophobic society. One might query some of the comments on poems: the equation of cross-class marriages in Jane Austen and "The Lord of Burleigh," for instance, or the negative judgment drawn from the fact that the woman in "Dover Beach" — like most addressees of love poems and dramatic monologues — is not allowed to speak. But the virtues of this fresh and invigorating book are thrown into relief by comparison with *English Literature and the Wider World, Vol. 3, 1830–1876: Creditable Warriors*, edited by Michael Cotsell (London-Atlantic Highlands, NJ: Ashfield Press, 1990), which includes essays by Susan Shatto noting Tennyson's interest in sexy savages and his belief in the civilizing potential of free trade, Park Honan on Arnold's Europeanism, Simon Gatrell on Clough's Italian poems, Jacob Korg on Browning and Italy, and Deborah Phelps on Barrett Browning. Without a guiding vision, Cotsell's book as a whole (or at any rate the part of it that deals with poetry) is less than the sum of its parts. When Victorian poets withdrew from their age, Cotsell says, they were inclined to go abroad, where "they found natural beauty and ancient culture, and explored tensions of distance and displacement, a more suggestive European sense of history and modernity, wider but subtly emptied prospects" (19). What this means in political terms, however, especially in relation to imperialism, remains mostly to be explored.

The trend away from single-author and single-genre studies has been beneficial to Victorian poets, especially those who do not currently rate books of their own. *Amours de Voyage*, for instance, gets extensive attention in Slinn, Shaw, and Cotsell. Long poems, which lend themselves well to modes of analysis more commonly applied to the novel, are particularly popular in such books. *The Victorian Serial*, by Linda K. Hughes and Michael Lund (Charlottesville: UP of Virginia, 1991), indeed requires long works: not just long enough to have been serialized, but also to meet Hughes's and Lund's focus on works that "treat a central subject of the age: home, history, empire, doubt" (14). The authors of this well-contextualized study are particularly interested in the dynamics of serial reading: encountering *The Ring and the Book* in four monthly parts was like attending a trial, they say, or like a journey towards Pompilia, whereas *The Angel in the House* required the patience and mimicked the developmental processes of marriage. *The Idylls of the King* (considered under the category of Empire) offers an especially rich field for such analysis by analogy, and there are also chapters on Morris's *Earthly Paradise* and *Pilgrims of Hope* and Hardy's *The Dynasts*.

Hughes again discusses Patmore (a poet scorned too readily and read too seldom) in her contribution to Judith Kennedy's *Victorian Authors and Their Works: Revision Motivations and Modes* (Athens: Ohio UP, 1991). This collection includes Susan Shatto on *Maud* (a synopsis of the introduction to her 1986 edition of the poem), an essay on D. G. Rossetti and Morris by Frederick Kirchhoff which offers suggestive analogies between poetic revisions and the painter's and weaver's arts, and an analysis by Ashley Bland Crowder of one of Browning's least-read poems, "Pachiarotto and How He Worked in Distemper." Edward H. Cohen's very detailed if untheorized account of the evolution of Henley's *In Hospital* made me want to look at the poem again. The contributors to this volume are editors and biographers, and their short essays demonstrate how much critical interest can be derived from highly traditional work with texts, especially those of lesser-known works.

Michael Wheeler's *Death and the Future Life in Victorian Literature and Theology* (Cambridge: Cambridge UP, 1990) casts an exceptionally wide net in the sea of poetry (as well as of theological and other prose, including fiction), drawing up some texts I had never even heard of. There are brief discussions of Christina Rossetti, Browning, Patmore, Swinburne, *Modern Love, The City of Dreadful Night*, and chapters on *In Memoriam* and "The Wreck of the Deutschland"; but there is also a chapter on Newman's *Dream of Gerontius* and Elgar's oratorio setting of it, as well as discussion of Bailey's *Festus*. Robert Pollok's *The Course of Time* (1827) and E. H. Bickersteth's *Yesterday, Today and For Ever* (1866), epic poems on the Last Judgment, are instructive and amusing to read about, although they would be hellish, no doubt, actually to read. The chapter on *In Memoriam* rescues the poem from charges of vagueness (that recurrent theme), tracing a "specifically religious rather than vaguely spiritual" movement (255) and anchoring it in Broad Church specificity. Unlike critics who celebrate poetic mystery, Wheeler works to dispel it, and his persistently up-beat reading of *In Memoriam* is rather flat, missing the notes of terror and of darkness.

While Wheeler's magisterial work of scholarship could have been produced, one feels, at almost any time in the last decades, Richard Dellamora's *Masculine Desire: The Sexual Politics of Victorian Aestheticism* (Chapel Hill: U of North Carolina P, 1990) belongs precisely to this moment. The transgressive edge of criticism has passed to gay studies, which will find its best nineteenth-century ground, I think, not in the novel as feminist criticism has done, but in Victorian poetry. Critics until very recently have ignored or explained away what seem to be traces of homoeroticism in Victorian poetry, most notably in *In Memoriam*. Wheeler, for instance, predictably dismisses such suggestions when he reads "Descend, and touch, and enter; hear / The wish too strong for words to name" (*In Memoriam* 93) in theological terms

(250), whereas Dellamora hears less a reference to "sexual practices than [to] the terms of Greek pederastic tradition in which the 'hearer,' Tennyson, appeals to the 'inspirer,' Hallam" (38). But one reading need not exclude the other. Here if anywhere, acknowledgment of mystery and a refusal of "either/ or" (not to mention "did they/didn't they") readings seems appropriate, and the work of Foucault, Eve Sedgwick, and historians of homosexuality have made it possible to discuss these issues in more nuanced and historically precise terms than ever before. Dellamora provides evidence for what is evident to common sense: that poets whose all-male schools and universities encouraged romantic attachments, and who were educated in the Greek classics, were likely to have had some awareness of, and anxiety about, homosexuality. The nature of their awareness, however, usually remains unclear, and while Dellamora gives evidence of homosexual activity among Hallam's and Tennyson's circle of friends, he assumes that whatever voices of forbidden desire may speak in the poetry of Tennyson, Arnold, Swinburne, and Hopkins, with whatever degree of consciousness, such desire did not issue in extra-poetic action.

The importance of Dellamora's book, which documents and analyzes social contexts as well as reading poems, is that it considers male homosocial desire not just as a biographical issue but as a source of poetry. He is appropriately tentative, to the point that it is sometimes unclear what he is saying. "Conclusive answers to questions about the sexual self-awareness of the men whom I discuss here may never be forthcoming," he says in a typical formulation. "Nonetheless [a word typical of the book's mode of argument], I believe that they responded to their situations not simply in panic, self-ignorance, or confusion but in resourceful and creative, even if circumscribed and at times painful, fashion" (22). The appearance of *Leaves of Grass* in 1855, he points out, which marked a watershed in the conscious awareness of homosexuality, opened new poetic possibilities. He gives compelling readings of Hopkins: "God's Grandeur," he argues, "constructs an ideology of bodily practices in which a male-identified virginity is seen as natural, loving, and (paradoxically) creative while bodily expression in voluntary emission and copulation are derogated" (54). He finds homoerotic energies and repressions, surprisingly but not unpersuasively (his tentativeness is contagious), in the ventless suffering of Arnold's Empedocles and suggests that for Swinburne aberrant "sexual practices marked not by dominance and subordination but by reciprocity" are means of escaping "the impasse of male gender norms" (71). The varying instabilities of gendered subject positions and the effects on poetry of feelings that cannot be named — that remain mysterious — call for further exploration.

"When the [Cambridge] Apostles in their correspondence advert to base passions for *women*, they tend to do so in a light vein" (Dellamora 22), and some of the deepest mysteries of Victorian poetry may be more accessible to gay studies — or a more broadly conceived gender studies — than to feminist criticism, which has had relatively little to say even about long quasi-novelistic poems. Gender issues are connected with biography, close textual analysis, and the wider political arena in Frederick Kirchhoff's *William Morris: The Construction of a Male Self, 1856–1872* (Athens: Ohio UP, 1990). Kirchhoff reads sexual anxiety in fantasies like "The Blue Closet" and the absence of a stable self (rather than hidden motives) in "The Defense of Guenevere," and he traces the development in Morris's poetry of a relatively firm identity that does not depend on male bonding through the sexual domination of women. Morris's Marxism, Kirchhoff concludes, was built on his rejection of a social order "privileging . . . male individualism and romantic passion" (237). In other studies, though, while oppressive attitudes towards women are sometimes dutifully noted, issues of gender usually remain peripheral when they are raised at all. David Shaw takes domestic life and two female characters to illustrate the virtues of silence: "what a family feels it does not express, and what it expresses it does not fully feel. Wise people like Dorothea and Mrs. Bulstrode [who moves mysteriously through Shaw's book, a most unlikely heroine] learn to feel and live their truths without speaking them" (195). But this implicit domestication and gendering of silence does not interest Shaw any more than the absence of women among his ironists interests Ryals.

The impulse of feminist criticism runs along the threads of Gerhard Joseph's web, and is duly recorded by Joseph Bristow. But for feminist analysis of male poets we have to go back a few years to work by women. Isobel Armstrong's "Tennyson's 'The Lady of Shalott': Victorian Mythography and the Politics of Narcissism," in *The Sun Is God: Painting, Literature, and Mythology in the Nineteenth Century*, edited by J. B. Bullen (Oxford: Clarendon P, 1989, 49–107), considers, among many other things, the politics of the gaze and the various significances of weaving. As Armstrong puts it, "The beauty of the poem is the inconspicuous ease with which it defamiliarizes the cotton weaver and his exploitation by making the Lady a proxy who carries the meaning of estranged labour" (82). Ann Brady's *Pompilia: A Feminist Reading of Robert Browning's The Ring and the Book* (Athens: Ohio UP, 1988) works in the style of early feminism, tracking down misogyny (classical, Christian, Renaissance, Victorian, one as bad as the other) and celebrating a self-directed moral heroine. Marion Shaw's *Alfred Lord Tennyson* (Atlantic Highlands, NJ: Humanities P International, 1988) considers in psychoanalytic terms the formation of the masculine subject and the place of the feminine in that formation, taking the gender of female figures in the poetry more seriously than critics usually do.

Recent work on women poets is disappointingly scant, especially in light of the powerful work that has been done on Victorian women novelists and the substantial flurry of books on Barrett Browning and Rossetti that appeared in 1988 and 1989. Kathleen Jones's *Learning Not to Be First: The Life of Christina Rossetti* (Gloustershire: Windrush, 1991) is not a book for scholars. Rod Edmond's *Affairs of the Hearth: Victorian Poetry and Domestic Narrative* (London: Routledge, 1988), which considers long poems of contemporary life in terms of the "institution and ideology of the middle-class family" (vii), has excellent chapters on *Aurora Leigh* and *Goblin Market* as well as *The Bothie of Tober-na-Vuolich, The Princess,* and *Modern Love.* But in the books under review here Barrett Browning appears only in Cotsell and, paired with Christina Rossetti, in Harrison. Shaw and Wheeler focus on Rossetti's religious poetry, which unlike narratives of contemporary life need not raise issues of gender. And no one seems interested in the poems of Emily Brontë.

Arnold, out of tune with our ruling preoccupations, trails even behind the women. The fifth edition of *The Norton Anthology of English Literature,* which largely controls the canon in America, makes more room for women, takes a little from Tennyson and Browning, but cuts a full quarter of the poems by Arnold in the fourth edition (Morris and the poets of the nineties are even more drastically cut). Ryals includes Arnold among ironists, Dellamora includes him among homoerotic poets, and David G. Riede demonstrates in *Matthew Arnold and the Betrayal of Language* (Charlottesville: UP of Virginia, 1988) that his "simultaneous mystification and demystification of poetic language" (25) "leaves him with no possible arguments — no possible language — for setting forth the faith in poetic language that he nevertheless clings to" (24). But Lucas finds him authoritarian and W. David Shaw dismisses him for profaning mystery with reductive speech. In contrast, Clough's long poems of modern life are valued for being less dogmatic and more attuned to contemporary concerns.

Morris's poetry seems especially to raise questions about literature and the wider world: besides Kirchhoff's book, there are two essays on his poems in *Socialism and the Literary Artistry of William Morris,* edited by Florence S. Boos and Carole G. Silver (Columbia: U of Missouri P, 1990). In "Morris's 'Chants' and the Problems of Socialist Culture," Christopher Waters studies his socialist songs, drawing on Victorian ideas about the use of music for the moral elevation of the workers and noting the contradiction implied in writing songs for the people whose creativity the socialists hoped to inspire. Boos writes on "Narrative Design in *The Pilgrims of Hope*" — the only major Victorian poem, she points out, with a hero who belongs to the urban poor — and suggests that the blend of "romantic pastoralism and aggrieved realism" (149) and the "balance of interior vision and historical reality" (166) are intimately related to Morris's socialist vision.

Books on other poets, often resolutely and sometimes defensively un-trendy, are still doing the basic work of literary scholarship and attempting to situate their poets on the Victorian scene. Swinburne is becoming a less peripheral, more serious and congenial presence. Margot K. Louis's engaged and informative *Swinburne and His Gods: The Roots and Growth of an Agnostic Poetry* (Montreal and Kingston: McGill-Queens UP, 1990) shows how — having been well instructed in Christian doctrine before losing his faith at Oxford — he moved from demonic parody, with the "divine whore" as "emblem of the formidably free human imagination" (22), through the anti-sacramental pessimism of *Atalanta in Calydon*, to a new radical Romanti-cism. Trevor Johnson's *A Critical Introduction to the Poems of Thomas Hardy* (New York: St. Martin's Press, 1991) is a counterpart to Bristow's Browning volume, an introduction for students rather than scholars, lively and apprecia-tive but disengaged from contemporary critical concerns. Katherine Kearney Maynard's *Thomas Hardy's Tragic Poetry: The Lyrics and The Dynasts* (Iowa City: U of Iowa P, 1991) attempts to define tragedy as well as to survey nineteenth-century plays, verse drama, and poems which embody (or more often, Maynard concludes, do not) a truly tragic vision, with *The Dynasts* appearing as the culmination of a century of failures. Through analysis of the lyrics Maynard maps "the Hardyean tragic landscape," which is character-ized by "immediacy, isolation, and [that word again!] mystery" (124). May-nard brings in a very wide range of nineteenth-century works and writers, some more to the point than others, and concludes that "If Hardy . . . gave authentic voice to a tragic feeling that others reached only intermittently, he did so by responding fully to the thought and emotion of his time" (186).

Hopkins has been reinstituted as a Victorian (rather than twentieth-cen-tury) poet by the fifth edition of the *Norton Anthology*. Being a Jesuit made him an outsider in Victorian culture, however (rather like being a woman), and Hopkins criticism remains its own world — one which sometimes reminds me of my student days, when we were all expected to be, or pretend to be, male, Anglo-Saxon, and Episcopalian. In her introduction to a collec-tion of new and older essays, *Critical Essays on Gerard Manley Hopkins* (Boston: G. K. Hall, 1990), Alison G. Sulloway speaks of the need to rectify the "simplistic judgments" and "careless assumptions" of "[i]mmature or biased readers" (3) who might neglect, for instance, the essential importance to Hopkins's poetry of Loyola's *Spiritual Exercises* (2). Virginia Ridley El-lis's contribution to the general delight in mystery, *Gerard Manley Hopkins and the Language of Mystery* (Columbia: U of Missouri P, 1991), announces a common-sensical adherence to intentionality and the biographical author, which she turns to particularly good account in her use of manuscripts. Ellis's Hopkins is not a baffled seeker for certainty, but accepts mystery both as priest and as poet. As it does for David Shaw, the topic produces sensitive, finely-nuanced readings of poems. The substantial flow of books on Hopkins (partly induced by the recent centenary) also includes two major biographies — Robert Bernard Martin's *Gerard Manley Hopkins: A Very Private Life* (New York: G. P. Putnam's, 1991) and Norman White's *Hopkins: A Literary Biography* (Oxford: Clarendon P, 1992).

Scholars have given us some excellent editions, especially of letters. Cecil Y. Lang and Edgar F. Shannon, Jr.'s *Letters of Alfred Lord Tennyson*, 3 vols. (Oxford: Clarendon P, 1981–90) is now complete. *The Brownings' Correspondence*, edited by Philip Kelley and Ronald Hudson (Winfield, KS: Wedgestone Press, 1984–), printing all known letters to and from both poets, with contemporary reviews and other documents, has reached its seventh volume and the year 1843, with both poets in their twenties and Robert (six years younger than his wife, with much less surviving youthful correspondence) now getting more space. *Selected Letters of William Michael Rossetti*, edited by Robert W. Peattie (University Park: Pennsylvania State UP, 1990) shows the letter-writer's famous brother and sister, as well as Swinburne, Meredith, and others, through the eyes of a kind, patient, generous man who cared about and took care of poets and their reputations (Dante Gabriel's servants, he wrote, in 1872, must be paid off but not "exasperated, or they might spread many rumours abroad *on more subjects than one*, of a very unpleasant kind," 292). *The Oxford Diaries of Arthur Hugh Clough*, edited by Anthony Kenny (Oxford: Clarendon P, 1990), is a sad document, its increasingly laconic, often enigmatic entries chronicling self-doubt, worries about not working hard enough, attacks of unbelief, "foolish" behavior in society, masturbation, problems with his Balliol tutor, W. G. Ward, who made inordinate demands on his time and emotions, and uneasiness about affectionate relations with men. There is a well-annotated new edition of *Aurora Leigh*, edited by Margaret Reynolds (Athens: Ohio UP, 1992), which one would like to see in paperback. An odd but pleasant work is F. B. Pinion's *A Tennyson Chronology* (Boston: G. K. Hall, 1990), which tells where Tennyson is in any given month, what is going on in his life, who his visitors are and what he is reading aloud to them, who invites him to dinner and whether or not he accepts; its usefulness is somewhat limited, however, because usually the source of information is not given.

It will be evident from this survey that the move to enlarge the canon has not made much headway here. A notable exception is John Gray, who moved from the working class (one of his best poems describes the making of a wheel) to the civil service and the circle of Oscar Wilde and ended as a Roman Catholic priest. Gray is a fascinating example of poetic self-making and the uses of homoeroticism in verse, and Jerusha Hull McCormack's critical biography, *John Gray: Poet, Dandy, and Priest, (Hanover:* Brandeis UP, 1991) provides background for Ian Fletcher's scholarly edition of Gray's published and unpublished works, *The Poems of John Gray* (Greensboro: ELT Press, 1988). Christopher Ricks's *New Oxford Book of Victorian Verse* (1987) introduces many unfamiliar voices, but an anthology necessarily favors short poems (Ricks's taste is for urbane and witty ones), and it is hard to establish new perspectives in so small a compass. Bernard Richards's topically organized *English Poetry of the Victorian Period 1830–1890* (London: Longman, 1988), which is written for "the modern reader" — "A central question that will intrigue modern readers is: what do Victorian poets do with sexuality in marriage?" (132) — draws attention to some recently neglected poems; the section on courtship in the chapter on love poetry begins with an enthusiastic description of Meredith's "Love in the Valley." But we can learn most about neglected poets from Paul Turner's *Victorian Poetry, Drama and Miscellaneous Prose 1832–1890* (Oxford: Clarendon P, 1989). This mellow, genial survey sometimes reminds us where we have come from: Christina Rossetti's poetry "seems neither cerebral nor calculated, but totally spontaneous" (122), as in pre-feminist days; Swinburn gives us "a mood of great intensity, enjoyable but almost devoid of intellectual meaning" (136); and among thirty-seven "other" (as opposed to major and "lesser") poets, only two — Emily Brontë and Jean Ingelow — are women. But despite a pleasant tartness Turner contrives with just a few exceptions — Martin Tupper, Alfred Austin — to find something nice to say about everyone. Edwin Arnold's *The Light of Asia*, which most of us know only through its proximity on the shelves to Matthew Arnold, is declared "still worth reading" (173); Owen Meredith's *Lucile* and *King Poppy* sound quite attractive; and there is a chapter on comic verse, parody, and nonsense. There is still a lot more out there, after all.

Cornell University

NEW DIRECTIONS IN VICTORIAN ART HISTORY

By Joseph A. Kestner

THE FIELD OF VICTORIAN ART recently has been marked by several intriguing, provocative, if not always successful, productions, including exhibitions, art historical studies, and monographs, the last category with but few examples. The major focus has been on the exhibition, whether broadly ranging or challengingly focused on specific movements and practices. The most important of these exhibitions were in Britain and did not travel to the United States. All, however, are represented by extremely fine catalogues which researchers will find quite significant.

Several exhibitions covered considerable chronological spans, none more so than *The Queen's Pictures: Royal Collectors through the Centuries* (October 1991–January 1992) in the Sainsbury Wing of the National Gallery of Art. The exhibition included nearly 100 works from the Royal Collection of nearly 7,000 works of art, constituting the greatest private collection of art in the world. Although the gallery at Buckingham Palace has periodic displays of material from the Royal Collection, this was the greatest assemblage of works to be exhibited outside a royal palace for fifty years. The accompanying catalogue (London: National Gallery Publications, 1991) includes several excellent essays by Christopher Lloyd and Sir Oliver Millar. Every canvas is accompanied by a full-color plate as well as an individual catalogue essay. Particularly significant for the present situation of the Royal Collection was the intervention of Prince Albert in preserving the canvases, which in 1842 Anna Jameson saw at Hampton Court, where she praised the collection but lamented its condition. The Prince Consort was instrumental in rectifying the situation. Since Queen Victoria and the Prince Consort both drew and painted, their involvement in art matters was not superficial. The Queen visited the annual exhibitions at the Royal Academy, and Prince Albert was responsible for the detailed inventory of the Royal Collection undertaken in 1857 by Richard Redgrave.

The most stimulating dimension of the exhibition was the opportunity to observe rarely-exhibited canvases, and many important Victorian pictures were in evidence. William Dyce's *The Virgin and Child* (1845) and *Saint Joseph* (1847), brought from Osborne House, are crucial in grasping the career of this artist in his "Raphaelite" rather than "Pre-Raphaelite" period. Dyce's Madonna is painted in silhouette holding the infant Jesus against a generalized landscape, not detailed in the manner of the artist's later work, such as *George Herbert at Bemerton*. Both these paintings indicate Dyce's contact with and influence by German Nazarene artists like Overbeck and Schnorr von Carolsfeld, especially in "their simplicity of design, purity of outline and restricted colour" (238). Edwin Landseer was represented by two paintings, each expressing a different dimension of his career. *The Sanctuary* (1842) is a magnificent achievement, showing a stag gaining refuge from hunters and based on "The Stricken Deer" by Landseer's friend William Russell. Landseer's treatment of light, combining sunset with emerging moonlight, creates an ethereal effect that is balanced by extraordinary detail, such as the water dripping from the stag's neck or the diagonals of its trail through the water. *Queen Victoria and Prince Albert at the Bal Costumé of 12 May 1842* (1846) shows the Queen and Consort in medieval fancy dress in the Throne Room, she as Queen Philippa and he as Edward III. Mark Girouard in *The Return of Camelot* (1981) has demonstrated the power of such medievalism in Victorian culture, but no more striking image of its force exists than this canvas.

The Queen was attracted to canvases embodying a narrative or reflecting contemporary events, and this exhibition included a range of such subjects: Frith's *Ramsgate Sands* (1854), Paton's *Home: The Return from the Crimea* (1859), Holl's "*No Tidings from the Sea*" (1870), and Elizabeth Thompson's *The Roll Call* (1874). The latter three were exhibited in close proximity to considerable advantage, with Paton's sentimental image (wounded veteran, hearth fire, baby in cradle) contrasting with Thompson's stupendous representation of a roll call (bloody snow, dazed survivors, wounded sufferers). The fact that this canvas and a work such as Holl's of women desolate after the loss of a fisherman were acquired after the Consort's death reflects the precision of the Queen's taste and her willingness to confront harsh realities of her reign. *The Queen's Pictures* was an outstanding exhibition, and for Victorianists, the opportunity to study the canvases of Dyce, Holl, Thompson, Landseer and Paton, among others, was not to be missed.

A similar opportunity was provided with the exhibition *The Portrait in British Art* (November 1991–February 1992) at the National Portrait Gallery, which included works purchased through the National Art Collections Fund, ranging from Elizabethan canvases to the early twentieth century. The accompanying catalogue by John Hayes (London: National Portrait Gallery, 1991)

Sir John Everett Millais. "Effie Millais" (1873). Reproduced by kind permission of the National Portrait Gallery, London.

John Singer Sargent. "C. E. Harrison" (1888). Reproduced by kind permission of the National Portrait Gallery, London.

included excellent entries on each of the 66 exhibits. The juxtaposition of Watts's portrait of Millais (1871) with Millais's portrait of Effie (1873) was only one example of the judicious hanging of the exhibition: Watts's treatment is stark, showing the artist in profile, with no background accessories; Millais's study of Effie shows the loose brushwork of his post Pre-Raphaelite period, although interestingly he painted out the child in her lap and substituted an issue of the *Cornhill* magazine, not dwelling on the couple's endless progeny. Rossetti's *Monna Vanna* (1866) from the Tate was the sole truly Pre-Raphaelite canvas in the show, an advantage because it permitted outstanding portraits such as Herkomer's *Anne Herkomer* (1876) to shine. The artist's first wife was already dying when this portrait was painted, and the poignant emphasis on her wedding ring and drawn and withdrawn countenance is revelatory. The opposite tendency was noticeable in Sargent's *C. E. Harrison* (1888), a depiction of the son of a stockbroker, decked in sailor suit against a rich crimson background. Sickert's famous portrait of Beardsley (1894) showed the emergence of new technique in his sketchy laying on of paint, with the canvas scarcely concealed. Its elongated format conveys the essence of Beardsley's own emphasis on line. In juxtaposing so many styles, *The Portrait in British Art* confirmed the rich tradition of portraiture in British painting, with the Victorian exhibits more than able to hold their own in terms of innovation and psychological insight.

If *The Queen's Pictures* provided one opportunity to view canvases rarely seen, a similar opportunity was presented with *American Originals: Selections from Reynolda House, Museum of American Art*, an exhibition of forty-one masterpieces from one of the finest small collections in America, the former country estate of R. J. Reynolds at Winston Salem, North Carolina. Again traversing a chronological range (eighteenth through twentieth centuries), a range of artists (among them Bierstadt, Eakins, Copley, Church, Cole, O'Keefe, Stella), and an array of artistic movements (folk art, realism, impressionism, futurism, cubism), this was the first tour this collection has ever sponsored, presented at seven venues in the United States. The installation at the Gilcrease Museum was marked by outstanding hanging, with a large gallery devoted to the show, each canvas separated from its adjacent exhibits. Since each of these paintings was chosen to hang in a domestic setting at Reynolda House, the chance to view these works apart from the domestic interior was invaluable.

The nineteenth-century canvases included masterpieces with strong affiliation with British movements, for example, Frederic Church's *The Andes of Ecuador* (1855), strongly reflecting in its luminosity the influence of Turner as well as nineteenth-century debates about geology (for example, Lyell and Humboldt), the Victorian interest in biblical creation (the Argument by Design), and the apocalyptic canvases of John Martin. Asher Durand's *Rocky*

Cliff (c. 1860) shows the effect not only of Lyell but also of Ruskin in its minute record of rock striations, while Elihu Vedder's *Dancing Girl* (1871) shows the power of Whistler's example in *The White Girl* as well as the "Orientalism" of Fitzgerald's *Rubaiyat*, which Vedder illustrated in 1884. The Aesthetic movement in America is indicated by Chase's *In the Studio* (c. 1884), with its figurines, Japanese print, and Turkish incense burner. The catalogue (New York: Abbeville, 1991) with an essay by Charles C. Eldredge and entries by Barbara B. Millhouse provides a discussion of each exhibit, and the color plates are excellent, particularly because many plates of details are included. The exploration of Anglo-American art relations, now much in the forefront, can profit by consideration of these canvases.

The influence of Japan on Victorian art was the focus of a major exhibition, *Japan and Britain: An Aesthetic Dialogue 1850–1930*, held at the Barbican Art Gallery and the Setagaya Art Museum in 1991, with a fine catalogue by Tomoko Sato and Toshio Watanabe (London: Lund Humphries, 1991). The exhibition is a successor to such key exploratory shows of the 1980s as *Japanese Influences in American Art 1853–1900* at the Clark Institute in 1981 and the revolutionary *Shigeru Aoki and the [sic] Late Victorian Art* of 1983 at Ishibashi, with its excellent essay by John Christian, "Shigeru Aoki and the Pre-Raphaelites." The latter was the first exhibition in Japan of works by Rossetti, Crane, Stanhope, Watts, Burne-Jones, and Moore, and the predecessor of major exhibitions of Victorian art in Japan initiated by Christian in 1985, 1987, and 1989. The 1991 exhibition explores myriad ramifications of what Philippe Burty called Japonisme in his essay of 1872, translated in 1875 for *The Academy*.

The catalogue essays discuss the British presence in Japan in the nineteenth century, the influence of Western-style art on Japanese painting, and Japan's participation in international exhibitions, but the indispensable essay, by Sato and Watanabe, is "The Aesthetic Dialogue Examined: Japan and Britain 1850–1930," a superb appraisal of a variety of subjects, among them Japonisme and mid-Victorian painting, Japonisme and Victorian design, and late Victorian and Edwardian painting and Japan. As the authors note, the process of japanning (imitation lacquer) and the vogue for porcelain had existed prior to the nineteenth century, but it was with the arrival of *HMS Furious* in Edo in August 1858 that the intense influence of Japan on British taste originated.

The context of such an exhibition enabled one to note with a new awareness the effect of Japanese art on a host of British Victorian artists. For example, the background of Frederick Sandys's *Medea* (1868) deploys cranes and dragons; the green kimono in Rossetti's *The Beloved* (1866) provides strong color accent; Moore's *Azaleas* (1868) uses the scattered flower petals and fishbowl for aesthetic effect, as does his *A Venus* (1869) with its vases and flowers. The work of an artist not associated with Japonisme, for example Frederic Leighton's *Mother and Child* (1865), partakes of such influence with its gilt screen of cranes, their legs and feathers providing a powerful diagonal against the horizontality of the principal figure. A strong feature of the exhibition was its emphasis on Victorian architecture and design, including works by Burges, Godwin, Nesfield, and Jeckyll.

The inclusion of sixteen works by Whistler was a great advantage and naturally crucial, but in these contexts such familiar works as *The Little White Girl* (1864) or *Old Battersea Bridge* (1875) gained a striking resonance. To associate Whistler with artists such as Moore is predictable, but the exhibition also included canvases by Poynter, Grimshaw, Greiffenhagen, Orchardson, and Kate Hayllar, which extended the influence of Japonisme by presenting either non-canonical artists or works by those associated with different movements. The subdivision of the exhibition into fourteen inter-related but discrete sections was a major advantage in assessing the trajectory of the influence of Japonisme. The large political context of the debate about Eurocentrism, initiated by Edward Said's *Orientalism* in 1978, is made explicit in this exhibition. It is within these parameters that such exhibitions must advance in the 1990s if they wish to challenge comparison with *Japan and Britain*.

Another exhibition with a correspondingly incisive focus was *Pre-Raphaelite Sculpture: Nature and Imagination in British Sculpture 1848–1914*, at Birmingham City Museum and Art Gallery after a venue at the Matthiesen Gallery in London (October 1991–March 1992). Like *Japan and Britain*, this exhibition derives from the scholarship of the 1980s devoted to Victorian sculpture, such as Dorment's *Alfred Gilbert* (1985), Manning's *Marble and Bronze* [on Hamo Thornycroft] (1982), Read's *Victorian Sculpture* (1982), and Beattie's *The New Sculpture* (1983). The catalogue for the exhibition (London: Lund Humphries, 1991) includes essays by Benedict Read, Christian, Leonée Ormond, and Katharine Macdonald, with emphasis on the careers of Thomas Woolner and Alexander Munro.

There was a genuine advantage to viewing the exhibition in Birmingham, since the sculpture was exhibited in two rooms, one of which contains some of Birmingham's most celebrated Pre-Raphaelite canvases by Hughes, Hunt, Millais, Rossetti, Brown, Brett, and Brune-Jones. Locating this sculpture in the PRB picture gallery provoked central questions about the nature of Pre-Raphaelite influence in sculpture and its relationship with painting. Apart from the canvases, the effect of the exhibition would surely have been quite different — arid, dated, and peripheral. In Birmingham its significance could be evaluated and its importance assessed. The inclusion of twenty-two works by Munro and thirty-eight by Woolner, virtual mini-exhibitions within the larger one, made it the most important such show in this century.

Throughout the catalogue essays, the two elements of this sculpture denominated Pre-Raphaelite are its attention to detail and its poetic truth of imagination. Woolner, of course, was one of the seven original PRB members, and there is no denying that, as Read notes, much of his work exhibits an "almost infinitesimal truth to nature" (26). In Woolner's portraits especially, there is "a relentless truth to nature" (8). The difficulty of the classification "Pre-Raphaelite sculpture," however, rests on the danger, as Read points out, of "pressing too far in expanding the field of Pre-Raphaelite sculpture" (9). It is here that the exhibition presented its greatest problem. One can make the term Pre-Raphaelite so broad as to include works merely inspired by PRB examples, at which point the category disintegrates. The inclusion of a bronze (post 1900) by Sargent derived from Rossetti's *How They Met Themselves*, for instance, albeit surprising, blurs the category itself. Nor is it sufficient to regard Gilbert's *St. George* (1898–99) as a subject inspired by Burne-Jones *and therefore* Pre-Raphaelite. While it partakes of Burne-Jones's chivalric medievalism, its technique cannot be credited with a close affiliation, even if Gilbert's "colouristic tendencies" (86), as John Christian notes, reflect Gilbert's contact with Burne-Jones. Is Pre-Raphaelitism in sculpture a question of subject or of technique or of both? Medievalism was so pervasive in Victorian culture (again see Girouard) that such subject matter does not seem a sufficient basis for expanding the category Pre-Raphaelite. It is worth noting that Gilbert was the only sculptor included in the 1978 *Victorian High Renaissance* exhibition, where his affiliation with an alternative Victorian category was advanced.

The strongest case for PRB sculpture is of course made by Woolner, whose work dominates the exhibition and to whom three catalogue essays are devoted. Read's essay is an excellent survey of Woolner's career, for his focus on detail is unquestionably at one with that of his painting comrades-in-arms: bulging arteries, bags under the eyes, and crows' feet contribute an astonishing realism to his work, as in the bronzes of James Macarthur (1854) or Browning (1856). Woolner completed at least ninety-six portraits during his career, in addition to "ideal" works derived from mythology or history, although the latter were never so lucrative as portraits. These "ideal" conceptions, presumably because size precluded their inclusion, were under-represented in the exhibition, although one wonders why Woolner's *Godiva* at Coventry could not have been transported.

Alexander Munro's work was also a major focus of the exhibition. Munro was a close associate of Arthur Hughes, and he served as the model for *April Love*; it was supposedly Munro who passed on the meaning of the initials PRB to Angus Reach, who proceeded to publish it. In his early career, Munro came under the influence of Flaxman, and there is in all his work a restraint not demonstrated by Woolner. His famous *Paolo and Francesca*

(1852) suggests Rossetti's watercolor, but it is not known whose was the inspiration for the pose. While it and his great marble of Josephine Butler (1855) exhibit detail, in the work of the 1850s it is not the relentless detail of Woolner because moderated by the influence of Flaxman. In later portraits, such as that of William Henry Hunt from 1861, a sharper realism emerges.

As good as are many of the entries and essays in the catalogue, much of it betrays an emphasis on what the art is *of* rather than what it is *about*. The concentration on portraits, for instance, brings to mind Victorian hero-worship and the effect of Carlyle's writings, but only Read (24) mentions this aspect, which merited an essay in itself. Likewise, the *a priori* category of "detail" in PRB sculpture might have been differentiated from the emphasis on detail in the New Sculpture. While the Gothic appears elusively in several passages, an entire essay might be devoted to this subject, linking the sculpture with architecture in a more decisive manner. One might usefully ask what is gender-inflected about the choice of subjects, with so much emphasis on public men. There will probably not be another exhibition with such a focus for some time, and undoubtedly Munro and Woolner will never be accorded separate exhibits, so *Pre-Raphaelite Sculpture* will remain important as much for the problems it raised as for the works it included. If there are monographs on sculptors like Gilbert and Thornycroft, however, there is a need for one devoted to Woolner, whose importance is at least as great.

A final exhibition concentrating on a very tight focus yielded brilliant results, *John Singer Sargent's El Jaleo* at the National Gallery of Art in Washington (March 1 through August 2, 1992), with a superb catalogue (Washington: National Gallery of Art, 1992). As Nicolai Cikovsky observes: "There have been no major exhibitions on the subject of hispanism [the term for the fascination with Spain] as there have been several on the influence of Japan, nor any comprehensive accounts of its depth and scope" (13). As part of its series of Focus Exhibitions, the Gallery organized an absorbing exhibition around Sargent's masterpiece, exhibited at the Salon in 1882 and an overnight sensation. Adding to the sensation of the Washington show was the exhibition of *Spanish Dancer*, a full-length study for the central gypsy figure in *El Jaleo*, rediscovered in Grenoble in 1988. The vogue of *espagnolisme* was extensive, producing Merimée's *Carmen* in 1847 and earlier Hugo's *Ernani* (1830) and *Ruy Blas* (1832), and of course Byron's *Don Juan* is the most conspicuous memorial to hispanism in the early nineteenth century in England, propelled by the Peninsular War of 1808–1813. Manet, Cassatt, Eakins, and Whistler, as well as Sargent, were profoundly moved by Spanish painting, particularly by Velázquez. The Englishman Richard Ford's *Handbook for Travellers in Spain* (1845) became the bible of Victorian travellers to the Iberian peninsula.

The National Gallery's installation was superb, confined to two large galleries and including virtually every sketch and drawing related to Sargent's interest in Spanish dance during the 1879–1880 excursion to Spain. Of particular interest were the oil studies for *The Spanish Dance* of 1880, where Sargent manipulates flecks of paint to create a mysterious atmosphere of impassioned couples against a night sky. It is possible that Whistler's nocturnes influenced Sargent in this attraction to such effects. The rediscovered *Spanish Dancer* exhibits Sargent's strong attraction to Velázquez as he envelops the dancer in gray areas.

El Jaleo [the name means ruckus or uproar] is, as Mary Volk asserts in her exceptional essay, Sargent's "first undisputed materpiece" (21), with its bravura, loose brushstrokes reinforcing the dynamism of the gypsy flamenco dancer. The work is startling because it demonstrates Sargent's movement away from the tightly controlled brushwork that constituted his study at the École des Beaux-Arts. As Volk observes: "Instead of closing and smoothing the edges of objects . . . Sargent left them irregular" to emphasize "the sensation of dynamic transitory effect inherent to the subject the painting presents" (52–53). Every exhibit in the show is included in color in the catalogue, making the book indispensable as a basis for examining *espagnolisme* in European culture. Above all, the concentration on a single masterpiece and its attendant sketches, drawings, and sources demonstrates the great value of a series such as the Focus Exhibitions at the National Gallery. There can be little doubt that study of Sargent and Whistler will receive a genuinely new impetus from this splendid exhibition.

Several of the sculptures in the PRB exhibition at Birmingham involved Arthurian themes, which are the focus for Muriel Whitaker's *Legends of King Arthur in Art* (Woodbridge, Suffolk: Boydell and Brewer, 1990). Of the book's thirteen chapters, nearly half are devoted to the nineteenth century or later, important for Victorianists interested in medievalism, art illustration, and architecture. Whitaker's study is a thorough analysis of the ramifications of the Arthurian legend in Victorian culture, nowhere more so than in the chapter focusing on "the art of moral buildings," in which she investigates the Westminster competition, concentrating on the influence of Pugin and William Dyce. As she observes, "Dyce's Robing Room programme had great significance. It affirmed that Arthurian chivalry could provide valid models for Victorian society" (183). Whitaker relates this decoration to other practices of the same kind, including the Oxford Union mural project of the young PRBs and Philip Webb's Red House.

One of the strongest parts of Whitaker's study is its reinvestigation of the Tristan stained glass for Harden Grange executed by Morris and Company in 1862 (now preserved at Bradford and all reproduced in color here). This project involved Hughes, Rossetti, Burne-Jones, and Madox Brown, and because it is not frequently studied, Whitaker's examination is particularly significant. Whitaker discusses the influence of Tennyson on artists, noting that "between 1860 and 1869 alone fifty or sixty paintings on Arthurian subjects were exhibited and though some derive from Malory, Tennyson's influence in popularising the material was paramount" (214). Works by Rossetti, Watts, Archer, Paton, Siddal, Waterhouse, and Victorian photographers such as Robinson and Cameron are juxtaposed. Even if this material is familiar, Whitaker manages to find new dimensions, as in her analysis of Sandys's *Vivien* (1863), where she notes that every detail signifying an enchantress may also indicate the Virgin Mary. Several sculptures, by Woolner and Reynolds-Stephens, are also studied.

A particularly interesting chapter is devoted to Arthurian motifs in American and Canadian art. Her discussion of artists such as Homer Watson and architects such as Ralph Adam Cram, who designed many buildings at Princeton, is unusual and original, the only caveat being that this part of the book needed many more illustrations. Whitaker alludes to the survival of chivalric images in memorials of the Boer War and World War I, territory previously canvassed by Girouard. Whitaker's study with its thorough bibliography is to be recommended for its Anglo-American focus, its concentration on the unexpected, and the color plates of such rarely-reproduced items as the Bradford Tristan panels.

If Whitaker's proposition is to emphasize the medievalizing and Gothic dimension of Victorian culture, Richard Jenkyns in *Dignity and Decadence* (London: HarperCollins, 1991) intends to correct a concentration on medievalism by his own focus on the dimensions of Victorian classicism: architectural, sculptural, pictorial, even musical. These chapters originated as lectures at the University of Hull, and Jenkyns takes pride in asserting that he has "not sought wholly to disguise the book's origins" (ix). Indeed. The result is a book replete with outrageous assertions and superficial, glancing comments, facile readings guaranteed to sound authoritative for the moment as the slides click forward. Throughout the book, Jenkyns constantly refers to artists and writers as practicing a "game" (for example, 263, 272, 275, 282, 289), but the persistently flippant tone and the dismissive asides render Jenkyns himself the genuine gamester. If the book has a merit, it is to emphasize the importance of the classical for Victorian culture; the many black and white photographs, especially of buildings not often reproduced, provide a good compendium. Three or four gins later, this is all amusing and engaging, but in sober light it is anything but. While seeking to instantiate the importance of classicism, Jenkyns repeatedly denigrates it, especially its pictorial manifestation in the work of Leighton, Poynter, Waterhouse, and Alma-Tadema. This kind of smug and self-satisfied leering and bashing ought to have gone out with the Edwardians and Georgians.

Jenkyns opens his study with a chapter on the Victorian metier, but already the wildly inaccurate opinions are flying. He can assert that Kenelm Digby's *Broad Stone of Honour* "had no real importance" (18) and that Tennyson was but "lightly" touched by the "anaemic romanticism" of the "limp cult of knightliness" (18). To make such an assertion after Girouard's work or that of Joanna Banham in *William Morris and the Middle Ages* (1984) is absurd: one does not need to overthrow the medieval to establish the classical. Jenkyns blithely goes on to state that in the nineteenth century "Britain develops from oligarchy to representative democracy, a profound transformation achieved with remarkably little fuss" (34). Oh really? This blindness to history continues: "The Greeks and Romans, despite brilliant science and mathematics, did not produce a technological revolution" (39). But this casual attitude to history is merely preparation for what follows.

The first part of the chapter dealing with sculpture usefully emphasizes the influence of Flaxman (note the equivalent significance in the study of Munro in *Pre-Raphaelite Sculpture*, although Munro is not discussed by Jenkyns). However, the ensuing discussion of Pygmalion contains such insights as "the birch tree [in Millais's *The Knight-Errant*] is beautifully painted" albeit the canvas is "very large and remarkably embarrassing" (118), which scarcely qualifies as analysis. Burne-Jones's two series on the Pygmalion theme are addressed in one paragraph, with no concern that the artist painted the theme twice.

Jenkyns's discussion of Victorian neoclassical (High Renaissance) painting, however, is the epitome of his flippant, dismissive attitude. A sampling of opinions will demonstrate this tenor:

> This is a scene of high tragedy — literally, indeed, since Andromache is lifted above the onlookers. (212, on Leighton's *Captive Andromache*)
> We are supposed to think that [the wild beasts] have been tamed by the bride's beauty and chastity; it is unfortunate that they seem merely to be stuffed. (203, on Leighton's *The Syracusan Bride*)
> In England a run-of-the-mill imitator [of Alma-Tadema] who achieved great popular success was Sir Edward Poynter. (245)
> A talented painter without strong individuality. . . . His *Mariamne* . . . offered another opportunity to depict a woman in chains. (281, 283, on Waterhouse)
> A fantasy of girlish lust. (285, on Draper's *Ulysses and the Sirens*)
> Rather as Regent Street separates Mayfair from Soho without quite having the character of either, so it is tempting to see Watts as the point where the artistic establishment and bohemia met. (295)

The one artist who escapes this treatment is Albert Moore, about whom Jenkyns has some useful observations, for example that his "handling is almost anti-sculptural" (271) despite his influence by Greek statuary. But this calibre of observation is lost amid the mockery of Victorian classical art. No attempt is made to link such art with gender studies or Victorian legislation. In addition, the book is devoid of theory: for example, Jenkyns can refer to gazes (138) without the slightest recognition of the theory of the gaze (Lacan, Mulvey, and others). At the conclusion of his book Jenkyns notes "how mockery of the Victorians has modulated into a humorous appreciation of period charm. Humour is indeed the key" (335).

But while such "humour" may be fleetingly engaging to undergraduates and popular audiences, it is not a substitute for analysis and rigor. If Jenkyns wishes to demonstrate the pervasive influence of the classical in Victorian culture, it does little good to denigrate, mock, and dismiss the very manifestations of that movement. In its alignment of painting, sculpture, and architecture, the book (via its illustrations) demonstrates this manifestation, but the analyses do not represent current evaluations of the movement. (See, for instance, John Christian's catalogue for the exhibition *Victorian Dreamers*, Tokyo 1989; or the catalogue for *Victorian High Renaissance*, Manchester 1978; or the monograph *Lord Leighton* by Richard and Leonée Ormond, 1975.)

Equally problematic as Jenkyns's discussion is that of Lynne Pearce in *Woman/Image/Text: Readings in Pre-Raphaelite Art and Literature* (Toronto: U of Toronto P, 1991), a series of essays focusing on female figures (Beatrice, Mariana, Lady of Shalott, Isabella, Madeline and others) depicted in PRB canvases. In her "Introduction" Pearce sets herself to study discourses of power as inscribed in a number of nineteenth-century canvases, asking usefully: "What can the twentieth-century feminist reader/viewer actually *do* with male-produced nineteenth-century images of women?" (2). Pearce surveys succinctly a number of recent feminist critiques of Victorian art by critics such as Pollock and Nead. The difficulty arises as one reads Pearce's assertion: "As a twentieth-century feminist I feel that I have the capacity to make of a text what I will, while at the same time acknowledging that such readings may wilfully ignore and excuse the patriarchal discourses out of which it was created" (25). This solipsism mars a number of readings which might otherwise be provocative rather than only tendentious.

In her analysis of Rossetti's *Girlhood of Mary Virgin*, Pearce investigates the degree to which a text related to or affixed to a canvas controls interpretation, leaving no sutures for deconstructive readings. The printed text, she argues, if "read *before* the painting itself has been surveyed . . . would . . . control the *order* in which it was to be read" (37), and Pearce concludes "there are few of the *aporia* necessary for a more productive feminist reading" (42). By the second chapter, an analysis of *Beata Beatrix*, however, Pearce's method becomes bizarre as even she begins to recognize: "With a little tortured meditation . . . we have arrived at a point where the twentieth-century feminist reader/viewer can, if she wishes, claim Beatrice as her own'' (56). Unfortunately, this position is maintained by ignoring such evidence as the importance of the *dolce stil nuovo* or Rossetti's translations in the *Early Italian Poets*. By the time Pearce writes of Millais's *Mariana*, she can only conclude that ''her textual self is hard to recover or reclaim for any radical purposes beyond a simple exemplification of her in terms of the prevailing 'myths of sexuality' '' (68), which is to say that unless a canvas can be recuperated by Pearce's strategy, it has little merit. Waterhouse's *Lady of Shalott*, Pearce concludes, ''is not a sensible text for the feminist to fall in love with'' (82), as if this were a legitimate critical standard for assessing a canvas. (Pearce is unaware that Waterhouse painted this subject three times.) Devoting an entire chapter to ''Guenevere,'' Pearce assumes Morris's canvas is of Arthur's Queen rather than of Iseult, when of course this is much disputed, a conflict she dismisses: ''Since sufficient evidence exists for it to be thought of as the former, it has obviously been in my own interest to make that assumption'' (114).

The most startling part of Pearce's work is its conclusion, in which she concedes ''that feminist intervention is, for the most part, limited to a fairly basic sexual political critique,'' since the texts allow ''few 'gaps' into which we can insert ourselves'' (146). Her final position appears to undermine her own project: ''It is now my opinion that 'reading against the grain' of a text cannot ever legitimate reading against its *contexts* . . . we cannot ever override the hierarchy of those discourses (i.e., ignore the 'dominant ideology' present in a text)'' (148). One may well ask, why undertake such an experiment in the first place? Such procrustean practice is doomed to myopia. A number of errors in the text (Wordsworth for Wadsworth, 85; a misattribution, 83; a misspelling of Hardy's *Tess*, 107) do not instill confidence. Most astonishing of all, the one major icon not studied, and the one which would permit the greatest amount of intervention by a feminist critique, is *La Belle Dame sans Merci* (for example, by Waterhouse, Hughes, Crane, Dicksee).

While the number of monographs published recently is few, two might be noted for special significance, the first concerning Thomas Eakins. *Writing About Eakins: The Manuscripts in Charles Bregler's Thomas Eakins Collection* by Kathleen A. Foster and Cheryl Leibold (Philadelphia: U of Pennsylvania P, 1989) is the volume which formed the basis of the exhibition *Thomas Eakins Rediscovered* (December 1991–April 1992) at the Pennsylvania Academy of the Fine Arts. Bregler, a student of Eakins, assembled 1600 items by and concerning the artist, including paintings, oil sketches, photographs, drawings, and hundreds of letters. This archive collected in *Writing About Eakins* is an inventory of the manuscript materials, many relevant to several scandals which marked Eakins's career, particularly the suicide of his niece Ella Crowell, who shot herself in 1897 after studying with Eakins but not before she contended to her parents that Eakins had molested her.

Eakins had already paid a heavy price for his insistence on having his students draw from the nude. In 1886 he had resigned as director of the Pennsylvania Academy because of his position. Subsequently, Eakins's former student and brother-in-law Frank Stephens prompted his dismissal from the Philadelphia Sketch Club. The Bregler Collection contains much valuable correspondence about these disputes, which even involved accusations of "bestiality and incest" (84).

Of particular interest to British Victorianists is the fact that in the two years prior to Ella Crowell's suicide, Eakins's sexual behavior was linked with that of Oscar Wilde, since her accusation of "unnatural sexual excitements" (114) occurred during the period of the Wilde trials in 1895. Foster discusses this affiliation with cautious objectivity, noting that such an invocation "must make us look again at the parade of beautiful male bodies that passed across Eakins's canvases and in front of his camera" (115). As the authors note, Eakins's known relations were heterosexual and "his reportedly happy and stable married life . . . all tend to counterbalance innuendoes of homosexuality. However, the existence of such strong currents of appreciation of both male and female beauty confirms the presence of a powerful sexual awareness in Eakins" (115). The authors note, significantly, that the central question is the role of the artist and his or her estimation by society: "Eakins and Wilde were united by their marginality. . . . In his advocacy of a painter's prerogatives and his willingness to confront popular opinion, Eakins was no less militant than Wilde, and his personal style was no less unconventional and mannered" (116). In appraising Anglo-American artistic relations in the nineteenth century, the issue of the status of the artist remains to be explored, with the Eakins/Wilde analogy one instance of such comparative assessments. This volume is illustrated by fifty photographs, has a biographical index, and much additional material now essential for research on this artist. Monographs written about Eakins prior to the publication of this volume will have to be reconsidered, not only in terms of the appraisal of his life but also of his paintings. By including transcriptions of key documents and summarizing many others, the authors have enabled researchers to have an excellent vade mecum.

There has been no biographical study of Ford Madox Brown since that produced by his grandson, Ford Madox Ford, in 1896, although recent exhibitions (Liverpool 1964; Tate 1984) and the publication of his *Diary* (1981) have provided opportunities to explore his career. There can be no denying Brown's central place in Victorian art, and much was to be hoped from *Ford Madox Brown and the Pre-Raphaelite Circle* by Teresa Newman and Ray Watkinson (London: Chatto and Windus, 1991). While the book is valuable as a modern assessment, it fails to be the major biographical study, the need for which remains. Although the work addresses some new material — such as Brown's poetry (151 ff) or his infatuation with his pupil Marie Spartali (150) — in general the book does not illuminate Brown beyond the material one could assemble from Ford's biography, the *Diary*, and exhibition catalogues.

The authors essentially record the major events of Brown's life, varying the depth of analysis given to his paintings. Their emphasis seems to be on the politics of the Victorian art world, and indeed, considering Brown's many fractious experiences with the establishment, this focus is merited. With the exception of remaining Rossetti's heroic friend, Brown had quarrels with all the circle: Millais (with whom he had little in common), Burne-Jones, Hunt, and of course the loathed Ruskin, who paid him back by discouraging dealers from purchasing Brown's work. As the *Diary* indicates, Brown was an irascible man, given to suspicion and even paranoia. Brown always was an exile in England, not moving there permanently until 1846. In addition, his continental training set him apart from his contemporaries.

The writers periodically throw some intriguing light on the canvases, for example in their discussion of *The Pretty Baa-Lambs* (58–60) or the influence of Hogarth on *Work* (67) or the evolution of that canvas (119–129). More frequently, however, they tend to ignore key elements of Brown's canvases, such as the fact that *Manfred on the Jungfrau* (1839–40) is an experiment in light or that *Waiting* (1851–54) reflects this same ambition. Although *Carrying Corn* (1854–55) is described as "revolutionary" (82), the authors fail to do justice to Brown's landscapes.

The genuine strength of the book is its superb collection of black and white and some color plates, 187 in all, an archive of material, much of it rarely or never reproduced. Plates 90 through 95 demonstrate Brown's intense involvement with Morris, Marshall Faulkner & Company from its founding in 1861. There is genuine frustration in the fact, unfortunately, that nowhere in the book are dimensions of pictures given, which means that one has to consult the Liverpool, Tate, or even earlier catalogues for such information. The picture credits, moreover, are hopelessly confused (no credits at all for plates 140–187), therefore making it difficult to trace the location of the canvases except by reference to exhibition catalogues. The absence of a bibliography is a fault, since source material must be gleaned from notes. A complete bibliography of material as well as current critical appraisals (see this reviewer's essay in *Contemporary Literature* 30: 224–39) would have provided the necessary basis for future research. As it stands, *Ford Madox Brown and the Pre-Raphaelite Circle* is a competent study but not a definitive monograph, valuable for its plates but incomplete in its assessments.

Considering the lacunae of monographs about specific artists, it is hoped that the production of monographs about many important figures (Merritt, Poynter, Rae, to name a few) will be part of future research projects. The

Eakins/Wilde question indicates the value of additional explorations of Anglo-American artistic relations. Furthermore, as the example of Jenkyns's study illustrates, there is much room for application of theory to the appraisal of artistic discourses during the Victorian period.

University of Tulsa

ROBERT AND ELIZABETH BARRETT BROWNING: AN ANNOTATED BIBLIOGRAPHY FOR 1990

By Sandra M. Donaldson

The following abbreviations appear in this year's bibliography:

BIS   *Browning Institute Studies*
BSN   *Browning Society Notes*
DAI   *Dissertation Abstracts International*
SBHC   *Studies in Browning and His Circle*
TLS   *Times Literary Supplement*
VIJ   *Victorians Institute Journal*
VN   *Victorian Newsletter*
VP   *Victorian Poetry*
VR   *Victorian Review*
VS   *Victorian Studies*

An asterisk* indicates that we have not seen the item or have seen only a clipping or abstract. Cross references with citation numbers between 51 and 70 followed by a colon (e.g., C68:) refer to William S. Peterson's *Robert and Elizabeth Barrett Browning: An Annotated Bibliography, 1951–1970*, New York: The Browning Institute, 1974; higher numbers refer to *Robert Browning: A Bibliography 1830–1950*, compiled by L. N. Broughton, C. S. Northup, and Robert Pearsall, Ithaca: Cornell UP, 1953.

Readers are encouraged to send abstracts or offprints to Sandra Donaldson, Department of English/7209, University of North Dakota, Grand Forks, ND 58202. I especially need articles that have appeared in less familiar journals.

A. Primary Works

A90:1. Forster, Margaret, ed. and introduction. *Elizabeth Barrett Browning: Selected Poems*. [See A88:4.] ¶Rev. by Alice Falk, *VS* 33(1990):328–30; Rupert Christiansen, *The Listener* 23 June 1988:32.

A90:2. Jack, Ian, and Rowena Fowler, eds. *The Poetical Works of Robert Browning, Volume 3. Bells and Pomegranates I–VI*. [See A88:5.] ¶Rev. by Stefan Hawlin, *Review of English Studies* 41(1990):134–36; Lynne Pearce, *Year's Work in English Studies* 69(1988):419.

A90:3. Karlin, Daniel, ed. and introduction. *Robert Browning and Elizabeth Barrett: The Courtship Correspondence, 1845–1846, A Selection*. [See A89:4.] ¶Rev. by Deirdre David, *VS* 34(1990):112–13; Chris Jones, *Notes and Queries* 37(March 1990):108–9; Kenneth M. McKay, *Modern Language Review* 85(1990):702–3.

A90:4. Kelley, Philip, and Ronald Hudson, eds. *The Brownings' Correspondence*, Volume 4. [See A86:5.] ¶Rev. by Philip Drew, *Yearbook of English Studies* 20(1990):301–2.

A90:5. Kelley, Philip, and Ronald Hudson, eds. *The Brownings' Correspondence*, Volume 5. [See A87:4.] ¶Rev. by Stefan Hawlin, *Review of English Studies* 41(1990):412–13.

A90:6. Kelley, Philip, and Ronald Hudson, eds. *The Brownings' Correspondence*, Volume 6. [See A88:8.] ¶Rev. by Stefan Hawlin, *Review of English Studies* 41(1990):412–13; Lynne Pearce, *Year's Work in English Studies* 69(1988):420; Suzanne Raitt, *TLS* 4 May 1990:470.

A90:7. Kelley, Philip, and Ronald Hudson, eds. *The Brownings' Correspondence*, Volume 7. [See A89:7.] ¶Rev. by Danny Karlin, *London Review of Books* 11 January 1990:17–18; Suzanne Raitt, *TLS* 4 May 1990:470.

A90:8. Kelley, Philip, and Ronald Hudson, eds. *The Brownings' Correspondence*, Volume 8: October 1843–May 1844. Winfield, KS: Wedgestone P, 1990. xii + 447 pp.

A90:9. King, Roma A., Jr., and Susan Crowl, eds. *The Ring and the Book, Books V–VIII*. Volume VIII of *The Complete Works of Robert Browning with Variant Readings & Annotations*. Ed. Jack W. Herring, et al. [See A89:9.] ¶Rev. by Stefan Hawlin, *Review of English Studies* 41(1990):134; John Bayley, *London Review of Books* 4 August 1988:20–21.

*A90:10. Reynolds, M[argaret] L. "*Aurora Leigh* by Elizabeth Barrett Browning: An Edition with Textual Variants, Explanatory Annotation and Critical Introduction." *Index to Theses with Abstracts Accepted for Higher Degrees by the Universities of Great Britain and Ireland and the Council for National Academic Awards* 39:0196. London, Birkbeck College [1986].

A90:11. Stack, V. E., ed. *The Love Letters of Robert Browning and Elizabeth Barrett*. [See A87:9.] ¶Rev. by *Listener* 17 March 1988:22.

B. *Reference and Bibliographical Works and Exhibitions*

B90:1. Champeau, Donesse. "Robert and Elizabeth Barrett Browning: An Annotated Bibliography for 1988." *BIS* 18(1990):157–71.

B90:2. Cohen, Edward H., ed. "Brownings," "Browning, E.," and "Browning, R." in "Victorian Bibliography for 1989." *VS* 33(1990):772–75.

B90:3. Drew, Philip. *An Annotated Critical Bibliography of Robert Browning*. Hemel Hempstead: Harvester Wheatsheaf, 1990. xxvii + 106 pp. ¶Selects and annotates editions of poems, bibliographical aids, and biographies and criticism on RB. Criticism includes general works (on technique, subject, and reputation), particular (organized by major work or decade), and collections. A short section on letters follows. Selection criteria are that works be helpful and "first-rate"; undergraduates are intended audience. Detailed studies of single poems are numerous, but many are "pedestrian and ill-written" and therefore not included; a broader critical estimate of RB's work is needed. Literary critics who are not RB specialists tend to neglect his work.

B90:4. Maynard, John. "Guide to the Year's Work in Victorian Poetry: 1989: Robert Browning." *VP* 28(1990):193–201.

B90:5. Mermin, Dorothy. "Guide to the Year's Work in Victorian Poetry: 1989: Elizabeth Barrett Browning." *VP* 28(1990):190–93.

C. *Biography, Criticism, and Miscellaneous*

C90:1. Anderson, Amanda Sara. "Tainted Souls and Painted Faces: The Rhetoric of Fallenness in Victorian Literature." *DAI* 50.11(1990):3597A. Cornell University, 1989. ¶Argues that representations of fallen women and prostitutes express social attitudes as well as offer structural cues for reading character. Marian Earle's character heightens the tensions of genre in EBB's *Aurora Leigh*.

C90:2. Anderson, John Dennis. "Performing Consciousness in the Novel of Voices." *DAI* 51.2(1990):342A. University of Texas at Austin, 1990. Locates the beginning of the modernist novel of multiple first-person narratives in RB's *The Ring and the Book*.

C90:3. Barker, Nicolas, and John Collins. *A Sequel to An Enquiry into the Nature of Certain Nineteenth Century Pamphlets by John Carter and Graham Pollard. The Forgeries of H. Buxton Forman & T. J. Wise Re-examined*. London and Berkeley: Scolar P, 1983. 394 pp. ¶Follows leads from Carter and Pollard (see below) regarding the forgeries of T. J. Wise, including the "Reading" edition of EBB's *Sonnets from the Portuguese*, and examines the role played by Forman and his son Maurice. Rev. by John Pafford, *Notes and Queries* March 1990:122–24.

C90:4. Blondel, Jacques. "Du periple des sots à la quête de 'Childe Roland'." *Le Voyage Romantique et ses Reécritures*, ed. Christian La Cassagnère. N.s. 26. Centre du Romantisme Anglais. Clermont-Ferrand (France): Association des Publications de la Faculté des Lettres et Sciences Humaines, 1987. 119–28. ¶Compares Satan's passage through the "Paradise of Fools" in book 3 of Milton's *Paradise Lost* with the quest in RB's "Childe Roland to the Dark Tower Came." Both poets use the grotesque, but whereas Milton's allegory is a parody, RB's poem is a symbolic autobiography, a search for identity in the face of modern despair. Childe Roland's non-voyage is a heroic refusal; the knight-poet endures. In French.

C90:5. Bornstein, George. *Poetic Remaking: The Art of Browning, Yeats and Pound.* [See C88:6.] ¶Rev. by Lionel Kelly, *Year's Work in English Studies* 69(1988):608.

C90:6. Brady, Ann P. *Pompilia: A Feminist Reading of Robert Browning's "The Ring and the Book".* [See C88:8.] ¶Rev. by Alice Falk, *VS* 33(1990):328–30.

C90:7. Bristow, Joseph, and Paul Kenny, eds. *BSN* 17.1–3(1987/88). [See C88:31 & 39.] ¶Rev. by Lynne Pearce, *Year's Work in English Studies* 69(1988):418–19.

C90:8. Byrd, Deborah. "Combating an Alien Tyranny: Elizabeth Barrett Browning's Evolution as a Feminist Poet." *Courage and Tools: The Florence Howe Award for Feminist Scholarship 1974–1989.* Ed. Joanne Glasgow and Angela Ingram. New York: Modern Language Association of America, 1990. 203–17. ¶Reprint of C87:5, with afterword.

C90:9. Calcraft, R. P. "Jorge Guillén's Homage to the Brownings." *BSN* 20.2(1990):46–47. ¶Introduces a printing of "Al Margen de los Browning: El Amor Valeroso" by Spanish poet Jorge Guillén.

C90:10. Carter, John, and Graham Pollard. *An Enquiry into the Nature of Certain Nineteenth Century Pamphlets.* 2nd edition. Ed. Nicolas Barker and John Collins. London and Berkeley: Scolar P, 1983. 10 + xii + 400 + 41 pp. ¶Corrected reprint of C4118 (1934), including a transcription of marginalia and annotations, as well as an epilogue. See above, Barker and Collins. Rev. by John Pafford, *Notes and Queries* March 1990:122–24.

C90:11. Cervo, Nathan. "Sara Coleridge: The Gigadibs Complex." *VN* 78(Fall 1990):3–9. ¶Draws connections between Sara Coleridge's life and ideas about faith in her *Memoirs and Letters* and the figure of Gigadibs in RB's "Bishop Blougram's Apology," particularly his insistence on "pure faith." She read, translated, and wrote about German philosophers; the writings of her father, Samuel Taylor Coleridge; and the Tractarians, Newman, and other ecclesiastical writers.

C90:12. Chamberlain, Harriet Sue. "Existential Perspectives and Victorian Literature: Browning, Arnold, and Hopkins." *DAI* 50.12(1990):3960A. University of California at Santa Cruz, 1989. ¶Applies concepts from existential philosophy and psychology to RB's "Childe Roland to the Dark Tower Came," especially Martin Heidegger's paradigm for authentic being. These poets relinquish self-deception, sustain anxiety, and acknowledge the joys and risks accompanying freedom.

C90:13. Chappell, M. Debnam. "Women Perceived and Women Perceiving: Characterizations of Women and Womanhood in Robert Browning's 'The Ring and the Book'." *DAI* 50.9(1990):2903A–2904A. New York University, 1989. ¶Identifies the relation of the sexes as the central subject of RB's poem. A basic human experience, this relationship is both ordinary and grand.

C90:14. Cheskin, Arnold. " ' 'Tis Only the Coat of a Page to Borrow': Robert Browning's Hebraic Borrowings and Concealments for 'Jochanan Hakkadosh'." *BSN* 20.1(1990):31–38. ¶Details RB's borrowings from Rev. B. Gerrans's translation of *Travels of Rabbi Benjamin* (1784) to explain the ungrammatical Hebrew and other Hebraic references in the poem. The "missionizing theology" in his source, however, is not congruent with RB's mature respect for Jewish tradition.

C90:15. Cooper, Helen. *Elizabeth Barrett Browning, Woman and Artist.* [See C88:13.] ¶Rev. by Thomas J. Collins, *Nineteenth-Century Literature* 44(1990):560–63; Alice Falk, *VS* 33(1990):328–30; Lynne Pearce, *Year's Work in English Studies* 69(1988):418; Richard Tobias, *English Language Notes* 28(September 1990):79–81; Joyce Zonana, *Tulsa Studies in Women's Literature* 9(1990):160–63.

C90:16. Cronin, Richard. *Colour and Experience in Nineteenth-Century Poetry.* Macmillan P, 1988. 81–167. ¶Examines poetic use of words for color as they merge with value and suggest metaphor. RB uses color rather than pure white light in his need to not look directly; his work is limned by the contests of dualism, "the defining condition of human experience"; and he studies optics (the atmosphere) and chemistry (the spectroscope). The colors he uses in *The Ring and the Book* and other poems are white (good), black (evil), and red (human experience). Rev. by Lynne Pearce, *Year's Work in English Studies* 69(1988):412.

C90:17. Dally, Peter. *Elizabeth Barrett Browning: A Psychological Portrait.* [See C89:20.] ¶Rev. by Kenneth Millard, *TLS* 30 March 1990:354.

C90:18. David, Deirdre. *Intellectual Women and Victorian Patriarchy: Harried Martineau, Elizabeth Barrett Browning, George Eliot.* [See C87:11.] ¶Rev. by Katharine M. Rogers, *Signs* 9(1990):878–80.

C90:19. David, Deirdre. "The Old Right and the New Jerusalem: Elizabeth Barrett Browning's Intellectual Practice." *Intellectuals: Aesthetics, Politics,*

Academics. Ed. Bruce Robbins. Cultural Politics 2. Minneapolis: U of Minnesota P, 1990. 201–23. ¶Extends her discussion in C87:11, examining the contradictory aspects of EBB's intellectual production: her political writings seem at odds with "an increasingly secularized and materialistic society," they denounce "English middle-class liberalism and glorify France's Second Empire," and she advocates political conservatism and even patriarchal politics.

C90:20. Desaulniers, Mary. "Names and Usury: An Economy of Reading in *The Ring and the Book.*" *Nineteenth-Century Literature* 45.3(1990):317–38. ¶Reads the ring trope in RB's poem as its being a commodity and thus associated with money and value, which Guido connects with names and therefore language. The ring then relates more than just truth and illusion; it connects reading and words. In the course of the poem RB reverses sign and signified, making an arc, a wholeness.

C90:21. Dillon, Steven C. "Browning and the Figure of Life." *Texas Studies in Literature and Language* 32.2(1990):169–86. ¶Argues that the idea of life in RB's poetry often appears in relationship to the figure of death, and its location is strange. A "humanistic, 'naive' interpretation and a skeptical, demystifying reading" are both needed. Deconstruction, which "handles margins and oppositional reversals," illuminates readings of RB's poems. In contrast to thin Shelleyan life, RB doubles life with his complex figures.

C90:22. Duban, James, and William J. Scheick. "The Dramatis Personae of Robert Browning and Herman Melville." *Criticism* 32(Spring 1990):221–40. ¶Examine asymmetry and disorder; hesitation, ellipsis, and evasion; and betraying verbal traces in the narrative voices in Melville and RB, focusing on *Billy Budd* and "Pictor Ignotus." These techniques signal readers that the narrators are unreliable, that their words are "poetical, self-referential projections."

C90:23. Dupras, Joseph. "Dispatching 'Porphyria's Lover'." *Conversations: Contemporary Critical Theory and the Teaching of Literature*, ed. Charles Moran and Elizabeth F. Penfield. Urbana: National Council of Teachers of English, 1990. 179–86.¶Describes "a pedagogical 'texticide' " committed in teaching RB's poem and offers better approaches to teaching it than by explication: examining the interpretive process itself, reading aloud, and allowing the text to continue to perplex.

C90:24. Dupras, Joseph. "The Word's Dispersion: Two Letters and a Parchment in Browning's Poetry." *BIS* 18(1990):95–111. ¶Reads "An Epistle of Karshish," "Cleon," and "A Death in the Desert" for ways RB presents the philological and interpretive changes happening within Christianity and also for ways of reading and writing.

C90:25. Duvall, Scott. "The Importance of Collecting Presentation and Inscribed Copies: An Example From the Browning Books in BYU's Victorian

Collection.'' *The Best for the Patron: Proceedings of the Research Forum, Academic Library Section, Mountain Plains Library Association*, ed. Randy J. Olsen and Blaine H. Hall. Emporia, KS: University Press, 1990. 17–30. ¶Uses a selection from Brigham Young University's collection of first editions of RB's and EBB's works to demonstrate the usefulness of doing research on inscriptions. They offer knowledge not often found otherwise. Appendix describes the 25 books of RB's and 13 of EBB's in the University's holdings.

C90:26. Edmond, Rod. '' 'A printing woman who has lost her place': Elizabeth Barrett Browning's *Aurora Leigh*.'' *Affairs of the Hearth: Victorian Narrative Poetry and the Ideology of the Domestic*. [See C88:18.] ¶Rev. by Thomas J. Collins, *VS* 33(1990):679; Lynne Pearce, *Year's Work in English Studies* 69(1988):412; Marion Shaw, *Review of English Studies* 41(1990):414–15.

C90:27. Elmore, Phyllis Lavonia Pearson. ''Elizabeth Barrett Browning: Argumentative Discourse in 'Sonnets from the Portuguese'.'' *DAI* 51.3(1990):861A. Texas Woman's University, 1989. ¶Applies Aristotelian and classical rhetorical theory to EBB's sonnet cycle, showing her use of argumentative strategy and the poems' toughmindedness.

C90:28. Faas, Ekbert. *Retreat into the Mind: Victorian Poetry and the Rise of Psychiatry*. [See C89:25.] ¶Rev. by Thomas J. Collins, *VS* 33(1990):678.

C90.29. Forster, Margaret. *Elizabeth Barrett Browning: A Biography*. [See C88.21.] ¶Rev. by Rupert Christiansen, *The Listener* 23 June 1988:32; Deirdre David, *VS* 34(Autumn 1990):112–13; Lynne Pearce, *Year's Work in English Studies* 69(1988):418.

C90:30. Forster, Margaret. *Elizabeth Barrett Browning: The Life and Loves of a Poet*. New York: St. Martin's P, 1990. 416 pp. ¶Paperback reprint of above [C88.21].

C90:31. Forster, Margaret. *Lady's Maid*. London: Chatto & Windus, 1990. 536 pp. ¶Fictionalizes the life of Elizabeth Wilson, EBB's maid. Rev. by Nicola Beauman, *Spectator* 7 July 1990:31; Barbara Hardy, *TLS* 20 July 1990:781; Danny Karlin, *London Review of Books* 27 September 1990:20; *Kirkus Reviews* 15 December 1990:1694–95; Anne Smith, *The Listener* 12 July 1990:29.

C90:32. Fowler, Rowena. ''William Rothenstein Reads Browning.'' *BIS* 18(1990):1–14. ¶Examines some of the few pictures of or about RB's works, those by Rothenstein, especially ''The Browning Readers.'' The painter does not imagine anecdotal or picturesque subjects of the poems but instead creates ''the formal and visual equivalent to the psychological and intellectual experience of reading him.''

C90:33. Fredeman, William E. ''Thomas J. Wise's Last Word on the Reading *Sonnets*.'' *Book Collector* 37(1990):422–23. ¶Notes that Wise indirectly acknowledged forging an early copy of EBB's *Sonnets from the Portuguese* when he listed in a volume of the *Ashley Library Catalogue* a gift to him of William Andrews Clark's edition of her poems as "A facsimile of the spurious 'Reading' edition."

C90:34. Freiwald, Bina. "Of Selfsame Desire: Patmore's *Angel in the House.*" *Texas Studies in Language and Literature* 30.4(1988):538–61. ¶Analyzes the textual sexual politics in Coventry Patmore's poem, contrasting it to EBB's *Aurora Leigh,* in which the female subject is present and heroic, not effaced.

C90:35. Gibson, Mary Ellis. "The Criminal Body in Victorian Britain: The Case of *The Ring and the Book.*" *BIS* 18(1990):73–93. ¶Analyzes RB's poem as a text from his culture, despite its excesses, its seeming to be an anomaly, and its historical claims. The poem is embedded in the context of the sensation novel and the social discourse on the criminal body, including interest in trials and morbid anatomy. Its focus on body, text, and trial raises questions about language, truth, and history.

C90:36. Gibson, Mary Ellis. *History and the Prism of Art: Browning's Poetic Experiments.* [See C87:20.] ¶Rev. by Peter A. Dale, *Clio* 19.1(1989):73–76; Philip Drew, *Modern Language Review* 35(1990):928–29.

C90:37. Gray, Donald. "Victorian Comic Verse; or, Snakes in Greenland." *VP* 26(1988):211–30. ¶Examines how in "Fra Lippo Lippi" and "Mr. Sludge, 'The Medium,' " among others, RB uses the tactics of comic poetry and achieves similar effects. Victorian readers likely enjoyed linquistic play, audacity, and variety of sounds and styles; conventional poets used these devices for more transcendental effects than did comic poets.

C90:38. Greenberg, Nathan A. "Browning and *Alcestis.*" *Classical and Modern Literature* 8/9(1989):131–52. ¶Assesses RB's accomplishment as a translator of Euripides' *Alcestis,* which seemed "creative" in his time but anticipated current ways of looking at the play. *Balaustion's Adventure* and "Apollo and the Fates" are treated.

C90:39. Griffiths, Eric. *The Printed Voice of Victorian Poetry.* [See C89:33.] ¶Rev. by Thomas J. Collins, *VS* 33(1990):678–79.

C90:40. Habgood, John S., Archbishop of York. "An Old Friend." *BSN* 20.1(1990):9–12. ¶Observes that RB's dramatic monologues address moral and intellectual issues that trouble us today. He was "a poet for an age of doubt and questioning" whom some saw as a prophet.

C90:41. Harrison, Antony H. " 'Cleon' and Its Contexts." *Victorian Poets and Romantic Poems: Intertextuality and Ideology.* Charlottesville: U of Virginia P, 1990. 44–68. ¶Extends discussion in C81:25 to include besides Arnold's *Empedocles on Etna,* the Spasmodic poets, whose poetic practices RB attacks, defending his own in *Men and Women.* Wordsworth's "Intimations of Immortality" and *The Prelude* also figure in forming RB's response. Rev. by Kathryn Burlinson, *Times Higher Education Supplement* 5 October

1990:19; Hans Ostrom, *VR* 16.2(1990):93–95; W. David Shaw, *Nineteenth-Century Literature* 45(1990):371–74.

C90:42. Harrison, Antony H. "In the Shadow of E.B.B.: Christina Rossetti and Ideological Estrangement." *Victorian Poets and Romantic Poems: Intertextuality and Ideology.* Charlottesville: U of Virginia P, 1990. 108–43. ¶Views EBB as Christina Rossetti's most important female precursor, not competitor. Rossetti admired EBB's outspokenness and reserved for herself a defiant silence. She exercised revisionist appropriation of EBB's work. They both treated power, the image of Eve and motherhood, and love in their poetry. Rossetti was alienated from the dominant value systems and their critiques, whereas EBB sought power and change. Rev. by Kathryn Burlinson, *Times Higher Education Supplement* 5 October 1990:19; Hans Ostrom, *VR* 16.2(1990):93–95.

C90:43. Hawlin, Stefan. "Browning, Shelley and 'On Worming Dogs'." *Essays in Criticism* 40.2(1990):136–55. ¶Discusses how RB in *Men and Women* justifies his aesthetic of dramatic naturalism. "Fra Lippo Lippi," " 'Transcendentalism'," "How It Strikes a Contemporary," and "Protus" follow a pattern of setting up something elevated or significant, which expectation is then undermined by a shift to "a humbler, stouter vision."

C90:44. Hawlin, Stefan. "Browning's 'A Toccata of Galuppi's': How Venice Once Was Dear." *Review of English Studies* 41(1990):496–509. ¶Examines RB's renegotiations of Romantic themes, particularly Keats's questioning of art and reality and his opposing poetry to philosophy, as well as the example of Byron's life in and poetry on Venice. Alfred Domett's "Venice" participates in the construction of RB's scene and poetic voice. The speaker is also Paracelsus reimagined, working through the Promethean questions. Music is the speaker's Grecian Urn.

C90:45. Hawlin, Stefan. "Browning's Voice." *BSN* 20.2(1990):7–21. ¶Describes the "ghosts of personality and voice" that can be discerned from the printed text of RB's poems and letters, then examines "Love in a Life," "A Woman's Last Word," and "Love Among the Ruins."

C90:46. Hawlin, Stefan. "A Note on 'A Toccata of Galuppi's' and Thackeray's 'King Canute'." *VP* 28(1990):147–50. ¶Notes that RB's poem and Thackeray's ballad share verse form, use of the caesura, rhythmic rise and fall, and underlying content. The latter poem employs serious humor.

C90:47. Honan, Park. "Browning and the Lyric Test." *Authors' Lives: On Literary Biography and the Arts of Language.* New York: St. Martin's P, 1990. 159–76. ¶Examines the character lyric, the musical lyric, and the lyric of dramatized thought and feeling, looking at the synthesis of style and subject. RB's experiments indicated a shift in the nineteenth century away "from a closed decorum of style and genre." Disruptions of meter, syntax, and sound are for expressive effect and reflect "a new realism."

C90:48. Honan, Park. "Historical Privilege: Ezra Pound, Robert Browning, and 'Kit Marlowe'." *Authors' Lives: On Literary Biography and the Arts of Language*. New York: St. Martin's P, 1990. 211–19. ¶Suggests that Pound admired RB in part because RB's intimacy with historical facts allowed him to invent in his poetry. His history poems respect verifiable facts but are not built out of them. Instead his immersion in such facts allows him "to explain history by imagining its life and blood."

C90:49. Huston, Nancy. "A Tongue Called Mother." *Raritan* 9.3(1990):99–108. ¶Explores the idea of maternal language and its use by artists. As children we create a family romance in order to reinvent our origins, "to transform a creation of the body into a creation of the mind." Women writers, among them EBB, often have difficulty reconciling motherhood and artistic creativity. EBB raises the question in the "superb poetry" of *Aurora Leigh*; by traveling and writing, she renounced "the family roof."

C90:50. Ingersoll, Earl G. "Lacan, Browning, and the Murderous Voyeur: 'Porphyria's Lover' and 'My Last Duchess'." *VP* 28(1990):151–57. ¶Examines Lacan's interpretations of the Freudian concepts of scopophilia (the love of looking) and exhibitionism. RB's two poems are concerned with seeing and being seen, speaking and listening. Porphyria's lover narrates an act within which he was silent; the illogic of strangling his beloved reveals defiance of God. In "My Last Duchess" the Duke may encourage his guest to gaze at the portrait in order to read how its painter saw the duchess, how much it involved desire.

C90:51. Jacobik, Gray. "Emily Dickinson and Power." *DAI* 51.4(1990):1229A. Brandeis University, 1990. ¶Examines ways Dickinson used opposition and affiliation to enable her to become a strong woman poet. EBB's "A Vision of Poets" led Dickinson to develop a myth of poetic election, a transcendence that legitimated her work.

C90:52. Karlin, Daniel. *The Courtship of Robert Browning and Elizabeth Barrett*. [See C85:31.] ¶Rev. by J. R. Watson, *DUJ* 80(1990):352–53.

C90:53. Karlin, Daniel. "Saving the City: The Case for Comedy in Browning's *Aristophanes' Apology*." *BSN* 20.2(1990):21–31. ¶Argues that the classical aspects of RB's *Aristophanes' Apology* disguise a contemporary debate, relying on the affinity the Victorians felt with Athenian culture. Opposing comedy with tragedy, like the social and political perspectives they reflect, reveals them to be self-divided.

C90:54. Knoepflmacher, U. C. "Projection and the Female Other: Romanticism, Browning, and the Victorian Dramatic Monologue." *Out of Bounds: Male Writers and Gender(ed) Criticism*, ed. Laura Claridge and Elizabeth Langland. Amherst: U of Massachusetts P, 1990. 148–68. ¶Reprint of C84:38.

C90:55. Korg, Jacob. "Robert Browning and Italy." *Creditable Warriors:1830–1876*, ed. Michael Cotsell. Vol. 3, English Literature and the Wider World. London: Ashfield P, 1990. 209–23. ¶Traces the idea of Italy in RB's poetry, both as subject and influence. His experiences in and thoughts about Italy contributed to his poetic theory of resuscitation and to his objective mode, a significant form in modern poetry. Revision of C83:38.

C90:56. Kowal, Michael. "An Allusion to Goethe in Browning." *Notes and Queries* 37(March 1990):33–34. ¶Cites lines in the last two stanzas of "The Last Ride Together" translated from Goethe's *Faust* regarding happiness of the moment and eternal happiness. RB sees a state of perpetual promise as the way to join time and eternity, that is, happiness and hope.

C90:57. Kozicki, Henry. "Browning, *Pauline*, and Cornelius Agrippa: The Protagonist as Magus." *VP* 28(1990):17–38. ¶Approaches RB's poem as being cogent and unified when seen in terms of his knowledge of occultist thought, a type of neoplatonism. The speaker, an imaginary person, resembles Cornelius Agrippa, author of *De Occulta Philosophia* (1533), and seeks to mediate between the higher spirit and the fallen world.

C90:58. Kozlowski, Liza M. "Tracking McSwine's Fiendish Spoor: Robert Browning's 'Soliloquy of the Spanish Cloister' in *Lolita*." *Nabokovian* 23(Fall 1989):28–35. ¶Compares pig or hog imagery and lecherous behavior in Nabokov's novel with that in RB's poem, alluded to several times in the novel.

C90:59. Lane, Maggie. "Elizabeth Barrett Browning 1806–61." *Literary Daughters*. New York: St. Martin's P, 1989. 11–24, 75–101. ¶Describes EBB's relationship with her father before her marriage. She recorded this period in autobiographical essays, a diary, letters, and stories, used here to construct an account of her early life. Her father encouraged her talent and individuality in childhood, stifled her spirit in young adulthood "when she threatened to set up her will in rivalry to his," rewarded her "with an unhealthy, selfish, demoralizing love when she became suitably quiescent," and cast "a fearsome shadow over her courtship and marriage." Her strong character and intellect fed her determination to resist injustice and repression generally; his cruelties and withdrawal paradoxically also made her a better poet. She was the inspiration for other women writers, including Emily Dickinson, George Eliot, and Virginia Woolf.

C90:60. Leighton, Angela. *Elizabeth Barrett Browning*. [See C86:34.] ¶Rev. by Susan Shatto, *Yearbook of English Studies* 20(1990):300–1.

C90:61. Lerner, Laurence. "A Centenary Tribute to Robert Browning." *Times Higher Education Supplement* 15 December 1989:13. ¶Recounts the story of RB's life and discusses "A Grammarian's Funeral." RB is "so incontestably the finer poet" and EBB "the better letter-writer," perhaps because letters are personal and domestic. RB's poetry is important for demonstrating the possibility of being some other person and for creating the presence of the listener in the dramatic monologues, rather than for being self expressive.

C90:62. Lucas, John. "A Note on Browning's 'A Toccata of Galuppi's'." *Critical Survey* 2.1(1990):42–48.¶Examines the form of RB's poem, noting that it is trochaic octameter, a long line meant to challenge harmony and orthodoxy. The narrator is disheartened because a scientist, not a sensualist; however, readers, "less timorous or orthodox," may be heartened by his experience.

C90:63. de Manuel, Maria Dolores. "Muses, Voices, Poetic Selves: The Image of the Muse as a Form of Self-Reference in the Poetry of John Milton, Elizabeth Barrett Browning and Stevie Smith." *DAI* 51.5(1990):1618A. Fordham University, 1990. ¶Considers how Milton, EBB, and Smith construct a poetic voice, looking at poems that reflect on their own making, that operate within a visionary and prophetic tradition, and that figure each poet's "needs, experiences and strengths." The figure of Milton does not inhibit or silence EBB and Smith but is rather "part of the tradition against which they and other women poets situate themselves and define their voices."

C90:64. Mermin, Dorothy. *Elizabeth Barrett Browning: The Origins of a New Poetry.* [See C89:51.] ¶Rev. by Deirdre David, *VS* 34(1990):112–14; Elaine Jordan, *Essays in Criticism* 40(1990):77–88; Kenneth Millard, *TLS* 30 March 1990:354.

C90:65. Morlier, Margaret M. "The Death of Pan: Elizabeth Barrett Browning and the Romantic Ego." *BIS* 18(1990):131–55. ¶Views EBB's "The Dead Pan" as a feminist revision of Christian materials in which EBB substitutes self-connection for self-projection. Pan in "A Musical Instrument" is not an egocentric and Romantic Christ, nor is Pan as artist a violent representation of intuition.

C90:66. Munich, Adrienne Auslander, ed. *BIS* 14(1986). ¶Rev. by Rosemary T. VanArsdel, *SBHC* 16(1988):135–39.

C90:67. Munich, Adrienne Auslander, and John Maynard, eds. *BIS* 15(1987).¶Rev. by Rosemary T. VanArsdel, *SBHC* 16(1988):135–39.

C90:68. Netland, John Thomas. "Coleridge, Hermeneutics, and Victorian Poetry." *DAI* 50.9(1990):2910A. University of California at Los Angeles, 1989. ¶Explores influence of Coleridge's hermeneutic theory in RB's work which deconstructs and reconstructs biblical texts.

C90:69. Nichols, Ashton. "Dialogism in the Dramatic Monologue: Suppressed Voices in Browning." *VIJ* 18(1990):29–51. ¶Finds RB's dramatic monologues to be multivocal and thus never finalized or completed. Readers construct potential texts in response to the monologist's claims and to speak for the silenced side of the monologue. Bakhtin views dialogism in literature as a result of the rise of a world culture. RB's speakers attempt to authorize their own ways and feel undercut by the emerging threats.

C90:70. Pathak, Pratul Chandra. "The Infinite Passion of Finite Hearts: A Study of Failure in the Love Poems of Robert Browning." *DAI* 50.8(1990):2501A. University of Wisconsin at Milwaukee, 1989. ¶Argues that lack of understanding between lovers is a major theme in RB's poetry. The frustrations of his characters contrast with his own happy marriage; however, throughout his life love relations were problematic. Also, this focus is seen in light of his doctrine of the imperfect, his philosophy of success in failure, and his ability to imaginatively experience the struggles of lovers.

C90:71. Phelps, Deborah. " 'At the Roadside of Humanity': Elizabeth Barrett Browning Abroad." *Creditable Warriors:1830–1876*, ed. Michael Cotsell. Vol. 3, English Literature and the Wider World. London: Ashfield P, 1990. 225–42. ¶Argues that in most of EBB's political poetry, her female speakers identify with the political situation but are socially sequestered from direct action; they have an "almost supernatural, witch-like power," mainly to curse and denounce. She uses domestic space in an undomestic way and presents the child "as a matriarchal instrument of action." The political woman, confined and frustrated by disenfranchisement, acts through harsh words as a "roadside commentator." EBB's own position "as an enclosed champion of action" was admittedly contradictory. Her later women characters transcend traditional roles and perform symbolic political acts. Her poems' rhetorical force is to be "always looking outward as it works within," fusing the European struggle for freedom with "the intensities of a woman's circumscribed world."

C90:72. Plasa, Carl Andrew. "The Economy of Revision: Keats, Browning and T. S. Eliot." *Index to Theses with Abstracts Accepted for Higher Degrees by the Universities of Great Britain and Ireland and the Council for National Academic Awards* 39:0195. University of Southampton, 1988. *DAI* 50.12(1990):3964A. ¶Counters Bloom's theory of influence through an examination of specific linguistic transformations performed by later texts upon earlier ones. The later texts are systematically narcissistic and consider their shifting relations with the past. RB's relation to Wordsworth may be seen in "Pauline."

C90:73. Posnock, Ross. *Henry James and the Problem of Robert Browning.* [See C86:48.] ¶Rev. by Alan W. Bellringer, *Modern Language Review* 83(1988):173–74.

C90:74. Pritchett, V. S. "Pioneer." *Lasting Impressions: Essays 1961–1987.* New York: Random House, 1990. 35–41. ¶Reprint of C74.44 (review of Irvine and Honan).

C90:75. Redmond, James. "Action, Character, and Language: Dickens, His Contemporaries, and the Lure of the Stage." *Dramatic Dickens*, ed. Carol Hanbery MacKay. New York: St. Martin's P, 1989. 125–38. ¶Describes the falling out of RB and W. C. Macready as a paradigmatic example of the tension between conventional attitudes toward stage action and modern interest in the depiction of psychological states.

C90:76. Reeves, Carol. "Browning's Don Juan: Libertine or Victorian?" *University of Mississippi Studies in English* 7(1989):154–60. ¶Suggests that the Don Juan character in RB's *Fifine at the Fair* — a combination of mythic ethos and Victorian sensibility — creates "the possibility for the tension between the physical and the philosophical" in the poem, as well as the poem's ironic ambiguity. Questions of fidelity, sincerity, and stability are explored.

C90:77. Rigg, Patricia D. "Legal 'Repristination' in *The Ring and the Book*." *BIS* 18(1990):113–30. ¶Explores RB's ideas of historicity and artistic creativity. Both dramatic irony and romantic irony operate here. The monologues of the two lawyers, Archangeli and Bottini, require the reader to be a judge; the structure of the poem involves "Browning-speaker-listener-reader." Art is "objectified experience" realized by the artist through "active imaginative striving"; so too, for the reader, the poem is the process of reading it.

C90:78. Roberts, Adam. "Euripidaristophanizing: Browning's *Aristophanes' Apology*." *BSN* 20.2(1990):32–45. ¶Examines RB's poem's classical details and allusions, identifying scatological and sexual expressions neglected by Victorian critics. In the debate between Aristophanes and Balaustion, he defends the principle of sexual freedom and she advocates a more decorous vision; both sides are heard.

C90:79. Roberts, Adam. "Using Myth: Browning's *Fifine at the Fair*." *BSN* 20.1(1990):12–30. ¶Examines mythic references, especially the fatal woman, in RB's poem, seeking a coherent pattern and a message regarding sexuality and male-female relations. The poem uses the angel/whore dichotomy as image and theme. The sequence of mythic characters appears to represent a progression but instead reflects the poem's circular rhythm.

C90:80. Ryals, Clyde de L. " 'Development' and the Philosophy of Inadequacy." *BIS* 18(1990):23–31. ¶Reads RB's last publication, *Asolando*, for its philosophy, seeing development as "a series of provisional resting places" which are serviceable when needed but from which one must eventually move. This theme is apparent throughout RB's life. He attempted to experience alterity and "to examine to what extent it is possible to think differently," rather than to legitimate the known.

C90:81. Ryerse, Barbara Ruth. "Some Aspects of Browning's Satire: Browning, Donne, and Mandeville." *DAI* 50.10(1990):3238A-39A. University of

Western Ontario, 1989. ¶Explores religious, aesthetic, and satiric elements in RB's poems. His use of Christian satire may be seen in comparing "Christmas-Eve and Easter-Day" with Donne's "Satyres," and his use of Menippean satire in "With Bernard de Mandeville" may be seen in comparisons with Mandeville's "Fable of the Bees."

C90:82. Shaw, W. David. "Browning and Mystery: *The Ring and the Book* and Modern Theory." *Victorians and Mystery: Crises and Representation.* Ithaca: Cornell UP, 1990. 300–21. ¶Revised from C89:68.

C90:83. Shaw, W. David. "Browning's Unheard Words: The Poetry of Silence." *Victorians and Mystery: Crises of Representation.* Ithaca: Cornell UP, 1990. 196–220. ¶Explores the silence of reserve, the silence of emptiness, and a silence of "the amazed possession of all words" in RB's poems. The first assumes that meaning is recoverable but as yet unspeakable; the second that it cannot ever be expressed but may be intimated. Other meanings may be unspeakable because they are too full; these take the poet to the brink.

C90:84. Sherwood, Dolly. "The Brownings in Florence." *House & Garden* May 1990:88, 90, 95. ¶Describes the furnishings and artwork of the Brownings' home in Florence, Casa Guidi.

C90:85. Simons, Judy. "Behind the Scenes: The Early Diary of Elizabeth Barrett Browning." *Diaries and Journals of Literary Women from Fanny Burney to Virginia Woolf.* Iowa City: U of Iowa P, 1990. 83–105. ¶Considers the EBB of the 1831–32 diary "a lonely and frustrated woman" who is analyzing a particularly trying year in her life. Scholarly interests she shared with H. S. Boyd at this time allowed her to develop an independent spirit and mind, and she was freed from his influence by translating Aeschylus' *Prometheus.* Rev. by Lindsay Duguid, *TLS* 20 July 1990:770.

C90:86. Smith, Laura Frances. "The Externalization of the Quest Romance in Nineteenth Century British Literature." *DAI* 51.03(1990):869A. Indiana University, 1989. ¶Traces poets' use of the quest motif from internal (representing emotional and psychological states) to external (having social significance). RB's "Childe Roland to the Dark Tower Came," at a midpoint in the century, questions the ability of the hero to transfer personal gains to lasting social gains.

C90:87. Smulders, Sharon G. M. "Christina Rossetti: Response and Responsibility." *DAI* 49.12(1989):3736A-37A. University of Sussex, 1987. ¶Compares EBB's *Sonnets from the Portuguese* and Christina Rossetti's "Monna Innominata." Both poets were concerned about the lack of a female literary tradition. EBB's philanthropic and political themes arise from her principle of adoration. EBB influenced Rossetti to extend her range of subjects and, like EBB, to reform gender conventions within the genre.

C90:88. Spender, Stephen. "Centenary Address: Westminster Abbey, December 12 1989." *BSN* 20.1(1990):8–9. ¶Views RB's poetry as a journey from Romantic lyricism, through Victorian clutter, to learned modernism. He saw the roots of the modern age in the past, incorporated prose and journalism, and played with language.

C90:89. Starzyk, Lawrence J. "Remodeling Models: The Recursive Element in Victorian Poetry and Poetics." *The Arnoldian* 15(1988):1–21. ¶Includes RB's "Paracelsus," "Cleon," and "Childe Roland to the Dark Tower Came" in a discussion of some Victorian poets' use of recursive elements and their relation to belief or despair. Repetitions in RB's poems demonstrate "the past's ongoing transformation in the present." Shadow or representation may mock reality (the object), but, unlike Tennyson for whom discontinuity prompts regret and Arnold who despairs at spiritual loss, RB delights in the present and its mimics.

C90:90. Steiner, Robert. "The Double Death of Eurydice: A Discussion of Browning and Mythology." *Sex and Death in Victorian Literature*, ed. Regina Barreca. Bloomington and Indianapolis: Indiana UP, 1990. 211–26. ¶Considers "Eurydice to Orpheus. A Picture by Leighton" as a heretical reading of the myth, seeing Orpheus suspended "between reflection and event, between representation and the thing itself." In Eurydice's speech, "she does not commit suicide, she exhorts her husband to murder, . . . [RB's] defeat of mythic barbarism and a victory for Eros."

C90:91. Stephenson, Glennis. *Elizabeth Barrett Browning and The Poetry of Love.* [See C89:70.] ¶Rev. by Deirdre David, *VS* 34(1990):112–14; Kenneth Millard, *TLS* 30 March 1990:354.

C90:92. Stonum, Gary Lee. "The Influence of Elizabeth Barrett Browning." *The Dickinson Sublime.* Madison: U of Wisconsin P, 1990. 34–46. ¶Examines EBB's influence on Emily Dickinson and her poetry, arguing that Dickinson expressed a sense of filiation, particularly just after EBB's death.

C90:93. Thomas, Donald, ed. and introduction. *The Post-Romantics.* London: Routledge, 1990. 1–18, 67–113, 187–89. ¶Selects and reprints reviews and critical essays on five nineteenth-century poets, including RB, showing "the progress of the Victorian romantic soul." These poets "collectively inspired some of the best criticism of poetry in the nineteenth century." Items are mainly from the nineteenth century; a final chapter surveys twentieth-century books, editions, and overviews. Reprint in part of C82:47.

C90:94. Vance, Norman. "Ovid and the Nineteenth Century." *Ovid Renewed: Ovidian Influences on Literature and Art from the Middle Ages to the Twentieth Century.* Ed. Charles Martindale. Cambridge: Cambridge UP, 1988. 215–31. ¶Cites RB's *The Ring and the Book* as sharing elements of Ovid's *Art of Love* and *Metamorphoses*, but largely by suggestion. He more overtly established a Greek atmosphere in *Balaustion's Adventure* and *Aristophanes' Apology*; in *Pauline* his references to Ovid are more apparent. Rev. by Lynne Pearce, *Year's Work in English Studies* 69(1988):413.

*C90:95. Weikert, Heidrun-Edda. *Robert Brownings kunstthematische Dichtung: Ihr Epochenkontext zwischen Spatgotik und Viktorianismus.* Stuttgart: Franz Steiner, 1989. 318 pp. ¶In German.

C90:96. White, Leslie. "Meaning 'beyond the facts' and Saving 'the soul besides': Culture Transcendence in the Opening Triad of *The Ring and the Book.*" *Publications of the Arkansas Philological Association* 15(1989):109–20. ¶Sees books 2, 3, and 4 of RB's poem dramatizing his argument: the poem transforms history into poetry and explores "the potential of the human will as a way of shaping and defining modes of existence, and of transcending the increasingly corrosive pressures of a complex industrialized society."

C90:97. Woodring, Carl. *Nature into Art: Cultural Transformations in Nineteenth-Century Britain.* Cambridge, MA: Harvard UP, 1989. 143–44. ¶Cites RB as a major Victorian poet who anticipates stances and characteristics of the Pre-Raphaelites and urges scholars to consider the ways he "looked first to his own day" for characters.

C90:98. Woolford, John. *Browning the Revisionary.* [See C87:64.] ¶Rev. by Thomas J. Collins, *Nineteenth-Century Literature* 44(1990):560–63; Lynne Pearce, *Year's Work in English Studies* 69(1988):419.

*C90:99. Yoshikado, Makio. " 'A Death in the Desert' as a Christian Mock-Document." *Shiron* 27(1988):58–72.

BIBLIOGRAPHY INDEX

INDEX

429

Eakins, Thomas, 398, 403, 404, 406
East India Company, 161
Eastlake, Charles, 158n.2
Ecole des Beaux-Arts, 399
Edinburgh Review, 157n.1, 199, 200,
    205–06, 208, 304
Edmond, Rod, 386
Edmonds, Jill, 344
Ehrenreich, Barbara, 366–67
Eigner, Edwin M., 141
Eldredge, Charles C., 395
Eliot, George, 45, 60, 157, 250, 253, 260,
    262–63, 287, 289–90, 348–49, 351–55
Elliot, Maude Howe, 192
Ellis, Havelock, 51n.14, 340–41, 345
Ellis, Sarah Stickney, 235–36
Ellis, Virginia Ridley, 387–88
Emerson, Ralph Waldo, 132, 144, 149,
    157n.1
Empire Theatre, 339, 341
Empson, William, 259, 271n.4
Engels, Friedrich, 70, 92
L'Epee, Abbe de, 181
Erasmus, Desiderius, 26
Erebus, 121
Essay Club, 142
D'Etavigny, Azy, 180
Ethardo, Emmaline, 345
Ethnographic Society, The, 43
Evangelicals, 55–56
Evans, Marian, *see* Eliot, George
Evolutionists, 26, 307

Farewell, Lt. Francis, 118
Farrar, Dean, 144
Farrell, John, 185
Fawkes, Guy, 245
Fee, Elizabeth, 27
Femme Moderne, la, 344
Fernseed, Frank, 31–32
Ferrero, George, 39
Feuerbach, Ludwig, 276–77, 286
Finot, Jean, 48
Fish, Stanley, 314
Fishbane, Jonathan, 20n.9
Fitzgerald, Edward, 395
Fitzsimmons, Linda, 343
Flaxman, 397–98, 401
Fletcher, Ian, 388–89
Foakes, R. A., 96n.15

Fontenay, Saboureux de, 180
Foote, G. W., 94n.1, 95n.10
Ford, Ford Maddox, 404–05
Ford, Richard, 398
Forster, John, 361, 364
Fortnightly Review, 3
Foster, Kathleen A., 403–04
Foucault, Michel, 206, 369–70
Fox, William J., 296–97, 308, 379
Franklin Expedition, 100
Franklin, Lady, 121
Franklin, Sir John, 120–22, 125, 129,
    131–32, 136n.3, n.4, 137n.10
Fraser's Magazine, 3, 87–88, 96n.14,
    207–08
French, Daniel Chester, 180
French Sign Language, 194n.1
Freud, Sigmund, 190, 192, 272n.20
Frye, Northrop, 271n.15
Fuller, Margaret, 11, 352
Furnival, Fredrick, 306

Gallagher, Catherine, 236
Gallaudet, Thomas, 180–81
Galton, Francis, 73, 94n.3, 284
Gamble, Elizabeth Burt, 47–48, 51n.16,
    n.17
Gardener, Helen, 30–31, 38, 47
Gardner, Vivien, 343, 345
Gaskell, Elizabeth, 208, 222
Gatrell, Simon, 382
Gay and Lesbian Studies, 366–68, 377
Geddes, Patrick, 42
Gelpi, Barbara Charlesworth, 374
Gender Studies, 377
Genette, Gerard, 311
Gibbon, Edward, 101, 138n.12
Gibbon, Perceval, 350
Gilbert, Eliot L., 374–75
Gilbert, Sir John, 397–98
Gilbert, Sandra, 19, 20n.2, 194n.5, 353,
    375–76
Gilbert, William Schwenck, 135
Gilcrease Museum, 394
Gillet, Paula, 374
Gilman, Charlotte Perkins, 38–39, 50n.9
Gilmore, David D., 371–72
Girouard, Mark, 391, 400–01
Gladstone, William Ewart, 56, 149, 224,
    238n.10, n.13